Research Methods for the Behavioral Sciences

Second Edition

SAGE was founded in 1965 by Sara Miller McCune to support the dissemination of usable knowledge by publishing innovative and high-quality research and teaching content. Today, we publish over 900 journals, including those of more than 400 learned societies, more than 800 new books per year, and a growing range of library products including archives, data, case studies, reports, and video. SAGE remains majority-owned by our founder, and after Sara's lifetime will become owned by a charitable trust that secures our continued independence.

Los Angeles | London | New Delhi | Singapore | Washington DC

Research Methods for the Behavioral Sciences

Second Edition

Gregory J. Privitera
St. Bonaventure University

Los Angeles | London | New Delhi
Singapore | Washington DC

Los Angeles | London | New Delhi
Singapore | Washington DC

FOR INFORMATION:

SAGE Publications, Inc.
2455 Teller Road
Thousand Oaks, California 91320
E-mail: order@sagepub.com

SAGE Publications Ltd.
1 Oliver's Yard
55 City Road
London EC1Y 1SP
United Kingdom

SAGE Publications India Pvt. Ltd.
B 1/I 1 Mohan Cooperative Industrial Area
Mathura Road, New Delhi 110 044
India

SAGE Publications Asia-Pacific Pte. Ltd.
3 Church Street
#10-04 Samsung Hub
Singapore 049483

Acquisitions Editor: Reid Hester
Associate Editor: Nathan Davidson
eLearning Editor: Lucy Berbeo
Editorial Assistant: Morgan Shannon
Production Editor: Kelly DeRosa
Copy Editor: Christina West
Typesetter: C&M Digitals (P) Ltd.
Proofreader: Theresa Kay
Indexer: Jeanne Busemeyer
Cover Designer: Scott Van Atta
Marketing Manager: Shari Countryman

Printed in the United States of America

Library of Congress Cataloging-in-Publication Data

Privitera, Gregory J., author.

Research methods for the behavioral sciences/
Gregory J. Privitera. — 2e [edition].

pages cm
Includes bibliographical references and index.

ISBN 978-1-5063-2657-3 (hardcover : alk. paper)

1. Psychology—Research—Methodology. 2. Social sciences—Research—Methodology. 3. Psychology—Statistical methods. 4. Social sciences—Statistical methods. I. Title.

BF76.5.P65 2016
150.72'1—dc23   2015029690

This book is printed on acid-free paper.

16 17 18 19 20 10 9 8 7 6 5 4 3 2 1

BRIEF CONTENTS

SECTION IV: QUASI-EXPERIMENTAL AND EXPERIMENTAL RESEARCH DESIGNS

SECTION V: ANALYZING, INTERPRETING, AND COMMUNICATING RESEARCH DATA

DETAILED CONTENTS

SECTION III: NONEXPERIMENTAL RESEARCH DESIGNS

SECTION IV: QUASI-EXPERIMENTAL AND EXPERIMENTAL RESEARCH DESIGNS

SECTION V: ANALYZING, INTERPRETING, AND COMMUNICATING RESEARCH DATA

ABOUT THE AUTHOR

Gregory J. Privitera is an associate professor of psychology at St. Bonaventure University. Dr. Privitera received his PhD in behavioral neuroscience in the field of psychology at the State University of New York at Buffalo. He went on to complete postdoctoral research at Arizona State University before beginning his tenure at St. Bonaventure University. He is an author of multiple books on statistics, research methods, and the psychology of eating, in addition to authoring over two-dozen peer-reviewed scientific articles aimed at advancing our understanding of health and promoting the intake of healthier diets for children and adults. He oversees a variety of undergraduate student research projects at St. Bonaventure University, where over two-dozen students, many of whom are now earning graduate degrees at various institutions, have coauthored research in his laboratories. For his research work, Dr. Privitera was recognized by St. Bonaventure University as Advisor of the Year in 2013, and he was awarded an Early Career Professional award by the American Psychological Association in 2015. For his work with students and fruitful record of teaching, Dr. Privitera was recognized in 2014 with the Award for Professional Excellence in Teaching—the highest teaching award at St. Bonaventure University. The first edition of this text was a recipient of the "Most Promising New Textbook" National Award from the Text and Academic Authors Association. In addition to his teaching, research, and advisement, Dr. Privitera is a veteran of the U.S. Marine Corps, and he is married with two children: a daughter, Grace, and a son, Aiden. Dr. Privitera is also the author of *Statistics for the Behavioral Sciences, 2nd Edition*, and *Essential Statistics for the Behavioral Sciences*.

ACKNOWLEDGMENTS

I want to take a moment to thank all those who have been supportive and endearing throughout my career. To my family, friends, acquaintances, and colleagues—thank you for contributing to my perspective in a way that is indubitably recognized and appreciated. In particular, to my son, Aiden Andrew, and daughter, Grace Ann—every moment I am with you, I am reminded of what is truly important in my life. As a veteran of the U.S. Marine Corps, I also want to thank all those who serve and have served—there is truly no greater honor than to serve something greater than yourself. Semper Fidelis.

To all those at SAGE Publications, I am so very grateful to share in this experience and work with all of you. It is your vital contributions that have made this book possible and so special to me. Thank you.

I especially want to thank the thousands of research methods students across the country. It is your pursuit of scientific inquiry that has inspired this contribution. My hope is that you take away as much from reading this book as I have in writing it.

Last, but certainly not least, I would also like to thank the following reviewers who gave their time to provide me with valuable feedback during the development process:

George Alder, Simon Fraser University

Elizabeth Krumrei Mancuso, Pepperdine University

Evan M. Kleiman, Harvard University

Gary Popoli, Stevenson University

Mary E. Saczawa, University of Florida

Vincent Trofimoff, California State University, San Marcos

Shulan Lu, Texas A&M University–Commerce

Bryan Raudenbush, Wheeling Jesuit University

Christopher J. Ferguson, Stetson University

PREFACE

Research Methods for the Behavioral Sciences uses a problem-focused approach to introduce research methods in a way that fully integrates the decision tree—from identifying a research question to choosing an appropriate analysis and sharing results. This book begins with an introduction to the general research process, ethics, identifying and measuring variables, conducting literature reviews, selecting participants, and more. Research designs are then introduced in a logical order, from the least controlled (nonexperiments and quasi-experiments) to the most controlled (experiments). Throughout each chapter, students are shown how to structure a study to answer a research question (design) and are navigated through the challenging process of choosing an appropriate analysis or statistic to make a decision (analysis). This book integrates statistics with methods in a way that applies the decision tree throughout the book and shows students how statistics and methods fit together to allow researchers to test hypotheses using the scientific method. The following are unique features in this book to facilitate student learning:

- **Strengthened organization of research design:**
  - **Follows a problem-focused organization.** This book is organized into five main sections. Each section builds upon the last to give a full picture of the scientific process. In Section I, Scientific Inquiry, students are introduced to the process and ethics of engaging in the scientific method. In Section II, Defining and Measuring Variables, Selecting Samples, and Choosing an Appropriate Research Design, students are shown how to define and measure scientific variables, and methods used to select samples and choose an appropriate research design are described (Chapters 4–6). Sections III and IV fully introduce each type of research design from Nonexperimental Research Designs (Chapters 7–8) to Quasi-Experimental and Experimental Research Designs (Chapters 9–12), respectively. In Section V, Analyzing, Interpreting, and Communicating Research Data, students are shown how to summarize and describe statistical outcomes in words (using American Psychological Association [APA] style) and graphs. Also included is a full chapter that introduces how to use APA style to write manuscripts and gives an introduction to creating posters and giving talks (Chapters 13–15). The organization of this

book is "problem focused" in that it introduces the scientific process as it would be applied from setting up a study, to conducting a study, to communicating the outcomes observed in that study—all while applying the decision tree to engage further the critical thinking skills of students.

o **Ethics in Focus sections in each chapter.** Ethical considerations are often specific to a particular research design or methodology. For this reason, the topic of ethics is not only covered in Chapter 3, but at least one Ethics in Focus section is also included in each chapter. These sections review important ethical issues related to the topics in each chapter. This allows professors the flexibility to teach ethics as a separate section and integrate discussions of ethics throughout the semester. This level of organization for ethics is simply absent from most comparable research methods textbooks.

o **Introduces three broad categories of research design.** In truth, research design is complex. Many designs are hybrids that cannot be neatly fit into a single type of category or research design. For this reason, I simplify research designs into those that do not show cause (nonexperimental and quasi-experimental) and those that can show cause (experimental). For example, other books may introduce correlational designs as being separate from a nonexperiment. However, such a distinction is often unnecessary. The correlational design is an example of a nonexperiment—it does not show cause. Instead, the organization in this book focuses on understanding how, when, and why research designs are used, and the types of questions each design can and cannot answer.

o **Chapters organized from least control to most control.** This book transitions from research designs with the least control (nonexperimental) to those with the most control (experimental). There is a logical progression as research designs are introduced in this book that is clearer than the organization you will find in many comparable textbooks. Students can clearly distinguish between the types of research designs they read, and this level of clarity can make it easier for students to understand how to appropriately select research designs to answer the many research questions that researchers ask.

- **Reduced bias in language across research designs:**

  o **Research design is introduced without bias.** Research designs are introduced as being used to answer different types of questions. I avoid referring to all studies as "experiments." In that spirit, experiments are instead introduced as answering different types of research questions. It is emphasized throughout this book that the ability to demonstrate cause does not make a design superior to other designs; it simply allows researchers to answer different types of questions (i.e., research questions pertaining to cause).

  o **The qualitative research design and perspective is given fair coverage.** While many textbooks appropriately focus on quantitative methods that make up most of the research conducted in the behavioral sciences, many omit or even are dismissive of qualitative methodology. This bias can mislead students into thinking that all research is quantitative. Although this book does emphasize quantitative methods because these methods are the most used methodology in the behavioral sciences, fair coverage of qualitative methods is also included. In Chapter 7, for example, a section is included to introduce qualitative research, and in Chapter 15, an overview for reporting qualitative outcomes is included.

- **Emphasis on statistical technologies:**
  - **Guide for how to use IBM® SPSS® Statistics* with this book**. It can be difficult to teach from a textbook and a separate SPSS manual. The separate manual often does not include research examples or uses language that is inconsistent with language used in the textbook, which can make it difficult for students to learn. This book corrects for this problem by incorporating SPSS coverage into the book, which begins with the guide at the front of the book, "How to Use SPSS With This Book." The guide provides students with an easy-to-follow, classroom-tested overview of how SPSS is set up, how to read the Data View and Variable View screens, and how to use the SPSS in Focus sections in the book. This guide gives students the familiarization they need to be able to apply the SPSS instructions given in the book.
  - **SPSS in Focus sections in the chapters**. Most research methods textbooks for the behavioral sciences omit SPSS, include it in an appendix separate from the main chapters in the book, or include it in ancillary materials that often are not included with course content. In this book, SPSS is included in each appropriate chapter, particularly for experimental design chapters where specific designs are generally associated with specific statistical tests. These SPSS in Focus sections provide step-by-step, classroom-tested instruction using practical research examples for how the data measured using various research designs taught in each chapter can be analyzed using SPSS. Students are supported with annotated screenshot figures and explanations for how to read and interpret SPSS outputs.

- **Engages student learning and interest:**
  - **Conversational writing style**. I write in a conversational tone that speaks to the reader as if he or she is the researcher. It empowers students to view research methods as something they are capable of understanding and applying. It is a positive psychology approach to writing that involves students in the process and decisions made using the scientific process. The goal is to motivate and excite students by making the book easy to read and follow without "dumbing down" the information they need to be successful.
  - **Written with student learning in mind**. There are many features in this book to help students succeed. Many figures and tables are given in each chapter to facilitate student learning and break up the readings to make the material less intimidating. Key terms are bolded and defined on a separate text line, as they are introduced. Each defined term is included in a glossary, and these terms are also restated at the end of each chapter to make it easier for students to search for key terms while studying. In addition, margin notes are included

---

*SPSS is a registered trademark of International Business Machines Corporation.

in each chapter to summarize key material, and many reviews and activities are included at the end of each chapter to test learning and give students an opportunity to apply the knowledge they have learned.

o **Learning objectives and learning objective summaries.** Learning objectives are stated in each chapter to get students focused and thinking about the material they will learn, and to organize each chapter and to allow students to review content by focusing on those learning objectives they struggle with the most. In addition, a chapter summary organized by learning objective is provided at the end of each chapter. In this summary, each learning objective is stated and answered. Hence, not only are learning objectives identified in each chapter, but they are also answered at the end of each chapter.

o **Learning Checks** are inserted throughout each chapter for students to review what they learn, as they learn it. Many research methods textbooks give learning check questions, with no answer. How can students "check" their learning without the answers? Instead, in this book, all learning checks have questions with answer keys to allow students to actually "check" their learning before continuing their reading of the chapter.

o **MAKING SENSE sections** support critical and difficult material. A research methods course can have many areas where students can struggle, and the MAKING SENSE sections are included to break down the most difficult concepts and material in the book—to make sense of them. These sections, included in most chapters in the book, are aimed at easing student stress and making research methods more approachable to students. Again, this book was written with student learning in mind.

o **APA Appendices** support student learning of APA style. The appendices include an APA writing guide (A.1), an APA guide to grammar, punctuation, and spelling (A.2), a full sample APA-style manuscript from a study that was published in a peer-reviewed scientific journal (A.3), and instructions for creating posters using Microsoft PowerPoint, with a sample poster and poster template given (A.4). Also included are instructions for using randomization (B.1) and constructing a Latin square (B.2), a general instructions guide for using SPSS (C.1), and statistical tables for common tests (C.2). Hence, this book provides the necessary support for students who are asked to complete a research project, and complete an APA-style paper, poster, or talk. Few books provide this level of comprehensive supportive materials.

In addition, there is one more overarching feature that I refer to as *teachability*. Although this book is comprehensive and a great reference for any undergraduate student, it sometimes can be difficult to cover every topic in this book. For this reason, the chapters are organized into sections, each of which can largely stand alone, to give professors the ability to more easily manage course content by assigning students particular sections in each chapter when they cannot teach all topics covered in a chapter. Hence, this book was written with both the student and the professor in mind. Here are some brief highlights of what you will find in each chapter:

Chapter 1 is a traditional introductory chapter. Students are introduced to scientific thinking, the steps of the scientific method, the goals of science, and more. A key feature in this chapter is the distinction made between qualitative and quantitative research and between basic and applied research, as well as tips provided to help students distinguish between pseudoscience and science. These distinctions are not often made in a Chapter 1, if at all, but can be important in helping students identify key perspectives in conducting research.

Chapter 2 introduces students to what constitutes scientific ideas and provides guidelines for developing these ideas into hypotheses and theories. A full introduction to using online databases is provided, with suggestions provided for conducting an effective literature review. In addition, difficult concepts such as induction versus deduction and confirmational versus disconfirmational strategies are introduced, with many illustrations included to guide student learning.

Chapter 3 provides a full overview of key historic events related to ethics in behavioral research that led to the Nuremberg Code and the Belmont Report. Examples of historical events in psychology are also included. Students are further introduced to the standards and procedures set by institutional review boards for humans and institutional animal care and use committees for animals. A key feature in this chapter is the inclusion of each APA ethical standard stated in the APA code of conduct.

Chapter 4 identifies the types of variables researchers measure and the scales of measurement for data, and describes ways to identify the reliability and validity of scientific measures. Note that validity and reliability of research design (e.g., internal and external validity) are not discussed in this chapter in order to focus chapter content only on the validity and reliability of measurement to avoid confusion.

Chapter 5 introduces sampling procedures, including nonprobability and probability sampling methods. Although the types of sampling are often included as a section within a chapter, this book devotes a full chapter to this topic—doing so allows for full coverage of sampling techniques, along with the many advantages and limitations associated with each sampling method. The concept of sampling error is also identified, with a section showing how to identify this error in SPSS output tables.

Chapter 6 establishes an organization for introducing research design in subsequent chapters. A tree diagram for experimental, quasi-experimental, and nonexperimental designs is provided. These figures outline the different types of research design that fall into each category—and each design is introduced in the book. In addition, extensive illustrations associated with introducing common threats to internal and external validity are included to facilitate student learning on a topic that is often difficult for students. In addition, concepts such as manipulation, randomization, control, and individual differences are defined and explained because these concepts will be used in later chapters to distinguish between different research designs.

Chapter 7 introduces three nonexperimental designs: naturalistic designs, qualitative designs (phenomenology, ethnography, and case study), and existing data designs (archival, content, and meta-analysis). Qualitative and existing data designs often use techniques that build on those used with a naturalistic design, which is why these designs are grouped in the same chapter. For clarity, each design is described under a separate heading. A key feature for this chapter is the introduction of the qualitative perspective prior to introducing qualitative designs, which clearly distinguishes it from the quantitative perspective.

Chapter 8 introduces two more nonexperimental designs: survey designs and correlational designs. These designs are grouped in the same chapter because surveys are often used in correlational research. Suggestions are provided to help students write good survey items, and a section focused on issues related to sampling bias is included. For clarity, each design is described in a separate heading.

Chapter 9 introduces many quasi-experimental designs: one-group, time series, nonequivalent control group, and developmental designs. Quasi-experimental designs are clearly defined in that each design includes a quasi-independent variable and/or lacks a control group. In a separate heading, the first experimental design is introduced: single-case designs (reversal, multiple-baseline, and changing-criterion designs). The single-case designs are taught as experimental designs because they can demonstrate unambiguous cause and effect, which is the traditional way to introduce such designs.

Chapter 10 introduces the between-subjects experimental design for two groups and more than two groups. Also, this chapter begins by introducing what criteria must be met to qualify a study as an experiment (randomization, manipulation, and control/comparison). These criteria are used to distinguish the types of experimental designs introduced in the book. This chapter is unique in that statistical methods are introduced with research design in order to distinguish between methodological control (of individual differences) and statistical control (of statistical error). Each design is introduced in the full context of a research example so that students can clearly see how a research problem or hypothesis is tested from design to analysis.

Chapter 11 introduces the within-subjects experimental design for two groups and more than two groups. The chapter begins with a clear description of the conditions that must be met for such a design to qualify as an experiment. Issues related to counterbalancing and order effects are discussed. As in Chapter 10, statistical methods are introduced with research design in order to distinguish between methodological control (of order effects and individual differences) and statistical control (of statistical error). Each design is introduced in the full context of a research example so that students can clearly see how a research problem or hypothesis can be tested from design to analysis.

Chapter 12 introduces the factorial experimental design for the between, within, and mixed factorial designs. To illustrate the features of this design, many examples in the chapter are for the between-subjects factorial design. As in Chapters 10 and 11, statistical methods are introduced with research design in order to distinguish between methodological control (of order effects and/or individual differences) and statistical control (of statistical error), which is particularly useful for identifying main effects and interactions. Each design is introduced in the full context of a research example so that students can clearly see how a research problem or hypothesis can be tested from design to analysis.

Chapter 13 introduces descriptive statistics, graphing data, and statistical measures of reliability. The chapter introduces measures of frequency, central tendency, and variability and also shows how to graph such measures. Calculations of measures of reliability (i.e., Cronbach's alpha and Cohen's kappa) are also introduced to reinforce topics first introduced in Chapter 4.

Chapter 14 introduces the logic of significance testing, each major test of significance, effect size, and confidence intervals. Each significance test is introduced with a decision tree diagram to support how to choose among the many parametric and nonparametric tests available for analyzing data. Effect size is introduced for t tests, analysis of variance (ANOVA), correlations, and the chi-square test. How to compute and interpret effect size is also discussed. In addition, estimation and the use of confidence intervals are described, with particular emphasis placed on how to read and interpret confidence intervals.

Chapter 15 includes a full introduction to writing an APA-style manuscript. Each section of the manuscript is described and illustrated using a sample manuscript. Suggestions for how to organize and write APA-style manuscripts are included. In addition, writing and presenting posters is discussed, with a final section providing suggestions for giving good presentations. Hence, this chapter meaningfully introduces each way of communicating research.

Appendix A fully supports the content covered in Chapter 15. It includes an APA writing guide (A.1), an APA guide to grammar, punctuation, and spelling (A.2), a full sample APA-style manuscript from a study that was published in a peer-reviewed scientific journal (A.3), and instructions for creating posters using Microsoft PowerPoint, with a sample poster and poster template given (A.4). These resources give students guidelines to support their APA writing.

Appendix B includes a random numbers table (B.1) with directions for using this table to randomly sample or randomly select participants in a study. The random numbers table supports concepts taught in Chapter 5 (random sampling) and Chapter 6 (random assignment). Also given are directions for constructing a Latin square (B.2) to support concepts taught in Chapter 11 (within-subjects designs).

Appendix C includes a general instructions guide for using SPSS (C.1). Throughout this book, these instructions are provided with an example for how to analyze and interpret data. However, it would be difficult for students to thumb through the book to find each test when needing to refer to these tests later. Therefore, this appendix provides a single place where students can go to get direction for any statistical test taught in this chapter. Also given with each instruction is where in the book they can go to find an example of how to compute each test. Also included are statistical tables for the t test, ANOVA, Pearson correlation, and chi-square (C.2) to support statistical material taught in Chapters 5, 7, 10, 11, 12, and 14.

Supplements

Visit **edge.sagepub.com/priviteramethods2e** for a complete set of ancillary resources, including:

SAGE edge for Instructors

The following chapter-specific assets are available on the teaching site:

- **An author-created test bank** provides a diverse range of 2,200+ pre-written questions and answers tied to learning objectives from the book, as well as the opportunity to edit any question and/or insert personalized questions to effectively assess students' progress and understanding

- Editable, chapter-specific **PowerPoint® slides** offer complete flexibility for creating a multimedia presentation for the course

- **Sample course syllabi** for semester and quarter courses provide suggested models for structuring one's course

- An **Instructor's Manual** provides chapter-by-chapter lecture notes, discussion questions, class activities, and more to ease preparation for lectures and class discussions

- **SPSS in Focus Screencasts** that accompany each SPSS in Focus section from the book show you how to use SPSS step-by-step

- **Answer keys** for all problems featured in the book and in the SPSS Workbook assist in grading student work

- EXCLUSIVE! Access to full-text **SAGE journal articles** that have been carefully selected to support and expand on the concepts presented in each chapter to encourage students to think critically

- **Multimedia content** includes videos that appeal to students with different learning styles

- A **Course cartridge** provides easy LMS integration

SAGE edge for Students

The open-access study site includes the following:

- **SPSS in Focus Screencasts** that accompany each SPSS in Focus section from the book show you how to use SPSS step-by-step

- A customized online **action plan** includes tips and feedback on progress through the course and materials, allowing students to individualize their learning experience

- **Learning objectives** reinforce the most important material

- Mobile-friendly **eFlashcards** strengthen understanding of key terms and concepts

- **Web resources** are included for further research and insights.

- **Multimedia content** includes audio and video resources that appeal to students with different learning styles

- EXCLUSIVE! Access to full-text **SAGE journal articles** that have been carefully selected to support and expand on the concepts presented in each chapter

Thank you for choosing *Research Methods for the Behavioral Sciences*, and best wishes for a successful semester.

Gregory J. Privitera
St. Bonaventure, New York

TO THE STUDENT— HOW TO USE SPSS WITH THIS BOOK

The Statistical Package for the Social Sciences (SPSS), acquired by IBM in January 2010, is an innovative statistical computer program used to compute most statistics taught in this book. This preface provides you with an overview to familiarize you with how to open, view, and understand this software. The screenshots in this book show SPSS version 22.0 for the PC. Still, even if you use a Mac or different version, the figures and instructions should provide an effective guide for helping you use this statistical software (with some minor differences, of course). SPSS will be introduced throughout this book, so it will be worthwhile to read this preface before moving into future discussions of SPSS. Included in this preface is a general introduction to familiarize you with this software.

Understanding this software is especially important for those interested in research careers because it is the most widely used statistical program in the social and behavioral sciences. For students who will be working through a research project this semester, knowing how to enter, analyze, and interpret statistics using SPSS is instrumental to your success. The SPSS in this book is an essential complement to your reading and work because it will help you better understand and interpret the output from SPSS software.

P.1 Overview of SPSS: What Are You Looking At?

When you open SPSS, you will see a window that looks similar to an Excel spreadsheet. (In many ways, you will enter and view the data similar to that in Microsoft Excel.) At the bottom of the window, you will see two tabs as shown in Figure P.1. The **Data View** tab is open by default. The **Variable View** tab to the right of it is used to view and define the variables being studied.

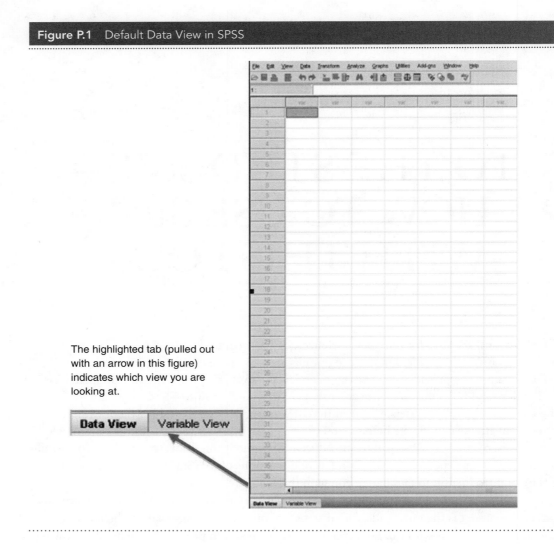

The highlighted tab (pulled out with an arrow in this figure) indicates which view you are looking at.

Data View

The Data View screen includes a **menu bar** (located at the top of the screen), which displays the following commands that perform most functions that SPSS provides: **File**, **Edit**, **View**, **Data**, **Transform**, **Analyze**, **Graphs**, **Utilities**, **Window**, and **Help**. Each command will be introduced as needed in each chapter in the SPSS in Focus sections.

Below the menu bar is where you will find the **toolbar**, which includes a row of icons that perform various functions. We will use some of these icons, whereas others are beyond the scope of this book. The purpose and function of each icon will be introduced as needed in each chapter (again, in the SPSS in Focus sections).

Within the spreadsheet, there are **cells** organized in columns and rows. The rows are labeled numerically from 1, whereas each column is labeled *var*. Each column will be used to identify your variables, so *var* is short for *variable*. To label your variables with something other than *var*, you need to access the Variable View tab—this is a unique feature to SPSS.

Variable View

When you click the Variable View tab, a new screen appears. Some features remain the same. For example, the menu bar and toolbar remain at the top of your screen. What changes is the spreadsheet—notice that the rows are still labeled numerically beginning with 1 but the labels across the columns have changed. There are 11 columns in this view, as shown in Figure P.2: **Name, Type, Width, Decimals, Label, Values, Missing, Columns, Align, Measure**, and **Role**. We will describe each column in this section.

Figure P.2 Variable View Page With 11 Columns

	Name	Type	Width	Decimals	Label	Values	Missing	Columns	Align	Measure	Role
1											
2											
3											
4											
5											

Each column allows you to label and characterize variables.

Name. In this column, you enter the names of your variables (but no spaces are allowed). Each row identifies a single variable. Also, once you name a variable, the columns label in the Data View will change. For example, while in Variable View, enter the word *stats* in the first cell of this column. Now click on the Data View tab at the bottom left. Notice that the label for column 1 has now changed from *var* to *stats*. Also, notice that once you enter a name for a variable, the row is suddenly filled in with words and numbers. Do not worry; this is supposed to happen.

Type. This cell identifies the type of variable you are defining. When you click in the box, a small gray box with three dots appears. Click on the gray box and a dialog box appears, as shown in Figure P.3. By default, the variable type selected is numeric. This is because your variable will almost always be numeric, so we usually just leave this cell alone.

Figure P.3 Variable Type Dialog Box

	Name	Type	Width	Decimals	Label
1	stats	Numeric	8	2	

Variable Type

- ● Numeric
- ○ Comma
- ○ Dot
- ○ Scientific notation
- ○ Date
- ○ Dollar
- ○ Custom currency
- ○ String

Width: 8
Decimal Places: 2

OK   Cancel   Help

The dialog box shown here appears by clicking the small gray box with three dots in the Type column. This allows you to define the type of variable being measured.

Width. The Width column is used to identify the largest number or longest string of your variable. For example, grade point average would have a width of 4: one digit to the left of the decimal, one space for the decimal, and two digits to the right. The default width is 8. So if none of your variables are longer than 8 digits, you can just leave this alone. Otherwise, when you click in the box, you would select the up and down arrows that appear to the right of the cell to change the width.

Decimals. This cell allows you to identify the number of places beyond the decimal point in your variables. Like the Width cell, when you click in the decimal box, you can select the up and down arrows that appear to the right of the cell to change the decimals. If you enter whole numbers, for example, you would simply set this to 0.

Label. The Label column allows you to label any variable whose meaning is not clear. For example, we can label the variable name *stats* as *statistics* in the label column, as shown in Figure P.4. This clarifies the meaning of the *stats* variable name.

Figure P.4 Column for Labeling Variables

	Name	Type	Width	Decimals	Label
1	stats	Numeric	8	2	statistics

In this example, we labeled the variable name *stats* as *statistics* in the Label column.

Values. This column allows you to identify the levels of your variable. This is especially useful for coded data. Nominal data are often coded numerically in SPSS because SPSS recognizes numeric values. For example, sex could be coded as 1 (*male*) and 2 (*female*); seasons could be coded as 1 (*spring*), 2 (*summer*), 3 (*fall*), and 4 (*winter*).

Figure P.5 Value Labels Dialog Box

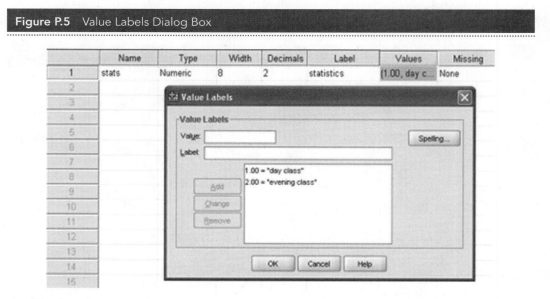

The dialog box shown here appears by clicking the small gray box with three dots in the Values column. This function allows you to code data that are not numeric.

Click on the small gray box with three dots to display a dialog box where we can label the variable, as shown in Figure P.5. To illustrate, we will label *day class* as 1 and *evening class* as 2 for our *stats* variable. To do this, enter *1* in the value box and *day class* in the label box, then click the **add** option. Follow these same instructions for the *evening class* label. When both labels have been entered, click **OK** to finish.

Missing. It is at times the case that some data researchers collect are missing. In these cases, you can enter a value that, when entered, means the data are missing. *99* is a common value used to represent missing data. To enter this value, click on the small gray box with three dots that appears to the right of the cell when you click in it. In the dialog box, it is most common to click on the second open circle and enter a *99* in the first cell. When this has been entered, click **OK** to finish. Now, whenever you enter *99* for that variable in the Data View spreadsheet, SPSS will recognize it as missing data.

Columns. The Columns column lets you identify how much room to allow for your data and labels. For example, the *stats* label is 5 letters long. If you go to the Data View spreadsheet, you will see *stats* as the column label. If you wrote *researchcourse* in the name column, then this would be too long because the column's default value is only 8. You can click the up and down arrows to increase or decrease how much room to allow for your column name label.

Align. The Align column allows you to choose where to align the data you enter. You can change this by selecting the dropdown menu that appears after clicking in the cell. The alignment options are right, left, and center. By default, numeric values are aligned to the right, and string values are aligned to the left.

Measure. This column allows you to select the scale of measurement for the variable (scales of measurement are introduced in Chapter 4). By default, all variables are considered scale (i.e., an interval or ratio scale of measurement). If your variable is an ordinal or nominal variable, you can make this change by selecting the dropdown menu that appears after clicking in the cell.

Role. The Role column is one that has been added in recent versions. The dropdown menu in the cell allows you to choose the following commands: input, target, both (input and target), none, partition, or split. Each of these options in the dropdown menu generally allows you to organize the entry and appearance of data in the Data View tab. Although each option is valuable, these are generally needed for data sets that we will not work with in this book.

P.2 Preview of SPSS in Focus

This book is unique in that you will learn how to use SPSS in the context of the research designs that require its use (this instruction is provided in the SPSS in Focus sections in many chapters). Most research methods textbooks omit this information, include it in an appendix separate from the main chapters in the book, or include it in ancillary materials that often are not included with course content. The reason SPSS is included in this book is simple: Most researchers use some kind of statistical software to analyze data, and in the social and behavioral sciences, the most common statistical software utilized by researchers is SPSS. So, this textbook brings research methods to the 21st century, giving you both the theoretical and the applicable instruction needed to understand how, when, and why to analyze data using appropriate technologies.

SCIENTIFIC INQUIRY

Identify a problem

- Determine an area of interest.
- Review the literature.
- Identify new ideas in your area of interest.
- Develop a research hypothesis.

Generate more new ideas

- Results support your hypothesis—refine or expand on your ideas.
- Results do not support your hypothesis—reformulate a new idea or start over.

Develop a research plan

- Define the variables being tested.
- Identify participants or subjects and determine how to sample them.
- Select a research strategy and design.
- Evaluate ethics and obtain institutional approval to conduct research.

After reading this chapter, you should be able to:

1 Define science and the scientific method.

2 Describe six steps for engaging in the scientific method.

3 Describe five nonscientific methods of acquiring knowledge.

4 Identify the four goals of science.

5 Distinguish between basic and applied research.

6 Distinguish between quantitative and qualitative research.

7 Delineate science from pseudoscience.

Communicate the results

- Method of communication: oral, written, or in a poster.
- Style of communication: APA guidelines are provided to help prepare style and format.

Conduct the study

- Execute the research plan and measure or record the data.

Analyze and evaluate the data

- Analyze and evaluate the data as they relate to the research hypothesis.
- Summarize data and research results.

chapter one

INTRODUCTION TO SCIENTIFIC THINKING

Are you curious about the world around you? Do you think that seeing is believing? When something seems too good to be true, are you critical of the claims? If you answered yes to any of these questions, the next step in your quest for knowledge is to learn about the methods used to understand events and behaviors—specifically, the methods used by scientists. Much of what you think you know is based on the methods that scientists use to answer questions.

For example, on a typical morning you may eat breakfast because it is "the most important meal of the day." If you drive to school, you may put away your cell phone because "it is unsafe to use cell phones while driving." At school you may attend an exam review session because "students are twice as likely to do well if they attend the session." In your downtime you may watch commercials or read articles that make sensational claims like "scientifically tested" and "clinically proven." At night you may try to get your "recommended 8 hours of sleep" so that you have the energy you need to start a new day. All of these decisions and experiences are related in one way or another to the science of human behavior.

This book reveals the scientific process, which will allow you to be a more critical consumer of knowledge, inasmuch as you will be able to critically review the methods that lead to the claims you come across each day. Understanding the various strengths and limitations of using science can empower you to make educated decisions and confidently negotiate the many supposed truths in nature. The idea here is that you do not need to be a scientist to appreciate what you learn in this book. *Science* is all around you—for this reason, being a critical consumer of the information you come across each day is useful and necessary across professions.

1.1 Science as a Method of Knowing

This book is a formal introduction to the scientific method. **Science** is one way of knowing about the world. The word *science* comes from the Latin *scientia*, meaning knowledge. From a broad view, science is any systematic method of acquiring knowledge apart from ignorance. From a stricter view, though, science is specifically the acquisition of knowledge using the **scientific method**, also called the **research method**.

Science is the acquisition of knowledge through observation, evaluation, interpretation, and theoretical explanation.

The **scientific method**, or **research method**, is a set of systematic techniques used to acquire, modify, and integrate knowledge concerning observable and measurable phenomena.

Science is one way of knowing about the world by making use of the scientific method to acquire knowledge.

To use the scientific method we make observations that can be measured. An observation can be direct or indirect. For example, we can directly observe how well a student performs on a test by counting the number of correct answers on the test. However, learning, for example, cannot be directly observed. We cannot "see" learning. Instead, we can indirectly observe learning by administering tests of knowledge before and after instruction, or by recording the number of correct responses when applying the knowledge to a new situation. In both cases, we indirectly observe learning by defining how we measure learning. The number of correct responses when applying the knowledge, for example, is not learning, but we can infer that more correct responses are associated with greater learning. Hence, we can make direct or indirect observations of behavior by defining how we exactly measure that behavior.

The scientific method requires the use of systematic techniques, many of which are introduced and discussed in this book. Each method or design comes with a specific set of assumptions and rules that make it *scientific*. Think of this as a game. A game, such as a card game or sport, only makes sense if players follow the rules. The rules, in essence, define the game. The scientific method is very much the same. It is defined by rules that scientists must follow, and this book is largely written to identify those rules for engaging in science. To begin this chapter, we introduce the scientific method and then introduce other nonscientific ways of knowing to distinguish them from the scientific method.

LEARNING CHECK 1 ✓

1. Define the scientific method.

2. Engaging in the scientific method is like a game. Explain.

Answers: 1. The scientific method is a set of systematic techniques used to acquire, modify, and integrate knowledge concerning observable and measurable phenomena; **2.** Science is defined by rules that all scientists must follow in the same way that all players must follow rules defined for a game or sport.

1.2 The Scientific Method

To engage in the scientific method, we need to organize the process we use to acquire knowledge. This section provides an overview of this process. The remainder of this book will elaborate on the details of this process. The scientific method is composed of six general steps, which are shown in Figure 1.1. The steps are:

Identify a problem

Develop a research plan

Conduct the study

Analyze and evaluate the data

Communicate the results

Generate more new ideas

Step 1: Identify a Problem

The research process begins when you identify the problem to be investigated, or a problem that can be resolved in some way by making observations. For example, Painter, Wansink, and Hieggelke (2002) found that placing candies in closer proximity to a participant (i.e., within arm's reach) increased the number of candies participants ate. From this study, Privitera and Creary (2013) identified a problem to be investigated. Specifically, they asked if it matters what you put in the bowl. For example, would placing a bowl of fruits or vegetables closer to participants show a similar result? This was the problem to be investigated that could be resolved by observing participants with a bowl of fruits and vegetables placed far versus near them.

In Step 1, we determine what to observe in a way that will allow us to answer questions about the problem we are investigating. In the behavioral sciences, we often investigate problems related to human behavior (e.g., drug abuse; diet and health factors; social, moral, political views), animal behavior (e.g., mating, predation, conditioning, foraging), or processes and mechanisms of behavior (e.g., cognition, learning and memory, consciousness, perceptions of time). Step 1 is discussed in greater detail in Chapter 2.

(1) DETERMINE AN AREA OF INTEREST.

The scientific process can take anywhere from a few days to a few years to complete, so it is important to select a topic of research that interests you. Certainly, you can identify one or more human behaviors that interest you.

(2) REVIEW THE LITERATURE.

The literature refers to the full database of scientific articles, most of which are now accessible using online search engines. Reviewing the scientific literature is important

Figure 1.1 The Six Steps of the Scientific Method

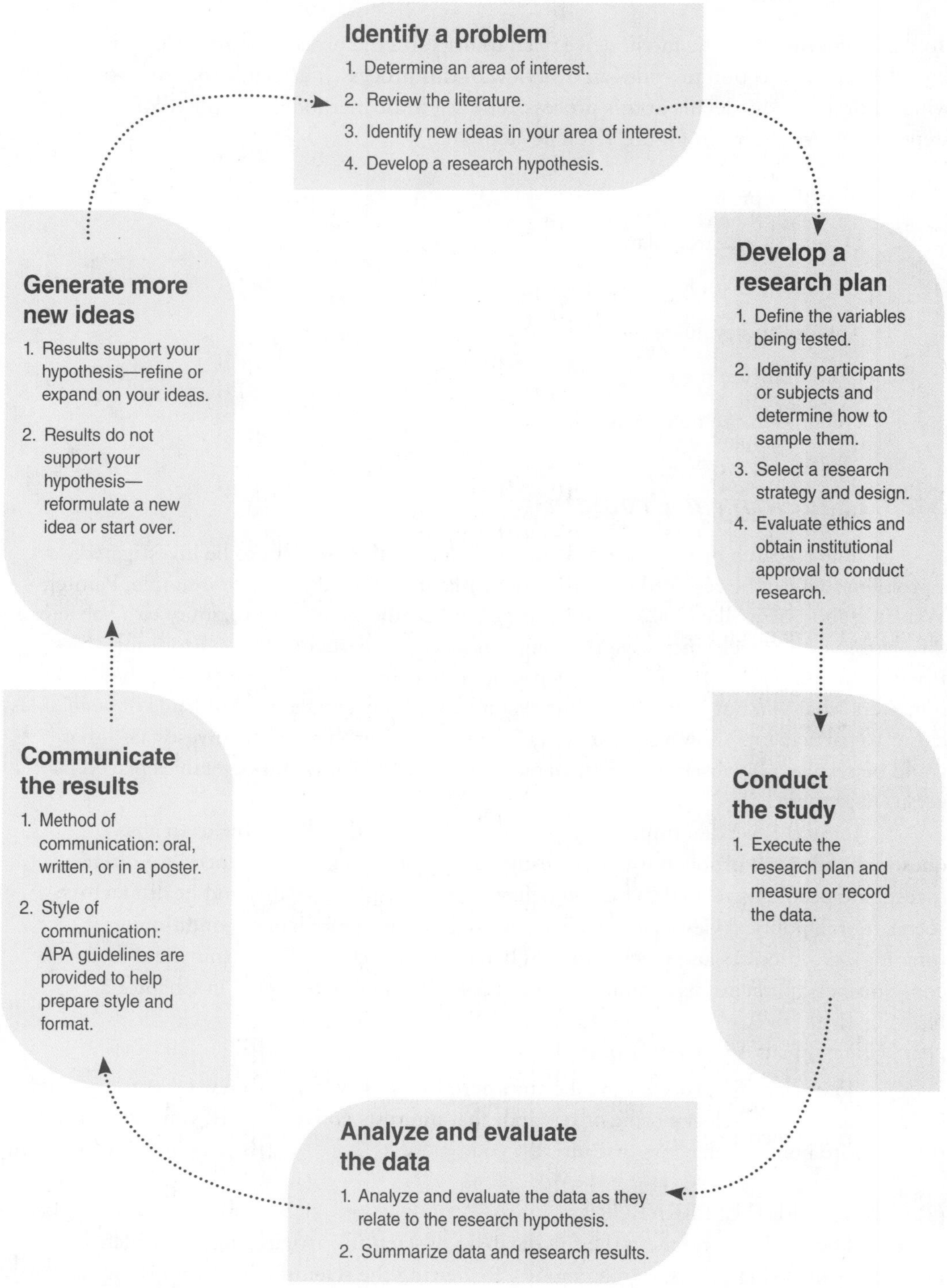

Identify a problem

1. Determine an area of interest.
2. Review the literature.
3. Identify new ideas in your area of interest.
4. Develop a research hypothesis.

Develop a research plan

1. Define the variables being tested.
2. Identify participants or subjects and determine how to sample them.
3. Select a research strategy and design.
4. Evaluate ethics and obtain institutional approval to conduct research.

Generate more new ideas

1. Results support your hypothesis—refine or expand on your ideas.
2. Results do not support your hypothesis—reformulate a new idea or start over.

Communicate the results

1. Method of communication: oral, written, or in a poster.
2. Style of communication: APA guidelines are provided to help prepare style and format.

Conduct the study

1. Execute the research plan and measure or record the data.

Analyze and evaluate the data

1. Analyze and evaluate the data as they relate to the research hypothesis.
2. Summarize data and research results.

because it allows you to identify what is known and what can still be learned about the behavior of interest to you. It will be difficult to identify a problem without first reviewing the literature.

(3) IDENTIFY NEW IDEAS IN YOUR AREA OF INTEREST.

Reviewing the literature allows you to identify new ideas that can be tested using the scientific method. The new ideas can then be restated as predictions or expectations based on what is known. For example, below are two outcomes identified in a literature review. From these outcomes we then identify a new (or *novel*) idea that is given as a statement of prediction, called a **research hypothesis**:

> A **research hypothesis** or **hypothesis** is a specific, testable claim or prediction about what you expect to observe given a set of circumstances.

> *Scientific Outcome 1:* Grade school children make food choices influenced by images on packaging.

> *Scientific Outcome 2:* Grade school children can readily understand expressions of emotion displayed as emoticons.

> *Research hypothesis:* Using emoticons on foods to indicate health (happy = healthy, sad = not healthy) will increase healthy food choices among grade school children.

(4) DEVELOP A RESEARCH HYPOTHESIS.

The research hypothesis is a specific, testable claim or prediction about what you expect to observe given a set of circumstances. We identified the research hypothesis that placing emoticons on food packaging to indicate health (happy = healthy, sad = not healthy) will increase healthy food choices among grade school children, similar to a hypothesis tested by Privitera, Phillips, Zuraikat, and Paque (2015)—we will revisit this study at the end of this section. In their study, they identified "healthy" foods as low-calorie foods (i.e., vegetables and fruits), so we will likewise use this criterion. We use Steps 2 to 6 of the scientific process to test this hypothesis. Note also that we used the literature review to develop our research hypothesis, which is why we must review the literature before stating a research hypothesis.

Step 2: Develop a Research Plan

Once a research hypothesis is stated, we need a plan to test that hypothesis. The development of a *research plan*, or a strategy for testing a research hypothesis, is needed to be able to complete Steps 3 and 4 of the scientific process. The chapters in Sections II, III, and IV of this book discuss Steps 2 to 4 in greater detail. Here, we will develop a research plan so that we can determine whether our hypothesis is likely to be correct or incorrect.

> To make a testable claim, or hypothesis, it is appropriate to then develop a plan to test that claim.

(1) DEFINE THE VARIABLES BEING TESTED.

A **variable**, or any value that can change or vary across observations, is typically measured as a number in science. The initial task in developing a research plan is to define or *operationalize* each variable stated in a research hypothesis in terms of how each variable is measured. The resulting definition is called an **operational definition**. For example, we can define the variable identified in the research hypothesis we developed: Placing emoticons on food packaging to indicate health (happy = healthy, sad = not healthy) will increase healthy food choices among grade school children.

In our research hypothesis, we state that healthy food choices will increase if emoticons are placed on the packaging. The term *choice*, however, is really a decision made when faced with two or more options. We need a way to measure this phenomenon in such a way that it is numeric and others could also observe or measure food choice in the same way. How we measure food choice will be the operational definition we use. The following are two ways we could measure or operationalize liking:

Operational Definition 1: The number of healthy/low-calorie food options chosen.

Operational Definition 2: The difference in the number of healthy foods chosen with vs. without the emoticons added.

To operationally define a variable, you define it in terms of how you will measure it.

Each operational definition clearly identifies how *choice* will be measured—either as a count (i.e., the number of healthy/low-calorie foods chosen) or as a difference (in choices made with vs. without emoticons). Both operational definitions make *choice* a suitable variable for scientific study because we identified how it will be objectively measured. We typically need to choose one operational definition, which can influence the type of study we conduct in Step 3.

MAKING SENSE—OBSERVATION AS A CRITERION FOR "SCIENTIFIC"

In science, only observable behaviors and events can be tested using the scientific method. Figure 1.2 shows the steps to determine whether a phenomenon can be tested using the scientific method. Notice in the figure that we must be able to observe and measure behaviors and events. Behaviors and events of interest (such as liking for a food) must be observable because we must make observations to conduct the study (Step 3). Behaviors and events must be measurable because we must analyze the observations we make in a study (Step 4)—and to analyze observations, we must have defined the specific way in which we measured those observations.

The scientific method provides a systematic way to test the claims of researchers by limiting science to only phenomena that can be observed and measured. In this way, we can ensure that the behaviors and events we study truly exist and can be observed or measured by others in the same way we observed them by defining our observations operationally.

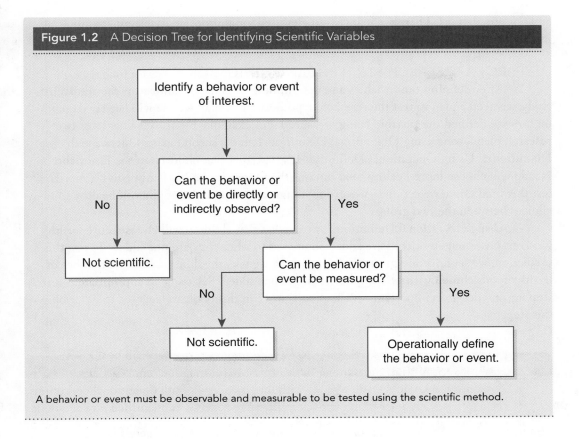

Figure 1.2 A Decision Tree for Identifying Scientific Variables

Identify a behavior or event of interest.

Can the behavior or event be directly or indirectly observed?

No → Not scientific.

Yes → Can the behavior or event be measured?

No → Not scientific.

Yes → Operationally define the behavior or event.

A behavior or event must be observable and measurable to be tested using the scientific method.

(2) IDENTIFY PARTICIPANTS OR SUBJECTS AND DETERMINE HOW TO SAMPLE THEM.

Next we need to consider the population of interest, which is the group that is the subject of our hypothesis. A **population** can be any group of interest. In our research hypothesis, we identify how grade school children make food choices (by using images on the foods). The population of interest to us, then, is grade school children. We need to define this population further so that we can define the exact group of children of interest to us. For example, we could define this group by an age range. In this case, we can define the population as children between 5 and 11 years of age, which is roughly kindergarten through fifth grade in U.S. schools.

Of course, we cannot readily observe every 5- to 11-year-old child. For this reason, we need to identify a sample of 5- to 11-year-old children that we will actually observe in our study. A **sample** is a subset or portion of individuals selected from the larger group of interest. Observing samples instead of entire populations is more realistic. It also requires less time, money, and resources than observing entire populations. Indeed, most scientific research is conducted with samples,

A **population** is a set of *all* individuals, items, or data of interest about which scientists will generalize.

A **sample** is a set of *selected* individuals, items, or data taken from a population of interest.

and not populations. There are many strategies used for appropriately selecting samples, as introduced in Chapter 5.

(3) SELECT A RESEARCH STRATEGY AND DESIGN.

After defining the variables and determining the type of sample for the research study, we need a plan to test the research hypothesis. The plan we use will largely depend on how we defined the variable being measured. For example, Figure 1.3 illustrates two research plans—one using Operational Definition 1, and a second using Operational Definition 2. Using Operational Definition 1, we predict that children in the Emoticon Group will choose more healthy food options than those in the No Emoticon Group. To test this prediction, we set up a two-group design to compare the number of healthy food choices between the two groups.

Using Operational Definition 2, we predict that children will choose more healthy food options when emoticons are added compared to when they are not added. To test this prediction, we set up a one-group design in which we take the difference in the number of healthy foods chosen with vs. without the emoticons added. Selecting an appropriate research strategy and design is important, so Chapters 6 to 12 in this book are devoted to describing this step.

Figure 1.3 Two Research Plans to Test the Same Hypothesis

Research Plan 1 (Two-group study)

Groups:	*Emoticons Group:* Children choose foods from a list with emoticons added to inform them about health. vs.	*No Emoticons Group:* Children choose foods from a list without emoticons added to inform them about health.
Measurements:	Operational Definition 1: The number of healthy/low-calorie food options chosen.	
Prediction from research hypothesis:	Children in the Emoticon Group will choose more healthy food options than those in the No Emoticon Group.	

Research Plan 2 (One-group study)

Groups:	*Choice Group:* Children are shown two identical lists of foods, one with and one without emoticons added to inform them about health.
Measurements:	Operational Definition 2: The difference in the number of healthy/low-calorie foods chosen with vs. without the emoticons added.
Prediction from research hypothesis:	More healthy food options will be chosen with versus without emoticons added to inform the children about health.

Two ways that scientists could design a study to test the same research hypothesis. The type of design we implement influences how the dependent variable will be defined and measured.

(4) EVALUATE ETHICS AND OBTAIN INSTITUTIONAL APPROVAL TO CONDUCT RESEARCH.

While a research design can be used to test a hypothesis, it is always important to make considerations for how you plan to treat participants in a research study. It is not acceptable to use unethical procedures to test a hypothesis. For example, we cannot force children to choose any foods. Hence, participation in a study must be voluntary. Because the ethical treatment of participants can often be difficult to assess, research institutions have created ethics committees to which a researcher submits a proposal that describes how participants will be treated in a study. Upon approval from such a committee, a researcher can then conduct his or her study. Because ethics is so important to the research process, this topic is covered in the Ethics in Focus sections in subsequent chapters, and it is also specifically described in detail in Chapter 3.

LEARNING CHECK 2 ✓

1. What three tasks should a researcher perform before stating a research hypothesis?

2. A researcher studying attention measured the time (in seconds) that students spent working continuously on some task. Longer times indicated greater attention. In this study, what is the variable being measured, and what is the operational definition for the variable?

3. A psychologist wants to study a small population of 40 students in a local private school. If the researcher is interested in selecting the entire population of students for this study, then how many students must the psychologist include?

   A. None, because it is not possible to study an entire population in this case.

   B. At least half, because 21 or more students would constitute most of the population.

   C. All 40 students, because all students constitute the population.

Answers: 1. Determine an area of interest, review the literature, and identify new ideas in your area of interest; 2. Variable measured: Attention, Operational definition: Time (in seconds) spent continuously working on some task; 3. C.

Step 3: Conduct the Study

The goal of Step 3 is to execute a research plan by actually conducting the study. In Step 2, we developed a plan that led to two ways we could conduct a study to test our hypothesis, as illustrated in Figure 1.3. Now we pick one. In other words, we will execute only one of the plans shown in Figure 1.3. For example, let us execute Research Plan 2. Using this plan, we would select a sample of 5- to 11-year-old children, show the children an identical list of foods (one with and one without emoticons added), and record the difference in the number of healthy foods chosen between the two lists. By doing so, we have conducted the study.

Step 4: *Analyze and Evaluate the Data*

(1) ANALYZE AND EVALUATE THE DATA AS
THEY RELATE TO THE RESEARCH HYPOTHESIS.

Data are typically analyzed in numeric units, such as the counts we analyzed for Research Plan 2 (i.e., the difference in the number of healthy foods chosen between the two lists). In Step 4, we analyze the data to specifically determine if the pattern of data we observed in our study shows support for the research hypothesis. In Research Plan 2, we start by assuming that there will be 0 difference in healthy food choices between the two lists if emoticons do not influence food choice, and then we test this assumption. To make this test, we make use of *statistics*, which will be introduced throughout this book to provide a more complete understanding of how researchers make decisions using the scientific method.

> Evaluating data, typically using statistical analysis, allows researchers to draw conclusions from the data they observe.

(2) SUMMARIZE DATA AND REPORT THE RESEARCH RESULTS.

Once the data are evaluated and analyzed, we need to concisely report the data. Data are often reported in tables, or graphically as shown in Figure 1.4 later on this chapter. Also, statistical outcomes are reported by specifically using guidelines identified by the American Psychological Association (APA). The exposition of data and the reporting of statistical analyses are described throughout the book beginning in Chapter 5 and also specifically reviewed in Chapters 13 and 14.

> **Data** (plural) are measurements or observations that are typically numeric. A **datum** (singular) is a single measurement or observation, usually called a **score** or **raw score**.

Step 5: *Communicate the Results*

To share the results of a study, we must decide how to make our work available to others, as identified by the APA.

(1) METHOD OF COMMUNICATION.

Communicating your work allows other professionals to review your work to learn about what you did, test whether they can replicate your results, or use your study to generate their own new ideas and hypotheses. The most typical ways of sharing the results of a study are orally, in written form, or as a poster.

Oral and poster presentations are often given at professional conferences, such as national conferences held by the APA, the Society for Neuroscience, and the Association for Psychological Science. The strongest method for communication, however, is through publication in a peer-reviewed journal. To publish in these journals, researchers describe their studies in a manuscript and have it reviewed by their peers (i.e., other professionals in their field of study). Only after their peers agree that their study reflects high-quality scientific research can they publish their manuscript in the journal. Chapter 15 provides guidelines for writing manuscripts using APA style, as well as for writing posters and giving talks. Several examples of posters and an APA manuscript that has been published are given in Appendix A.

(2) STYLE OF COMMUNICATION.

Written research reports often must conform to the style and formatting guidelines provided in the *Publication Manual of the American Psychological Association* (APA, 2009), also called the *Publication Manual*. The *Publication Manual* is a comprehensive guide for using ethics and reducing bias, writing manuscripts and research reports, and understanding the publication process. It is essential that you refer to this manual when choosing a method of communication. After all, most psychologists and many scientists across the behavioral sciences follow these guidelines.

For our research hypothesis, we chose Research Plan 2. Privitera et al. (2015) also used a plan similar to Research Plan 2 except that children in their study chose from actual foods displayed on shelves, and not from a list of choices. These researchers published their results in the peer-reviewed journal *Appetite*. Their results, a portion of which are shown in Figure 1.4, show support for the hypothesis—children at each grade level chose more healthy/low-calorie food options with versus without emoticons on the food packaging. The researchers call this strategy *emolabeling*, and it is one of the first efforts to develop a strategy that can effectively communicate information about health (and influence healthy food choices) to early literacy children.

Step 6: *Generate More New Ideas*

When your study is complete, you can publish your work and allow other researchers the opportunity to review and evaluate your findings. You have also learned something from

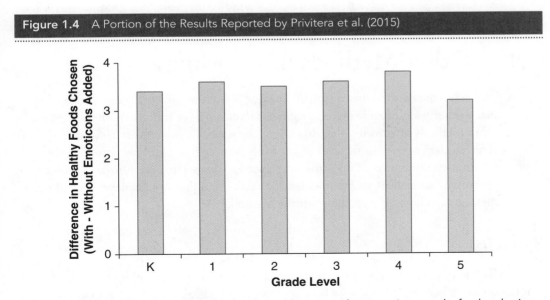

Figure 1.4 A Portion of the Results Reported by Privitera et al. (2015)

Children chose more healthy/low-calorie food options with versus without emoticons on the food packaging at each grade level. The healthy/low-calorie foods were fruits and vegetables; the less healthy/high-calorie foods were cakes, cookies, and chips. The results are adapted from those reported by Privitera, Phillips, Zuraikat, and Paque (2015).

your work. If you found support for your research hypothesis, you can use it to refine and expand on existing knowledge. If the results do not support your research hypothesis, then you propose a new idea and begin again.

Steps 1 to 6 of the scientific process are cyclic, not linear, meaning that even when a study answers a question, this usually leads to more questions and more testing. For this reason, Step 6 typically leads back to Step 1, and we begin again. More importantly, it allows other researchers to refute scientific claims, and question what we think we know. It allows researchers to ask, "If your claim is correct, then we should also observe this," or "If your claim is correct, then this should not be observed." A subsequent study would then allow other researchers to determine how confident we can be about what we think we know of that particular behavior or event of interest.

LEARNING CHECK 3 ✓

1. A researcher measures the following weights of four animal subjects (in grams): 90, 95, 80, and 100. An individual weight is referred to as a _____, whereas all weights are referred to as _____.

2. State three methods of communication. What style of communication is used in psychology and much of the behavioral sciences?

Answers: 1. datum, data; 2. Oral, written, and as a poster. APA style is used in psychology and much of the behavioral sciences.

1.3 Other Methods of Knowing

The scientific method is one way of knowing about the world. There are also many other ways of knowing, and each has its advantages and disadvantages. Five other methods of knowing that do not use the scientific process are collectively referred to as nonscientific ways of knowing. Although not an exhaustive list, the five nonscientific ways of knowing introduced in this section are tenacity, intuition, authority, rationalism, and empiricism. Keep in mind that at some level each of these methods can be used with the scientific method.

The scientific process is cyclic, not linear; it is open to criticism and review.

Tenacity

Tenacity is a method of knowing based largely on habit or superstition; it is a belief that exists simply because it has always been accepted. Advertising companies, for example, use this method by creating catchphrases such as Budweiser's slogan "King of Beers," Nike's slogan "Just Do It," or Geico's much longer slogan "15 minutes could save you 15% or more on car

Tenacity is a method of knowing based largely on habit or superstition.

insurance." In each case, tenacity was used to gauge public belief in a company's product or service. A belief in superstitions, such as finding a penny heads up bringing good luck, or a black cat crossing your path being bad luck, also reflects tenacity. Tenacity may also reflect tradition. The 9-month school calendar providing a 3-month summer vacation originated in the late 1800s to meet the needs of communities at the time (mostly due to heat, not farming). While the needs of our society have changed, the school calendar has not. The key disadvantage of using tenacity, however, is that the knowledge acquired can often be inaccurate, partly because tenacity is mostly assumed knowledge. Hence, there is no basis in fact for beliefs using tenacity.

Intuition

Intuition is an individual's subjective hunch or feeling that something is correct. Intuition is sometimes used synonymously with instincts. For example, stock traders said to have great instincts

> **Intuition** is a method of knowing based largely on an individual's hunch or feeling that something is correct.

may use their intuition to purchase a stock that then increases in value, or gamblers said to have great instincts may use their intuition to place a bet that then wins. Parents often use their intuition when they suspect their child is getting into trouble at school, or students may use their intuition to choose a major that best fits their interests. The disadvantage of using intuition as a sole method of knowing is that there is no definitive basis for the belief. Hence, without acting on the intuition, it is difficult to determine its accuracy.

Intuition also has some value in science in that researchers can use their intuition to some extent when they develop a research hypothesis, particularly when there is little to no information available concerning their area of interest. In science, however, the researchers' intuition is then tested using the scientific method. Keep in mind that we use the scientific method to differentiate between hypotheses that do and do not accurately describe phenomena, regardless of how we initially developed our hypotheses. Hence, it is the scientific method, and not intuition, that ultimately determines what we know in science.

Authority

Authority is knowledge accepted as fact because it was stated by an expert or respected source in a particular subject area. In faith-based practices, it is the Bible, the Koran, the Torah, or another text that is the authority in a given faith-based practice.

> **Authority** is a method of knowing accepted as fact because it was stated by an expert or respected source in a particular subject area.

Preachers, pastors, rabbis, and other religious leaders teach about God using the authority of those texts, and the teachings in those texts are accepted based solely on the authority of those texts. Education agencies such as the National Education Association often lobby for regulations that many educators will trust as benefiting them without reviewing in detail the policies being lobbied for. As another example, the U.S. Food and Drug Administration (FDA) was the second most trusted government agency behind only the Supreme Court around the turn of the 21st century (Hadfield, Howse, & Trebilcock, 1998), and the FDA likewise makes policy decisions that many Americans trust without detailed vetting. The disadvantage of using authority as a sole method of knowing is that, in many cases, there is little effort to challenge this type of knowledge, often leaving authoritative knowledge unchecked.

Like intuition, authority has value in science. Einstein's general theory of relativity, for example, requires an understanding of mathematics shared by perhaps a few hundred scientists. The rest of us simply accept this theory as accurate based on the authority of the few scientists who tell us it is. Likewise, many scientists will selectively submit their research for publication in only the most authoritative journals—those with a reputation for being the most selective and publishing only the highest-quality research compared to other presumably less selective journals. In this way, authority is certainly valued to some extent in the scientific community.

Rationalism

Rationalism is any source of knowledge that requires the use of reasoning or logic. Rationalism is often used to understand human behavior. For example, if a spouse is unfaithful to a partner, the partner may reason that the spouse does not love him or her; if a student receives a poor grade on a homework assignment, the professor may reason that the student did not put much effort into the assignment. Here, the spouse and professor rationalized the meaning of a behavior they observed—and in both cases they could be wrong. This is a disadvantage of using rationalism as a sole method of knowing, in that it often leads to erroneous conclusions.

> **Rationalism** is a method of knowing that requires the use of reasoning and logic.

Even some of the most rational ideas can be wrong. For example, it would be completely rational to believe that heavier objects fall at a faster rate than lighter objects. This was, in fact, the rational explanation for falling objects prior to the mid-1500s until Galileo Galilei proposed a theory and showed evidence that refuted this view.

Rationalism certainly has some value in science as well inasmuch as researchers can use rationalism to develop their research hypotheses—in fact, we used reasoning to develop our research hypothesis about food packaging. Still, all research hypotheses are tested using the scientific method, so it is the scientific method that ultimately sorts out the rationally sound from the rationally flawed hypotheses.

Empiricism

Empiricism is knowledge acquired through observation. This method of knowing reflects the adage "seeing is believing." While making observations is essential when using the scientific method, it can be biased when used apart from the scientific method. In other words, not everyone experiences or observes the world in the same way—from this view, empiricism alone is fundamentally flawed. One way that the scientific method handles this problem is to ensure that all variables observed in a study are *operationally defined*—defined in terms of how the observed variable is measured such that other researchers could observe that variable in the same way. An operational definition has the advantage of being more objective because it states exactly how the variable was observed or measured.

> **Empiricism** is a method of knowing based on one's experiences or observations.

There are many factors that bias our perception of the behaviors and events we observe. The first among them is the fact that human perception can be biased. To illustrate, Figure 1.5 depicts the Poggendorff illusion, named after the physicist who discovered it in a drawing published by German astrophysicist Johann Zöllner in 1860. The rectangles in Parts A and B are the same, except that the rectangle in Part A is not transparent. The lines going through the rectangle in Part A appear to be continuous, but this is an illusion. Viewing them through the transparent rectangle, we observe at once that they are not. There are many instances in which we do not see the world as it really is, many of which we still may not recognize or fully understand.

Figure 1.5   The Poggendorff Illusion

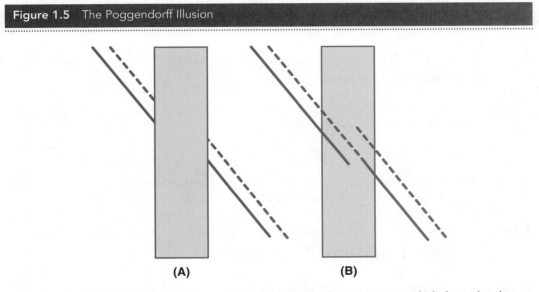

(A)   **(B)**

In Part A, both lines appear to be continuous. In Part B, the rectangle is transparent, which shows that the lines are, in fact, not continuous.

Human memory is also inherently biased. Many people are prone to forgetting and to inaccurate recollections. Memory is not a bank of recordings to be replayed; rather, it is a collection of representations for the behaviors and events we observe. Memory is an active process, and you are unlikely to accurately recall what you observed unless you make a conscious effort to do so. If you have ever entered a room and forgot why you wanted to go there in the first place, or you forgot someone's name only minutes (often seconds) after being introduced, then you have experienced some of the vagaries of memory. Many factors influence what we attend to and remember, and many of these factors work against our efforts to make accurate observations.

In all, tenacity, intuition, authority, rationalism, and empiricism are called the nonscientific methods of knowing. While some of these methods may be used during the scientific process, they are only used in conjunction with the scientific method. Using the scientific method ultimately ensures that only the most accurate hypotheses emerge from the observations we make.

The nonscientific ways of knowing are ways of acquiring knowledge that are commonly applied but not based in science.

1. State the five nonscientific methods of knowing.

2. State the method of knowing illustrated in each of these examples.

   A. Your friend tells you that he likes fried foods because he saw someone enjoying them at a buffet.

   B. You close up the store at exactly midnight because that is when the store always closes.

   C. A teacher states that students do not care about being in school because they are not paying attention in class.

   D. Your mother locks up all of the alcohol in the house because she has a feeling you may throw a party while she is at work.

   E. You believe that if you do not read your textbook you will fail your research methods class because your professor said so.

Answers: 1. The five methods of knowing are tenacity, intuition, authority, rationalism, and empiricism; 2. A. empiricism, B. tenacity, C. rationalism, D. intuition, E. authority.

1.4   The Goals of Science

Many people will seek only as much knowledge as they feel will satisfy their curiosity. For instance, people may conclude that they know about love because they have experienced it themselves (empiricism) or listened to stories that others tell about their experiences with love (authority). Yet science is a stricter way of knowing about the world. In science, we do not make observations for the sake of making observations. Instead we make observations with the ultimate goal to describe, explain, predict, and control the behaviors and events we observe. Each goal is described in this section and listed in Table 1.1.

Describe

To understand the behaviors and events we study, we must describe or define them. Often, these descriptions are in the literature. We can even find descriptions for behaviors and events quite by accident, particularly for those that are not yet described in the literature or not fully understood. For example, a young boy named John Garcia had his first taste of licorice when he was 10 years old. Hours later he became ill with the flu. Afterward, he no longer liked the taste of licorice, although he was fully aware that the licorice did not cause his illness. As a scientist, Garcia tried to describe his experience, which eventually led him to conduct a landmark study showing the first scientific evidence that we learn to dislike tastes

Table 1.1 The Four Goals of Science

Goal	Question asked to meet the goal
Describe	What is the behavior or event?
Explain	What are the causes of the behavior or event?
Predict	Can we anticipate when the behavior or event will occur in the future?
Control	Can we manipulate the conditions necessary to make a behavior or event occur and not occur?

associated with illness, known as *taste aversion learning* (Garcia, Kimeldorf, & Koelling, 1955). Scientific knowledge begins by describing the behaviors and events we study, even if that description originates from a childhood experience.

Explain

To understand the behaviors and events we study, we must also identify the conditions within which they operate. In other words, we identify what causes a behavior or event to occur. Identifying cause can be a challenging goal in that human behavior is complex and often caused by many factors in different situations. Suppose, for example, that we want to understand what makes people view someone as being *competent*, which we describe as the ability to successfully master some task or action. Some obvious causes for being viewed as competent are someone's rank or position at work, and education and income level. Less obvious, though, is that an individual will be viewed as more competent if he or she is simply more attractive (see Langlois et al., 2000). Imagine now how many less obvious factors exist but have not yet been considered. Explaining behavior is a cautious goal in science because there are so many variables to consider.

Predict

Once we can describe and explain a particular behavior or event, we can use that knowledge to predict when it will occur in the future. Knowing how to predict behavior can be quite useful. For example, if a parent wants a child to take a long nap, the parent may take the child to the park for an hour before naptime to tire the child out. In this case, the parent predicts that greater activity increases sleepiness (for review, see Horne, 1988). However, as with most behaviors, sleep is caused by many factors, so parents often find that this strategy does not always work. Predicting behavior, then, can be challenging because to predict when a behavior will occur depends on our ability to isolate the causes of that behavior.

Control

The central, and often most essential, goal for a scientist is control. Control means that we can make a behavior occur and not occur. To establish control, we must be able to describe the behavior, explain the causes, and predict when it will occur and not occur. Hence, control is only possible once the first three goals of science are met.

The ability to control behavior is important because it allows psychologists to implement interventions that can help people improve their quality of life and establish control over aspects of their lives that are problematic. Levitt, Malta, Martin, Davis, and Cloitre (2007), for example, used their knowledge of a variety of factors related to symptoms of depression and post-traumatic stress disorder (PTSD) to implement a behavioral therapy that reduced symptoms of depression and PTSD among 9/11 survivors. As another example, Maynard, Kjellstrand, and Thompson (2014) used their knowledge of a variety of factors related to school completion and drop-out prevention to implement a program for middle and high school students at risk for dropping out of school. Their work found that monitoring school attendance, disciplinary referrals, and academic performance and building relationships with students to problem-solve these issues led to greater academic achievement and attendance and a decrease in disciplinary referrals. Hence, the intervention allowed students to control their academic performance by controlling the factors related to their previous poor academic performance. Control, then, is a powerful goal of science because it means that researchers are able to establish some control over the behaviors that they study.

> The four goals of science serve to direct scientists toward a comprehensive knowledge of the behaviors and events they observe.

LEARNING CHECK 5 ✓

1. State the four goals of science.

2. If researchers can make a behavior occur and not occur, then which goal of science have they met?

Answers: 1. Describe, explain, predict, control; 2. Control.

1.5 Approaches in Acquiring Knowledge

There are many approaches that lead to different levels of understanding of the behaviors and events we study using the scientific method. In this section we introduce research that is basic or applied, and research that is qualitative or quantitative.

Basic and Applied Research

> Basic research uses the scientific method to answer questions that address theoretical issues about fundamental processes and underlying mechanisms related to the behaviors and events being studied.

Basic research is an approach where researchers aim to understand the nature of behavior. Basic research is used to answer fundamental questions that address theoretical issues, typically regarding the mechanisms and processes of behavior. Whether there are practical applications for the outcomes in basic research is not as important as whether the research builds upon existing theory. Basic research is used to study many aspects of behavior such as the influence of biology, cognition, learning, memory, consciousness, and development on behavior.

Applied research, on the other hand, is an approach in which researchers aim to answer questions concerning practical problems that require practical solutions. Topics of interest in applied research include issues related to obesity and health, traffic laws and safety, behavioral disorders, and drug addiction. In the classroom, for example, applied research seeks to answer questions about educational practice that can be generalized

> **Applied research** uses the scientific method to answer questions concerning practical problems with potential practical solutions.

across educational settings. Examples of educational applied research include implementing different instructional strategies, character development, parental involvement, and classroom management. Researchers who conduct applied research focus on problems with immediate practical implications in order to apply their findings to problems that have the potential for immediate action.

While basic and applied research are very different in terms of the focus of study, we can use what is learned in theory (basic research) and apply it to practical situations (applied research), or we can test how practical solutions to a problem (applied research) fit with the theories we use to explain that problem (basic research). As an example, basic research using rats to test learning theories in the 1970s showed that adding sugar to a flavored drink increased how much the rats would consume of the flavor subsequently given without the added sugar (Holman, 1975). A similar result was shown with preschool-aged children in an applied research study in which researchers showed that adding sugar to grapefruit juice a few times enhanced liking for the grapefruit juice, even when it was subsequently consumed without the added sugar (Capaldi & Privitera, 2008; Privitera, 2008a). The applied research study in 2008, which was developed from basic research studies over 30 years earlier, proposed immediate solutions that could be applied to strategies for enhancing how much children like consuming low-sugar drinks.

Qualitative and Quantitative Research

Quantitative research uses the scientific method to record observations as numeric data. Most scientific research in the social sciences is quantitative because the data are numeric, allowing for a more objective analysis of the observations

> **Quantitative research** uses the scientific method to record observations as numeric data. Most research conducted in the behavioral sciences is quantitative.

made in a study. Researchers, for example, may define *mastery* as the time (in seconds) it takes to complete a presumably difficult task. By defining mastery in seconds (a numeric value), the analysis is more objective—other researchers can readily measure mastery in the same way. Numeric values can also be readily entered into statistical formulas, from which researchers can obtain measurable results. Statistical analysis is not possible without numeric data.

Qualitative research uses the scientific method to make nonnumeric observations, from which conclusions are drawn without the use of statistical analysis.

Qualitative research is different from quantitative research in that qualitative research does not include the measurement of numeric data. Instead, observations are made, from which conclusions are drawn. The goal in qualitative research is to describe, interpret, and explain the behaviors or events being studied. As an example, a qualitative researcher studying attraction may interview a small group of participants about their experiences with attraction. Each participant is allowed to respond however he or she wants. From this, the researcher will look at how the participants described attraction in order to interpret and explain what attraction is. Whereas in quantitative research the researcher defines the variable of interest (e.g., attraction) and then makes observations to measure that variable, in qualitative research the participants describe the variable of interest, from which researchers interpret and explain that variable.

Quantitative and qualitative research can be effectively used to study the same behaviors, so both types of research have value. For example, quantitative research can be used to determine how often and for how long (in minutes, on average) students study for an exam, whereas qualitative research can be used to characterize their study habits in terms of what they study, why they study it, and how they study. Each observation gives the researcher a bigger picture of how to characterize studying among students. In this way, both types of research can be effectively used to gauge a better understanding of the behaviors and events we observe.

1.6 Distinguishing Science From Pseudoscience

Throughout this book, you will be introduced to the scientific process, the general steps for which were elaborated in this chapter. As is evident as you read further, science requires that a set of systematic techniques be followed to acquire knowledge. However, sometimes knowledge can be presented as if it is scientific, yet it is nonscience, often referred to as *pseudoscience*; that being said, all nonscience is not pseudoscience (Hansson, 2015; Mahner, 2007).

The term **pseudoscience** is not to be confused with other terms often inappropriately used as synonyms, which include "unscientific" and "nonscientific." A key feature of pseudoscience is intent to deceive: it is nonscience posing as science (Gardner, 1957; Hansson, 2015). For example, there are ways of knowing that do not at all purport to be based in science, such as those described in Section 1.3 in this chapter. These are not pseudoscience. As another example, an individual may engage in science, but the science itself is incorrect or rather poorly conducted (e.g., the individual misinterprets an observation or runs a careless experiment). Even if the "bad" science is intentional or fraudulent, "bad" science is rarely called pseudoscience. Therefore, to clarify we can adopt two criteria here to define pseudoscience that delineates it as a narrower concept, adapted from Gardner (1957) and Hansson (2015):

1. it is not scientific, and

2. it is part of a system or set of beliefs that try to deceptively create the impression that the knowledge gained represents the "final say" or most reliable knowledge on its subject matter.

> **Pseudoscience** is a set of procedures that are not scientific, and it is part of a system or set of beliefs that try to deceptively create the impression that the knowledge gained represents the "final say" or most reliable knowledge on its subject matter.

As an example to illustrate, consider the following three scenarios:

Scenario 1: A psychologist performs a study and unknowingly analyzes the data incorrectly, then reports erroneous conclusions that are incorrect because of his or her mistake.

Scenario 2: A psychologist makes a series of impromptu observations, then constructs an explanation for the observations made as if his or her conclusions were scientific.

Scenario 3: A psychologist reports that he or she has a personal belief and faith in God, and believes that such faith is important.

> Pseudoscience is often described as nonscience that looks like science, but it is not.

In the cases above, only Scenario 2 meets the criteria for pseudoscience in that it is not scientific, and the psychologist tries to deceivingly leave the impression that his or her conclusions have scientific legitimacy, when they do not. Scenario 1 is a basic case of "bad" science, and Scenario 3 is simply a nonscientific way of knowing—there was no intent to give the impression that such faith is rooted in science. Being able to delineate science from pseudoscience can be difficult, and the demarcation between science and pseudoscience is often a subject of debate among philosophers and scientists alike. The examples given in this section provide some context for thinking about science versus pseudoscience, which should prove helpful as you read about science in this book.

LEARNING CHECK 6 ✓

1. Distinguish between basic and applied research.

2. What is the difference between quantitative and qualitative research?

3. Identify if the following is an example of pseudoscience; explain: A psychologist makes a series of observations while in a waiting room, then constructs an explanation for his observations as if his conclusions were scientific.

Answers: 1. Basic research is used to address theoretical questions regarding the mechanisms and processes of behavior, whereas applied research is used to address questions that can lead to immediate solutions to practical problems; 2. In quantitative research, all variables are measured numerically, whereas qualitative research is purely descriptive (variables are not measured numerically); 3. It is an example of pseudoscience because it is not scientific (i.e., there are no systematic procedures followed), and he tries to deceivingly leave the impression that his conclusions are scientific, when they are not.

LO 1 Define science and the scientific method.

- **Science** is the acquisition of knowledge through observation, evaluation, interpretation, and theoretical explanation.
- Science is specifically the acquisition of knowledge using the **scientific method**, which requires the use of systematic techniques, each of which comes with a specific set of assumptions and rules that make it *scientific*.

LO 2 Describe six steps for engaging in the scientific method.

- The scientific process consists of six steps:

  Step 1: Identify a problem: Determine an area of interest, review the literature, identify new ideas in your area of interest, and develop a research hypothesis.

  Step 2: Develop a research plan: Define the variables being tested, identify participants or subjects and determine how to sample them, select a research strategy and design, and evaluate ethics and obtain institutional approval to conduct research.

  Step 3: Conduct the study. Execute the research plan and measure or record the data.

  Step 4: Analyze and evaluate the data. Analyze and evaluate the data as they relate to the research hypothesis, and summarize data and research results.

  Step 5: Communicate the results. Results can be communicated orally, in written form, or as a poster. The styles of communication follow standards identified by the APA.

  Step 6: Generate more new ideas. Refine or expand the original hypothesis, reformulate a new hypothesis, or start over.

LO 3 Describe five nonscientific methods of acquiring knowledge.

- **Tenacity** is a method of knowing based largely on habit or superstition. A disadvantage of tenacity is that the knowledge acquired is often inaccurate.
- **Intuition** is a method of knowing based largely on an individual's hunch or feeling that something is correct. A disadvantage of intuition is that the only way to determine the accuracy of an intuition is to act on that belief.
- **Authority** is a method of knowing accepted as fact because it was stated by an expert or respected source in a particular subject area. A disadvantage of authority is that there is typically little effort to challenge an authority, leaving authoritative knowledge largely unchecked.
- **Rationalism** is a method of knowing that requires the use of reasoning and logic. A disadvantage of rationalism is that it often leads to erroneous conclusions.

- **Empiricism** is a method of knowing based on one's experiences or observations. Disadvantages of empiricism are that not everyone experiences or observes the world in the same way, perception is often illusory, and memory is inherently biased.

LO 4 Identify the four goals of science.

- The four goals of science are to **describe** or define the variables we observe and measure, **explain** the causes of a behavior or event, **predict** when a behavior or event will occur in the future, and **control** or manipulate conditions in such a way as to make a behavior occur and not occur.

LO 5–6 Distinguish between basic and applied research, and between quantitative and qualitative research.

- **Basic research** uses the scientific method to answer questions that address theoretical issues about fundamental processes and underlying mechanisms related to the behaviors and events being studied. **Applied research** uses the scientific method to answer questions concerning practical problems with potential practical solutions.
- **Quantitative research** is most commonly used in the behavioral sciences and uses the scientific method to record observations as numeric data. **Qualitative research** uses the scientific method to make nonnumeric observations, from which conclusions are drawn without the use of statistical analysis.

LO 7 Delineate science from pseudoscience.

- **Pseudoscience** is a set of procedures that are not scientific, and it is part of a system or set of beliefs that try to deceptively create the impression that the knowledge gained represents the "final say" or most reliable knowledge on its subject matter.
- Being able to delineate science from pseudoscience can be difficult, and the demarcation between science and pseudoscience is still a subject of debate among philosophers and scientists alike.

KEY TERMS

science

scientific method or
  research method

research hypothesis or
  hypothesis

variable

operational definition

population

sample

data or datum

score or raw score

tenacity

intuition

authority

rationalism

empiricism

basic research

applied research

quantitative research

qualitative research

pseudoscience

1. Science can be any systematic method of acquiring knowledge apart from ignorance. What method makes science a unique approach to acquire knowledge? Define that method.

2. The scientific method includes a series of assumptions or rules that must be followed. Using the analogy of a game (given in this chapter), explain why this is important.

3. State the six steps for using the scientific method.

4. A researcher reviews the literature and finds that taller men earn greater incomes than shorter men. From this review he hypothesizes that taller men are more intelligent than shorter men. What method of knowing did he use to develop this hypothesis? Which method of knowing is used to determine whether this hypothesis is likely correct or incorrect?

5. A social psychologist records the number of outbursts in a sample of different classrooms at a local school. In this example, what is the operational definition for classroom interruptions?

6. Identify the sample and the population in this statement: A research methods class has 25 students enrolled, but only 23 students attended class.

7. True or false: Samples can be larger than the population from which they were selected. Explain your answer.

8. A friend asks you what science is. After you answer her question she asks how you knew that, and you reply that it was written in a textbook. What method of knowing did you use to describe science to your friend? Define it.

9. You go out to eat at a restaurant with friends and have the most delicious meal. From this experience, you decide to go to that restaurant again because the food is delicious. What method of knowing did you use to make this decision? Define it.

10. State the four goals of science.

11. Studying the nature of love has proven challenging because it is difficult to operationally define. In this example, which of the four goals of science are researchers having difficulty meeting?

12. State which of the following is an example of basic research, and which is an example of applied research.

    A. A researcher is driven by her curiosity and interest to explore the theoretical relationship between socioeconomic status and political affiliation.

    B. A researcher is interested in exploring the extent to which voters of different socioeconomic status and political affiliation are likely to vote for a particular candidate.

13. Which research, basic or applied, is used to study practical problems in order to have the potential for immediate action?

14. State whether each of the following is an example of quantitative or qualitative research.

    A. A researcher interviews a group of participants and asks them to explain how they feel when they are in love. Each participant is allowed to respond in his or her own words.

    B. A researcher records the blood pressure of participants during a task meant to induce stress.

    C. A psychologist interested in attention injects rats with a drug that enhances attention and then measures the rate at which the rat presses a lever.

    D. A witness to a crime describes the suspect to police.

15. Is the following an example of pseudoscience? Explain.

    A researcher enters a home and uses a device that shows that some areas of the house have higher electromagnetic fields (EMFs) than others. He concludes that these EMF readings show scientific proof that ghosts or spirits are present in the rooms where the EMFs were highest.

ACTIVITIES

1. Recall that only behaviors and events that can be observed and measured (operationally defined) are considered scientific. Assuming that all of the following variables are both observable and measurable, state at least two operational definitions for each:

   The morality of politicians

   A participant's ability to remember some event

   A mother's patience

   The effectiveness of a professor's teaching style

   The quality of life among elderly patients

   The level of drug use among teens

   The amount of student texting during class time

   The costs of obtaining a college education

2. We developed the following three hypotheses using Step 1 of the scientific method. Choose one of the ideas given, or use one of your own, and complete Step 2 of the scientific method.

   (a) *Scientific Outcome 1:* The typical student obtains a C+ in difficult courses.

       Scientific Outcome 2: The typical student obtains a C+ in relatively easy courses.

       Research hypothesis: Students will do less work in an easy course than in a difficult course.

   (b) *Scientific Outcome 1:* The more education a woman has obtained, the larger her salary tends to be.

Scientific Outcome 2: Today, more women earn a PhD in psychology than men.

Research hypothesis: Women in fields of psychology today earn higher salaries than their male colleagues.

(c) *Scientific Outcome 1:* Distractions during class interfere with a student's ability to learn the material taught in class.

Scientific Outcome 2: Many students sign on to social networking sites during class time.

Research hypothesis: Students who sign on to social networking sites during class time will learn less material than those who do not.

3. Historically there has been great debate concerning the authority of scientific knowledge versus religious knowledge. What methods of knowing are used in science and religion? What are the differences between these methods, if any? What are the similarities, if any?

Identify a problem

- Determine an area of interest.
- Review the literature.
- Identify new ideas in your area of interest.
- Develop a research hypothesis.

Generate more new ideas

- Results support your hypothesis—refine or expand on your ideas.
- Results do not support your hypothesis— reformulate a new idea or start over.

Develop a research plan

- Define the variables being tested.
- Identify participants or subjects and determine how to sample them.
- Select a research strategy and design.
- Evaluate ethics and obtain institutional approval to conduct research.

Communicate the results

- Method of communication: oral, written, or in a poster.
- Style of communication: APA guidelines are provided to help prepare style and format.

Conduct the study

- Execute the research plan and measure or record the data.

After reading this chapter, you should be able to:

1 Explain what makes an idea interesting and novel.

2 Distinguish between a hypothesis and a theory.

3 Distinguish between induction and deduction.

4 Describe the process of conducting a literature review.

5 Identify four ethical concerns for giving proper credit.

6 Describe the "3 Cs" of conducting an effective literature review.

7 Distinguish between a confirmational and a disconfirmational strategy.

8 Explain the issue of publication bias.

Analyze and evaluate the data

- Analyze and evaluate the data as they relate to the research hypothesis.
- Summarize data and research results.

chapter
two

GENERATING TESTABLE IDEAS

Hearsay, gossip, scuttlebutts, and rumors are a common phenomenon. A friend tells you that someone else likes you, or a classmate tells you that she heard that class is canceled today. Yet how can you trust your friend or classmate? One way would be to confirm that your friend heard it from the person who likes you, or your classmate heard it directly from the professor who canceled the class. In other words, the best information "comes straight from the horse's mouth." This idiomatic expression made popular in horse racing in the early 1900s is synonymous with reliability and observation.

The phrase is also synonymous with the reliability of one's sources. In horse racing, a person who was so close to a horse that he or she could see inside the horse's mouth must have been a trusted source. This phrase is also synonymous with observation. Throughout history, unscrupulous horse traders falsified equine health records and ages, in hopes of persuading potential buyers to overpay for horses. The only way to know the health and age of a horse for sure was to look inside the horse's mouth for the truth. A horse's health and age could be estimated quite accurately by looking at the number and condition of his or her teeth. Consequently, to appraise a horse's worth, one must make an observation "straight from the horse's mouth."

In the same way that horse traders relied on trustworthy sources and observations to make judgments of a horse's worth, scientists develop their ideas or hypotheses based on the reliability of their sources and on their observations of phenomena. In this chapter we will introduce the types of sources from which researchers generate ideas and the ways in which researchers can identify these sources based on whether the information reported in them "came straight from the horse's mouth."

2.1 Generating Interesting and Novel Ideas

It was the German-born American physicist Albert Einstein who once said, "I am neither especially clever nor especially gifted. I am only very, very curious." While it is more likely that Einstein was clever, gifted, and curious, his insight marks an important feature in science: Knowledge is only possible through inquiry. One characteristic of all good scientists is that they ask good questions. Einstein, for example, asked, "Are time and space the same thing?" His research was to answer this question, which led to his theory of relativity—a mathematical proof that the answer to his question is yes. For all of the complexities of the theory of relativity, imagine that this research was inspired by such a simple question.

The object of research is to extend human knowledge beyond what is already known. Once a research study is complete, researchers will try to publish the results in a scientific journal called a **peer-reviewed journal**. After all, the scientific community will not know about a research study that is not published. To publish your work, you should be considerate of the aims of peer-reviewed scientific journals as you develop your ideas. Two criteria of importance to publishing a work can be met by answering the following two important questions regarding your idea:

> A **peer-reviewed journal** is a type of publication that specifically publishes scientific articles, reviews, or commentaries only after the work has been reviewed by peers or scientific experts who determine its scientific value or worth regarding publication. Only after acceptance from peer reviewers will a work be published.

- *Is my idea interesting?* An interesting idea can potentially benefit society, test a prediction, or develop areas of research where little is known. Peer-reviewed journals have a readership, and your idea must appeal to those who read that journal if you are to publish your ideas. In other words, journals prefer to publish papers that are going to be widely read and useful to their readers. The webpage for most peer-reviewed journals has an *aims and scope* section that you should read before deciding to submit your work to a particular journal. Not meeting the aims and scope of a journal can be grounds alone for rejection of a work.

- *Is my idea novel?* A novel idea is one that is original or new. You must be able to show how your idea adds to or builds upon the scientific literature. If you can demonstrate what we learn from your idea, then it is novel. It is valuable to replicate or repeat the results of other works; however, replication alone, without appreciable advancement of a fundamental new understanding or knowledge in an area, is often not sufficient to publish a work. Instead, the editors at peer-reviewed journals will prefer scientific reports of "original and significant" findings that extend, not simply repeat, scientific understanding or knowledge.

For any idea you have, the answer to both of these questions should be yes. Ultimately, it is your peers (i.e., other researchers in a field related to your idea) who will review your work before it can be published in a scientific journal. By answering yes to both questions you should be able to effectively communicate the value of your idea to a broad scientific audience. Table 2.1 gives three examples of how the authors of a peer-reviewed article studying alcohol use among college students communicated what made their ideas interesting and novel.

In this chapter, we specifically describe how scientists develop interesting and novel ideas—ideas that are based upon the review of reliable sources and can be tested; that is, we can make observations to confirm or disconfirm if the new idea is correct using the scientific method.

Table 2.1 Three Articles Concerning Alcohol Intake Among College Students

Reference	Description	Is the idea interesting?	Is the idea novel?
Barnett, Wei, & Czachowski (2009)	Researchers measured alcohol content of mixed drinks served at college parties during a single semester.	"[T]he highest rates of alcohol use [are among] college students . . . [which] puts students at risk for experiencing significant negative consequences . . . [with] alcohol-service parties [being a] popular source of alcoholic beverages for college students" (p. 152).	This research will "provide basic information about the extent to which mixed drinks [are mixed properly] . . . and would contribute an understanding of student alcohol consumption at these parties" (p. 152).
Butler & Correia (2009)	Researchers tested the effectiveness of face-to-face and computerized intervention techniques among heavy-drinking college students.	"Computerized intervention could offer several advantages [over face-to-face intervention]; they allow for anonymity, allow users to proceed at their own pace, and can be designed to be appealing, engaging, and personalized . . . [and] both time and cost effective" (p. 163).	This research will "compare the efficacy of [face-to-face and computerized interventions]—in reducing alcohol use and related problems among undergraduates" (p. 164).
Abar & Turrisi (2008)	Researchers looked at the extent to which parents continue to influence the choices their children make (including alcohol use) during the college years.	"In response to the breadth of research coupling college alcohol misuse with a range of negative outcomes, both scientists and administrators have increased their efforts in addressing college heavy drinking tendencies" (p. 1360).	This research will determine the extent to which "parental approval of alcohol use, parental monitoring, and parental knowledge of their teens' activities outside the home are each facets of parenting that are associated with college drinking" (p. 1361).

The citation for where the authors of each article explicitly state what makes their research interesting and novel is given.

2.2 Converting Ideas to Hypotheses and Theories

In many ways, science may appear to be the search for new information. However, the information itself is of little value without organization. Imagine, for example, trying to find a book in a library that places books on shelves in a random order. The information is in the library; however, it will be difficult to find the information you seek. Moreover, we must do more than just catalog the information we obtain; we must also understand it. In other words, we identify the relevance or usefulness of information. Specifically, we identify the relevance of information by identifying how information can broaden our understanding of the phenomena we study.

The process of organizing information in science is similar to working on a puzzle. You begin with scattered pieces and guessing which pieces fit where. Once you have enough puzzle pieces in place, you can begin to organize other puzzle pieces based on what you know about the pieces in place. Some regions of the puzzle have a similar color and some have a similar design, and this organization can help you ultimately organize the remaining pieces until they all fit the puzzle. The pieces of the puzzle are like the observations we make. And the strategies we use to complete the puzzle are like the hypotheses and theories that researchers state.

An idea should be interesting (appeal to others) and novel (provide new information).

A **hypothesis**, also defined in Chapter 1, is a specific, testable claim or prediction about what you expect to observe given a set of circumstances. For example, researchers tested the hypothesis that placing foods in McDonald's packaging will increase how much children like eating those foods (Robinson, Borzekowski, Matheson, & Kraemer, 2007). The hypothesis was a prediction that specifically identified the outcome they expect to observe (increased liking for foods) given a specified set of circumstances (the foods are wrapped in McDonald's packaging). Using the puzzle analogy, each attempt to place puzzle pieces together is like an attempt to test a hypothesis. As we start to "put the pieces together," a theory can then develop.

A **hypothesis** is a specific, testable claim or prediction about what you expect to observe given a set of circumstances.

A **theory** is a broad statement used to account for an existing body of knowledge and also provide unique predictions to extend that body of knowledge. A theory is not necessarily correct; instead, it is a generally accepted explanation for evidence, as it is understood.

A **theory** is a broad statement used to account for or explain an existing body of knowledge and also provide unique predictions to advance that body of knowledge. A theory essentially organizes evidence that has been rigorously tested and supported by scientific observations. If the findings of research studies point to a collective explanation for the observations made, then a theory develops. Returning to the puzzle analogy, imagine that we put together a puzzle without knowing what the image is that we are constructing. As we group pieces by colors and patterns we will start to see an image appear in a similar way; as we gain evidence we begin to "see" the nature of the phenomena we study. From that information, we can theorize what the puzzle image is. As we continue to fit pieces of the puzzle together we can then modify and refine our theory for what is in the image, similar to how we modify and refine theories of natural or behavioral phenomena as we gather more evidence about these phenomena.

While not exhaustive, there are three key criteria to consider when developing a good hypothesis or theory that is regarded as scientific:

1. Testable/Falsifiable. A good theory or hypothesis must be stated in a way that makes it possible to reject it (i.e., it must be falsifiable). For example, we can state the theory that a belief in God leads to better health outcomes (Rosmarin, Krumrei, & Andersson, 2009). This theory does lead to falsifiable predictions that researchers can readily test. However, we cannot state the theory that God exists because the existence of God cannot be falsified, and therefore cannot be accepted as a good theory. That is not to say science says God does not exist; that is to say that such a claim cannot be tested using the scientific process.

2. Replicable/Precise. The mechanisms (i.e., presumed causes) and outcomes in a hypothesis or theory should be clearly defined and should be precise. For example, consider the theory that feelings of attraction promote commitment to a long-term relationship (see Frank, 1988, 2001). This theory is scientific if feelings of attraction (the mechanism) and what constitutes a long-term relationship (the outcome) are specifically defined, such that other researchers could also readily observe, measure, and repeat the procedures used to test this theory. Feelings of attraction may be measured using rating scales or perhaps by recording time spent holding hands in public, for example. It should also be explicitly defined how long is long enough to constitute a long-term relationship (e.g., 3 months? 1 year?). This needs to be clearly defined and precise so that other researchers could readily set up similar measures and procedures to see if they get similar results.

3. Parsimonious. **Parsimony** is a canon of science that simpler explanations should be preferred to more complex ones. For example, one poor theory popularized by television is the ancient alien theory,

> **Parsimony** is a canon of science that states that, all else being equal, simpler explanations should be preferred to more complex ones.

which posits that aliens have visited Earth in the past and influenced human civilizations. The theory, among other flaws, is unnecessarily complex. A simpler explanation is simply that Man influenced human civilization. Evidence such as pyramid building and cultural norms such as burial practices can be explained without the need to appeal to ancient aliens visiting Earth and interacting with humans. Thus, one reason it is a poor theory for science is that simpler explanations can just as readily explain the evidence purported to support the theory itself.

The advantage of a theory is that it not only states unique predictions, but it can also explain an existing body of research. Figure 2.1 shows the general pattern of developing hypotheses and theories. Notice in the figure that a theory is just as open to testing as a hypothesis. Specifically, a theory is often tested in one of two ways:

Conduct a literature review.

State or modify hypotheses to explain some behavior or event.

Test the predictions made by the new or modified hypotheses.

After working through various predictions, convert the hypotheses to a new or modified theory that can explain some behavior or event.

Test new predictions made by the theory.

State or modify the theory to explain some behavior or event. Discard the theory if the central tenets of the theory fail to be supported.

- **The predictions made by a theory can be tested.** For example, the familiarity theory states that the more familiar children are with a food, the more they will eat the food (Pliner, 1982; Privitera, 2008b). We can test a "healthy" prediction of the theory to see if increasing a child's familiarity with vegetables will increase how much he or she eats vegetables.

- **The limitations of a theory can be tested.** For example, the familiarity theory is stated largely for children, with the assumption that adults have had too much prior experience with foods. Thus, one limitation of the theory is age. We could test this limitation by testing if adults will eat more foods they have never previously consumed before with greater familiarity to those foods. Or we could test a possible limitation by food type, by testing if children will eat more of any food with greater familiarity, and if not, to identify the food types where familiarity does not influence eating.

Hypotheses and theories allow researchers to organize a large body of research in a way that explains an understanding for evidence, as it is understood, and also provides predictions to organize the expectations for what we should observe. From this platform we can state hypotheses to test our ideas, and we can also revise and develop our theories to better explain our observations—all with the hope of one day "completing the puzzle" of understanding human behavior.

> Researchers state hypotheses that, after being rigorously tested, can develop into a theory.

LEARNING CHECK 1 ✓

1. Explain why it is important for an idea to be interesting and novel.

2. Distinguish between a hypothesis and a theory.

3. State three key criteria to consider when developing a good hypothesis or theory that is regarded as scientific.

Answers: 1. An idea should be interesting because peer-reviewed journals have a readership and the idea must appeal to those who read that journal in order to be published. An idea should be novel because you must be able to show how your idea adds to or builds upon the scientific literature; 2. A hypothesis is a specific, testable claim or prediction about what you expect to observe given a set of circumstances, whereas a theory is a broad statement used to account for an existing body of knowledge and also provide unique predictions to extend that body of knowledge; 3. Testable/falsifiable, replicable/precise, parsimonious.

2.3 Developing Your Idea: Deduction and Induction

The reasoning that scientists often use to develop their ideas is to begin with a theory or to begin with an observation, referred to as deductive and inductive reasoning, respectively. To some extent, many scientists use a combination of both types of reasoning to develop their ideas. Each type of reasoning is introduced here and illustrated in Figure 2.2.

Figure 2.2 A Comparison of Deductive and Inductive Reasoning

Deduction. A "top-down" or "theory-driven" approach in which researchers begin with a specific claim or theory that generates predictions from which observations can be made to refute or support the claim or theory.

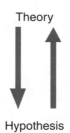

Theory

Hypothesis

Observations

Induction. A "bottom-up" or "data-driven" approach in which researchers begin by making general observations that lead to patterns from which they formulate hypotheses that make testable predictions—leading to the development of a new theory.

Deductive Reasoning

Many scientific reports will explicitly state theories that have been developed to explain a body of knowledge. A useful theory is one that leads to logical predictions of what we should and should not observe if the theory is correct. The reasoning we use to develop ideas to test those predictions is called **deductive reasoning.** Using deductive reasoning, you begin with a hypothesis or theory, then use that claim to deduce what you believe should occur, or not occur, if the claim is correct. The prediction you deduce will be used to refute or support the claim. Hence, using deductive reasoning, you start with an idea (the hypothesis or theory) to generate your ideas (predictions made by the hypothesis or theory). Using deductive reasoning, the hypothesis or theory guides the ideas you generate and observations you make.

> **Deductive reasoning** is a "top-down" type of reasoning in which a claim (a hypothesis or theory) is used to generate ideas or predictions and make observations.

To illustrate deductive reasoning, imagine that, based on a literature review, you state the following theory, which you call the "front row theory": Students who sit in the front row are smarter than students who sit in the back row. From this starting point, you deduce predictions of what will be observed if your theory is correct. One prediction, for example, is that students who sit in the front row will score higher on an exam than students who sit in the back row. You can test this prediction by recording the grades of students and recording where they sat in class. In this way, your theory guides what you choose to observe. Figure 2.3 illustrates the "front row theory" example using deductive reasoning.

Inductive Reasoning

Sometimes, you may find that your initial ideas are developed by your own data or observations. The type of reasoning you use to generate ideas from observations is called **inductive reasoning**. Using inductive reasoning, you make a casual observation (e.g., you see that students always attend a psychology class) or collect and measure data (e.g., you record total class attendance for one week). You then generate an idea to explain what you observed or measured (e.g., students attend class because the professor gives quizzes each day). The idea you generate to explain the observation is your hypothesis. Hence, using inductive reasoning, you start with an observation to generate new ideas; you generalize beyond the limited observations you made. Using inductive reasoning, then, the data or observations guide the ideas you generate and observations you make.

> **Inductive reasoning** is a "bottom-up" type of reasoning in which a limited number of observations or measurements (i.e., data) are used to generate ideas and make observations.

To illustrate the distinction between deductive and inductive reasoning, we can revisit the "front row theory" example to show how inductive reasoning could lead to the same idea we developed using deductive reasoning. Suppose you observe that three students sitting in the front row always score highest on exams. From this starting point, you hypothesize that all students who sit in the front row will score higher on exams than those who sit in the back row. You record the grades of all students and record where they sat in class. Notice that we arrive at the same idea and the same study to test that idea using both types of reasoning. Figure 2.3 illustrates the "front row theory" example using inductive reasoning.

> Inductive and deductive reasoning represent two ways in which researchers develop ideas for scientific testing.

LEARNING CHECK 2 ✓

1. Which of the following situations is an example of deductive reasoning, inductive reasoning, or both?

   A. You observe two of your friends arguing. About 2 minutes into the argument, a comedy special airs on TV that makes both of them laugh. After that, they no longer argue. From this you conclude that humor can alleviate conflict.

   B. While reading a professional paper you come across a theory stating that increased violence during children's television programming leads to an increase in violence among children. You resolve that if this is true, then it is also true that an increase in nonviolent children's television programming will lead to a decrease in violence among children.

   C. You observe a friend praying while he is sick. Soon afterward he recovers. You conclude that spiritual faith has a positive impact on health. If this is true, you resolve, then people who express spiritual faith have a shorter duration of common illnesses than those who do not.

Answers: 1. A. Induction; B. Deduction; C. Both.

Figure 2.3 The Process of Deduction and Induction for the Same Problem

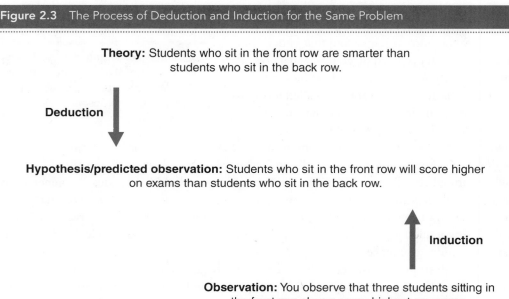

Theory: Students who sit in the front row are smarter than students who sit in the back row.

Deduction

Hypothesis/predicted observation: Students who sit in the front row will score higher on exams than students who sit in the back row.

Induction

Observation: You observe that three students sitting in the front row always score highest on exams.

In this example, both types of reasoning led to the same hypothesis.

2.4 Performing a Literature Review

To develop an idea you must perform a **literature review**. The *literature* is the general body of published scientific knowledge. The *review* is the search you perform of this general body of knowledge. The literature is most often published in peer-reviewed journals and academic books. Other sources, such as newspapers, popular magazines, and Internet websites, are not part of the scientific literature because the information provided in these sources is not typically subjected to a peer review.

A key objective of the literature review is to develop new ideas that can be converted into a hypothesis that is both interesting and novel. Research is not an isolated process; rather, it is one of collaboration and peer review. Therefore, reviewing the general body of knowledge in your topic area is important to determine what is known and to develop ideas for what is yet to be discovered. In this section, we will explain how to get started with your literature review to develop new ideas and select a research topic. We will then explain how to use searchable databases and organize your search results.

> A **literature review** is a systematic search for and recording of information identified in the general body of published scientific knowledge.

Getting Started: Choosing a Research Topic

Inquiry begins with a question. What topics interest you? What questions do you want to ask about those topics? When choosing a research topic, be sure to select one that interests you. The research process can be tedious. Asking questions about topics that interest you can make this process fun. Certainly, topics involving food, sports, physical fitness, relationships, video game playing, drug addiction, politics, or even shopping interest you. A researcher is probably studying just about any topic or behavior you can think of. It will be difficult to stay committed to a research project if you are not interested in the topic you are studying.

> Choose a research topic that interests you.

Getting Organized: Choosing Appropriate Sources

After you find an interesting research topic, you will review the literature about that topic. Keeping track of the types of sources you come across as you perform your review is important. A *source* is any published or printed article, chapter, or book from which information can be obtained. There can be thousands of sources for even a single research topic, and reviewing them all can be challenging. To organize the sources you come across and make a literature review more efficient:

- Begin with a search of review articles.

- Search only from peer-reviewed or other scientific sources.

You can categorize sources as primary and secondary. A **secondary source** is any source in which an author describes research or ideas that are not necessarily his or her own. Secondary sources can include textbooks, newspaper and magazine articles, online sources, and review articles. *Review articles* provide a full summary of a research topic by an author who is regarded as an expert on that topic. It is good to begin with these types of articles for the following two reasons:

- Key sources pertaining to a topic of interest are described in a review article.

- Review articles are typically published in peer-reviewed journals.

Review articles include dozens of the most up-to-date findings in an area of research. To summarize the literature for a topic, an author will review many sources from other researchers in that topic area. Each source reviewed in the article that was not the actual work of the author is called a secondary source. In a review article, the author or authors provide a thorough review of sometimes hundreds of secondary sources. By reading review articles, you can quickly review a diverse number of sources that you can be confident are related to your topic of interest.

Each time you come across a secondary source that interests you, you can find the reference cited in that review article and read it for yourself. As you review secondary sources, be sure to record the full reference of each source that interests you. For most sources, you should write down the author, publication year, title, journal, issue, and page numbers. Or you can create an electronic file or spreadsheet with this information to keep your search organized. You can be more efficient by having this information ready when it comes time to find the secondary sources that interest you.

The original source of an idea or research is called a **primary source**. In an *empirical article*, in which the authors conduct a firsthand study, the introduction for these articles is

> A **secondary source** is any publication that refers to works, ideas, or observations that are not those of the author.
>
> A **primary source** is any publication in which the works, ideas, or observations are those of the author.

a great place to find secondary sources. Empirical articles can often be readily identified because these include a detailed method and results section, in addition to a concluding discussion section. These additional sections are a primary source (or the original ideas/design of the authors). In your review, keep track of secondary sources so that you can find the primary source later. It is important to find and read a primary source from the original author of a work. You should not develop your ideas based upon secondary sources because a secondary source is someone (e.g., the author of the review article) telling you what someone else (e.g., the original author of the work) observed. You need to check your sources. Find the primary source and read what the original author of that work did. You do this to check that what was reported in the review article was accurate and to be more confident in the ideas you develop from your review.

> It can be more efficient to review secondary sources, and then primary sources, in a literature review.

Most of the primary and secondary sources you find in your review can be found using online databases. Many databases for searching only peer-reviewed and scientific works are available at colleges throughout the world. If you have access to these library databases, then this will make your search far easier and more efficient.

MAKING SENSE—PRIMARY AND SECONDARY SOURCES

A common misconception is that a source is either primary or secondary. In fact, most journal articles, especially those published in peer-reviewed journals, are a mix of both. Review articles mostly consist of secondary sources. However, secondary sources can also be found in original research articles from primary sources. For any research, authors must explain how their research is novel, and to do so authors must show how their research study (primary source) builds upon the known body of research typically published by various different authors (secondary sources). For this reason, most articles published in peer-reviewed journals begin with an introduction, which is where authors will explain what is known (typically by reviewing secondary sources) and what is yet to be explained and so tested in their study (primary source).

After you spend days or weeks reviewing a research topic, it is often all too easy to forget whether the information you have came from primary or secondary sources. One contributing factor to this problem is that you can find secondary sources in most articles you read, even in articles you list as being a primary source. Keeping track of primary and secondary sources as you review them can minimize this problem.

Getting Searching: Using Online Databases

Online databases allow researchers to search for, save, and print thousands of primary and secondary sources in all topic areas in the behavioral sciences. Popular databases in the behavioral sciences, the contents of which are described in Table 2.2, include PsycINFO, PsycARTICLES, PubMed, ERIC, and JSTOR. Many of these databases offer peer-reviewed articles in **full text**, meaning that the full article is provided and can be downloaded and saved on your computer, usually as a PDF.

> A **full-text article** is any article or text that is available in its full or complete published version.
>
> A **full-text database** is any online database that makes full-text articles available to be downloaded electronically as a PDF or in another electronic format.

When searching for peer-reviewed articles it is important to recognize the types of articles you can find. Searching in the databases suggested here is the safest way to ensure that you are finding only peer-reviewed articles. However, if you are ever uncertain as to whether your source is peer reviewed—whether using the databases suggested here or other databases such as Google Scholar—it is often beneficial to check that your source is indeed peer reviewed. You can do this by visiting the website for the journal and viewing the *about this journal* or *aims and scope* sections. For inexperienced students, it can also be a good idea to check with your professor or other more experienced professional.

In the remainder of this section, we will describe the general process for navigating online databases using PsycINFO as an example. Note that the screenshots for this database can vary from those shown in Figures 2.4 and 2.5 depending on the type of computer system you use to search PsycINFO.

After logging on to a database, typically using access provided by a college or research institution, you will see several search options under the advanced search tab. To illustrate the use of PsycINFO, we will use this database to perform a literature review on the relationship between studying and student grades. Figure 2.4 shows the upper section of

Table 2.2 Descriptions for Five Widely Used Online Databases in the Behavioral Sciences

Database	Description
PsycINFO	An abstract database containing more than 2.7 million records updated weekly, from more than 49 countries and in 29 languages. Ninety-nine percent of journals covered are peer reviewed from areas in psychology and related disciplines (American Psychological Association [APA], 2013b).
PsycARTICLES	A full-text database containing more than 142,000 full-text articles in HTML or PDF updated weekly. Full-text articles cover 66 journals from 1894 to present in areas of psychology and related disciplines (APA, 2013a).
PubMed	A comprehensive bibliographic and full-text database that contains nearly 19 million records updated weekly in the biomedical and life sciences from 1949 to present (U.S. National Library of Medicine, 2013).
ERIC	A bibliographic and full-text database that contains more than 1.2 million records, updated twice weekly for journal articles, books, conference and policy papers, technical reports, and other education-related materials (Educational Resource Information Center, n.d.).
JSTOR	A multidisciplinary database established in 1997, JSTOR covers disciplines in the arts and sciences, including 112 titles in psychology and related fields (ITHAKA, 2013).

| Logout | Quick Search | Advanced Search | Search Tools | Browse |

(GPA	or		or	)	Keywords, KW=
and (study habits	or		or	)	Keywords, KW=
and (	or		or	)	Keywords, KW=

Search Tips: e.g., wildcar*, exact phrase; use Keywords for a single search of Title, Abstract, Descriptors

[Search]   [Clear]

Now Selected: ⓘ PsycINFO

Change: [--- Subject Area ---] or Specific Databases

Date Range: [Earliest] to [2009]

Limited to: ☐ Latest Update ☑ Journal Articles Only ☑ English Only

Psycinfo

In our search we chose to search for the keywords "GPA" and "study habits" in "Journal Articles Only" and "English Only."

Database PsycINFO

Title **Exploring cramming: Student behaviors, beliefs, and learning retention in the Principles of Marketing course.**

Author McIntyre, Shelby H.[1]; Munson, J. Michael[1]

Affiliation (1)Santa Clara University, Santa Clara, CA, US

Source Journal of Marketing Education. Vol 30(3), Dec 2008, pp. 226-243

ISSN 0273-4753

Descriptors ☐ Business Education* ☐ Rating Scales* ☐ Student Attitudes* ☐ *Study Habits* ☐ Test Construction* ☐ Learning ☐ Marketing ☐ Retention

New Search Using Marked Terms: ⦿ Use AND to narrow ○ Use OR to broaden
Add to Current Search: ○ Use AND to narrow ○ Use OR to broaden (Go)

Abstract Cramming for finals is common on college campuses, and many students seem to cram for their final in the Principles of Marketing course. This article addresses the question of defining and measuring a àcramming *study* strategy.à Scales are developed to assess (a) cramming for courses in general and (b) cramming specifically in the Principles of Marketing course relative to two other *study* strategies. Several research questions about cramming are addressed, including (a) How widespread is the practice? (b) How effective do students perceive it to be? (c) How effective is it actually, both in the short and long term, for studentsà *GPA* and grade in the Principles of Marketing course? and (d) Is there a deterioration in retention, as measured by a master test, of content learned in the Principles course from using more of a cramming *study* strategy? Implications are discussed, particularly in light of various pedagogical approaches to combating learning decay, and areas for future research are suggested. (PsycINFO Database Record (c) 2009 APA, all rights reserved) (journal abstract)

Psycinfo

These are the results of selecting the article authored by McIntyre and Munson (2008).

the screen for this search. To begin a search you need to select keywords for the database to search. For this example, the keyword "GPA" was entered in the top left cell, and the keyword "study habits" was entered in the cell below it. Be thoughtful when choosing keywords. It is unlikely that there is "no research on your topic." It is more likely that you are not using appropriate terms to search for your topic. So before giving up your search, use a thesaurus or check if you are using the correct technical jargon for your topic. It is likely that articles for your topic will appear once you start using more appropriate terms.

In the keyword search, you have the option to search GPA *or* study habits if you enter these terms across the rows. As they are entered now, the database will search for GPA *and* study habits, which will narrow the search a bit. Note that the *and/or* options may appear as a dropdown menu in other database displays. You can also limit your search to find keywords anywhere in an article, by publication year, by author, and according to many other search options. At the bottom of the screen are additional search options. Notice in Figure 2.4 that by checking two boxes at the bottom of the screen, our search was limited to "Journal Articles Only" and "English Only." To perform the search using the keywords and criteria you selected, click the "Search" option to the left.

Clicking "Search" for the information entered in Figure 2.4 will display a list of sources related to the keywords you entered. Because the database is updated weekly, these results will change. Each article is listed with the title, year, author, journal, issue, and page information given.

> An **abstract** is a brief written summary of the purpose, methods, and results of an article, a chapter, a book, or another published document. The length of an abstract can vary; however, abstracts are usually 250 words or less.

Many sources are full text, and all should include at least an **abstract** or brief overview of the article. If you selected the article authored by McIntyre and Munson (2008), for example, you would see the information shown in Figure 2.5. If the full-text article is available, then download and save it. If it is not, then saving the abstract and reference information will make it easier for you to find the full-text article later. If a source is not available electronically, then it can likely be found using the interlibrary loan process at your college or university library.

> Online databases, such as PsycINFO, make research more accessible by allowing users to search thousands of articles in a single search.

Section 2.6 expands on this general description of working with a database by describing some common practices for conducting an effective literature review. We turn first to a discussion in Section 2.5 for how to properly cite research that is used in your research study.

LEARNING CHECK 3 ✓

1. What is a literature review?

2. Distinguish between primary and secondary sources.

3. List five online databases used by behavioral scientists.

2.5 Ethics in Focus: Giving Proper Credit

One important reason for organizing your sources when conducting a literature review is to avoid confusion when giving credit for sources cited in your research study. Ethical problems arise if you cite these sources incorrectly or without reference to the primary source. Four ways to avoid such ethical problems are the following:

- **Always double-check your sources for accuracy.** When referring to a secondary source, be sure to cite it properly and accurately so that your readers can find the source should they wish to pursue the subject you are writing about. Readers may become frustrated if they try to locate the source and cannot find it. Accuracy in citations is a concern for you and even among researchers who publish in peer-reviewed scientific journals—Siebers and Holt (2000), for example, found many reference errors in leading medical journals, as shown in Table 2.3.

- **Obtain the primary source of an article you cite.** One way to find the primary source is to check the references of secondary sources, particularly review articles. In that way, you can find the original work that should be given proper credit. After all, "Citing the original article ensures that the person with priority for the discovery is provided proper credit. To cite a later source misallocates that credit" (Zigmond & Fischer, 2002, p. 231).

- **Avoid "abstracting."** Abstracting in this sense refers to instances in which an individual cites the full reference of some work after simply skimming through an abstract. This is poor practice because "citing references without scrutiny of the entire paper may lead to misrepresentation of the paper's actual findings" (Taylor, 2002, p. 167). When you cite a reference, be sure that you have read it in full to ensure that you properly represent the work.

Table 2.3 Error Rates in Articles Published by Five Leading Medical Journals in March 1999

Total references checked	1,557
References with any error	300
Reference error rate (%)	19
Author errors	206
Title errors	101
Journal errors	20
Volume errors	15
Year errors	20
Page errors	49

Data adapted from those presented by Siebers and Holt (2000).

- **Be aware of citation bias.** Citation bias occurs when an author or authors cite only evidence that supports their view and fail to cite conflicting evidence. For example, Ferguson (2010) identified such a problem in the video game violence literature. He noted that "a close look at the research on violence in video games reveals that findings are far less consistent than have been reported by some sources" (p. 72). What he revealed was that many articles in this area of research only cited one side for or against the dangers of video game violence. Make sure you cite sources for all findings in your area of interest, and be aware of possible citation biases when reviewing the work of others.

In this section, we described four ethical concerns related to giving accurate and proper credit. The Office of Research Integrity offers a more exhaustive list of ethical considerations. To access the list, go to http://ori.dhhs.gov/education/products/ and select the "Misconduct" tab.

> **Citation bias** is a misleading approach to citing sources that occurs when an author or authors cite only evidence that supports their view and fail to cite existing evidence that refutes their view.

LEARNING CHECK 4 ✓

1. State the ethical pitfall that is described for each example given below:

   A. A student reads an interesting abstract of an article. He tries to find the full article but is unable to locate it. He still cites the full article in his research paper.

   B. A professor reads an interesting review article stating that other researchers have shown a link between diet and addiction. She later writes about this link and gives credit to the review article, but not the original researchers who showed this link.

   C. An author makes a claim that watching television reduces the attention span of a child and cites only those sources that support his view even though some evidence exists that refutes his view.

   D. A researcher reads an article that includes a study that piques his interest. When he goes to find the reference cited he notices that the publication year is wrong.

Answers: 1. A. The student is guilty of abstracting; B. The professor has failed to obtain the primary source of an article cited; C. The work has a citation bias; D. The author of the article failed to double-check the sources for accuracy.

2.6 The "3 Cs" of an Effective Literature Review

This section presents some additional strategies for conducting an effective literature review. You can remember them as the "3 Cs," or being comprehensive, critical, and clever.

Be Comprehensive

Most of the sources available using online databases are peer-reviewed research journals, which are considered very reliable sources. These journals specialize; that is, they tend to publish articles only in a particular area of research. If you find an article relevant to your research topic in one journal, then it is likely that there are additional articles on that topic in other issues of that journal. To search the journal's archive, enter the journal title in an online database keyword search and search by journal.

Searching multiple databases can also enhance your search. Each database, such as PsycINFO or PubMed, includes a different list of journals to search from. It is very possible that an online search in one database will produce different results than an online search in another database. Hence, searching multiple databases can increase the total number of possible results to review for your topic of interest.

Keep in mind that each journal article follows a particular format. While many follow an APA (2009)–style format, not all journals will do so. Regardless of the formatting style used, each article will include a title, followed by an abstract, an introduction, method, results, discussion, and references. Table 2.4 lists and describes each of these sections. Usually, reading select portions of an article is sufficient to determine whether it is relevant to your research topic. Examining each article in the following order will help you search most efficiently.

Title. In many cases, if the title of an article does not pique your interest, then neither will the article.

Abstract. The abstract summarizes, typically in fewer than 250 words, the purpose and results of some work. Reading the title and abstract takes about one minute and allows you to discard many of the articles that are not

Table 2.4 The Sections of Articles in Peer-Reviewed Journals

Section	Description
Title	A single sentence that captures the topic of a study
Abstract	A brief summary of the purpose and results of a study
Introduction	An overview of the research topic that explains how it is interesting and novel and identifies the hypotheses being tested
Method	A description of the materials, procedures, and participants or subjects in a study
Results	A summary of the statistical analyses that often includes figures and tables to summarize data
Discussion	The conclusion of the study that explains how the results of a study answered the hypotheses tested and sometimes offers ideas for future research
References	A listing for every source that was cited in the body of the article

relevant to your research topic. Many online databases give you a minimum of the title and abstract of an article, making it easy to distinguish the articles you do need from those you do not.

Introduction and discussion. For the articles that you like, you can print and save the full text; if you are unable to access the article, see your librarian to learn how you can obtain a copy. Reading the introduction and discussion sections can allow you to determine if an article is truly relevant. If the article is relevant, then its list of secondary sources will identify other articles of possible interest.

Method and results. Once you have determined that an article is relevant to your research topic, carefully read through it. Be critical of the methods and results published in an article and make sure that both are consistent with the conclusions drawn in the article.

References. Once you have fully reviewed articles of interest, you can search through the references listed at the end of each article to double-check that you have exhausted all articles related to your research topic of interest.

Also, keep in mind that one study rarely is sufficient to answer a research question or prove a claim, so you should not base your entire literature review on a single article or viewpoint. Scientists hold many opposing views and often present data that contradict scientific evidence published earlier. To be comprehensive, you should identify some of these opposing viewpoints and the contradictory evidence in those studies. Doing so can actually help you develop your own ideas to generate stronger hypotheses and theories.

Be Critical

To be critical means that you ask questions, know your sources, and are objective as you conduct your literature review. Each aspect of being critical is described here.

> Being comprehensive means performing an effective literature review in a minimum amount of time.

Ask questions. As you read an article, ask yourself questions about the participants that the researchers used, the methods or procedures employed, and the conclusions drawn. The article itself will provide most of the answers. Also, many researchers identify potential limitations or drawbacks to their study in the discussion section. As you read through this section, think of ways you could address them. Asking questions will help you generate your own ideas, and those ideas could eventually become part of your hypothesis.

Know your sources. Know where your information comes from. Know whether the information you find comes from a secondary or a primary source and whether it is peer reviewed. Most journals disclose their review policies in each issue. Also, be cautious when using online sources because they are often not subjected to a peer review. You must check the credibility of online sources closely, as a few may be peer reviewed, such as articles from open access publishers (e.g., BioMed Central).

Remain objective. Be aware of your own biases. You may have some ideas before starting the literature review, which may affect what you decide to read and pay attention to during your search. If you keep an open mind, you may find sources that contradict your point of view. Knowing the opposing views may even help you generate some of your best ideas. After all, if you disagree with a point of view, then you should be able to explain why you disagree, which can often lead to new ideas or explanations.

Being critical means that you ask challenging questions rooted in the scientific literature.

Be Clever

Being clever means that you actively think of unique ways to advance the research you read about in your literature review; be innovative in your approach to advance scientific research. The following are five strategies you can use to be clever in your approach to generate new ideas for your research topic.

Identify flaws. There is some probability of an error in all published scientific data. Additionally, scientists are not infallible—on some occasions they can, without intention, misinterpret, mislead, or misrepresent the data they publish. Consequently, some of the research you come across can be wrong or inaccurate. Identify these inaccuracies and conduct a study without them.

Identify contradictions. You may come across two or more studies with contradictory hypotheses or data. If you read these articles closely, you can develop hypotheses of your own that make predictions that can lend support to one or both studies. Your work will help clarify possible confusion in the published work.

Identify anomalies. Look for conclusions, interpretations, or data presented in articles that are inconsistent. For example, researchers often disregard scores called *outliers* that do not fit with most of the data as anomalies or errors. Often, anomalies are not errors, and they can lead to new ideas that result in new directions of research.

Consider subtleties. You may find that subtle changes to a study can make a big difference in a research result. An important issue, particularly in laboratory research, is whether research studies generalize to situations beyond those observed. Making subtle changes, such as observing participants with different demographic characteristics, or measuring different variables, can have a significant impact on the results observed.

Think beyond the research. Physiologist Ivan Pavlov, who won the 1904 Nobel Prize in Physiology or Medicine, is just as well known for his work on classical conditioning, research that merged his Nobel Prize–winning work in physiology with psychology. Princeton University psychologist Daniel Kahneman won the 2002 Nobel Prize in Economic Sciences for his landmark research applying psychology to economic theory. Both of these scientists combined two previously unrelated areas of research and observed very new and interesting results. Perhaps you can use a similar strategy to generate new ideas of your own by merging two different research topics to resolve the same problem.

> Being clever means that you are innovative in your approach to advance scientific research.

This brief list of strategies aims to help you see how knowing what to look for and how to generate new ideas can help you select a research topic. Your goal should be to generate your own new ideas, and the "3Cs" can help guide you in the right direction for achieving that goal.

LEARNING CHECK 5 ✓

1. List the order in which you should read sections of a research article as part of your literature review.

2. For each of the following examples, state the aspect of being critical that the student is ignoring.

   A. A student reads through an article and just accepts every argument in the article without question.

   B. A student cites an article as key evidence to justify her hypothesis, but does not know whether the source is peer reviewed.

   C. A student gets upset at a relevant article that contradicts his point of view, so he decides to put it aside and not include it in his paper.

3. State five clever strategies for generating new ideas that can help you select a research topic.

Answers: 1. Title, abstract, introduction and discussion, method and results, and references; 2. A. The student neglected to ask questions; B. The student failed to know the sources; C. The student did not remain objective; 3. Identify flaws, identify contradictions, identify anomalies, consider subtleties, and think beyond the research.

2.7 Testing Your Idea: Confirmation and Disconfirmation

Any idea you develop must be testable—it must make specific predictions that can be observed under specified conditions. In this section, we consider two ways to test a theory or hypothesis: a confirmational strategy in which a researcher tests *anticipated* outcomes, and a disconfirmational strategy in which *unanticipated* outcomes are tested by a researcher.

Confirmational Strategy

A **confirmational strategy** is a method of testing a theory or hypothesis in which a positive result confirms the predictions made by that theory or hypothesis. A *positive result* confirms a hypothesis or theory and occurs when an effect or a difference is observed. A confirmational strategy is often used to test a new theory or hypothesis in terms of the predictions that it anticipates will occur if the theory or hypothesis is correct. Using an "if . . . then" logic statement, a confirmational strategy can be represented as follows:

> A **confirmational strategy** is a method of testing a theory or hypothesis in which a positive result confirms the predictions made by that theory or hypothesis.

If A is true, then B is true.

B is true.

Therefore, A is true.

The problem with using this type of logic, referred to as *affirming the consequent*, is that it can be fallacious or not true, as the following example demonstrates:

If you are a scientist (A), then you are educated (B).

You are educated (B).

Therefore, you are a scientist (A).

The conclusion that you are a scientist is not always true. While scientists are certainly educated, not all educated people are scientists. Thus, the logic is not valid. This problem of logical fallacy means that using the confirmational strategy alone to test theories and hypotheses is not good practice. To balance this major limitation, researchers also use a disconfirmational strategy.

Disconfirmational Strategy

A **disconfirmational strategy** is a method of testing a theory or hypothesis in which you test an outcome that is not predicted by the theory or hypothesis you are testing. A *positive result* in this case disconfirms a hypothesis or theory. Using this strategy, for example, suppose we hypothesize that rat subjects will consume less of a flavored solution if it is associated with feeling sick, which is called an *aversion*. To test this theory we first have rats consume two flavored solutions and record how much is consumed in a baseline phase. In a training phase, rats consume one flavored drink and are immediately injected with lithium chloride (LiCl), which makes rats feel sick. Rats consume a different flavored drink and are injected with a saline solution, which has no effect on the body. On a test day, subjects are given each flavored solution to drink. The amount consumed of each flavor after 30 minutes is measured and compared to the amount consumed of these solutions in baseline.

> A **disconfirmational strategy** is a method of testing a theory or hypothesis in which a positive result disconfirms the predictions made by that theory or hypothesis.

In this example, we applied both a confirmational and a disconfirmational strategy. Our hypothesis predicts that on test day, rats will consume less of the flavored solution paired with an injection of LiCl because it made the rats feel sick. As illustrated in Figure 2.6, this test is a confirmational strategy: If A, then B. For our hypothesis to be correct, we also must observe that rats do not consume less of the flavored solution paired with an injection of saline because that solution did not cause sickness. As illustrated in Figure 2.6, this test is a disconfirmational strategy: If A, then not C. If we do observe C, then sickness is not likely causing reduced intake of a flavored solution.

A benefit of using the disconfirmational strategy is that we can refute a theory or hypothesis with a positive result. Alternatively, to refute a theory or hypothesis using a confirmational strategy, we would need to observe a *negative result*, meaning no effect or difference. As discussed in Section 2.8, because of problems related to statistical power (i.e., the likelihood of detecting an effect or a difference), negative results alone are rarely published in peer-reviewed journals. For this reason, a disconfirmational strategy is the best strategy for refuting a theory.

Figure 2.6 Using Confirmational and Disconfirmational Strategies to Test a Theory

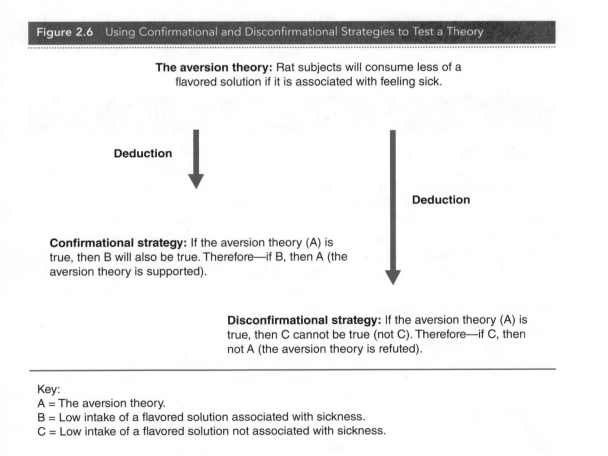

The aversion theory: Rat subjects will consume less of a flavored solution if it is associated with feeling sick.

Deduction

Deduction

Confirmational strategy: If the aversion theory (A) is true, then B will also be true. Therefore—if B, then A (the aversion theory is supported).

Disconfirmational strategy: If the aversion theory (A) is true, then C cannot be true (not C). Therefore—if C, then not A (the aversion theory is refuted).

Key:
A = The aversion theory.
B = Low intake of a flavored solution associated with sickness.
C = Low intake of a flavored solution not associated with sickness.

In this example, the aversion theory anticipates B—a confirmational strategy is used to test this outcome. But the aversion theory does not anticipate C—a disconfirmational strategy is used to test this outcome.

1. A researcher proposes the following theory: The more often students miss class, the worse their class grade will be. The following two studies, A and B, tested this claim. State the type of strategy, confirmational or disconfirmational, used in each study.

   A. You select a sample of research methods students who have missed at least six classes during the semester. Half the students work full-time, and half do not work. You record the GPA of all students to see if there is a difference between groups. Because all students sampled in this study missed the same number of classes, the theory does not predict a difference between groups.

   B. You obtain school records from a random sample of college freshmen attending a small university. You record the semester GPA and the number of classes missed during the semester for each student sampled. If the theory is true, then it should also be true that the more classes students miss during the semester, the lower their semester GPA will be.

Answers: 1. A. Disconfirmational strategy; B. Confirmational strategy.

2.8 Ethics in Focus: Publication Bias

Researchers conduct studies to observe an effect. An *effect* is any difference or significant outcome observed in a study. The failure to observe an effect in a study, particularly when the study is associated with low statistical power to detect the effect, means that few, if any, peer-reviewed journals will allow the study to be published (Dickersin, 1990; McCambridge, 2007). The response from reviewers for these journals is usually to tell the researchers to increase their statistical power and conduct the study again. For this reason, much of the peer-reviewed literature is biased in favor of studies showing positive results, a situation described as the publication bias. The **publication bias** is the tendency for editors of peer-reviewed journals to preferentially accept articles that show positive results and reject those that show only negative results.

Because editors of peer-reviewed journals and the peer reviewers themselves often reject a manuscript on the basis of a failure to show positive results (Liesegang, Albert, & Schachat, 2008), researchers are often deterred from even trying to submit negative results for publication (Calnan, Smith, & Sterne, 2006; Olson et al., 2002). As a result, many researchers do not even try to publish negative findings, instead choosing to file them away, a situation described as the **file drawer problem**.

The publication bias means that the size of an effect could be overstated for many behavioral phenomena reported in the peer-reviewed literature. For example, suppose you read a few studies showing that a new behavioral therapy for depression significantly reduces symptoms of depression in patients. If a researcher tests the

Positive results are more likely to be published in peer-reviewed journals than negative results.

effectiveness of this same behavioral therapy and finds no effect, it is likely that no peer-reviewed journal will accept it, so you will never find it or read about it. It is therefore possible that the effectiveness of this therapy is overstated because studies failing to show an effect are not included in the published peer-reviewed literature. Howard, Lau, et al. (2009) stated that "scientific progress is made by trusting the bulk of current knowledge" (p. 117), and the publication bias compromises this trust. Keep in mind that while positive results reported in the peer-reviewed literature can certainly be trusted, also take caution in knowing that many negative results may not be included in your search.

Publication bias is the tendency for editors of peer-reviewed journals to preferentially accept articles that show positive results and reject those that show only negative results.

The publication bias is also called the **file drawer problem** because researchers have a tendency to file away studies that show negative results, knowing that most journals will likely reject them.

CHAPTER SUMMARY

LO 1 Explain what makes an idea interesting and novel.

- An interesting idea is any idea that appeals to the readership of **peer-reviewed journals**. A novel idea is one that is original or new.

LO 2 Distinguish between a hypothesis and a theory.

- A **hypothesis** is a specific, testable claim or prediction about what you expect to observe given a set of circumstances. A **theory** is a broader statement used to account for an existing body of knowledge and also provide unique predictions to extend that body of knowledge.
- Three key criteria to consider when developing a good hypothesis or theory that is regarded as scientific are as follows: testable/falsifiable, replicable/precise, and parsimonious.

LO 3 Distinguish between induction and deduction.

- **Deductive reasoning** is a "top-down" type of reasoning in which a claim (hypothesis or theory) is used to generate ideas or predictions and make observations.
- **Inductive reasoning** is a "bottom-up" type of reasoning in which a limited number of observations or measurements (i.e., data) are used to generate ideas and make observations.

LO 4 Describe the process of conducting a literature review.

- Getting started: Find a research topic that interests you because it will make the scientific process more worthwhile.

- Getting organized: Review **secondary sources** to identify primary sources that are most relevant to your research topic. Then follow up and read the **primary sources** to check what is reported in those sources.
- Getting searching: Use online databases, such as PsycINFO, PsycARTICLES, PubMed, ERIC, and JSTOR. Each online database allows you to use keyword searches to review thousands of articles and books.

LO 5 Identify four ethical concerns for giving proper credit.

- These concerns are as follows: incorrectly citing reference articles, failing to obtain or give proper credit to a primary source, citing a source after only reading the abstract for that source, and citation bias.
- **Citation bias** occurs when citing only evidence that supports your view without also citing existing evidence that refutes your view.

LO 6 Describe the "3 Cs" of conducting an effective literature review.

- Be comprehensive. Journals specialize, so search a journal name if you know it contains articles that interest you. Read sections of research articles in the following order: title, abstract, introduction and discussion, method and results, and references. Also, be aware that one study rarely is sufficient to answer a research question or prove a hypothesis, so you should not base your entire literature review on a single article or viewpoint.
- Be critical. Ask questions as you read, know the types of sources you are using, and remain as objective as possible.
- Be clever. Some clever strategies are to identify flaws, identify contradictions, identify anomalies, consider subtleties, and think beyond the research.

LO 7 Distinguish between a confirmational and a disconfirmational strategy.

- A **confirmational strategy** is a method of testing a theory or hypothesis in which a positive result confirms the predictions made by that theory or hypothesis.
- A **disconfirmational strategy** is a method of testing a theory or hypothesis in which a positive result disconfirms the predictions made by that theory or hypothesis.

LO 8 Explain the issue of publication bias.

- **Publication bias** is the tendency for editors of peer-reviewed journals to preferentially accept articles that show positive results and reject those that show only negative results.
- The publication bias is also called the **file drawer problem** because researchers have a tendency to file away studies that show negative results, knowing that most journals will likely reject them. The publication bias means that the size of an effect could be overstated for many behavioral phenomena reported in the peer-reviewed literature.

peer-reviewed journal	literature review	citation bias
hypothesis	secondary source	confirmational strategy
theory	primary source	disconfirmational strategy
parsimony	full-text article	publication bias
deductive reasoning	full-text database	file drawer problem
inductive reasoning	abstract	

REVIEW QUESTIONS

1. Why is it important for a research idea to be novel?

2. Researchers conducted a hypothetical study concerning self-image, parenting, and popular magazines. In their article they stated the following:

   > Popular magazines, such as *Cosmopolitan* (Cosmo), tend to portray women as the "fun, fearless female" (Machin & Thornborrow, 2003, p. 462). Considering that millions of girls in the United States read these popular magazines (Magazine Publishers of America, 2013), it is important to understand how this portrayal influences self-image among girls. In this study, the authors advance current knowledge by testing (1) the extent to which parents are aware of and approve of the content in these magazines, and (2) the extent to which girls actively incorporate this portrayal into their own self-image.

   A. Identify the portion of this excerpt that describes what makes this research interesting.

   B. Identify the portion of this excerpt that describes what makes this research novel.

3. Is a theory or a hypothesis described as a statement that has been rigorously tested and supported by scientific observations?

4. Which type of source, primary or secondary, should you use to begin your literature review search? Why?

5. Name five databases used to perform a literature review. What article information is typically provided for available articles in these databases?

6. Which scenario listed below is ethical, and which is not? (Hint: Refer to Section 2.4.) Explain your answer.

A. A student attends a conference and reads an abstract on a poster that she finds interesting as a source for her own paper. The presenter of the poster tells her that the research described in the abstract has been published in the *Journal of Neuroscience*. The student finds the full-text article, reads it, and cites it in her paper.

B. A student conducts a literature review by searching articles in PsycINFO. In his search he finds three secondary sources that give many interesting primary sources. He is unable to find these primary sources; however, he still cites them in his own paper.

7. State the "3Cs" of an effective literature review.

8. What is the advantage of reading through the title and abstract of an article before reading further?

9. Which of the following terms best describes inductive or deductive reasoning?
   A. Top-down
   B. Bottom-up

10. The explanation below describes the reasoning you used to develop a theory. Identify the portion of the excerpt that (A) describes the use of inductive reasoning and (B) describes the use of deductive reasoning.

    You notice that among your college friends, those who are the most outgoing always seem to be dating. You conclude that being outgoing is necessary to get a date. Using this conclusion as your theory, you predict that more outgoing individuals are more likely to date.

11. Distinguish between a confirmational and a disconfirmational strategy.

12. Explain why using a confirmational strategy alone to test a theory or hypothesis is poor practice.

13. What is the concern regarding publication bias?

ACTIVITIES

1. Choose a research topic that interests you and conduct a literature review as described in this chapter. In your search, find at least three articles that are relevant to your topic, and do the following:
   A. Without restating the abstract, briefly describe the study in each article you chose. Indicate whether the article is a primary or a secondary source.
   B. What information in the title and abstract of each source made it obvious to you that the source was a good reference for your topic?
   C. Include the following reference information for each source: author or authors, publication year, title, journal name, issue, and page numbers.

2. The three hypotheses listed below have been tested in the published literature. You can use the citations to search for the full articles using PsycINFO. Choose one hypothesis and answer the questions that follow.

   Hypothesis 1: Increased eye contact between musician and audience leads the audience to better appreciate the music of the musician (Antonietti, Cocomazzi, & Iannello, 2009).

   Hypothesis 2: Some athletes may practice "disordered restriction" [in terms of diet] as a way to enhance their performance (Thompson & Sherman, 2010).

   Hypothesis 3: Exposure to prosocial media—that is, media that foster caring in ways that benefit others—promotes prosocial outcomes (Greitemeyer, 2009).

   A. Deduce one prediction that is generated from the hypothesis you chose. Devise a study to test this prediction using a confirmational strategy.

   B. Deduce one outcome that is not anticipated by the hypothesis you chose. Devise a study to test this unanticipated outcome using a disconfirmational strategy.

3. Over the course of the next week, observe the behavior and events you encounter. From your observations, use inductive reasoning to develop a research hypothesis and describe the behaviors or events that led to your hypothesis.

Identify a problem

- Determine an area of interest.
- Review the literature.
- Identify new ideas in your area of interest.
- Develop a research hypothesis.

Develop a research plan

- Define the variables being tested.
- Identify participants or subjects and determine how to sample them.
- Select a research strategy and design.
- Evaluate ethics and obtain institutional approval to conduct research.

Generate more new ideas

- Results support your hypothesis—refine or expand on your ideas.
- Results do not support your hypothesis—reformulate a new idea or start over.

After reading this chapter, you should be able to:

1. Define research ethics.

2. Trace the history leading to the Nuremberg Code and state the 10 directives listed in the code.

3. Trace the history leading to the Belmont Report and state the three ethical principles listed in the report.

4. Identify the ethical concerns for three landmark studies in psychology: the Robbers Cave experiment, Milgram's obedience experiments, and the Stanford prison study.

5. Describe the role of the IRB in regulating ethical research with human participants.

6. Describe the standards in the APA code of conduct relating to human participant research.

7. Describe the role of an IACUC in regulating ethical research with animal subjects.

8. Describe the standards in the APA code of conduct relating to animal subject research.

9. Describe the standards in the APA code of conduct relating to scientific integrity.

Communicate the results

- Method of communication: oral, written, or in a poster.
- Style of communication: APA guidelines are provided to help prepare style and format.

Conduct the study

- Execute the research plan and measure or record the data.

Analyze and evaluate the data

- Analyze and evaluate the data as they relate to the research hypothesis.
- Summarize data and research results.

RESEARCH ETHICS

Ethics is often thought of as the distinction between right and wrong, such as the Golden Rule: "Do unto others as you would have them do unto you." Sometimes ethics can even be confused with common sense; however, issues of ethics are far more difficult to resolve than common sense. The reason is that many concerns of ethics are universally recognized, but the interpretation or application for resolving these issues can vary based on the perspective of an individual.

One's perspective is shaped in different ways often depending on one's values and life experiences. The perspective an individual takes can have a substantial impact on the actions of an individual to address ethical concerns. Consider academic dishonesty, for example. Being a dishonest student is an ethical concern; however, the debate to address this concern can differ in perspective. A student may assess the consequences of cheating in the classroom with pressures for academic scholarships and college enrollment status; a professor may assess the consequences of cheating on class grading; an administrator may assess the fairness of awarding degrees to students who cheat. In each case, the issue of academic honesty is addressed, but from divergent perspectives.

Researchers also have divergent perspectives regarding ethical conduct in behavioral research. The information we obtain using the scientific method is typically important. For example, studying academic dishonesty is important. However, how we obtain information about academic dishonesty is also of ethical concern. For example, would it be ethical to tell a student to cheat in order to observe cheating? Is it ethical to video record a classroom to check for possible cheating during a test without making students aware that they are being recorded? The evaluation of these types of ethical questions and many more in scientific research is introduced in this chapter.

3.1 Ethics in Behavioral Research

The term *ethics* describes appropriate human action in areas such as business, medicine, health, religion, and research. In addition, most schools have ethical guidelines about cheating, academic dishonesty, and showing respect to classmates. In behavioral research, the term has special meaning. The term **research ethics** is used to identify the actions that a researcher must take to conduct responsible and moral research. Engaging in responsible research requires a researcher to anticipate what might happen, react to what is happening, and reflect on what did happen. Researchers must be aware of how a study will affect others in any positive or negative way.

> **Research ethics** identifies the actions that researchers must take to conduct responsible and moral research.

> Research ethics provide guidelines for responsible and moral research throughout the research process.

The research process begins with an idea or hypothesis from which researchers devise a research plan. In the plan, the researcher must make ethical considerations such as to anticipate what type of sample is needed (human or animal) and how to treat those in the sample. The difficulty of anticipating what will happen in a study is the biggest ethical challenge that researchers face. After all, the best-case scenario is to avoid ethical problems altogether, and the best way to do that is to fully anticipate concerns before the study is actually conducted.

We begin this chapter with an overview of the history of ethics in research that can also be found by taking the free certification Protecting Human Research Participants course at http://phrp.nihtraining.com. This course is offered by the National Institutes of Health specifically for researchers who receive federal funding to cover the costs of their research. We suggest that all individuals who plan to conduct human participant research complete this course prior to conducting research.

LEARNING CHECK 1 ✓

1. Define research ethics. What is the biggest ethical challenge that researchers face?

Answer: 1. Research ethics identifies the actions researchers must take to conduct responsible and moral research. The biggest ethical challenge that researchers face is to anticipate what will happen in a study.

3.2 The Need for Ethics Committees in Research: A Historical Synopsis

Guidelines for conducting ethical research are relatively new, particularly in the behavioral sciences. Researchers in the past were seldom required to consider the effects of their research on participants, and abuses often caused much pain and suffering. In this section, we describe two past events in which research caused harm to human subjects. These two events were instrumental in establishing ethical guidelines for behavioral research and shaped our modern views of how to treat research participants.

The Nuremberg Code

The ethical conflict in research arises from researchers' desires to achieve *outcomes* regardless of the *means* required to achieve those outcomes. That is, before there were ethics committees, a few researchers valued what they learned from their study more than what they had to do to gain that knowledge. Hence, they favored the outcomes of their research over the means needed to achieve those results. Examples of harmful research on unwilling participants in which researchers sought outcomes above all else include the Nazi medical experiments in concentration camps during World War II. These experiments were unprecedented in the scope and degree of harm to unwilling participants.

These experiments, which took place between 1939 and 1945, included exposing prisoners to harmful gases, infecting them with diseases such as tuberculosis, immersing them in icy waters, placing them in compression chambers deprived of oxygen, and even cutting them with slivers of glass. These experiments, which often resulted in death, were conducted to learn something: the outcomes. The compression chamber experiments, for example, were conducted to determine the altitudes at which aircraft crews could survive without oxygen. However, these experiments were conducted with no concern for how prisoners were treated (the means) to gain that knowledge.

From 1945 to 1947, the individuals and physicians responsible for conducting the Nazi medical experiments were tried in international courts. Because of the enormous amount of evidence, shown in a file photo in Figure 3.1, and the number of defendants involved, many trials were required to investigate all of the claims of misconduct. The first trial was held before the International Military Tribunal, which tried the most important and high-ranking criminals. Subsequent trials held under the Control Council Law No. 10 at the U.S. Nuremberg Military Tribunals prosecuted lesser war criminals. Among these trials included the Doctors' Trial between December 1946 and July 1947. In August 1947, the verdict from this trial included a section called Permissible Medical Experiments, which has come to be known as the **Nuremberg Code**—the first international code of research ethics. Table 3.1 lists the 10 directives of the Nuremberg Code.

> The **Nuremberg Code** (published in 1947) is the first international code for ethical conduct in research consisting of 10 directives aimed at the protection of human participants.

The Tuskegee Syphilis Study

A second event of unethical research behavior was the Tuskegee Syphilis Study. This study, which began in 1932, was performed on 600 Black men, 399 who had syphilis and 201 who did not. The health of the men was compared between the two groups for many decades. Most of those in the study were illiterate sharecroppers from one of the poorest counties in Alabama. Researchers told the men that they would be treated at no cost for "bad blood," a local term used to describe ailments ranging from fatigue to syphilis. In truth, the men did

Figure 3.1 The Nuremburg Trials

The International Military Courtroom (top) and U.S. Army staffers organizing documents that were presented as evidence against the defendants (bottom).

Sources: National Archives and Records Administration, College Park (top); National Archives and Records Administration, College Park Harry S. Truman Library United States Holocaust Memorial Museum, courtesy of Robert Kempner/Photographer Charles Alexander (bottom).

not receive proper treatment, and the researchers conducting the study never intended to treat the men. Their true purpose was to determine the course of the disease through death, the outcome.

Table 3.1 The Nuremberg Code

	Ten Directives
1	The voluntary consent of the human subject is absolutely essential.
2	The experiment should be such as to yield fruitful results for the good of society, unprocurable by other methods or means of study, and not random and unnecessary in nature.
3	The experiment should be so designed and based on the results of animal experimentation and a knowledge of the natural history of the disease or other problem under study that the anticipated results will justify the performance of the experiment.
4	The experiment should be so conducted as to avoid all unnecessary physical and mental suffering and injury.
5	No experiment should be conducted where there is an a priori reason to believe that death or disabling injury will occur; except, perhaps, in those experiments where the experimental physicians also serve as subjects.
6	The degree of risk to be taken should never exceed that determined by the humanitarian importance of the problem to be solved by the experiment.
7	Proper preparations should be made and adequate facilities provided to protect the experimental subject against even remote possibilities of injury, disability, or death.
8	The experiment should be conducted only by scientifically qualified persons. The highest degree of skill and care should be required through all stages of the experiment of those who conduct or engage in the experiment.
9	During the course of the experiment the human subject should be at liberty to bring the experiment to an end if he has reached the physical or mental state where continuation of the experiment seems to him to be impossible.
10	During the course of the experiment the scientist in charge must be prepared to terminate the experiment at any stage, if he has probable cause to believe, in the exercise of the good faith, superior skill, and careful judgment required of him, that a continuation of the experiment is likely to result in injury, disability, or death to the experimental subject.

Source: Reprinted from *Trials of War Criminals before the Nuremberg Military Tribunals under Control Council Law No. 10,* Vol. 2, pp. 181–182. Washington, DC: U.S. Government Printing Office, 1949.

In the 1940s, penicillin became widely available as an effective treatment for syphilis; one such common advertisement used to promote the use of penicillin is shown in Figure 3.2. Yet, with little apparent concern for the health and well-being of participants in this study, the researchers denied the men access to penicillin, and the study continued for another quarter-century. It was not until 1968 that a researcher would voice concerns about the study, ultimately leading to the termination of the study in 1972. Over the 40 years that this study continued, it was supported at one time or another by such government agencies as the U.S. Public Health Service (USPHS), the Centers for Disease Control and Prevention (CDC), and local chapters of the American Medical Association (AMA) and the National Medical

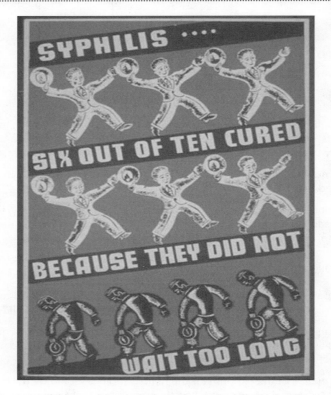

Although treatments were available, participants in the Tuskegee Syphilis Study were prevented from receiving treatment.

Source: Library of Congress; http://www.loc.gov/pictures/item/98514735/

Association (NMA). Table 3.2 shows a synopsis for this study, and lists the changes that were made once the details of the study came to light.

LEARNING CHECK 2 ✓

1. Why were researchers prosecuted in the Nuremberg trials?

2. The _____ is the first international code of research ethics.

3. In the 1940s, penicillin became widely available to treat syphilis. How did researchers of the Tuskegee Syphilis Study respond to this?

Answers: 1. Nazi physicians were prosecuted for conducting harmful experiments on concentration camp prisoners between 1939 and 1945; 2. Nuremberg Code; 3. The researchers denied treating the participants who had syphilis with penicillin, and they continued the study for another quarter-century.

Table 3.2 Synopsis of the Tuskegee Syphilis Study

1932 Tuskegee Syphilis Study begins with a sample of 399 men with syphilis and 201 without. The men are told they are being treated for "bad blood," although none of the participants receive treatment.

1934 First papers are published suggesting health issues related to untreated syphilis.

1936 Local physicians insist that the men in the study not be treated. The decision is made to follow the men until death.

1940 Researchers hinder men from getting treatment ordered by the military draft effort.

1945 Penicillin accepted as an effective treatment for syphilis; USPHS researchers choose not to treat study participants with syphilis.

1947 USPHS establishes "Rapid Treatment Centers" to treat syphilis, although they continue to deny men in the study from being treated.

1968 Peter Buxtun, a venereal disease researcher with the USPHS, and others raise concerns about the ethics of the study.

1969 CDC reaffirms the need to continue the study and gains local support from the AMA and NMA chapters.

1972 The Associated Press publishes a newspaper report condemning the study, leading to public outrage; the Tuskegee Syphilis Study ends.

1973 Congress holds hearings, and a class-action lawsuit is filed by the National Association for the Advancement of Colored People on behalf of the study participants.

1974 A $10 million out-of-court settlement is reached, and the U.S. government promises to give lifetime medical benefits and burial services to all living participants; Congress establishes the National Commission for the Protection of Human Subjects of Biomedical and Behavioral Research to review the study and provide recommendations.

1979 The national commission drafts its recommendations in the Belmont Report.

1997 On May 16, President Bill Clinton formally apologizes on behalf of the nation.

Source: Adapted from McCallum, J. M., Arekere, D. M., Green, B. L., Katz, R. V., & Rivers, B. M. (2006). Awareness and knowledge of the U.S. Public Health Service syphilis study at Tuskegee: Implications for biomedical research. *Journal of Health Care for the Poor and Underserved, 17,* 716–733; and Centers for Disease Control and Prevention. (2011). *U.S. Public Health Service Syphilis Study at Tuskegee: The Tuskegee timeline.* Atlanta (GA): Author. Available at http://www.cdc.gov/tuskegee/timeline.htm.

The Belmont Report

Public outrage following the first published accounts of the Tuskegee Syphilis Study by the Associated Press in 1972 led Congress to establish a National Commission for the Protection of Human Subjects of Biomedical and Behavioral Research in 1974. This national commission was charged with identifying and developing ethical guidelines for all human participant research; in 1979, the commission drafted its recommendations in what is called the **Belmont Report**. The Belmont Report identifies three principles for the ethical conduct of research using human participants:

The **Belmont Report** (published in 1979) is a published document that recommends three principles for the ethical conduct of research with human participants: respect for persons, beneficence, and justice.

- Respect for persons
- Beneficence
- Justice

The Belmont Report provides three principles upon which all researchers must follow to engage in ethical research.

Respect for persons means that participants in a research study are treated as autonomous agents. That is, participants in a study must be capable of making informed decisions concerning whether to participate in a research study. A *capable* participant is one with the physical and mental capacity to participate. An *informed* participant is one with the ability to comprehend his or her potential role in a research study.

In addition to being capable and informed, all potential participants in research must be free of coercion or undue influence. In order to adhere to this recommendation, researchers must provide certain protections for special populations. For example, to protect children less than 18 years of age, a parental waiver to participate in a research study is required; parents give consent for their underage children. This protection is especially important for protecting children who participate in sensitive areas of research such as those investigating possible pharmacological treatments for drug abuse (see Curry, Mermelstein, & Sporer, 2009) or research requiring the disclosure of health diagnoses such as HIV (see Barfield & Kane, 2009).

Beneficence means that it is the researcher's responsibility to minimize the potential risks and maximize the potential benefits associated with a research study. Anticipating the risks and benefits in a study is also called a **risk-benefit analysis**. To apply a risk-benefit analysis, you must determine whether the benefits of a research study outweigh the risks. If not, then the study is potentially unethical.

The principle of beneficence can be subjective and difficult to assess. Researchers must anticipate potential risks, including the potential for physical and psychological harm, stress and health concerns, and loss of privacy or confidentiality. They must also anticipate potential benefits including the potential for monetary gain, the acquisition of new skills or knowledge, and access to treatments for psychological or physical illnesses. To meet the challenges of anticipating potential risks and benefits in research, all research institutions appoint ethics committees that consist of many trained professionals from diverse educational backgrounds who provide additional review of the risks and benefits anticipated in a study before any research is conducted.

Justice refers to the fair and equitable treatment of all individuals and groups selected for participation in research studies in terms of the benefits they receive and the risks they bear from their participation in research. Justice is applied to ensure equality in the selection of potential participants in research. Researchers often select participants based on such criteria as age, gender, level of education, ethnicity, or body weight. The principle of justice ensures that any decision to include or exclude certain individuals or groups from participating in a research study is scientifically justified. For example, a study on the effects of menstruation on mood can include only women. The scientifically justifiable reason to exclude men is that men do not have menstruation cycles.

> **Justice** is an ethical principle listed in the Belmont Report that states that all participants should be treated fairly and equitably in terms of receiving the benefits and bearing the risks in research.

LEARNING CHECK 3 ✓

1. Name the study conducted from 1932 to 1972 that caused public outrage eventually leading to the Belmont Report.

2. State the principle of the Belmont Report that best describes each of the following:

   A. In a study on female gender roles, researchers justify that men can be excluded from participating.

   B. Researchers decide not to conduct a study because the risks to participants outweigh the benefits.

   C. Researchers inform participants of the true purpose and intent of their study.

Answers: 1. The Tuskegee Syphilis Study; 2. A. Justice; B. Beneficence; C. Respect for persons.

3.3 Ethics in Focus: Examples From Psychology

There are classic examples of ethically problematic studies in psychology, many of which are landmark studies. Three such studies are described: the Robbers Cave experiment, the Milgram obedience experiments, and the Stanford prison study.

> Ethical concerns extend beyond medicine to examples in psychology, and are as relevant today as they were in the past.

Robbers Cave Experiment

In 1954, Muzafer Sherif conducted the Robbers Cave experiment, in which two groups of boys were brought to Robbers Cave State Park in Oklahoma (Sherif, Harvey, White, Hood, & Sherif, 1961/1988). The aim of the study was to understand prejudice and intergroup conflict. The researchers created the camp to manipulate prejudice. To accomplish this, for about the first week of camp each group created a name and flag to identify itself (group identity) and group members did all activities together (group cohesion), but the two groups remained apart to create animosity between them. After this time, the two groups finally interacted only in competitive tasks such as baseball, tug-of-war, and tent pitching—all to strengthen the animosity between the groups. The result was dramatic in that the two groups became violent: burning each other's flags, ransacking each other's cabins, and erupting in near riot-like food fights. The manipulation worked, but now the groups were aggressive toward each other because of prejudice that the researchers manipulated.

To resolve the ethical concerns of fostering prejudice in children, the researchers tried to eliminate prejudice between the groups before the camp ended. To achieve this, they staged a situation that required the two groups to work together for a shared goal. As shown in Figure 3.3, the researchers staged a broken-down camp truck that needed to be pulled up a steep hill that required cooperation between the groups in order to make it back to camp (the shared goal). Although the two groups resisted at first, they ultimately worked together, and the prejudice between them dissipated. In fact, many children made "best friends" across group lines.

Figure 3.3 The Robbers Cave Experiment

To alleviate prejudice created by the researchers, the two groups of children had to work together to pull a camp truck that the researchers arranged to be broken down (Sherif et al., 1961/1988).

Source: Image from *The Robber's Cave Experiment: Intergroup Conflict and Cooperation* © 1988 by Muzafer Sherif. Reprinted by permission of Archives of the History of American Psychology, The Drs. Nicholas and Dorothy Cummings Center for History of Psychology, The University of Akron.

Milgram's Obedience Experiments

Beginning in the 1960s, Stanley Milgram conducted his obedience experiments that were staged to make the participant think that he or she was causing harm to another participant by administering electric shocks (Milgram, 1963). In his classic study conducted at Yale University, Stanley Milgram was the authority figure. He assigned one participant as a "teacher" and another person, who unbeknownst to the participant was paid to act as a participant, as the "learner." The general setup of the experiment is shown in Figure 3.4. The task of the learner (the actor) was to memorize word pairs. The task of the teacher was to state one word and wait for the learner to respond with the correct second word in the pair. For each incorrect response, the teacher was told by Milgram (the authority figure) to administer shocks to the learner in increments of 15 volts for each successive incorrect response. The experiment was set up to appear real to the participant. For example, the apparatus for administering shock was realistic and labeled with the different shock levels; the learner was prearranged to give incorrect answers and respond or act as if painful shocks were being administered. However, in truth, no shocks were ever administered. The results were astonishing: 100% of participants shocked the learner up to 300 volts, and 65% of participants shocked the learner to the maximum 450 volts—enough to kill a human being.

The key ethical concern of this study involved the significant stress placed on the participant. Although most participants followed the orders of the authority figure, most

Figure 3.4 Milgram Obedience Experiment

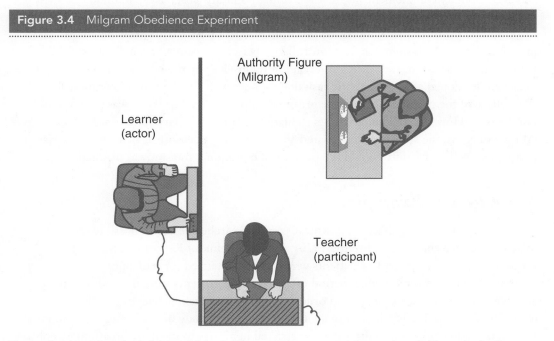

The teacher (participant) administered "shocks" from another room to a learner (actor). The authority figure gave orders to the participant to continue as the experiment progressed.

Source: http://www.ocf.berkeley.edu/~wwu/psychology/compliance.shtml

also complained and pleaded with the authority figure to stop the experiment very early on. For example, one participant complained: "He's [the learner] banging in there! I'd like to continue, but I can't do that to a man… I'll hurt his heart" (Milgram, 1963, p. 376). Clearly, participants experienced great stress in this experimental setting. To alleviate the stress caused by his manipulation, Milgram disclosed to participants the true intent of his experiment and that no shocks were ever administered, after the experiment was completed.

Stanford Prison Study

In the summer of 1971, Philip Zimbardo conducted the Stanford prison study (Haney & Zimbardo, 1977; Zimbardo, 1975). The aim of this study was to understand how social roles influence behavior. Participants were randomly assigned to be a prisoner or a guard. The prisoners were "arrested" and brought in by police, read their *Miranda* rights, and fingerprinted before being brought to the prison. The "prison" was constructed in the basement of the psychology building at Stanford University. The guards wore official uniforms and sunglasses and followed 8-hour shifts throughout the day. Once all "inmates" were in their cells, the study began, and the prison guards were left to run the prison. It did not take long for things to get out of hand. The guards became aggressive whenever a prisoner was disobedient in any way. At first they took away prisoner privileges such as the opportunity to read or talk to other prisoners. It progressed later to taking away meals and bedding, tedious work such as cleaning toilets with bare hands, physical work such as doing push-ups while a guard stepped on the prisoner's back, and even "solitary confinement" in what was actually a utility closet. Keep in mind that these punishments were developed by the guards (not the researchers) during the study.

The prisoners faced increased psychological and physical harm as the guards' actions progressed. Some prisoners cried uncontrollably, became violent and rebellious, suffered from severe depression, and started referring to themselves by their "prison number," and one even developed a psychosomatic rash due to the stress. The ethical concern was for the welfare of the participants, and the prisoners in particular. The study was planned to last 2 weeks. However, the punishments escalated in only a few days. Therefore, to resolve ethical concerns, the study was terminated after only 6 days because at that point, the risks to participant welfare far outweighed the benefits of continuing the study as planned.

More Recent Examples

Despite the best efforts of lawmakers and researchers, cases of possible ethical misconduct have continued since the 1970s when the Belmont Report was issued. In 1994, for example, researchers had 23 patients who were hospitalized for schizophrenia taken off their medication for a median period of 30 days. The patients were then administered amphetamines to induce psychosis in order to measure metabolic changes (Wolkin et al., 1994). In 2001, a participant in an asthma treatment study died after agreeing to take hexamethonium and inhale a drug that constricted her lungs to see if, by breathing deeply, she could overcome its effects without the need of common asthma treatments (see Edwards, Kirchin, & Huxtable, 2004). The methodology and clarity of the risks involved to participants have been questioned in these studies.

A more recent example involved a study that manipulated the algorithms on News Feeds of almost 700,000 Facebook users for one week in January 2012, to see whether a mostly positive or negative News Feed would elicit different types of status updates (Kramer, Guillory, & Hancock, 2014). The authors concluded: "When positive expressions were reduced, people produced fewer positive posts and more negative posts; when negative expressions were reduced, the opposite pattern occurred. These results indicate that emotions expressed by others on Facebook influence our own emotions" (p. 8788). The key ethical concern for this study was that, while the information collected "was consistent with Facebook's Data Use Policy" (Verma, 2014; p. 10779), participants did not have an option to opt out of participating in the study, which violates the respect for persons principle of the Belmont Report. Other ethical concerns were also evident. Indeed, the ethical concerns for this study were so apparent that the editor for the journal that published these findings formally printed an "expression of concern" regarding the ethics of the study, and the authors of the study further issued a formal apology via popular media.

These examples are a reminder that ethical responsibility is a modern concern—as relevant now as it was in the past. Although the development of ethical standards in behavioral research aims to prevent human participants from being used simply as a means to an end, the standards of ethical responsibility are dynamic and evolving as technologies advance and research methods improve. For this reason, ethical behavior and responsibility require action on the part of each individual. Future generations must learn from the mistakes of the past to generate contributions in science using ethically responsible actions.

3.4 Human Participant Research: IRBs and the APA Code of Conduct

The ethical principles outlined in the Belmont Report are included in the Code of Federal Regulations issued by the U.S. Department of Health and Human Services (2007). Under these regulations, every institution receiving federal funding must have an **institutional review board (IRB)** for human participant research. IRBs have at least five members, one of whom comes from outside the institution. A primary function of the IRB is to review **research protocols** submitted by researchers at that institution. In a research protocol the researchers provide details of a human participant study they wish to perform and describe how they will respond to any potential ethical conflicts. An IRB then categorizes the research as involving no risk, minimal risk, or greater-than-minimal risk and will make the final determination pertaining to the level of risk potentially involved in the research study. Only upon the IRB's approval are researchers permitted to conduct their research study.

An **institutional review board (IRB)** is a review board with at least five members, one of whom comes from outside the institution. These members review for approval research protocols submitted by researchers prior to the conduct of any human participant research. Every institution that receives federal funding must have an IRB.

A **research protocol** is a proposal, submitted by a researcher to an IRB, outlining the details of a study he or she wishes to complete and how he or she will address potential ethical concerns. Only upon approval by an IRB is a researcher allowed to conduct his or her study, and all researchers are bound to follow the protocol once it is approved.

The American Psychological Association (APA), the largest association of psychologists worldwide, has adopted a method of assessing risk in its publication of the *Ethical Principles of Psychologists and Code of Conduct* (APA, 2010). This code extends the ethical principles outlined in the Belmont Report to include two others:

- Fidelity and responsibility
- Integrity

First published in 1953 (APA, 1953), Section 8 of this code identifies expected standards of ethical conduct in research and publication. This section has 15 subheadings that detail the ethical principles. The remainder of this chapter will discuss the important features of each subheading in numerical order from 8.01 to 8.15, as they apply to ethical conduct in behavioral research.

MAKING SENSE—GETTING RESEARCH IN ORDER

The code of conduct published by the APA is arranged to match the typical order in which human participant research is conducted. Figure 3.5 shows this sequence of steps. The standards identified in the APA code of conduct begin with IRB approval and end with full disclosure of a study, as does all federally funded research in the behavioral sciences.

Figure 3.5 The Order in Which Most Human Participant Research Is Conducted

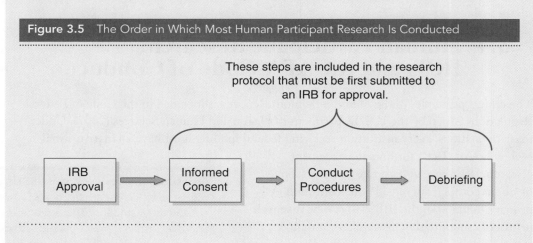

Institutional Approval

When institutional approval is required by an IRB, researchers must do the following:

- Provide accurate information concerning the proposed program of research.
- Obtain approval from an IRB *before* conducting the research.
- Conduct the research in accordance with the approved version of the research protocol.

Once approved, the research protocol acts as a legal document to which the researcher(s) and the institution(s) must comply. Approval by an IRB ensures that any research that is conducted has been fully reviewed for ethical conduct beforehand.

Informed Consent to Research

In research, it is the right of every person to make informed decisions regarding whether to participate in a research study, as required in the Belmont principle of respect for persons. The APA applies this principle by requiring that all participants give **informed consent** *prior* to participating in a research study. Informed consent is typically provided using an informed consent form that is read aloud and signed by participants before a study begins. Table 3.3 shows an annotated example of an informed consent form, describing each of its key sections. Although more sections can be added to an informed consent form, the 10 sections shown in Table 3.3 are typically sufficient to meet the requirement of obtaining informed consent.

> **Informed consent** is a signed or verbal agreement in which participants state they are willing to participate in a research study after being informed of all aspects of their role in the study.

The 10 sections shown in Table 3.3 are meant to meet APA requirements, which are that participants must be informed of the following:

- The purpose of the research
- The expected duration and procedures being used
- The participant's right to decline or withdraw participation at any time
- Foreseeable consequences for declining or withdrawing
- Potential risks of participation
- Potential benefits of participation
- Limits of confidentiality
- Incentives of participation
- Information for whom to contact with regard to any questions a participant may have regarding the research and research participants' rights

Table 3.3 Informed Consent Form

Introduction: State the purpose of requesting informed consent using this form.

> *Example for a hypothetical food intake study:*
>
> If you decide to participate, then as a study participant you will join a study examining food intake and perception involving at least 100 participants. You will be asked to taste foods located in cubicles and rate the foods you eat in this study. You will rate these foods by filling out questionnaires. Each cubicle will contain five plates of food, plastic eating utensils, napkins, a 16-ounce cup of water, and a rating packet. Please taste one food at a time and rate each food before going on to the next food and drink water between foods. If you do not feel comfortable eating a food in front of you, then you may skip it and move on to the next food. You will have 20 minutes to consume and rate these foods. Your participation in this study will take no more than half an hour.

> *Example for introduction:*
>
> The purpose of this form is to provide you as a potential participant with information to help you decide whether or not to participate in this research and to record the consent of those who agree to participate in the study.

Invitation/identification: Invite potential participants and identify the researchers who are involved in this study by name.

> *Example invitation line:*
>
> [Insert name of each researcher involved] at [insert university/institution name] invites you to participate in a research study.

Purpose: In two or three sentences, state what area of research you are investigating and why you are studying this area.

> *Example for a hypothetical food intake study:*
>
> The purpose of this study is to understand how perception influences how we learn about food. Your participation in this study can help us better understand the nature of this learning in humans.

Description of research study: Describe exactly what you will do and what you require of participants in terms of their time and effort. In this section you should also identify the approximate number of participants involved in the study.

Risks and benefits: This part of the consent form can be split into two sections, but all potential risks and benefits associated with participation in the research must be clearly stated.

Confidentiality: A statement should be made with regard to protecting each participant's privacy and confidentiality. This description should explicitly state how you will protect the participant's identity and for how long.

> *Example confidentiality paragraph:*
>
> All information obtained in this study is strictly confidential unless required by law. The results of this research may be used in reports, presentations, and publications, but the researchers will not identify you. In order to protect your privacy and identity, all records of your participation will be given a group number that does not allow anyone (including the project staff) to personally identify you. These records will be kept in a locked cabinet in a locked room where they will remain for at least 3 years following the completion of this research study or until the records can be safely destroyed.

Compensation: To recruit participants it is often necessary to compensate them. The most common types of compensation are financial reimbursement and credit toward a college course. If the study does not involve compensation, then state it here.

Questions/contact information: The researcher must offer to answer any questions about the research and the participants' rights. When appropriate, it is advisable to include whom to contact in the event of a research-related injury or question. In all cases, the telephone number or address of a researcher must be provided.

> *Example questions/contact information paragraph:*
>
> Please ask any questions you may have at this time. If you have questions following your participation, they can be answered by [insert name and contact information]. If you have questions about your rights as a participant in this research, or if you feel you have been placed at risk, please contact [insert name and contact information].

Disclaimer: Explicitly state that participation is voluntary and that participants can quit or withdraw from the study at any time without penalty. When appropriate, also inform participants that they can refuse any portions of the study without withdrawing from the entire study.

Signature lines: A participant must sign the informed consent form to be recognized as an individual voluntarily consenting to participate in a research study. For this reason it is necessary to have each participant sign the form. The researcher should also sign the form. A statement similar to this should precede the signature and date lines:

> *Example signature line paragraph:*
>
> Participant statement: This form explains the nature, demands, benefits, and any risks associated with this research. I have read the informed consent form, have had all my questions answered to my satisfaction, and voluntarily agree to participate in this research study.
>
> _____   _____   _____
> Participant signature   Printed name   Date
>
> Researcher statement: I certify that I have orally explained to the above individual the nature and purpose of, as well as the potential benefits and possible risks associated with participation in, this research study; have answered any questions that have been raised; and have witnessed the above signature. I have provided (offered) the participant a copy of this signed consent document.
>
> _____   _____   _____
> Researcher signature   Printed name   Date

Assent is the consent of a minor or other legally incapable person to agree to participate in research only after receiving an appropriate explanation in reasonably understandable language.

A copy of the informed consent form must be submitted to an IRB as part of a research protocol. The APA code of conduct also provides special provisions for persons who are legally incapable of giving informed consent, including minors. For example, researchers must attain **assent** when children are participants in research. In other words, for minors to participate in research, they must agree to participate only after receiving an appropriate explanation in reasonably understandable language. Obtaining consent from a child's parent or other legal guardian is also necessary.

The purpose of obtaining informed consent is to demonstrate the Belmont principle of respect for persons by providing all pertinent information in an informed consent form. Some additional guidelines for preparing and writing an informed consent form are as follows:

- Avoid exculpatory language. That is, participants should not be asked to waive or appear to waive any legal rights, or to release the institution or its agents from liability for negligence.

- Use numeric values (such as <1%) to describe the probability of "rare" risks when possible. The more severe the potential risks, the less likely participants think they will occur, even when the same word is used to describe their probability (Fischer & Jungermann, 1996; Mazur & Merz, 1994; Rector, 2008).

- For participants requiring or requesting a translator, one must be provided to them, and the translator in addition to the participant should sign the form.

- Avoid technical jargon. Write in simple language at less than a high school level throughout the form.

- Write as if you are speaking to the participant. Use the second person using the pronoun "you" throughout the form.

- Use black, nonitalicized, 11-point font (or larger if appropriate) throughout the form.

An important, yet often overlooked, concern is what participants actually recall about a research study—particularly with regard to communicating risks (Lipkus, 2007; Parascandola, Hawkins, & Danis, 2002; Sieber, 2007). Evidence appears to indicate that participants actually recall very little (Flory & Emanuel, 2004). In one study intended to determine how researchers could improve participants' recall, the researchers paid participants $5 for each item correctly recalled in an informed consent form. As the data shown in Figure 3.6 indicate, this financial incentive increased recall of the items in the form (Festinger et al., 2009). Also, the finding that participants in this study recalled less than 20% of risks and benefits listed in an informed consent is somewhat concerning, particularly for research with the potential of severe risks to participants.

Informed consent appeals to the Belmont principle of respect for persons.

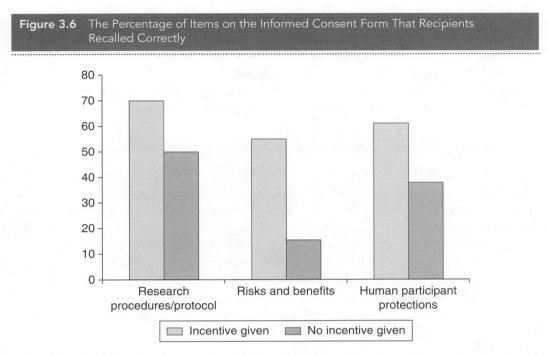

Figure 3.6 The Percentage of Items on the Informed Consent Form That Recipients Recalled Correctly

Notice that participants who received an incentive of $5 for each item correctly recalled significantly increased their recall in each section of the form. Data are adapted from Festinger et al. (2009).

Informed Consent for Recording Voices and Images in Research

Some research uses video or voice recorders. Recording devices such as these are particularly useful in interviews and to observe social behaviors in naturalistic settings. Before making recordings, however, researchers must obtain informed consent, with two exceptions. Researchers do not need to obtain informed consent when either of the following occurs:

- The research is conducted strictly in naturalistic settings and poses no anticipated risk of personal identification or harm.

- The research requires *deception*, and consent is obtained after the recordings have been made (the use of deception in research is described later in this section).

Client/Patient, Student, and Subordinate Research Participants

Researchers must also protect potential participants from adverse consequences associated with declining or withdrawing participation in a research study. For example, college students often participate in research. As an incentive for students to participate, researchers often offer credits toward a particular college course. To avoid potential adverse consequences, these credits must be granted in full so long as the student shows up to participate; granting these credits must *never* be contingent on the student's actual participation in a study. All potential participants have the right to decline or withdraw participation at any time without undue influence or coercion.

Dispensing With Informed Consent for Research

To minimize bias and ensure the integrity of the data collected in a research study, it is sometimes permissible to initially exclude information in an informed consent form, or dispense with or waive the need for an informed consent. An informed consent can sometimes "give away" what the study is about, which could bias participant responses during a study. To overcome this or a related concern, a researcher may wish to withhold specific information that is critical to a research hypothesis, or seek a consent waiver. However, for an IRB to approve this action (i.e., not being fully forthcoming or waiving informed consent), the researcher must show that the potential of distress or harm to participants in a proposed study is minimal to none, and that it is permitted by law and federal or institutional regulations.

While informed consent can be waived or information in an informed consent can be withheld or deceiving, such actions must never put a participant at greater-than-minimal risk and must be approved by an IRB.

Offering Inducements for Research Participation

Sometimes research participants will receive incentives to participate. Incentives can include monetary compensation, gift cards, or entry into a prize drawing. Whatever the incentive, researchers must ensure that it is not excessive or inappropriate. The idea here is that if a researcher made the incentive large enough, participants may participate in a study because the "payoff is too good to pass up," even when their actual intention would be to decline participation. Excessive incentives are viewed as a type of coercion or undue influence on the part of the researcher in order to gain participation. Therefore, excessive incentives should never be offered for participation in a study.

Deception in Research

Deception is a strategy used by researchers in which participants are deliberately misled concerning the true purpose and nature of the research being conducted. Deception can be active (deliberately untruthful) or passive (omission of key information).

A cover story is a false explanation or story intended to prevent research participants from discovering the true purpose of a research study.

Deception in research occurs when participants are deliberately misled about the purpose or nature of a research study. Deception can be active (deliberately untruthful; e.g., telling a lie, often by using a **cover story**) or passive (omission of key information about a study; e.g., not telling participants that one study participant is a confederate). For an IRB to approve the use of deception, the researcher must show the following:

- The deception is necessary, and the use of nondeceptive alternatives is not feasible.

- There is no reasonable expectation for causing physical pain or severe emotional distress to participants as a result of the deception.

- Participants are informed of the deception as early as possible, meaning at the end of the study, but no later than at the end of the data collection.

The use of deception is sometimes unavoidable. For example, when participants expect a drug treatment to cause some change, such as to relieve stress, they often report experiencing that change even if the drug treatment they received was actually fake. This response to the fake drug is called a *placebo effect*. To avoid a placebo effect, researchers do not let participants know whether they will actually receive a treatment (Kaptchuk, 1998; Miller, Wendler, & Swartzman, 2005), and this practice of deception in science is rather common (Wendler & Miller, 2004). Determining if the use of deception is justified can still be subjective, which is why researchers must include any use of deception in their research protocol for an IRB to review.

Debriefing

At the conclusion of a study, all participants receive a **debriefing** in which the researcher discloses the true purpose of the study. The debriefing form can be read aloud to participants by the researcher. When no deception is used, participants can often be given a printed debriefing form to read on their own. The debriefing is included at the end of a study to meet the Belmont principle of respect for persons by being upfront with participants regarding their role in a research study. As part of a debriefing, the researcher must do the following:

- Take appropriate steps to answer participant questions and address any misconceptions or concerns the participants may have.

- Take reasonable steps to reduce risk or harm to participants if the researcher can justify delaying or withholding information in a debriefing.

- Take reasonable steps to protect participants if or when the researcher becomes aware that research procedures have harmed a participant.

The debriefing is especially important for studies that use deception because the debriefing informs the participant of the deception used. Consider, for example, the study conducted by Hermans, Larsen, Herman, and Engels (2008). Their cover story to participants was that the study was intended to evaluate television commercials. In truth, female participants were recruited to study social modeling of food intake. Each female participant was paired with a female **confederate**

> A **debriefing** is the full disclosure to participants of the true purpose of a study and is typically given at the end of a study.
>
> A **confederate** is a co-researcher or actor who pretends to be a participant in a research study for the purposes of scientific investigation.

Whether or not deception is used, participants have a right to know the true purpose of a study prior to the conclusion of a study.

who worked with the researchers by pretending to be a participant. The women first watched TV commercials to make the cover story plausible. During a "break," the women were given a bowl of M&M's to snack on. The confederate was directed prior to the study to eat a large amount, a small amount, or no M&M's. As shown in Figure 3.7, the more M&M's the confederate ate, the more a female participant ate during the break.

Suppose that the researchers let the female participants leave without disclosing the cover story. This is an unethical situation researchers want to avoid; the debriefing is a researcher's opportunity to "come clean," so to speak, when deception is used in a study. Interestingly, participants are rarely offended by being misled and instead often feel it is justified (Christensen, 1988; Resnick & Schwartz, 1973).

3.5 Ethics in Focus: Anonymity and Confidentiality

In the APA code of conduct, researchers are required to protect the privacy of research participants. Consequently, researchers take steps to protect the anonymity and confidentiality of participants. **Anonymity** is the stricter standard in which the identity of a participant remains unknown to all people throughout a study. Hence, not even those involved in the study, including the researchers, can identify participants. This standard is often hard to meet, though, particularly for research that requires observing participants at multiple times, thereby requiring researchers to keep track of participants.

Figure 3.7 The Intake in Kilocalories of M&M's

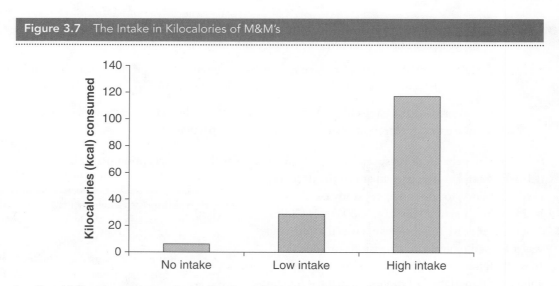

In a "break" (the observation session), a female confederate modeled no, low, or high intake of the candies. Results show that the more M&M's a confederate ate, the more female participants ate. Data adapted from Hermans et al. (2008).

When anonymity is not possible, researchers instead take steps to protect the **confidentiality** of participants by ensuring that the identity of a participant is not made available to anyone who is not directly involved in a study. The researchers are able to identify participant information, and they promise not to share that information with anyone. Confidentiality allows researchers to track participants using personal identifiers, and also protect participant information from being seen by anyone else, such as parents, friends, and other participants. Unfortunately, the terms *anonymity* and *confidentiality* are often used interchangeably, especially in ordinary speech. Be sure you are aware of the distinction between these terms when conducting research studies.

Anonymity is a protection of individual identity in which the identity of a participant remains unknown throughout a study, even to those involved in a study.

Confidentiality is a protection of individual identity in which the identity of a participant is not made available to anyone who is not directly involved in a study. Those involved in a study, however, are able to identify participant information.

LEARNING CHECK 5 ✓

1. State the principle in the Belmont Report that best describes the need for an informed consent and debriefing in human participant research.

2. A researcher informs participants of their rights as research participants prior to asking them to participate in a research study. By doing so, what APA ethical standard does the researcher meet?

3. A researcher studying spousal abuse deceives participants and tells them that they are being asked to participate in a study on marital satisfaction. What must the researcher do at the conclusion of the study?

4. Which protection of participant identity, anonymity or confidentiality, ensures that not even the researchers can identify participants?

Answers: 1. Respect for persons; 2. Informed consent to research; 3. They must give a debriefing in which they disclose the true intent or purpose of the study; 4. Anonymity.

3.6 Animal Subject Research: IACUCs and the APA Code of Conduct

Many behavioral researchers also study animals, such as rats, mice, hamsters, guinea pigs, birds, insects, and even primates. An advantage of using animals in research is that the entire life of an animal can be controlled from birth to death. Researchers can breed animals to control genetic differences, and they control an animal's living environment to control factors such as the animal's diet, day/night sleep cycle, and contact with conspecifics—this level of control is not possible in human research. Protections for the use of animals in research actually have a longer history than protections afforded to humans. In the United States, for example, the American Society for the Prevention of Cruelty to Animals (ASPCA) was established in 1866 (ASPCA, 1996), over 100 years before the Belmont Report was drafted.

To protect animals in research, a research study must be reviewed and approved by an **institutional animal care and use committee (IACUC)** prior to conducting a study. An IACUC includes at least one veterinarian, one scientist with experience using animals, and one public member from the community. The IACUC serves to ensure that all researchers adhere to the guidelines for the protections of animals provided in the *Guide for the Care and Use of Laboratory Animals* (National Research Council, 2011) and other applicable laws and regulations, including federal animal welfare regulations, and USPHS policies. Researchers using animal subjects must submit a research protocol to an IACUC prior to conducting a study. Table 3.4 shows many of the questions that researchers must answer in the protocols they submit to an IACUC. Only upon approval by an IACUC is a researcher allowed to conduct his or her research study.

IACUCs were established to protect the ethical care and use of animals in research.

The APA code of conduct has guidelines for the ethical care and use of animals in research. Separate from the code of conduct guidelines reviewed in this section, the APA provides more detailed guidelines in the *Guidelines for Ethical Conduct in the Care and Use of Nonhuman Animals in Research* (APA, 2012). Researchers must adhere to the guidelines provided by the APA for the ethical care and use of animals in research.

Humane Care and Use of Animals in Research

The APA code of conduct includes a list of researcher responsibilities to protect the care and use of animals. In this list, researchers who use animals in research must do the following:

- Comply with federal, state, and local laws in the care and use of animals.

- Use experienced professionals to supervise animals.

- Train all individuals who will handle animals.

- Make a reasonable effort to minimize discomfort, infection, illness, and pain in animals.

- Use justified procedures (including surgical procedures) that minimize pain to animals.

- Use appropriate anesthesia in a timely manner to minimize pain to animals.

Table 3.4 Animal Care and Use Protocols

The following basic questions should be answered before proposing a research study using animal subjects:
1. What is the rationale and purpose of the research?
2. Can the researchers justify the species and number of animals requested?
3. Are other less invasive research procedures available or appropriate?
4. Have the researchers been trained in the procedures used?
5. What are the housing and husbandry (i.e., care) requirements? Are there any unusual requirements?
6. Are any studies unnecessary, such as duplicating research already conducted?
7. What is the timeline for the study for the duration of time animal subjects are under the researchers' care, not just the timeline for the research study?
8. What is the plan for caring for animals following the research procedure?
9. What is the method of euthanasia or disposal of animals?
10. Is the working environment for personnel safe?
11. For surgical studies, are sedation, analgesia, and anesthesia appropriate?
12. For surgical studies, how will multiple major operative procedures be conducted on the same animals?

Source: Adapted from the *Guide for the Care and Use of Laboratory Animals* (National Research Council, 2011).

Keep in mind that protections for animals extend for the full duration of time that they are under the care of a researcher. This responsibility begins when the animals arrive in a research lab before the study, and ends when the animals leave the research lab at the conclusion of a study. Hence, the researcher is responsible for the care and use of animal subjects around the clock, and not just during the conduct of a research study.

LEARNING CHECK 6 ✓

1. What is the role of an institutional animal care and use committee (IACUC) in animal subject research?

2. True or false: Animal researchers are responsible for the care and use of animals only for the duration of time that a study is actually conducted.

Answers: 1. An IACUC is a review board that has at least three members who review research protocols involving the use of animal subjects; 2. False. Animal researchers are responsible for the care and use of animals for the full duration of time that they are under the researchers' care, and not only during a study.

3.7 Additional Ethical Considerations: Scientific Integrity

> In ethics, **scientific integrity** is the extent to which a researcher is honest and truthful in his or her actions, values, methods, measures, and dissemination of research.

The remaining APA code of conduct provides ethical guidelines for **scientific integrity**, which reflects the personal and professional conduct of the researcher. These additional considerations are discussed in this section.

Reporting Research Results

Researchers are expected to truthfully report data and never fabricate research results by making up data that were never observed or measured. If or when researchers make a mistake regarding the data they report, they must correct the mistake as soon as the mistake is discovered. Recent examples of **fabrication** include a graduate student who, by her own admission, fabricated a series of articles in the field of personality and social psychology; a clinical researcher in the area of cancer prevention and treatment who fabricated patient data; and a researcher from an elite Ivy League medical school who fabricated up to 50% of reported data on sleep apnea in severely obese patients (Office of Research Integrity, 2011b). However infrequent, examples such as these occur each year.

> In research, **fabrication** is to concoct methods or data that misrepresent aspects of a research study with the intent to deceive others.

Plagiarism

Researchers are expected to represent their own ideas in published work and, when they use ideas from other people, to appropriately give credit to others. If a researcher represents someone else's ideas as his or her own, then the researcher is guilty of **plagiarism**. In 2009, researchers reviewing articles available on the search engine MEDLINE found 9,120 entries of research articles with "high levels of citation similarity and no overlapping authors" (Long, Errami, George, Sun, & Garner, 2009, p. 1293), making it possible that many researchers were using sources from other articles without giving proper credit (see also Errami & Garner, 2008; Office of Research Integrity, 2011a). Keep in mind that you should feel free to use the work of others, so long as you acknowledge the source of those ideas. To avoid plagiarism, do not represent it as your own work. Indeed, you will read about the work of others throughout this book, but the sources and credits are given.

> **Plagiarism** is an individual's use of someone else's ideas or work that is represented as the individual's own ideas or work.

Publication Credit

When publishing or professionally presenting research data, all individuals who "have substantially contributed" (APA, 2010) to the work should be recognized as an author. In addition, those who made minor contributions should be acknowledged appropriately, such as in a footnote or an introductory statement. Authors should be listed in order of their relative contribution to the work, with the first author listed being recognized as the individual having made the largest contribution. The APA recommends that all potential authors discuss authorship prior to conducting a study in order to avoid possible concerns later.

> Researchers have an ethical responsibility to accurately and truthfully disclose the ideas and outcomes of a study.

Duplicate Publication of Data

The same work should never be published twice without recognition of what is being republished and why. It is unethical to duplicate or republish previously published data as original data. Long et al. (2009) identified 212 pairs of duplicate articles in a review of those available on the search engine MEDLINE. Among the pairs of duplicate articles, on average the overlap between the original and the duplicate copy was 86.2% in the text and 73.1% among references cited. Also reported was that 71.4% of the duplicate pairs had a similar or identical table or figure. Avoiding **duplication** like this is an ethical concern.

> **Duplication** is the republication of original data that were previously published.

Sharing Research Data for Verification

Researchers are expected to share their data upon request from others for the purposes of inspection, reanalysis, and **replication**, which is one reason that researchers are expected to maintain their research data for years. The data upon which researchers base their conclusions should be made available to other scientists upon request in the following situations:

> **Replication** is the reproduction of research procedures under identical conditions for the purposes of observing the same phenomenon.

- The data do not compromise the confidentiality of participants.

- Sharing the data is permitted by law.

Individuals who request to review another researcher's data may only use these data for the purposes of verification and replication. Any other use of research data, such as manipulating or altering data, requires written permission from the researcher.

> **Peer review** is a procedure used by scientific journals in which a manuscript or work is sent to peers or experts in that area to review the work and determine its scientific value or worth regarding publication.

Researchers have a responsibility to protect data and confidentiality during and after the time in which a study is conducted.

Reviewers

To publish a scientific work, researchers can submit their work for publication in a scientific journal where their peers review their work. Once a **peer review** is complete, then an article can be rejected or accepted for publication in a scientific journal. As part of this process, peer reviewers can sometimes have access to information that should be protected. For this reason, the last principle in the APA code of conduct requires peer reviewers to respect the confidentiality and propriety rights of those who submit their work for review.

LEARNING CHECK 7 ✓

1. A researcher uses ideas described in another work and submits them as if they were his own ideas or work. What has the researcher done?

2. A researcher conducts a study and loses the data. She decides to make up the data instead and defends them as original data. What has the researcher done?

3. True or false: A peer reviewer is responsible for maintaining the confidentiality of those who submit their work for review.

Answers: 1. He plagiarized; 2. She fabricated data; 3. True.

CHAPTER SUMMARY

LO 1 Define research ethics.

- **Research ethics** identifies the actions that researchers must take to conduct responsible and moral research. In science, researchers must *anticipate* ethical considerations in a research plan, *react* to ethical concerns during a study, and *reflect* on what did happen in their study after the plan is executed.

LO 2 Trace the history leading to the Nuremberg Code and state the 10 directives listed in the code.

- The individuals and physicians responsible for the conduct of harmful experiments on concentration camp prisoners were put on trial between 1945 and 1947. Many trials were held during this time. The Doctors' Trial was prosecuted between December 1946 and July 1947. In August 1947, the verdict from this trial included a section that has come to be known as the **Nuremberg Code**, the first international code of research ethics.

LO 3 Trace the history leading to the Belmont Report and state the three ethical principles listed in the report.

- In 1932, the Tuskegee Syphilis Study began in which 600 Black men—399 with syphilis and 201 who did not have the disease—were studied to determine the course of the disease through death. The true purpose of the study was not revealed to the men. In the 1940s, penicillin became widely available as an effective treatment for syphilis; however, participants in the study were denied treatment, and the study continued for another quarter-century. In response to public outrage, the study ended in 1972; in 1974, Congress established the national commission that drafted the **Belmont Report** in 1979, which states three ethical principles: respect for persons, beneficence, and justice.

  - **Respect for persons:** Participants in a research study must be autonomous agents capable of making informed decisions concerning whether to participate in research.
  - **Beneficence:** It is the researcher's responsibility to minimize the potential risks and maximize the potential benefits associated with conducting a research study.
  - **Justice:** All participants should be treated fairly and equitably in terms of receiving the benefits and bearing the risks in a research study.

LO 4 Identify the ethical concerns for three landmark studies in psychology: the Robbers Cave experiment, Milgram's obedience experiments, and the Stanford prison study.

- Muzafer Sherif conducted the Robbers Cave experiment in 1954. Two groups of boys were brought to Robbers Cave State Park in Oklahoma. The aim of the study was to understand prejudice and intergroup conflict. However, the two groups of boys were aggressive toward each other because of prejudice that the researchers manipulated. To resolve the ethical concerns of fostering prejudice in children, the researchers staged a situation that required the two groups to work together for a shared goal. Although the two groups resisted working together at first, they ultimately worked together, and the prejudice between them dissipated.
- Stanley Milgram at Yale University studied obedience using a manipulation in which participants thought they were administering significant levels of shock to another participant. One participant was told by Milgram (the authority figure) to administer shocks in increments of 15 volts to another participant (the confederate) for each incorrect response to a series of word pairs. The experiment was set up to appear real to the participant. However, in truth, no shocks were ever administered. The key ethical concern of this study involved the significant stress placed on the participant. To alleviate the stress caused by his manipulation, Milgram disclosed to participants that no shocks were ever administered, after the experiment was completed.

- Philip Zimbardo conducted the Stanford prison study in 1971. The aim of this study was to understand how social roles influence behavior. Participants were randomly assigned to be a prisoner or a guard. However, the guards began to use excessive force once the study began; the guards became aggressive whenever a prisoner was disobedient in any way, and the prisoners began to show signs of significant stress. The prisoners faced increased psychological and physical harm as the guards' actions progressed. The main ethical concern was for the welfare of the participants, and the prisoners in particular. Because the potential for serious harm to participants escalated in only a few days, the study was terminated after only 6 days.

LO 5 Describe the role of the IRB in regulating ethical research with human participants.

- An **institutional review board (IRB)** is a review board with at least five members, one of whom comes from outside the institution. These members review for approval research protocols submitted by researchers prior to the conduct of any research. Every institution that receives federal funding must have an IRB.

LO 6 Describe the standards in the APA code of conduct relating to human participant research.

- All research requiring institutional approval is bound by the information in a research protocol, and the research can only be conducted after receiving approval.
- **Informed consent** is obtained prior to the conduct of research, and it must provide full information regarding all aspects of a research study.
- In most cases, informed consent must be obtained prior to the recording of voices or images obtained during research.
- Client/patient, student, and subordinate research participants must be protected from adverse consequences associated with declining or withdrawing from participation.
- In some situations, it is permissible to initially exclude information from an informed consent form so long as the potential harm to participants is minimal.
- Researchers should avoid offering excessive or inappropriate incentives that are likely to coerce participants.
- The use of **deception** is allowable in research in certain circumstances outlined by the APA aimed to protect human participants from harm.
- Researchers must disclose to participants the true purpose or intent of a study in a **debriefing**.

LO 7 Describe the role of an IACUC in regulating ethical research with animal subjects.

- An **institutional animal care and use committee (IACUC)** is a review board that consists of at least one veterinarian, one scientist with experience using animals, and one public member from the community. These members review animal research protocols submitted by researchers prior to the conduct of any research. Every institution that receives federal funding must have an IACUC.

LO 8 Describe the standards in the APA code of conduct relating to animal subject research.

- Researchers are responsible for the welfare of animal subjects for the duration of time that they are under the researchers' care. This includes all aspects of care before, during, and after the completion of a study.

LO 9 Describe the standards in the APA code of conduct relating to scientific integrity.

- Researchers must not **fabricate** research data and methods.
- Researchers must not **plagiarize**.
- All individuals making substantial contributions to a work must be recognized as authors; those making minor contributions must also be recognized.
- Researchers must not **duplicate** work published by them or another author.
- Researchers must store and maintain their data for the purposes of **replication**.
- Peer reviewers must respect the confidentiality and propriety rights of those who submit their work for **peer review**.

KEY TERMS

research ethics

Nuremberg Code

Belmont Report

respect for persons

beneficence

risk-benefit analysis

justice

institutional review board (IRB)

research protocol

informed consent

assent

deception

cover story

debriefing

confederate

anonymity

confidentiality

institutional animal care and use committee (IACUC)

scientific integrity

fabrication

plagiarism

duplication

replication

peer review

REVIEW QUESTIONS

1. Define research ethics and explain how researchers must anticipate, react, and reflect to conduct ethical research.

2. The conflict between ethics and research stems from the focus on *outcomes* versus *means*. Explain what this means.

3. Among the many trials held for harmful experiments on concentration camp prisoners was the Doctors' Trial, which led to what code? What is significant about this code?

4. In the 1940s, penicillin became widely available as an effective treatment for syphilis. Did the researchers in the Tuskegee Syphilis Study end the study and provide penicillin to the men with syphilis at this time?

5. Based on the timeline in Table 3.2, place the following events (A–E) in order of when they occurred.

   A. The Tuskegee Syphilis Study begins with a sample of 399 men with syphilis and 201 without.

   B. The Associated Press publishes a newspaper report condemning the study, leading to public outrage.

   C. The national commission drafts its recommendations in the Belmont Report.

   D. Researchers hinder men from getting treatment ordered by the military draft effort.

   E. President Bill Clinton formally apologizes on behalf of the nation.

6. State the principle of the Belmont Report that best describes each of the following:

   A. A psychologist requests permission from jurors to record their voices during deliberations prior to making the recordings.

   B. Researchers studying the influence of play behavior in early development justify that only preschool-aged children can be included in the study.

   C. A study investigating the effects of a treatment to relieve symptoms of depression is approved by an IRB after the board determines that the benefits in the study outweigh the risks involved.

7. The APA code of conduct requires that all research be approved prior to the conduct of the research.

   A. What is the name of the committee that is charged with reviewing research that uses human participants?

   B. What is the name of the document that researchers must submit to the review board committee?

8. State the five ethical principles incorporated in the APA code of conduct. Three of these principles were published in which 1979 report?

9. Referring to Table 3.3, state 10 sections that should be included in an informed consent form.

10. Are researchers ever permitted to exclude information from an informed consent? Explain.

11. A researcher studying academic dishonesty uses a cover story in an informed consent form that tells participants that they are being asked to participate in a study concerning school pride.

    A. Is this type of deception allowed?

    B. What must researchers do at the end of the research study to disclose their deception?

12. What is the name of a committee that is charged with reviewing research that uses animal subjects?

13. How does a researcher's duration of care for animal subjects differ from that with human participants?

14. State whether each of the following is an example of fabrication or plagiarism.

    A. A researcher submits a manuscript to a research journal that includes two figures summarizing data that were not actually recorded.

    B. A student uses the ideas from a book review to write a paper on the role of psychology in child development. She does not cite the book in her paper.

    C. A student notices a cool graphic that he decides to include in his research paper without giving credit to the original author of the graphic.

    D. A researcher notices that there are data missing, so she fills in the missing data with (made-up) scores that help show that her hypothesis is correct.

ACTIVITIES

1. For each of the following research situations, state whether it is an ethical study. If you consider the study unethical, state how the hypothesis could potentially be studied in an ethical manner.

    A. Researchers hypothesize that louder music leads to greater alcohol consumption. To test this idea, they place students in a social setting where alcohol is served with low-, moderate-, or high-volume music playing in the background. They measure the amount of alcohol consumed during a 1-hour session, debrief the students, and dismiss them from the study.

    B. A psychologist hypothesizes that murder suspects will show mostly a remorseful body posture when taking the stand in their own defense. To test this idea, she records the body language of the defendant during the testimony of his or her crime at six different trials. This study was conducted in the natural setting of a courtroom trial.

    C. An animal researcher hypothesizes that rats will associate a sweet taste with illness if they are made sick. To test this idea, he allows rat subjects to drink a sweet-tasting solution for 10 minutes, then immediately injects them with a dosage of lithium chloride to make them sick. The next day he records how much of the sweet solution the rats consume.

    D. Researchers studying psychosexual development hypothesize that exposure to sexual content in television commercials will lead to lower self-image among teenage girls. To test this idea, they recruit teenage girls with positive self-image to participate. Half the girls are shown commercials with sexual content; the other half are shown commercials with neutral content. After the participants view the commercials the researchers measure self-image in both groups, debrief the girls, and dismiss them from the study.

2. Suppose you are interested in testing the following hypothesis using the following research design:

Hypothesis: Both men and women will rate promiscuous females as having less attractive personality characteristics, such as being more selfish, egotistical, lazy, and greedy, or being less ambitious, loving, and nurturing, than promiscuous males.

Research design: You select a sample of 30 men and 30 women. You then randomly assign the participants to one of three groups so that there are 10 men and 10 women in each group. Each group reads a vignette describing a promiscuous partner and rates the personality characteristics of the person the group members read about. In one group the promiscuous partner in the vignette is male (Group Male); in a second group the promiscuous partner is female (Group Female); and in a third group the sex of the promiscuous partner is not identified (Group Neutral).

A. For this study, do you think a cover story is needed? Explain your answer and state a cover story you would use to distract from the true intent or purpose of the study.

B. What precautions would you take to ensure minimal harm or psychological distress to participants? Include a justification of the use of deception.

C. What information would you include in the debriefing? Explain each part of your answer.

3. Within the U.S. Department of Health and Human Services, the Office of Research Integrity is responsible for promoting integrity and monitoring research misconduct primarily in the behavioral and biomedical sciences. On the Office of Research Integrity website, there is a list of recent case summaries for research misconduct: http://ori.dhhs .gov/misconduct/cases/. Examine at least three cases of research misconduct posted on this website. Summarize the ethical misconduct for each case, and explain how you feel this type of misconduct could have been prevented or discovered sooner.

DEFINING AND MEASURING VARIABLES, SELECTING SAMPLES, AND CHOOSING AN APPROPRIATE RESEARCH DESIGN

Identify a problem

- Determine an area of interest.
- Review the literature.
- Identify new ideas in your area of interest.
- Develop a research hypothesis.

Develop a research plan

- Define the variables being tested.
- Identify participants or subjects and determine how to sample them.
- Select a research strategy and design.
- Evaluate ethics and obtain institutional approval to conduct research.

Generate more new ideas

- Results support your hypothesis—refine or expand on your ideas.
- Results do not support your hypothesis—reformulate a new idea or start over.

Communicate the results

- Method of communication: oral, written, or in a poster.
- Style of communication: APA guidelines are provided to help prepare style and format.

Conduct the study

- Execute the research plan and measure or record the data.

Analyze and evaluate the data

- Analyze and evaluate the data as they relate to the research hypothesis.
- Summarize data and research results.

After reading this chapter, you should be able to:

1 Describe two criteria that make variables suitable for scientific investigation.

2 Delineate the need for constructs and operational definitions in research.

3 Distinguish between continuous and discrete variables, and between quantitative and qualitative variables.

4 State the four scales of measurement, and provide an example for each.

5 Describe the following types of reliability: test-retest reliability, internal consistency, and interrater reliability.

6 Describe the following types of validity: face validity, construct validity, criterion-related validity, and content validity.

7 Identify the concerns of participant reactivity, experimenter bias, and sensitivity and range effects for selecting a measurement procedure.

8 Explain why the failure to replicate a result is not sufficient evidence for fraud.

9 Enter data into SPSS by placing each group in a separate column and each group in a single row (coding is required).

chapter
four

IDENTIFYING SCIENTIFIC VARIABLES

While driving, you have probably asked, "How fast am I going?" While at work, maybe you have asked, "How much longer until I get out of work?" As a student, you may ask, "How much does college tuition cost?" In each case, the question you ask requires a definition and measurement of the variables (speed, time, tuition) about which you are asking a question.

To answer a question, you need a way to understand how that question can be answered. For example, to determine how "fast" you are going, you need to know how speed is measured—in miles or kilometers per hour. You can then use this measure of speed to find a measurable answer to the question "How fast am I going?" Similarly, you can measure time in seconds, minutes, or hours to answer the question "How much longer until I get out of work?" The expenses of tuition can likewise be measured in dollars to answer the question "How much does college tuition cost?" For each variable stated here, you define the variable in terms of how you will measure that variable—that is, speed is current miles per hour, time is minutes until work ends, and tuition is cost in dollars.

Defining how variables are measured is important because it ensures that others clearly understand how the questions of researchers are answered. In the example above, you know how to answer each question because you identified how you will measure or observe speed, time, and tuition. Similarly, scientists ask questions about behaviors, such as love, happiness, and stress. They then identify how they will measure or observe these variables so that others can clearly understand how their questions will be answered. We begin this chapter by further illustrating the importance and need for defining and measuring variables in science.

4.1 Criteria for Defining and Measuring Variables

Using the scientific method, we typically need to first define the variables we will observe and measure in order to test a hypothesis. We can use an example to illustrate. Textbooks will often highlight or color key terms to emphasize their importance in a text. Suppose you hypothesize that placing key terms in color increases the attention readers give to those words. To test this hypothesis using the scientific method, you must first ask the following questions:

- How will I observe or measure attention?

- Can other people observe attention in the same way I did?

To test this hypothesis, you must determine what you will observe, how you will observe it, and under what conditions it will be observed. In this example, you will measure or observe attention. You could create two conditions: In Group Color, students read a text with key terms given in color; in Group No Color, students read the same text with key terms given in plain black font. You hypothesize that Group Color will spend more time attending to the key terms in the text than Group No Color. In this example, the measured variable, attention, must meet two criteria to make it suitable for scientific investigation: The variable must be observable and must be replicable.

> A **variable** (also defined in Chapter 1) is any value or characteristic that can change or vary from one person to another or from one situation to another.

A variable that is *observable* is one that can be directly or indirectly measured. A variable that is *replicable* is one that can be consistently measured. To meet both criteria, you must explain how the variable was measured (observable) and under what conditions the variable was measured so that other researchers can re-create the same conditions to measure the same variable you did (replicable). To measure attention, for example, you can use a device that tracks eye movements and record the amount of time a student's eyes orient toward the key terms in the text. The longer a student's eyes orient toward a key term, the greater his or her attention to that word. As long as other researchers have a similar eye-tracking device, they can also measure attention in the same way that you did. Hence, as illustrated in Figure 4.1, attention is measured as time in milliseconds (observable) and could be observed again with an eye-tracking device (replicable), which makes the variable suitable for scientific study.

> For a variable to be suitable for scientific study, it must be observable and replicable.

In this chapter, we introduce the types of variables that researchers measure, how they measure them, and the extent to which a measure is informative. We then describe techniques researchers use to determine the reliability and validity of their measurements and some potential concerns or cautions for selecting a measurement procedure. Finally, we introduce how to enter data and code the variables you measure using SPSS statistical software.

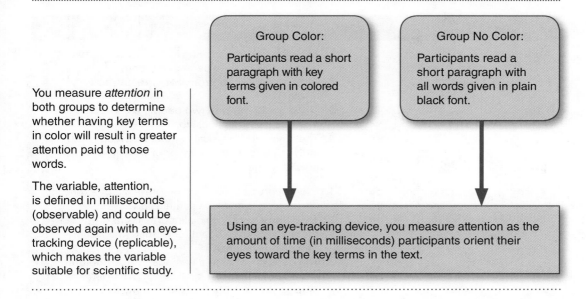

You measure *attention* in both groups to determine whether having key terms in color will result in greater attention paid to those words.

Group Color:

Participants read a short paragraph with key terms given in colored font.

Group No Color:

Participants read a short paragraph with all words given in plain black font.

The variable, attention, is defined in milliseconds (observable) and could be observed again with an eye-tracking device (replicable), which makes the variable suitable for scientific study.

Using an eye-tracking device, you measure attention as the amount of time (in milliseconds) participants orient their eyes toward the key terms in the text.

4.2 Constructs and Operational Definitions

An important challenge for researchers is to clearly explain how they will measure the variables they wish to study. To illustrate, consider the following three variables that researchers can measure: attraction, anxiety, and recall. Table 4.1 lists a description for each variable and three or four operational definitions that could be used to measure or define each variable. Recall from Chapter 1 that an operational definition describes a variable in terms of how it is measured.

The reason we use operational definitions is because it minimizes ambiguity caused by observing otherwise arbitrary phenomena. For example, we could describe *attraction* as the appeal of a person's physical appearance. However, this description is ambiguous because one person may think of the appeal of a person's physical appearance very differently from another person. After all, does "appeal" refer to the clothes a person wears, the person's body type, or a specific feature of the person's body such as his or her hair or eye color? A general description of a variable is simply not good enough. Instead researchers need to specifically define variables in terms of those variables will be measured. As shown in Table 4.1, a single variable can have many operational definitions.

Keep in mind that many of the behaviors and events researchers observe are actually not observed at all—not directly anyway. For example, the first operational definition listed for *recall* in Table 4.1 is the number of errors made on an exam. The more errors made on the exam, the worse the recall. Using this operational definition, we will observe the number

Table 4.1 A Description and Operational Definitions for Three Constructs Studied in the Behavioral Sciences: Attraction, Anxiety, and Recall

Variable	Description	Operational Definitions
Attraction	The appeal of a person's physical appearance.	1. The physical proximity (in inches) between two participants in an experimental room. 2. A rating on a scale (from *not attractive* to *very attractive*). 3. The duration of time two people are involved in a monogamous relationship. 4. The amount of physical contact between two individuals (e.g., the number of times they touch or how long they touch).
Anxiety	A state or feeling of worry and nervousness.	1. Exam scores obtained in the presence of a teacher (the anxiety-provoking stimulus). 2. The number of times male participants stutter in the presence of a beautiful woman (the anxiety-provoking stimulus). 3. The duration of time a teenager pauses before answering a personal question in front of his or her parents (the anxiety-provoking stimulus).
Recall	The ability to bring a thought or experience back to mind or memory.	1. The number of errors made on an exam. 2. The time it takes to accurately complete a previously learned task. 3. The time it takes participants to reorient themselves to a previously experienced environment. 4. The percent of participants able to correctly identify a photo of a confederate they saw earlier.

A **construct** or **hypothetical construct** is a conceptual variable that is known to exist but cannot be directly observed.

An **external factor of a construct** is an observable behavior or event that is presumed to reflect the construct itself.

of errors on an exam. *Recall*, then, is the word or **construct** we use to describe what we actually observed. In other words, we observe errors on an exam, and we infer that this observation reflects the ability for participants to *recall* items on the exam.

Most of the behaviors and events researchers study are constructs. To identify or observe a construct, we identify the observable components or **external factors** of the construct. The operational definition of a construct is the external factor of that construct that we will observe. For example, the external factor of *recall* was the number of errors made on an exam, and three other ways we could observe *recall* are also given in Table 4.1. Many constructs are studied in the behavioral sciences, including learning, anxiety, motivation, alertness, resilience, consciousness, cognition, intelligence, personality, achievement, and love. Each construct must be operationally defined to identify the external factor that will be observed for each construct.

Constructs are often a central component to an explanation provided by a theory. To illustrate, consider the following theory concerning the construct *attraction:* Feelings of attraction promote commitment to a long-term relationship (see Frank, 1988, 2001). This theory uses a construct (attraction) as a mechanism to explain another construct (commitment). The *mechanism* in a theory is the behavior or event that is believed to lead to, or make possible, the *outcome* or occurrence of another behavior or event. Hence, the attraction theory states that feeling attracted to another person (the mechanism) will result in greater commitment to a long-term relationship (the outcome). It is fairly common to find theories that use one construct (the mechanism) to explain another construct (the outcome). Being able to recognize the constructs that are central to a theory is important because constructs can be observed in many different ways—and each way you observe the construct should support the theory. If not, then the theory can be refuted.

> A construct is operationally defined to identify the external factor that will be observed or measured.

MAKING SENSE: OBSERVING CONSTRUCTS

How we define a construct depends on how we will observe it, and there are often many different ways to observe a construct. To illustrate, consider the following two studies used to measure the same construct, fear, which is a commonly studied factor in behavioral research (Brach, 2015; Fanselow & Sterlace, 2014):

Study 1: Suppose we create an experimental situation where participants must walk past a presumably scary portion of campus after dark. To measure fear, we measure how quickly (in seconds) participants walk through the scary portion of campus after dark. We assume that faster times indicate greater fear.

Study 2: Suppose we select a sample of participants in which half have a fear of snakes, and half do not. Participants are brought into an experimental room one at a time. Soon a confederate enters the room and tells participants that in a few minutes they will need to briefly hold a snake as part of the study. A few minutes later a staff nurse measures the blood pressure of each participant. No snake is actually brought in. We assume that higher blood pressure indicates greater fear.

These studies are the same in that both studies measure fear. However, the external factors of fear are very different in each study. In Study 1, we observed how quickly (in seconds) participants walked through a portion of campus, which was the external factor of fear in Study 1. In Study 2, we measured each participant's blood pressure, which was the external factor of fear in Study 2. These hypothetical studies describe different experimental situations, each with a very different external factor that is presumed to measure the same construct, *fear.* Because the same construct can be measured in very different ways, it is important to know not only what was measured in a study, but also how it was measured.

1. State two criteria that make a variable suitable for scientific investigation.

2. Which definition is an operational definition for hunger? Explain.

   A. A physical state of energy deprivation signaled by the body.

   B. The duration of time (in hours) since a previous meal.

3. For the following hypothetical research study state (a) the construct and (b) the external factor for the construct.

   A researcher places sexually inexperienced male rat subjects in one end of an experimental chamber with either a nonestrous (not sexually responsive) or an estrous (sexually responsive) female rat placed in the other end of the chamber. To get to the female, male rats must cross an electrical grid that administers moderate shocks. The researcher measures the difference in time (in seconds) it takes each male rat to cross the electrical grid. He hypothesizes that male rats will be more motivated (i.e., show faster times) to reach the estrous versus nonestrous female rat.

Answers: 1. A variable must be observable and replicable; 2. B is correct because it is defined in terms of how hunger will be measured; 3. (a) Motivation, (b) The time (in seconds) it takes male rats to cross the electrical grid.

4.3 Types of Variables

Every variable or construct we study is defined in terms of how it is measured. The different types of variables we can measure fall into two categories:

- Continuous or discrete

- Quantitative or qualitative

> Constructs are often a central component to an explanation provided by a theory.

Each category is discussed in this section. Many examples for how variables fit into each of these categories are given in Table 4.2.

Continuous and Discrete Variables

Variables can be categorized as continuous or discrete. A **continuous variable** is measured along a continuum, meaning that continuous variables can be measured at any

A **continuous variable** is measured along a continuum at any place beyond the decimal point, meaning that it can be measured in whole units or fractional units.

place beyond the decimal point. Consider, for example, that Olympic sprinters are timed to the nearest hundredths place (in seconds), but if the Olympic judges wanted to clock them to the nearest millionths place, they could.

Table 4.2 A List of 20 Variables and How They Fit Into the Three Categories Used to Describe Them

Variables	Continuous vs. Discrete	Qualitative vs. Quantitative	Scale of Measurement
Gender (male, female)	Discrete	Qualitative	Nominal
Seasons (spring, summer, fall, winter)	Discrete	Qualitative	Nominal
Number of dreams recalled	Discrete	Quantitative	Ratio
Number of errors	Discrete	Quantitative	Ratio
Duration of drug abuse (in years)	Continuous	Quantitative	Ratio
Ranking of favorite foods	Discrete	Quantitative	Ordinal
Ratings of satisfaction (1 to 7)	Discrete	Quantitative	Interval
Body type (slim, average, heavy)	Discrete	Qualitative	Nominal
Score (0% to 100%) on an exam	Continuous	Quantitative	Ratio
Number of students in your class	Discrete	Quantitative	Ratio
Temperature (in degrees Fahrenheit)	Continuous	Quantitative	Interval
Time (in seconds) to memorize a list	Continuous	Quantitative	Ratio
The size of a reward (in grams)	Continuous	Quantitative	Ratio
Position standing in line	Discrete	Quantitative	Ordinal
Political affiliation (Republican, Democrat)	Discrete	Qualitative	Nominal
Type of distraction (auditory, visual)	Discrete	Qualitative	Nominal
A letter grade (A, B, C, D, F)	Discrete	Qualitative	Ordinal
Weight (in pounds) of an infant	Continuous	Quantitative	Ratio
A college student's SAT score	Discrete	Quantitative	Interval
Number of lever presses per minute	Discrete	Quantitative	Ratio

A **discrete variable**, on the other hand, is measured in whole units or categories, meaning that discrete variables are not measured along a continuum. For example, the number of brothers and sisters you have and your family's socioeconomic class (working class, middle class, upper class) are examples of discrete variables. Refer to Table 4.2 for more examples of continuous and discrete variables.

> A **discrete variable** is measured in whole units or categories that are not distributed along a continuum.

Quantitative and Qualitative Variables

Whereas quantitative variables can be continuous or discrete, qualitative variables can only be discrete.

Variables can be categorized as quantitative or qualitative. A **quantitative variable** varies by amount. These variables are measured in numeric units, so both continuous and discrete variables can be quantitative. For example, we can measure food intake in calories (a continuous variable), or we can count the number of pieces of food consumed (a discrete variable). In both cases, the variables are measured by amount (in numeric units).

A **qualitative variable**, on the other hand, varies by class. These variables are often labels for the behaviors we observe, so only discrete variables can be categorized as qualitative. For example, socioeconomic class (working class, middle class, upper class) is discrete and qualitative; so are many categories of mental disorders, such as depression (unipolar or bipolar) and drug use (none, experimental, abusive). Refer to Table 4.2 for more examples of quantitative and qualitative variables.

> A **quantitative variable** varies by amount. A quantitative variable is measured as a numeric value and is often collected by measuring or counting.
>
> A **qualitative variable** varies by class. A qualitative variable is often a category or label for the behaviors and events researchers observe, and so describes nonnumeric aspects of phenomena.

LEARNING CHECK 2 ✓

1. State whether each of the following is continuous or discrete.

   A. The time (in seconds) it takes a driver to make a left-hand turn after a traffic light turns green.

   B. The number of questions that students ask during a seminar.

   C. Type of drug use (none, infrequent, moderate, or frequent).

   D. Season of birth (spring, summer, fall, or winter).

2. State whether the variables listed in Question 1 are quantitative or qualitative.

Answers: 1. A. Continuous, B. Discrete, C. Discrete, D. Discrete; 2. A. Quantitative, B. Quantitative, C. Qualitative, D. Qualitative.

4.4 Scales of Measurement

Researchers can measure data using one of four **scales of measurement**. In the early 1940s, Harvard psychologist S. S. Stevens coined the terms *nominal*, *ordinal*, *interval*, and *ratio* to classify the scales of measurement (Stevens, 1946). Scales of measurement are rules that describe the informativeness of measured data. In this section, we discuss the extent to which data are informative

> **Scales of measurement** are rules for how the properties of numbers can change with different uses.

on each scale of measurement. In all, scales of measurement are characterized by three properties: order, differences, and ratios. Each property can be described by answering the following questions:

1. *Order:* Does a larger number indicate a greater value than a smaller number?

2. *Differences:* Does subtracting one set of numbers represent some meaningful value?

3. *Ratio:* Does dividing, or taking the ratio of, one set of numbers represent some meaningful value?

Table 4.3 gives the answers to the questions for each scale of measurement. In this section, we begin with the least informative scale (nominal) and finish with the most informative scale (ratio).

Table 4.3 Different Scales of Measurement and the Information They Provide Concerning the Order, Difference, and Ratio of Numbers

		Scale of Measurement			
		Nominal	Ordinal	Interval	Ratio
Property	Order	NO	YES	YES	YES
	Difference	NO	NO	YES	YES
	Ratio	NO	NO	NO	YES

Nominal

Numbers on a **nominal scale** identify something or someone; they provide no additional information. Common examples of nominal numbers include ZIP codes, license plate numbers, credit card numbers, country codes, telephone numbers, and Social Security numbers. These numbers identify locations, vehicles, or individuals and nothing more. One credit card number, for example, is not greater than another; it is simply different.

In science, numbers on a nominal scale are typically categorical variables that have been **coded**—converted to numeric values. Examples of nominal variables include a person's race, gender, nationality, sexual orientation, hair and eye color, season of birth, marital status, or other demographic or personal information. Researchers may code men as 1 and women as 2. They may code the seasons of birth as 1, 2, 3, and 4 for spring, summer, fall, and winter, respectively.

Nominal scales are measurements in which a number is assigned to represent something or someone. Numbers on a nominal scale are often coded values.

Coding is the procedure of converting a categorical variable to numeric values.

These numbers are used to identify gender or the seasons and nothing more. We often code words with numeric values when entering them into statistical programs such as SPSS. Coding is largely done because it is often easier to compute data using statistical programs, such as SPSS, when data are entered as numbers, not words.

> The four scales of measurement are nominal, ordinal, interval, and ratio.

Ordinal

An **ordinal scale** of measurement is one that conveys order alone. Examples of variables on an ordinal scale include finishing order in a competition, education level, and ranking. Ordinal scales indicate only that one value is greater than or less than another, so differences between ranks do not have meaning. Consider, for example, the Princeton Review's *Gourman Report* rankings for the top psychology PhD programs in the United States. Table 4.4 shows the rank, college, and actual score of the top 20 ranked colleges according to the report. Based on ranks alone, can we say that the difference between the psychology graduate programs ranked 2 and 4 is the same as the difference between those ranked 8 and 10? In both cases, two ranks separate the schools. Yet, if you look at the actual scores for determining rank, you find that the difference between

> **Ordinal scales** are measurements that convey order or rank only.

Table 4.4 A List of the Top 20 Psychology PhD Programs in the United States, According to the Princeton Review's *Gourman Report of Graduate Programs*

Rank	College Name	Actual Score
1	Stanford University	4.72
2	Yale University	4.70
3	University of Pennsylvania	4.69
4	University of Michigan, Ann Arbor	4.68
5	University of Minnesota, Twin Cities	4.66
6	Harvard University	4.65
7	University of California, Berkeley	4.63
8	University of Illinois, Urbana-Champaign	4.60
9	University of California, Los Angeles	4.58
10	University of Chicago	4.55
11	University of California, San Diego	4.53
12	Carnegie Mellon University	4.52
13	Indiana University, Bloomington	4.48
14	Columbia University	4.47

Rank	College Name	Actual Score
15	Princeton University	4.45
16	University of Wisconsin, Madison	4.43
17	University of Oregon	4.42
18	University of Virginia	4.41
19	University of Texas, Austin	4.40
20	University of Washington	4.39

Source: http://www.socialpsychology.org/ggradgen.htm.

ranks 2 and 4 is 0.02 point, whereas the difference between ranks 8 and 10 is 0.05 point. So the difference in points is not the same. Ranks alone do not convey this difference. They simply indicate that one rank is greater or less than another rank.

Interval

An **interval scale** of measurement can be understood readily by two defining principles: equidistant scales and no true zero. A common example for this in behavioral science is the rating scale. Rating scales are taught here as an interval scale because most researchers report these as interval data in published research. This type of scale is a numeric response scale used to indicate a participant's level of agreement or opinion with some statement. An example of a rating scale is given in Figure 4.2. Here we will look at each defining principle.

> **Interval scales** are measurements that have no true zero and are distributed in equal units.

An equidistant scale is a scale distributed in units that are equal distance from one another. Many behavioral scientists assume that scores on a rating scale are distributed in equal intervals. For example, if you are asked to rate your satisfaction with a spouse or job on a 7-point scale from 1 (*completely unsatisfied*) to 7 (*completely satisfied*), like in the scale shown in Figure 4.2, then you are using an interval scale. Because the distance between each point (1 to 7) is assumed to be the same or equal, it is appropriate to compute differences between scores on this scale. So a statement such as "The difference in job satisfaction among men and women was 2 points" is appropriate with interval scale measurements.

Figure 4.2 An Example of a 7-Point Rating Scale for Satisfaction Used for Scientific Investigation

Satisfaction Ratings

| 1 | 2 | 3 | 4 | 5 | 6 | 7 |

Completely
Unsatisfied

Completely
Satisfied

However, an interval scale does not have a **true zero**. A common example of a scale with no true zero is temperature. A temperature equal to zero for most measures of temperature does not mean that there is no temperature; it is just an arbitrary zero point. Values on a rating scale also have no true zero. In the example shown in Figure 4.2, a 1 was used to indicate no satisfaction, not 0. Each value, including 0, is arbitrary. That is, we could use any number to represent none of something. Measurements of latitude and longitude also fit this criterion. The implication is that without a true zero, there is no absolute value to indicate the absence of the phenomenon you are observing; so a zero proportion is not meaningful. For this reason, stating a ratio such as "Satisfaction ratings were 3 times greater among men compared to women" is not appropriate with interval scale measurements.

Ratio

Ratio scales are similar to interval scales in that scores are distributed in equal units. Yet, unlike interval scales, a distribution of scores on a ratio scale has a true zero. That is, a ratio scale value includes a value equal to 0 that indicates the absence of the phenomenon being observed. This is an ideal scale in behavioral research because any mathematical operation can be performed on the values that are measured.

Common examples of ratio scale measurements include length, height, weight, and time. For scores on a ratio scale, order is informative. For example, a person who is 30 years old is older than another who is 20. Differences are also informative. For example, the difference between 70 and 60 seconds is the same as the difference between 30 and 20 seconds (the difference is 10 seconds). Ratios are also informative on this scale because a true zero is defined—it truly means nothing. Hence, it is meaningful to state that 60 pounds is twice as heavy as 30 pounds.

In science, researchers often go out of their way to measure variables on a ratio scale. For example, if they measure hunger, they may choose to measure the amount of time between meals, or the amount of food consumed (in ounces). If they measure memory, they may choose to measure the amount of time it takes to memorize some list, or the number of errors made. In these examples, hunger and memory were measured using ratio scales, thereby allowing researchers to draw conclusions in terms of the order, differences, and ratios of values on those scales—there are no restrictions for variables measured on a ratio scale.

A ratio scale is the most informative scale of measurement.

LEARNING CHECK 3 ✓

1. Participants ranked their favorite beverages in order from least to most preferred. Beverage rankings are on what scale of measurement?

2. State the two defining principles of interval scales.

3. State the scale of measurement for each variable listed below.

   A. Gender (male, female)

   B. Speed (in seconds)

   C. The latitude and longitude coordinates of a person's place of birth

   D. Movie ratings (1 to 4 stars)

4. Which scale of measurement is the most informative?

4.5 Reliability of a Measurement

Recall that a variable must be observable and replicable for it to be suitable for scientific investigation. The second criterion, that a variable be replicable, is most closely related to **reliability**—a replicable variable is one that has a reliable measurement. A measure is reliable inasmuch as it is consistent, stable, or repeatable across measures or across observations. We will introduce three types of reliability in this section:

> **Reliability** is the consistency, stability, or repeatability of one or more measures or observations.

- Test-retest reliability
- Internal consistency
- Interrater reliability

Test-Retest Reliability

One type of reliability is the extent to which measurements or observations are consistent across time, called **test-retest reliability**. This type of reliability is shown when a measure or observation demonstrated at "Time 1" is again demonstrated using the same measure or observation procedure at "Time 2." When a measure is consistent over time, it is called a *stable* measure. Hence, test-retest reliability is the stability of a measure over time, with more stable measures being more reliable.

> **Test-retest reliability** is the extent to which a measure or observation is consistent or stable at two points in time.

To demonstrate test-retest reliability, we can give participants the same measure at two times. The more consistent each participant's score from Time 1 to Time 2, the higher the test-retest reliability. To illustrate, Taylor and Sullman (2009) measured the test-retest reliability of the Driving and Riding Avoidance Scale (DRAS). A portion of items in the DRAS is given in Table 4.5. The DRAS is a 20-item scale used to measure driving and riding avoidance, with higher scores indicating greater avoidance (Stewart & St. Peter, 2004; see also Taylor, 2008). In the Taylor and Sullman (2009) study, 219 participants completed the DRAS during class and again 2 months later through the mail. The results, given in Table 4.6, showed that many items in the DRAS were stable or consistent at both times. The researchers used a correlation to identify the stability or test-retest reliability of the scale; correlations are discussed in Chapter 8. The key advantage of test-retest reliability is that you can determine the extent to which items or measures are replicable or consistent over time.

Table 4.5 A Portion of the Driving and Riding Avoidance Scale (DRAS)

Items and Subscales
Avoidance of traffic or busy roads
5 I avoided driving on residential streets.
6 I avoided driving on busy city streets.
7 I avoided driving on the motorway.
8 I avoided driving through busy intersections.
9 I traveled a longer distance to avoid driving through heavy traffic or busy streets.
10 I rescheduled making a drive in the car to avoid traffic.
15 I avoided riding in a car if I knew the traffic was heavy.
Avoidance of weather or darkness
11 I avoided driving the car because the weather was bad (e.g., fog, rain, or ice).
12 I avoided driving the car after dark.
13 I avoided riding in a car because the weather was bad (e.g., fog, rain, or ice).
14 I avoided riding in a car after dark.
17 I rescheduled making a drive in the car to avoid bad weather (e.g., fog, rain, or ice).

Participants rate their avoidance of each item in the past week on a 4-point scale from 0 (*avoid rarely or none of the time*) to 3 (*avoid most or all of the time*). Total scores range from 0 to 60, with higher scores indicating greater avoidance. Items are adapted from those given in Taylor and Sullman (2009).

Table 4.6 The Mean and Standard Deviation (*M* ± *SD*) Total Score on Two Subscales of the DRAS from Time 1 to Time 2 in a Sample of 219 Participants

Subscales of the DRAS	Time 1 During Class	Time 2 Two Months Later
Avoidance of traffic or busy roads	5.27 ± 4.45	5.05 ± 4.37
Avoidance of weather or darkness	1.40 ± 2.48	1.50 ± 2.59

Total scores remained stable over time. Data based on those presented by Taylor and Sullman (2009).

Internal Consistency

A type of reliability used to determine the extent to which multiple items for the same variable are related is called **internal consistency**. This type of reliability is shown when participants respond similarly to each item used to measure the same variable. Hence, internal consistency reflects the extent to which multiple items for the variable give the same picture of the behavior or event being measured.

> **Internal consistency** is a measure of reliability used to determine the extent to which multiple items used to measure the same variable are related.

To demonstrate internal consistency, we must show that scores or items for a single test or measure are related using a statistic called *Cronbach's alpha*, which is introduced in Chapter 13 with instructions for how to compute this statistic using SPSS. In short, this statistic "splits" all items for the same measure every possible way and computes a correlation value for them all. The larger the value of Cronbach's alpha, the higher the internal consistency will be.

To illustrate the interpretation of internal consistency, suppose we gave the avoidance of traffic or busy roads subscale of the DRAS to five participants. The results for this hypothetical study are shown in Table 4.7. Because each item measures the same phenomenon—avoidance of traffic or busy roads—we expect the participants to show a consistent pattern in their responses to each item. Indeed, a consistent pattern does emerge from the responses in Table 4.7. For example, notice that Andrew consistently responded on the high end of each item on the scale (i.e., five 3s and one 2); Joseph consistently responded on the low end (i.e., all 0s). When scores for each participant are consistent across items for the same measure, then the items give a consistent picture of the behavior being measured—avoidance of traffic or busy roads—and the measure is associated with high internal consistency.

Table 4.7 An Example of High Internal Consistency

Participants	Subscale: Avoidance of traffic or busy roads						
	#5	#6	#7	#8	#9	#10	#15
Andrew	3	3	3	2	3	3	2
Gregory	3	3	2	2	3	3	2
Rachel	2	2	2	2	2	2	2
Stephen	2	1	1	2	1	2	2
Joseph	0	0	0	0	0	0	0

The data are for five hypothetical participants who responded to the *avoidance of traffic or busy roads* subscale of the DRAS.

Interrater Reliability

A type of reliability used to compare the consistency of ratings or judgments of a behavior or event is called **interrater reliability (IRR)**. This type of reliability is shown when observers make similar judgments of the same behavior or event. Hence, IRR is the extent to which the raters or observers are in agreement with what they observed.

> **Interrater reliability (IRR)** or interobserver reliability is a measure for the extent to which two or more raters of the same behavior or event are in agreement with what they observed.

To demonstrate IRR, we must show that scores or ratings are similar across raters using a statistic called *Cohen's kappa*, which is introduced in Chapter 13 with instructions for how to compute this statistic using SPSS. In short, this statistic gives an estimate of the consistency in ratings of two or more raters. The more consistent the ratings, the higher the IRR will be. In behavioral research, raters are used to observe a behavior in a contrived or natural social situation or evaluate written or oral summaries created by participants. Multiple raters are used any time different people could interpret an observation differently. To make sure that the observations made are reliable, the researcher uses multiple raters who independently observe the same behavior or event to get a consensus about what was observed. High IRR shows that observations made in a study reflect those that other observers would agree with. Low IRR, on the other hand, indicates a misunderstanding or confusion concerning the behavior or event being observed inasmuch as a consensus was not reached.

> Reliability is important inasmuch as we make consistent measurements or observations of a construct of interest.

LEARNING CHECK 4 ✓

1. Which of the following describes the reliability of a measure?

   A. Consistency

   B. Stability

   C. Repeatability

   D. All of the above

2. State the type of reliability measured for each of the following examples.

   A. A researcher has participants complete a 7-item personality survey and measures the extent to which responses for those 7 items are consistent or the same for each participant.

   B. A health psychologist asks a sample of participants who are obese to rank their favorite foods before and after a buffet-style meal and measures the extent to which participant rankings are consistent at both times.

C. A researcher has two observers rate the same social situation and measures the extent to which the two raters agree in their judgments.

4.6 Validity of a Measurement

Reliability is important; however, it does not indicate the accuracy of a measure. For example, a clock that is 10 minutes off will consistently be 10 minutes off. In this case, the clock is not accurate but gives a reliably wrong estimate of time. For this reason, it is important to determine the extent to which a variable measures what it is intended to measure, which leads us to consider the validity of a measurement.

Recall that a variable must be observable and replicable for it to be suitable for scientific investigation. The first criterion that a variable be observable is most closely related to **validity**—a valid variable is one that is correctly or accurately observed. A measure is valid inasmuch as we measure what we intended to measure. For example, if we claim to be measuring attraction, then the measure is valid if we are indeed measuring attraction. We will introduce the following four types of validity in this section:

- Face validity

- Construct validity

- Criterion-related validity

- Content validity

> The **validity** of a measurement is the extent to which a measurement for a variable or construct measures what it is purported or intended to measure.

Face Validity

The most basic type of validity is to make a judgment as to whether a measure "looks like" it is measuring what we think it should be measuring, called **face validity**. This type of validity is a quick judgment of what we think the measure is measuring at "face value," so to speak. For example, suppose we have a beautiful female confederate sit in the middle of a room. We then ask male participants to take any seat they want in that room. We measure attraction as the distance between the beautiful confederate and the male participant. The closer the male participant sits to the confederate, the more attracted he is to the confederate. Face validity, in this example, is the extent to which we think the distance between the confederate and the participant is actually a measure of attraction. If we have doubts, then the measure lacks face validity. For example, might the distance between the confederate and the participant also measure shyness or confidence,

> **Face validity** of a measurement is the extent to which a measure for a variable or construct appears to measure what it is purported to measure.

with male participants sitting closer to the female confederate being less shy or more confident? If so, then the measure has low face validity.

Face validity is a preliminary step; it is a judgment by a researcher to determine if his or her measure for a variable or construct "looks like" it will measure what it was intended to measure. Face validity does not involve the use of statistics or scientific decisions. To obtain face validity, we get a general consensus among our peers that the measure we are using for a variable appears to be valid. In a way, face validity reflects how transparent or obvious a measure is for a variable or construct.

Construct Validity

Construct validity of a measurement is the extent to which an operational definition for a variable or construct is actually measuring that variable or construct.

Another type of validity is used to determine the extent to which an operational definition for a construct is valid, called **construct validity**. This type of validity is shown when we determine that the operational definition for a variable or construct is actually measuring that variable or construct. For example, to measure the construct *learning*, an instructor may distribute a one-dimensional exam, such as multiple-choice only. In this case, the operational definition for learning is an exam score, with higher scores indicating greater learning. However, scores on one-dimensional exams often do not measure learning, but instead measure other factors, such as exam anxiety or stress (Dunn & Dunn, 1978; Morgan, Umberson, & Hertzog, 2014). Hence, one-dimensional exams often have low construct validity—it is not always true that low exam scores (the measure) reflect poor learning (the construct the exam is intended to measure).

Criterion-Related Validity

Criterion-related validity of a measurement is the extent to which scores obtained on some measure can be used to infer or predict a criterion or expected outcome.

Different types of criterion-related validity include predictive validity, concurrent validity, convergent validity, and discriminant validity. Each type of criterion-related validity is described in Table 4.8.

Another type of validity, called **criterion-related validity**, examines the relationship between scores obtained on a measure for a construct and some criterion, outcome, or indicator of the construct. Criterion-related validity is the extent to which scores obtained on a measure for a variable or construct can be used to infer or predict a criterion or expected outcome of that variable or construct. This type of validity has many different subtypes, including *predictive validity, concurrent validity, convergent validity*, and *discriminant validity*. Table 4.8 defines and gives an example for each subtype of criterion-related validity.

Criterion-related validity is demonstrated when scores for a measure are related to, or predictive of, a certain outcome or criterion that is expected if, in fact, that measure is valid. Demonstrating any one of the subtypes of criterion-related validity is sufficient to demonstrate criterion-related validity. Although a detailed discussion of each subtype of

Table 4.8 Four Subtypes of Criterion-Related Validity

Subtype of Criterion-Related Validity	Definition	Example
Predictive	The extent to which scores obtained by a measure predict outcomes it should predict.	SAT scores (measure) predict later academic performance (criterion).
Concurrent	The extent to which a measure can distinguish between groups it should be able to distinguish between.	An assessment for social development in girls (measure) is related to social development in girls (criterion) but not boys.
Convergent	The extent to which two or more different measures for the same construct are related or "converge."	Blood pressure (one measure) and cholesterol levels (second measure) similarly predict risk of heart disease (criterion).
Discriminant	The extent to which one measure can be "discriminated" from another measure that it should not be related to.	Affection (measure) predicts long-term commitment (criterion). This measure is unrelated to hate (a measure that it should not be related to).

criterion-related validity goes beyond the scope of this book, it is important to be familiar with the subtypes of criterion-related validity listed in Table 4.8. Examples demonstrating each subtype are also given in Table 4.8.

> **Content validity** of a measurement is the extent to which the items or contents of a measure adequately represent all of the features of the construct being measured.

Content Validity

A fourth type of validity, called **content validity**, determines whether the contents of a measure are adequate to capture or represent that construct. Content validity is the extent to which the items or contents of a measure adequately reflect all of the features of the construct being measured. Hence, the more thorough a measure for a construct, the higher the content validity of the measure will be.

To demonstrate content validity, we must show that the items we use to measure a construct are representative of the construct as a whole. For example, a final exam should test an adequate sample of all topics taught during the semester; an exam of basic math skills should include more than just addition problems; an assessment for personality should measure more than just one personality trait. In each example, the validity of the measure reflected the extent to which an appropriate number of items were included to measure the construct as a whole.

> Validity is important in that we want to confirm that our measurements are indeed measuring what we intended to measure.

1. What is face validity?

2. A researcher operationally defines nervousness as the time (in seconds) that a participant paces around a hospital waiting room. To demonstrate construct validity, what must the researcher show?

3. Name four subtypes of criterion-related validity.

4. A researcher measures depression using a multidimensional assessment that encompasses all symptoms of the disorder. For this reason, the researcher likely has high _____ validity.

Answers: 1. Face validity is the extent to which a measure "looks like" it will measure what it is intended to measure; 2. The researcher must show that the time spent pacing (the operational definition) is actually measuring nervousness (the construct); 3. Four subtypes of criterion-related validity are predictive validity, concurrent validity, convergent validity, and discriminant validity; 4. content.

4.7 Selecting a Measurement Procedure

There are many things a researcher can do to help ensure that a measure for a variable or construct is reliable (repeatedly observed) and valid (actually measures what it was intended to measure). Researchers can be aware of, and control for, problems that can arise in the measurement procedures used. We will introduce four potential concerns that researchers should be aware of and control:

- Participant reactivity

- Experimenter bias

- Sensitivity

- Range effects

Participant Reactivity

In many research studies, particularly those held in a research laboratory, the participants know that they are being observed. For most studies, participants are given an informed consent form that directly tells them that they are volunteering to participate in a study. The behavior of a participant can change in response to knowing that he or she is being observed, which is a phenomenon referred to as **participant reactivity**.

Participants most often react to their environment in one of three ways, as described in Table 4.9. Participants can be overly cooperative

> **Participant reactivity** is the reaction or response participants have when they know they are being observed or measured.

Table 4.9 Three Types of Participant Reactivity in Behavioral Research

Type of Participant Reactivity	Synopsis	Full Description
Participant expectancy	"The overly cooperative participant"	Plays the role of the "good participant" and behaves in ways he or she feels are consistent with the intent of the research study.
Evaluation apprehension	"The overly apprehensive participant"	Plays the role of the "shy participant" and conceals or withholds information he or she considers private or personal.
Participant reluctance	"The overly antagonistic participant"	Plays the role of the "bad participant" and behaves in ways he or she feels will disconfirm or contradict the intent of the research study.

by behaving as if they are trying to please the researcher by acting in ways that they think are consistent with how the researcher wants them to behave—called **participant expectancy**. Participants can be overly apprehensive and withhold information the researcher is trying to study—called **evaluation apprehension**. Participants can also be overly antagonistic by behaving in ways that they think contradict how the researcher wants them to behave—called **participant reluctance**. In each example, the participant's behavior is a reaction to the knowledge that he or she is being observed, and it is not a reflection of the manipulation or construct the researcher is trying to measure.

Three types of participant reactivity are **participant expectancy** (a participant is overly cooperative), **evaluation apprehension** (a participant is overly apprehensive), and **participant reluctance** (a participant is overly antagonistic).

To avoid participant reactivity, researchers can simply not let participants know that they are being observed. However, for many research studies, this is not possible because participants are given an informed consent form prior to the conduct of the research procedures. In situations in which participants know that they are being observed, the following strategies can be used to minimize participant reactivity:

- **Reassure confidentiality.** A statement of confidentiality or anonymity is included in an informed consent form. Most research situations will protect the confidentiality of participants, and this point should be emphasized to remind participants that their responses will not be revealed. Reassuring confidentiality is especially effective for minimizing evaluation apprehension.

- **Use deception when ethical.** Participant expectancy and participant reluctance occur because the participant thinks that he or she has figured out the research hypothesis. To conceal the research hypothesis and therefore the true intent or purpose of the research study, it is often justified to use deception, especially when the true intent of the research study is transparent or obvious.

- **Measure less obvious variables.** To avoid the use of deception, a researcher can measure less obvious variables that indirectly measure the construct of interest. Indirect variables for a construct are called *nonreactive* or *unobtrusive* measures. For example, you could measure linguistic style (e.g., ratings of self-related words) to study patients with eating disorders because linguistic style is a less obvious measure that is related to eating disorders (see Wolf, Sedway, Bulik, & Kordy, 2007), which can minimize the likelihood of participant reactivity.

- **Minimize demand characteristics.** The research setting itself can sometimes give participants clues (usually unintentionally) about how to behave or react, typically in ways that promote the research hypothesis—such biases should be minimized or assessed to ensure that responding is due to the manipulation or construct being measured, and not due to these "clues" (Robinson-Cimpian, 2014). Clues in the research setting that participants may use to decide how to behave are called **demand characteristics**. For example, suppose that a researcher studies preferences for a food reward. In asking which reward the participant prefers, the researcher may inadvertently give the participant a clue as to which choice is consistent with the research hypothesis, such as by pointing to one reward and not the other. To eliminate demand characteristics, participants should experience a similar research setting across conditions or groups. For example, the researcher could instead point to both rewards or to none at all and be consistent for all groups.

A **demand characteristic** is any feature or characteristic of a research setting that may reveal the hypothesis being tested or give the participant a clue regarding how he or she is expected to behave.

Participant reactivity is problematic inasmuch as it can interfere with efforts to measure or observe a construct of interest.

Experimenter Bias

Experimenter bias is the extent to which the behavior of a researcher or experimenter intentionally or unintentionally influences the results of a study.

Expectancy effects are preconceived ideas or expectations regarding how participants should behave or what participants are capable of doing. Expectancy effects can often lead to experimenter bias.

In many research studies, the researcher knows the predicted outcome of interest. The extent to which a researcher uses his or her knowledge of the predicted outcome to influence the results of a study is called **experimenter bias**. This type of bias, which is most often unintentional, often results from **expectancy effects**, which are preconceived ideas or expectations that researchers have regarding how participants should behave or what participants are capable of doing.

To illustrate an experimenter bias, suppose you hypothesize that men are more likely to help others in need than women. To test this hypothesis, you stage a scene where a male confederate appears to have a broken-down car in a parking lot in the late evening. The confederate asks men and women who pass by for help—and you find that men are twice as likely to help than women. While your results show that men were more willing to help, this result was likely influenced by an experimenter bias. The confederate was male, it was late evening, and he needed help with his car. Women were probably less likely to help for many reasons, most importantly because they were concerned for their personal safety. After all, the study was conducted in late evening, and it was a male confederate asking for help. Also, "fixing cars" is a male-stereotyped job, which further biased the study. The study was designed to all but ensure that the hypothesis would be confirmed, which was an experimenter bias.

Experimenter bias occurs anytime the researcher behaves or sets up a study in a way that facilitates results in the direction that is predicted. The following strategies can help minimize the problem of experimenter bias:

- **Get a second opinion.** It is often difficult to criticize yourself or your research plan. It could be that your plan is somehow biased and you do not notice it. A simple solution is to ask another colleague or friend for feedback first, before conducting the research study.

- **Standardize the research procedures.** To standardize the research procedures, you must ensure that all participants are treated the same. For example, you can read from a script verbatim, prerecord instructions for a study, or thoroughly train confederates prior to their participation in a study when appropriate to ensure that you treat participants similarly in a study.

- **Conduct a double-blind study.** A *blind* study is one in which the researcher or participants are unaware of the condition that participants are assigned. In a **double-blind study**, both the researcher and the participants are unaware of the conditions that participants are assigned. When the researcher is blind to the predicted outcome or results of a study, the potential for experimenter bias is minimal.

> A **double-blind study** is a type of research study in which the researcher collecting the data and the participants in the study are unaware of the conditions that participants are assigned.

Sensitivity and Range Effects

The measure you choose for a construct or variable can sometimes limit your ability to observe that variable or construct. One limitation is the **sensitivity of a measure**, which is the extent to which a measure can change in the presence of a manipulation. For example, suppose we measure eating behavior (the construct) in participants who are lean and obese as the amount consumed (in grams) in a meal and the calories consumed in a meal. Many studies reveal that participants who are lean and obese show no difference in the amount consumed (in grams) in a meal. Hence, amount consumed (in grams) may not be a sensitive measure for observing differences in eating. However, because participants who are obese tend to consume higher-fat diets, they do tend to consume more calories in a meal than participants who are lean (see Privitera, 2008b; Rolls, 2014).

> The **sensitivity of a measure** is the extent to which a measure can change or be different in the presence of a manipulation.

Hence, in this example, while eating behavior measured in grams may not reveal differences between groups, eating behavior measured in calories consumed in a meal is a more sensitive measure for eating behavior because it can change or be different between the lean and obese groups.

Another possible limitation is **range effect**, which typically occurs when scores for a measure are clustered at one extreme. Scores can be clustered very high, called a **ceiling effect**, which can occur when a measure is too easy or obvious. This may occur, for example, if you give students 5 minutes to memorize only five items. Most people will likely be able to memorize the five items. Scores can also be clustered very low, called a **floor effect**, which typically occurs when a measure is too difficult or confusing. This may occur, for example, if you measure how much participants like stale popcorn at home or at a movie. If the stale popcorn tastes bad, then most participants will likely rate it very low no matter where they eat it.

A range effect can limit the sensitivity of a measure because scores will cluster very low or high for all groups, making it difficult to detect differences between groups. The following strategies can help maximize the sensitivity of a measure and minimize range effects:

- **Perform a thorough literature review.** There is a very good possibility that other researchers have already used a measure for the construct you wish to study. Review the literature to find what measures for the construct have been used and whether or not they were sensitive to detecting differences between groups. Then you can use the same measure in your study with the confidence of knowing that it will be a sensitive measure.

- **Conduct a pilot study.** If you are using a new measure, then start small. Begin with a **pilot study**, which is a small preliminary study. In the pilot study, you can evaluate whether the measure is sensitive to detecting changes in the presence of a manipulation before spending the time and money on a full-scale study.

- **Include manipulation checks.** You should consider that maybe the manipulation, and not the measure, is the reason that you are not detecting differences between groups. To check that a manipulation has the effect you intend, you can include a **manipulation check**. If, for example, you measure the speed of decision making when participants are hungry or full, you can check that participants are hungry or full (the manipulation) by asking participants to rate their hunger.

- **Use multiple measures.** Many constructs have more than one measure. Using two or more measures for the same variable can be more informative and make it more likely that at least one measure will detect differences between groups.

> Experimenter bias can be problematic inasmuch as the researcher conducting the study is aware of the predicted outcomes of interest.

A **range effect** is a limitation in the range of data measured in which scores are clustered to one extreme. Scores can be clustered very low (**floor effect**) or very high (**ceiling effect**) on a given measure.

A **pilot study** is a small preliminary study used to determine the extent to which a manipulation or measure will show an effect of interest.

A **manipulation check** is a procedure used to check or confirm that a manipulation in a study had the effect that was intended.

For example, you could measure memory recall as the number of items correctly identified and the speed at which participants correctly identify items. The more measures you use, the more likely it is that at least one of them will be sensitive to detecting changes or group differences in your study.

LEARNING CHECK 6 ✓

1. Participants are asked to choose from a mock lineup a person whom they previously encountered. One participant thinks the hypothesis is that most people will make the wrong choice. To appease the researcher, this participant intentionally picks out the wrong person from the mock lineup, which is an example of what type of participant reactivity?

2. State four strategies used to minimize participant reactivity.

3. State three strategies used to minimize experimenter bias.

4. A researcher uses a measure that participants in all groups scored very high on. What type of range effect should the researcher be concerned with?

5. State four strategies used to maximize the sensitivity of a measure and minimize range effects.

Answers: 1. Participant expectancy; 2. Reassure anonymity, use deception when ethical, measure less obvious variables, and minimize demand characteristics; 3. Get a second opinion, standardize the research procedures, and conduct a double-blind study; 4. Ceiling effect; 5. Perform a thorough literature review, conduct a pilot study, include manipulation checks, and use multiple measures.

4.8 Ethics in Focus: Replication as a Gauge for Fraud?

Many researchers assume that a replicable measure should be observed each time a researcher conducts a study. Researchers, who are ethically obligated to share their data for verification (see Chapter 2), can be subjected to criticism and even accused of fraud if other researchers reconduct their research procedures from an original study and do not obtain the same results as they did. However, a failure to replicate a result could likely be due to statistical error and not fraud. Any measure consists of a true score and a possible error that causes variability in that measure:

$$\text{Behavioral Measure} = \text{True Score} + \text{Error}$$

An *error* is any influence in the response of a participant that can cause variability in his or her response. For example, a measure of life satisfaction can vary depending on a variety of factors including a participant's current mood, relationship status, mental state, health, and even the time of day that the participant responds. Each factor can potentially contribute to an error in measurement inasmuch as each factor can cause responses on the life satisfaction measure to vary. Unfortunately, the potential errors of a measure are often not well understood and therefore are difficult to anticipate. For this reason, when a result is not replicated, always first consider potential sources of error in measurement that can likely explain why a result was not replicated.

4.9 SPSS in Focus: Entering and Coding Data

This book provides instructions for using the IBM SPSS® statistical software program by showing you how this software can make all of the work you do by hand as simple as point and click. Before you read this SPSS in Focus section, please take the time to read the section titled "How to Use SPSS With This Book" at the beginning of this book. This introductory section gives an overview of the different views and features of SPSS statistical software.

In this chapter, we discussed the types of variables that researchers measure, how they measure them, and the extent to which a measure is informative. In this section, we will use SPSS to enter data. When entering data, make sure that all values or scores are entered in each cell of the Data View spreadsheet. The biggest challenge is making sure you enter the data correctly. Entering even a single value incorrectly can alter the data analyses that SPSS computes. For this reason, always double-check the data to make sure the correct values have been entered.

We will use the following general example: Suppose you record the following grade point average (GPA) scores for each of three research methods classes, given in Table 4.10.

Table 4.10 GPAs of Students in Three Research Methods Classes

Class 1	Class 2	Class 3
3.3	3.9	2.7
2.9	4.0	2.3
3.5	2.4	2.2
3.6	3.1	3.0
3.1	3.0	2.8

There are two ways you can enter these data: by column or by row. To **enter data by column:**

1. Open the **Variable View** tab. In the **Name column**, enter your variable names as *class1*, *class2*, and *class3* (note that spaces are not allowed) in each row. Three rows should be active, as shown in Figure 4.3.

2. Because the data are to the tenths place, go to the **Decimals column** and reduce that value to 1 in each row.

Figure 4.3 SPSS Variable View

Name	Type	Width	Decimals
class1	Numeric	8	1
class2	Numeric	8	1
class3	Numeric	8	1

3. Open the **Data View** tab. Notice in Figure 4.4 that the first three columns are now labeled with the group names. Enter the data for each class, as shown in Figure 4.4. The data are now entered by column.

Figure 4.4 Data Entry in Data View for SPSS

class1	class2	class3
3.3	3.9	2.7
2.9	4.0	2.3
3.5	2.4	2.2
3.6	3.1	3.0
3.1	3.0	2.8

Another way to enter these data in SPSS is to **enter data by row**, which will require *coding* the data. To begin, open a new SPSS data file and follow the instructions given here:

1. Open the **Variable View** tab. Enter *classes* in the first row in the **Name column.** Enter *GPA* in the second row in the Name column, as shown in Figure 4.5.

2. Go to the **Decimals column** and reduce that value to 0 for the first row. You will see why we did this in the next step. Reduce the Decimals column to 1 in the second row because we will enter GPA scores for this variable.

Figure 4.5 SPSS Variable View

Name	Type	Width	Decimals	Label	Values
classes	Numeric	8	0		{1, class 1}...
GPA	Numeric	8	1		None

3. Go to the **Values column** and click on the small gray box with three dots. In the **dialog box** enter *1* in the **Values cell** and *class 1* in the **Label cell**, and then select **Add**. Repeat these steps by entering *2* for *class 2* and *3* for *class 3*; then select **OK**. When you go back to the Data View tab, SPSS will now recognize the codes you entered for each class.

4. Open the **Data View** tab. In the first column, enter *1* five times, *2* five times, and *3* five times, as shown in Figure 4.6. This tells SPSS that there are five students in each group. In the second column, enter the GPA scores for each class by row, as shown in Figure 4.6. The data are now entered by row.

Figure 4.6 Data Entry in Data View for SPSS

	classes	GPA
1	1	3.3
2	1	2.9
3	1	3.5
4	1	3.6
5	1	3.1
6	2	3.9
7	2	4.0
8	2	2.4
9	2	3.1
10	2	3.0
11	3	2.7
12	3	2.3
13	3	2.2
14	3	3.0
15	3	2.8

The data are now labeled, coded, and entered. In this book, you will learn many research designs used to observe behaviors and events. For most designs, statistical analysis of the behaviors or events observed is essential. If you master how to enter data correctly into SPSS, this statistical software will make summarizing, computing, and analyzing any data set fast and simple.

Section II: Variables, Samples, and Design

CHAPTER SUMMARY

LO 1 Describe two criteria that make variables suitable for scientific investigation.

- A variable that is "observable" is one that can be directly or indirectly measured. A variable that is "replicable" is one that can be consistently measured. To meet both criteria, you must explain how the variable was measured (observable) and under what conditions the variable was measured so that other researchers can re-create the same conditions to measure the same variable you did (replicable).

LO 2 Delineate the need for constructs and operational definitions in research.

- **Constructs** are conceptual variables that are known to exist but cannot be directly observed. To observe a construct, we identify the observable components or **external factors** of the construct. The operational definition of a construct is the external factor or how we will observe the construct.

LO 3 Distinguish between continuous and discrete variables, and between quantitative and qualitative variables.

- A **continuous variable** is measured along a continuum, whereas a **discrete variable** is measured in whole units or categories. Continuous but not discrete variables are measured at any place beyond the decimal point.

- A **quantitative variable** varies by amount, whereas a **qualitative variable** varies by class. Continuous and discrete variables can be quantitative, whereas qualitative variables can only be discrete.

LO 4 State the four scales of measurement, and provide an example for each.

- The **scales of measurement** refer to how the properties of numbers can change with different uses. They are characterized by three properties: order, differences, and ratios. There are four scales of measurement: **nominal, ordinal, interval,** and **ratio.** Nominal values are typically coded (e.g., seasons, gender), ordinal values indicate order alone (e.g., rankings, grade level), interval values have equidistant scales and no true zero (e.g., rating scale values, temperature), and ratio values are equidistant and have a true zero (e.g., weight, height).

LO 5 Describe the following types of reliability: test-retest reliability, internal consistency, and interrater reliability.

- **Reliability** is the consistency, stability, or repeatability of one or more measures or observations. Three types of reliability are test-retest reliability, internal consistency, and interrater reliability.

- **Test-retest reliability** is the extent to which a measure or observation is consistent or stable at two points in time. **Internal consistency** is a measure of reliability used to determine the extent to which multiple items used to measure the same variable are related. **Interrater reliability** is a measure for the extent to which two or more raters of the same behavior or event are in agreement with what they observed.

LO 6 Describe the following types of validity: face validity, construct validity, criterion-related validity, and content validity.

- The **validity** of a measurement is the extent to which a measurement for a variable or construct measures what it is purported or intended to measure. Four types of validity are face validity, construct validity, criterion-related validity, and content validity.

- **Face validity** is the extent to which a measure for a variable or construct appears to measure what it is intended to measure. **Construct validity** is the extent to which an operational definition for a variable or construct is actually measuring that variable or construct. **Criterion-related validity** is the extent to which scores obtained on some measure can be used to infer or predict a criterion or expected outcome. Four types of criterion-related validity, described in Table 4.8, are predictive validity, concurrent validity, convergent validity, and discriminant validity. **Content validity** is the extent to which the items or contents of a measure adequately represent all of the features of the construct being measured.

LO 7 Identify the concerns of participant reactivity, experimenter bias, and sensitivity and range effects for selecting a measurement procedure.

- **Participant reactivity** is the reaction participants have when they know they are being observed or measured. To minimize participant reactivity, you can reassure confidentiality, use deception when ethical, measure less obvious variables, and minimize **demand characteristics**.

- **Experimenter bias** is the extent to which the behavior of a researcher influences the results of a study. To minimize experimenter bias, you can get a second opinion, standardize the research procedures, and conduct a **double-blind study**.

- The **sensitivity** of a measure is the extent to which it changes in the presence of a manipulation. A **range effect** is when scores on a measure all fall extremely high (**ceiling effect**) or low (**floor effect**) on the scale. To maximize the sensitivity of a measure and minimize possible range effects, you can perform a thorough literature review, conduct a **pilot study**, include **manipulation checks**, and use multiple measures.

LO 8 Explain why the failure to replicate a result is not sufficient evidence for fraud.

- Researchers can be subjected to criticism and even accused of fraud if other researchers reconduct their research procedures from an original study and do not obtain the same results as they did. However, a failure to replicate a result could be due to statistical error and not fraud. Any measure consists of a true score and a possible error that causes variability in that measure. An *error* is any influence in the response of a participant that can cause variability in his or her response. The error that causes variability, and not fraud, therefore could explain why a result was not replicated.

LO 9 Enter data into SPSS by placing each group in a separate column and each group in a single row (coding is required).

- SPSS can be used to enter and define variables. All variables are defined in the **Variable View** tab. The values recorded for each variable are listed in the **Data View** tab. Data can be entered by column or by row in the Data View tab. Listing data by row requires coding the variable. Variables are coded in the Variable View tab in the **Values column** (for more details, see Section 4.9).

KEY TERMS

variable

construct

hypothetical construct

external factor of a construct

continuous variable

discrete variable

quantitative variable

qualitative variable

scales of measurement

nominal scale

coding

ordinal scale

interval scale

true zero

ratio scale

reliability

test-retest reliability

internal consistency

interrater reliability (IRR)

interobserver reliability

validity

face validity

construct validity

criterion-related validity

content validity

participant reactivity

participant expectancy

evaluation apprehension

participant reluctance

demand characteristics

experimenter bias

expectancy effects

double-blind study

sensitivity of a measure

range effect

ceiling effect

floor effect

pilot study

manipulation check

REVIEW QUESTIONS

1. State two criteria that make variables suitable for scientific investigation, and explain how to meet each criterion.

2. Which of the following choices is not an operational definition for a funny joke?

   A. Duration of time (in seconds) spent laughing during a 1-minute comedy skit.

   B. Ratings on a scale from 0 (*not funny*) to 5 (*very funny*).

   C. The extent to which a joke or comment causes laughter.

3. Below is a brief description of a rather clever study conducted by Hannover and Kühnen (2002):

> A study tested the hypothesis that wearing different clothing can influence how people describe their personality. Researchers first gained consensus on a list of personality traits associated with individuals in formal wear (e.g., cultivated, accurate) and casual wear (e.g., easygoing, tolerant). They then asked some participants to arrive in formal wear and some to arrive in casual wear, and then had them rate their own personality traits. As predicted, they found that participants in formal wear rated themselves with more "formal-appropriate traits," whereas those in casual wear rated themselves with more "casual-appropriate traits."

A. What is the construct being measured in this study?

B. What is the operational definition for the construct?

C. Was the hypothesis confirmed? Explain.

4. For each of the following examples, (1) name the variable being measured, (2) state whether the variable is continuous or discrete, and (3) state whether the variable is quantitative or qualitative.

A. A researcher records the month of birth for patients with schizophrenia.

B. A professor records the number of students who were absent for a final exam.

C. A researcher asks children to choose which type of cereal they prefer (one with a toy inside the box or one without). He records the choice of cereal for each child.

D. A therapist measures the time (in seconds) that a mother ignores a crying child before giving the child attention.

5. Rank the scales of measurement in order from least informative to most informative.

6. State the scale of measurement for each of the following variables.

A. Duration (in seconds) of blushing following an embarrassing mishap.

B. The type of drug used during a clinical trial (brand name or generic).

C. Rating of risk-taking on a scale from –2 (*not likely*) to +2 (*very likely*).

D. The ranking of a participant's top five favorite music artists.

7. A psychologist measures sleepwalking behavior using a new assessment she constructed with two subscales. Describe two ways the researcher could show that her new measure is reliable.

8. A researcher tests the hypothesis that women are better at multitasking than men. During an experimental session, women and men completed as many household tasks as they could in 5 minutes. Three raters made judgments concerning the number of completed tasks for each participant. What type of reliability should the researcher demonstrate?

9. State four types of validity for research design.

10. A researcher operationally defines helping behavior as the amount of time (in seconds) that participants volunteer for a local charity during one summer. To demonstrate construct validity, what must the researcher show?

11. A researcher shows that students' self-efficacy, or belief in their abilities, can predict future college academic performance. Which type of criterion-related validity does this illustrate?

12. State whether each of the following examples is likely to have high or low content validity.

    A. A friend places a posting on an online dating website and completely and honestly fills in the required fields concerning his personal information.

    B. You find a job posting that does not explain key information concerning salary, benefits, and hours of availability required.

    C. A researcher measures the construct love by having participants rate a group of characteristics known to be associated with it (e.g., caring, trustworthiness, commitment).

13. Explain three strategies that can minimize participant reactivity.

14. To avoid experimenter bias, a researcher conducts a double-blind study. Why is this is a good strategy to minimize experimenter bias?

15. Explain four strategies that can maximize the sensitivity of a measure and minimize range effects.

ACTIVITIES

1. Choose three of the following constructs and answer the questions below for each.

Attractiveness	Satisfaction	Obsession
Bravery	Intelligence	Spirituality
Resilience	Creativity	Persuasiveness
Success	Popularity	Patriotism
Athleticism	Loyalty	Recklessness

    A. State two operational definitions for each construct. The operational definition for each construct must be on a different scale of measurement.

    B. State whether each external factor or operational definition is continuous or discrete, and quantitative or qualitative.

    C. State the scale of measurement for each external factor or operational definition.

2. Write down the five most important characteristics you look for in a romantic partner. For example, characteristics that typically top these lists include financial potential, faithfulness, sense of humor, intelligence, and attractiveness. For each characteristic you list, state whether it is a construct, and describe at least one way you would operationally define it.

3. The three hypotheses listed below have been tested in the published literature. You can use the citations to search for the full articles using PsycINFO. Choose one hypothesis, and answer the questions that follow.

   Hypothesis 1: Blushing after a transgression or mishap leads to being judged more favorably by others (Dijk, de Jong, & Peters, 2009).

   Hypothesis 2: Cues associated with drug use (e.g., context, paraphernalia) promote nicotine dependence and relapse (Wing & Shoaib, 2008).

   Hypothesis 3: Thinking about or simulating social contact can reduce prejudice toward other groups (Crisp & Turner, 2009).

   A. Devise a research study to test one hypothesis and explain whether your study has face validity. How might you assess the reliability of your measure?

   B. Explain two strategies you will use to minimize participant reactivity and to minimize experimenter bias.

   C. Explain one strategy you will use to maximize the sensitivity of your measure.

Identify a problem

- Determine an area of interest.
- Review the literature.
- Identify new ideas in your area of interest.
- Develop a research hypothesis.

Develop a research plan

- Define the variables being tested.
- Identify participants or subjects and determine how to sample them.
- Select a research strategy and design.
- Evaluate ethics and obtain institutional approval to conduct research.

Generate more new ideas

- Results support your hypothesis—refine or expand on your ideas.
- Results do not support your hypothesis— reformulate a new idea or start over.

After reading this chapter, you should be able to:

1   Explain why researchers select samples that are representative of a population of interest.

2   Distinguish between *subjects* and *participants* as terms used to describe those who are subjected to procedures in a research study.

3   Distinguish between probability sampling methods and nonprobability sampling methods.

4   Delineate two nonprobability sampling methods: convenience sampling and quota sampling.

5   Delineate four probability sampling methods: simple random sampling, stratified random sampling, systematic sampling, and cluster sampling.

6   Define and explain sampling error and the standard error of the mean.

7   Define and explain sampling bias and nonresponse bias.

8   Identify potential ethical concerns related to sampling from subject pools in human participant research.

9   Compute an estimate for the standard error of the mean, and compute the one-sample *t* test using SPSS.

Conduct the study

- Execute the research plan and measure or record the data.

Communicate the results

- Method of communication: oral, written, or in a poster.
- Style of communication: APA guidelines are provided to help prepare style and format.

Analyze and evaluate the data

- Analyze and evaluate the data as they relate to the research hypothesis.
- Summarize data and research results.

chapter
five

SAMPLING FROM POPULATIONS

As a student, you have surely had a teacher hand out grades for an exam you took earlier. Given the strong tendency for students to compare themselves to other students, you have likely on occasion asked students sitting near you to tell you their grade on the same exam—to get a better sense of how you performed on the exam. If the few people you ask all did worse than you on the exam, then you will probably feel much better; if they all did better than you, then you will probably feel worse.

The reason you did not ask all students in the class how they did on the exam is because of the constraints of the class. When you received your grade, your class was in session. You certainly could not walk to the front of the class and take a poll. Instead, the only students who could be quickly polled without disrupting the class were the students near where you were sitting. In this example, the population was all students in class who took the exam, and the sample was the few students who told you their grade. In science we likewise have constraints that require us to select samples to understand behavior in a population. For example, human behaviors, such as love or depression, are expressed in all people. We certainly cannot ask all people how they experience these behaviors, so we ask only a few of them who are accessible or close by.

Now of course we still need to consider that only a few people were asked. Why, for example, did asking only a few students make you feel so much more confident in how well or poorly you performed on the exam? An answer requires an understanding of how samples are selected from populations, as is explored in this chapter. Specifically, in this chapter we explore approaches that scientists take to select samples from populations so that we can be confident that the observations made in a sample will also be observed in the larger population.

5.1 Why Do Researchers Select Samples?

A population can be identified as any group of interest. In the behavioral sciences, a population is specifically a group that a researcher is interested in answering a question about. For example, suppose you ask why college students join fraternities and sororities. In this case, students who join fraternities and sororities make up the group, called the population, that you are interested in. You identified a population of interest just as researchers identify populations they are interested in.

Remember that researchers select samples mostly because they do not have access to all individuals in a population. Imagine having to identify every person who has fallen in love, experienced anxiety, been attracted to someone else, suffered from depression, or taken a college exam. It is not possible for us to identify all individuals in such populations. So researchers use data gathered from samples (a portion of individuals from the population) to make inferences concerning a population.

To make sense of this, suppose you want to get an idea of how people in general feel about a new pair of shoes you just bought. To find out, you put your new shoes on and ask 20 people at random throughout the day whether or not they like the shoes. Now, do you really care about the opinion of only those 20 people you asked? Not really—you actually care more about the opinion of people in general. In other words, you only asked the 20 people (your sample) to get an idea of the opinions of people in general (the population of interest). Sampling from populations follows a similar logic, and in this chapter, we introduce strategies that researchers use to select samples from populations. We then describe many of the errors, biases, and ethical concerns related to sampling, particularly when we select human participants.

> Researchers select samples to learn more about populations of interest to them.

5.2 Subjects, Participants, and Sampling Methods

Sampling from populations is unique in that researchers thoughtfully determine what groups to study and how to select them for a study. To begin, we distinguish between *participants* and *subjects* based on ethics guidelines provided by the American Psychological Association (APA, 2010). We also introduce the categories of sampling that are described in this chapter.

Subjects and Participants

The term **participant** is used to describe a human who volunteers to be subjected to the procedures in a research study.

The term **subject** is used to describe a nonhuman that is subjected to procedures in a research study and to identify the names of research designs.

Using the APA (2010) guidelines provided in the code of conduct, we refer to humans as **participants** and nonhuman groups as **subjects**. The reason for this distinction is in the semantics of how we use language. A "subject of research" implies that an individual is subjected to the study, regardless of his or her consent. This is not the case with human groups because humans provide informed consent prior to participation, and only upon signing the consent form will they participate in a study. Therefore, humans are participants in a study inasmuch as they voluntarily choose to participate. Nonhuman groups, however, do not volunteer. Instead, the researchers and ethics review boards (i.e., an institutional animal care and use committee; see Chapter 3) decide for these groups whether or not they will be subjected to the procedures in a study. In this way, then, nonhuman groups are subjects in research, and humans are participants. This distinction is made throughout the book.

The term *subject* is also used to identify the names of research designs. For example, as will be described in Chapters 10 and 11, when different participants or subjects are observed in each group, the research design is called a *between-subjects design*; when the same participants or subjects are observed in each group, the research design is called a *within-subjects design*. *Subjects* is used to identify each research design, regardless of whether human or nonhuman groups are studied.

Selecting Samples From Populations

When researchers identify a population of interest, the population they identify is typically very large. For this reason, researchers often categorize populations as being a target population or an accessible population.

The **target population** is all members of a group of interest to a researcher. The target population of interest to a researcher is typically very large—so large that we can rarely select samples directly from it. For example, suppose we want to study what is most important to prospective U.S. students in choosing a college to attend. In this example, the target population of interest is prospective U.S. students. The size of that population is very large and spread out across the country. We could not possibly give all members of this group an opportunity to participate in our study.

> A **target population** is all members of a group of interest to a researcher.
>
> The **accessible population**, also called the **sampling frame**, is the portion of the target population that can be clearly identified and directly sampled from.

By contrast, an **accessible population** is a portion of the target population that can be clearly identified and directly sampled from. The accessible population is a smaller group that is part of the target population. This group is generally in close proximity to the researcher, such that all members of the accessible population could potentially have an opportunity to participate in a study. For example, we could identify prospective U.S. students at one or more local high schools (the accessible population) and select a sample from that portion of the larger target population.

While most samples are selected from accessible populations, the goal is still to describe characteristics in the target population. In other words, researchers select samples to learn more about the characteristics of individuals in a target population. However, as illustrated in Figure 5.1, most samples are selected from an accessible population, and characteristics in an accessible population are not always the same as those in the larger target population. For this reason, researchers must use careful

Researchers typically select samples from an accessible population and generalize observations made with samples to the target population of interest.

Figure 5.1 The Process of Nonprobability Sampling

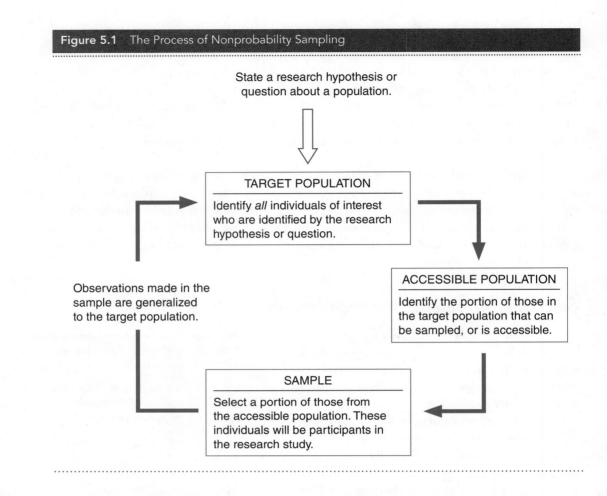

State a research hypothesis or
question about a population.

TARGET POPULATION

Identify *all* individuals of interest
who are identified by the research
hypothesis or question.

ACCESSIBLE POPULATION

Identify the portion of those in
the target population that can
be sampled, or is accessible.

Observations made in the
sample are generalized
to the target population.

SAMPLE

Select a portion of those from
the accessible population. These
individuals will be participants in
the research study.

A **representative sample** is one in which the characteristics of individuals or items in the sample resemble those in a target population of interest.

procedures that allow them to select samples from accessible populations that mimic or have similar characteristics as those in the target population.

If researchers want to generalize the results they observe in a sample to those in the target population, then they need to make certain that the sample is representative of the target population. A **representative sample** is a sample that has characteristics that resemble those in the target population. This can be difficult when we know little about the characteristics of individuals in a target population. However, when we do know about characteristics in the target population, then we can use a sampling procedure that ensures that those characteristics will also be represented or included in the sample that is selected from that population.

The methods that researchers use to select samples from one or more populations can be categorized as probability and nonprobability sampling. **Probability sampling** is a category of sampling in which a sample is selected directly from the target population; **nonprobability sampling** is a category of sampling in which a sample is selected from the accessible population. Sampling directly from the target population using probability sampling is possible in situations in which the exact probability of selecting each individual in a target population is known.

However, it is rare that researchers know the exact probability of selecting each individual in a target population because it is difficult to identify all individuals in very large populations, let alone know the exact probability of selecting each individual. For this reason, nonprobability sampling methods, which are discussed in the next section, are most commonly used to select samples in behavioral research.

> **Probability sampling** is a category of sampling in which a sample is selected directly from the target population. Probability sampling methods are used when the probability of selecting each individual in a population is known and every member of the population has an equal chance of being selected.
>
> **Nonprobability sampling** is a category of sampling in which a sample is selected from the accessible population. Nonprobability sampling methods are used when it is not possible to select individuals directly from the target population.

5.3 Methods of Sampling: Nonprobability Sampling

Researchers can rarely identify all members of a target population, which is why they often select samples from an accessible population that can be identified. For example, suppose a study investigates neural response patterns in the brain of participants as the participants pray. In this example, the target population is all people who pray. It would be difficult to identify this entire group, so an accessible population—of a group at local churches or other places of worship, for example—would be identified and sampled from. Hence, researchers use nonprobability sampling, as illustrated in Figure 5.1, when it is not possible to identify all members of a target population. Two types of nonprobability sampling methods discussed in this section are convenience sampling and quota sampling.

Convenience Sampling

A **convenience sample**, as indicated in the name, is selected out of convenience or ease, meaning that participants are selected based on their availability to participate. A commonly used sampling method in experimentation is to select college students, who are the most convenient sample available to many behavioral researchers. Recognizing this trend as early as the 1940s, one researcher even characterized experimentation as "the science of the behavior of [college] sophomores" (McNemar, 1946, p. 333). The reason that college students are the most convenient group to sample from is because many college professors conduct their research at the university or college by which they are employed.

> **Convenience sampling** is a method of sampling in which subjects or participants are selected for a research study based on how easy or convenient it is to reach or access them and based on their availability to participate.
>
> A **participant pool**, or **subject pool**, is a group of accessible and available participants for a research study. In college or university settings, a participant pool is created using policies that require students to participate in academic research, typically as a condition for receiving grades or credits in introductory-level classes.

Many college departments create a **participant pool** (also commonly referred to as a **subject pool**) of college students using policies that require students to participate in academic research, typically as a condition for receiving grades or credits in introductory-level classes. The reason these participant pools are created is so that researchers can have access to a group that is available to participate in behavioral research. Selecting a sample from a participant pool of college students is an example of convenience sampling. The ethical implications of creating participant pools for the purposes of research are described in Section 5.8.

A drawback of convenience sampling is that it does not ensure that a sample will be representative of the target population because the sample was selected out of convenience—a "first come, first serve" kind of approach. In a convenience sample, more convenient individuals have a better chance of being selected than those who are less convenient. Because we cannot know how "convenient" and "inconvenient" individuals are different, we cannot know whether the sample we selected is representative of the target population. To make a convenience sample representative of a larger target population of interest, researchers can use the following two strategies:

> Convenience sampling is the most common method of sampling in behavioral research.

1. Researchers can use *quota sampling*, in which they select subgroups of the population that resemble or represent characteristics in a target population of interest.

2. Researchers can use a *combined sampling method*, in which they combine convenience sampling with a probability sampling method.

We begin by describing quota sampling, which is a common sampling method using nonhuman subjects. In Section 5.4, we describe four probability sampling methods that can be combined with convenience sampling to ensure that a sample is representative of the target population of interest to a researcher.

Quota Sampling

A **quota sample** is selected based on known or unknown criteria or characteristics in the target population. Researchers use quota sampling to ensure that the characteristics upon which subjects or participants are selected are represented in a sample.

For situations in which little is known about the characteristics of a target population, researchers use **simple quota sampling**. For example, Daniulaityte, Falck, Li, Nahhas, and Carlson (2012) used a type of simple quota sampling to select a group of participants who were nondependent illicit drug users. This group is difficult to sample because the individuals in this group do not seek treatment and tend to be discrete about their drug use. For these types of samples, a simple quota sampling method can be useful to select participants to ensure that the sample is representative of the target population of nondependent illicit drug users.

> **Quota sampling** is a method of sampling in which subjects or participants are selected based on known or unknown criteria or characteristics in the target population.
>
> **Simple quota sampling** is a type of quota sampling used when little is known about the characteristics of a target population. Using this type of quota sampling, an equal number of subjects or participants are selected for a given characteristic or demographic.

Using simple quota sampling, an equal number of subjects or participants are selected based on a characteristic or demographic that they share. For example, as illustrated in Figure 5.2 (left side), in a brain imaging study we may be concerned that men and women process information differently and we will thus select an equal number of men and women to participate in the research study. Other characteristics of interest can include age, education level, marital status, and any other demographic characteristic believed to be representative of the target population. Simple quota sampling is often used when the target population is not well understood, such as sampling students who cheat on exams—this group would be unlikely to admit cheating, and therefore would be difficult to identify.

For situations in which certain characteristics are known in the population, researchers use **proportionate quota sampling**. Using proportionate quota sampling, subjects or participants are selected such that known characteristics or demographics are proportionately represented in the sample. For example, we know that approximately 25% of the American population is obese and 75% is not obese. Based on these known proportions, we could select a sample in which 25% of participants were obese, and 75% were not, as illustrated in Figure 5.2. Assuming the target population of interest was the American population, we have now proportionately represented health categories (obese, not obese) in our sample.

> **Proportionate quota sampling** is a type of quota sampling used when the proportions of certain characteristics in a target population are known. Using this type of quota sampling, subjects or participants are selected such that the known characteristics or demographics are proportionately represented in the sample.

Quota sampling is often used to study human and nonhuman behavior, but it is specifically a standard method of sampling for studies that use nonhuman subjects. For example, animal research laboratories routinely select animal subjects from a single supplier and order the same species, strain, sex, age, and even weight of animals from these suppliers. Hence, researchers select—or order from a supplier—nonhuman subjects

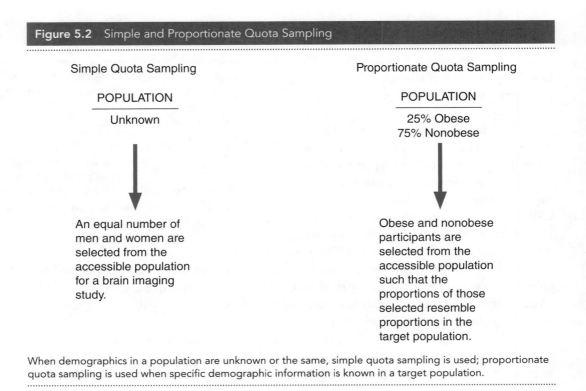

Figure 5.2 Simple and Proportionate Quota Sampling

Simple Quota Sampling

POPULATION

Unknown

An equal number of men and women are selected from the accessible population for a brain imaging study.

Proportionate Quota Sampling

POPULATION

25% Obese
75% Nonobese

Obese and nonobese participants are selected from the accessible population such that the proportions of those selected resemble proportions in the target population.

When demographics in a population are unknown or the same, simple quota sampling is used; proportionate quota sampling is used when specific demographic information is known in a target population.

that are equal or proportionate on many characteristics of interest to a researcher. In this way, researchers use nonprobability sampling methods to conduct research using nonhuman subjects in behavioral research.

Quota sampling is one method of sampling used to ensure that a sample is representative of the target population of interest to a researcher. Another strategy used to ensure that a sample is representative of the target population is to combine convenience sampling with probability sampling methods—four probability sampling methods are introduced in the next section.

LEARNING CHECK 2 ✓

1. Name two types of nonprobability sampling methods.

2. Name two strategies that researchers use to ensure that characteristics in a convenience sample are representative of characteristics in a target population.

3. Which type of quota sampling is used when characteristics in a target population are unknown?

5.4 Methods of Sampling: Probability Sampling

Probability sampling methods, as illustrated in Figure 5.3, are used when the probability of selecting each individual in a target population is known. Four probability sampling methods introduced in this section are simple random sampling, simple and proportionate stratified random sampling, systematic sampling, and cluster sampling.

Probability sampling and nonprobability sampling methods are ways in which samples are selected to inform us about a target population.

Figure 5.3 The Process of Probability Sampling

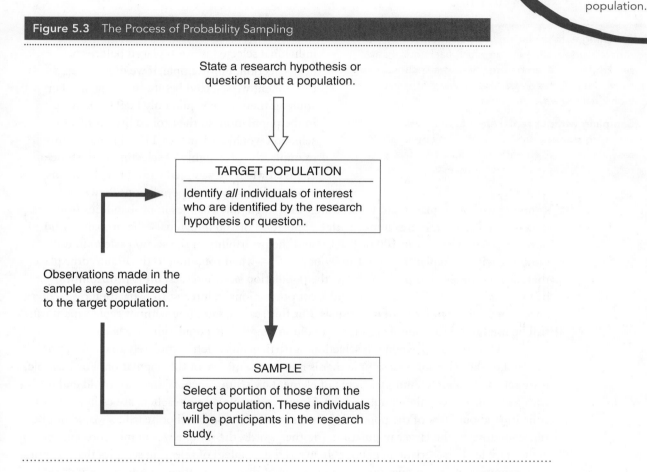

Simple Random Sampling

For small populations of interest, a simple random sample can be selected because each individual can be identified and the likelihood of selecting each individual is known. Using **simple random sampling**, the likelihood of selecting each individual in the population is known, so we can use a random procedure to select individuals from the population, such as using the random numbers table, which is given in Appendix B.1 with instructions for how to use it.

> **Simple random sampling** is a method of sampling subjects and participants such that all individuals in a population have an equal chance of being selected and are selected using sampling with replacement.

To ensure that the probability of selecting each individual is always the same, researchers use **sampling with replacement**. To use sampling with replacement, each individual selected is replaced before the next selection. To illustrate how this works, suppose we have a population of a college class of 10 students. The probability of selecting the first student is 1 in 10 or 10%. If we return the student we selected back into the class before selecting again, then 10 students will remain in the class when we select again, and the probability of the next selection will again be 1 in 10 or 10%.

> **Sampling with replacement** is a strategy used with simple random sampling in which each individual selected is replaced before the next selection to ensure that the probability of selecting each individual is always the same.
>
> **Sampling without replacement** is a nonrandom sampling strategy most often used by behavioral researchers in which each individual selected is not replaced before the next selection.

However, most researchers use **sampling without replacement**, which means that each individual selected is not replaced before the next selection. For example, if we did not replace the student we selected before selecting another student, then there would only be 9 students left in the population, so the probability of the next selection would be 1 in 9 or 11%. Hence, in this example, the probability of selecting each student changed when we sampled without replacement.

For very large populations, however, sampling without replacement is associated with negligible changes in probabilities from one selection to the next. For example, with a population of 100 individuals, the probability (p) of the first selection is 1 in 100 or $p = .01$, and the probability of the second selection using sampling without replacement is 1 in 99 or $p = .01$—when rounding to the hundredths place, there is no difference in probability. As the population size increases, these probabilities become more and more negligible, and most populations of interest to behavioral researchers have thousands or millions of individuals. For this reason, sampling without replacement can still be used to select a simple random sample so long as the population size is large.

Unfortunately, when the selection of participants is left completely to chance, this can lead to the selection of a sample that is not representative of the population. For example, if we selected a simple random sample of elementary schoolteachers, then we could end up with a sample of 20 male schoolteachers. However, female schoolteachers are estimated to constitute about 80% of the population, so a sample of 20 male schoolteachers would not be representative of the larger population. In other words, the sample would misrepresent the demographic characteristic of gender. To avoid the problem of selecting samples that are not representative of the population, we can use one of three alternative sampling methods that are described in this section.

Stratified Random Sampling

One sampling method used to obtain a representative sample, called **stratified random sampling**, involves dividing the population into subgroups or "strata," then randomly selecting participants from each subgroup using a simple random sampling procedure. Participants selected from each subgroup are then combined into one sample that is representative of each stratum from which participants have been selected. Populations should be divided into strata based on characteristics that are relevant to the research hypothesis. For example, Balk, Walker, and Baker (2010) stratified undergraduate students at a university by their academic year (freshman, sophomore, junior, senior), and then selected students to participate in each stratum in a study examining the characteristics of college students who were grieving a death within 24 months of their study.

> **Stratified random sampling** is a method of sampling in which a population is divided into subgroups or strata; participants are then selected from each subgroup using simple random sampling and are combined into one overall sample.
>
> Stratified random sampling can involve selecting an equal number of participants in each subgroup, called **simple stratified random sampling**, or selecting a different proportion of participants in each subgroup, called **proportionate stratified random sampling**.

To represent a certain characteristic of a population in a sample, researchers could use **simple stratified random sampling** by selecting an equal number of participants in each subgroup or stratum. For example, to stratify students by academic year, researchers can split the population of students into four strata (freshmen, sophomores, juniors, seniors), and then randomly select the same number of students from each stratum. Participants selected in each stratum can then be combined into one large sample that has an equal number of students from each academic year.

> With stratified random sampling, the strata are subgroups in a target population of interest.

As another strategy to represent a certain characteristic of a population in a sample, researchers could use **proportionate stratified random sampling**. Using this strategy, researchers select participants in each subgroup or stratum, such that the numbers in each stratum are proportionately represented similar to proportions in the population. For example, suppose that 30% of students are freshmen, 30% sophomores, 20% juniors, and 20% seniors at a given college. In this case, illustrated in Figure 5.4, the researcher can split the population into four strata (freshmen, sophomores, juniors, seniors), then randomly select participants such that 30% of those selected are freshmen, 30% are sophomores, 20% are juniors, and 20% are seniors. When the four strata are combined, the proportion of those from each academic year in the sample will be identical to the proportions that exist in the population of students at that college.

Notice that stratified random sampling is similar to quota sampling in that an equal or proportionate number of subjects or participants can be selected based on known characteristics in a population. Notice also the similarity in Figures 5.2 and 5.4. The difference is that quota sampling uses convenience sampling and not random sampling to select participants; however, both strategies ensure that certain characteristics in a sample are representative of the population.

Systematic Sampling

A probability sampling method that begins with random sampling and then switches to a systematic procedure is called **systematic sampling**. Using this sampling method, a researcher randomly selects the first participant, and then selects every nth person until all participants have been selected. Hence, the researcher uses simple random

Figure 5.4 Simple and Proportionate Stratified Random Sampling

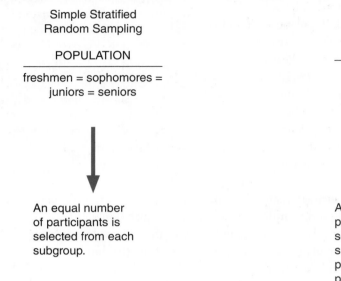

Simple Stratified
Random Sampling

POPULATION

freshmen = sophomores =
juniors = seniors

An equal number
of participants is
selected from each
subgroup.

Proportionate Stratified
Random Sampling

POPULATION

30% freshmen
30% sophomores
20% juniors
20% seniors

A proportion of
participants is
selected from each
subgroup to resemble the
proportion of those in the
population.

When subgroups contain similar numbers of persons in the population, then simple stratified random sampling is used; proportionate stratified random sampling is used when subgroups are not equal.

Systematic sampling is a method of sampling in which the first participant is selected using simple random sampling, and then every *n*th person is systematically selected until all participants have been selected.

sampling to select the first participant, and then uses a systematic sampling procedure to select all remaining participants (i.e., by selecting every *n*th person). For example, Muliira, Nalwanga, Muliira, and Nankinga (2012) used a systematic sampling procedure to select male participants at a local university by selecting one student residence room at random, and then selecting students living in every fifth room until all eligible students were selected to participate.

To further illustrate systematic sampling, suppose that a professor has a class of 90 students. The professor wants to select a sample of 30 students from this class. To achieve this sample size, the professor will need to select every third student (90 ÷ 30 = 3). The first participant is selected using simple random sampling, such as by using the random numbers table given in Appendix B.1 to select the first participant. The next 29 participants in the sample are chosen systematically, meaning that every third person is selected until 30 participants are in the sample. One way to use the systematic procedure would be to have students count off by threes starting with the randomly selected first participant saying "Three" and the next student beginning back at "One." The students who say "Three" will then be the remaining 29 participants in the sample.

Cluster Sampling

For situations in which the population of interest is spread out across a wide region, researchers can use cluster sampling. When a population is spread out across a wide region, this can make random and systematic sampling very difficult because the population is hard to access and efforts to select a sample would be too time-consuming and costly. A solution to this problem is to sample from smaller segments or clusters within the population using a probability sampling method called **cluster sampling**. Using cluster sampling, we divide the population into clusters (or subgroups), and then select all individuals in some of those clusters who we think are representative of the population as a whole. Hence, some clusters (or subgroups) will be completely omitted from the sample.

> **Cluster sampling** is a method of sampling in which subgroups or clusters of individuals are identified in a population, and then a portion of clusters that are representative of the population are selected such that all individuals in the selected clusters are included in the sample. All clusters that are not selected are omitted from the sample.

Cluster sampling is different from stratified random sampling in that some subgroups are omitted from a sample using cluster sampling, whereas a random sample of individuals in each subgroup is included in a sample using stratified random sampling, as illustrated in Figure 5.5. The advantage of using cluster sampling is that it breaks down a population into clusters when it is difficult to reach all clusters in such a way that the clusters selected are representative of all clusters in the population.

As an example to illustrate cluster sampling, suppose we want to study concerns of bullying behavior in New York State (NYS) public high schools. The difficulty is that the population of public high school students in NYS is spread out over a wide region. To use cluster sampling, we first break up the population into clusters, such as by district. Then we choose a sample of districts by selecting three or four districts (we could choose any number of districts) that we think are representative of the characteristics of students in the larger population of NYS public schools. Once those districts have been selected, all students in those districts will be selected for the sample. All districts that were not selected will be omitted from the sample.

A limitation of cluster sampling is that it limits a sample to individuals in the chosen clusters, and there can be substantial variation between clusters within one population. For instance, bullying behavior in Queens, New York, will likely be different from bullying behavior in Buffalo, New York; bullying behavior will likely be different for schools in wealthier neighborhoods as well. Other important factors include race, gender, and school size. To select a representative sample, each of these characteristics should be represented in the selected clusters because only individuals in those clusters will be included in the sample.

> With cluster sampling, the clusters are subgroups in the target population of interest.

In all, the six sampling methods described in this chapter are some of the most common methods used in behavioral research to select participants for research studies. Table 5.1 summarizes each of the probability and nonprobability sampling methods described in Sections 5.3 and 5.4.

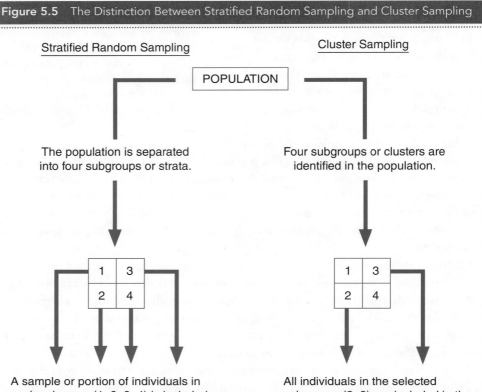

Using stratified random sampling, a portion of individuals in each subgroup is selected in a sample. Using cluster sampling, all individuals in a sample or portion of subgroups are included in a sample.

LEARNING CHECK 3 ✓

1. To use simple random sampling, a researcher should use sampling with replacement or sampling without replacement?

2. What sampling method involves selecting all individuals from a portion of subgroups in a population?

3. A researcher investigates how political attitudes (Republican, Democrat) are related to attitudes toward teaching evolution in a school classroom. To select the sample, she is given access to a database identifying the political affiliations and mailing addresses

for all local residents in her area. She splits the list into two subgroups (Republican, Democrat), and then selects a sample or portion of individuals from each subgroup. To select participants from each subgroup, she uses a random procedure to select the first address and then selects every sixth address after that until 300 participants from each subgroup are selected. What three sampling methods has she combined to select this sample?

Answers: 1. Sampling with replacement; 2. Cluster sampling; 3. Convenience sampling (only local residents have a chance of being selected), simple stratified random sampling (the list is separated into subgroups, and an equal number of participants are selected from each subgroup), and systematic sampling (she chooses every sixth address on the list after a random start).

Table 5.1 The Probability and Nonprobability Sampling Methods Described in 5.3 and 5.4

Type of sampling	Description	Population sampled from	Expected quality of the sample
Nonprobability Sampling Methods			
Convenience sampling	A sampling method in which participants are selected based on availability or convenience.	Accessible population	The sample is not random and not representative.
Quota sampling	A sampling method in which available or convenient subgroups of participants are selected, typically in a way that resembles the target population.	Accessible population	The sample is not random but can be representative.
Probability Sampling Methods			
Simple random sampling	A sampling method in which all individuals in a population have an equal chance of being selected.	Target population	The sample is random but not always representative.
Stratified random sampling	A sampling method in which a population is divided into subgroups or strata, then a random sample of participants is selected from each subgroup and combined into one overall sample.	Target population	The sample is random and representative, particularly for proportionate stratified sampling.

(Continued)

Table 5.1 (Continued)

Type of sampling	Description	Population sampled from	Expected quality of the sample
Systematic sampling	A sampling method in which the first participant is randomly selected, then every *n*th person is systematically selected from there until all persons have been selected.	Target population	The sample is systematic (not random), and not always representative.
Cluster sampling	A sampling method in which subgroups or clusters of individuals are identified in a population. A sample of clusters is then selected, and all individuals in those clusters are included in the sample.	Target population	The sample is not random, but can be representative with the careful selection of clusters.

MAKING SENSE—REPRESENTATIVE VERSUS RANDOM SAMPLES

Using random sampling does not always mean that the sample selected is representative of characteristics in a population. For researchers, the larger concern is for a sample to be representative because they want to be able to describe characteristics in a population based on observations they make with samples. The more the characteristics in the sample resemble those in the population, the more representative of the population the sample will be.

The convenience sampling method is often used in the behavioral sciences but does not use a random sampling procedure. However, if we know characteristics in the target population, then we can represent them in our sample by combining convenience sampling with a probability sampling method. For example, to study class behavior among college students, we can select a convenience sample of local college students and use stratified sampling to split the pool of potential participants by class year (freshman, sophomore, junior, senior), as illustrated in Figure 5.6. We can then randomly select participants from each class year among those available in the convenience sample. In this example, class year is now represented in the convenience sample.

In a published study, Cohn, Fredrickson, Brown, Mikels, and Conway (2009) used a similar strategy in a study on the relationship between positive emotions and life satisfaction. The researchers selected a convenience sample of local participants recruited through newspaper ads and posters offering up to $100 for participation, which produced an eligible pool of 214 potential participants. Then they used a simple stratified random sampling method by separating the eligible pool of 214 people into two subgroups (men and women), and then randomly selecting 60 men and 60 women to participate in their study. Hence, the researchers combined a convenience sampling method (a convenient pool of qualified individuals who responded to ads) with a probability sampling method (simple stratified random sampling) to ensure that the characteristic of gender (men, women) was represented in their sample.

Figure 5.6 Probability Sampling Used With Convenience Sampling to Make the Sample More Representative of the Population

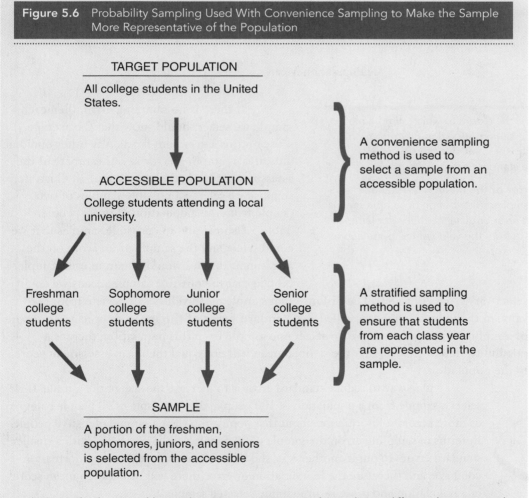

TARGET POPULATION

All college students in the United States.

ACCESSIBLE POPULATION

College students attending a local university.

A convenience sampling method is used to select a sample from an accessible population.

Freshman college students

Sophomore college students

Junior college students

Senior college students

A stratified sampling method is used to ensure that students from each class year are represented in the sample.

SAMPLE

A portion of the freshmen, sophomores, juniors, and seniors is selected from the accessible population.

In this example, the accessible population (a convenience sample) is split into different class years, and then participants are randomly selected from each group (a stratified sample) to ensure that class year is represented in the sample.

5.5 Sampling Error and Standard Error of the Mean

Regardless of the sampling strategy we use to select a sample, there is always a probability of error. Hence, the characteristics we observe in a sample are not always the same or representative of those in the population from which the sample was selected. This difference between what we observe in a sample and what is true in the population is called **sampling error**. The implication of sampling error is that two random samples selected from the same population can produce very different scores or outcomes.

To illustrate sampling error, suppose that a small hypothetical population of three people (A, B, C) scored an 8, 5, and 2, respectively, on some assessment. The mean or average score on the assessment in this population, then, is the sum of each score divided by the total number of scores summed:

$$\text{Population Mean} = \frac{8 + 5 + 2}{3} = 5.0$$

Sampling error is the extent to which sample means selected from the same population differ from one another. This difference, which occurs by chance, is measured by the standard error of the mean.

The **standard error of the mean** is the standard deviation of a sampling distribution of sample means. It is the standard error or distance that sample mean values can deviate from the value of the population mean.

The standard error of the mean is a measure of sampling error.

If there is no sampling error, then each sample we select should show that the average score on this assessment is 5.0. Any other outcome indicates a sampling error in our estimate of the assessment score in the population. To illustrate, suppose we select all possible samples of two people from this population of three people. Table 5.2 shows all nine possible samples that we could select and the sample mean score on the assessment that we would obtain in each sample. Notice that the possible sample means we could select vary from 2.0 to 8.0. The distance that sample mean values can deviate from the value of the population mean, called the **standard error of the mean**, is used as a measure of sampling error. Hence, if we do select one sample from this population, there is a possibility, due to chance, that the sample mean will not equal the mean assessment score in the population.

One way to reduce standard error is to increase the size of the sample. If we select a sample from a population of 100 people, then a sample of 90 people will give us more accurate information about that population than a sample of just 10 people. In terms of sampling error, the sample of 90 people will be associated with a smaller standard error. To put it another way, the larger the sample, the more information you have, and therefore the less variation or error there will be between mean scores in a population and those in a randomly selected sample.

Table 5.2 The Participants, Individual Scores, and Sample Mean for Each Possible Sample of Size 2 From This Population of Size 3

> Although the population mean is 5.0, average scores in each sample can vary from 2.0 to 8.0.

Participants Sampled ($n = 2$)	Scores for Each Participant	Sample Mean for Each Sample
A,A	8,8	8.0
A,B	8,5	6.5
A,C	8,2	5.0
B,A	5,8	6.5
B,B	5,5	5.0
B,C	5,2	3.5
C,A	2,8	5.0
C,B	2,5	3.5
C,C	2,2	2.0

5.6 SPSS in Focus: Estimating the Standard Error of the Mean

SPSS can be used to estimate the standard error. (For an overview of SPSS, please refer to the preface titled "How to Use SPSS With This Book.") Standard error can be any value from 0 to ∞, with larger values indicating greater variability among possible sample means that could be selected from a given population. Suppose, for example, that we measure the individual reaction times (in seconds) for a team of 10 firefighters to respond to an emergency call: 93, 66, 30, 44, 20, 100, 35, 58, 70, and 81. We will follow the steps to estimate the standard error of the mean using SPSS statistical software.

1. Click on the **Variable View** tab and enter *reaction* in the **Name column.** We will enter whole numbers, so reduce the value to 0 in the **Decimals column.**

2. Click on the **Data View** tab and enter the 10 values in the column labeled *reaction.*

3. Go to the menu bar and click **Analyze**, then **Descriptive Statistics**, and **Descriptives,** to display a dialog box.

4. In the **dialog box**, select the *reaction* variable and click the arrow to move it into the box labeled **Variable(s)** to the right. Click the **Options...** tab to bring up a new dialog box, shown in Figure 5.7 (top).

5. In the new dialog box, select **S.E. mean** in the **Dispersion** box and click **Continue**.

6. Select **OK**, or select **Paste** and click the **Run** command.

The SPSS output table, shown in Figure 5.7 (bottom), gives the value for the standard error as 8.596. This value indicates the standard distance or error by which sample means can deviate from the population mean.

Figure 5.7 The SPSS Dialog Box in Step 5 (Top), and the Output Table (Bottom)

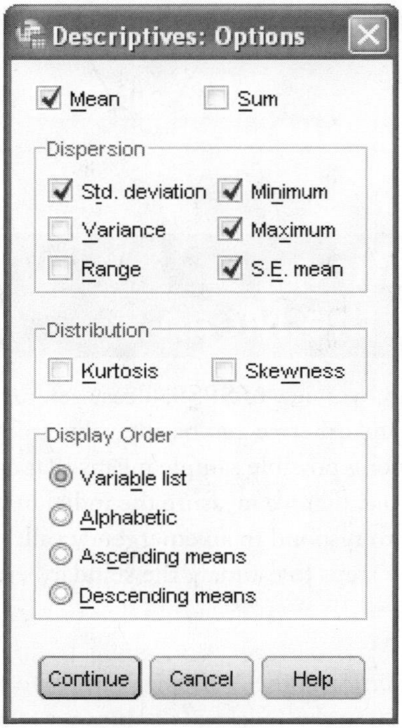

The value of standard error

Descriptive Statistics

	N	Minimum	Maximum	Mean		Std. Deviation
	Statistic	Statistic	Statistic	Statistic	Std. Error	Statistic
reaction	10	20	100	59.70	8.596	27.183
Valid N (listwise)	10					

1. How is standard error related to sampling error?

2. Name one way to reduce sampling error.

Answers: 1. Sampling error, which occurs by chance, is measured numerically by the standard error of the mean; 2. Increase the sample size.

5.7 Potential Biases in Sampling

Selecting a sample can be prone to bias either due to the fault of the researcher, *sampling bias*, or due to the fault of the participants, *nonresponse bias*. Both biases, which are introduced in this section, can limit the extent to which researchers can use observations in a sample to describe characteristics in a population.

Sampling Bias

One source of bias can result from the research procedures developed by the researcher. This type of bias, called **sampling bias**, occurs when sampling procedures employed in a study favor certain individuals or groups over others. Sampling bias can lead to the selection of a sample that is not representative of the target population but is instead representative of only the overrepresented groups in the sample. Suppose, for example, that we study

> **Sampling bias**, or **selection bias**, is a bias in sampling in which the sampling procedures employed in a study favor certain individuals or groups over others.

attitudes toward gun control by sampling individuals from a list of registered National Rifle Association members. Whatever the result, it is likely to be biased in favor of those who favor less government oversight of gun ownership and distribution.

Sampling bias can be particularly problematic for research that uses online surveys or computer-based surveys, which have increased significantly in use among researchers over the past decade. Using online surveys is easier and more cost-effective; however, problems with the sampling procedures include the technology aptitude of participants, system incompatibilities (e.g., potential respondents cannot open the survey), and institutional gatekeeping policies that recognize the survey as spam (Hartford, Carey, & Mendonca, 2007; LaRose & Tsai, 2014). Each problem with the sampling procedures leads to sampling bias, in that these problems limit the potential portion of the population that is sampled in favor of participants with greater aptitude and experience with computers and those with access to more compatible computer systems.

Nonresponse Bias

Another source of bias can result from the nonresponsiveness of participants. This type of bias, called **nonresponse bias**, occurs when participants choose not to respond to

Nonresponse bias is a bias in sampling in which a number of participants in one or more groups choose not to respond to a survey or request to participate in a research study.

a survey or request to participate in a study. The reason that nonresponse bias can be a problem is that individuals in a population who respond to surveys or postings asking for participants, such as in a newspaper or poster, are likely to be systematically different from those who do not. Hence, nonresponse bias could limit a sample to be representative of only the portion of the population that is willing to respond to a survey or request to participate in a study.

To illustrate nonresponse bias, suppose we select a sample of children who are obese. One problem we will face is that the parents of these children are less likely to give their written or verbal authorization, called *active consent*, to allow their children to participate (see Mellor, Rapoport, & Maliniak, 2008), largely due to the perceived negative stereotype associated with being obese. If many parents choose not to give active consent, then any results we observe in a sample may be limited to only that portion of the population of children who are obese who also have parents who are willing to give consent. It is not possible to know for sure if the results we observe in our sample would also be observed with children who are obese who have parents who are not willing to give consent.

5.8 Ethics in Focus: Participant Pools

In colleges and universities across the country, academic departments in the social sciences create participant pools by establishing policies that require students to participate in academic research. These policies typically require research participation as a condition to receive grades or credits in introductory-level classes. College students are often observed as participants in behavioral research, so the question is whether or not it is fair to establish policies that create participant pools. The concern is the ethical principle of justice in that creating participant pools for introductory-level college courses may place the burden of participation in research too heavily on the population of college students who take these courses. To address this concern, academic departments include the following two rules in their policies to ensure that participant pools are filled only with students willing to volunteer as participants in research.

- **Class grades are never contingent on actual participation in a research study.** Students must receive full credit for simply showing up to a research study on time. In fact, the researcher must state on an informed consent form that there is no penalty for choosing not to participate in the study. Students have the right to decline or withdraw participation at any time without penalty or consequence, as required by the APA code of conduct (see Chapter 3). Hence, students will get full research participation credit even when they choose not to participate in any of the studies they attend.

- **Students are given alternative options to receive a grade.** Students are also not required to even volunteer to participate in a research study. All students have the option to complete an alternative assignment to receive a grade. This alternative assignment, which is typically a research paper or article review, should require about the same amount of time as participation in a research study. The requirements for alternative assignments will be described in a course syllabus provided by the professor.

These two rules ensure that the burden of participation on college students in behavioral research is not coercive or mandatory because all students in a participant pool can opt out of participation in research without penalty. Hence, participant pools consist of volunteers who willingly give informed consent to participate in research—no student is ever required to actually participate in a research study.

> Participant pools are accessible populations of students available and willing to participate in research.

5.9 SPSS in Focus: Identifying New Populations Using the One-Sample *t* Test

As a prelude to research design, one type of design that is specifically applied to identify new populations or subgroups within a larger population can be described here. To identify new populations, researchers can compare a value measured in a sample to a known parameter in a population. This type of research is often used to identify at-risk populations. For example, we could test if a group who eats an unusually high-fat diet is at risk of high blood pressure by comparing mean blood pressure in a sample to known healthy levels of blood pressure in the population. To make a comparison, the mean value in a population must be known so that we can compare that value to the value obtained in the sample we select from that population. For this reason, parameters of interest tend to be physiological measures or standardized measures such as the IQ, SAT score, or grade point average, in which we know the mean score in the general population of interest.

To apply this type of research, we can select a random sample from a larger known population, either directly from a target population, as illustrated in Figure 5.3, or from an accessible population, as illustrated in Figure 5.1. We then compare the mean value in our sample to the mean for that measure in

> The **one-sample *t* test** is a statistical procedure used to test hypotheses concerning the mean of interval or ratio data in a single population with an unknown variance.

a population of interest. We make this comparison using a *test statistic* called the **one-sample *t* test**, which determines if a sample comes from a truly unique population or if any differences between the sample and the population are likely due to chance.

To illustrate the utility of the one-sample *t* test, we can consider an example from the area of mental health and family caregivers (Lollar & Talley, 2014; Umberson, Thomeer, & Williams, 2013). Albert, Salvi, Saracco, Bogetto, and Maina (2007) asked if relatives of patients with obsessive-compulsive disorder (OCD) are as healthy as those in the general healthy population. In their study, they recorded the social functioning of relatives of patients with OCD using a 36-item Short-Form Health Survey (SF-36), with scores ranging from 0 (*worst possible health*) to 100 (*best possible health*). They cited that the mean social functioning score in the general healthy population of interest was 77.43. Using a sample data set that approximates their findings, we will use SPSS

> A one-sample *t* test compares differences between a sample mean and a population mean.

Table 5.3	SF-36 Scores for a Sample of 18 Relatives of a Patient With Obsessive-Compulsive Disorder

Social Functioning Scores (SF-36)
20
60
48
92
50
82
48
90
30
68
43
54
60
62
94
67
52
85

to compute the one-sample t test to compare the social functioning scores given in Table 5.3 to the mean value in the population, 77.43.

1. Click on the **Variable View** tab and enter *health* in the **Name column**. We will enter whole numbers for this variable, so reduce the value in the **Decimals column** to 0.

2. Click on the **Data View** tab and enter the 18 values in Table 5.3 in the column labeled *health*.

3. Go to the menu bar and click **Analyze**, then **Compare Means**, and **One-Sample T Test** to display the dialog box shown in Figure 5.8.

4. In the **dialog box**, select the variable *health* and click the arrow in the middle to move this variable to the **Test Variable(s):** box.

5. The **Test Value:** box has a default value equal to 0. The value in this box is the value of the score in the general population. Type the value *77.43* in the **Test Value:** box.

6. Select **OK**, or select **Paste** and click the **Run** command.

The SPSS output table, shown in Table 5.4, gives the key values for this test. The top table gives the value of the sample mean, 61.39. The bottom table gives the results of the one-sample t test. The first two columns give the value of the test statistic, –3.230, and the value of degrees of freedom, which for a one-sample t test is one less than the sample size, or 18 – 1 = 17. The value of particular interest is in the **Sig.** column, which states the likelihood that we could have selected a sample with a mean SF-36 score of 61.39 from a population

Figure 5.8 SPSS Dialog Box for Steps 3 to 5

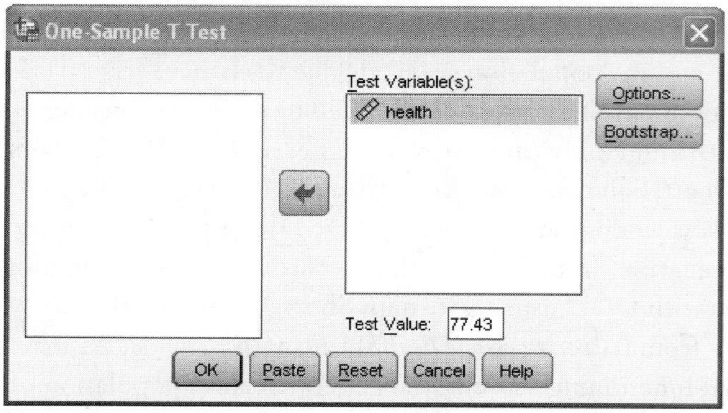

Table 5.4 SPSS Output Table for the One-Sample *t* Test

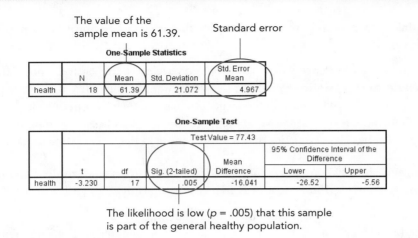

The value of the sample mean is 61.39.

Standard error

One-Sample Statistics

	N	Mean	Std. Deviation	Std. Error Mean
health	18	61.39	21.072	4.967

One-Sample Test

	Test Value = 77.43					
					95% Confidence Interval of the Difference	
	t	df	Sig. (2-tailed)	Mean Difference	Lower	Upper
health	-3.230	17	.005	-16.041	-26.52	-5.56

The likelihood is low (*p* = .005) that this sample is part of the general healthy population.

with a mean score of 77.43. In this study, the likelihood is low, *p* = .005, that relatives of patients with OCD (the sample) with a mean SF-36 score of 61.39 are part of the general healthy population with a mean score of 77.43.

In the behavioral sciences, the typical criterion is to conclude that a sample represents a unique group or population when *p* ≤ .05. Hence, we conclude that relatives of patients with OCD are a unique population because the likelihood that the sample we selected is part of the general healthy population is less than .05 in this study. To report the results of a one-sample *t* test in a research journal, we use the guidelines provided in the *Publication Manual of the American Psychological Association* (APA, 2009). Using these guidelines, we state the value of the test statistic, the degrees of freedom, and the *p* value as shown (all values are given in the SPSS output table):

> A one-sample *t* test showed that relatives of a patient with OCD are a unique population with lower mean SF-36 social functioning scores compared to the general healthy population, *t*(17) = −3.230, *p* = .005.

LEARNING CHECK 5 ✓

1. Distinguish between sampling bias and nonresponse bias.

2. State two rules that make the creation of participant pools an ethical practice.

3. State a statistical test specifically applied to identify new populations or subgroups within a larger population.

Answers: 1. Sampling bias is a bias in sampling in which the sampling procedures employed in a study favor certain individuals or groups over others, whereas nonresponse bias is a bias in sampling in which a number of participants in one or more groups choose not to respond to a survey or request to participate in a study; 2. Class grades are never contingent on actual participation in a research study, and students are given alternative options to receive a grade; 3. One-sample *t* test.

LO 1 Explain why researchers select samples that are representative of a population of interest.

- Researchers select samples from a population to learn more about the population from which the samples were selected. If researchers want to generalize the results they observe in a sample to those in the target population, then they need to make certain that the sample is representative of the target population. A **representative sample** is a sample that has characteristics that resemble those in the target population.

LO 2 Distinguish between *subjects* and *participants* as terms used to describe those who are subjected to procedures in a research study.

- The term **participant** is used to describe a human who volunteers to be subjected to the procedures in a research study. The term **subject** is used to describe a nonhuman that is subjected to procedures in a research study and it is also used to identify the names of research designs.

LO 3 Distinguish between probability sampling methods and nonprobability sampling methods.

- **Probability sampling** is a category of sampling in which a sample is selected directly from the target population; **nonprobability sampling** is a category of sampling in which a sample is selected from the accessible population. Sampling directly from the target population using probability sampling is possible in situations in which the exact probability of selecting each individual in a target population is known. However, it is rare that researchers know the exact probability of selecting each individual in a target population, so nonprobability sampling methods are most commonly used to select samples in behavioral research.

LO 4 Delineate two nonprobability sampling methods: convenience sampling and quota sampling.

- A **convenience sample**, as indicated in the name, is selected out of convenience or ease, meaning that participants are selected based on their availability to participate. A drawback of convenience sampling is that it does not ensure that a sample will be representative of the target population. To make a convenience sample representative of a target population of interest, researchers can use quota sampling, or they can use a combined sampling method.
- **Quota sampling** is a method of sampling in which subjects or participants are selected based on the characteristics they share in order to ensure that these characteristics are represented in a sample. For situations in which little is known about the characteristics of a target population, researchers use **simple quota sampling**. For situations in which certain characteristics are known in the population, researchers use **proportionate quota sampling**.

LO 5 Delineate four probability sampling methods: simple random sampling, stratified random sampling, systematic sampling, and cluster sampling.

- **Simple random sampling** is a method of sampling subjects and participants such that all individuals in a population have an equal chance of being selected and are selected using sampling with replacement.
- **Stratified random sampling** is a method of sampling in which a population is divided into subgroups or strata; participants are selected from each subgroup using simple random sampling and are combined into one overall sample. We can select an equal number of participants from each subgroup (**simple stratified random sampling**) or a number of participants from each subgroup that is proportionate with those in the population (**proportionate stratified random sampling**).
- **Systematic sampling** is a method of sampling in which the first participant is randomly selected, and then every nth person is systematically selected until all participants have been selected.
- **Cluster sampling** is a method of sampling in which subgroups or clusters of individuals are identified in a population, and then a portion of clusters that are representative of the population are selected such that all individuals in the selected clusters are included in the sample. All clusters that are not selected are omitted from the sample.

LO 6 Define and explain sampling error and the standard error of the mean.

- The extent to which sample means selected from the same population differ from one another is called **sampling error**. This difference, which occurs by chance, is measured by the **standard error of the mean**, which is the standard error or distance that sample mean values can deviate from the value of the population mean.

LO 7 Define and explain sampling bias and nonresponse bias.

- **Sampling bias** is a bias in sampling in which the sampling procedures employed in a study favor certain individuals or groups over others, whereas **nonresponse bias** is a bias in sampling in which a number of participants in one or more groups choose not to respond to a survey or request to participate in a study. Both biases can result in the selection of samples that are not representative of the population.

LO 8 Identify potential ethical concerns related to sampling from "participant pools" in human participant research.

- The creation of participant pools could place the burden of participation too heavily on the population of college students. There are two reasons why this is not the case: class grades are never contingent on actual participation in a research study, and students are given alternative options to receive a grade.

LO 9 Compute an estimate for the standard error of the mean and compute the one-sample *t* test using SPSS.

- An estimate for the standard error is computed in SPSS using the **Analyze, Descriptive Statistics**, and **Descriptives** options in the menu bar. These actions will bring up a dialog box that will allow you to identify your variable, select **Options**, and choose the **S.E. mean** option to compute an estimate of the standard error (for more details, see Section 5.6).
- The one-sample *t* test is computed in SPSS using the **Analyze, Compare Means**, and **One-Sample T Test** options in the menu bar. These actions will display a dialog box that allows you to identify the variable, enter the comparison value for the test, and run the test (for more details, see Section 5.9).

KEY TERMS

participant	quota sampling	proportionate stratified random sampling
subject	simple quota sampling	systematic sampling
target population	proportionate quota sampling	cluster sampling
accessible population	simple random sampling	sampling error
sampling frame	sampling with replacement	standard error of the mean
representative sample		
probability sampling	sampling without replacement	sampling bias
nonprobability sampling	stratified random sampling	selection bias
convenience sampling	simple stratified random sampling	nonresponse bias
participant pool		one-sample *t* test
subject pool		

REVIEW QUESTIONS

1. Which of the following best describes the reason why researchers select samples from populations of interest?

   A. Researchers make observations with samples to learn about, or generalize to, populations.

   B. Researchers select samples to avoid having to describe the characteristics of an entire population.

   C. Researchers make observations in populations to learn about the samples they will select.

2. Distinguish between a target population and an accessible population.

3. Which method of sampling requires that the probability of selecting each individual in a population is known?

4. Identify the target population, the accessible population, and the sample for the following hypothetical study.

    A consultant is hired by a national firm to test the hypothesis that "casual days" (any days where employees can wear casual clothing) improve employee satisfaction and productivity on the job. To test this hypothesis, the consultant obtains a list of all of the employees at a local branch of the firm and randomly selects 60 employees to participate in the study.

5. Identify the target population, the accessible population, and the sample for the following hypothetical study.

    A professor who teaches three sections of a research methods class tests the hypothesis that his research methods class prepares students for a career in research. To test this hypothesis, the professor obtains a list of all students in each of his three sections and randomly selects 25 students from each section to participate in a study.

6. A researcher selects a sample from an accessible portion of a target population. What sampling method, probability sampling or nonprobability sampling, is described in this example?

7. What is the most common nonprobability sampling method used to select human participants for a research study? Which nonprobability sampling method is typically used to obtain animal subjects in behavioral research?

8. State the nonprobability sampling method described in each example.

    A. A researcher studies student perceptions of global warming by selecting college participants from a participant pool at the local college and has each student complete a global warming attitudes survey.

    B. A researcher conducts a study on eating in a movie theater by asking patrons as they enter a movie theater if they are willing to participate in a study while they watch their movie. The researcher selects the first 50 women and the first 50 men who volunteer to participate in the study.

9. State the probability sampling method described in each example.

    A. To determine why many residents at a local nursing home are not eating their full meals, a researcher obtains a list of all residents at the nursing home and separates the list into two subgroups: residents who eat their full meals and residents who do not. The researcher randomly selects 12 residents from each subgroup to be in her sample.

    B. A professor obtains a list of all registered students in his class and randomly selects 40 students from the list to participate in a course evaluation.

C. An administrator at a local elementary school identifies that 24 classes are taught throughout the day at her school. From this list, she selects 12 classes and measures preparedness among all students in those 12 classrooms.

D. A psychologist randomly selects one athlete to participate in a study from a list of all athletes on campus. Then, beginning with the randomly selected athlete, he selects every fourth athlete on the list to also participate in the study.

10. What is sampling error, and how is it measured?

11. Distinguish between sampling bias and nonresponse bias.

12. Which ethical principle was a concern for the creation of participant pools? Explain.

ACTIVITIES

1. Researchers select samples from populations to learn more about the populations from which they selected the samples. Give an analogy from an everyday experience you have had to illustrate why researchers select samples from populations.

2. Choose any research topic that interests you and develop a research hypothesis. Answer the following items, which should be part of your research plan.

   A. Identify the target population and accessible population addressed by your research hypothesis.

   B. Describe the sampling method you will use. If you plan to use a combined sampling method, then identify each method you plan to combine. Make sure you identify your exact procedure for selecting participants.

   C. Explain how the sample you select is, or is not, representative of the target population.

Identify a problem

- Determine an area of interest.
- Review the literature.
- Identify new ideas in your area of interest.
- Develop a research hypothesis.

Develop a research plan

- Define the variables being tested.
- Identify participants or subjects and determine how to sample them.
- Select a research strategy and design.
- Evaluate ethics and obtain institutional approval to conduct research.

Generate more new ideas

- Results support your hypothesis—refine or expand on your ideas.
- Results do not support your hypothesis—reformulate a new idea or start over.

After reading this chapter, you should be able to:

1. Identify three categories of research design: experimental, quasi-experimental, and nonexperimental.

2. Explain how a gradient of control can be used to understand research design.

3. Define and explain internal and external validity.

4. Describe three elements of control required in an experiment.

5. Distinguish between a laboratory experiment and a field experiment.

6. Describe factors that threaten the internal validity of a research study.

7. Describe factors that threaten the external validity of a research study.

8. Define and explain mundane and experimental realism.

Conduct the study

- Execute the research plan and measure or record the data.

Communicate the results

- Method of communication: oral, written, or in a poster.
- Style of communication: APA guidelines are provided to help prepare style and format.

Analyze and evaluate the data

- Analyze and evaluate the data as they relate to the research hypothesis.
- Summarize data and research results.

CHOOSING A RESEARCH DESIGN

Behavioral science is about understanding behavior. You are in many ways a behavioral scientist in that you ask questions about human behavior and seek to answer those questions. For example, if you are struggling in a course, you may ask, "How can I improve my studying to increase my grade?" While you may not have considered the formal scientific process to answer your question, it can nonetheless be used to answer your question.

One way to think of research design is as a set of rules for how to make observations to answer questions. Each research design has a unique set of rules to help you control, manage, and organize what will be observed and how it will be observed. In this way, research design is similar to a board game, which has many rules to control, manage, and organize how you are allowed to move game pieces on a game board. Most board games, for example, have rules that tell you how many spaces you can move on the game board at most at a time, and what to do if you pick up a certain card or land on a certain spot on the game board. The rules, in essence, define the game. Each board game only makes sense if players follow the rules.

Likewise, in science, the rules stated in a research design allow us to make sense of the conclusions we draw from the observations we make. In a board game, we follow rules to establish a winner; in science, we follow rules to establish conclusions from the observations we make. There are many ways in which you could observe yourself studying—for example, alone, in groups, while using a specific memory strategy, in a dorm room, or in a more controlled setting such as a library. In this chapter, we will explore the basic nature of the major categories of research design introduced in this book and organize how these research designs differ based on the types of conclusions they allow you to draw from the observations you make.

6.1 Designing a Study to Answer a Question

Conducting a study is important because it allows you to make observations using the scientific process to answer your research question. The type of study you conduct depends largely on the type of question you are asking. To conduct a research study, you need to be thoughtful of the extent to which you are actually answering your question. To illustrate, suppose you ask if people have different emotional responses to negative versus positive movie poster images—a similar type of question was tested by Baumgartner and Laghi (2012). To answer this question, you show one group of participants a movie poster with mostly negative images (Group Negative) and another group a movie poster with mostly positive images (Group Positive). If you find that Group Positive has a more positive emotional response to the movie poster, then can we conclude that the images caused this difference between groups?

The answer to your question depends on how thoughtful your research design was. For example, color influences emotion, so the colors displayed in each poster should be the same. Otherwise, if the positive images also displayed softer colors (e.g., light blue or yellow), then maybe the colors and not the images themselves caused the differences in emotional responsiveness between groups. Other factors that could also influence emotion include the size of the posters or the genre of movies that participants prefer watching. These additional factors should also be controlled to clearly show that the images themselves caused the differences between groups. In other words, designing a study is a careful, thoughtful, and often clever endeavor.

A research study applies specific methods and procedures, called the **research design**, to answer a research question. The types of research questions that you can ask are generally categorized as *exploratory*, *descriptive*, or *relational* questions. Each type of question is described with examples given in Table 6.1. In this chapter, we introduce many types of research designs used in the behavioral sciences. In this book, Chapters 7 to 12 will describe in greater detail each type of research design introduced in this chapter.

> A **research design** is the specific methods and procedures used to answer a research question.

LEARNING CHECK 1 ✓

1. State the type of question being asked for each example.

   A. How often do college students change their major on average?

   B. What if the way that animals learn is similar to the way that humans learn?

   C. Is personal income related to happiness?

Answers: 1. A. Descriptive. B. Exploratory. C. Relational.

Table 6.1 The Three Types of Questions That Researchers Ask

Type of Question	Question Stated	Description/Goal	Examples
Exploratory	"What if"	To "get an idea of" or "explore" an area of research that is not well understood. Rarely do these questions provide definitive answers; rather, they lead to a stronger focus for subsequent research.	1. What if a high-fat, high-sugar diet is physically addictive? 2. What if human memory has an infinite capacity for storage?
Descriptive	"What is" "How"	To characterize, explain, or "describe" variables that are related to a specific group of individuals. These questions are not concerned with relationships between variables; rather, they are concerned with simply describing variables.	1. What is the average time spent watching TV per year? 2. How many pounds does a college student typically gain in his or her freshman year?
Relational	"Does" "Is"	To determine the extent to which specified relationships exist between variables. These questions provide (1) causal explanations or (2) descriptions of the relationship between two or more variables.	1. Do low levels of serotonin in the brain cause depression? 2. Is personal income related to life satisfaction?

6.2 Categories of Research Design

To answer a research question, you can choose a research design that falls into one of the following three categories, summarized in Figure 6.1:

> **Control** in research design is (a) the manipulation of a variable and (b) holding all other variables constant. When control is low, neither criterion is met; when control is high, both criteria are met.

- Experimental research design

- Quasi-experimental research design

- Nonexperimental research design

Each type of research design is distinguished by the level of control that is established in the design. The term **control** is used in research design to describe (a) the manipulation of a variable and (b) holding all other variables constant. When control is low, neither criterion (a nor b) is met. For example, suppose we observe play behavior among children at a park. The variable is play behavior; some children play quietly, and others play loudly. The children determine how loudly they play—the play behavior, then, is not manipulated or controlled by the researcher. Also, many other factors (e.g., the types of toys available to play with or the behavior of other children) can influence a child's play behavior at a park. Because the researcher does not manipulate the variable or hold these other variables constant, the study has low control.

Alternatively, when control is high, both criteria (a and b) are met. For example, to study play behavior, a researcher can have the children play one at a time on a playground. In one group, the children are told to play quietly; in another group, the children are told to play loudly. By manipulating the play behavior of the children (quiet play, loud play), the researcher establishes greater control. In addition, because all of the children play alone on the same playground, factors such as the types of toys available to play with or the behavior of other children are now held constant—all children, whether they play quietly or loudly, play alone with the same playground of toys. In this example, the researcher has established greater control by meeting both criteria (a and b) needed to establish control in a research design.

In this section, we introduce each research category and we briefly describe the types of research designs that fall into each category. We will specifically distinguish between the levels of control established with each design because *control* is the key feature that can distinguish between categories of research design.

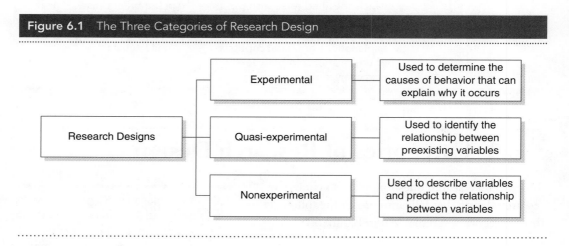

Figure 6.1 The Three Categories of Research Design

Experimental Research Designs

An **experimental research design** is the use of methods and procedures to make observations in which the researcher fully controls the conditions and experiences of participants by applying three required elements of control: randomization, manipulation, and comparison/control.

The staple of all designs is the experimental research design. The **experimental research design** is the use of methods and procedures to make observations in which the researcher fully controls the conditions and experiences of participants by applying three required elements of control: randomization, manipulation, and comparison/control. Each element of control is discussed in greater detail in Section 6.4. Figure 6.2 identifies many experimental research designs introduced in this book—each design will be introduced in greater detail in Chapters 9 through 12.

A key strength of the experimental research design is that it is the only research design capable of demonstrating cause and effect. To demonstrate that one factor causes changes in a dependent variable, the conditions and experiences of participants must be under the full control of the researcher. This often means that an experiment is conducted in a laboratory and not in the environment where a behavior naturally operates. Suppose, for example, we study the effects of winning and losing on the desire to gamble. In a natural environment, it would be difficult to know if winning or losing causes changes in a person's desire to gamble because many other factors can vary in that setting. Some factors include the person's reasons for gambling that day, the amount of money available to gamble, the number of gamblers in a group, the types of games being played, and even the bright lights and sounds in the casino. We may be able to observe differences related to one's desire to gamble, but identifying the specific causes in that natural environment would be very difficult. To identify if winning or losing causes changes in a person's desire to gamble, Young, Wohl, Matheson, Baumann, and Anisman (2008) conducted an experiment by bringing students into a laboratory and having them experience a "virtual reality" casino in which the events, including winning and losing, were specifically controlled by the researchers. In this controlled setting of a virtual casino, the researchers specifically identified that high-risk gamblers have a much greater desire to gamble following a large win than following a series of small wins in a virtual casino setting.

A key limitation of the experimental research design is that behavior that occurs under controlled conditions may not be the same as behavior that occurs in a natural environment. For example, it is certainly possible that how a person behaves in a virtual setting (a virtual casino) will be different from how a person behaves in a natural setting (a real casino). In the Young et al. (2008) study, observations in the virtual casino setting clearly identified that the size of a win (large vs. small) causes changes in a dependent

Figure 6.2 Experimental Research Designs

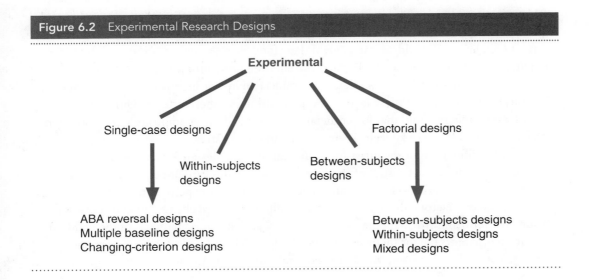

variable (desire to gamble). However, observations in their experiment were made in that virtual setting only, and not in a real casino setting. For this reason, it will be difficult to generalize their findings beyond a virtual casino setting—that is, until such observations are made in an actual casino setting.

Quasi-Experimental Research Designs

An alternative to the experimental research design for situations in which it is difficult or impossible to manipulate a factor is the quasi-experimental research design. The **quasi-experimental research design** is the use of methods and procedures to make observations in a study that is structured similar to an experiment, but the conditions and experiences of participants are not under the full control of the researcher. The conditions and experiences of participants are not under the full control of the researcher when the factor is not manipulated (i.e., it is "quasi-independent"), or when the research design lacks a comparison/control group. A **quasi-independent variable** is any factor in which the levels of that factor are preexisting. Quasi-independent variables typically of interest to researchers include characteristics of participants, such as their gender (man, woman), health status (lean, overweight, obese), or political affiliation (Democrat, Republican). When a factor is preexisting, participants cannot be randomly assigned to each level of that factor.

A **quasi-experimental research design** is the use of methods and procedures to make observations in a study that is structured similar to an experiment, but the conditions and experiences of participants lack some control because the study lacks random assignment, includes a preexisting factor (i.e., a variable that is not manipulated), or does not include a comparison/control group.

A **quasi-independent variable** is a variable with levels to which participants are not randomly assigned and that differentiates the groups or conditions being compared in a research study.

A key strength of the quasi-experimental research design is that it allows researchers to study factors related to the unique characteristics of participants. For example, Roemmich, Lambiase, Lobarinas, and Balantekin (2011) investigated how two preexisting quasi-independent factors (i.e., dietary restraint and adiposity) were related to food intake during stress among 8- to 12-year-old children. Dietary restraint (i.e., how well children can control their food choices) and adiposity (i.e., body fat percentage) are preexisting factors because the children came into the study having good or poor control of their food choices (dietary restraint) and low or high body fat percentage (adiposity)—hence, each of these factors was preexisting or inherent to the children. In this study, the researchers found that lower dietary restraint and lower adiposity were associated with consuming 123 fewer kilocalories in a meal after being stressed.

A key limitation of the quasi-experimental research design is that researchers do not manipulate the characteristics of the participants and thus cannot demonstrate cause and effect. Referring back to the Roemmich et al. (2011) quasi-experiment, it is not possible to know if the two factors (dietary restraint and adiposity) *caused* changes in kilocalories consumed after being stressed because other factors, such as eating patterns of the children or what their parents taught them about food, could also be related to these factors and therefore could also be causing the increased intake observed. Anytime a factor is preexisting (i.e., quasi-independent), then any other factors related to it could also be causing changes in a dependent variable. Figure 6.3 identifies the many quasi-experimental research designs introduced in this book. Each research design listed in Figure 6.3 will be described in greater detail in Chapter 9.

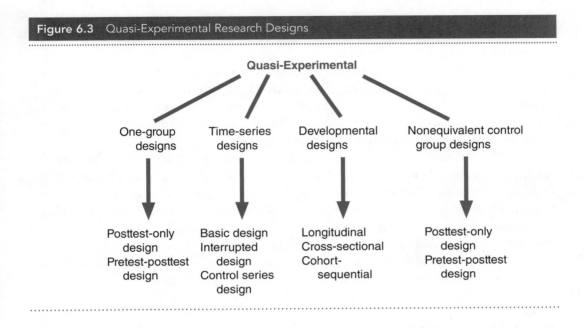

Figure 6.3 Quasi-Experimental Research Designs

Nonexperimental Research Designs

The third category of research design used in the behavioral sciences is the nonexperimental research design. The **nonexperimental research design** is the use of methods and procedures to make observations in which the conditions or experiences of participants are not manipulated.

> A **nonexperimental research design** is the use of methods and procedures to make observations in which the behavior or event is observed "as is" or without an intervention from the researcher.

A *manipulation* occurs when the researcher creates the conditions in which participants are observed; however, this is not always possible to study behavior. For example, we cannot manipulate the content of existing documents at different times in history, such as an analysis of presidential speeches in times of war. Another example is that we often cannot manipulate interactions in natural settings, such as those between a prisoner and a guard or between an athlete and a coach. Situations such as these are certainly worthy of scientific investigation, so nonexperimental research designs have been adapted to study these types of situations.

There are many situations in which we want to study behavior in settings where the behavior or variables being observed cannot be manipulated. Figure 6.4 identifies many nonexperimental research designs introduced in this book—each design will be introduced in greater detail in Chapters 7 and 8. A key characteristic that differentiates nonexperimental designs from all other research designs is that the behavior or event being observed is observed "as is" or without intervention from the researcher. For example, Chapman, Struhsaker, Skorupa, Snaith, and Rothman (2010) used 26 to 36 years of data for five species of primates living in Kibale National Park, Uganda, to understand potential changes in population density and habitat and community dynamics. In this study, the members of each species lived out their lives as usual, and the researchers applied research techniques to study the dynamics of their lives in that natural setting.

A key strength of the nonexperimental research design is that it can be used to make observations in settings in which the behaviors and events being observed naturally operate. Referring back to the Chapman et al. (2010) study, these researchers observed five species of primates in their natural environment of the national park. Likewise, we can observe other situations in natural settings—that is, a prisoner and a guard in a prison or an athlete and a coach during a game. In each example, we make observations in a setting where the subjects or participants being observed would naturally interact.

A key limitation of the nonexperimental research design is that it lacks the control needed to demonstrate cause and effect. For example, if the number of primates in a certain area of the park diminished after humans began populating that area, we cannot know for sure that "human presence" caused that change, because other factors (e.g., possible changes in weather, food availability, or even competition from other primates) could also explain the change. It is often difficult to anticipate all alternative explanations for what is observed in a natural setting. Using a nonexperimental research design, then, we can speculate about potential causes for the observations we make, but we cannot know for sure without greater control.

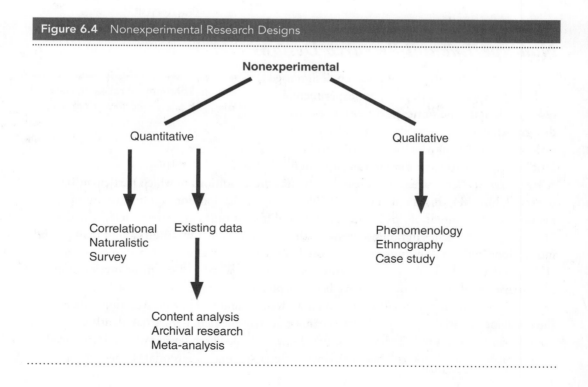

Figure 6.4 Nonexperimental Research Designs

As shown in Figure 6.5, we could characterize a research design as either having demonstrated cause and effect (i.e., experimental research design) or having failed to establish the control needed to do so (i.e., nonexperimental and quasi-experimental designs). This characterization can lead to the erroneous conclusion that the best or superior research designs are those that demonstrate cause—this conclusion is not true.

Figure 6.5 Classifying Research Designs by Whether They Can Demonstrate Cause and Effect

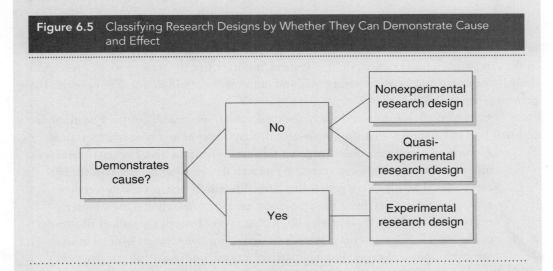

Certainly, one of the goals in science discussed in Chapter 1 is to *explain* the causes of the behaviors and events we observe. An experimental research design is the only design capable of meeting this goal. However, it is also a goal in science to *describe* the behaviors and events we observe, and to determine the extent to which we can *predict* their occurrence in different situations. Nonexperimental and quasi-experimental research designs are well adapted to meet these goals. Studying behavior is complex, and we must understand that not all behaviors and events can be brought under the full control of a researcher. Therefore, nonexperimental and quasi-experimental research designs are an essential and valuable tool that allows researchers to meet the goals of science and add to an understanding of the behaviors and events they observe.

6.3 Internal and External Validity

Categorizing research design is rather difficult. Indeed, there is not even full agreement among scientists about what types of research designs fit into each category. In other research methods textbooks, for example, many of the quasi-experimental designs listed in Figure 6.3

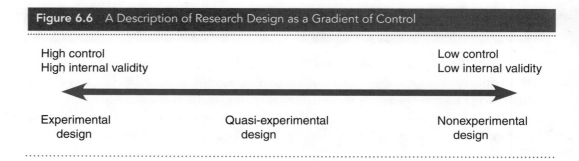

Figure 6.6 A Description of Research Design as a Gradient of Control

High control
High internal validity

Low control
Low internal validity

Experimental
design

Quasi-experimental
design

Nonexperimental
design

are instead taught as being nonexperimental designs. However, try not to get bogged down in the categorization of research design. Instead, use the three main categories of research design—experimental, quasi-experimental, and nonexperimental—as a way to organize the general types of designs used.

Categorization can oversimplify the complexity of research design. For example, you will find in Chapter 9 that the single-case design is taught as a type of experiment; however, not all researchers agree on this categorization. In Chapter 12, you will find that sometimes we can combine research designs that belong to different categories. The idea here is that thinking of research design only in terms of categories takes away from the true complexity of research design. A better approach is to think of research design along a gradient of control, as illustrated in Figure 6.6. Experimental research designs have the greatest control in that the conditions and experiences of participants are under the full control of the researcher. This control is less in a quasi-experimental research design and can be absent in a nonexperimental research design.

> Internal validity is higher with greater control; external validity is higher with fewer constraints.

The level of control in a research design directly relates to **internal validity** or the extent to which the research design can demonstrate cause and effect. The more control in a research design, the higher the internal validity. Experimental research designs have the greatest control and therefore the highest internal validity; nonexperimental research designs typically have the least control and therefore the lowest internal validity.

A second validity for research design, called **external validity**, relates to the constraints in a study. A *constraint* is any aspect of the research design that can limit observations to the specific conditions or manipulations in a study. A psychologist, for example, may measure a participant's response time by measuring how fast, in seconds, he or she presses a computer key after an image of a specific shape or color appears on the screen. The constraint is that a computer program is used to measure the behavior (i.e., response time). Would the speed of a response in this situation be the same in other situations, such as reading words in an e-mail or identifying a person in a crowd? The more an observation generalizes

Internal validity is the extent to which a research design includes enough control of the conditions and experiences of participants that it can demonstrate a single unambiguous explanation for a manipulation—that is, cause and effect.

External validity is the extent to which observations made in a study generalize beyond the specific manipulations or constraints in the study.

beyond the specific conditions or constraints in a study, the higher the external validity. The fewer the constraints or the more natural the settings within which observations are made, the higher the external validity of a research study tends to be.

6.4 Demonstrating Cause in an Experiment

Any study that demonstrates cause is called an **experiment**. To demonstrate cause, an experiment must follow strict procedures to ensure that all other possible causes have been minimized or eliminated. Therefore, researchers must control the conditions under which observations are made to isolate cause-and-effect relationships between variables. Figure 6.7 uses an example to show the steps of a typical experiment. We will work through this example to describe the basic structure of an experiment.

> An **experiment** is the methods and procedures used in an experimental research design to specifically control the conditions under which observations are made in order to isolate cause-and-effect relationships between variables.
>
> Three required elements of control in an experiment are randomization, manipulation, and comparison/control. Each element of control is described further in this section.

General Elements and Structure of Experiments

An experiment includes three key elements of control that allow researchers to draw cause-and-effect conclusions:

1. Randomization (random sampling and random assignment).

2. Manipulation (of variables that operate in an experiment).

3. Comparison/control (a control group).

Figure 6.7 illustrates a hypothetical experiment to determine the effect of distraction on student test scores. To employ **randomization**, we use **random sampling** by selecting a sample at random from a population of students, and we

> **Randomization** is the use of methods for selecting individuals to participate in a study and assigning them to groups such that each individual has an equal chance of being selected to participate and assigned to a group.

then use **random assignment** to assign students to one of two groups at random. In one group, the professor sits quietly while students take an exam (low-distraction condition); in the other group, the professor rattles papers, taps her foot, and makes other sounds during an exam (high-distraction condition).

> Researchers use randomization to ensure that individuals are selected to participate at random (**random sampling** or **random selection**) and are assigned to groups at random (**random assignment**).

Random sampling is a method of selecting participants such that all individuals have an equal chance of being selected to participate. *Random assignment* is a method of assigning participants to groups such that each participant has an equal chance of being assigned to each group. To use random assignment, we identify the **independent variable** or **factor** that will be manipulated in an experiment (note that *manipulation* is the second element of control in an experiment). We then assign participants to each **level** of that factor using a random procedure, such as using a random numbers table to assign participants to groups. (Note that a random numbers table is given in Appendix B.1 with instructions for how to use it.) As shown in Figure 6.7, in our experiment we manipulated "distraction" (the factor), which has two levels (low, high). We then randomly assigned participants to one level or the other. Each level of the independent variable is a group in our design.

> An **independent variable** or **factor** is the variable that is manipulated in an experiment. The levels of the variable remain unchanged (or "independent") between groups in an experiment. It is the "presumed cause."
>
> The **levels of a factor** are the specific conditions or groups created by manipulating that factor.

Random assignment was first introduced in research with plant seeds (Fisher, 1925, 1935) and has since been applied to research with humans. What was learned in studies with plants is that random assignment controls for the **individual differences** in the characteristics of plants, and the same principle can be applied to human participants. An individual difference is any characteristic that can differentiate people, including their eye color, gender, style of clothing, eating habits, sleeping patterns, employment status, or any other characteristic that may differ between people in a study.

> In an experiment, random assignment is used to control for individual differences.

We use random assignment with humans to control for individual differences in participant characteristics by ensuring that the characteristics of participants in each group of an experiment vary entirely by chance. If we do not control for individual differences, then any number of participant characteristics could differ between groups and explain an observed difference between groups. The individual differences would be a **confound**, or an alternative explanation for an observation in an experiment.

> **Individual differences** are the unique characteristics of participants in a sample that can differ from one participant to another.
>
> A **confound** or **confound variable** is an unanticipated variable not accounted for in a research study that could be causing or associated with observed changes in one or more measured variables.
>
> The **dependent variable** is the variable that is believed to change in the presence of the independent variable. It is the "presumed effect."

We create at least two groups in an experiment so that a presumed cause (high distraction) can be compared to a group where it

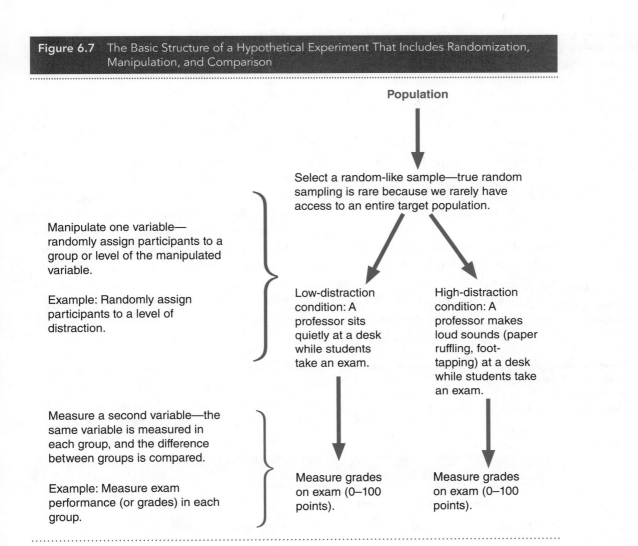

Population

Select a random-like sample—true random sampling is rare because we rarely have access to an entire target population.

Manipulate one variable—randomly assign participants to a group or level of the manipulated variable.

Example: Randomly assign participants to a level of distraction.

Low-distraction condition: A professor sits quietly at a desk while students take an exam.

High-distraction condition: A professor makes loud sounds (paper ruffling, foot-tapping) at a desk while students take an exam.

Measure a second variable—the same variable is measured in each group, and the difference between groups is compared.

Example: Measure exam performance (or grades) in each group.

Measure grades on exam (0–100 points).

Measure grades on exam (0–100 points).

is absent or minimal (low distraction). We can then compare grades in each group to determine the difference or effect that distraction had on exam grades. The measured variable in an experiment is called the **dependent variable**. If a difference is observed between the low- and high-distraction groups, then we conclude that distraction levels caused the difference because we used randomization, manipulation, and comparison/control to design the experiment. Additional factors to be considered in order to draw cause-and-effect conclusions are described in Section 6.6.

In an experiment, the independent variable is manipulated to create groups; the dependent variable is measured in each group.

Laboratory and Field Experiments

Two types of experiments in the behavioral sciences are laboratory and field experiments. The strength of an experiment is that it can demonstrate cause and effect, meaning that it has high internal validity. A **laboratory experiment** is an experiment

> A **laboratory experiment** is an experiment that takes place in a laboratory setting in which the researcher has greatest control over variables, regardless of whether it is made to look natural or not.

that takes place in a laboratory setting. Although a laboratory setting can be made to appear as if it is a natural environment, this setting often does not resemble the environment within which the behavior or event being observed would naturally operate. Regardless of whether it appears natural or not, however, a laboratory experiment is typically associated with the highest internal validity because the researcher has the greatest control over variables in this environment.

As an example of a laboratory experiment, suppose we study racial attitudes and have White participants read a vignette about a White roommate (same-race condition) or a Black roommate (different-race condition). Participants in each group then rate whether they have positive or negative attitudes toward the roommate described in the vignette. In this example of a laboratory experiment, also illustrated in Figure 6.8, we manipulated race (White, Black) by giving participants different vignettes to read. We cannot be certain that a difference between groups would generalize to a real situation in which participants actually live with a same- or opposite-race roommate because we conducted the experiment in a laboratory and not in a dormitory. Hence, laboratory experiments tend to be associated with low external validity.

> A **field experiment** is an experiment that takes place in an environment within which the behavior or event being observed would naturally operate.

To increase the external validity of an experiment, we can conduct a **field experiment**, or an experiment conducted in the natural setting within which the behavior of interest naturally operates. For example, to study racial attitudes,

---

Figure 6.8 Two Types of Experiments to Study Racial Attitudes

Laboratory Experiment

Manipulation (create two conditions):

White participants read a vignette about a roommate and rate their attitudes of the roommate described.

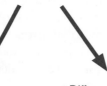

Same-race condition: The roommate is described as White.

Different-race condition: The roommate is described as Black.

Field Experiment

Manipulation (create two conditions):

White freshmen are randomly assigned to live with a roommate in a college dormitory and rate their attitudes of the roommate.

Same-race condition: The roommate assigned is White.

Different-race condition: The roommate assigned is Black.

In the laboratory experiment, racial conditions were manipulated in a lab. In the field experiment (Shook & Fazio, 2008), the manipulation took place in a natural setting.

Shook and Fazio (2008) randomly assigned White freshman college students to live with a White (same-race) or Black (different-race) roommate in a college dormitory. Because the students lived with the roommate in a college dormitory (a natural setting for living with roommates), this is an example of a field experiment. This field experiment is also illustrated in Figure 6.8. Field experiments typically increase the external validity of an experiment because the study takes place in a natural setting where we would naturally expect the behavior—that is, the development of racial attitudes—to occur. However, field experiments do lose some control. In this case, for example, we have little control over the actual interactions of the roommates. For this reason, we typically lose some level of internal validity in a field experiment in order to strengthen external validity.

It should be noted that external validity is relative. In other words, the field experiment described in this section is associated with greater external validity *compared to* the laboratory experiment. However, the field experiment was conducted on a college campus with college students; these are constraints. It is not possible to know the extent to which such findings would generalize to other campuses, or to participants of similar age who chose not to attend college. In other words, field experiments tend to have higher external validity compared to laboratory experiments. However, this is not meant to imply that field experiments are associated with no constraints that can limit external validity. Instead, laboratory and field experiments are both likely to be associated with constraints in terms of generalizability across people and settings. Field experiments simply tend to be associated with fewer constraints, and thus have higher external validity, compared to laboratory experiments.

MAKING SENSE—DISTINGUISHING BETWEEN AN EXPERIMENT AND A QUASI-EXPERIMENT

A researcher must manipulate the independent variable or factor in an experiment. Manipulating the factor means that the researcher creates the levels of that factor so that participants can then be assigned to a level or group at random. If the researcher does not manipulate the levels of the factor, then participants cannot be randomly assigned to groups, and the study is not an experiment. When a factor is not manipulated, the factor is called a quasi-independent variable.

Quasi-independent variables can be readily identified because these factors are typically characteristics that are unique to participants. For example, suppose we measure differences in the number of tasks completed by men and women. Figure 6.9 illustrates this study, which at first glance appears to be an experiment. However, gender is a characteristic of the participants and cannot be randomly assigned, which makes this factor a quasi-independent variable and makes this study a quasi-experimental research design. Be careful, therefore, to identify when the levels of

(Continued)

(Continued)

a factor are manipulated because this one change can influence whether a study is experimental (demonstrates cause and effect) or quasi-experimental (does not demonstrate cause and effect).

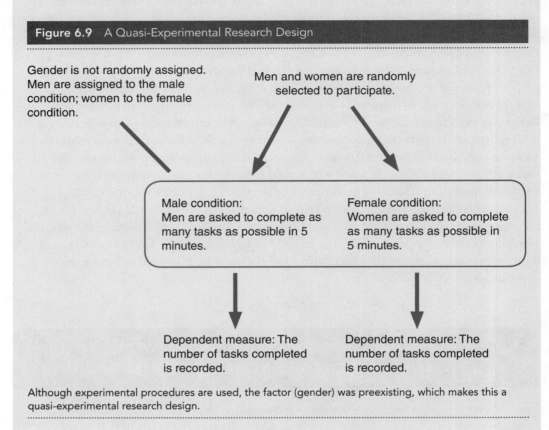

Figure 6.9 A Quasi-Experimental Research Design

Gender is not randomly assigned. Men are assigned to the male condition; women to the female condition.

Men and women are randomly selected to participate.

Male condition:
Men are asked to complete as many tasks as possible in 5 minutes.

Female condition:
Women are asked to complete as many tasks as possible in 5 minutes.

Dependent measure: The number of tasks completed is recorded.

Dependent measure: The number of tasks completed is recorded.

Although experimental procedures are used, the factor (gender) was preexisting, which makes this a quasi-experimental research design.

6.5 Ethics in Focus: Beneficence and Random Assignment

In an experiment, researchers manipulate the levels of an independent variable and randomly assign participants to groups in order to establish control. Researchers also include a control or comparison group. In the example illustrated in Figure 6.7, a high-distraction condition was compared to a low-distraction condition. This example is likely associated with little ethical concern because manipulating the levels of distraction did not necessarily result in significant benefits or risks to participants. However, some situations may produce big differences in how participants are treated in each group. In these situations, there can be an ethical concern that relates to *beneficence*, which is the equal distribution of potential costs and benefits of participation (see Chapter 3).

Random assignment ensures that all participants in the research study have an equal chance of being assigned to a group and, therefore, an equal chance of receiving whatever benefits and costs are associated with participation in that group. Random assignment, however, may not be sufficient when one group has obviously greater benefits than another group. For example, clinical trials can have significant benefits for those participants receiving a superior treatment; thus, the control group (standard treatment condition) can be viewed as relatively disadvantaged. In these situations, researchers will often compensate the disadvantaged group, such as giving the control group access to the superior treatment at some time after the study, referred to as *compensatory equalization of treatments* (see Kline, 2008). Such compensation is provided to participants in order to meet the ethical standard of beneficence, as required in the American Psychological Association (2010) code of conduct.

> Random assignment ensures that participants have an equal chance of receiving the benefits or taking the risks associated with participation in a group.

LEARNING CHECK 3 ✓

1. State three elements of control in an experiment that allow researchers to draw cause-and-effect conclusions.

2. A social scientist tests whether attitudes toward morality differ based on emotional state (positive or negative). Identify the independent variable and the dependent variable in this example.

3. Which type of experiment, laboratory or field experiment, is associated with higher internal validity? Which is typically associated with higher external validity?

Answers: 1. Randomization, manipulation, and comparison/control; 2. Independent variable: Emotional state. Dependent variable: Attitudes toward morality; 3. Laboratory experiments typically have higher internal validity. Field experiments typically have higher external validity.

6.6 Threats to the Internal Validity of a Research Study

Validity was first introduced in Chapter 4 to describe measurement, or the extent to which a variable measures what it is intended to measure. In this chapter, we introduce validity to describe research design, or the extent to which the claim of a researcher fits with what was actually observed in a research study. Factors that threaten (i.e., decrease) the internal validity of a research study are those factors that vary systematically with an independent variable. (Internal validity was introduced in Section 6.3 in this chapter.) Therefore, any threat to the internal validity of a study is a potential confound that must be controlled.

The following is a list of common threats to the internal validity of a research study, which are introduced in this section:

- History and maturation
- Regression and testing effects
- Instrumentation and measurement
- Heterogeneous attrition
- Environmental factors

History and Maturation

One threat to internal validity, called a **history effect**, refers to an unanticipated event that co-occurs with a treatment or manipulation in a study. History effects threaten internal validity when the event itself can also explain a research finding. For example, suppose researchers in New York City wanted to study the benefits of reading and so measured well-being on September 7, 2001, and again on September 14, 2001, among a group of participants who read each day for 1 hour during that time. A history effect, or unanticipated event, may have been the 9/11 terrorist attacks, which occurred during the study. If well-being scores decreased, it was just as likely due to the 9/11 attacks (history effect) as it was to the reading manipulation. Other more subtle examples include holidays (e.g., measuring candy vs. vegetable intake during Halloween), weather (e.g., measuring mood changes in areas with different climates), and public policy (e.g., measuring stress levels before and after a presidential election or change in bankruptcy laws). In each case, 9/11, a holiday, weather, or public policy (history effects) can also explain any changes in well-being, intake, mood, or stress, respectively.

A **history effect** is a possible threat to internal validity in which an unanticipated event co-occurs with a treatment or manipulation in a study.

Maturation is a possible threat to internal validity in which a participant's physiological or psychological state changes over time during a study.

Another concern relates to **maturation**, which is a threat to internal validity in which a participant's physiological or psychological state changes over time during a study. Maturation refers to internal changes that exist within an individual and are not related to external events. Maturation includes factors such as age, learning, hunger, physical development, and boredom. As an example, suppose that a speech therapist shows that 3- to 4-year-old children improve their speech following her therapy, as illustrated in Figure 6.10. However, 3- to 4-year-old children develop speech naturally during that age period. Some changes during the therapy, then, could simply be due to natural development and not to her specific therapy. One way to eliminate this problem would be to conduct an experiment that includes a no-therapy control condition, also illustrated in Figure 6.10.

Figure 6.10   Maturation

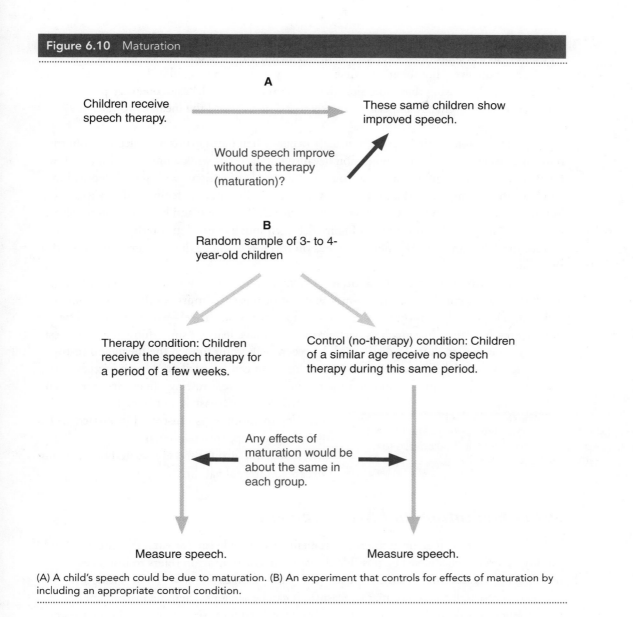

A

Children receive speech therapy. → These same children show improved speech.

Would speech improve without the therapy (maturation)?

B

Random sample of 3- to 4-year-old children

Therapy condition: Children receive the speech therapy for a period of a few weeks.

Control (no-therapy) condition: Children of a similar age receive no speech therapy during this same period.

Any effects of maturation would be about the same in each group.

Measure speech.   Measure speech.

(A) A child's speech could be due to maturation. (B) An experiment that controls for effects of maturation by including an appropriate control condition.

Regression and Testing Effects

Some possible threats to internal validity are related to performance. Two examples of this are regression toward the mean and testing effects. **Regression toward the mean** occurs when unusually high or low performance at one time

Regression toward the mean is a change or shift in a participant's performance toward a level or score that is closer to or more typical of his or her true potential or mean ability on some measure, after previously scoring unusually high or low on the same measure.

shifts toward a level or score that is more typical or closer to the mean of an individual's true ability at a second time. You see this firsthand anytime you obtain a better score on a makeup exam after "bombing" the first exam, or you watch a pro golfer hit a great shot after completely missing that same shot the previous day. In both cases, one very possible explanation for the change in performance is regression toward the mean or toward one's true abilities.

Regression toward the mean usually occurs when participants are selected from the bottom or top percentile in a population because initial scores will be unusually high or low for that group. For example, suppose you select a sample of patients with severe depression and have them complete a test in which lower scores indicate lower feelings of self-worth. You then give them a cognitive behavioral therapy (CBT) session and have them complete this same test again. As illustrated in Figure 6.11, without a control group that does not receive the CBT, any improvement in scores on this test could be due to regression toward the mean.

A **testing effect** may be another explanation for the results in the CBT study. Testing effects occur when performance on a test or measure improves the second time it is taken. In the CBT study, the improvement in scores on the self-worth test could be due to a testing effect inasmuch as participants may have learned something about the test the first time they took it. To distinguish between regression toward the mean and testing effects, keep in mind that regression toward the mean can be attributed to an increase or a decrease in performance from one time to another, whereas testing effects are attributed primarily to an increase in performance from one time to another. As illustrated in Figure 6.11, including an appropriate control group (i.e., a no-CBT group) can eliminate both as being threats to internal validity.

A **testing effect** is the improved performance on a test or measure the second time it is taken due to the experience of taking the test.

Instrumentation and Measurement

Sometimes an error in the measurement of a variable can threaten the internal validity of a research study. The possible threat of **instrumentation** refers to instances in which the measurement of the dependent variable changes due to an error during the course of a research study. For many measures it can be obvious when the instrument of measurement breaks or has an error. For example, we can measure differences in the weight of participants, the time it takes to complete a task, or body temperature during the day. The instruments are a scale, a timer, and a thermometer, and it would likely be noticeable if one of them broke during the course of a study. The researcher would notice the problem, and then correct it and continue the research study.

Instrumentation can be problematic when it is inherently prone to error, such as when a rater makes judgments regarding the behaviors he or she observes. For example, suppose three raters rate the time a participant held eye contact with a male or female interviewer during a mock

Instrumentation is a possible threat to internal validity in which the measurement of the dependent variable changes due to an error during the course of a research study.

Figure 6.11   Regression Toward the Mean and Testing Effects

Is the improvement due to prior experience taking the assessment (testing effect)?

Depression scores are measured in a sample of patients with depression.

The sample participates in a cognitive behavioral therapy (CBT) session.

Scores on the depression assessment improve.

Is the improvement due to the tendency for scores to shift toward the mean (regression)?

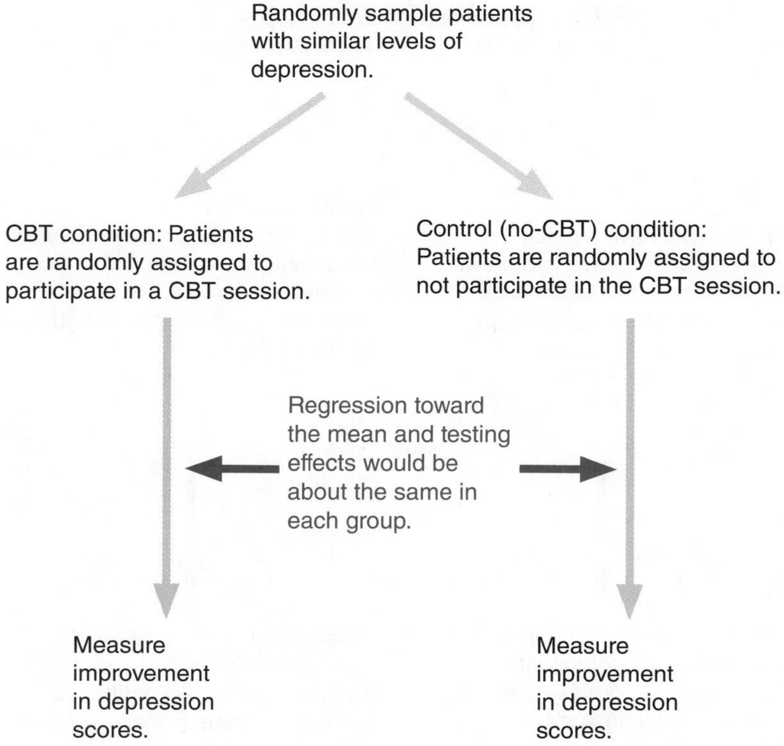

Randomly sample patients with similar levels of depression.

CBT condition: Patients are randomly assigned to participate in a CBT session.

Control (no-CBT) condition: Patients are randomly assigned to not participate in the CBT session.

Regression toward the mean and testing effects would be about the same in each group.

Measure improvement in depression scores.

Measure improvement in depression scores.

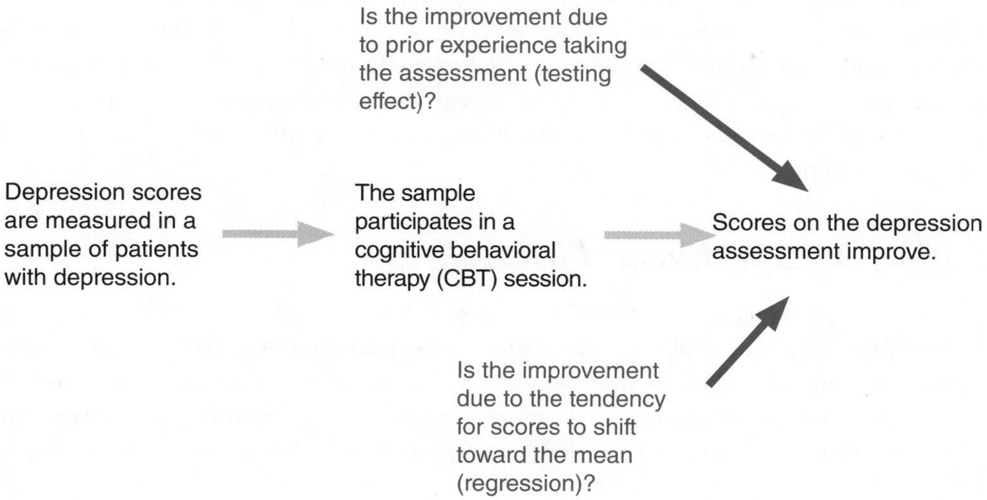

(A) Improved depression scores could be due to regression or testing effects. (B) An experiment that controls for the effects of both factors by including an appropriate control condition.

interview. Because the raters will get better at rating the dependent variable (duration of eye contact) over time, the researchers should intermix the order of the observations such that all of one condition is not run before another. If all participants in the female interviewer group, for example, were observed prior to those in the male interviewer group, then it is possible that ratings were better for the group that was observed last (the male interviewer group). In this case, instrumentation can threaten the internal validity of the study because the experience of the raters varies systematically with the levels of the factor, as illustrated in Figure 6.12.

Attrition or Experimental Mortality

A common threat to internal validity can arise when a study is conducted across multiple trials or days. The problem of **attrition**, or **experimental mortality**, occurs when a participant does not show up for a study at a scheduled time or fails to complete the study. A type of attrition that specifically threatens internal validity is called **heterogeneous attrition**, which occurs when attrition rates in one group are more or less than attrition rates in another

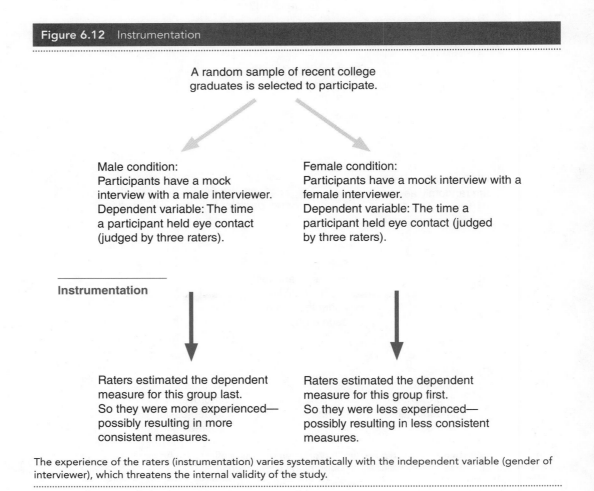

Figure 6.12   Instrumentation

A random sample of recent college graduates is selected to participate.

Male condition:
Participants have a mock interview with a male interviewer.
Dependent variable: The time a participant held eye contact (judged by three raters).

Female condition:
Participants have a mock interview with a female interviewer.
Dependent variable: The time a participant held eye contact (judged by three raters).

Instrumentation

Raters estimated the dependent measure for this group last.
So they were more experienced— possibly resulting in more consistent measures.

Raters estimated the dependent measure for this group first.
So they were less experienced— possibly resulting in less consistent measures.

The experience of the raters (instrumentation) varies systematically with the independent variable (gender of interviewer), which threatens the internal validity of the study.

group. Heterogeneous attrition is a threat to internal validity because attrition rates are different in each group. To illustrate, suppose you randomly assign children with a behavioral disorder to receive or not receive an intervention. In this case, the intervention group is likely to be a more tedious or demanding group for the children. If more children in the intervention than the no-intervention group drop out of the study, then attrition rates are now different between groups, and thus attrition rates vary systematically with the levels of the independent variable, as shown in Figure 6.13. Hence, the different rates of attrition can also potentially explain differences between groups in this example.

> **Attrition**, or **experimental mortality**, is a possible threat to validity in which a participant does not show up for a study at a scheduled time or fails to complete the study.
>
> **Heterogeneous attrition** is a possible threat to internal validity in which rates of attrition are different between groups in a study.

Another type of attrition, called *homogeneous attrition*, occurs when rates of attrition are the same in each group. Because attrition rates are the same in each group, homogeneous attrition does not threaten internal validity. It can, however, threaten the external validity of the study as defined and described further in Section 6.7.

Figure 6.13 Heterogeneous Attrition

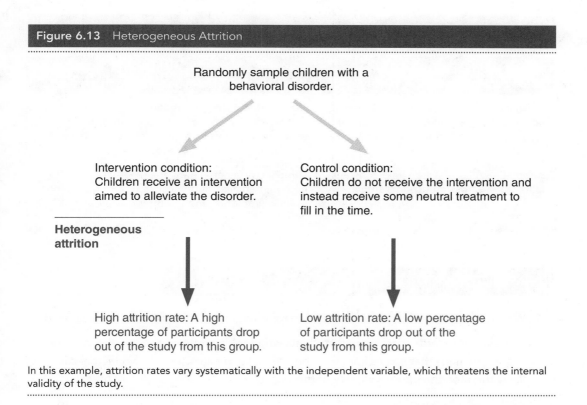

In this example, attrition rates vary systematically with the independent variable, which threatens the internal validity of the study.

Environmental Factors

Often, it is characteristics or dynamics of the study itself and the actions of the researchers that can be the most critical threats to internal validity. These types of threats are collectively referred to as *environmental factors*. Environmental factors include the time of day that a study is conducted, how researchers treat participants, and the location of the study. Environmental factors can vary from one research design to another, so these factors should be carefully considered before conducting a study.

An environmental factor can only threaten the internal validity of a study when it varies systemically with the levels of an independent variable. Suppose, for example, you conduct a study to determine how participants judge the portion size of their meals. In one group, participants eat a meal placed on a large plate; in a second group, participants eat the same meal placed on a small plate. In this case, if participants in one group ate the meal at a different time of day than those in a second group, then this new factor (time of day) could threaten the internal validity of the study because it varies systematically with the levels of the independent variable (the size of the plate). Other environmental factors include how participants are observed (alone or in a group) and where they eat the meal. Each environmental factor should be held constant so that only the size of the plate varies between groups. Table 6.2 summarizes the threats to internal validity that were described in this section, and it also describes the threats to external validity that will be introduced in Section 6.7.

Table 6.2 Internal and External Validity

Type of validity	What is common among threats to this validity?	What are the common threats to this validity?
Internal validity	All threats vary systematically with the levels of the factor or independent variable.	History, maturation, regression toward the mean, testing effects, instrumentation, heterogeneous attrition, and environmental factors that vary or are different between groups.
External validity	All threats are held constant across groups in a study.	Sampling and participant characteristics, homogeneous attrition, research settings, timing of measurements, and the operationalization of constructs.

LEARNING CHECK 4 ✓

1. What is characteristic of a factor that threatens the internal validity of a research study?

2. A professor records scores for 10 students who took a midterm and a makeup midterm exam. She finds that scores improved on the makeup exam. Which two factors can likely threaten the internal validity of this result?

3. Explain why heterogeneous attrition, and not homogeneous attrition, is a threat to internal validity.

Answers: 1. Factors that threaten the internal validity of a research study vary systematically with the levels of the independent variable; 2. Regression toward the mean and testing effects; 3. Heterogeneous attrition, but not homogeneous attrition, occurs when attrition rates differ between groups; therefore, only heterogeneous attrition is a threat to internal validity because it varies systematically with the levels of an independent variable.

6.7 Threats to the External Validity of a Research Study

Threats to internal validity vary systematically with the levels of an independent variable. However, it can also be problematic when factors that are held constant between groups threaten the external validity of a study. Factors that threaten the external validity of a study limit the extent to which observations made by a researcher generalize beyond the constraints of the study. (External validity was introduced in Section 6.3 in this chapter.) Hence, the factor that is held constant becomes the constraint to which observations are limited.

External validity is a broad term and can be subcategorized into at least four validities, each of which is described in Table 6.3. The following common threats to the external validity of a research study are described in this section:

- Population validity
- Ecological validity
- Temporal validity
- Outcome validity

Population Validity: Sampling and Participant Characteristics

Results observed in a study can sometimes be constrained to the sample. The extent to which results generalize to the population from which a sample was selected is called

Table 6.3 Four Subcategories for External Validity

Subcategory of external validity	Description	Threats to this subcategory of external validity
Population validity	The extent to which results observed in a study will generalize to the target population.	Sampling methods and participant characteristics
Ecological validity	The extent to which results observed in a study will generalize across settings or environments.	Research settings
Temporal validity	The extent to which results observed in a study will generalize across time and at different points in time.	Timing of measurements
Outcome validity	The extent to which results observed in a study will generalize across different but related dependent variables.	Operationalization of constructs

population validity. Researchers select samples to learn more about the populations from which the samples were selected. Sampling directly from the target population will result in the highest population validity. However, this sampling method is often too difficult, so researchers more often select a sample of participants from a portion of the target population that is accessible, as was illustrated in Figure 5.1 in Chapter 5. When researchers select samples from an accessible population, they use strategies to ensure that characteristics in the sample are similar to those in the larger population, which will increase the population validity of a study.

> **Population validity** is the extent to which results observed in a study will generalize to the population from which a sample was selected.

One threat to population validity is **homogeneous attrition**, which occurs when the same number of participants do not show up for a study at a scheduled time or fail to complete a study. In these cases, it is possible that participants who drop out or do not show up for a study are systematically different from those who do participate in the full study. Hence, the observations we make in the study will have low population validity, in that results may be limited to only those participants who show up to participate and may not generalize to those who do not. If differences between participants who complete and do not complete a study are related to changes in the dependent variable, this can lead to bias in the study (Goldkamp, 2008; Scott, Sonis, Creamer, & Dennis, 2006).

The key concern for population validity is that an effect that is observed in a study will only occur in that study. However, keep in mind that even when researchers use appropriate sampling methods, many results in a study can be constrained to a variety of factors even within a given population. For example, food preferences vary by culture, and crime rates vary by gender, ethnicity, and age. If we study food preferences or crime rates in the United States, then we must recognize that differences exist for these factors within the U.S. population. Issues of population validity, then, extend far beyond the methods used to select samples from populations. For this reason, it is important to be cautious in the extent to which we generalize observations to a larger population.

> **Homogeneous attrition** is a threat to population validity in which rates of attrition are about the same in each group.

Ecological Validity: Research Settings

Results observed in a study can be constrained to the research setting in which observations were made. The extent to which results observed in a study will generalize across settings or environments is called **ecological validity**. For example, suppose a researcher has participants in a laboratory listen to a list of words spoken in a monotone or dynamic voice and finds that participants recall more of the words when the words are spoken in a dynamic voice. Whether the results will generalize to other settings, such as in a college classroom during a lecture, determines the ecological validity of the research study.

> **Ecological validity** is the extent to which results observed in a study will generalize across settings or environments.

Research conducted in a natural setting typically has high ecological validity because it is conducted in the same setting in which the behavior or event being measured would normally operate. Laboratory research, on the other hand, is often not conducted in a natural setting. As a consequence, laboratory research is typically associated with low ecological validity. In general, ecological validity is high so long as observations are not dependent on, or limited to, specific features of the research setting itself, such as the lab, the equipment used in the study, or the presence of the researcher.

Temporal Validity: Timing of Measurements

Results observed in a study can be constrained to the timing of observations made in a study. The extent to which results observed in a study will generalize across time and at different points in time is called **temporal validity**. The timing of measurements refers to the passage of time and to different points in time. The passage of time is illustrated by the phrase "Let me think about it." For example, college students may change their mind about their choice of an academic major, or they may forget key information tested on an exam only to recall that information moments later. Temporal validity is the extent to which these observations (i.e., choice of college major and recall on an exam) are stable, constant, or steady over time.

Temporal validity is also the extent to which a result observed in a study is stable at different points in time (Willson, 1981). For example, the timing of depression and aggression varies with the seasons: Depression is more common in winter months, and aggression is more frequent in summer months. Also, many factors in women, such as stress levels, emotional state, and sexual responsiveness, can vary at different stages of the menstrual cycle. Therefore, for the examples given here, researchers must consider the timing of their measurement of depression, aggression, and measures of stress, emotion, and sexual desire in women. Such factors should be considered to increase the temporal validity of a research result.

> **Temporal validity** is the extent to which results observed in a study will generalize across time and at different points in time.

Outcome Validity: Operationalization of Constructs

Results observed in a study can be constrained to how the researcher defines the dependent variable. The extent to which results observed in a study generalize across related dependent measures for a variable or construct is called **outcome validity**. For example, if a study showed that a new behavioral intervention helped children stay on task, then it would have high outcome validity if it also showed that it reduced the number of times children disrupted the class. Disrupting class (outcome) is a different but related dependent variable to staying on task (outcome). As another example, if a study showed an effect of increased hunger, then it would have high outcome validity if it also showed an effect of increased calories consumed in a meal, for example. In this example,

> **Outcome validity** is the extent to which the results or outcomes observed in a study will generalize across different but related dependent variables.

calories consumed in a meal (outcome) are a different but related dependent variable to hunger (outcome). Outcome validity, then, is the extent to which the outcomes or results of a research study can be generalized across different but related dependent variables. Hence, high outcome validity allows researchers to generalize a result or outcome beyond the specific measures used in a study.

LEARNING CHECK 5 ✓

1. What is characteristic of a factor that threatens the external validity of a research study?

2. State four subcategories of external validity.

3. A researcher conditions animal subjects to swim to a platform located at a fixed point. Subjects show strong conditioning for weeks after the conditioning. This study has high _____, which is a subcategory of external validity.

Answers: 1. Factors that threaten external validity are held constant across conditions in a study; 2. Population validity, ecological validity, temporal validity, and outcome validity; 3. Temporal validity.

6.8 External Validity, Experimentation, and Realism

Researchers who conduct laboratory studies are aware that studies conducted in laboratories generally have low external validity, so they make efforts to increase the external validity of their studies. Because researchers can control all aspects of the study in the laboratory, laboratory studies tend to have high internal validity. To increase the external validity of laboratory studies, researchers can take additional steps to make the experimental situation *look* and *feel* as "real" as possible.

Mundane realism is the extent to which a research setting physically resembles or looks like the natural or real-world environment being simulated.

Experimental realism is the extent to which the psychological aspects of a research setting are meaningful or feel real to participants.

The extent to which an experimental situation *looks* real is called **mundane realism**. Suppose, for example, that you want to study gambling behavior. To establish mundane realism, you could create a casino-like setting in a laboratory with flashing lights, coin slots, and other games of risk. If the appearance of the setting looks real to participants, then the study has high mundane realism. Although field experiments, like one in an actual casino, will have higher mundane realism than laboratory experiments, efforts to mimic a "real" setting, such as a casino setting, can substantially increase the external validity of laboratory experiments.

The extent to which an experimental situation *feels* real is called **experimental realism**. In the casino gambling study, the more that participants feel as if they are in a casino during the study, the higher the experimental realism will be. If you set up a "real" casino-like setting in the laboratory, then it would likely have high mundane realism in that it *looks* like a real casino. However, if the study was conducted in a laboratory or academic building, then participants may not entirely *feel* like they are at a real casino—because they realize where they are. In this way, it is important to reflect on both types of realism, as each type is distinct.

To enhance the experimental realism in a study, it is important that the manipulations in a study are meaningful to participants. For example, inherent physical abilities are meaningful to athletes, so we could manipulate high and low self-esteem by manipulating whether an athlete receives positive or negative feedback concerning his or her physical abilities. This manipulation would increase the experimental realism of the study because the manipulation is personally meaningful to participants. In all, making such considerations to increase the mundane realism, the experimental realism, or both in a study will increase the external validity of a research result.

> Increasing the mundane and experimental realism of a study will increase the external validity of the study.

6.9 A Final Thought on Validity and Choosing a Research Design

Selecting a research design requires careful thoughtful planning, and some creativity. Be aware that few, if any, research designs will demonstrate high internal and high external validity in the same design. Indeed, some research designs have low internal validity, such as nonexperimental research designs, whereas others have low external validity, such as laboratory experiments. However, the goal in behavioral research is not to solve the world's problems in one study; this goal may not even be possible or realistic. Instead, the goal in behavioral research is to move forward and advance our knowledge of the world and the behaviors and events that operate within it. Researchers are responsible for stating a question and choosing a research design that can answer their question. Researchers must choose an appropriate research design that can answer their question, and they must recognize the limitations of the research designs they choose.

Each research design used in behavioral research has strengths and limitations. Whether a study has high or low internal or external validity will vary from one study to another. For this reason, the greatest advancement of knowledge is found when many different types of research designs, with a complement of strengths and weaknesses, are employed to address the same problem. To advance knowledge, then, you do not have to design the perfect experiment; instead you must choose an appropriate research design and be cautious to understand its strengths and weaknesses when drawing conclusions from the observations you make. In this way, to advance scientific knowledge, it is as important to be aware of the limitations, and strengths, of the research designs used to answer a research question.

> High internal and external validity is not a prerequisite for "good" research designs. All research designs have limitations, and it is important that researchers recognize them.

Section III (Chapters 7 and 8) and Section IV (Chapters 9 to 12) will describe the research designs listed for each category of research design in Figures 6.2 to 6.4 in this chapter. You can revisit these figures as you read to help you organize how to think about research design in the chapters ahead.

1. What are two types of realism that can influence external validity?

2. True or false: All research designs in science must have high internal and high external validity to be considered good research designs.

Answers: 1. Mundane realism and experimental realism; 2. False. A single research design rarely, if ever, has high internal and high external validity.

CHAPTER SUMMARY

LO 1 Identify three categories of research design: experimental, quasi-experimental, and nonexperimental.

- A **research design** is the specific methods and procedures used to answer research questions. The types of research questions that researchers ask are generally categorized as exploratory, descriptive, or relational questions.

  o An **experimental research design** is the use of methods and procedures to make observations in which the researcher fully controls the conditions and experiences of participants by applying three required elements of control: randomization, manipulation, and comparison/control.

  o A **quasi-experimental research design** is the use of methods and procedures to make observations in a study that is structured similar to an experiment, but the conditions and experiences of participants are not under the full control of the researcher. Specifically, the study includes a preexisting factor (i.e., a variable that is not manipulated: a **quasi-independent variable**) or lacks a comparison/control group.

  o A **nonexperimental research design** is the use of methods and procedures to make observations in which the behavior or event being observed is observed "as is" or without any intervention from the researcher.

LO 2 Explain how a gradient of control can be used to understand research design.

- Categorizing research can oversimplify the complexity of research design. Another way to approach research design is to think of it along a gradient of control. The more control present in a study, the more suited the design will be to demonstrate that one variable causes a change in a dependent variable. Studies with high control will be experimental; the less control in a study, the more quasi-experimental or nonexperimental the research design.

LO 3 Define and explain internal and external validity.

- **Internal validity** is the extent to which a research design includes enough control of the conditions and experiences of participants that it can demonstrate cause and effect.

- **External validity** is the extent to which observations made in a study generalize beyond the specific manipulations or constraints in the study.

LO 4 Describe three elements of control required in an experiment.

- An **experiment** has the following three elements of control that allow researchers to draw cause-and-effect conclusions:
  - Randomization (random sampling and random assignment).
  - Manipulation (of variables that operate in an experiment).
  - Comparison/control (a control group).

- Randomization is used to ensure that individuals are selected to participate and assigned to groups in a study using a random procedure. Manipulation means that a researcher created the levels of the **independent variable**, thereby allowing the researcher to randomly assign participants to groups in the study. A comparison or control group is used to allow researchers to compare changes in a **dependent variable** in the presence and in the absence of a manipulation.

LO 5 Distinguish between a laboratory experiment and a field experiment.

- A **laboratory experiment** is conducted in a setting that does not resemble the environment within which the behavior or event being observed would naturally operate; a **field experiment** is conducted in an environment within which the behavior or event being observed would naturally operate.

LO 6 Describe factors that threaten the internal validity of a research study.

- Factors that threaten the internal validity of a research study will vary systematically with the levels of an independent variable. These factors include **history effects**, **maturation, regression toward the mean, testing effects, instrumentation, heterogeneous attrition**, and environmental factors that can vary between groups in a study.

LO 7 Describe factors that threaten the external validity of a research study.

- Factors that threaten the external validity of a research study are those that are held constant across groups in a study. These factors include four subcategories of external validity:
  - **Population validity**, or the extent to which observations generalize beyond a sample to the population.
  - **Ecological validity**, or the extent to which observations generalize across settings.
  - **Temporal validity**, or the extent to which observations generalize across time or at different points in time.
  - **Outcome validity**, or the extent to which observations generalize across different but related dependent variables.

LO 8 Define and explain mundane and experimental realism.

- **Mundane realism** is the extent to which a research setting physically resembles or *looks* like the natural environment being simulated. **Experimental realism** is the extent to which the psychological aspects of a research setting are meaningful or *feel* real to participants. A study with high mundane and experimental realism will have high external validity.

KEY TERMS

research design	random sampling	regression toward the mean
control	random assignment	testing effect
experimental research design	independent variable	instrumentation
	factor	attrition
quasi-experimental research design	levels of a factor	experimental mortality
quasi-independent variable	individual differences	heterogeneous attrition
nonexperimental research design	confound	population validity
	confound variable	homogeneous attrition
internal validity	dependent variable	ecological validity
external validity	laboratory experiment	temporal validity
experiment	field experiment	outcome validity
randomization	history effect	mundane realism
random selection	maturation	experimental realism

REVIEW QUESTIONS

1. Choose the category of research design that best fits with the description given.

   A. Generally associated with high external validity.

   B. Associated with the highest internal validity.

   C. Structured as an experiment but lacks the control needed to demonstrate cause and effect.

2. State the only category of research design that can demonstrate a cause-and-effect relationship between two factors.

3. In terms of controlling the conditions and experiences of participants:

   A. Which category of research design has the least control?

B. Which has the most control?

C. What is the relationship between control and internal validity?

4. State three elements of control that allow researchers to draw cause-and-effect conclusions.

5. Based on the following description of a hypothetical study, identify (a) the independent variable and (b) the dependent variable.

   A cognitive psychologist believes that chess players will be better at memorizing where chess pieces are on a board when the pieces are placed in locations on the board that could occur in a standard game. To test this, a random sample of chess players are randomly assigned to memorize chess pieces that are placed either in logical or in illogical locations on a chessboard. Each chess player has 5 minutes to memorize the board, and the number of chess pieces correctly recalled is recorded.

6. State whether each factor listed below is an example of an independent variable or a quasi-independent variable. Only state "quasi-independent variable" for participant variables that cannot be manipulated.

   A. Marital status

   B. Political affiliation

   C. Time of delay prior to recall

   D. Environment of research setting

   E. Level of work experience

   F. Type of feedback (negative, positive)

7. Laboratory experiments are associated with higher _____ validity than field experiments, whereas field experiments are associated with higher _____ validity than laboratory experiments.

8. What is characteristic of threats to internal validity? What is characteristic of threats to external validity?

9. A researcher measures the effectiveness of an antidoping advertisement campaign by measuring the number of arrests for doping before and after the campaign. One problem is that police initiate a crackdown on doping during this same time. What is the history effect in this example?

10. A researcher measures responsiveness to a drug treatment in patients who volunteered or were mandated to participate. One problem that arises is that many patients drop out of the program before the study is completed.

    A. What type of threat to validity does this example illustrate if dropout rates are the same among volunteer and mandated patients? Is this a threat to internal or external validity?

    B. What type of threat to validity does this example illustrate if dropout rates differ between volunteer and mandated patients? Is this a threat to internal or external validity?

11. Distinguish between regression toward the mean and testing effects as threats to internal validity.

12. Which subcategory of external validity is most likely threatened by homogeneous attrition? Explain.

13. A researcher uses an intervention program at a local youth center to help children with behavioral disorders. The researcher finds that the program was effective in an urban community but not in a rural community. What subcategory of external validity is low in this example? Explain.

14. A researcher measures a student's motivation to succeed as the amount of time spent studying. In a second study, the researcher conducts the same study but instead measures a student's motivation to succeed as the percentage of classes attended during a semester. Different results were observed in each study. What subcategory of external validity is low in this example? Explain.

15. State whether the following study has high mundane realism, high experimental realism, or both. Explain.

A researcher measures gambling behavior among addicted gamblers. The study is conducted at a local casino (the researcher reserved a portion of the casino for the duration of the study). She manipulated whether participants won or lost a predetermined game and recorded the amount of money participants gambled for 1 hour after this manipulation.

ACTIVITIES

1. A researcher hypothesizes that married men will be more patient if they are also a parent. (a) Describe a research design to test this hypothesis. (b) Explain why you cannot choose an experimental research design for this example. Hint: Consider characteristics of quasi-independent variables.

2. Suppose you choose to conduct a study on fighting at nightclubs, eating behavior in movie theaters, or safety concerns in college dormitories. Choose one topic, select and describe a research design, and explain how you would ensure your study has high mundane realism and high experimental realism.

3. Choose any behavioral research topic that interests you and state a research hypothesis. Identify the following information:

   A. Identify whether or not you will use an experimental research design to test your hypothesis. Explain.

   B. Identify factors that may threaten the internal validity of your study. Explain how your research design controls, or fails to control, for these threats to internal validity.

   C. Identify factors that may threaten the external validity of your study. Explain how your research design controls, or fails to control, for these threats to external validity.

NONEXPERIMENTAL RESEARCH DESIGNS

Identify a problem

- Determine an area of interest.
- Review the literature.
- Identify new ideas in your area of interest.
- Develop a research hypothesis.

Develop a research plan

- Define the variables being tested.
- Identify participants or subjects and determine how to sample them.
- Select a research strategy and design.
- Evaluate ethics and obtain institutional approval to conduct research.

Generate more new ideas

- Results support your hypothesis—refine or expand on your ideas.
- Results do not support your hypothesis—reformulate a new idea or start over.

After reading this chapter, you should be able to:

1   Identify and define the naturalistic research design.

2   Distinguish between natural and contrived research settings.

3   Identify and describe how researchers make unobtrusive observations.

4   Describe how researchers operationalize, quantify, and manage observation periods in a naturalistic or contrived setting.

5   Describe the philosophy of qualitative research, and explain how trustworthiness relates to validity and reliability.

6   Identify and describe three qualitative research designs: phenomenology, ethnography, and case study.

7   Identify and describe three existing data research designs: archival research, content analysis, and meta-analysis.

Conduct the study

- Execute the research plan and measure or record the data.

Communicate the results

- Method of communication: oral, written, or in a poster.
- Style of communication: APA guidelines are provided to help prepare style and format.

Analyze and evaluate the data

- Analyze and evaluate the data as they relate to the research hypothesis.
- Summarize data and research results.

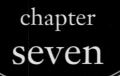

seven

NATURALISTIC, QUALITATIVE, AND EXISTING DATA RESEARCH DESIGNS

Imagine you are sitting on a bench "people watching" on campus as you wait for your next class. What might you observe? A couple passing by you holding hands? A professor sharing a conversation with a student? A student reading a book alone under a tree? These are not uncommon observations one could make on a college campus, yet rarely do we consider *how* we make such observations—that is, how do we decide what we are observing?

Recall that science is a process with rules for how we make observations. In the natural setting of a college campus, we could begin considering these rules. For example, how do you decide that the couple strolling by you holding hands is in love? How might you observe the nature of the relationship between the professor and the student? Or how might you evaluate the content of the book that the student reads under the tree? In other words, how do you define the constructs you observe each day—constructs such as love, interactions, and content? Specifically, how do we define our observations so that others will see and interpret our observations the same way? In this chapter, we introduce research designs that allow us to answer these questions.

In our examples here, you may identify love by recording how long the couple holds hands; the nature of the relationship between the professor and student could be determined by evaluating the types of classes that the student takes with the professor; content of a book could be evaluated by genre or subject matter. "People watching" can be a great exercise in applying the rules that scientists use to make observations. Many rules for observing behavior in natural settings and for assessing data that already exist (such as books) are introduced in this chapter.

NATURALISTIC OBSERVATION

Many research designs can be used to test the same hypotheses. This chapter is separated into three major sections; each section describes a nonexperimental research design: the naturalistic, qualitative, and existing data designs. To introduce how each research design can be used to test the same hypothesis, we begin each major section by developing a new research design to test the same hypothesis.

Suppose we hypothesize that fruits will be eaten more if they are made more convenient, as has been tested in the published literature (Privitera & Creary, 2013; Privitera & Zuraikat, 2014; Wansink, Painter, & Lee, 2006). We could use a naturalistic observation to test this hypothesis by observing a buffet-style meal at a local restaurant. Before we make observations in this setting, we categorize the fruits as being in a convenient or an inconvenient location in the buffet and then record the number of fruits chosen in the buffet. This is a naturalistic design because we will make observations in a natural setting (i.e., a restaurant) and observe the behavior of patrons as they would naturally behave in that setting. If we set up the study correctly, we can use the observations we make at the restaurant to test the hypothesis that fruits will be eaten more if they are made more convenient.

We will return to this hypothesis with a new way to test it when we introduce qualitative research designs, and again for the existing data designs that are introduced in this chapter. We begin this chapter, however, with an introduction to the research design that was illustrated here: the naturalistic research design.

7.1 An Overview of Naturalistic Observation

A nonexperimental research design can be used to make observations in natural settings, or in places where the behaviors being observed naturally operate. For example, we could observe buying behavior in a grocery store, parenting behavior in a residential home, employee relations in a place of business, or the interactions of children at a local day care facility. In each example we make a **naturalistic observation**, meaning that we make an observation in the natural setting where we would expect to observe those behaviors.

The naturalistic research design is associated with high external validity. Recall that external validity is the extent to which observations made in a study generalize beyond the specific manipulations or constraints in the study. Because we do not attempt to overtly manipulate the conditions of the environment using a naturalistic observation, we do not limit or constrain the observations we make. Hence observations made in natural settings will generalize beyond the limited constraints of the study because we do not limit or constrain the environment using a naturalistic observation.

Naturalistic observation is the observation of behavior in the natural setting where it is expected to occur, with limited or no attempt to overtly manipulate the conditions of the environment where the observations are made.

However, also keep in mind that in certain cases, the external validity of observations in a natural setting can still be limited. For example, the reasons why young people join gangs in Los Angeles may be very different from why they join gangs in Honduras. In this example, external validity is limited to the region in which the observations are made.

While external validity is generally high using the naturalistic research design, this design is also associated with low internal validity. Recall that internal validity is the extent to which a research design has enough control of the conditions and experiences of participants that it can demonstrate a single unambiguous explanation for an observed effect—that is, cause and effect. Because we do not overtly manipulate the conditions in a natural environment, we typically have limited control over other possible factors that could be causing the observations we make. Therefore, we cannot necessarily determine what is causing the behaviors that we observe using a naturalistic observation.

> The naturalistic research design is generally associated with high external validity, but low internal validity.

7.2 The Research Setting: Natural and Contrived Settings

A **natural setting** is a location that is, or appears to be, the environment where the behavior or event being observed typically occurs. When the natural setting is the location where the behavior typically occurs, the researcher does not have to arrange or manipulate the setting in any way. However, making observations in this setting can be difficult. It can be expensive in that the researcher has to travel to locations where the behaviors naturally occur. It can be time-consuming in that the researcher has to wait for the behaviors to occur, which can also be frustrating because the researcher can spend days or weeks waiting to observe a behavior, such as waiting to observe mating displays among animal species.

> A **natural setting** is a location or site where a behavior of interest normally occurs.
>
> A **contrived setting**, or **structured setting**, is a location or site arranged to mimic the natural setting within which a behavior of interest normally occurs, in order to facilitate the occurrence of that behavior.

An alternative to making observations in natural settings is to instead observe behavior in an arranged or **contrived setting**. A contrived setting is one that is arranged or manipulated to appear the same as the natural environment within which a behavior of interest naturally occurs. A contrived setting should have high mundane and experimental realism, meaning that the setting should *look* and *feel* natural in order to increase the external validity of the observations made in that setting—the more a contrived setting looks and feels real, the more likely we are to observe that behavior as it would naturally occur in a natural setting.

> Researchers make naturalistic observations in a natural or contrived setting.

To illustrate a research situation in which a contrived setting could be used, we can use the naturalistic observation design to study how children experience fear of a dentist (see Fareedi, Prasant, Safiya, Nashiroddin, & Sujata, 2011; Gao, Hamzah, Yiu, McGrath, & King, 2013; Gow, 2006; Milgrom, Mancl, King, & Weinstein, 1995). Suppose we measure

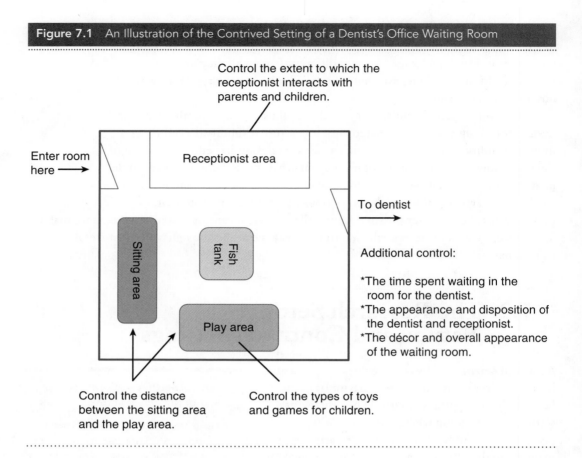

Figure 7.1 An Illustration of the Contrived Setting of a Dentist's Office Waiting Room

play behavior among children as they wait to see a dentist in a waiting room. An example of a contrived waiting room is illustrated in Figure 7.1. We could create this waiting room setting in a laboratory or any other location. To make observations in this setting, we could ask parents to tell their children that they are going to the dentist, then observe the children as they wait in the contrived waiting room setting. Creating a contrived setting, such as the one illustrated in Figure 7.1, has two important advantages.

- We can control many factors that are otherwise impossible to control in a natural setting. In a dentist's waiting room, for example, we cannot control how many children are in the waiting room at a time; where the toys, if any, are located; the appearance of the waiting room; or the disposition of the receptionist. However, in a contrived setting, we can control all of these factors, as described in Figure 7.1. This greater level of control allows us to increase the internal validity of the observations we make in a contrived setting.

- Second, we can structure the setting to facilitate the occurrence of a behavior. In the dentist's waiting room, for example, we can place the toys near the children, as illustrated in Figure 7.1, to facilitate the chance of observing play behavior among the children in the waiting room. We could also place more popular toys in that area to further enhance our chance of observing play behavior.

1. Define naturalistic observation.

2. State whether each of the following describes a natural or a contrived setting:

   A. A study on athletic ability in a room arranged to look like a gym.

   B. A study on the quality of child care conducted at three local preschools.

   C. A study on employee performance conducted at the place of business.

Answers: 1. Naturalistic observation is the observation of behavior in the natural setting where it is expected to occur, with limited or no attempt to overtly manipulate the conditions of the environment where the observations are made; 2. A. Contrived, B. Natural, C. Natural.

7.3 Techniques for Conducting Naturalistic Observation

Researchers use many techniques to make naturalistic observations. These techniques are used to ensure that observations are unobtrusive and measurable, and that the time period of observations is managed. Each technique is described in this section.

Making Unobtrusive Observations

We use a naturalistic observation to observe a behavior as it would naturally occur, so we typically do not want participants to know that they are being observed. In other words, we want to make **unobtrusive observations**, which are observations that do not interfere with or change a participant's behavior. If participants knew that they were being observed, or were influenced by the observations made, then their behavior would not be a natural response in a natural setting—instead, their behavior would be a reaction to being observed. Making unobtrusive observations, then, can minimize or eliminate participant reactivity because participants do not know they are being observed using unobtrusive observation strategies. Four strategies used to make unobtrusive observations are introduced here.

> An **unobtrusive observation** is a technique used by an observer to record or observe behavior in a way that does not interfere with or change a participant's behavior in a research setting.

- *Remain hidden.* To remain hidden, we can never be seen by participants. We could hide behind a curtain or one-way mirror, or we could place hidden cameras in a research setting so that observations can be recorded surreptitiously. In both cases, we remain hidden and out of view of the participants.

- *Habituate participants to the researcher.* In some situations we may need to be physically in the research setting. One strategy is to allow participants to habituate to, or get used to, our presence. For example, to observe students or a professor in the classroom, we can sit quietly in a classroom for a few class days before actually recording data. This allows for unobtrusive observations inasmuch as those in the classroom habituated to our presence.

- *Use a confederate.* To be present in a research setting, we can also employ a confederate or coresearcher. The confederate would play a role in the study, such as pretending to be a participant. If the confederate is convincing in that role, then he or she can make unobtrusive observations while being present in the research setting. The observations would be unobtrusive so long as participants viewed the confederate as "one of them."

Making unobtrusive observations minimizes participant reactivity in a setting.

- *Use indirect measures.* A clever strategy is to indirectly measure some behavior in a way that does not make obvious what it is that we are measuring. For example, we could measure recycling behavior by rummaging through trash or recycling bins, which is probably not fun, but effective nonetheless. In this way we can make unobtrusive observations in that our research does not "tip off" participants that they are being observed.

Operationalizing Observations

The challenge of observing behaviors in a natural setting is being able to know when you actually observed the behavior. In our previous example, illustrated in Figure 7.1, we studied play behavior among children in a dentist's office waiting room. In order to know when we are observing play behavior, we need to define exactly what "counts" as play behavior, which means that we need to anticipate all of the different ways that the children could play. To do this, we define **behavior categories** to identify the specific types of behaviors we intend to measure in the research setting.

To list behavior categories, we first identify all of the categories of the construct we are measuring, and we then list examples of what "counts" in each category. In the waiting room study, we could anticipate the following categories of play behavior: aggressive play, nonaggressive play, cooperative play, solitary play, and no play. To define each category of play behavior, we then need to list examples of how we think the children will behave in the waiting room so that an observer can recognize that behavior when he or she sees it. For example, we could list "A child pulls a toy away from another child" as an example of aggressive play. We would need as exhaustive of a list as possible for all of the behavior categories we created.

Once the researcher has identified the behavior categories and the examples of behaviors that "count" in each category, he or she can make observations. In many cases, what "counts" in each category can be a subjective interpretation, even with the most careful preparation. For example, suppose a child starts to pull a toy away from another child, but then stops abruptly—does that still "count" as aggressive play? To ensure that observations made in a naturalistic observation are reliable, multiple observers are

Behavior categories are the specific types of behaviors that researchers want to measure in the research setting, and they are typically organized as a list of examples that "count" in each category or for each type of behavior.

often used to observe the same research setting. Then the level of agreement of each rater, called *interrater reliability*, can be measured. To improve interrater reliability, each rater or observer should be formally trained and have time to prepare and learn the behavior categories that he or she is being asked to observe. One way to accomplish this is to make sure all raters have a list of the examples in front of them with a checklist for coding or recording each occasion that they observed the behavior, similar to the checklist shown in Figure 7.2.

> Researchers define behavior categories using examples that operationalize, or make measurable, each category.

Quantifying Observations

When researchers make an observation, they need to record or quantify that observation in terms of how it was measured. Researchers can use many methods to quantify observations. The following are four such methods.

- An **interval method** is used by dividing an observational period into intervals of time, and then recording whether or not certain behaviors occur in each interval. The interval method is illustrated in the checklist in Figure 7.2. Notice in the figure that observations are split into 10-second time intervals. We use this method to break down long observation intervals of time into smaller units of time.

- A **frequency method** is used by counting the number of times a behavior occurs during a fixed period of time. We use this method when the behavior we observe occurs often because if it did not, then we would not have enough observations of the behavior. For example, the frequency method could be used to count the number of times a teenager uses profanity around other friends; however, this behavior may occur much less around the teen's parents, so a frequency method may not be the best method to quantify observations in this case.

- A **duration method** is used by recording the amount of time or duration that a participant engages in a certain behavior during a fixed period of time. We use this method to record behaviors that participants engage in over a period of time. For example, we can use the duration method to record the amount of time people spend at an art exhibit to determine which exhibit is most preferred, or the amount of time it took a participant to solve a puzzle, or to complete a task at work. For this method, the behavior being observed must have a clearly defined start and end before we make observations. For example, we define "completing a puzzle" as starting when the pieces are laid out on the table, and finishing when the final piece is correctly fit into the puzzle.

> An **interval method** is a method used to quantify observations made in a study by dividing an observational period into equal intervals of time, and then recording whether or not certain behaviors occur in each interval.
>
> A **frequency method** is a method used to quantify observations made in a study by counting the number of times a behavior occurs during a fixed or predetermined period of time.
>
> A **duration method** is a method used to quantify observations made in a study by recording the amount of time or duration that participants engage in a certain behavior during a fixed period of time.

Time intervals		Aggressive play	Nonaggressive play	Cooperative play	Solitary play	No play
Min	Sec					
0	10					
	20					
	30					
	40					
	50					
1	0					
	10					
	20					
	30					
	40					
	50					
2	0					
	10					
	20					
	30					
	40					
	50					
3	0					

Participant _____
Observer _____
Date/Time _____

Observers rate or place a checkmark in the appropriate box as they observe the behaviors over time.

- A **latency method** is used by recording the time or duration between behaviors during a fixed period of time. We use this method to record behaviors that are repeated. For example, we may record the time (i.e., latency) in seconds between each play in a football game, or the latency between each time a student looks at his or her phone during a class. Like the duration method, the behavior being observed using the latency method must have a clearly defined start and end before we make observations.

> A **latency method** is a method used to quantify observations made in a study by recording the time or duration between the occurrences of behaviors during a fixed period of time.

The four methods of quantifying behaviors described here are among the most common methods applied in the behavioral sciences, but they are not the only methods used. Other methods for quantifying behaviors include the *topography method* (the shape or style of a behavior is recorded), the *force method* (the intensity of a behavior is recorded), and the *locus method* (the location of a behavior is recorded). Ultimately, each method is used to quantify or make measurable the behaviors observed in a natural setting.

Managing the Observational Period

A naturalistic observation requires strong time management on the part of the researcher because behaviors can occur at any time and at different rates. Having strong time management becomes even more important when the researcher needs to observe multiple behaviors during a single observation period. To minimize any possible stress on the part of the observer or researcher, he or she must plan for how observations will be made. The most effective strategy is often to use a recording device, such as a video or audio device, when possible. This allows researchers to view the observation setting as often as they need, thereby giving them more time to make their judgments because recordings can be replayed repeatedly.

However, the use of recording devices may not always be possible due to ethical concerns (e.g., putting cameras in a person's home) or perhaps a lack of funding to afford expensive video equipment. Whatever the reason, many naturalistic observations do not use recording devices; in those cases, we can use one of the following three strategies to manage the observation period:

- **Time sampling** is used by splitting a fixed period of time into smaller intervals of time, and then making observations during alternating intervals. For example, suppose we record behaviors that occur during a 5-minute period. Using a time sampling strategy we could first divide the 5-minute observation period into intervals of 30 seconds. We then record observations for the first 30-second interval; take a break for the next 30-second interval, maybe using that time to check that all behaviors were accurately recorded; and again record observations for a 30-second interval, repeating this pattern until the 5-minute observational period has ended.

> **Time sampling** is a strategy used to manage an observation period by splitting a fixed period of time into smaller intervals of time, and then making observations during alternating intervals until the full observation period has ended.

- **Event sampling** is used by splitting a fixed period of time into smaller intervals of time, and then recording a different behavior in each time interval. In the dentist's office waiting room study, for example, we could split a 5-minute observation period into ten 30-second intervals, and then record each of the five types of play behavior twice over the full 5-minute observation period: once in the first half and again in the second half of the observation period. Using event sampling, we want to make sure that each event is recorded for the same duration (each type of play behavior will be observed for 1 minute total) and spread out at different points in time (each type of play behavior will be observed in the first and second half of the 5-minute observation period).

> **Event sampling** is a strategy used to manage an observation period by splitting a fixed period of time into smaller intervals of time, and then recording a different behavior in each time interval.
>
> **Individual sampling** is a strategy used to manage an observation period by splitting a fixed period of time into smaller intervals of time, and then recording the behaviors of a different participant in each time interval.

- **Individual sampling** is used by splitting a fixed period of time into smaller intervals of time, and then recording the behavior of a different participant in each time interval. This strategy is similar to event sampling, except that we switch from one participant to another instead of from one event to another. For example, to observe two participants during a 4-minute interval, we could split the observation period into four intervals of 1 minute each and then alternate recording the behavior of each participant in each interval until the 4-minute period is complete. Similar to event sampling, it is important that all participants be recorded for the same duration and spread out at different points in time. This strategy can be most useful when we want to preserve the order in which participants behave over time (e.g., she did this first, then she did this…).

Minimizing Bias in Observation

Interpreting what we observe can be difficult because each person is inherently biased inasmuch as each person has a unique perspective. This is one reason why we compare the reliability of ratings made by multiple observers in a study—to check that each rater had similar ratings or interpretations of the behaviors or events observed in a study. One particular concern is observer or experimenter bias, which was introduced in Chapter 4. Observer bias occurs anytime the observer knows the intent or purpose of a research study because this knowledge of the purpose of the study could influence how he or she observes or interprets a research situation, often unknowingly. A solution, when possible, is for a primary investigator to train observers and not reveal the purpose of the study to the observers. So long as the observers are *blind* to the purpose of the study, then the influence of observer bias is unlikely.

Another caution is to only record behaviors as they were quantified and not to make interpretations during an observation. It is a human tendency to interpret or find a cause of what was observed. As an example of this tendency, paranormal investigators will often infer changes in polarity and unexplained noises in a dark room as evidence of activity from spirits. In truth, the polarity of the earth naturally fluctuates, and unexplained noises are just that—unexplained. An interpretation of these observations as being caused by the presence of spirits is unnecessary; however, this typically will not stop many from trying to infer meaning from these observations.

In a research situation, an observer is rarely needed to interpret behavior. Instead the job of an observer is typically to record the occurrence or absence of a behavior, and that is all. For an observer, interpretations should be considered at a later time and not during an observational period.

> Observer bias can lead to misinterpretation of what is observed.

7.4 Ethics in Focus: Influencing Participant Behavior

In many situations, a researcher may find that making naturalistic observations can be an ethical alternative to conducting an experiment. Barnett, Wei, and Czachowski (2009), for example, conducted a study in which they attended on-campus college parties to record the amount of alcohol consumed by those attending the party and to collect mixed-drink samples. In this case, they observed alcohol consumption among college students. Such a study would be largely unethical in an experiment because we would need to randomly assign college students to consume varying amounts of alcohol. Randomly assigning participants to consume alcohol, possibly at dangerous mixtures, would be a serious ethical concern.

The ethical concern pertains to what is being asked of participants due to the direct influence of the researcher. If potentially dangerous behavior is observed, then the researcher should have no influence over the behavior of participants, if at all possible. In our example, the researchers attended parties that they had no part in organizing and observed drinking behavior with no influence over what alcohol was served, how it was served, and whether or not patrons consumed the alcohol. Because the researchers conducted this study at college parties and made unobtrusive observations at the parties, the behaviors of attendees were not influenced in any way by the actions of the researchers. Randomly assigning participants to different drinking conditions would have been dangerous, so this study was an ethical alternative that allowed the researchers to study drinking behavior in this setting.

LEARNING CHECK 2 ✓

1. State four ways that a researcher can make unobtrusive observations.

2. How are behavior categories typically defined in naturalistic research?

3. To measure nervousness, a researcher counts the number of times that a presenter says the word *um* during a brief talk. Which method was used to quantify nervousness?

4. A researcher records the attentiveness of students in a classroom setting for 10 minutes, then takes a break for 10 minutes. This pattern is repeated for a 60-minute observation period. Which method of sampling was used to manage the observation period?

5. What are two sources of bias during an observation period?

Answers: 1. Remain hidden, habituate participants to the researcher, use a confederate, and use indirect measures. 2. As a list of examples that "count" in each behavior category; 3. Frequency method; 4. Time sampling; 5. Observer or experimenter bias, and the tendency of observers to infer meaning from what was observed.

QUALITATIVE DESIGNS

In the chapter opening, we stated the following hypothesis: Fruits will be eaten more if they are made more convenient. To answer the hypothesis, we used a naturalistic observation. However, a qualitative analysis could provide insight into the validity of this hypothesis as well. For example, suppose we spend time in a weight loss clinic for a few weeks and interview some of the patients about their experiences eating food. If many of the patients describe that they eat foods that are easier to prepare, such as fruits, then we can describe their experiences in this way. If we set up the study correctly, we can use this qualitative analysis to show support for the hypothesis that fruits will be eaten more if they are made more convenient.

We will return to this hypothesis with a new way to test it when we introduce existing data designs later in this chapter. First, we introduce the research design that was illustrated here: the qualitative research design.

7.5 An Overview of Qualitative Designs

In Chapter 1, we introduced the **qualitative research design** as a method used to make nonnumeric observations, from which conclusions are drawn without the use of statistical analysis. Qualitative or nonnumeric data can include many types of information, such as data presented in words or pictures. In this section, we introduce the philosophy of conducting qualitative research, which is rather different from other research designs taught in this book.

> The **qualitative research design** is the use of the scientific method to make nonnumeric observations, from which conclusions are drawn without the use of statistical analysis.

A Holistic Perspective

A core assumption in science is that of **determinism**, which is an assumption that all actions in the universe have a cause. In quantitative research—that is, all research described in this book, except that described in this section—we observe the behavior of many individuals, and measure that behavior exactly the same way for all individuals. By doing so, we must assume that there is a single reality or truth in nature that can be measured the same way for all people. Behavior, then, is a measurable phenomenon that can be understood independent of the context in which any one individual experiences it. That is, behavior is a universal phenomenon.

> **Determinism** is an assumption in science that all actions in the universe have a cause.

Qualitative research also adopts the assumption of determinism; however, it does not assume that behavior itself is universal. Instead, qualitative research identifies behavior as something experienced differently by each individual, so behavior cannot be measured independent of how the individual experiences it. In all, the perspective of qualitative research is based on a holistic, or "complete picture," view that emphasizes the following two principles:

1. There is no single reality in nature; hence, *reality changes.* Reality, or the truth about behavior that science is used to discover, is in the eye of the beholder. In other words, each person experiences a slightly different reality. From this view, the participant is no longer an object of study used to measure behavior, as is the case in quantitative research. Instead, the participant is an expert in his or her own life because we aim to understand the participant's unique experiences in order to study the causes of his or her behavior. The focus, then, is not on behavior itself, but specifically on people's perceptions and interpretations of their experiences.

2. Behavior does not occur independent of context; hence, *behavior is dynamic.* Context is the individual, psychological, social, political, historical, and cultural setting within which an individual behaves at any given time. From a qualitative perspective, people's perceptions and interpretations of their experiences, which we call behavior, can only be understood in the specific context within which the behavior occurs. Hence, behavior operates differently in different contexts; an analysis of behavior outside of the particular context in which it occurs, then, will be incomplete.

From the perspective described here, Table 7.1 distinguishes between the quantitative and qualitative approaches. Unlike quantitative research, which is guided mostly by the hypotheses and theories stated by a researcher, the research procedures for qualitative

Table 7.1 The Distinction Between Quantitative and Qualitative Philosophies

	Quantitative Research	Qualitative Research
Participants	An object of study whose identity is to be protected.	A coresearcher; an expert in his or her own life.
Relationship between the researcher and the participant	Directional. The researcher directs the progression of a study. Researcher → Participant	Interactive. The participant is regarded as a "coresearcher" in a study. Researcher ← → Participant
The role of theory in measurement	A theory or hypothesis is used to justify what will be observed or measured in a study.	Any participant response is recorded in a study. A theory or hypothesis is often modified as data are collected.
Data collection	Numeric. Behavior is operationalized in terms of how it is measured.	Words. Participant perceptions and experiences are described in words as the participant describes them.
Data analysis	Occurs after data collection.	Occurs concurrently with data collection.
Conclusion	Statistical. Summarizes only those scores that were measured.	Descriptive. Summarizes all responses provided by participants.

research can be guided as much by the participant as by the researcher. As described in the next section, using a qualitative approach can limit a researcher's ability to establish the reliability and validity of an observation.

Criteria of Trustworthiness

To engage in qualitative research, we describe the experiences of individuals in words or narratives and not as values that can be subjected to statistical analysis. This creates problems in comparisons across studies, in that it is difficult to determine the validity and reliability of an outcome without using statistics. For this reason, qualitative research uses different criteria that can parallel validity and reliability.

Indeed, many qualitative researchers flat out reject the notion of validity and reliability because such measures presume that a singular external reality exists, which contradicts the philosophy of a qualitative approach. As an alternative to using validity and reliability, many qualitative researchers instead use four criteria of **trustworthiness**, which are the credibility, transferability, dependability, and confirmability of a qualitative analysis (Guba & Lincoln, 1989; Krefting, 1991; Lincoln & Guba, 1985). Each criterion is described in Table 7.2. Creditability and transferability parallel internal and external validity, respectively; dependability parallels reliability; and confirmability parallels the objectivity of a qualitative analysis.

Trustworthiness is the credibility, transferability, dependability, and confirmability of a qualitative analysis.

Table 7.2 The Four Criteria of Trustworthiness in Qualitative Research

Criteria of Trustworthiness	Parallel	Description
Credibility	Internal validity	Truthfulness—the extent to which observed results reflect the realities of the participants in such a way that the participants themselves would agree with the research report.
Transferability	External validity	Applicability—the extent to which observed results are useful, applicable, or transferable beyond the setting or context of the research.
Dependability	Reliability	Consistency—the extent to which observed results would be similar if similar research were conducted in the same or a similar context.
Confirmability	Objectivity	Neutrality—the extent to which observed results reflect the actual context of participant experiences, rather than simply the researcher's perspective.

Adapted from Guba and Lincoln (1989) and Lincoln and Guba (1985).

Section III: Nonexperimental Research Designs

Although these criteria parallel concepts of validity, reliability, and objectivity, these criteria do not conform well to quantitative research. Without statistical analyses, it is not possible to compare the significance of observed results or generalize beyond the experiences of a few individuals or studies. This makes it difficult to integrate knowledge gained from both perspectives of research. However, qualitative research does provide a unique understanding of behavior from the perspective of the individual. Also, it is a new perspective, compared to quantitative research, and continues to develop and gain recognition in the scientific community.

> Trustworthiness provides alternative criteria for validity, reliability, and objectivity, and is utilized in qualitative research.

LEARNING CHECK 3 ✓

1. State the two principles emphasized by the holistic view of qualitative research.

2. Quantitative research assesses the internal and external validity of a research study. What parallel criteria are assessed for qualitative research?

3. The credibility, transferability, dependability, and confirmability of a qualitative analysis are four criteria of _____.

Answers: 1. Reality changes and behavior is dynamic; 2. Credibility and transferability, respectively; 3. trustworthiness.

7.6 Qualitative Research Designs

Qualitative research designs can use techniques from the naturalistic observation design in addition to those unique to this design. Three qualitative designs described here are phenomenology, ethnography, and the case study.

Phenomenology

One qualitative research design, called **phenomenology**, is the study of the conscious experiences of phenomena from the first-person point of view. A *conscious experience* is any experience that a person has lived through or performed and can bring to memory in such a way as to recall that experience. To use this research design, the researcher interviews a participant who gives a first-person account (e.g., "I did/see/think...") of his or her conscious experiences. The researcher then constructs a narrative to describe or summarize the experiences described in the interview. Other methods used to collect data include observation and videotaping, although in-depth interviews are the primary method for the phenomenology research design.

> **Phenomenology** is the qualitative analysis of the conscious experiences of phenomena from the first-person point of view of the participant.

The narrative a researcher constructs is used to describe any type of conscious experience such as interacting with coworkers, being in college, surviving 9/11, or experiencing different emotions such as love, guilt, disgust, and jealousy. To write a qualitative narrative, the researcher must be considerate of the *intentionality* or meaning of a participant's conscious experiences. It is often easiest to identify the intentionality of a participant's conscious experiences by first identifying *objects of awareness*, which are those things that bring an experience to memory or consciousness. Objects of awareness tend to direct conscious experiences and also illuminate the intentionality of a participant's conscious experiences. To illustrate, consider the following narrative described in a phenomenological study published by Horton (2009):

> Elisabeta [the participant or "coresearcher"] speaks about her son with the sparkling eyes of a new mother, although she has not seen him for 2 years now. She came to the United States after her marriage broke up and left her unable to support him and her elderly mother. She carries two photos of her son in the front of her wallet—the one she brought with her when she left him and the one her mother took of him on his fifth birthday—and regularly sends him money and gifts. As Elisabeta describes it, the transnational space her family inhabits is an intimately shared space of loss and grief. As she puts it, "I work here but my heart lies there." This compartmentalization of Elisabeta's life—a worker "here" but a mother in El Salvador—speaks to a division at the very core of her personhood. While women such as Elisabeta have become the new braceras of the twenty-first century (see Hondagneu-Sotelo 2002), their children's lives continue to unfold in El Salvador in their absence. (pp. 21–22)

In this narrative, the object of awareness is Elisabeta's son. Notice that the object of awareness is the focus or main theme of the narrative. By focusing on Elisabeta's son, the author is able to describe the intentionality of how she presents, thinks, and conceives of her son, which conveys the intentionality, meaning, or content of her experience. From this description, for example, we learn that Elisabeta's experience is one of sadness and division, in that she describes her experience as "I work here but my heart lies there." This narrative provides insight into the intentionality of her experiences of motherhood by focusing on how she specifically experiences the distance that separates her and her son.

Phenomenology is used to describe first-person accounts of conscious experiences.

In writing narratives, the author should make additional considerations that increase the trustworthiness of the research. These additional considerations should account for the context within which participants self-describe their experiences. Table 7.3 describes seven key considerations that should be made in order to account for the context of the experiences described by a participant. Being able to consistently make each consideration in your writing is very important and requires a great deal of practice and training. In all, constructing narratives that identify the intentionality of conscious experiences and the context of those experiences will strengthen the trustworthiness of the research. In this way, phenomenology allows for the detailed analysis of individual conscious experience in a way that conforms to criteria of trustworthiness.

Table 7.3 Key Considerations of the Context of Self-Description That Can Influence How Participants Self-Describe Their Conscious Experiences

Context of Self-Description	Description (Example)
Historical	Relevant political, societal, geographic, temporal, and personal histories (e.g., pre- vs. post-9/11).
Political/Governmental	Current political and legal issues that impact an individual (e.g., legality of same-sex marriage).
Societal/Cultural/Religious	Social, cultural, or religious idiosyncrasies (e.g., current obesity rates, cultural norms of eating, or common religious practices).
Geographic	Different social settings or localities (e.g., urban vs. rural settings).
Temporal	Individuals adapt or change over time, even during a research study (e.g., an interviewer changes his or her demeanor during the course of an interview).
Gender	This applies to both the researcher and the participant (e.g., a male interviewer asks questions of a sexual nature to female participants).
Familiarity	We often can only describe experiences when we reflect on them (e.g., a state of fear or anger clouds intention at the time of an experience).

MAKING SENSE—DATA COLLECTION IN QUALITATIVE RESEARCH

A key distinction between quantitative and qualitative research is in the data collection process. Unlike quantitative research, which tends to measure only those variables that are relevant to a hypothesis, qualitative research describes characteristics of phenomena without numeric measurement. For example, a quantitative researcher may hypothesize that the longer a student studies, the better the student will perform on an exam. Based on this hypothesis, the researcher will measure minutes spent studying and the score on an exam. However, a qualitative researcher would observe studying and record anything that is observed or self-described by a participant as helping him or her do well on an exam. In other words, the participant's responses, and not always some hypothesis, guide the direction of qualitative research. There is little effort to fully structure, control, or predetermine the data collection process using qualitative research. Instead, the participant is regarded as a coresearcher or expert in his or her own life. Hence, as illustrated in Figure 7.3 for qualitative research, participants have greater control in the data collection process.

(Continued)

(Continued)

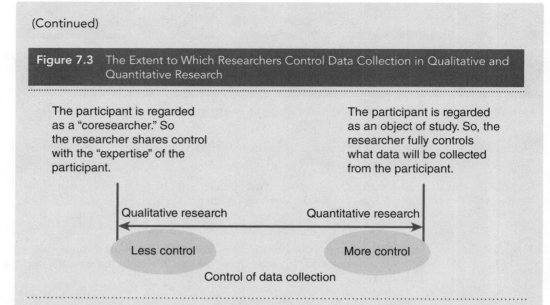

Figure 7.3 The Extent to Which Researchers Control Data Collection in Qualitative and Quantitative Research

The participant is regarded as a "coresearcher." So the researcher shares control with the "expertise" of the participant.

The participant is regarded as an object of study. So, the researcher fully controls what data will be collected from the participant.

Qualitative research   Quantitative research

Less control   More control

Control of data collection

A qualitative researcher does not predetermine measures or theories within which the data must fit. Instead, the researcher plays the role of a learner in that the researcher aims to learn about the participant who is an expert in his or her own life. From this view, then, the participant is allowed greater control during the research study, such as being allowed to ask questions him- or herself in an interview, because the participant's expert descriptions are valued as part of the data collection process. As described in Section 7.7, the value placed on the participant can be thought of as an ethical position in that it shows high regard for the Belmont principle of respect for persons.

Ethnography

A qualitative research design used to describe and characterize the behavior and identity of a group or culture is called **ethnography**. The perspective for this research is that groups of people will eventually evolve a culture over time, meaning that they will form an identity that will guide some worldview or way of life for the members of that culture. Ethnography is used to understand the intricacies of culture as it is defined and described by members of that culture. A culture is a "shared way of life" that includes patterns of interaction (e.g., norms), shared beliefs and understandings (e.g., beliefs about God), adaptations to the environment (e.g., housing and agriculture), and many more factors that can lead to a group or

Ethnography is the qualitative analysis of the behavior and identity of a group or culture as it is described and characterized by the members of that group or culture.

cultural identity. Ethnography is used to describe the culture (e.g., the shared beliefs, values, and worldview); members of that group or culture are regarded as experts in their lives, and researchers conduct the study, in part, to learn from and about them.

Ethnography is used to study macro-level and micro-level groups and cultures. Macro-level cultures or groups are those with large membership, such as all members of a country, government, or continent. For example, we could use ethnography to study dream interpretations among individualistic (e.g., American, Australian) and collectivistic (e.g., Indonesian, Japanese) cultures. Micro-level cultures or groups are those with small membership, such as members of a college fraternity, a first-grade classroom, or a sports team. For example, we could use ethnography to study the dynamics of communication between prisoners and guards in a penitentiary. In sum, any type of group, culture, or subculture can be studied using ethnography.

To observe a group or culture, it is often necessary to get close to or participate in that group or culture. To do this, researchers use **participant observation**, which means that the researcher becomes a participant in or member of the group or culture for the length of the study. Researchers use participant observation to study a group or culture similar to the way that an investigative reporter joins a group or culture to investigate its members' actions. When researchers use participant observation to make observations, they need to remain neutral in how they interact with members of the group. If they show a bias, then any observations may be specific to the bias and may not be characteristic of the group or culture as a whole. Three types of bias in how researchers can interact with members of a group or culture are described in Table 7.4.

> **Participant observation** is a method of observation in which researchers participate in or join the group or culture that they are observing.

Table 7.4 Three Common Pitfalls Associated With Participant Observation

Type of Bias	Description
The "eager speaker" bias	The researcher tends to focus on or speak mostly with those who are eager to speak to them, while largely ignoring those who do not. This is poor practice inasmuch as those who do not speak with the researcher do make important contributions to the overall identity of a given group or culture.
The "good citizen" bias	The researcher assumes that he or she knows how members should contribute to the group or culture. As a result, members who actively participate with the researcher tend to be held in higher regard, or as "good citizens," than those who do not. This is poor practice inasmuch as the researcher shows bias against members who do not actively participate.
The "stereotype" bias	The tendency for a researcher to positively or negatively regard a group or culture in a way that influences how the researcher treats members of the group. Researchers can be overly positive toward members if they hold the group in high regard (e.g., police officers) or overly negative to members if they hold the group in low regard (e.g., criminals in prison).

Source: Adapted in part from suggestions made by Parker (2005).

An added challenge of using participant observation to study a group or culture is that many of the members can be aware of the researcher's presence, which can then lead to *participant reactivity* (see Chapter 4). Researchers typically use one of two strategies to gain entry into a group or culture without causing participants to react or change their behavior in reaction to the researchers' presence:

- Researchers can covertly or secretly enter a group. This strategy can work for larger groups; however, the physical presence of a "new" member, covert or not, in a small group can result in participant reactions that are not always obvious or predictable.

- Researchers can announce or request entry into a group. This strategy is used when it is not possible to enter a group covertly. By being up front and honest with members of a group, the researcher can try to get the group to habituate to his or her presence or accept him or her as a member of the group.

Participant observation is often used to observe groups and cultures in ethnographic research.

In an ethnographic study on immigrant day laborers, Purser (2009) used the second strategy by asking members of an immigrant day laborer group if she could "hang around and watch as they sought work" (p. 124). To record her observations, she used field notes and conducted individual and group interviews, which are commonly used to record observations in ethnography research. The field notes and interviews are used to identify themes or recurring topics that emerge in the descriptions and observations made during a study. The Purser study was a 5-month study, during which time the researcher spent 2 to 3 days a week on streets where the day laborers waited for potential employers to drive by and pick them up. During one informal interview the researcher casually sipped coffee with Margarito, a day laborer, and recorded how Margarito said he felt about searching for work on the street:

> The work is hard and you never know what you are going to get, but I can come and go when I want and I can negotiate the pay. The truth is that I have autonomy. If a guy comes by here looking for someone to work for $6 an hour, I can say "never." I am a hard worker and know I can earn more than that. So, if you are ambitious, a little creative, and you work hard, it is really good on the corner because you can start building up clients who come back for you regularly. I have five clients now. (Purser, 2009, p. 126)

In her analysis, Purser (2009) also noted two recurring themes in her conversations with Margarito in that "his emphasis on *autonomy* and *negotiation* was something that [she] heard over and over again throughout the course of [her] research" (p. 126). Hence, the need for autonomy and the ability to negotiate were recurring themes or focal points of the experiences of the day laborer. The overall analysis published by Purser of course required her to review the transcripts from all her interviews and field notes over the full five-month duration of the study. Because studies of this length are not uncommon, a qualitative analysis using the ethnography research design can require a lot of time, thought, and effort on the part of the researcher.

Case Study

Another research design, the **case study**, can be used to analyze one individual (e.g., the president of the United States), group (e.g., military veterans), organization (a small business), or event (e.g., 9/11). The name *case study* is used because the focus of study (e.g., the individual, group, organization, or event) is called a "case." The following are three types of case studies; each type is further described in Table 7.5:

- An **illustrative case study** investigates rare or unknown cases, such as the behavioral effects of serious trauma or strokes by looking at patients who happened to suffer from these serious cases. Hence, we use this case study to understand a particular case or person (e.g., a person who suffered a serious trauma or stroke).

- An **exploratory case study** is a preliminary analysis that explores potentially important hypotheses, such as possible concerns regarding the methods used to study adult education programs in a local community. Hence, we use a case or person to better understand a more general phenomenon (e.g., methods to study adult education).

> A **case study** is the qualitative analysis of an individual, a group, an organization, or an event used to illustrate a phenomenon, explore new hypotheses, or compare the observations of many cases.
>
> Three types of case studies are the **illustrative case study** (used to investigate rare or unknown phenomena), the **exploratory case study** (used to explore or generate hypotheses for later investigation), and the **collective case study** (used to compare observations of many cases).

Table 7.5 Three Types of Case Studies in Behavioral Research

Type of Case Study	Description
Illustrative	Pertains to rather unique cases where little is known about an individual, a group, or an organization. This can provide new insights and a better understanding of rare or largely unknown phenomena, and often leads to the introduction of a common language for describing the phenomena being studied.
Exploratory	A preliminary or pilot study conducted prior to the conduct of a large-scale research study. This type of study explores or provides important information pertaining to the selection of research questions, measurements, and potential limitations that may arise when the large-scale study is conducted.
Collective	The review and analysis of several cases. For example, researchers may conduct a case study on behavior problems associated with three children with autism in the classroom. The collective description for each case (or child) can provide insights into the extent to which observations will generalize to other cases, but not to the general population.

- A **collective case study** compares the individual analysis of many related cases, such as comparing behavioral symptoms expressed by three children with autism in a classroom.

A **case history** is an in-depth description of the history and background of the individual, group, or organization observed. A case history can be the only information provided in a case study for situations in which the researcher does not include a manipulation, a treatment, or an intervention.

The case study is often used to record qualitative and quantitative data.

In each example, the level of analysis is to make observations one individual or group at a time. For each type of case study, researchers can use field notes, interviewing, naturalistic and participant observation, and the retrieval of records or documents related to the case being studied to make observations. Most researchers will use a combination of these methods to increase the trustworthiness of the research.

As part of an analysis, a case study typically includes a **case history** of the individuals, groups, or organizations being observed. Case histories give a history and background of the individual, group, or organization observed, such as age, family history, and what makes the case interesting to the researcher. A case history can often be the only information provided in a case study for situations in which the researcher does not include a manipulation, such as a learning assessment given to a child with a learning disorder.

In all, case studies have the following two common applications in behavioral science:

1. *General inquiry.* In this sense, researchers tend to ask a lot of questions instead of stating hypotheses. The purpose or intent of the case study, then, is to learn about certain cases of interest. For example, Alvarez and Schneider (2008) observed interactions between members of the lesbian, gay, bisexual, transgender, and queer (LGBTQ) community and other campus groups during efforts to strengthen safety and inclusion for this group. Their research was not theory driven in that they did not set up the study to test an idea they had. Rather, the researchers made observations to record and learn about potential issues and concerns related to the diversity and inclusion of this group on college campuses. Case studies are often used to advance knowledge regarding naturally occurring social groups, such as the LGBTQ community, and rare or unknown cases, such as individuals suffering from trauma or mental disease.

2. *Theory development.* In this sense, researchers state hypotheses to develop new theories or to test existing theories. For example, Sarkar, Klein, and Krüger (2008) observed the case of Mrs. Y, a 46-year-old woman with a case history of obsessive-compulsive disorder (OCD). The researchers tested the hypothesis that administering two drug treatments (i.e., escitalopram and aripiprazole) for OCD would significantly attenuate symptoms of the disorder, so they tested that hypothesis with Mrs. Y as their participant. Case studies are particularly effective for testing the effectiveness of a new treatment or therapy because it is often more ethical to conduct these tests on a case-by-case basis.

A case study, while qualitative in design, can be used to measure quantitative data. For example, Shepherd and Edelmann (2007) conducted a collective case study of four individuals with a social phobia. While the researchers described many qualitative analyses, such as the case histories with social phobia for each individual, they also reported each individual's average alcohol intake (in units consumed) and scores on numeric assessments for substance abuse and depression. Case studies like the one described here are common because the case study can be used to make qualitative and quantitative analyses.

7.7 Ethics in Focus: Anonymity in Qualitative Research

A unique characteristic of qualitative research is that the identity of participants is not entirely concealed. Instead the real name or pseudo name for a participant is often published and directly linked to the data collected. Of the qualitative studies described in this chapter, for example, recall that Horton (2009) identified Elisabeta in the phenomenology study, Purser (2009) identified Margarito in the ethnography study, and Sarkar et al. (2008) identified the pseudo name Mrs. Y in the case study. In contrast with qualitative research, participant identities are concealed and rarely, if ever, linked to the data measured in quantitative research. The reason for concealing participant identities is to protect the participants from being identified by others, particularly when the data measured are potentially harmful to participants, such as survey studies asking participants to indicate their level of drug use on the job. Concealing participant identities therefore shows high regard for the Belmont principle of respect for persons.

However, the same argument can be made that revealing participant identities is an ethical position. McLaughlin (2003) argued that the view that all participants are "fragile beings" in need of protection is itself an ethical position. Also, the anonymity of participant responses conceals participants from the data, and therefore from being able to challenge how the researcher interprets their responses. Parker (2005) explains that protecting the identity of participants "may operate all the more efficiently to seal off the researcher[s] from those they study, actually serving to protect the researcher[s] . . . [from] interpretations that have been made in a report" (p. 17). In this way, revealing the identity of participants also shows high regard for the Belmont principle of respect for persons in that researchers are more accountable, particularly to those they observe, for their part or role in a research study.

LEARNING CHECK 4 ✓

1. Which qualitative research design is used to study the conscious experiences of phenomena from the first-person point of view?

2. State the type of qualitative research design described in each of the following examples.

A. A researcher joins a local neighborhood crime watch group for 6 months to study how these groups operate.

B. A researcher conducts an in-depth interview of a fraternity president and asks him to reflect on his experiences in college. She reports his first-person accounts in a narrative.

C. A researcher completes a full qualitative analysis of a patient who shows signs of amnesia following a sudden stroke.

3. How can revealing the identity of participants show high regard for the Belmont principle of respect for persons?

Answers: 1. Phenomenology; 2. A. Ethnography, B. Phenomenology, C. Case study; 3. Revealing the identity of participants can make researchers more accountable for their part in a research study.

EXISTING DATA DESIGNS

In the chapter opening, and again to introduce qualitative designs, we stated the following hypothesis: Fruits will be eaten more if they are made more convenient. To answer the hypothesis, we could also use an existing data design. For example, suppose we reviewed online testimonials provided by individuals who successfully lost weight. We could analyze the content of those testimonials to find whether there are themes or recurring phrases in the content. If we find, for example, that a high percentage of testimonials indicate that individuals ate more fruits when they were in more convenient locations around their house, then this would lend support to the hypothesis that fruits will be eaten more if they are made more convenient. If we set up the study correctly, we can use this existing data analysis to show support for the hypothesis that fruits will be eaten more if they are made more convenient.

In this final section, we introduce the research design that was illustrated here: the existing data design.

7.8 An Overview of Existing Data Designs

An **existing data design** is the collection, review, and analysis of any type of existing documents or records, including those that are written or recorded as video, as audio, or in other electronic form.

In many cases, researchers can analyze data that have already been recorded in some form. **Existing data designs** are research designs for handling and analyzing data that already exist, usually as a written document or as an electronic or audio recording. Existing data can be qualitative, such as written records of the words in a presidential speech, or they can be quantitative, such as voting records that reveal how often a president voted for or against different policies.

As noted earlier in this chapter for naturalistic observations, obtaining data that already exist is one strategy used to make unobtrusive observations. For example, to study food preferences, you could obtain copies of grocery store receipts. In this example, researchers obtain grocery store receipts, so data are never obtained directly from a participant. Obtaining existing data can also be more economical than selecting samples used to measure data, in that it can save time and money. When the data already exist, researchers do not need to spend their time and money selecting a sample and observing participants in the sample because the data that will be analyzed already exist.

> Existing data designs are used to analyze data that already exist.

7.9 Existing Data Designs

Existing data designs are used to describe behavior based on an analysis of data that already exist in some form. Two particular cautions should be made anytime you select data from existing records:

1. Existing records can provide a selective record of behaviors observed, called **selective deposit**. For example, a detective may screen a host of records to admit into evidence, including some (e.g., phone records) but excluding others (e.g., letters written by a defendant).

2. Only certain types of records may survive over time, called **selective survival**. For example, some government documents of previously classified events may have been shredded, so the surviving records are biased in favor of only those records that were kept.

> **Selective deposit** is the process by which existing records are selectively recorded or deposited into document files that can be accessed for analysis.
>
> **Selective survival** is the process by which existing records survive or are excluded/decay over time.

Each caution can limit the generalizability of your results inasmuch as the selective records of behavior and the selective survival of existing records represent only those data that remain over time; it is not possible to draw conclusions about data that are not available for analysis. Three existing data designs described in this section are archival research, content analysis, and meta-analysis.

Archival Research

One type of existing data design, called **archival research**, is used to characterize or describe existing archives or historical documents. Archival research, which is becoming increasingly utilized in the social sciences (Tamboukou, 2014), involves the collection of documents that are then described

> **Archival research** is a type of existing data design in which events or behaviors are described based on a review and analysis of relevant historical or archival records.

or summarized in terms of how they address a research hypothesis. As one example from research on gender biases in the peer-reviewed literature (Engqvist & Frommen, 2008; Moon & Hoffman, 2000; Mutz, Bornmann, & Daniel, 2012), Moon and Hoffman (2000) entered 105 search terms into the PsycINFO database to test the hypothesis that there is a gender bias in the published literature. The researchers searched for online articles published between 1887 and 1997 and recorded the number of articles that made reference to women and men. The results of their study showed that women were overrepresented in the literature, particularly since 1974. Figure 7.4 shows evidence to support their hypothesis in that there was a disproportionately larger number of references to women than men in the psychological literature.

Existing data can be obtained from any recorded document, including newspapers, books, magazines, medical reports, voting records, store receipts, criminal records, and historical or government documents. These records can be used to study anything from alcohol sales at sporting events to the likelihood of pregnancy risk or even risk of cancer. The biggest challenge often is obtaining a copy of the existing data you need. For example, many government documents are confidential, and rare historical records may be protected from public viewing. In addition, many archives may be inherently biased, such as the gender bias demonstrated by Moon and Hoffman (2000). Once the document is obtained, the data can be recorded and analyzed.

Figure 7.4 Proportion of Total References to Women and Men From 1974 to 1997

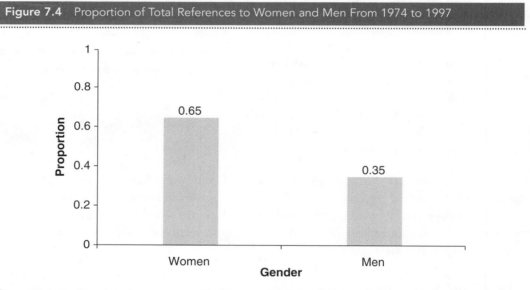

Source: Data are based on those presented by Moon and Hoffman (2000).

Content Analysis

Another type of existing data design, called **content analysis**, uses archival records to analyze the content of specific events or behaviors, such as penalties called in a game or the advice given by academic advisors. Unlike archival research, which is used mostly to describe existing data as summary statistics, content analysis is used to analyze or interpret the detailed content in the records. For example, to analyze strategies that politicians use during political campaigns, we could review autobiographies or qualitative interviews of politicians in a local area or state. Using a content analysis, we can analyze the content of the autobiographies or interviews by recording the types of words used by politicians to describe their constituents, or how often and where they campaigned. In order to describe these data, we must analyze the actual content of the materials. To use a content analysis, the following must be identified:

> A **content analysis** is a type of existing data design in which the content of written or spoken records of the occurrence of specific events or behaviors is described and interpreted.

- The unit of analysis in the document or existing record. What information or content in the document will you specifically analyze, code, or interpret?

- The operational definition for the content analyzed. What words or features in the content are of interest? How will you be able to identify that content?

As an example, Grabe, Trager, Lear, and Rauch (2006) analyzed the content of criminal reporting in *The Herald Times* (a small newspaper in Bloomington, Indiana) for a 6-month period from November 1, 2001, to April 30, 2002. In this study, the existing data were from the newspaper. To use a content analysis, the researchers needed to identify the unit of analysis in the newspaper. In their study, the unit of analysis was an individual crime story. They also needed to give an operational definition for what content they would analyze in the individual crime story. In their study, they defined a crime story as "one that featured violent or nonviolent crime, excluding minor offenses such as parking, speeding, and city ordinance violations" (Grabe et al., 2006, p. 143). Using this definition, the researchers analyzed the content of each story, including the crimes, criminals, and victims depicted in each story.

Similar to archival research, a content analysis is typically used to test some hypothesis. In the Grabe et al. (2006) study, the content analysis was used to test the chivalry hypothesis (Anderson, 1976; Pollak, 1950), which predicted "female criminals [would] receive more lenient treatment in the criminal justice system and in [newspaper] coverage of their crimes than [males]" (p. 137). To test this hypothesis, multiple raters read each newspaper and coded the gender of the criminal, the type of crime committed (violent or nonviolent), and the extent to which the criminal was treated harshly by the media. As shown in Table 7.6, their findings show support for the chivalry hypothesis when nonviolent crimes occurred (women were treated *less* harshly by the media), but not when violent crimes and crimes committed against children occurred (women were instead treated *more* harshly by the media).

Table 7.6 Gender Differences for Reporting Crimes in *The Herald Times*

	Men (%)	Women (%)
Nonviolent crimes		
Main section	68.5	59.9
Front page	2.4	0.7
Violent crimes		
Main section	73.8	82.8
Front page	3.3	6.5
Crimes against children		
Main section	67.7	83.6
Front page	3.9	7.5

Source: Adapted from data presented by Grabe et al. (2006).

Meta-Analysis

An existing data design used to review findings from many research studies is called a **meta-analysis**. This type of analysis is often used when there are results across a series of studies that are not in agreement. Some studies may show evidence that a behavioral therapy is effective, for example, whereas others may not show this effect. A meta-analysis can help sort out these inconsistencies by summarizing the results across a large group of studies or research papers. Specifically, a meta-analysis is used to combine, analyze, and summarize data across a group of related studies to make statistically guided decisions about the strength or reliability of the reported findings in those studies.

> A **meta-analysis** is a type of existing data design in which data are combined, analyzed, and summarized across a group of related studies to make statistically guided decisions about the strength or reliability of the reported findings in those studies.

As a general outline for how to conduct a meta-analysis, the following three steps can provide a useful framework for conducting a meta-analysis:

1. Select the relevant variable(s) or topic(s). To operationalize a relevant variable or topic, we need to know what question we are asking. For example, suppose we ask if a new behavioral therapy is effective. We could identify the relevant topic in this example as all studies testing the utility of this new therapy.

2. Select a set of studies related to the relevant variable(s) or topic(s). Here we now need to refine our criteria for what "counts" as a study on this topic. The design and analysis used and even the participants observed may vary substantially from one study to another. What type of participants should be included? Should we exclude certain designs—such as qualitative designs that report nonnumeric data? What type of data do we need, and do the studies report sufficient data to include them in a meta-analysis? Also important is quality—both of the journal and the methodology. These should be evaluated, and data reported in higher-quality journals and data from studies with stronger methodology should be given greater weight or "count" more in the meta-analysis. These evaluations can be checked by an interrater reliability check.

3. Perform the meta-analysis. Once you have identified your topic and refined your criteria to collect data from the sample of studies that fit your topic, you can now apply meta-analytic techniques. In general, a meta-analysis is used to either compare studies or combine studies (Rosenthal, 1984). For example, we can compare if this new behavioral therapy produces significantly different effects for men compared to women. Or we could combine the data reported in the studies and report the overall utility or effect of this new behavioral therapy. While there are many statistical alternatives when evaluating data, a meta-analysis is most often reported as **effect size**.

> **Effect size** is a statistical measure of the size or magnitude of an observed effect in a population, which allows researchers to describe how far scores shifted in a population, or the percentage of variance in a dependent variable that can be explained by the levels of a factor.

Effect size, which is an estimate of the size of an observed effect or change in a population, is introduced in greater detail in Chapter 14 of this book. In a meta-analysis, effect size is used to describe the size of an effect for data reported across a series of related research studies. Researchers can compute effect size in many different ways, depending on the type of data available. Estimates of effect size, which differ in terms of how each is reported, can be interpreted in terms of the following:

> Effect size can be interpreted in terms of differences, proportions, and degree of association.

- Differences. An effect size measure for this interpretation is Cohen's *d*. The interpretation is typically in terms of how far scores shift in a population (e.g., how much greater benefit a patient gains from a new behavioral therapy), or how scores differ between two populations (e.g., the difference in benefits gained from a new behavioral therapy in men compared with women). This effect size measure, which is reported in standard deviation units, can be represented as follows:

$$\text{Effect size} = \frac{\text{Sample mean difference}}{\text{Sample standard deviation}}$$

- Proportions. The effect size measure for this interpretation is typically eta squared (η^2). The interpretation is in terms of the proportion of variance in a dependent variable that can be explained or accounted for by a manipulation or event (e.g., the proportion of variance in reduced symptoms for a disorder that can be explained by a new behavioral therapy). Proportion of variance ranges between 0 and 1, with larger values indicating greater effect size, and it can be represented as follows:

$$\text{Effect size} = \frac{\text{Varibility explained}}{\text{Total variability}}$$

- Degree of association. The effect size measure for this interpretation is typically the correlation coefficient (*r*). The interpretation is in terms of the degree of association or relationship between two factors, X and Y (e.g., the degree of association between a new behavioral therapy and improved quality of life outcomes). A correlation coefficient ranges between −1.0 and +1.0, with values further from 0 indicating a stronger relationship between two factors, and it can be represented as follows:

$$\text{Effect size} = \frac{\text{Variance of } X \text{ and } Y \text{ together}}{\text{Variance of } X \text{ and } Y \text{ separately}}$$

A meta-analysis uses these statistical measures to describe findings across many studies. As an example from published research, we can consider a meta-analysis that was conducted by Acevedo and Aron (2009) to test the relationship between types of love and relationship satisfaction using the correlation coefficient, *r*, as a measure of effect size. The

Statistical power, or **power**, is the likelihood that data in a sample can detect or discover an effect in a population, assuming that the effect does exist in the population of interest.

researchers reviewed the literature and selected 25 studies related to this topic. In their study, they computed the effect size of findings for all studies to measure how love types (e.g., romantic, obsessive) and relationship satisfaction in short- and long-term relationships were related. Their results, a portion of which are shown in Table 7.7, indicate that romantic love was strongly associated with relationship satisfaction in short- and long-term relationships, whereas obsessive love was not. These results were in contrast with the notion that romantic love fades over time.

Table 7.7 Estimates of Effect Size for Love Types With Relationship Satisfaction in Short- and Long-Term Relationships

Love Type	Short-Term Relationship			Long-Term Relationship		
	N	k	r	N	k	r
Romantic Love	3,256	13	0.55	1,419	7	0.56
Obsessive Love	2,958	12	0.08	889	6	−0.02

N = total sample size, k = number of studies, r = average effect size

Source: Adapted from data presented by Acevedo and Aron (2009).

A meta-analysis increases statistical power, but it is prone to publication bias.

A key advantage of a meta-analysis is that it increases **statistical power**, or the likelihood of detecting an effect or mean difference in one or more populations. A meta-analysis increases statistical power because it combines the sample sizes across many research studies, then computes effect size. Increasing sample size is one way to increase power. By combining many studies, a meta-analysis also combines the samples in those studies—thereby increasing, more than any individual study included in the analysis, the likelihood of detecting an effect (see H. Cooper & Rosenthal, 1980).

A key disadvantage of a meta-analysis is that it is prone to *publication bias*, which was defined in Chapter 2. Howard et al. (2009) drew an analogy of this problem to calculating a baseball player's batting average, which is the proportion of times at bat that a player hits the ball into fair play and gets on base. To illustrate this analogy, suppose you compute a player's batting average only on his "good hitting days" and do not count the days that he did not get a hit. In this case, you would overestimate a player's true batting average because you only counted days that the player got a hit. The same is true for a meta-analysis in that the editors of peer-reviewed journals have a tendency to publish positive results or results that show an effect, while omitting those studies that fail to show an effect. Hence, many studies that do not show an effect are possibly not included in calculations of effect size in a meta-analysis because such studies are not often published in peer-reviewed journals. In this way, a meta-analysis can be prone to overestimating the true size of an effect in a population.

7.10 Ethics in Focus: Existing Data and Experimenter Bias

A concern anytime you review existing data is to consider all data that are relevant to your research topic. Experimenter bias, intentionally or not, can occur when you selectively review only those records with data that fit with the conclusions you want to draw, so you disregard all other existing data. This can be a problem because, unlike sampling participants, researchers must often probe or sift through existing data records prior to including them in an analysis to make sure each record is relevant to the topic being studied. To avoid experimenter bias, you should have multiple researchers search existing data records during the initial review process. By doing so, you can reduce bias in that a consensus can be reached by many researchers prior to selecting which existing data records are included in or omitted from a research study.

LEARNING CHECK 5 ✓

1. State the type of existing data research design described in each example.

   A. A researcher selects 77 related studies that are published in peer-reviewed journals to analyze the extent to which student evaluations are related to student learning.

   B. A researcher analyzes the appropriateness of content in advertising themes during television programming aimed at children.

   C. A researcher reviews voting records to determine the demographic characteristics of those voting for each candidate in an election.

2. How does a meta-analysis increase statistical power?

Answers: 1. A. Meta-analysis, B. Content analysis, C. Archival research; 2. A meta-analysis increases statistical power because it combines the sample size from many studies.

CHAPTER SUMMARY

LO 1 Identify and define the naturalistic research design.

- The naturalistic research design applies a naturalistic observation strategy to make observations in natural settings. **Naturalistic observation** is the observation of behavior in the natural setting where it is expected to occur, with limited or no attempt to overtly manipulate the conditions of the environment where the observations are made.

LO 2 Distinguish between natural and contrived research settings.

- A **natural setting** is a location or site where a behavior of interest normally occurs. A **contrived setting** is a location or site arranged to mimic the natural setting within which a behavior of interest normally occurs, in order to facilitate the occurrence of that behavior.

LO 3 Identify and describe how researchers make unobtrusive observations.

- An **unobtrusive observation** is a technique used by an observer to record or observe behavior in a way that does not interfere with or change a participant's behavior in that observed research setting.
- To make unobtrusive observations, researchers can remain hidden, habituate participants to their presence, use a confederate, or use indirect measures.

LO 4 Describe how researchers operationalize, quantify, and manage observation periods in a naturalistic or contrived setting.

- Researchers operationalize observations by identifying behavior categories of interest. **Behavior categories** are the specific types of behaviors that researchers want to measure in the research setting, and they are typically organized as a list of examples that "count" in each category or for each type of behavior.
- To quantify observations, researchers can use the following methods:
  - **Interval method** (record whether or not certain behaviors occur in a given interval).
  - **Frequency method** (record the number of times a behavior occurs during a fixed period of time).
  - **Duration method** (record the amount of time that a participant engages in a certain behavior during a fixed period of time).
  - **Latency method** (record the time or duration between the occurrences of behaviors during a fixed period of time).
- To manage observation periods, researchers can use the following methods:
  - **Time sampling** (making observations in alternating intervals of an observation period).
  - **Event sampling** (recording different events or behaviors in each interval of an observation period).
  - **Individual sampling** (recording the behavior of different individuals in each interval of an observation period).

LO 5 Describe the philosophy of qualitative research, and explain how trustworthiness relates to validity and reliability.

- The philosophy of qualitative research is based on the holistic view that *reality changes* (each person experiences a unique reality or views the world from a different perspective) and *behavior is dynamic* (behavior can only be understood in the context within which it occurs).

- We cannot establish the validity and reliability of an outcome without the aid of statistics. For this reason, qualitative research uses different criteria that parallel validity and reliability. An alternative to validity and reliability is criteria of **trustworthiness** in qualitative research. The four criteria of trustworthiness are the *credibility*, *transferability*, *dependability*, and *confirmability* of a qualitative analysis. Credibility and transferability are similar to internal and external validity, respectively; dependability is similar to reliability; transferability is similar to objectivity.

LO 6 Identify and describe three qualitative research designs: phenomenology, ethnography, and case study.

- **Phenomenology** is the qualitative analysis of the conscious experiences of phenomena from the first-person point of view.
- **Ethnography** is the qualitative analysis of the behavior and identity of a group or culture as it is described and characterized by the members of that group or culture.
- **Case study** is the qualitative analysis of a single individual, group, organization, or event used to illustrate a phenomenon, explore new hypotheses, or compare the observations of many cases. Three types of case studies are illustrative, exploratory, and collective. A case study is unique in that it is often applied as a qualitative and a quantitative analysis.

LO 7 Identify and describe three existing data research designs: archival research, content analysis, and meta-analysis.

- **Archival research** is a type of existing data design in which events or behaviors are described based on a review and analysis of relevant historical or archival records.
- **Content analysis** is a type of existing data design in which the content of written or spoken records of the occurrence of specific events or behaviors is described and interpreted.
- A **meta-analysis** is a type of existing data design in which data are combined, analyzed, and summarized across a group of related studies to make statistically guided decisions about the strength or reliability of the reported findings in those studies.
  - Data are often reported as **effect size** in a meta-analysis. A meta-analysis increases **statistical power** by combining the sample sizes from many studies, but it is also prone to a publication bias because negative results, or those that do not show an effect, tend to be omitted from the peer-reviewed literature.

KEY TERMS

naturalistic observation	behavior categories	time sampling
natural setting	interval method	event sampling
contrived setting	frequency method	individual sampling
structured setting	duration method	qualitative research design
unobtrusive observation	latency method	determinism

trustworthiness

phenomenology

ethnography

participant observation

case study

illustrative case study

exploratory case study

collective case study

case history

existing data design

selective deposit

selective survival

archival research

content analysis

meta-analysis

effect size

statistical power

power

REVIEW QUESTIONS

1. Identify which statement, A or B, is false, and explain what makes the statement false.

   A. Naturalistic observation often involves the use of unobtrusive observations.

   B. Naturalistic observation is an experimental research design.

2. State four strategies that researchers use to make unobtrusive observations.

3. A researcher in a gym setting counts the number of times that individuals look at themselves in a mirror while they exercise during a 30-minute observation period. What method did the researcher use to quantify her observations?

4. State three sampling methods that researchers use to manage an observational period.

5. A researcher plays a video of an interview and records the behavior of the interviewer, and then replays the video and records the behavior of the interviewee. What sampling method did the researcher use to manage the observational period?

6. Many researchers reject the notion of validity and reliability for a qualitative analysis. What criteria do researchers use instead for qualitative analyses?

7. A researcher demonstrates that the participants in her study agree with her qualitative research report of that study.

   A. Which criteria of trustworthiness did the researcher demonstrate?

   B. What type of validity do the demonstrated criteria parallel?

8. A researcher states that he views each participant as a coresearcher and not as an object of study. Which perspective, qualitative or quantitative, does this statement describe? Explain.

9. State the type of qualitative research design that is most closely associated with the following terms:

   A. Conscious experience

   B. Cultural identity

   C. First-person narrative

   D. Participant observation

   E. Single case

   F. Case history

10. A young researcher joins a local fraternity posing as a student and becomes immersed in the fraternity lifestyle in order to study members of the fraternity.

    A. What method of observation did the researcher use?

    B. What type of qualitative research design often requires the use of this method of observation?

11. A researcher reviews academic transcripts to determine the percentage of high school students who enter college with at least some college credits. Which existing data research design did the researcher use?

12. To study whether a media bias exists, a researcher analyzes the content of the recordings of prime-time coverage for three major news networks (CNN, MSNBC, and Fox) during a 1-week period. Which existing data research design did the researcher use?

13. Name one advantage and one disadvantage of conducting a meta-analysis.

14. State three ways to interpret effect size.

ACTIVITIES

1. For any three of the following factors, identify a naturalistic and a contrived research setting that could be used to study the factor.

    A. Athletic performance

    B. Food choice among healthy adults

    C. Voting behavior during an election year

    D. Teaching style in the classroom

    E. Expressions of spirituality

2. Interview someone you know and want to learn about. Give a three- to five-question interview, and record the responses given by the interviewee using an audio recorder or a notebook. After the interview, analyze what you learned using a qualitative perspective by doing each of the following:

    A. Type a two- to three-page narrative summarizing the interview. The narrative should summarize common themes, if any, and identify the meaning of the responses given by the interviewee.

    B. Describe the extent to which your analysis of the interview meets the criterion of trustworthiness. Hint: To establish the credibility of your interview, you can have the interviewee read your narrative and state whether or not he or she agrees with your report.

3. Choose any behavioral research topic of interest, and state three different types of existing data you could obtain to study your topic.

Identify a problem

- Determine an area of interest.
- Review the literature.
- Identify new ideas in your area of interest.
- Develop a research hypothesis.

Develop a research plan

- Define the variables being tested.
- Identify participants or subjects and determine how to sample them.
- Select a research strategy and design.
- Evaluate ethics and obtain institutional approval to conduct research.

Generate more new ideas

- Results support your hypothesis—refine or expand on your ideas.
- Results do not support your hypothesis—reformulate a new idea or start over.

After reading this chapter, you should be able to:

1. Identify and construct open-ended, partially open-ended, and restricted survey items.

2. Identify nine rules for writing valid and reliable survey items.

3. Describe methods of administering written surveys and interview surveys.

4. Explain how response rates to surveys can limit the interpretation of survey results.

5. Identify how to appropriately handle and administer surveys.

6. Identify and describe the direction and strength of a correlation.

7. Explain how causality, outliers, and restriction of range can limit the interpretation of a correlation coefficient.

8. Explain how linear regression can be used to predict outcomes.

9. Compute the Pearson correlation coefficient and linear regression using SPSS.

Conduct the study

- Execute the research plan and measure or record the data.

Communicate the results

- Method of communication: oral, written, or in a poster.
- Style of communication: APA guidelines are provided to help prepare style and format.

Analyze and evaluate the data

- Analyze and evaluate the data as they relate to the research hypothesis.
- Summarize data and research results.

SURVEY AND CORRELATIONAL RESEARCH DESIGNS

You have probably made or heard the popular comment "Is it just me, or [fill in the blank here]?" This question is really a survey that asks others to indicate their level of agreement with some viewpoint—for example, "Is it just me, or is it hot in here?" or "Is it just me, or was this exam difficult?" We largely ask such questions to gauge the opinions of others. Many examples likely occur every day, from completing a customer satisfaction survey to asking your friends what they plan to order at a restaurant to get a better idea of what you might want to order. Really, we could survey people to measure all sorts of constructs, including love, attachment, personality, motivation, cognition, and many other constructs studied by behavioral scientists.

We can also identify how constructs such as love, attachment, personality, motivation, and cognition are related to other factors or behaviors such as the likelihood of depression, emotional well-being, and physical health. In everyday situations, you may notice relationships between temperature and aggression (e.g., the hotter it is outside, the more often you see people fighting at a sports stadium) or between class participation and grades (e.g., students with higher grades tend to also participate more in class). Hence, there is a natural tendency for us to engage the world under the assumption that behavior does not occur in isolation. Instead, behavior is related to or influenced by other factors in the environment.

It is therefore not uncommon at all for humans to observe the world by asking people to answer questions about themselves or by observing how human behavior is related to other factors such as health and well-being. The same is true in science. In this chapter, we describe how we can use the scientific method to evaluate or survey participant responses and identify relationships between factors.

SURVEY DESIGNS

Many research designs can be used to test the same hypotheses. This chapter is separated into two major sections; each section describes a nonexperimental research design: survey designs and correlational designs. To introduce how each design can be used to test the same hypothesis, we begin each major section by developing a new research design to test the same hypothesis.

Suppose we hypothesize that texting while driving is more prevalent among younger age groups, as has been tested in the published literature (Harrison, 2011; Ling, Bertel, & Sundsøy, 2012; Quisenberry, 2015). We could use a survey research design by asking a sample of young college students who drive to indicate in a questionnaire how often they use text messaging while driving (per month). If the hypothesis is correct and we set up this study correctly, we should find that a high percentage of young drivers use text messaging while driving.

We will return to this hypothesis with a new way to answer it when we introduce correlational designs. We begin this chapter with an introduction to the research design that was illustrated here: the survey research design.

8.1 An Overview of Survey Designs

> The **survey research design** is the use of a survey, administered either in written form or orally, to quantify, describe, or characterize an individual or a group.
>
> A **survey** is a series of questions or statements, called items, used in a questionnaire or an interview to measure the self-reports or responses of respondents.

A nonexperimental research design used to describe an individual or a group by having participants complete a survey or questionnaire is called the **survey research design**. A **survey**, which is a common measurement tool in the behavioral sciences, is a series of questions or statements to which participants indicate responses. A survey can also be called a *questionnaire* or *self-report* because many surveys specifically include questions in which participants report about themselves—their attitudes, opinions, beliefs, activities, emotions, and so on.

A survey can be administered in printed form, or it can be distributed orally in an interview. While a survey can be used as a measurement tool in many research designs, the survey research design specifically refers to the use of surveys to quantify, describe, or characterize an individual or a group. In this chapter, we introduce the types and writing of questions included in surveys, describe how to administer surveys, and discuss some limitations associated with using surveys in the behavioral sciences.

8.2 Types of Survey Items

A survey consists of many questions or statements to which participants respond. A survey is sometimes called a *scale*, and the questions or statements in the survey are often called *items*. As an example of a scale with many items, the estimated daily intake scale for sugar

(EDIS-S) (Privitera & Wallace, 2011) is identified as an 11-item scale, meaning that the scale or survey includes 11 items or statements to which participants respond on a 7-point scale from 1 (*completely disagree*) to 7 (*completely agree*). Notice that each item, listed in Table 8.1, is a statement about how much sugar participants consume in their diets.

There are three types of questions or statements that can be included in a survey: open-ended items, partially open-ended items, and restricted items. Each type of item is described here.

Open-Ended Items

When researchers want participants to respond in their own words to a survey item, they include an **open-ended item** in the survey. An open-ended item is a question or statement that is left completely "open" for response. It allows participants to give any response they feel is appropriate with no limitations. For example, the following three items are open-ended questions that were asked in a *focus group*, which is generally a guided discussion among a targeted group of participants to explore a topic. In this study, the aim was to identify what educators and students think about using patients as teachers in medical education (Jha, Quinton, Bekker, & Roberts, 2009, pp. 455–456):

> An **open-ended item** is a question or statement in a survey that allows the respondent to give any response in his or her own words, without restriction.

- What are your views on the role of patients teaching medical students?

- How do you think the role of patients as teachers in medical education will affect the doctor–patient relationship?

Table 8.1 The Eleven Items for the EDIS-S

Item	Statement
1	I tend to eat cereals that have sugar in them.
2	I tend to put a lot of syrup on my pancakes or waffles.
3	I often eat candy to snack on when I am hungry.
4	I tend to crave foods that are high in sugar.
5	I tend to snack on healthier food options.
6	I tend to consume a low-sugar diet.
7	I often snack on sugary foods when I am hungry.
8	When I crave a snack, I typically seek out sweet-tasting foods.
9	I tend to eat foods that are most convenient, even if they contain a lot of sugar.
10	I like consuming sweet-tasting foods and drinks each day.
11	I tend to avoid consuming a high-sugar diet.

- One potential plan is to bring "expert patients" (patients who are experts in their long-term conditions) into the classroom to deliver teaching on their condition. What are your views of this?

Open-ended items can also be given as a statement and not a question. For example, the researchers could have asked participants in the focus group to respond to the following survey item: "Describe an experience you had as a patient and whether you felt that experience was sufficient to deem you an 'expert' on your condition." In this example, the open-ended item is phrased as a statement and not a question; however, the response will still be open ended.

Open-ended items are most often used with the qualitative research design because the responses in the survey are purely descriptive. Indeed, the focus group study by Jha et al. (2009) was a qualitative research study. For all other research designs—those that are quantitative—the challenge is in coding the open-ended responses of participants. It is difficult to anticipate how participants will respond to an open-ended item, so the researcher must develop methods to code patterns or similarities in participant responses. Coding the responses to open-ended items, however, requires researchers to do both of the following:

- Tediously anticipate and list all possible examples of potential responses in terms of how participants might write or express their responses.

- Use multiple raters and additional statistical analyses to make sure the coding is accurate.

For the reasons listed here, open-ended survey items are not often used in quantitative research, with partially open-ended or restricted items being favored among quantitative researchers.

Partially Open-Ended Items

A **partially open-ended item** is a question or statement in a survey that includes a few restricted answer options and then a last one that allows participants to respond in their own words in case the few restricted options do not fit with the answer they want to give.

Researchers can include items, called **partially open-ended items**, which give participants a few restricted answer options and then a last one that allows participants to respond in their own words in case the few restricted options do not fit with the answer they want to give. The open-ended option is typically stated as "other" with a blank space provided for the participant's open-ended response. For example, the focus group study by Jha et al. (2009) also included the following partially open-ended item:

In what capacity do you (students or faculty or other) view the role of patients as teachers?

A. Teaching

B. Assessment

C. Curriculum development

D. Other _____ (p. 455)

In this item, participants either chose an option provided (teaching, assessment, or curriculum development) or provided their own open-ended response (other ___). For the researchers, it is easier to manage the participant responses, or data, when an open-ended item includes a few restricted options. To enter participant responses, researchers can code each answer option as a number. The last open-ended option could be coded further, or just analyzed without further coding. For example, we could report only the percentage of participants choosing the last open-ended option, without analyzing the specific open-ended responses given. In this way, coding and analyzing partially open-ended items can be less tedious than for open-ended items.

> Open-ended items are largely used in qualitative research; restricted items are largely used in quantitative research.

Restricted Items

The most commonly used survey item in quantitative research, called a **restricted item**, includes a restricted number of answer options. A restricted item does not give participants an option to respond in their own words; instead, the item is restricted to the finite number of options provided by the researcher. Restricted items are often given with a rating scale, which is often referred to as a **Likert scale** when the scale varies between 5 and 7 points. A Likert scale, named after Rensis Likert (1932) who was the first to use such a scale, is a finite number of *points* for which a participant can respond to an item in a survey, typically between 5 and 7 points.

> A **restricted item**, also called a **closed-ended item**, is a question or statement in a survey that includes a restricted number of answer options to which participants must respond.
>
> A **Likert scale** is a numeric response scale used to indicate a participant's rating or level of agreement with a question or statement.

Two common applications of rating scales are to have participants use the scale to describe themselves or to indicate their level of agreement. For example, Schredl, Fricke-Oerkermann, Mitschke, Wiater, and Lehmkuhl (2009) used the following 3-point rating scale to record how children describe their dreams (each number value is a "point" on the scale):

I have nightmares: (Circle one)

1	2	3
Never	Sometimes	Often

As another example of using a rating scale to indicate a level of agreement, Nagels, Kircher, Steines, Grosvald, and Straube (2015) used the following 5-point rating scale for an item included in an assessment of individual differences in gesture perception and production:

I like talking to people who gesture a lot when they talk. (Circle one)

1 2 3 4 5

Not   Fully
disagree   agree

A rating scale itself does not necessarily have to be numeric. For example, many young children cannot count, let alone use numeric scales to describe themselves. In these cases, pictorial scales, such as the "self-assessment manikin" (SAM) shown in Figure 8.1 (Bradley & Lang, 1994), can be used. This type of scale can be used with children, such as in a study in which children used the SAM scale to indicate how much they liked a grapefruit juice with versus without added sugar (Capaldi & Privitera, 2008). The scale can also be used with adults. For example, Kunze, Arntz, and Kindt (2015) used the SAM scale to evaluate participant responses to a variety of stimuli used in a study on fear conditioning. In each study, the researchers coded responses using a numeric scale from 1 (saddest) to 5 (happiest) so that responses with the images could be recorded as numeric values and then analyzed.

The main advantage of using restricted items is that survey responses can be easily entered or coded for the purposes of statistical analysis. The main limitation of using restricted items is that the analysis is restricted to the finite number of options provided to participants. However, when the options available to participants are exhaustive of all options they could choose, this limitation is minimal.

Figure 8.1 A Pictorial Rating Scale Used to Measure Emotion and Liking in Children

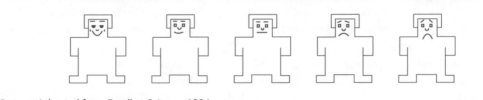

Source: Adapted from Bradley & Lang, 1994.

LEARNING CHECK 1 ✔

1. State the type of survey item for each of the following items:

   A. How do you feel about the effectiveness of your professor's teaching style?

   B. On a scale from 1 (*very ineffective*) to 7 (*very effective*), how would you rate your professor?

   C. Is your professor's greatest strength his or her (a) timeliness to class, (b) knowledge of the material, (c) concern for students, or (d) other ___ (please explain)?

2. A _____ is a numeric response scale used to indicate a participant's rating or level of agreement with a question or statement.

8.3 Rules for Writing Survey Items

Writing survey items is a thoughtful endeavor. The items that you write must be valid and reliable. In other words, the items must actually measure what you are trying to measure (valid), and the responses in the survey should be consistently observed across participants and over time (reliable). When an item or a measure is not valid and reliable, it is often due to a *measurement error*, or variability in responding due to poorly written survey items. In this section, we describe the following nine rules used to write valid and reliable survey items that can minimize the likelihood of measurement error:

1. Keep it simple.

2. Avoid double-barreled items.

3. Use neutral or unbiased language.

4. Minimize the use of negative wording.

5. Avoid the response set pitfall.

6. Use rating scales consistently.

7. Limit the points on a rating scale.

8. Label or anchor the rating scale points.

9. Minimize item and survey length.

Keep It Simple

Everyone who takes a survey should be able to understand it. The best strategy is to use less than a high school–level vocabulary in writing the survey items. We use this strategy to make sure that participants' responses reflect their actual responses and are not given because they are confused about what the question is asking. For example, we could have participants rate how full they feel by asking, "How *satiated* do you feel?" However, some participants may not know that *satiated* means to satisfy an appetite, so it would be better to plainly ask, "How *full* do you feel?" In sum, keep the language simple.

Use simple words or language in a survey.

Avoid Double-Barreled Items

Ask only one question or give only one statement for each item. **Double-barreled items** are survey items that ask participants for one response to two different questions or

> **Double-barreled items** are survey items that ask participants for one response to two different questions or statements.

statements. For example, to study relationship satisfaction, we could ask participants to indicate their level of agreement with the following statement:

I enjoy the time we spend together and dislike the time we are apart.

1	2	3	4	5
Strongly disagree				Strongly agree

This item for relationship satisfaction is double-barreled. It is not necessarily true that people who enjoy the time they spend with their partner also dislike the time they are apart. Anytime a sentence uses a conjunction, such as *and*, it is likely that the item is double-barreled. The solution is to split the question into separate items. For example, we can change the double-barreled item into two separate items, each with a separate rating scale. We could write the first item as "I enjoy the time we spend together" and the second item as "I dislike the time we are apart" to allow participants to give a separate response to each individual item.

Do not use double-barreled items in a survey.

Use Neutral or Unbiased Language

Do not use *loaded terms*, or words that produce an emotional reaction, such as language that is offensive or could potentially be considered offensive by a respondent. Offensive language is not only inappropriate, but it can also lead people to respond in reaction to the language used. In other words, responses may be caused by the choice of wording in a survey item and may not reflect the honest response of the participant.

Use appropriate and unbiased language in surveys.

To avoid the use of potentially offensive language, the American Psychological Association (APA, 2009) provides guidelines for using appropriate language. Some suggestions include identifying persons 18 years and older as *women* and *men* and capitalizing *Black* and *White* to identify racial and ethnic groups. More suggestions are provided in the publication manual (APA, 2009) and in Table 15.2 in Chapter 15.

Likewise, do not use *leading terms* or *leading questions*, or words or questions that indicate how people should respond to an item. For example, a leading question would be, "How bad are your problems with your boss?" In this example, it is implied that you have a problem, which may or may not be true. So the use of the word "bad" is a leading term in this sentence and it should be removed. A better way to phrase this question would be, "What is the nature of your relationship with your boss?" In this case, you are not implying what the nature of that relationship is, and the respondent is not being led toward one response or another. Thus, the solution for fixing survey items with loaded terms or leading questions is often to simply rephrase or rewrite the item to avoid this pitfall.

Minimize the Use of Negative Wording

The use of negative wording can trick participants into misunderstanding a survey item. *Negative wording* is the use of words in a sentence or an item that negates or indicates the opposite of what was otherwise described. The rule is to avoid asking participants in a survey item what they would *not* do, which can require rephrasing a sentence or survey item. For example, the survey item "How much do you *not* like working?" can be rephrased to "How much do you *dislike* working?" It may seem like a small change, but it can effectively reduce confusion.

> Avoid using negative wording in a survey item.

Avoid the Response Set Pitfall

When respondents notice an obvious pattern in the responses they provide, they will often use that same pattern to respond to future items in that survey. For example, suppose we ask participants to indicate their level of agreement with the following items on a 5-point scale to measure relationship satisfaction:

I enjoy the time I spend with my partner.

The time I spend with my partner makes me happy.

I look forward to the time I spend with my partner.

On the 5-point scale, suppose 1 indicates low satisfaction and 5 indicates high satisfaction. For each item, high satisfaction would be a rating of 5. If there were 20 questions like this, then participants would start to see a pattern, such as high ratings always indicate greater satisfaction. If participants are generally satisfied in their relationship, they may begin marking 5 for each item without reading many of the items because they know what the scale represents. However, the ratings participants give would reflect the fact that they saw a pattern and may not necessarily reflect their true ratings for each item. To avoid this problem, called a **response set**, mix up the items in a survey so that ratings are not all on the same end of the scale for a given measure.

> A **response set** is the tendency for participants to respond the same way to all items in a survey when the direction of ratings is the same for all items in the survey.

To illustrate how to avoid the response set pitfall, the following are four items from the EDIS-S (Privitera & Wallace, 2011), which is used to estimate how much sugar participants consume in their diet. Participants rate each item on a 7-point scale from 1 (*completely disagree*) to 7 (*completely agree*).

I tend to eat cereals that have sugar in them.

I often eat candy to snack on when I am hungry.

I tend to crave foods that are high in sugar.

I tend to consume a low-sugar diet.

> Do not include predictable response patterns in a survey.

Notice that the last item is flipped—if participants eat a lot of sugar, then they would rate on the low end of the scale for this last listed item only. Because a few items in the EDIS-S are flipped like this, responses on this scale are unlikely to result from a response set. However, for the scale to make sense, higher overall ratings must indicate greater daily intake of sugar. The first three items are stated such that higher scores do indicate greater daily intake of sugar. Suppose, for example, a participant rates the first three items a 7. The participant's total score so far, then, is 7 × 3 items = 21.

The fourth item is a **reverse coded item**, meaning that we need to code responses for the item in reverse order. The participant rates his or her response on the 1 to 7 scale, but when we score it, we will reverse it to a 7 to 1 scale. Hence, a 1 is scored as a 7, a 2 as a 6, a 3 as a 5, a 4 remains a 4, a 5 is scored as a 3, a 6 as a 2, and a 7 as a 1. By doing so, a 7 for the reverse coded item again indicates the highest intake of sugar, and a 1 indicates the lowest intake of sugar—consistent with the scale for the other items in the survey. Returning to our example, suppose that our participant rates the fourth item a 2. We reverse code this item and score it as a 6, then calculate the total score, which is 21 (first three items) + 6 (fourth item) = 27 (total score). Because the fourth item was reverse coded, the survey can now be scored such that higher scores indicate greater daily intake of sugar, and the survey can also be written so as to avoid a response set pitfall.

> A **reverse coded item** is an item that is phrased in the semantically opposite direction of most other items in a survey and is scored by coding or entering responses for the item in reverse order from how they are listed.

Use Rating Scales Consistently

Another rule is to use only one rating scale at a time. In the simplest scenario, use only one scale if possible. The EDIS-S, for example, uses a level of agreement scale for all items in the survey from 1 (*completely disagree*) to 7 (*completely agree*). Having only one response scale makes it clear how respondents must respond to all items in a survey. If a survey must use two or more different scales, then the items in the survey should be grouped from one type of scale to the next. Begin with all items for one scale (e.g., items with a scale rated from *very dissatisfied* to *very satisfied*); then give directions to clearly indicate a change in the scale for the next group of items (e.g., items with a scale rated from *not at all* to *all the time*). Consistent use of rating scales in a survey ensures that participants' responses reflect their true ratings for each item and not some confusion about the meaning of the scale used.

> Be clear about the rating scale(s) used in surveys.

Limit the Points on a Rating Scale

To construct a response scale, keep the scale between 3 and 10 points (Komorita & Graham, 1965; Matell & Jacoby, 1971). Experts in *psychometrics*, a field involved in the construction of measurement scales, suggest that response scales should have a midpoint or intermediate response level. Having fewer than 3 points on a response scale violates this suggestion, and response scales with more than 10 points can be too confusing.

There are two exceptions to the rule of limiting a rating scale to 3 to 10 points. One exception is that a 2-point scale is appropriate for dichotomous scales in which only two responses are possible. For example, dichotomous scales with true/false, yes/no, or agree/disagree as the response options are acceptable. A second exception is that **bipolar scales**, those that have points above and below a zero point, can be 3 to 10 points above and below the zero point. Hence, a bipolar scale, such as the one shown below with 11 points, can have up to 21 points, or 10 points above and 10 points below zero.

> **Bipolar scales** are response scales that have points above (positive values) and below (negative values) a zero point.

> As a general rule, use 3 to 10 points on the rating scale for each item in a survey.

How do you feel about your ability to find a job that will make you happy?

$-5 \quad -4 \quad -3 \quad -2 \quad -1 \quad 0 \quad 1 \quad 2 \quad 3 \quad 4 \quad 5$

| Extremely pessimistic | No opinion | Extremely optimistic |

> Anchor or label the end points of a rating scale.

Label or Anchor the Rating Scale Points

To clearly indicate what a rating scale means, we can use **anchors** or adjectives given at the end points of a rating scale. Anchors are often listed below the end points on a rating scale, such as those given for the bipolar scale for the previous rule. Notice also in the bipolar scale that the midpoint is labeled. Indeed, we can include anchors for the end points and label every other point on a scale if we choose.

> **Anchors** are adjectives that are given to describe the end points of a rating scale to give the scale greater meaning.

Minimize Item and Survey Length

As a general rule, you want to make sure that each item in a survey is as brief as possible. Being concise is important to ensure that respondents read the full item before responding. Likewise, a survey itself can be too long, although it is difficult to determine or define what constitutes "too long." The best advice is to write the survey to be as short and concise as possible, yet still able to convey or measure what it is intended to measure. Keep in mind that participants will fatigue or simply get tired of answering survey items. If this occurs, then a participant may start to "browse" survey items or even make up responses just to "get the survey over with." It is not to say that all participants will do this, but some will do this, and we want to avoid this problem of fatigue. The obvious solution is to make the survey and the items in the survey as brief or concise as possible. A survey that is not longer than 10 to 15 minutes is typically preferred to one that takes an hour to complete.

The time to complete a survey tends to be more important than the number of items in the survey. For example, a survey with a few open-ended items may take 15 to 20 minutes to complete, whereas a survey that has 30 restricted items may take only a minute or two to

Minimize item and survey length.

complete. To minimize survey length, then, the key goal is to minimize how long (over time) it takes a person to complete all items in a survey, and not necessarily to minimize the number items in the survey per se.

LEARNING CHECK 2 ✓

1. Which rule or rules for writing survey items does each of the following items violate? Note: Assume that each item is rated on a 5-point scale from 1 (*completely untrue*) to 5 (*completely true*):

    A. I am a likable person and enjoy the company of others.

    B. On a scale from 1 (*very unlikely*) to 13 (*very likely*), what are the chances you will win money in a casino?

    C. Reverse discrimination against white Americans is a big problem in America.

    D. Misogynistic men do not make good boyfriends.

2. True or false: How an item is worded can affect the reliability and validity of responses given for that item.

8.4 Administering Surveys

Once a survey is constructed, it is administered to participants who will respond to the survey. A survey can be written (in print or electronically) or spoken (such as in an interview). A written survey can be administered in person, by mail, or using the Internet. An interview survey can be administered face to face, by telephone, or in focus groups. Each method of administering a survey is described in this section.

Written Surveys

In-person surveys. A method that can effectively get participants to respond to a survey is to be physically present while participants complete the survey. The reason that more participants are willing to complete a survey administered in person is that you, the researcher, can be there to explain the survey, observe participants take the survey, and answer any questions they may have while they complete the survey. This method is more time-consuming, however, because it requires the researcher to be present while each and every participant completes the survey.

Mail surveys. An alternative that can require less of the researcher's time is to submit surveys in the mail. However, mail surveys are associated with higher rates of potential respondents choosing not to complete and return them to the researcher. Mail surveys can also be costly in terms of both the time it takes to prepare the surveys (e.g., printing and addressing surveys) and the money spent to send them out to potential respondents (e.g., postage stamps and envelopes). The following are four strategies that can increase how many people complete and return a mail survey:

- Include a return envelope with the return postage already paid.
- Let potential respondents know in advance that the survey is being sent.
- Include a cover letter detailing the importance of completing the survey.
- Include a gift for the potential respondent to keep, such as a pen or gift card.

Internet surveys. A popular and cost-effective survey option is to administer surveys online. This option is inexpensive in that a survey can be administered to a large group of potential respondents with little more than a click of a button. Online surveys can be administered via links provided in an e-mail or using online survey construction sites, such as *SurveyMonkey.com* (see Dillman, 2000). The main concern for using online surveys is that the results of these surveys may be limited to individuals who have access to computers with online capabilities, and to individuals who know enough about using computers that they can complete and submit the survey correctly.

> A written survey can be administered in person, by mail, or using the Internet.

Interview Surveys

Face-to-face interviews. A researcher could administer a survey orally to one participant at a time or to a small group. The advantage of a face-to-face interview is that the researcher can control how long it takes to complete the survey inasmuch as it is the researcher asking the questions. The drawback of face-to-face interviews is that they require the interviewer to be present for each survey and can be prone to **interviewer bias**, meaning that the interviewer's demeanor, words, or expressions in an interview may influence the responses of a participant. For this reason, face-to-face interviews, while used in quantitative research, tend to be more commonly applied in qualitative research for which interviewing is a primary method used to describe an individual or a group.

> **Interviewer bias** is the tendency for the demeanor, words, or expressions of a researcher to influence the responses of a participant when the researcher and the participant are in direct contact.

Telephone interviews. An interview can also be administered via the telephone. Phone interviews can be interpersonal (e.g., the researcher asks the questions) or automated (e.g., computer-assisted technology asks the questions). One advantage of automated telephone interviews is that they can save time and reduce the likelihood of interviewer bias. Another advantage is that telephone surveys can be administered at random by generating telephone numbers at random from within the area or region using **random digit dialing**. The key disadvantage of telephone interviews is that they often result in few people willingly agreeing to complete the survey. Also, the passage of new

Random digit dialing is a strategy for selecting participants in telephone interviews by generating telephone numbers to dial or call at random.

laws restricting telephone surveying has made this method of administering surveys less common in the behavioral sciences.

Focus-group interviews. Sometimes researchers use surveys that are aimed at getting people to share ideas or opinions on a certain topic or issue. A survey that is structured to get participants to interact is called a focus group, which is a small group of about three to eight people. Questions or survey items in a focus group are mostly open ended, and the researcher plays more of a moderator role than an interviewer role. The goal of a focus group is to get participants talking to each other to get them to share their ideas and experiences on a predetermined topic. The conversations are typically recorded and then analyzed. While focus groups can reveal new directions and ideas for a given research topic, they are associated with the same problems mentioned for face-to-face interviews.

Each survey administration method described here can vary substantially on how effectively researchers obtain representative samples. Obtaining representative samples is important because surveys are often used for the purpose of learning about characteristics in a population of interest. For example, we sample a few potential voters to identify the candidate who is likely to obtain the most votes in the population, not just among those sampled. Therefore, it is important that the sample we select to complete a survey is representative of the population. Administering a survey in person or face to face can make it more likely that we can obtain a representative sample. Administering the survey by mail, telephone, or Internet, on the other hand, can limit the representativeness of our sample because often only a small proportion of those who receive the survey will respond and actually complete the survey. Issues related to this problem of response rate are discussed in Section 8.5.

An interview survey can be administered face to face, by telephone, or in focus groups.

8.5 Surveys, Sampling, and Nonresponse Bias

Response rate is the portion of participants who agree to complete a survey among all individuals who were asked to complete the survey.

When administering a survey, it is important to obtain a high survey **response rate**, which is the portion of participants who agree to complete a survey among all those who were asked to complete the survey. When the response rate is low, the concern is that any results from the survey will be limited to only those people who were actually willing to complete the survey. When the response rate is high, we can be more confident that the sample of those who completed the survey is representative of the larger population of interest.

Issues related to response rates center on the possibility of a *nonresponse bias* (see Chapter 5), which occurs when participants choose not to complete a survey or choose not to respond to specific items in a survey. Although at least a 75% response rate should be obtained to minimize bias, the typical response rate to surveys in published peer-reviewed research is less than 50% (Baruch, 1999; Baruch & Holtom, 2008; Shih & Fan, 2008; Stoop, 2015). The problem of low response rates is that people who respond to surveys are probably different from those who do not respond. Because we cannot collect data from people who fail to respond, it is difficult to know the exact characteristics of this group of nonresponders. For this reason, we cannot know for sure whether survey results of those who do respond are representative of the larger population of interest, which includes those who do not respond to surveys.

While the low response rates in published research can be problematic, there is good reason to publish the results from these journals. Although low response rates can limit the population validity (a subtype of external validity; see Chapter 6) of results from a survey, researchers are not always interested in generalizing results to a population. To establish some external validity, researchers often use survey results to instead generalize to a theory, called **theoretical generalization**, or generalize to other observations, called **empirical generalization**. Each type of generalization is illustrated in Figure 8.2, with an example given for each type. As long as survey results are rooted in existing theories and data, researchers "can afford to be lenient [to some extent] about sample quality in academic research" (Blair & Zinkhan, 2006, p. 6).

> **Theoretical generalization** is the extent to which results in a survey or another research study are consistent with predictions made by an existing theory.
>
> **Empirical generalization** is the extent to which results in a survey or another research study are consistent with data obtained in previous research studies.

Figure 8.2 Two Types of Generalization for the Results in Survey Research

Theoretical generalization

Are survey results consistent with predictions made by an existing theory?

Example: We test a prediction of a theory of self-esteem by using a survey to identify if adults with low self-esteem also have greater self-doubt.

Empirical generalization

Are survey results consistent with data obtained in previous research studies?

Example: Studies show that certain job markets have grown substantially in the past year. We use a survey to identify if factors typically related to market growth (e.g., increased demand) are also present in these growing markets.

8.6 Ethics in Focus: Handling and Administering Surveys

To show respect for persons, which is a key principle in the Belmont report and the APA (2010) code of conduct, the researcher has certain ethical responsibilities regarding how to handle and administer surveys in a research study. The following are four responsible and appropriate ways to handle and administer surveys:

- The survey itself should not be offensive or stressful to the respondents. The respondents should, under reasonable circumstances, be satisfied or comfortable with their survey experience such that they would not feel distress if asked to complete the survey again. If they would feel distress, then the survey may pose potential psychological risks to the respondents.

- Do not coerce respondents into answering questions or completing a survey. All respondents should be informed prior to completing the survey (typically in an informed consent form) that they can skip or choose not to answer any survey items, or the entire survey, without penalty or negative consequence.

- Do not harass respondents in any way for recruitment purposes. Because of high nonresponse rates, researchers often actively recruit potential respondents through e-mail or phone call reminders. The potential respondents must not view these recruitment efforts as harassing or intrusive.

- Protect the confidentiality or anonymity of respondents. Personally identifiable information of respondents should be protected at all times. If the researcher requires respondents to provide personally identifiable information, then such information should be safeguarded while in the possession of the researcher.

LEARNING CHECK 3 ✓

1. State three ways that a written survey can be administered. State three ways that an interview survey can be administered.

2. Is the typical response rate for survey research that is published in the behavioral sciences less than or greater than 50%?

3. True or false: A survey should not be offensive or stressful to the respondent.

Answers: 1. A written survey can be administered in person, by mail, and over the Internet. An interview survey can be administered face to face, by telephone, and in focus groups. 2. Less than 50%; 3. True.

CORRELATIONAL DESIGNS

In the chapter opening, we stated the following hypothesis: Texting while driving is more prevalent among younger age groups. To answer the hypothesis, we used a survey design to begin this chapter. However, we could use a correlational research design to test this hypothesis as well. To use the correlational design, for example, we could ask a sample of participants who drive to indicate in a questionnaire their age (in years) and how often they use text messaging while driving (per month). If the hypothesis is correct and we set up this study correctly, then we should expect to find that increased texting is associated with younger drivers.

Notice that we used survey data (based on responses in a questionnaire) to record the data. Surveys are often used with a correlational research design. However, keep in mind that anytime we use data to determine whether two or more factors are related/correlated, we are using the correlational design, even if we used a survey or questionnaire to record the data. In this final section, we introduce the research design that was illustrated here: the correlational research design.

8.7 The Structure of Correlational Designs

It is often difficult to determine that one factor causes changes in another factor. For example, in the texting-while-driving study used to introduce each major section in this chapter, we cannot reasonably determine that being younger causes drivers to text more while driving because we cannot control for other possible factors that can cause a change in texting behavior. Other possible factors include how often people drive, how busy their daily lives are, how many friends they have, how good of a driver they think they are, or whether they believe texting while driving is dangerous. In these situations, when it is difficult to control for other possible factors that could be causing changes in behavior, we use the **correlational research design** to determine the extent to which two factors are related, not the extent to which one factor causes changes in another factor.

> A **correlational research design** is the measurement of two or more factors to determine or estimate the extent to which the values for the factors are related or change in an identifiable pattern.

To set up a correlational research design, we make two or more measurements for each individual observed. For the purposes of introducing the correlational research design, we will introduce situations in which only two measurements are made. Each measurement is for a different variable that we believe is related. For example, one economic factor, income, is related to obesity (Ogden, Lamb, Carroll, & Flegal, 2010; Su, Esqueda, Li, & Pagán, 2012) in that individuals with lower income tend to be more obese. The correlation establishes the extent to which two factors are related, such that values for one variable (income level) may predict changes in the values of a second variable (severity of obesity).

A correlation can be established in any setting. In a naturalistic setting, for example, we could measure the correlation between customer satisfaction in a restaurant

> The **correlation coefficient** is a statistic used to measure the strength and direction of the linear relationship, or correlation, between two factors. The value of *r* can range from −1.0 to +1.0.

and timeliness to serve patrons. In a laboratory setting, for example, we could expose participants to a fearful stimulus and record how fearful they rate the stimulus and their corresponding physiological stress response. Using existing data records, we could use legal documents to identify the correlation between duration of marriage (in years) and race, age, socioeconomic status, and any number of other demographic characteristics. In each example, we make two measurements for each individual (or document when using existing records), one measurement for each of the two variables being examined.

Once we measure two variables, we then compute a statistical measure called the **correlation coefficient** to identify the extent to which the values of the two variables or factors are related or change in an identifiable pattern. The correlation coefficient ranges from −1.0 (the values for two factors change in opposite directions) to +1.0 (the values for two factors change in the same direction), and it is used to identify a pattern in terms of the *direction* and *strength* of a relationship between two factors—each way of describing the relationship between two factors is introduced in this section.

In behavioral research, we mostly describe the linear (or straight-line) relationship between two factors. For this reason, we will limit this introduction to the direction and strength of a linear relationship between two factors.

8.8 Describing the Relationship Between Variables

The *direction* of a relationship between two factors is described as being positive or negative. The *strength* of a relationship between two factors is described by the value of the correlation coefficient, *r*, with values closer to $r = \pm 1.0$ indicating a stronger relationship between two factors. The direction and strength of correlation can be readily identified in a graph called a **scatter plot**. To construct a scatter plot (also called a **scatter diagram** or **scatter gram**), we plot each pair of values, called **data points**, along the *x*-axis and *y*-axis of a graph to see whether a pattern emerges.

> A **scatter plot**, also called a **scatter diagram** or **scatter gram**, is a graphical display of discrete data points (*x, y*) used to summarize the relationship between two factors.
>
> **Data points** are the *x*- and *y*-coordinates for each plot in a scatter plot.
>
> The **regression line** is the best-fitting straight line to a set of data points. A best-fitting line is the line that minimizes the distance that all data points fall from it.

The extent to which two factors are related is determined by how far data points fall from a **regression line** when the data points are plotted in a graph. The regression line is the best-fitting or closest-fitting straight line to a set of data points. The best-fitting straight line is the one that minimizes the distance of all data points that fall from it. We will use the regression line to illustrate the direction and strength of the relationship between two factors using the correlational research design.

The Direction of a Relationship

In a scatter plot, a **positive correlation** means that as values of one factor increase, values of a second factor also increase; as values of one factor decrease, values of a second factor also decrease. If two factors have values that change in the same direction, we can graph the correlation using a straight line. In Figure 8.3, values on the *y*-axis increase as values on the *x*-axis increase.

Figure 8.3a shows a *perfect* positive correlation, which occurs when each data point falls exactly on a straight line, although this is rare. More commonly, as shown in Figure 8.3b, a positive correlation is greater than 0 but less than 1.0, where

> The pattern of a set of data points can indicate the extent to which two factors are related.

> A **positive correlation** is a positive value of *r* that indicates that the values of two factors change in the same direction: As the values of one factor increase, values of the second factor also increase; as the values of one factor decrease, values of the second factor also decrease.

Figure 8.3 A Perfect Positive (a) and a Positive (b) Linear Correlation

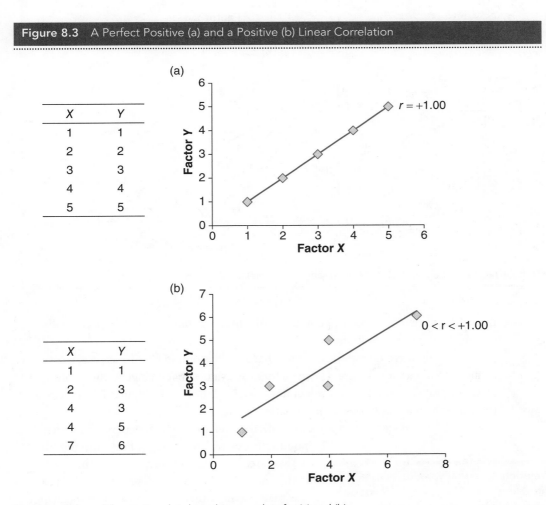

Both the table and the scatter plot show the same data for (a) and (b).

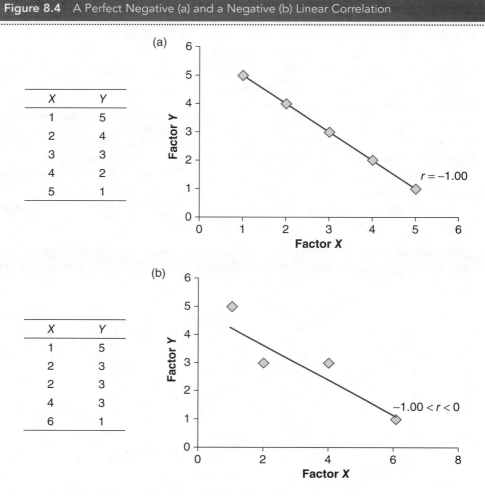

Figure 8.4 A Perfect Negative (a) and a Negative (b) Linear Correlation

(a)

X	Y
1	5
2	4
3	3
4	2
5	1

$r = -1.00$

(b)

X	Y
1	5
2	3
2	3
4	3
6	1

$-1.00 < r < 0$

Both the table and the scatter plot show the same data for (a) and (b).

the values of two factors change in the same direction but not all data points fall exactly on the regression line.

A **negative correlation** means that as values of one factor increase, values of the second factor decrease. If two factors have values that change in the opposite direction, we can graph the correlation using a straight line. In Figure 8.4, values on the y-axis decrease as values on the x-axis increase.

Figure 8.4a shows a *perfect* negative correlation, which occurs when each data point falls exactly on a straight line, although this is also rare. More commonly, as shown in Figure 8.4b, a negative correlation is greater than −1.0 but less than 0, where the values of two factors change in the opposite direction but not all data points fall exactly on the regression line.

A positive correction is given with a plus (+) sign; a negative correlation is given with a minus (–) sign.

A **negative correlation** is a negative value of *r* that indicates that the values of two factors change in different directions, meaning that as the values of one factor increase, values of the second factor decrease.

The Strength of a Relationship

A zero correlation ($r = 0$) means that there is no linear pattern or relationship between two factors. This outcome is rare because usually by mere chance at least some values of one factor, X, will show some pattern or relationship with values of a second factor, Y. The closer a correlation coefficient is to $r = 0$, the weaker the correlation and the less likely that two factors are related; the closer a correlation coefficient is to $r = \pm 1.0$, the stronger the correlation and the more likely that two factors are related.

The strength of a correlation reflects how consistently values for each factor change. When plotted in a graph, a stronger correlation means that the values for each factor change in a related pattern—the data points fall closer to a regression line, or the straight line that best fits a set of data points. Figure 8.5 shows two positive correlations between exercise (Factor X) and body image satisfaction (Factor Y), and Figure 8.6 shows two negative correlations between absences in class (Factor X) and quiz grades (Factor Y). In both figures, the closer a set of data points falls to the regression line, the stronger the correlation; hence, the closer a correlation coefficient is to $r = \pm 1.0$.

> The closer a set of data points falls to a regression line, the stronger the correlation.

The Correlation Coefficient

The most commonly used formula for computing r is the **Pearson correlation coefficient**, which is used to determine the strength and direction of the relationship between two factors on an interval or a ratio scale of measurement. Alternative formulas for computing a correlation with many scales of measurement exist,

> The **Pearson correlation coefficient** is used to measure the direction and strength of the linear relationship of two factors in which the data for both factors are on an interval or a ratio scale of measurement.

Figure 8.5 The Consistency of Scores for a Positive Correlation

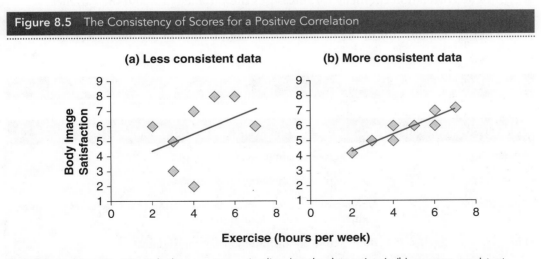

Both figures show approximately the same regression line, but the data points in (b) are more consistent because they fall closer to the regression line than in (a).

Figure 8.6   The Consistency of Scores for a Negative Correlation

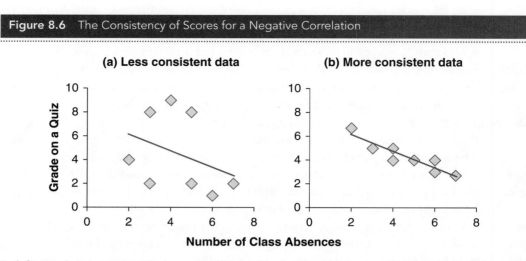

(a) Less consistent data   **(b) More consistent data**

Grade on a Quiz (y-axis, 0 to 10)

Number of Class Absences (x-axis, 0 to 8)

Both figures show approximately the same regression line, but the data points in (b) are more consistent because they fall closer to the regression line than in (a).

as identified in Table 8.2; however, each of these alternative formulas was derived from the formula for the Pearson correlation coefficient, so only the Pearson formula will be described in this section. The formula for the Pearson correlation coefficient is a measure of the variance of data points from a regression line that is shared by the values of two factors (X and Y), divided by the total variance measured:

$$r = \frac{\text{Variance shared by } X \text{ and } Y}{\text{Total variance measured}}$$

The correlation coefficient, r, measures the variance of X and the variance of Y, which constitutes the total variance that can be measured. The total variance is placed in the denominator of the formula for r. The variance in the numerator, called

Table 8.2   The Scales of Measurement for Factors Tested Using Correlation Coefficients

Correlation coefficient	Scale of measurement for correlated variables
Pearson	Both factors are interval or ratio data.
Spearman	Both factors are ranked or ordinal data.
Point-Biserial	One factor is dichotomous (nominal data), and a second factor is continuous (interval or ratio data).
Phi	Both factors are dichotomous (nominal data).

covariance, is the amount or proportion of the total variance that is shared by X and Y. The larger the covariance, the closer data points will fall to the regression line. When all data points for X and Y fall exactly on a regression line, the covariance equals the total variance, making

> **Covariance** is the extent to which the values of two factors (X and Y) vary together. The closer data points fall to the regression line, the more the values of two factors vary together.

the formula for r equal to +1.0 or −1.0, depending on the direction of the relationship between two factors. The farther that data points fall from the regression line, the smaller the covariance will be compared with the total variance in the denominator, resulting in a value of r closer to 0.

If we conceptualize covariance as circles, as illustrated in Figure 8.7, then the variance of each factor (X and Y) will be contained within each circle. The two circles, then, contain the total measured variance. The covariance of X and Y reflects the extent to which the total variance or the two circles overlap. In terms of computing r, the overlap or covariance is placed in the numerator; the total variance contained within each circle is placed in the denominator. The more the two circles overlap, the more the covariance (in the numerator) will equal the independent variances contained within each circle (in the denominator)—and the closer r will be to ±1.0.

Figure 8.7 Covariance Between X and Y

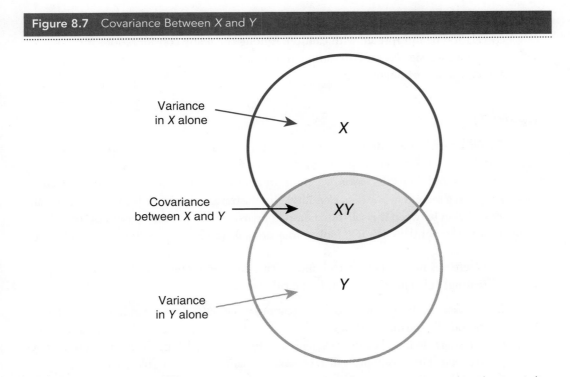

Each circle represents the variance of a factor. The variances of two factors covary inasmuch as the two circles overlap. The more overlap or shared variance of two factors, the more the two factors are related.

1. The value of the _____ provides an estimate of the strength and direction of the relationship between two factors.

2. A professor measures a negative correlation between time spent partying and grades. Interpret this result.

3. A researcher records a correlation of $r = +.02$.

   A. Identify the direction of this correlation.

   B. Identify the strength of this correlation.

4. How will the data points appear in a graph for two factors with values that change consistently?

Answers: 1. correlation coefficient (r); 2. As time spent partying increases, grades decrease; 3. A. The direction of the correlation is positive, B. The strength of the correlation is weak because .02 is close to 0; 4. The data points will fall close to the regression line.

8.9 Limitations in Interpretation

Fundamental limitations using the correlational method require that a significant correlation be interpreted with caution. Among the many considerations for interpreting a significant correlation, in this section we consider causality, outliers, and restriction of range.

Correlation does not demonstrate cause.

Causality

Using a correlational design, we do not manipulate an independent variable, and we certainly make little effort to control for other possible factors that may also vary with the two variables we measured. For this reason, a significant correlation does not show that one factor causes changes in a second factor (i.e., causality). To illustrate, suppose we measure a significant negative correlation between the self-rated mood of participants and the amount of food they eat daily (in calories per day). We will look at four possible interpretations for this correlation.

1. Decreases in how people feel (mood) can cause an increase in the amount they eat (eating). This possibility cannot be ruled out.

2. Increases in the amount people eat (eating) can cause a decrease in how people feel (mood). So the direction of causality can be in the opposite direction. Hence, instead of changes in mood causing changes in eating, maybe changes in eating cause changes in mood. This possibility, called **reverse causality**, cannot be ruled out either.

3. The two factors could be systematic, meaning that they work together to cause a change. If two factors are systematic, then Conclusions 1 and 2 could both be correct. The worse people feel, the more they eat, and the more people eat, the worse they feel. This possibility, that each factor causes the other, cannot be ruled out either.

4. Changes in both factors may be caused by a third unanticipated **confound** or **confound variable**. Perhaps biological factors, such as increased parasympathetic activity, make people feel worse and increase how much they want to eat. So, it is increased parasympathetic activity that could be causing changes in both mood and eating. This confound variable and any number of additional confound variables could be causing changes in mood and eating and cannot be ruled out either.

Reverse causality is a problem that arises when the direction of causality between two factors can be in either direction.

Reverse causality occurs when the direction of causality for two factors, A and B, cannot be determined. Hence, changes in Factor A could cause changes in Factor B, or changes in Factor B could cause changes in Factor A.

A **confound** or **confound variable** is an unanticipated variable not accounted for in a research study that could be causing or associated with observed changes in one or more measured variables.

Figure 8.8 summarizes each possible explanation for an observed correlation between mood and eating. The correlational design cannot distinguish between these four possible

Figure 8.8 Four Potential Explanations for a Significant Correlation

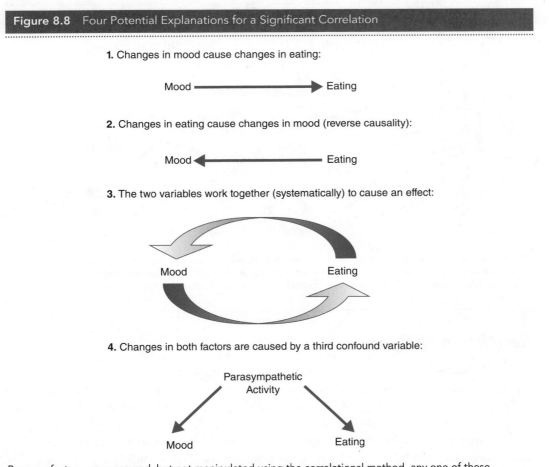

1. Changes in mood cause changes in eating:

Mood ⟶ Eating

2. Changes in eating cause changes in mood (reverse causality):

Mood ⟵ Eating

3. The two variables work together (systematically) to cause an effect:

Mood ⟷ Eating

4. Changes in both factors are caused by a third confound variable:

Parasympathetic Activity

Mood   Eating

Because factors are measured, but not manipulated using the correlational method, any one of these possibilities could explain a significant correlation.

An **outlier** is a score that falls substantially above or below most other scores in a data set.

explanations. Instead, a significant correlation shows that two factors are related. It does not provide an explanation for how or why they are related.

Outliers

Another limitation that can obscure the correlation or relationship between two factors is when an outlier is in the data. An **outlier** is a score that falls substantially above or below most other scores in a data set and can alter the direction and the strength of an observed correlation. Figure 8.9a shows data for the relationship between income and education without an outlier in the data. Figure 8.9b shows how an outlier, such as the income earned by a child movie star, changes the relationship between two factors. Notice in Figure 8.9 that the outlier changed both the direction and the strength of the correlation.

Figure 8.9   The Effects of an Outlier

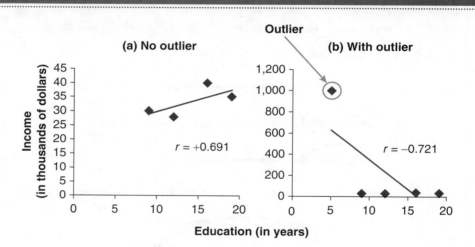

(a) The graph displays a typical correlation between income and education, with more education being associated with higher income. (b) The graph shows the same data with an additional outlier of a child movie star who earns $1 million. The inclusion of this outlier changed the direction and the strength of the correlation.

Restriction of Range

When interpreting a correlation, it is also important to avoid making conclusions about relationships that fall beyond the range of data measured. The **restriction of range** problem occurs when the range of data measured in a sample is restricted or smaller than the range of data in the general population.

Figure 8.10 shows how the range of data measured in a sample can lead to erroneous conclusions about the relationship between two factors in a given population. This figure

Figure 8.10   The Effects of Restriction of Range

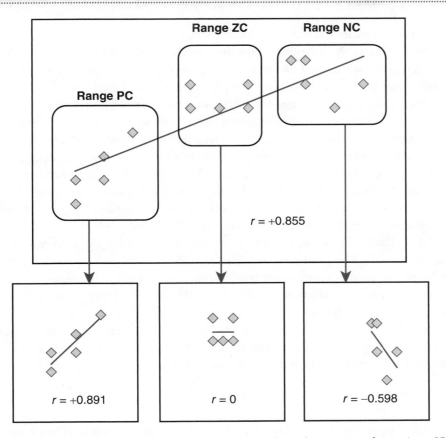

In this population, shown in the top graph, there is a positive correlation between two factors (r = +.855). Also depicted are three possible samples we could select from this population. Range PC shows a positive correlation (r = +.891), Range ZC shows a zero correlation (r = 0), and Range NC shows a negative correlation (r = −.598)—all within the same population. Because different ranges of data within the same population can show very different patterns, correlations should never be interpreted beyond the range of data measured in a sample.

shows the positive correlation for a hypothetical population (top graph) and the correlations in three possible samples we could select from this population (smaller graphs below). Notice that, depending on the range of data measured, we could identify a positive correlation, a negative correlation, or zero correlation from the same

Restriction of range is a problem that arises when the range of data for one or both correlated factors in a sample is limited or restricted, compared with the range of data in the population from which the sample was selected.

population, although the data in the population are actually positively correlated. To avoid the problem of restriction of range, the direction and the strength of a correlation should only be generalized to a population within the limited range of measurements observed in the sample.

8.10 Correlation, Regression, and Prediction

The correlation coefficient, r, is used to measure the extent to which two factors (X and Y) are related. The value of r indicates the direction and strength of a correlation. When r is negative, the values of two factors change in opposite directions; when r is positive, the values of two factors change in the same direction. The closer r is to ±1.0, the stronger the correlation, and the more closely two factors are related.

We can use the information provided by r to predict values of one factor, given known values of a second factor. Recall that the strength of a correlation reflects how closely a set of data points fits to a regression line (the straight line that most closely fits a set of data points). We can use the value of r to compute the equation of a regression line and then use this equation to predict values of one factor, given known values of a second factor in a population. This procedure is called **linear regression** (also called **regression**).

To use linear regression, we identity two types of variables: the predictor variable and the criterion variable. The **predictor variable** (X) is the variable with values that are known and can be used to predict values of the criterion variable; the predictor variable is plotted on the x-axis of a graph. The **criterion variable** (Y) is the variable with unknown values that we are trying to predict, given known values of the predictor variable; the criterion variable is plotted on the y-axis of a graph. If we know the equation of the regression line, we can predict values of the criterion variable, Y, so long as we know values of the predictor variable, X. To make use of this equation, we identify the following equation of a straight line:

$$Y = bX + a$$

In this equation, Y is a value we plot for the criterion variable, X is a value we plot for the predictor variable, b is the slope of a straight line, and a is the y-intercept (where the line crosses the y-axis). Given a set of data, researchers can find the values of a and b, and then use the equation they found to predict outcomes of Y.

To illustrate the use of the regression line to predict outcomes, consider a study conducted by Chen, Dai, and Dong (2008). In this study, participants completed a revised version of the Aitken Procrastination Inventory (API), and their level of procrastination was recorded. The researchers found that the following regression equation could be used to predict procrastination (Y) based on known scores on the API (X):

$$\hat{Y} = 0.146X - 2.922$$

> A correlation cannot describe data beyond the range of data observed in a sample.

Linear regression, also called **regression**, is a statistical procedure used to determine the equation of a regression line to a set of data points and to determine the extent to which the regression equation can be used to predict values of one factor, given known values of a second factor in a population.

The **predictor variable** (*X*) is the variable with values that are known and can be used to predict values of another variable.

The **criterion variable** (*Y*) is the to-be-predicted variable with unknown values that can be predicted or estimated, given known values of the predictor variable.

In this equation, $\hat{Y}$ is the predicted value of Y given known scores on the API, $a = 2.922$, and $b = 0.146$. Using this information, we could have a student complete the API, plug his or her API score into the equation for X, and solve for $\hat{Y}$ to find the procrastination level we predict for that student.

The advantage of using linear regression is that we can use the equation of the regression line to predict how people will behave or perform. A caution of using this procedure, however, is that smaller correlations, or those closer to $r = 0$, will produce inaccurate predictions using the equation of the regression line because the data points will fall far from it. Likewise, the stronger the correlation, or the closer to $r = \pm 1.0$, the more accurate the predictions made using the equation of the regression line because the data points will fall closer to it.

> The equation of the regression line can be used to predict outcomes of a criterion variable.

LEARNING CHECK 5 ✓

1. A correlational design does not demonstrate cause. Why?

2. True of false: An outlier can influence both the *direction* and the *strength* of an observed correlation.

3. _____ occurs when the range of data for one or both correlated factors in a sample is limited or restricted, compared with the range of data in the population from which the sample was selected.

4. What procedure is used to predict outcomes of one factor given known values of a second factor?

Answers: 1. Because we do not manipulate an independent variable, and we make little effort to control for other possible factors that may also vary with the two variables we measured; 2. True; 3. Restriction of range; 4. Linear regression.

8.11 SPSS in Focus: Correlation and Linear Regression

The correlational design will likely require the use of a correlation coefficient or linear regression to statistically analyze measured data. In this section, we describe how to compute each type of statistic using SPSS.

Pearson Correlation Coefficient

To compute a Pearson correlation coefficient using SPSS, suppose we test the hypothesis that greater mobile phone use is associated with increased stress, as has been tested in published research studies (see Murdock, Gorman, & Robbins, 2015; Reid et al., 2009; Thomée, Härenstam, & Hagberg, 2011). To measure mobile phone use, we can use the 27-item Mobile Phone Problem Use Scale (MPPUS; Bianchi & Phillips, 2005). To measure stress, we can use the 10-item Perceived Stress Scale (PSS; Cohen & Williamson, 1988). Using these measures, we will enter the data shown in Figure 8.11 to compute a Pearson correlation coefficient using SPSS.

1. Click on the **Variable View** tab and enter *MPPUS* in the **Name column**; enter *PSS* in the Name column below it. Reduce the value to 0 in the **Decimals column** for both rows.

2. Click on the **Data View** tab. Enter the data for MPPUS in the first column; enter the data for PSS in the second column.

3. Go to the menu bar and click **Analyze**, then **Correlate**, and then **Bivariate** to display a dialog box.

4. Using the arrows, move both variables into the **Variables** box.

5. Select **OK**, or select **Paste** and click the **Run** command.

The SPSS output table, shown in Table 8.3, is set up in a matrix with *MPPUS* and *PSS* listed in the rows and columns. Each cell in the matrix gives the direction and strength of the correlation ($r = .540$ for mobile phone use and stress; this value is shown with an asterisk for significant correlations), the significance ($p = .014$; how to interpret a p value is described in Chapters 10–12 and 14), and the sample size ($N = 20$). To make a decision: If a correlation is significant, then the decision is that the correlation observed in the sample will also be observed in the larger population from which the sample was selected. We can report a correlation in a research journal using the guidelines provided in the *Publication Manual of the American Psychological Association* (APA, 2009). Using these guidelines, we state the value of r, the p value, and the sample size as shown:

A Pearson correlation indicates that greater mobile phone use is associated with greater perceived stress, $r = .540$, $p = .014$, $N = 20$.

Linear Regression

For situations in which we want to know whether values for one factor predict values for a second factor, we use linear regression. As an example, suppose we conduct a test similar to that computed by Privitera and Wallace (2011). In that study, the researchers tested if scores on the 11-item EDIS-S predicted how much people like the taste of sugar. To measure liking for sugar, participants drank sugar water and rated how

MPPUS (Mobile Phone Use)	PSS (Perceived Stress)
142	25
115	23
127	25
122	28
137	20
103	22
85	20
198	23
95	12
131	16
158	30
142	15
140	25
111	20
137	19
153	22
132	17
192	30
160	28
180	29

The regression line is given in the scatter plot. Both the table and the scatter plot show the same data.

Table 8.3 SPSS Output Table for the Pearson Correlation Coefficient

Correlations

		MPPUS	PSS
MPPUS	Pearson Correlation	1	.540[*]
	Sig. (2-tailed)		.014
	N	20	20
PSS	Pearson Correlation	.540[*]	1
	Sig. (2-tailed)	.014	
	N	20	20

[*]. Correlation is significant at the 0.05 level (2-tailed).

much they liked the taste on a 100-millimeter line scale in which higher ratings indicated greater liking for the sugar water. Using data similar to those observed in the study by Privitera and Wallace (2011), we will enter the data shown in Figure 8.12 to compute linear regression using SPSS.

1. Click on the **Variable View** tab and enter *EDISS* in the **Name column**; enter *liking* in the Name column below it. Reduce the value to 0 in the **Decimals column** for both rows.

2. Click on the **Data View** tab. Enter the data for the EDIS-S in the first column; enter the data for liking in the second column.

3. Go to the menu bar and click **Analyze**, then **Regression**, then **Linear...** to display a dialog box.

4. Using the arrows, move the criterion variable, *liking*, in the **Dependent** box; move the predictor variable, *EDISS*, into the **Independent(s)** box.

5. Select **OK**, or select **Paste** and click the **Run** command.

The SPSS output table, shown in Table 8.4, displays three ways to analyze the data. The top table shows the proportion of variance, $R^2 = .797$, which is an estimate for how well EDIS-S scores predict ratings of liking for the sugar water. Values closer to 1.0 indicate better predictions. Results for the regression analysis are given in the middle

Figure 8.12 A Table and Scatter Plot Showing the Relationship Between EDIS-S Scores and Liking for Sugar Water

EDIS-S	Liking (rating)
45	62
55	70
47	60
54	68
28	45
77	82
34	36
56	48
72	88
45	54
65	80
55	70
76	98
68	90
50	50

The regression line is given in the scatter plot. Both the table and the scatter plot show the same data.

table. Based on the results in that table, we conclude that EDIS-S scores (the predictor variable) do significantly predict a liking for sugar water (the criterion variable), as indicated by the p value in the **Sig.** column (how to interpret a p value is described further in Chapters 10–12 and 14). To make a decision: If a regression analysis is significant, then the decision is that the predictive relationship observed in the sample will also be observed in the larger population from which the sample was selected. To determine the direction of the relationship between EDIS-S scores and liking for the sugar water, we look at the standardized beta coefficient given in the bottom table. In this example, the beta (β) coefficient is positive, $\beta = +.893$, indicating that higher scores on the EDIS-S predict higher ratings for the sugar water.

Based on guidelines in the *Publication Manual of the American Psychological Association* (APA, 2009), we report the results of a regression analysis with one predictor variable by including the value of R^2 (top table), the value of β (bottom table), and the results of the regression analysis (middle table; reported as an F value) as shown:

A regression analysis showed that EDIS-S scores significantly predicted ratings of liking for sugar water, $\beta = +.893$, $F(1, 13) = 50.978$, $p < .001$ ($R^2 = .797$).

Table 8.4 SPSS Output for Linear Regression

Model Summary

Model	R	R Square	Adjusted R Square	Std. Error of the Estimate
1	.893[a]	.797	.781	8.554

a. Predictors: (Constant), EDISS

ANOVA[a]

Model		Sum of Squares	df	Mean Square	F	Sig.
1	Regression	3729.789	1	3729.789	50.978	.000[b]
	Residual	951.145	13	73.165		
	Total	4680.933	14			

a. Dependent Variable: liking
b. Predictors: (Constant), EDISS

Coefficients[a]

Model		Unstandardized Coefficients		Standardized Coefficients	t	Sig.
		B	Std. Error	Beta		
1	(Constant)	4.674	8.968		.521	.611
	EDISS	1.126	.158	.893	7.140	.000

a. Dependent Variable: liking

LO 1 Identify and construct open-ended, partially open-ended, and restricted survey items.

- An *open-ended item* is a question or statement in a survey that allows the respondent to give any response in his or her own words, without restriction. This type of question is most often used in qualitative research.
- A *partially open-ended item* is a question or statement in a survey that includes a few restricted answer options and then a last option that allows participants to respond in their own words in case the few restricted options do not fit with the answer they want to give.
- A *restricted item* is a question or statement in a survey that includes a restricted number of answer options to which participants must respond. This type of question is most often used in quantitative research.

LO 2 Identify nine rules for writing valid and reliable survey items.

- Nine rules for writing valid and reliable survey items are as follows:
  - Keep it simple.
  - Avoid double-barreled items.
  - Use neutral or unbiased language.
  - Minimize the use of negative wording.
  - Avoid the response set pitfall.
  - Use rating scales consistently.
  - Limit the points on a rating scale.
  - Label or anchor the rating scale points.
  - Minimize item and survey length.

LO 3 Describe methods of administering written surveys and interview surveys.

- A survey can be written (in print or electronically) or spoken (such as in an interview). A written survey can be administered in person, by mail, or using the Internet. An interview survey can be administered face to face, by telephone, or in focus groups. In-person and face-to-face surveys have the best response rates. In addition, written surveys are preferred to interview surveys in quantitative research partly because interviews are prone to a possible interviewer bias.

LO 4 Explain how response rates to surveys can limit the interpretation of survey results.

- The problem of low response rates is that people who respond to surveys are probably different from those who do not respond. Because we cannot collect data from people who fail to respond, it is difficult to know the exact characteristics of this group of nonresponders. For this reason, we cannot know for sure whether survey results of those who do respond are representative of the larger population of interest, which includes those who do not respond to surveys.

LO 5 Identify how to appropriately handle and administer surveys.

- To appropriately handle and administer surveys, the survey itself should not be offensive or stressful to the respondent; do not coerce respondents into answering questions or completing a survey; do not harass respondents in any way for recruitment purposes; protect the confidentiality or anonymity of respondents.

LO 6 Identify and describe the direction and strength of a correlation.

- The **correlation coefficient**, r, is used to measure the extent to which two factors (X and Y) are related. The value of r indicates the direction and strength of a correlation. When r is negative, the values for two factors change in opposite directions; when r is positive, the values for two factors change in the same direction. The closer r is to ±1.0, the stronger the correlation, and the more closely two factors are related.
- When plotted in a graph, the strength of a correlation is reflected by the distance that data points fall from the **regression line**. The closer that data points fall to a regression line, or the straight line that best fits a set of data points, the stronger the correlation or relationship between two factors.

LO 7 Explain how causality, outliers, and restriction of range can limit the interpretation of a correlation coefficient.

- Three considerations that must be made to accurately interpret a correlation coefficient are as follows: (1) correlations do not demonstrate causality, (2) outliers can change the direction and the strength of a correlation, and (3) never generalize the direction and the strength of a correlation beyond the range of data measured in a sample (restriction of range).

LO 8 Explain how linear regression can be used to predict outcomes.

- We can use the information provided by r to predict values of one factor, given known values of a second factor using a procedure called **linear regression**. Specifically, we can use the value of r to compute the equation of a regression line and then use this equation to predict values of one factor, given known values of a second factor in a population. Using the following equation of the regression line, $Y = bX + a$, we can predict values of the criterion variable, Y, so long as we know values of the predictor variable, X.

LO 9 Compute the Pearson correlation coefficient and linear regression using SPSS.

- SPSS can be used to compute the Pearson correlation coefficient using the **Analyze, Correlate,** and **Bivariate** options in the menu bar. These actions will display a dialog box that allows you to identify the variables and to run the correlation (for more details, see Section 8.11).
- SPSS can be used to compute linear regression using the **Analyze, Regression,** and **Linear...** options in the menu bar. These actions will display a dialog box that allows you to identify the variables and to run the linear regression (for more details, see Section 8.11).

survey research design

survey

open-ended item

partially open-ended item

restricted item

Likert scale

double-barreled items

response set

reverse coded item

bipolar scales

anchors

interviewer bias

random digit dialing

response rate

theoretical generalization

empirical generalization

correlational research design

correlation coefficient

scatter plot

scatter diagram

scatter gram

data points

regression line

positive correlation

negative correlation

Pearson correlation coefficient

covariance

reverse causality

confound

confound variable

outlier

restriction of range

linear regression

regression

predictor variable

criterion variable

REVIEW QUESTIONS

1. Distinguish between an open-ended and a partially open-ended question.

2. Identify the problem or flaw with each of the following survey items. Assume that each item is rated on a 5-point scale from 1 (*strongly disagree*) to 5 (*strongly agree*).

   A. I hate driving behind old people.

   B. I am happy when I am alone, and I do not like to be visited.

   C. I have difficulty engaging in convoluted situations.

   D. My friends are not willing to participate in activities in which I am not willing to participate.

3. State two problems with the following scale for a survey item:

      1   2   3   4   5   6   7   8   9   10   11
               Somewhat Flawed

4. What are three reasons that more participants are willing to complete a survey administered in person?

5. Which type of bias can occur when a survey is administered in an interview?

6. State four responsible and appropriate ways to handle and administer surveys.

7. A researcher reports that the farther college students are from their parents, the more often they communicate with their parents (either by phone or by e-mail). Is this an example of a positive or a negative correlation?

8. An instructor reports that as the number of student interruptions during class decreases, student scores on in-class quizzes increase. Is this an example of a positive or a negative correlation?

9. The following graphs display the data points for a linear correlation. Based on the information provided in these graphs, answer the following questions.

   A. Which graph displays the negative correlation? Explain.

   B. Which graph displays the stronger correlation? Explain.

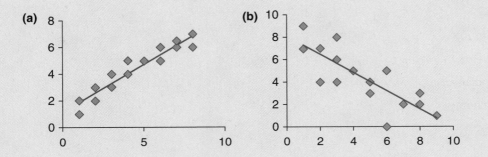

10. A researcher finds that the softer the tone that a parent uses to speak to his or her child, the less often the child has outbursts.

    A. Is this a positive or negative correlation?

    B. Is reverse causality possible for this example? Explain.

11. True or false: Outliers can change the direction and strength of a correlation.

12. When does restriction of range limit the interpretation of a significant correlation?

13. The equation of a regression line can be used to _____ values of one factor, given known values of a second factor.

14. What is the relationship between the predictor variable and the criterion variable?

ACTIVITIES

1. Follow the eight rules for writing valid and reliable survey items to construct a short 6- to 10-item survey to measure a behavior that you are interested in. Then give the survey to at least five people, and summarize the responses given for each item in your survey.

2. Think of two factors that you predict will be related. Measure each factor in a sample of at least 10 people. Enter the data you collect into SPSS, and follow the instructions for computing a Pearson correlation coefficient, given in this chapter. Summarize the results in terms of the direction and the strength of the correlation between the two factors you measured.

QUASI-EXPERIMENTAL AND EXPERIMENTAL RESEARCH DESIGNS

Identify a problem

- Determine an area of interest.
- Review the literature.
- Identify new ideas in your area of interest.
- Develop a research hypothesis.

Develop a research plan

- Define the variables being tested.
- Identify participants or subjects and determine how to sample them.
- Select a research strategy and design.
- Evaluate ethics and obtain institutional approval to conduct research.

Generate more new ideas

- Results support your hypothesis—refine or expand on your ideas.
- Results do not support your hypothesis—reformulate a new idea or start over.

After reading this chapter, you should be able to:

1 Define and identify a quasi-experiment and a quasi-independent variable.
2 Identify and describe two one-group quasi-experimental research designs: the posttest-only and pretest-posttest designs.
3 Identify and describe two nonequivalent control group quasi-experimental research designs: the posttest-only and pretest-posttest designs.
4 Identify and describe three time series quasi-experimental research designs: basic, interrupted, and control designs.
5 Identify and describe three developmental quasi-experimental research designs: longitudinal, cross-sectional, and cohort-sequential designs.
6 Define the single-case experimental design.
7 Identify and describe three types of single-case research designs: the reversal, multiple-baseline, and changing-criterion designs.
8 Identify in a graph the stability and magnitude of a dependent measure, and explain how each is related to the internal validity of a single-case design.
9 Identify three ways that researchers can strengthen the external validity of a result using a single-case design.

Conduct the study

- Execute the research plan and measure or record the data.

Communicate the results

- Method of communication: oral, written, or in a poster.
- Style of communication: APA guidelines are provided to help prepare style and format.

Analyze and evaluate the data

- Analyze and evaluate the data as they relate to the research hypothesis.
- Summarize data and research results.

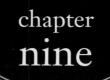

nine

QUASI-EXPERIMENTAL AND SINGLE-CASE EXPERIMENTAL DESIGNS

In the natural world, the environment or situation you find yourself in can be dynamic. You need look no further than a college classroom. Suppose, for example, that you take a college exam in which the average student scored a 50%. Why were the exam grades so low? Was the professor ineffective in his or her teaching? Did the students study for the exam? Was the exam itself not fair? Was the material being studied too difficult or at a too high a level? In this example, the answer can be difficult to identify because the environment is constrained by preexisting factors—the time, date, content, professor, and students enrolled in the course were not assigned by a researcher, but instead were determined by the school and students. Accounting for these preexisting factors is important to determine why the exam grades were low.

In other situations, we can have difficulty obtaining large samples of participants. If a company were a small business, then it would have few employees, or if a behavioral disorder were rare, then it would afflict few people. In these cases, we probably could not obtain a large sample, so it would be advantageous to observe the behavior of only one or a few individuals. For example, we could observe an employee after a merger as new policy changes successively go into effect, or we could observe a patient's health across multiple phases of treatment. In each case, we follow one participant and observe his or her behavior over time.

In this chapter, we introduce quasi-experimental designs used in science to make observations in settings that are constrained by preexisting factors. We also introduce many methods used to assess the behavior of a single participant or subject using single-case experimental designs, typically used when a large sample cannot be obtained.

QUASI-EXPERIMENTAL DESIGNS

Suppose we hypothesize that high school graduates who attend college will value an education more than those who do not attend college. To test this hypothesis, we could select a sample of high school graduates from the same graduating class and divide them into two groups: those who attended college (Group College) and those who did not attend college (Group No College). We could then have all participants complete a survey in which higher scores on the survey indicate a higher value placed on obtaining an education. If the hypothesis is correct and we set up this study correctly, then participants in Group College should show higher scores on the survey than participants in Group No College.

A **quasi-experimental research design** is the use of methods and procedures to make observations in a study that is structured similar to an experiment, but the conditions and experiences of participants lack some control because the study lacks random assignment, includes a preexisting factor (i.e., a variable that is not manipulated), or does not include a comparison/control group.

A **quasi-independent variable** is a preexisting variable that is often a characteristic inherent to an individual, which differentiates the groups or conditions being compared in a research study. Because the levels of the variable are preexisting, it is not possible to randomly assign participants to groups.

Notice in this example that participants controlled which group they were assigned to—they either attended college or did not. Hence, in this example, the factor of interest (whether or not students attended college) was a quasi-independent variable. When a factor in a study is not manipulated (i.e., quasi-independent), this typically means that the study is a type of quasi-experimental research design. In this chapter, we separate the content into two major sections: quasi-experimental designs and single-case experimental designs. We begin this chapter with an introduction to the type of research design illustrated here: the quasi-experimental research design.

9.1 An Overview of Quasi-Experimental Designs

In this major section, we introduce a common type of research design called the quasi-experimental research design. The **quasi-experimental research design**, also defined in Chapter 6, is structured similar to an experiment, except that this design does one or both of the following:

1. It includes a **quasi-independent variable** (also defined in Chapter 6).

2. It lacks an appropriate or equivalent control group.

In the example used to introduce this section, the preexisting factor was college attendance (yes, no). The researchers did not manipulate or randomly assign participants to groups. Instead participants were assigned to Group College or Group No College based on whether they attended college prior to the study. In other words, the participants, not the researcher, controlled which group they were assigned to. In this way, the study described to introduce this section was a quasi-experiment—the study was structured like an experiment in that differences in how students value college were compared between groups, but it lacked

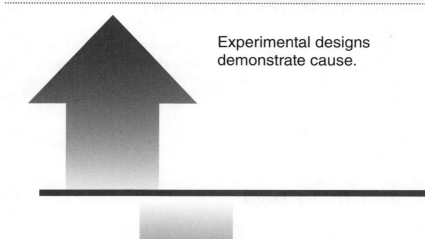

Experimental designs demonstrate cause.

Quasi-experimental and nonexperimental designs lack the control needed to demonstrate cause.

The line represents the requirements for demonstrating cause: randomization, manipulation, and comparison/control. A quasi-experiment lacks at least one of these requirements and so fails to demonstrate cause.

a manipulation (of the groups: whether students attended or did not attend college) and randomization (of assigning participants to each group).

Hence, a quasi-experiment is not an experiment because, as illustrated in Figure 9.1, the design does not meet all three requirements for demonstrating cause. In the college attendance study, for example, additional unique characteristics of participants, other than whether or not they attended college, could also be different between groups and therefore could also be causing differences between groups. For example, levels of motivation and academic ability may also be different between people who attend and do not attend college. When other possible causes cannot be ruled out, the design does not demonstrate cause.

In this major section, we introduce four categories of quasi-experimental research designs used in the behavioral sciences:

- One-group designs (posttest only and pretest-posttest)
- Nonequivalent control group designs (posttest only and pretest-posttest)
- Time series designs (basic, interrupted, and control)
- Developmental designs (longitudinal, cross-sectional, and cohort-sequential)

> Quasi-experiments include a quasi-independent variable and/or lack a control group.

9.2 Quasi-Experimental Design: One-Group Designs

In some situations, researchers ask questions that require the observation of a single group. When only one group is observed, the study lacks a comparison group and so does not demonstrate cause; that is, the study is a quasi-experiment. Two types of one-group quasi-experiments are the following:

One-group designs lack a control group.

- One-group posttest-only design

- One-group pretest-posttest design

One-Group Posttest-Only Design

The type of quasi-experiment most susceptible to threats to internal validity is the **one-group posttest-only design**, which is also called the *one-shot case study* (Campbell & Stanley, 1966). Using the one-group posttest-only design, a researcher measures a dependent variable for one group of participants following a treatment. For example, as illustrated in Figure 9.2, after a professor gives a lecture (the treatment), he may record students' grades on an exam out of 100 possible points (the dependent variable) to test their learning.

The major limitation of this design is that it lacks a comparison or control group. Consider, for example, the exam scores following the lecture. If exam scores are high following the lecture, can we conclude that the lecture is effective? How can we know for sure if scores would have been high even without the lecture? We cannot know this because we have nothing to compare this outcome to; we have no control group. Hence, the design is susceptible to many threats to internal validity, such as history effects (unanticipated events that can co-occur with the exam) and maturation effects (natural changes in learning). In all, these limitations make the one-group posttest-only design a poor research design.

A **one-group posttest-only design** is a quasi-experimental research design in which a dependent variable is measured for one group of participants following a treatment.

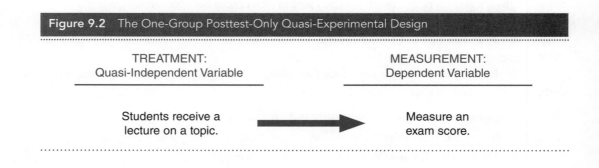

Figure 9.2 The One-Group Posttest-Only Quasi-Experimental Design

TREATMENT: Quasi-Independent Variable	MEASUREMENT: Dependent Variable
Students receive a lecture on a topic.	Measure an exam score.

One-Group Pretest-Posttest Design

One way to minimize problems related to having no control or comparison group is to measure the same dependent variable in one group of participants before (pretest) and after (posttest) a treatment. Using this type of research design, called a **one-group pretest-posttest design**, we measure scores before and again following a treatment, then compare the difference between pretest and posttest scores. The advantage is that we can compare scores after a treatment to scores on the same measure in the same participants prior to the treatment. The disadvantage is that the one-group design does not include a no-treatment control group and therefore is still prone to many threats to internal validity, including those associated with observing the same participants over time (e.g., testing effects and regression toward the mean).

> A **one-group pretest-posttest design** is a quasi-experimental research design in which the same dependent variable is measured in one group of participants before (pretest) and after (posttest) a treatment is administered.

To illustrate the one-group pretest-posttest design, we will look at the research example illustrated in Figure 9.3. Cooke, Holzhauser, Jones, Davis, and Finucane (2007) measured stress using the Perceived Occupational Stress Scale (POSS) among emergency department nurses before and after 12 weeks of aromatherapy massage treatment with music. Their results showed no change in occupational stress from before to after the treatment. A limitation of this design is that participants were not randomly assigned to groups. This means that any other factors related to stress, such as the extent to which nurses were short-staffed, how busy the emergency room was, or family problems among the nurses, were beyond the control of the researchers and could have also influenced the results. In addition, because the study lacked a control group with nurses who had no therapy at all, the design was susceptible to many threats to internal validity, as stated previously. Indeed, the authors of the study directly acknowledged that the use of "more rigorous randomization . . . and a control group would have enhanced analyses" (Cooke et al., 2007, p. 1701).

Figure 9.3 The One-Group Pretest-Posttest Quasi-Experimental Design

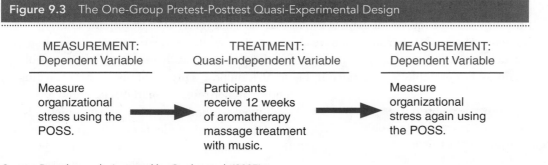

Source: Based on a design used by Cooke et al. (2007).

9.3 Quasi-Experimental Design: Nonequivalent Control Group Designs

A **nonequivalent control group** is a control group that is matched upon certain preexisting characteristics similar to those observed in a treatment group, but to which participants are not randomly assigned. In a quasi-experiment, a dependent variable measured in a treatment group is compared to that in the nonequivalent control group.

Selection differences are any differences, which are not controlled by the researcher, between individuals who are selected from preexisting groups or groups to which the researcher does not randomly assign participants.

Nonequivalent control group designs include a "matched" or nonequivalent control group.

In some cases, researchers can use nonequivalent control groups, when it is not possible to randomly assign participants to groups. A **nonequivalent control group** is a type of control group that is matched upon certain preexisting characteristics similar to those observed in a treatment group, but to which participants are not randomly assigned. For example, suppose a professor gives a new lecture method to your research methods class and gives a traditional method in another research methods class, then compares grades on the topic lectured. The classes are matched on certain characteristics: Both classes are on the same topic (research methods), offered at the same school, and taught by the same professor. However, the class taught using the traditional method is a nonequivalent control group because students in that class chose to enroll in the class, so they were not randomly assigned to that class. Any preexisting differences between students who tend to enroll for one class over another, called **selection differences**, could therefore explain any differences observed between the two classes. Two types of nonequivalent control group quasi-experiments are the following:

- Nonequivalent control group posttest-only design
- Nonequivalent control group pretest-posttest design

Nonequivalent Control Group Posttest-Only Design

Using the **nonequivalent control group posttest-only design**, a researcher measures a dependent variable following a treatment in one group and compares that measure to a nonequivalent control group that does not receive the treatment. The nonequivalent control group will have characteristics similar to the treatment group, but participants will not be randomly assigned to this group, typically because it is not possible to do so. For example, as illustrated in Figure 9.4, suppose a professor gives a new teaching method in her research methods class and gives a traditional method in another research methods class, then tests all students on the material taught. In this example, the nonequivalent control group was selected because it matched characteristics in the treatment group (e.g., all students were taking a research methods class). Students, however,

A **nonequivalent control group posttest-only design** is a quasi-experimental research design in which a dependent variable is measured following a treatment in one group and also in a nonequivalent control group that does not receive the treatment.

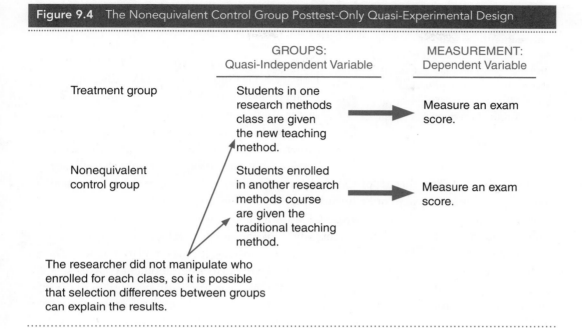

Figure 9.4 The Nonequivalent Control Group Posttest-Only Quasi-Experimental Design

GROUPS:
Quasi-Independent Variable

MEASUREMENT:
Dependent Variable

Treatment group

Students in one research methods class are given the new teaching method.

Measure an exam score.

Nonequivalent control group

Students enrolled in another research methods course are given the traditional teaching method.

Measure an exam score.

The researcher did not manipulate who enrolled for each class, so it is possible that selection differences between groups can explain the results.

enrolled themselves in each class; random assignment was not used, so the comparison is a nonequivalent control group.

A key limitation of this research design is that it is particularly susceptible to the threat of selection differences. In the example illustrated in Figure 9.4, because students enrolled in their college classes, they, and not the researcher, controlled which class they enrolled in. Therefore, any preexisting differences between students who choose one section of a class over another, such as how busy the students' daily schedules are or how motivated they are to attend earlier or later classes, may actually be causing differences in grades between classes. For this reason, the nonequivalent control group posttest-only design demonstrates only that a treatment is associated with differences between groups, and not that a treatment caused differences between groups, if any were observed.

Nonequivalent Control Group Pretest-Posttest Design

One way to minimize problems related to not having a comparison group is to measure a dependent variable in one group of participants observed before (pretest) and after (posttest) a treatment and also measure that same dependent variable at pretest and posttest in another nonequivalent control group that does not receive the treatment. This type of design is called the **nonequivalent control group pretest-posttest design**. The advantage of this design is that we can compare scores before and after a treatment in a group that receives the treatment and also in a nonequivalent control group that does not receive the treatment. While the nonequivalent control group will have characteristics similar to the treatment group, participants are not randomly assigned to this group, typically because it is not possible to do so. Hence, selection differences still can possibly explain observations made using this research design.

A **nonequivalent control group pretest-posttest design** is a quasi-experimental research design in which a dependent variable is measured in one group of participants before (pretest) and after (posttest) a treatment and that same dependent variable is also measured at pretest and posttest in another nonequivalent control group that does not receive the treatment.

To illustrate the nonequivalent control group pretest-posttest design, we will look at the research example in Figure 9.5. Reese and Miller (2006) used the Career Decision-Making Self-Efficacy Scale–Short Form (CDMSES-SF; Betz, Klein, & Taylor, 1996) to measure self-efficacy—that is, to measure how much students believed in their own ability to make decisions regarding their career. Reese and Miller hypothesized that a career development course would increase self-efficacy among students. To test this hypothesis, college students enrolled in a career development course (the treatment group) or an introductory psychology course (the nonequivalent control group) completed the CDMSES-SF during the first week and last week of their semester. As shown in Figure 9.6, students who took the career development course (the treatment group) showed a larger change or increase in self-efficacy compared with students in the nonequivalent control group who did not take the career development course.

A key limitation of this research design is that it is particularly susceptible to the threat of selection differences. In the example illustrated in Figure 9.5, because students enroll in college classes, they, and not the researcher, control what classes they will be in. Any preexisting differences between students who choose one class over another, then, could also

Figure 9.5 The Nonequivalent Control Group Pretest-Posttest Quasi-Experimental Design

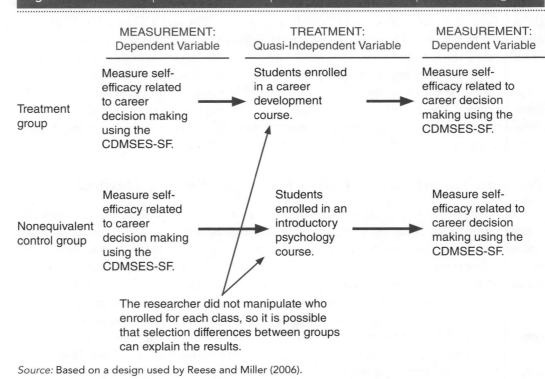

Source: Based on a design used by Reese and Miller (2006).

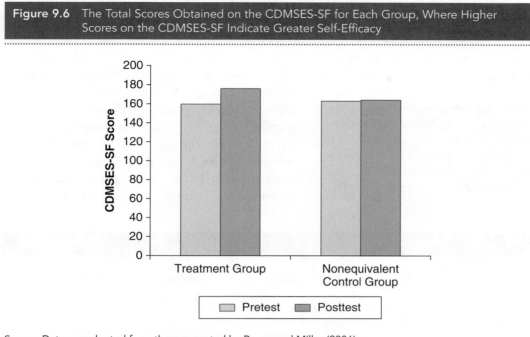

Source: Data are adapted from those reported by Reese and Miller (2006).

be causing differences between classes. For example, the authors of this study noted that some students in the career development course were forced to enroll due to academic probation, whereas enrollment in the introductory psychology course was entirely voluntary. This factor (forced vs. voluntary enrollment) also varied between the groups and therefore could be the cause or reason for the differences observed. Hence, the nonequivalent control group pretest-posttest design, like the posttest-only design, demonstrates only that a treatment is associated with differences between groups, and not that a treatment caused differences between groups, if any were observed.

9.4 Quasi-Experimental Design: Time Series Designs

In some situations, researchers observe one or two preexisting groups at many points in time before and after a treatment, and not just at one time, using designs called the time series quasi-experimental designs. Using these types of designs, we compare the pattern of change over time from before to following a treatment. Three types of time series quasi-experimental designs are as follows:

- Basic time series design
- Interrupted time series design
- Control time series design

Time series designs include many observations made before and after a treatment.

Basic Time Series Design

When researchers manipulate the treatment, they use a **basic time series design** to make a series of observations over time before and after a treatment. The advantage of measuring a dependent variable at multiple times before and after a treatment is that it eliminates the problem associated with only having a snapshot of behavior. To illustrate, suppose we test a treatment for improving alertness during the day. To use the basic time series design, we record alertness at multiple times before and after we give participants the treatment, as illustrated in Figure 9.7. Notice

A **basic time series design** is a quasi-experimental research design in which a dependent variable is measured at many different points in time in one group before and after a treatment that is manipulated by the researcher is administered.

Figure 9.7 The Time Series Quasi-Experimental Design

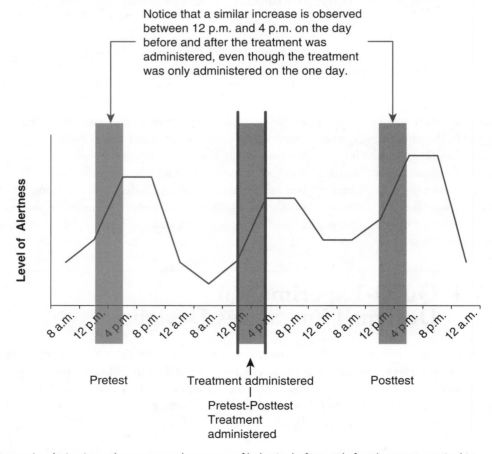

Notice that a similar increase is observed between 12 p.m. and 4 p.m. on the day before and after the treatment was administered, even though the treatment was only administered on the one day.

A time series design is used to compare the pattern of behavior before and after the treatment. In this example, the pattern that occurs before and after the treatment recurs at the same time of day, even without the treatment.

in the figure that a pretest (at 12 p.m.) and posttest (at 4 p.m.) measure can be misleading because the pattern observed before and after the treatment recurred without the treatment at the same time the day before and the day after the treatment was given. The basic time series design allows us to uniquely see this pattern by making a series of observations over time.

Using the basic time series design, the researcher manipulates or controls when the treatment will occur. The advantage of this design is that we can identify if the pattern of change in a dependent variable before and after the treatment occurs only during that period of time and not during other periods of time when the treatment is not administered. The disadvantage of this design is that only one group is observed, so we cannot compare the results in the treatment group to a group that never received the treatment.

> In a basic time series design, we manipulate the treatment; in an interrupted time series design, the treatment is naturally occurring.

Interrupted and Control Time Series Designs

In some situations, researchers will measure a dependent variable multiple times before and after a naturally occurring treatment or event. Examples of a naturally occurring treatment or event include a scheduled medical procedure, a wedding, a natural disaster, a change in public policy, a new law, and a political scandal. These events occur beyond the control of the researcher, so the researcher loses control over the timing of the manipulation. In these situations, when multiple measurements are taken before and after a naturally occurring treatment, researchers use the **interrupted time series design**.

> An **interrupted time series design** is a quasi-experimental research design in which a dependent variable is measured at many different points in time in one group before and after a treatment that naturally occurred.

As an example of the interrupted time series design, Khuder et al. (2007) measured hospital admission rates for coronary heart disease each month for 3 years before and 3 years after a smoking ban was implemented in Bowling Green, Ohio, in March 2002. For this study, the dashed line in Figure 9.8 shows that hospital admission rates for coronary heart disease declined in Bowling Green, 3 years following the implementation of the smoking ban.

An advantage of the interrupted time series design is that we can identify if the pattern of change in a dependent variable changes from before to following a naturally occurring treatment or event. The disadvantage of this design, like that for the basic time series design, is that only one group is observed, so we cannot compare the results in the treatment group to a group that never received a treatment. To address this disadvantage, we can include a matched or nonequivalent control group.

A basic or interrupted time series design that includes a matched or nonequivalent control group is called a **control time series design**. Khuder et al. (2007) included a matched control group by also recording hospital admission rates for coronary heart disease during the same time period in Kent, Ohio, which was a city determined to have

> A **control time series design** is a basic or interrupted time series quasi-experimental research design that also includes a nonequivalent control group that is observed during the same period of time as a treatment group, but does not receive the treatment.

Figure 9.8 Hospital Admission Rates for Coronary Heart Diseases per 10,000 Population (18 and Over) for 3 Years Before and 3 Years After Implementation of a Smoking Ban

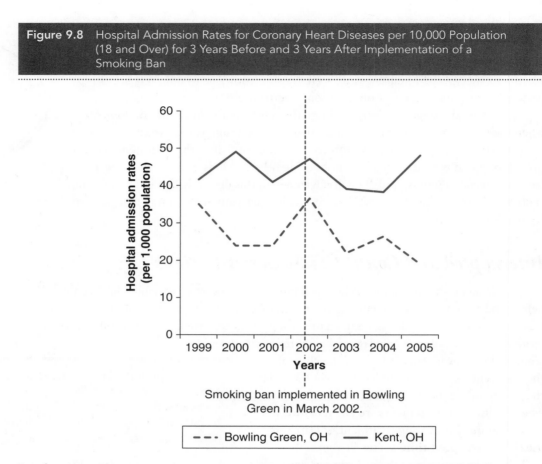

Smoking ban implemented in Bowling Green in March 2002.

--- Bowling Green, OH   —— Kent, OH

Data from Kent, Ohio, were used as a nonequivalent control group for comparison. Data are adapted from those reported by Khuder et al. (2007).

demographic characteristics that were comparable to those of Bowling Green. As shown in Figure 9.8 (solid line), hospital admission rates in the matched control city were rising while rates in Bowling Green were decreasing. The addition of this control group can increase how confident we are that the smoking ban was indeed effective.

As a caution, keep in mind that the residents in each city are preexisting groups in that residents chose to live in those locations; the researcher did not assign them to live in those locations. It is therefore possible, like for all other designs that use a nonequivalent control group, that selection differences, such as differences in eating and exercise habits between residents in each city, could have caused the different observed pattern of hospital admission rates, and not the smoking ban (the treatment). For this reason, we conclude that the smoking ban was associated with reduced hospital admission rates for coronary heart disease, and not that the smoking ban caused the reduction.

Table 9.1 summarizes each quasi-experimental research design described in this chapter. In the next section, we introduce a special case of quasi-experiments used in developmental research.

Table 9.1 The Quasi-Experimental Research Designs

Type of quasi-experimental design	Description	Key limitation
One-group posttest only	Observe one group after (posttest) a treatment.	No control group for comparison
One-group pretest-posttest	Observe one group before (pretest) and after (posttest) a treatment.	No control group for comparison
Nonequivalent control group posttest only	Observe treatment and nonequivalent control groups after (posttest) a treatment.	No random assignment between groups
Nonequivalent control group pretest-posttest	Observe treatment and nonequivalent control groups before (pretest) and after (posttest) a treatment.	No random assignment between groups
Basic time series design	Make many observations over a period of time before and after a treatment manipulated by the researcher.	No control group for comparison
Interrupted time series design	Make many observations over a period of time before and after a naturally occurring treatment.	No control group for comparison
Control series design	A time series design with a matched or nonequivalent control group.	No random assignment between groups

LEARNING CHECK 1 ✓

1. The quasi-experimental research design is structured similar to an experiment, except _____ [complete the sentence].

2. State the type of quasi-experimental research design described in each of the following examples:

   A. A researcher records the time (in seconds) it takes a group of participants to complete a computer-based task following an online "how-to" course.

   B. A researcher records the rate of traffic accidents on a section of highway each month for 2 years before and 2 years after the speed limit on that section of highway is reduced.

   C. A researcher records employee satisfaction before and after a training seminar. He compares satisfaction scores for employees at a local branch compared with the scores for those at the main branch who did not receive the seminar.

Answers: 1. the research design includes a quasi-independent variable and/or lacks an appropriate or equivalent control group; 2. A. One-group posttest-only design, B. Interrupted time series design, C. Nonequivalent control group pretest-posttest design.

9.5 Quasi-Experimental Design: Developmental Designs

An important area of research is used to study changes that occur across the life span. This type of research aims to understand how people or species change as they develop or age. The unique aspect of this area of research is that age, which is the factor being studied, is a quasi-independent variable. Age is a preexisting factor in that the researcher cannot manipulate the age of a participant. Because this design does not include a manipulation, it is also commonly categorized as a nonexperimental design. However, in this chapter, we describe this under the quasi-experimental category because, as you will see, each design is analogous to a quasi-experimental design already introduced in this chapter. Regardless of the category that developmental designs fit best with, it is most important to note that while developmental designs can demonstrate that variables differ by age, they do not demonstrate what causes variables to differ by age—more controlled procedures are needed, such as in an experiment.

The study of developmental changes across the life span is a special case, in that the focus of the field is on a factor that is inherent to the participants (their age). Therefore, researchers have developed research designs specifically adapted to study changes across the life span. Three types of developmental research designs are the following:

- Longitudinal design

- Cross-sectional design

- Cohort-sequential design

> Age is the quasi-independent variable using a developmental research design.

Longitudinal Design

Using a research design called the **longitudinal design**, we can observe changes across the life span by observing the same participants over time as they age. Using this design, researchers observe the same participants and measure the same dependent variable at different points in time or at different ages. The longitudinal design is similar to the *one-group pretest-posttest* quasi-experimental research design in that one group of participants is observed over time. In a strictly longitudinal design, however, changes at different ages are tested, but no treatment is administered.

To illustrate the longitudinal design, consider the research example illustrated in Figure 9.9. Vrangalova (2015) tested the hypothesis that casual sex among college students is related to their well-being. To test this hypothesis, the researchers had a sample of 528 undergraduate students complete an online survey at the beginning (Time 1) and again at the end (Time 2) of 1 academic year. In support of their hypothesis, students reporting having engaged in "genital

A **longitudinal design** is a developmental research design used to study changes across the life span by observing the same participants at different points in time and measuring the same dependent variable at each time.

Figure 9.9 The Longitudinal Design

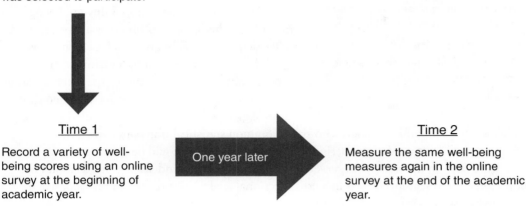

A sample of 528 students was selected to participate.

Time 1

Record a variety of well-being scores using an online survey at the beginning of academic year.

One year later

Time 2

Measure the same well-being measures again in the online survey at the end of the academic year.

Based on a design used by Vrangalova (2015). The structure of the longitudinal design is to observe the same participants across time.

hookups for anonymous reasons" (p. 945) between Time 1 and Time 2, had lower self-esteem, and had higher depression and anxiety scores compared with those who did not report engaging in this activity. This study highlights a key advantage of the longitudinal design in that changes in participant behavior can be recorded over extended periods of time (e.g., Hawkley, Thisted, & Cacioppo, 2009), even 1 year or more.

The disadvantage of the longitudinal design is that it is prone to many threats to internal validity associated with observing participants over time. For example, many participants may drop out of the study over time (attrition). One possibility is that those who are most motivated to complete the study will remain at the end, so it could be motivation to complete the study, and not age, that is associated with any changes observed. In addition, participants could learn how to take the assessments (testing effect) or settle down during the study so that assessments at Time 2 actually reflect their true score (regression toward the mean) on the measures recorded. Finally, the longitudinal design can require substantial resources, money, recruitment efforts, and time to complete, particularly for studies that last years or even decades.

Importantly, participant characteristics, referred to as individual differences, can further be used to explain any differences or changes observed in a longitudinal study. For this reason, many researchers who use this design will record additional measures at Time 1/Time 2 so that they can control for these factors prior to evaluating differences over time. For example, Vrangalova (2015) recorded a variety of participant characteristics, such as demographic background, personality traits, and prior casual and romantic sex (prior to the start of the study), to ensure that such factors could be controlled for (i.e., identified or eliminated as possible reasons or explanations for the results), prior to evaluating the differences described in her study. Measuring participant characteristics, then, is a practical way to control for factors that you anticipate may influence differences over time in a longitudinal study.

Cross-Sectional Design

A **cross-sectional design** is a developmental research design in which participants are grouped by their age and participant characteristics are measured in each age group.

A **cohort** is a group of individuals who share common statistical traits or characteristics, or experiences within a defined period.

An alternative developmental design that does not require observing the same participants over time is the **cross-sectional design**. Using this design, the researcher observes a cross-section of participants who are grouped based on their age. The cross-sectional design is similar to a *nonequivalent control group* quasi-experimental design in that the different age groups act as nonequivalent control groups. Each age group is called a **cohort**, which is any group of individuals who share common statistical traits or characteristics, or experiences within a defined period. For example, a cohort could be a group of people who were born in the same year, served in the same war, or attended the same school. For developmental research, cohorts in a cross-sectional analysis are related in terms of when participants were born.

To illustrate the cross-sectional design, we will look at the research example illustrated in Figure 9.10. Phillips (2008) selected a sample of 99 community college students and 320 middle school and high school students. Each group represented a different age group or cohort. The researcher measured the identity style of students in each cohort (community college vs. middle school and high school) using the Identity Style Inventory

---

Figure 9.10 The Cross-Sectional Design

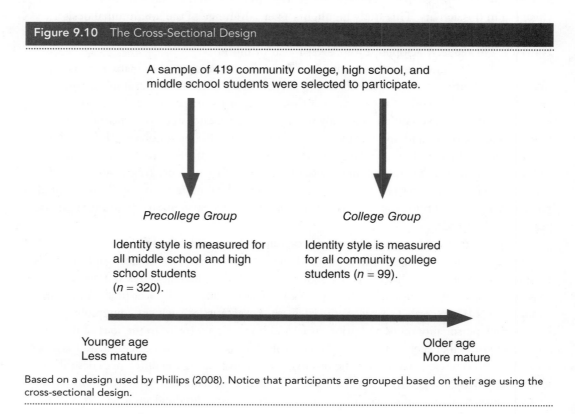

A sample of 419 community college, high school, and middle school students were selected to participate.

Precollege Group

Identity style is measured for all middle school and high school students (*n* = 320).

College Group

Identity style is measured for all community college students (*n* = 99).

Younger age
Less mature

Older age
More mature

Based on a design used by Phillips (2008). Notice that participants are grouped based on their age using the cross-sectional design.

Revised for a Sixth-Grade Reading Level (ISI-6G; White, Wampler, & Winn, 1998). Results showed that the identity style of a student is different for precollege and college-aged cohorts.

The advantage of a cross-sectional design is that participants are observed one time in each cohort. Observing participants one time eliminates many threats to internal validity associated with observing participants over time. Factors such as attrition, testing effects, and regression toward the mean are typically not a concern when participants are observed only one time.

However, a disadvantage of the cross-sectional design is the possibility of **cohort effects** (or **generation effects**), which occur when preexisting differences between members of a cohort can explain an observed result. For example, suppose we use a cross-sectional design to measure how often 20-year-olds, 40-year-olds, and 80-year-olds send text messages. In this example, we are likely to find that texting decreases with age. However, there is also a cohort effect due to the generational gap in advances of technology. An 80-year-old participant was raised when cell phones, and therefore texting, did not yet exist. This cohort effect of differences in experience or familiarity with texting across the life span can alternatively explain why texting appears to decrease with age, without appealing to age as the primary explanation. For this reason, researchers must be cautious to consider any possible cohort effects prior to the conduct of a cross-sectional study.

> A **cohort effect**, or a **generation effect**, is a threat to internal validity in which differences in the characteristics of participants in different cohorts or age groups confound or alternatively explain an observed result.

Table 9.2 summarizes the two developmental research designs described here. These two research designs, the longitudinal design and the cross-sectional design, can also be used together, as is described next.

Cohort-Sequential Design

To combine the advantages of longitudinal and cross-sectional developmental research designs, we can use a **cohort-sequential design**. Using the cohort-sequential design, two or more cohorts are observed from or at different points in time (cross-sectional design), and over time (longitudinal design). Figure 9.11 illustrates this design when three cohorts are observed, with each cohort also observed over time. Note that this design requires only that the longitudinal observations overlap across the cohorts. With only two cohorts observed, it is also common for some of the same participants to be represented in each cohort, as described in the following research example.

> A **cohort-sequential design** is a developmental research design that combines longitudinal and cross-sectional techniques by observing different cohorts of participants over time at overlapping times.

As an example of how the cohort-sequential design can be applied when the same participants are represented in each cohort, Pate et al. (2009) measured age-related changes in physical activity among adolescent girls. In their study, physical activity was measured in sixth-grade girls, and physical activity was again measured 2 years later when the girls were in eighth grade. Part of their sample was longitudinal in that the same girls from sixth grade were sampled again when they were in eighth grade. Also, by chance, some girls were sampled only one time because some sixth-grade girls did not participate in eighth grade and some

Figure 9.11 The Cohort-Sequential Design

Longitudinal (Time of Measurement)

	2000	2005	2010	2015
Cohort 1 (Generation X)	00	05	10	15
Cohort 2 (Millennials)	00	05	10	15
Cohort 3 (Generation Z)	00	05	10	15

Cross-Sectional (vertical axis)

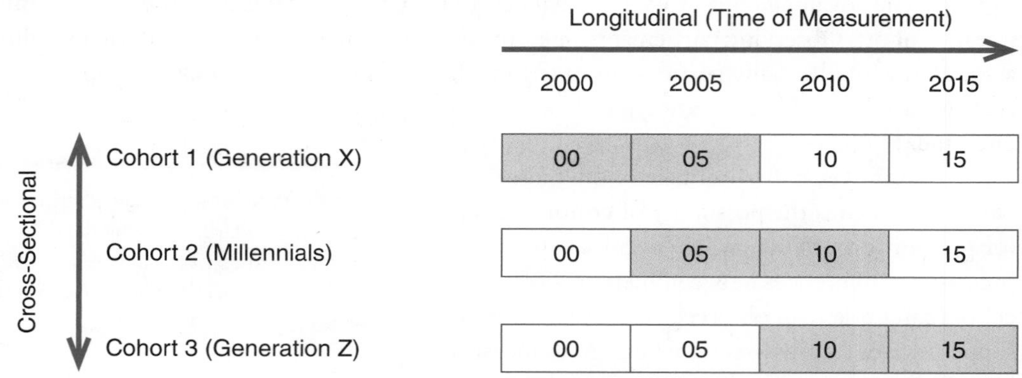

In this example of a cohort-sequential design, three cohorts of participants born as part of Generation X (oldest cohort), Millennials, or Generation Z (youngest cohort) are observed on some measure over time. The shaded boxes indicate when each group was observed. In this example, each cohort was observed twice, and the times of longitudinal observations overlapped.

Table 9.2 Potential Limitations of the Longitudinal and Cross-Sectional Research Designs

Potential Limitations	Developmental Research Design	
	Longitudinal	Cross-sectional
Threats to internal validity		
History and maturation?	Yes, because participants are observed more than one time, and the design lacks a control group.	Possibly, because the control groups (by age) are nonequivalent.
Regression and testing effects?	Yes, because participants are observed more than one time.	No, because participants are observed only one time.
Heterogeneous attrition?	Yes, because participants are observed more than one time.	Possibly, but not likely because participants are observed only one time.
Cohort effects?	No, because participants from the same cohort are observed over time.	Yes, because participants are grouped based on their age, which is a cohort.
Additional potential limitations		
Time-consuming?	Yes, studies can range from months to years in length.	No, a cross-section of the life span is observed at one time.
Costly/ expensive?	Yes, keeping track of participants costs time, recruitment, and money.	Possibly, but this design is typically less costly/expensive than a longitudinal study.

eighth-grade girls included in the study did not participate when they were in sixth grade. The advantage of using this cohort-sequential design is that researchers can do the following:

- Account for threats to internal validity associated with observing participants over time because part of the sample is a cross-section of age groups.

- Account for cohort effects because part of the sample includes the same participants observed over time in each age group or cohort.

9.6 Ethics in Focus: Development and Aging

Ethical concerns related to age are often focused on those who are very young and those who are very old. For younger participants, researchers must obtain consent from a parent or legal guardian to study minors, who are children under the age of 18 years. On the other extreme, older individuals require special permissions particularly when they are deemed no longer functionally or legally capable. Additional concerns also arise for the ethical treatment of clinical populations, such as those suffering trauma or disease at any stage of development. In all, you should follow three rules to ensure that such groups or cohorts are treated in an ethical manner:

- Obtain assent when necessary. In other words, ensure that informed consent is obtained from the participant only after all possible risks and benefits have been clearly identified.

- Obtain permission from a parent, a legal guardian, or another legally capable individual, such as a medical professional, when a participant is a minor or when a participant is functionally or legally incapable of providing consent.

- Clearly show that the benefits of a study outweigh the costs. For any group that is studied, that group (younger, older, or incapable) should specifically benefit from participating in the research with minimal costs.

LEARNING CHECK 2 ✓

1. State the developmental research design that is described by each of the following phrases:

   A. Observing participants over time

   B. Observing groups at one time only

   C. Prone to testing effects

   D. Prone to cohort effects

2. A _____ is a group of individuals who share common statistical or demographic characteristics.

Answers: 1. A. Longitudinal, B. Cross-sectional, C. Longitudinal, D. Cross-sectional; 2. Cohort.

SINGLE-CASE EXPERIMENTAL DESIGNS

In this section, we begin by identifying a new research design to test the following research hypothesis: Giving encouragement to students who are at risk of dropping out of school will keep them on task in the classroom. To answer this hypothesis, we could measure the time (in minutes) that an at-risk student stays on task. We could observe the student for a few days with no encouragement. Then we could observe the student for a few days with encouragement given as he or she works on the task. We could then again observe the student for a few more days with no encouragement. If the hypothesis is correct and we set up this study correctly, then we should expect to find that the time (in minutes) spent on task was high when the encouragement was given but low during the observation periods before and after when no encouragement was given. The unique feature of this design is that only one participant was observed.

In this final section, we introduce the research design that was illustrated here: the single-case experimental design.

9.7 An Overview of Single-Case Designs

A **single-case experimental design** is an experimental research design in which a participant serves as his or her own control and the dependent variable measured is analyzed for each individual participant and is not averaged across groups or across participants.

The single-case design, which is also called the *single-subject, single-participant,* or *small n design,* is most often used in applied areas of psychology, medicine, and education.

In some cases, often in areas of applied psychology, medicine, and education, researchers want to observe and analyze the behavior of a single participant using a research design called the **single-case experimental design.** A single-case design is unique in that a single participant serves as his or her own control; multiple participants can also be observed as long as each individual serves as his or her own control (Cooper, Heron, & Heward, 1987, 2007). In addition, the dependent variable measured in a single-case design is analyzed for each individual participant and is not averaged across groups or across participants. By contrast, all other experimental research designs, introduced in Chapters 10–12, are grouped designs.

For a single-case design to be an experimental design, it must meet the following three key elements of control required to draw cause-and-effect conclusions:

1. *Randomization* (random assignment). Using single-case designs, each participant can be randomly assigned to experience many phases or treatments controlled by the researcher.

2. *Manipulation* (of variables that operate in an experiment). The researcher must manipulate the phases or treatments that are experienced by each participant such that the factor or independent variable is not preexisting.

3. *Comparison/control group.* Each participant acts as his or her own control or comparison. For the single-case designs described here, comparisons can be made across multiple baseline phases (*reversal design*), participants (*multiple-baseline design*), or treatments (*changing-criterion design*).

An advantage of analyzing the data one participant at a time is that it allows for the critical analysis of each individual measure, whereas averaging scores across groups can give a spurious appearance of orderly change. To illustrate this advantage, suppose that a researcher measures the body weight in grams of four rat subjects before and after an injection of a drug believed to cause weight loss. The hypothetical data, provided in Table 9.3, show that rat subjects as a group lost 25 grams on average. However, Rat C actually gained weight following the injection. An analysis of each individual rat could be used to explain this outlier; a grouped design would often disregard this outlier as "error" so long as weight loss was large enough on average.

Table 9.3 The Value of an Individual Analysis

Subject	Baseline weight	Weight following drug treatment	Weight loss
Rat A	320	305	15
Rat B	310	280	30
Rat C	290	295	−5
Rat D	360	300	60

Average weight loss: 25 grams

Rat C was the only subject to gain weight. An individual analysis would investigate why, whereas a group analysis would mostly disregard this anomaly so long as average weight loss was large enough.

In this example, an individual analysis could be used to explain why Rat C was the only rat to gain weight following the treatment.

9.8 Single-Case Baseline-Phase Designs

Single-case designs are typically structured by alternating baseline and treatment phases over many trials or observations. In this major section, we introduce three types of single-case experimental research designs:

- Reversal design
- Multiple-baseline design
- Changing-criterion design

Reversal Design

One type of single-case design, called the **reversal design** (or **ABA design**), involves observing a single participant prior to (A), during (B), and following (A) a treatment or manipulation. The reversal design is structured into **phases**, represented alphabetically with an A or a B. Each phase consists of many observations or trials. The researcher begins with a **baseline phase (A)**, in which no treatment is given, then applies a treatment in a second phase (B), and again returns to a baseline phase (A) in which the treatment is removed. This type of research design can be represented as follows:

A (baseline phase) → B (treatment phase) → A (baseline phase)

A **reversal design**, or **ABA design**, is a single-case experimental design in which a single participant is observed before (A), during (B), and after (A) a treatment or manipulation.

A **phase** is a series of trials or observations made in one condition.

The **baseline phase (A)** is a phase in which a treatment or manipulation is absent.

If the treatment in Phase B causes a change in the dependent variable, then the dependent variable should change from baseline to treatment, then return to baseline levels when the treatment is removed. For example, we opened this section with the hypothesis that giving encouragement to students who are at risk of dropping out of school will keep them on task in the classroom. To test this hypothesis, we measured the time in minutes that an "at-risk" student spent on task in a class with no encouragement (baseline, A) for a few trials, then with encouragement (treatment, B) for a few trials, and again with no encouragement (baseline, A) for a few more trials. If the encouragement (the treatment) was successful, then the time (in minutes) spent on task would be higher when the encouragement was given but lower during the observation periods before and after when no encouragement was given. The second baseline phase minimizes the possibility of threats to internal validity. Adding another B and A phase would further minimize the possibility of threats to internal validity because the pattern of change would be repeated using multiple treatment phases.

A visual inspection of the data, and not inferential statistics, is used to analyze the data when only a single participant is observed. To analyze the data in this way, we look for two types of patterns that indicate that a treatment caused an observed change, as illustrated in Figure 9.12:

- A *change in level* is displayed graphically, as shown in Figure 9.12 (top graph), when the levels of the dependent variable in the baseline phases are obviously less than or greater than the levels of the dependent variable in the treatment phase.

- A *change in trend* is displayed graphically, as shown in Figure 9.12 (bottom graph), when the direction or pattern of change in the baseline phases is different from the pattern of change in the treatment phase. In the typical case, a dependent variable gradually increases or decreases in the treatment phase but is stable or does not change in the baseline phases.

The reversal design is typically conducted in applied areas of research to investigate possible solutions that can benefit individuals or society. For this reason, one advantage of the design is that it can be used to apply treatments that are beneficial to participants. Often this means that researchers will be asked by ethics committees to end their study with a treatment phase (B),

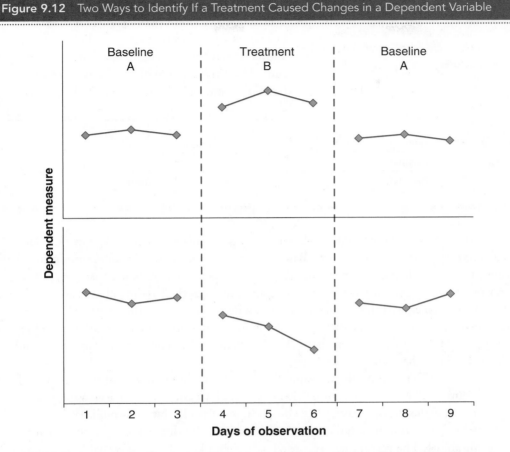

A change in level (top graph) and a change in trend (bottom graph) make it possible to infer that some treatment is causing an effect or a change in behavior.

which was the phase that was beneficial to the participant. For this reason, many reversal designs are at least four phases, or ABAB, so as not to return to baseline to end an experiment.

A limitation of the reversal design is that the change in a dependent variable in a treatment phase must return to baseline levels when the treatment is removed. However, in many areas of research, such as studies on learning, a return to baseline is not possible. When a participant is taught a new skill, for example, it is often not possible to undo what the participant learned—as fully expected, the behavior will not return to baseline. In these situations, when it is not possible for changes in a dependent variable to return to baseline, a reversal design cannot be used.

Multiple-Baseline Design

For situations in which it is not possible for changes in a dependent variable to return to baseline levels following a treatment phase, researchers can use the **multiple-baseline design**. The multiple-baseline design is a single-case design in

A and B indicate the phases in a reversal design.

A **multiple-baseline design** is a single-case experimental design in which a treatment is successively administered over time to different participants, for different behaviors, or in different settings.

which the treatment is successively administered over time to different participants, for different behaviors, or in different settings. This design allows researchers to systematically observe changes caused by a treatment without the need of a second baseline phase and can be represented as follows:

Case #1	Baseline _____	Treatment _____	
Case #2	Baseline _____	Treatment _____	
Case #3	Baseline _____	Treatment _____	

By representing the multiple-baseline design in this way, a *case* refers to a unique time, behavior, participant, or setting. Baseline periods are extended in some cases prior to giving a treatment. If the treatment causes an effect following a baseline phase for each case, then the change in level or pattern should begin only when the baseline phase ends, which is different for each case. If this occurs, then we can be confident that the treatment is causing the observed change. This design minimizes the likelihood that something other than the treatment is causing the observed changes if the changes in a dependent variable begin only after the baseline phase ends for each case.

To illustrate the multiple-baseline design, we will look at the research example illustrated in Figure 9.13. Dukes and McGuire (2009) used a multiple-baseline design to measure the effectiveness of a sex education intervention, which they administered to multiple participants with a moderate intellectual disability. The researchers recorded participant knowledge of sexual functioning using the Sexual Consent and Education Assessment (SCEA K-Scale; Kennedy, 1993), on which higher scores indicate greater ability to make decisions about sex. Each participant was given a baseline phase for a different number of weeks. Scores on the SCEA K-Scale were low in this baseline phase. As shown in Figure 9.13 for three participants, only after the baseline period ended and the intervention was administered did scores on the scale increase. Scores also remained high for 4 weeks after the program ended. Hence, the results showed a change in level from baseline to intervention for each participant.

The length of the baseline phase is varied using a multiple-baseline design.

Each participant in the sex education study received the intervention (or the treatment) in successive weeks: Tina (Week 11), Josh (Week 12), and Debbie (Week 13). Because the treatment was administered at different times, and changes in the dependent variable only occurred once the treatment was administered, the pattern showed that the treatment, and not other factors related to observing participants over time, caused the observed changes in SCEA K-Scale scores.

The advantage of a multiple-baseline design is that it can be used when we expect a treatment will not return to baseline, such as when we study learning on some measure, as illustrated in Figure 9.13 for our example. The limitation of a multiple-baseline design

Figure 9.13 Results From a Multiple-Baseline Design for Three Participants Receiving a Sex Education Intervention

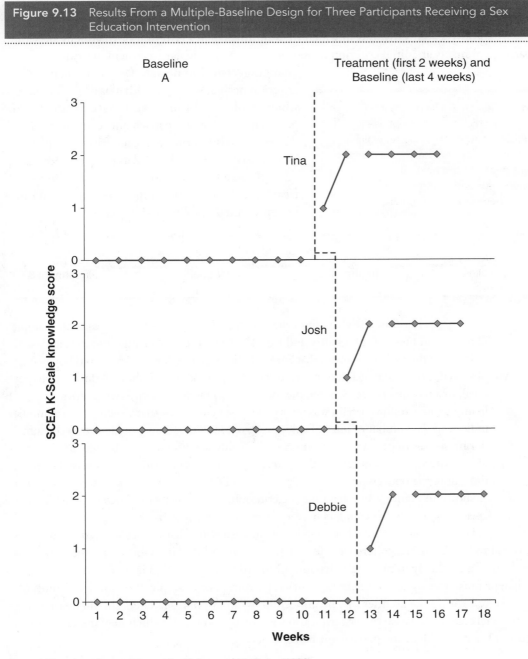

Source: Based on data presented by Dukes and McGuire (2009).

is that the design is used when only a single type of treatment is administered. This same limitation applies to the reversal design. For situations when we want to administer successive treatments, then, we require a different type of single-case experimental design.

Changing-Criterion Design

For research situations in which we want to change a criterion or treatment after the participant meets an initial criterion or responds to one particular treatment, we can use a changing-criterion design. Using the changing-criterion design, we begin with a baseline phase, which is followed by many successive treatment phases to determine if participants can reach different levels or criteria in each treatment phase. The criterion can be changed as often as necessary or until some final criterion is met. For a three-treatment study, the changing-criterion design can be represented as follows:

A **changing-criterion design** is a single-case experimental design in which a baseline phase is followed by successive treatment phases in which some criterion or target level of behavior is changed from one treatment phase to the next. The participant must meet the criterion of one treatment phase before the next treatment phase is administered.

To illustrate the changing-criterion design, we will look at the research example illustrated in Figure 9.14. Gentry and Luiselli (2008) used the changing-criterion design to increase the number of bites that Sam, a fictitious name for the 4-year-old boy being observed, would take of a nonpreferred food (i.e., a food he did not like) during a supper meal. In a baseline phase, Sam ate the food with no manipulation. Then a series of manipulations followed. Sam was instructed to spin an arrow that would fall on a number indicating the number of bites of a nonpreferred food that Sam would need to consume during supper to gain a reward, which in this study was his favorite play activity. The initial criterion was a spinner with a 1 and a 2 on it. This criterion was increased over time, until the options on the spinner were 5 and 6 (bites) to meet the criterion to gain a reward. As shown in Figure 9.14, each time the criterion, or the number of bites required to gain a reward, was increased, Sam's eating behavior correspondingly increased.

Each successive treatment phase in a changing-criterion design is associated with a change in criterion.

Two advantages of the changing-criterion design are that it does not require a reversal to baseline of an otherwise effective treatment and that it enables experimental analysis of a gradually improving behavior. A limitation of the design is that the target behavior must already be in the participant's repertoire. For example, the number of bites of food is well within the abilities of a healthy child. In addition, researchers should be cautious to not increase or decrease the criterion too soon or by too much, which may impede the natural learning rate of the participant being observed.

LEARNING CHECK 3 ✓

1. Why is the single-case design regarded as an experimental research design?

2. Identify whether each of the following is an example of a reversal design, a multiple-baseline design, or a changing-criterion design:

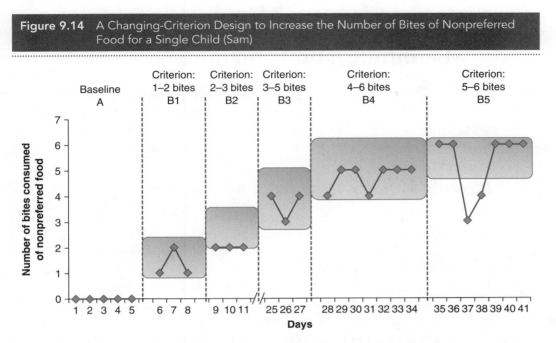

Figure 9.14 A Changing-Criterion Design to Increase the Number of Bites of Nonpreferred Food for a Single Child (Sam)

At baseline, Sam ate no bites, and then Sam spun an arrow that displayed different criteria for a reward. He began with 1–2 bites, then 2–3 bites, 3–5 bites, 4–6 bites, and finally 5–6 bites in order to receive the reward. The changing criterion is highlighted in each treatment phase. Notice that as the criterion was increased, so did Sam increase the number of bites he took of nonpreferred food. Data based on those presented by Gentry and Luiselli (2008).

A. A researcher gives a child successively greater levels of positive reinforcement after an initial baseline phase to reduce how often the child bites her nails. The successive treatments are administered until the child has reached a level where she is no longer biting her nails.

B. A researcher records the duration of time a participant stays on task in a dance recital 4 days before, 4 days during, and 4 days after a behavioral intervention strategy is implemented.

C. A researcher records the quality of artistic strokes made by three participants. Each participant was given a treatment phase after 3, 4, or 5 days of a baseline phase; no baseline phase was given after the treatment was administered.

3. For a single-case experimental study, why would a researcher use a multiple-baseline design instead of a reversal design?

Answers: 1. Because it meets the three key elements of control required to demonstrate cause and effect: randomization, manipulation, and comparison; 2. A. Changing-criterion design, B. Reversal design, C. Multiple-baseline design; 3. A multiple-baseline design would be used when it is not possible for changes in a dependent variable to return to baseline.

9.9 Validity, Stability, Magnitude, and Generality

The analysis of single-case experimental research designs is based largely on a visual inspection of the data in a graph and is not based on statistical analyses that require data to be grouped across multiple participants or groups. The specific visual features in a graph that indicate the validity of an observation are described in this section.

Internal Validity, Stability, and Magnitude

Recall from Chapter 6 that internal validity is the extent to which we can demonstrate that a manipulation or treatment causes a change in a dependent measure. Importantly, the extent to which we establish experimental control of all other possible causes is directly related to the internal validity of a research study. The greater the control we establish, the higher the internal validity.

A single-case design requires a visual analysis of the graphical data of a single participant. The level of control and therefore the internal validity of a single-case design can be determined when the following two features are observed in a graph using this type of analysis:

- The stability in the pattern of change across phases

- The magnitude or size of the change across phases

> **Internal validity is related to the stability and magnitude of change across phases in a single-case design.**

> **Stability** is the consistency in the pattern of change in a dependent measure in each phase of a design. The more stable or consistent changes in a dependent measure are in each phase, the higher the internal validity of a research design.

In a visual inspection of a graph, the **stability** of a measure is indicated by the consistency in the pattern of change in each phase. The stability of a dependent measure is illustrated in Figure 9.15. Data in a given phase can show a stable level (as in Figure 9.15a), can show a stable trend (as in Figure 9.15b), or can be unstable (as in Figure 9.15c). The stability of a measure in each phase is important because when a measure is unstable, changes are occurring in a dependent variable even when the researcher is not manipulating the behavior. When a dependent measure is stable, we can be confident that any changes in level or trend were caused by the manipulation, because changes only occurred between each phase and were otherwise stable or consistent within each phase. Therefore, the more stable a measure, the greater the control and the higher the internal validity in an experiment.

Another level of control can be demonstrated by the **magnitude** of change, which is the size of the change in a dependent measure observed between phases. When a measure is stable *within* each phase, we look at the magnitude of changes *between* phases. For a treatment to be causing changes in a dependent measure, we should observe immediate changes as soon as the treatment phase is administered. We can observe an immediate

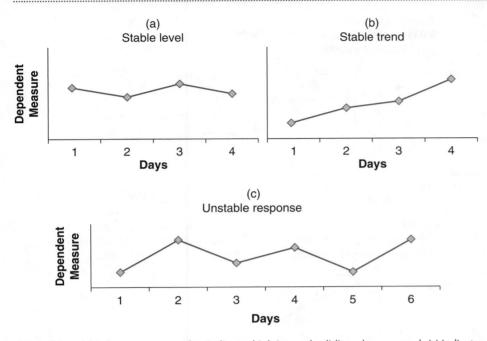

Graphs (a) and (b) show a response that indicates high internal validity, whereas graph (c) indicates low internal validity.

change in level (as shown in Figure 9.16a), or we can observe an immediate change in trend (as shown in Figure 9.16b). The greater the magnitude of changes between phases, the greater the control and the higher the internal validity in a single-case experiment.

Magnitude is the size of the change in a dependent measure observed between phases of a design. The larger the magnitude of changes in a dependent measure between phases, the higher the internal validity of a research design.

External Validity and Generality

Recall from Chapter 6 that external validity is the extent to which observations generalize beyond the constraints of a study. A single-case design is typically associated with low population validity, which is a subcategory of external validity. In other words, it is not possible to know whether the results in the sample would also be observed in the population from which the sample was selected because single-case experimental designs are associated with very small sample sizes. However, the results in a single-case design can have high external validity in terms of generalizing across behaviors, across subjects or participants, and across settings. The following is an example of each way to generalize results to establish the external validity of a single-case experiment:

Figure 9.16 Internal Validity and Control

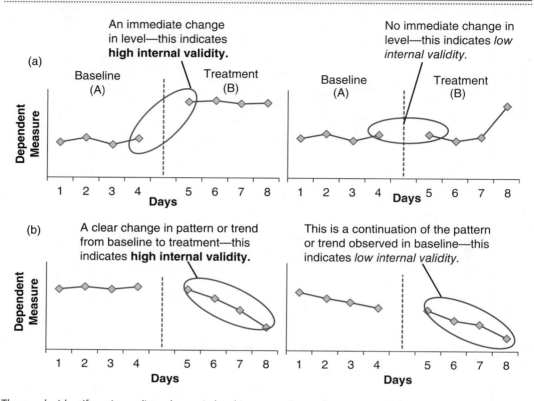

The graphs identify an immediate change in level (top row, a) or a change in trend (bottom row, b) that would indicate a high level of control and high internal validity.

- As an example of generalizing across behaviors, a psychotherapist may examine the extent to which causes of spousal abuse generalize to or also similarly cause child abuse. In this example, the therapist generalizes across behaviors, from spousal abuse (Behavior 1) to child abuse (Behavior 2).

- As an example of generalizing across subjects or participants, an animal researcher may examine the generality of foraging behavior across multiple rat subjects, or a clinical researcher may examine the effectiveness of a behavioral therapy to improve symptoms of depression across multiple participants. In each case, the researcher is generalizing across multiple subjects or participants.

- As an example of generalizing across settings, a child psychologist may want to determine the extent to which characteristics of child play behavior during recess generalize to characteristics of play behavior during class time. In this example, the researcher generalizes across settings, from child play behavior during recess (Setting 1) to child play behavior during class time (Setting 2).

> External validity is related to the generality of findings in a single-case design.

9.10 Ethics in Focus: The Ethics of Innovation

Many single-case experiments look at early treatments for behavioral disorders or simply bad habits such as smoking or nail biting. When these types of behaviors are studied using a single-case design, the treatment is typically hypothesized to have benefits, such as reducing symptoms of the behavioral disorder or reducing the frequency of bad habits. Researchers will end an experiment with the treatment phase that was most beneficial, so as to maximize the benefits that participants receive. In a reversal design, this means that researchers end the study in a B phase (e.g., ABAB). A multiple-baseline design and a changing-criterion design already end in a treatment phase. Adding a treatment phase or otherwise adapting a single-case design is quite manageable for researchers because they observe only one or a few subjects or participants in a single-case experiment. Observing such a small sample size allows researchers the flexibility to make changes, such as when they add or omit treatments to maximize benefits to participants.

The flexibility of a single-case design also allows for greater "investigative play" (Hayes, 1981, p. 193) or greater freedom to ask innovative or new questions about treatments with unknown causes or with unknown costs or benefits. Single-case designs allow for the conduct of such innovative research to rigorously evaluate potential, yet untested, treatments with small samples; this allows researchers to test the treatment without exposing such a treatment to large groups of participants, particularly when the potential costs of implementing such a treatment are largely unknown or untested. In this way, single-case designs can be used as an initial research design for testing some of the most innovative research in the behavioral sciences.

LEARNING CHECK 4 ✓

1. Perform a visual inspection of the following data. Does the graph illustrate a study with high internal validity? Explain.

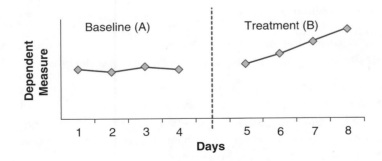

2. A researcher uses a single-case design to record the number of minutes spent studying in a baseline phase and a calming music treatment phase with a student who studied in a library and the same student who studied in a college dormitory room. Based on this description, can the researcher generalize across behaviors, across participants, or across settings?

3. Single-case designs allow for greater freedom to ask innovative or new questions about treatments with unknown causes or with unknown costs or benefits. Why can a single-case design be an ethically appropriate research design to test the effectiveness of such treatments?

Answers: 1. Yes, because the data in baseline are stable, and there is a change in trend from baseline to treatment; 2. Generalize across settings; 3. Because single-case designs are used with small samples, thereby testing the treatment without exposing such a treatment to large groups of participants.

CHAPTER SUMMARY

LO 1 Define and identify a quasi-experiment and a quasi-independent variable.

- A quasi-experimental research design is structured similar to an experiment, except that this design lacks random assignment, includes a preexisting factor (i.e., a variable that is not manipulated), or does not include a comparison/control group.
- A quasi-independent variable is a preexisting variable that is often a characteristic inherent to an individual, which differentiates the groups or conditions being compared in a research study. Because the levels of the variable are preexisting, it is not possible to randomly assign participants to groups.

LO 2 Identify and describe two one-group quasi-experimental research designs: the posttest-only and pretest-posttest designs.

- The **one-group posttest-only design** is a quasi-experimental research design in which a dependent variable is measured for one group of participants following a treatment.
- The **one-group pretest-posttest design** is a quasi-experimental research design in which the same dependent variable is measured in one group of participants before and after a treatment is administered.

LO 3 Identify and describe two nonequivalent control group quasi-experimental research designs: the posttest-only and pretest-posttest designs.

- A **nonequivalent control group** is a control group that is matched upon certain preexisting characteristics similar to those observed in a treatment group, but to which participants are not randomly assigned. When a nonequivalent control group is used, **selection differences** can potentially explain an observed difference between an experimental and a nonequivalent control group.

- The **nonequivalent control group posttest-only design** is a quasi-experimental research design in which a dependent variable is measured following a treatment in one group and is compared with a nonequivalent control group that does not receive the treatment.
- The **nonequivalent control group pretest-posttest design** is a quasi-experimental research design in which a dependent variable is measured in one group of participants before (pretest) and after (posttest) a treatment, and that same dependent variable is also measured at pretest and posttest in a nonequivalent control group that does not receive the treatment.

LO 4 Identify and describe three time series quasi-experimental research designs: basic, interrupted, and control designs.

- The **basic time series design** is a quasi-experimental research design in which a dependent variable is measured at many different points in time in one group before and after a treatment that is manipulated by the researcher is administered.
- The **interrupted time series design** is a quasi-experimental research design in which a dependent variable is measured at many different points in time in one group before and after a treatment that naturally occurs.
- A **control time series design** is a basic or interrupted time series quasi-experimental research design that also includes a nonequivalent control group that is observed during the same period of time as a treatment group, but does not receive the treatment.

LO 5 Identify and describe three developmental quasi-experimental research designs: longitudinal, cross-sectional, and cohort-sequential designs.

- A **longitudinal design** is a developmental research design used to study changes across the life span by observing the same participants over time and measuring the same dependent variable at each time.
- A **cross-sectional design** is a developmental research design in which participants are grouped by their age and participant characteristics are measured in each age group. Each age group is a **cohort**, so this design is prone to **cohort effects**, which occur when unique characteristics in each cohort can potentially explain an observed difference between groups.
- A **cohort-sequential design** is a developmental research design that combines longitudinal and cross-sectional techniques by observing different cohorts of participants over time at overlapping times.

LO 6 Define the single-case experimental design.

- The **single-case experimental design** is an experimental research design in which a participant serves as his or her own control and the dependent variable measured is analyzed for each individual participant and is not averaged across groups or across participants. This design meets the three requirements to demonstrate cause and effect: randomization, manipulation, and comparison/control.

LO 7 Identify and describe three types of single-case research designs: the reversal, multiple-baseline, and changing-criterion designs.

- The **reversal design** is a single-case experimental design in which a single participant is observed before (A), during (B), and after (A) a treatment or manipulation.
- The **multiple-baseline design** is a single-case experimental design in which a treatment is successively administered over time to different participants, for different behaviors, or in different settings.
- The **changing-criterion design** is a single-case experimental design in which a baseline phase is followed by successive treatment phases in which some criterion or target level of behavior is changed from one treatment phase to the next. The participant must meet the criterion of one treatment phase before the next treatment phase is administered.

LO 8 Identify in a graph the stability and magnitude of a dependent measure, and explain how each is related to the internal validity of a single-case design.

- The **stability** of a measure is the consistency in the pattern of change in a dependent measure in each phase of a design. The more stable or consistent changes in a dependent measure are in each phase, the higher the internal validity of a research design.
- The **magnitude** of change in a measure is the size of the change in a dependent measure observed between phases of a design. A measure can have a change in level or a change in trend. The larger the magnitude of change, the greater the internal validity of a research design.

LO 9 Identify three ways that researchers can strengthen the external validity of a result using a single-case design.

- A single-case design is typically associated with low population validity (a subcategory of external validity). However, three ways that researchers can strengthen the external validity of a result using a single-case design is to generalize across behaviors, across subjects or participants, and across settings.

KEY TERMS

quasi-experimental research design

quasi-independent variable

one-group posttest-only design

one-group pretest-posttest design

nonequivalent control group

selection differences

nonequivalent control group posttest-only design

nonequivalent control group pretest-posttest design

basic time series design

interrupted time series design

control time series design

longitudinal design

cross-sectional design

cohort

cohort effects

generation effects

cohort-sequential design

single-case experimental
  design

reversal design

ABA design

phases

baseline phase (A)

multiple-baseline
  design

changing-criterion
  design

stability

magnitude

REVIEW QUESTIONS

1. A quasi-experimental research design is structured similar to an experiment, with what two exceptions?

2. State whether each of the following factors is an example of an independent variable or a quasi-independent variable. Only state "quasi-independent variable" for participant variables that cannot be manipulated.

   A. The age of participants

   B. Time allotted for taking an exam

   C. A participant's work experience

   D. Time of day a study is conducted

   E. A participant's state of residence

   F. Amount of sugar added to a drink

3. How does a one-group pretest-posttest design improve on the posttest-only quasi-experimental design? What is the major limitation of all one-group designs?

4. What is a nonequivalent control group, and why does this type of group make it difficult to determine cause and effect using a nonequivalent control group quasi-experimental design?

5. What is the key difference between the basic and interrupted time series quasi-experimental research designs?

6. Name the developmental research design described in each of the following examples:

   A. A researcher measures job satisfaction in a sample of employees on their first day of work and again 1 year later.

   B. A researcher records the number of nightmares per week reported in a sample of 2-year-old, 4-year-old, and 8-year-old foster children.

7. (A) Cohort effects are a threat to what type of validity? (B) Which developmental research design is most susceptible to cohort effects?

8. Why is the single-case design regarded as an experimental research design?

9. A reversal design is used to test the hypothesis that low lighting in a room reduces how quickly students read. As shown in the figure for one student, a student reads passages of similar length in a room with normal lighting (baseline), then in the same room with dim lighting (treatment), and then again with normal lighting. Do the results shown in the figure support the hypothesis? Explain.

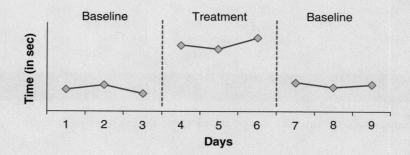

10. What is the most likely reason that a researcher uses a multiple-baseline design instead of a reversal design?

11. Define the changing-criterion design and explain when the design is used.

12. Are the baseline data shown in the following figure stable? Do the baseline data in the figure indicate high or low internal validity?

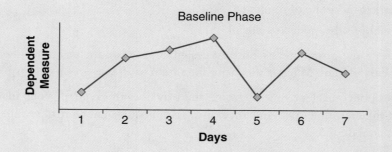

13. A researcher examines the generality of a behavioral treatment for overeating by testing the same treatment to treat overworking. In this example, is the researcher generalizing across behaviors, across participants, or across settings?

14. A researcher examines if the effectiveness of a new learning system used in a classroom is also effective when used in a home (for homeschooled children). In this example, is the researcher generalizing across behaviors, across participants, or across settings?

1. Use an online database, such as PsycINFO, to search scientific research articles for any topic you are interested in. Perform two searches. In the first search, enter a search term related to your topic of interest, and enter the term *longitudinal* to find research that used this design in your area of interest. Select and print one article. In the second search, again enter a search term related to your topic of interest, and this time enter the term *cross-sectional* to find research that used this design in your area of interest. Again, select and print one article. Once your searches are complete, complete the following assignment:

   A. Write a summary of each article, and explain how each research design differed.

   B. Describe at least two potential threats to internal validity in each study.

   C. Include the full reference information for both articles at the end of the assignment.

2. A researcher proposes that having a pet will improve health. (a) Write a research plan to test this hypothesis using a single-case experimental design. (b) What is the predicted outcome or pattern, if the hypothesis that having a pet will improve health were correct? (c) Graph the expected results. (d) Identify the extent to which your results demonstrate high or low internal validity.

Identify a problem

- Determine an area of interest.
- Review the literature.
- Identify new ideas in your area of interest.
- Develop a research hypothesis.

Generate more new ideas

- Results support your hypothesis—refine or expand on your ideas.
- Results do not support your hypothesis—reformulate a new idea or start over.

Develop a research plan

- Define the variables being tested.
- Identify participants or subjects and determine how to sample them.
- Select a research strategy and design.
- Evaluate ethics and obtain institutional approval to conduct research.

After reading this chapter, you should be able to:

1 Delineate the between-subjects design and the between-subjects experimental design.

2 Distinguish between an experimental group and a control group.

3 Distinguish between a natural and a staged experimental manipulation.

4 Explain how random assignment, control by matching, and control by holding constant can make individual differences about the same between groups.

5 Explain why it is important to measure error variance in an experiment.

6 Identify the appropriate sampling method and test statistic for independent samples to compare differences between two group means.

7 Identify the appropriate sampling method and test statistic for independent samples to compare differences among two or more group means.

8 Identify and give an example of three types of measures for a dependent variable.

9 Name two advantages and one disadvantage of the between-subjects design.

10 Compute a two-independent-sample t test and a one-way between-subjects analysis of variance using SPSS.

Communicate the results

- Method of communication: oral, written, or in a poster.
- Style of communication: APA guidelines are provided to help prepare style and format.

Conduct the study

- Execute the research plan and measure or record the data.

Analyze and evaluate the data

- Analyze and evaluate the data as they relate to the research hypothesis.
- Summarize data and research results.

chapter ten

BETWEEN-SUBJECTS EXPERIMENTAL DESIGNS

Imagine your friends want to play a pickup game of basketball. To pick teams, all your friends write their names on a piece of paper and place the paper in a hat. Names are drawn at random until all players have been picked for each team. Because names are picked at random, it is therefore only by chance that a given player is picked to play on a given team. Now suppose you end up on the winning team. Why did your team win? To answer this question, we could measure any number of statistics and compare differences between the two teams. For example, if we observe that your team had a higher percentage of jump shots made during the game, we may surmise that this statistic can explain why your team won the game.

In the example given here, we have two groups or basketball teams that were selected onto one or the other team at random. This way of creating groups is the basis for conducting experiments using *between-subjects* comparisons—we place participants in groups at random (so that their participation in any one group occurs by chance) and compare differences in some measure, such as the percentage of jump shots made, between groups. Because people can be different (i.e., each person has individual differences that make him or her unique), we select people for groups at random to ensure that differences between participants are about the same between groups—to control for the individual differences that make participants in each group unique.

In this chapter, we introduce the structure of the design described here in which different participants are observed one time in each group. The advantages of selecting participants at random and the structure of the between-subjects experimental design are introduced with examples given from published research.

10.1 Conducting Experiments: Between-Subjects Design

A **between-subjects design** is a research design in which different participants are observed one time in each group or at each level of a factor.

A **between-subjects experimental design** is an experimental research design in which the levels of a between-subjects factor are manipulated, then different participants are randomly assigned to each group or to each level of that factor and observed one time.

A **between-subjects factor** is a type of factor in which different participants are observed in each group, or at each level of the factor.

The most common reason for conducting an experiment is to identify factors that cause changes in behavior in a population. The term *experiment* is used almost synonymously with *science*. It is the staple for how researchers conduct research; however, keep in mind that other than the single-case design, to this point we have only introduced nonexperiments and quasi-experiments. In this chapter, we will introduce the **between-subjects design**, which is a research design in which different participants are observed at one time in each group. Specifically, we will introduce the **between-subjects experimental design** in which we manipulate the levels of a **between-subjects factor** and then randomly assign different participants to each group or to each level of that factor. The between-subjects experimental design, described in Figure 10.1, is a between-subjects design that meets the three requirements for demonstrating cause and effect (first introduced in Chapter 6):

1. Randomization (random sampling and random assignment)

2. Manipulation (of variables that operate in an experiment)

3. Comparison/control (or a control group)

In Figure 10.1, Steps 1 and 3 meet the requirements for randomization, and Step 2 meets the requirements for manipulation (of the levels of an independent variable) and comparison/control (by creating two or more groups). Steps 4 and 5 allow researchers to compare differences in a dependent variable between two or more groups, and use statistical analyses to determine if the differences observed in the sample are also likely to exist in the population from which the sample was selected. A decision in Step 6 is then made regarding the research hypothesis tested. In this chapter, we will introduce the procedures used in each step of the between-subjects experimental design, as described in Figure 10.1.

10.2 Experimental Versus Control Group

Each type of research design introduced in this book can be distinguished by the level of control that is established by a researcher. The term **control**, also defined in Chapter 6, is used in research design to describe (a) the manipulation of a variable and (b) holding all other variables constant. In an experiment, control is high, and therefore both criteria (a and b) must be met in a between-subjects experiment.

Figure 10.1   The Steps Used for a Between-Subjects Experimental Design

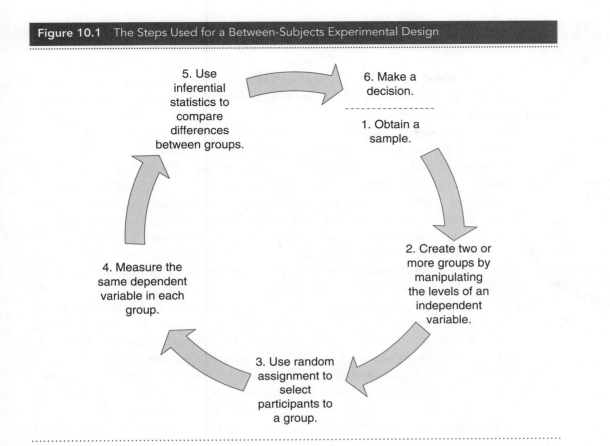

5. Use inferential statistics to compare differences between groups.

6. Make a decision.

1. Obtain a sample.

2. Create two or more groups by manipulating the levels of an independent variable.

3. Use random assignment to select participants to a group.

4. Measure the same dependent variable in each group.

A staple of the between-subjects experiment is that results in an experimental group can be compared with those in a control group. For this reason, we begin here by clarifying the distinction between a control group and an experimental group. The **experimental group**, or **treatment group**, is a group that receives a treatment or is exposed to a manipulation believed to cause changes in a dependent variable. The **control group** is a group that is treated the same as an experimental group, except that participants are not treated; that is, the manipulation is omitted.

Participants in a control group must be "matched" or treated exactly the same as those in the experimental group, minus the manipulation. For example, suppose we hypothesize that a new drug will reduce symptoms of depression. In an experiment, we administer the new drug to one group, and a placebo drug to a control group. The **placebo** is a fake version of the drug, typically in the form of a sugar pill, that has no real effect. In this way, two

Control in research design is (a) the manipulation of a variable and (b) holding all other variables constant. When control is low, neither criterion is met; when control is high, both criteria are met.

The **experimental group** or **treatment group** is a condition in an experiment in which participants are treated or exposed to a manipulation, or level of the independent variable, that is believed to cause a change in the dependent variable.

The **control group** is a condition in an experiment in which participants are treated the same as participants in an experimental group, except that the manipulation believed to cause a change in the dependent variable is omitted.

> A **placebo** is an inert substance, surgery, or therapy that resembles a real treatment but has no real effect.

groups are administered a drug, but only the experimental group has the real drug that is thought to reduce symptoms of depression. If we observe differences between groups, then it is likely due to the administration of the new drug treatment because both groups were otherwise treated the same.

As an added measure of control, it is also important to keep participants blind to the group to which they are assigned. In other words, do not let the participants know whether they took the real or the fake pill—any knowledge you divulge about the type of pill administered can lead to expectancy effects (Oldham, 2011), and some data even suggest that the side effects of drugs can enhance expectancy effects (Bjørkedal & Flaten, 2011). When expectancy effects occur, the behavior observed tends to be due to how participants think the drug works, and not due to the actual effects of the drug, which is why it is important to minimize expectancy effects in studies like these. The correct use of a control group is further described in the MAKING SENSE section.

> Participants in a control group are treated identical to those in a treatment group, minus the manipulation.

Keep in mind also that a control group is different from a comparison group. A comparison group is typically used in studies where a control group is not possible, often in educational or clinical settings in which behavioral therapies are tested. For example, Langer, Cangas, Salcedo, and Fuentes (2012) randomly assigned 18 patients with psychosis to receive a mindfulness-based cognitive therapy (MBCT; experimental group) or be placed on a waiting list to receive the MBCT (comparison group). The comparison group in this study is not a control group because this group received no treatment at all—this would be the same as giving a drug treatment to one group without also giving a placebo to the control group. Hence, participants in the group placed on the waiting list for MBCT were not treated exactly the same as those in the experimental group, minus the treatment, largely because it would be difficult to conceive of a way to accomplish this.

MAKING SENSE—CREATING APPROPRIATE CONTROL GROUPS

The control group must be treated exactly the same as an experimental group, except that the members of this group do not actually receive the treatment believed to cause changes in the dependent variable. As an example, suppose we hypothesize that rats will dislike flavors that are associated with becoming ill (see Capaldi, Hunter, & Privitera, 2004; Garcia, Kimeldorf, & Koelling, 1955). To test this hypothesis, the rats in an experimental group receive a vanilla-flavored drink followed by an injection of lithium chloride to make them ill. The rats in a control group must be treated the same, minus the manipulation of administering lithium chloride to make them ill. In a control group, then, rats receive the same vanilla-flavored drink also followed by an injection; however, in this group, the substance injected is inert, such as a saline solution (the placebo). The next day, we record how much vanilla-flavored solution rats consume during a brief test (in milliliters).

Note that simply omitting the lithium chloride is not sufficient. The control group in our example still receives an injection; otherwise, both being injected and the substance that is injected will differ between groups. Other important factors for experiments like these include some control of the diets rats consume before and during the study, and to ensure that many other environmental factors are the same for all rats, such as their day/night sleep cycles and housing arrangements. These added levels of control ensure that both groups are truly identical, except that one group is made ill and a second group is not. In this way, researchers can isolate all factors in an experiment, such that only the manipulation that is believed to cause an effect is different between groups.

LEARNING CHECK 1 ✓

1. What are the three requirements for demonstrating cause and effect in an experiment?

2. Identify the experimental group and the control group in the following description of an experiment:

   To test whether a new sleeping pill was effective at increasing the duration of time that people sleep uninterrupted, adults with insomnia were randomly assigned to receive the sleeping pill or a placebo pill. The duration (in minutes) of uninterrupted sleep was then recorded during a subsequent observation period.

Answers: 1. Randomization, manipulation, and comparison/control; 2. Experimental group: participants receiving the sleeping pill, Control group: participants receiving the placebo pill.

....

10.3 Manipulation and the Independent Variable

An important characteristic of an experiment is that participants are assigned to groups using a random procedure. To use random assignment, defined in Chapter 6, the researcher must manipulate the levels of an independent variable to create two or more groups. In this section, we introduce the types of manipulations used in an experiment, how researchers employ random assignment, and some additional strategies researchers use to control the assignment of participants to groups in an experiment.

Experimental Manipulations

To make an **experimental manipulation,** the researcher must identify an independent variable, then create the groups that constitute the levels of that independent variable. For example,

> An **experimental manipulation** is the identification of an independent variable and the creation of two or more groups that constitute the levels of that variable.

Figure 10.2 Identifying an Experimental Manipulation

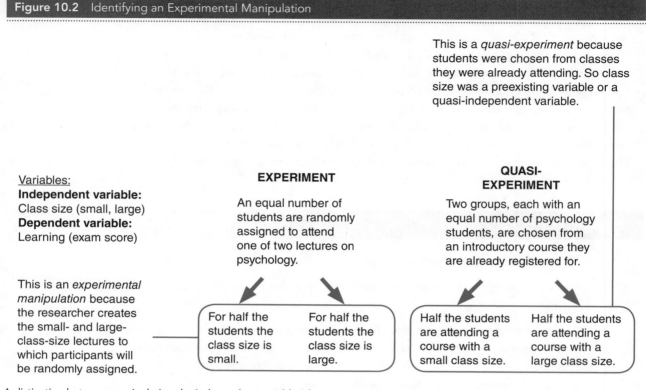

A distinction between manipulating the independent variable (class size) in an experiment and observing preexisting groups of students in classes of different size in a quasi-experiment.

suppose that we study the effects of class size on student learning. In this example, class size is our independent variable only if we manipulate the levels of that variable. As shown in Figure 10.2 for an experiment, we could create two lecture courses and randomly assign participants to one of two lectures. In this case, we created the lectures and controlled the assignment of participants to each lecture. As shown in Figure 10.2 for the quasi-experiment, however, if we observed students who were already enrolled in a class with a small or large class size, then the study would no longer be an experiment because we did not control which students attended each class; instead, the students controlled which class they attended when they enrolled.

Experimental manipulations can be described as natural or staged. **Natural manipulations** are those that can naturally be changed with little effort. A natural manipulation typically involves the manipulation of a physical stimulus. For example, Minamimoto, La Camera, and Richmond (2009) investigated how motivation in monkeys was changed during a task by manipulating the size of a reward (1, 2, 4, or 8 drops of 0.1 ml water) that was given at different delays (about 0, 3, or 7 seconds) following a correct

A **natural manipulation** is the manipulation of a stimulus that can be naturally changed with little effort.

response. Both manipulations were naturally measured as the number of drops (reward size) or time in seconds (reward delay). As other examples, we could study the effects of distraction on exam scores by creating a dimmed or brightly lit room (in watts), or a room with a soft or a loud sound (in decibels), or a room with different shades of color (e.g., bright colors, dark colors). In each example, we would manipulate a physical stimulus (e.g., light, sound, or color).

Staged manipulations require the participant to be "set up" to experience some stimulus or event. A staged manipulation often requires the help of a *confederate*, who is a coresearcher in cahoots with the researcher. For example, Hermans, Salvy, Larsen, and Engels (2012) studied how participants would model (i.e., copy or emulate) the eating behaviors of another person by exposing participants to a same-sex confederate who modeled eating of pastries or did not model eating. Results showed that participants did not eat more when exposed to the eating versus noneating confederate. As other examples of staged manipulations, to manipulate self-esteem, we could give a fake assessment to athletes and give them false feedback that they have low or high skill levels; to manipulate prejudice, we could have participants read a passage containing offensive versus neutral language; to manipulate participant expectations, we could create a cover story to mislead participants. In these examples, the manipulation would be staged with a fake assessment, an offensive passage, or a cover story.

> A **staged manipulation** is the manipulation of an independent variable that requires the participant to be "set up" to experience some stimulus or event.

Random Assignment and Control

An experimental manipulation allows researchers to create groups to which participants can be randomly assigned. Random assignment, defined in Chapter 6, is a procedure used to ensure that each participant has the same likelihood of being selected to a given group. One way to do this would be to refer to Appendix B.1 and follow the directions given for using random assignment.

The primary advantage of random assignment is that it makes the individual differences of participants about the same in each group. The key phrase in our statement is "*about* the same between groups." Random assignment is not always perfect—it can be extremely effective at making individual differences equivalent between groups, but it does not guarantee that such differences will be equivalent, particularly when your sample size is small. Individual differences, defined in Chapter 6, are the unique characteristics of participants that make them unique or different from other participants. Individual differences can include intelligence, marital status, income, education level, self-esteem, mood, age, political views, race, citizenship, genetic predispositions, and gender. If a researcher does not directly control such characteristics, then these characteristics (or individual differences), and not the levels of the independent variable, may be instead causing an effect or a difference between groups.

> Random assignment makes individual differences about the same between groups.

Random assignment ensures that participants, and therefore the individual differences of participants, are assigned to groups entirely by chance. When we do this, we can assume that the individual differences of participants in each group are about the same (Fisher, 1925, 1935). Hence, if we use random assignment, then we can be confident that any differences observed between groups can be attributed to the different levels of the independent variable that were manipulated by the researcher, and not to individual differences between participants.

Restricted Measures of Control

Keep in mind that when we use random assignment, we can *assume* that individual differences are about the same in each group. However, this is not necessarily always the case; sometimes we do not want to leave it to chance that individual differences are about the same between groups. In these cases, researchers can take steps to control the assignment of participant characteristics to each group by using **restricted random assignment**. Two strategies of restricted random assignment are as follows:

- Control by matching

- Control by holding constant

Researchers can match certain participant characteristics they wish to control in each group by using **control by matching**. Using this strategy, we assess or measure the characteristic we want to control, group or categorize participants based on scores on that measure, and then use a random procedure to assign participants from each category to a group in the study. For example, Corcos and Willows (2009) studied how a child's familiarity with words influenced recall of a set of words among children in Grades 4 and 6. To conduct their study, the researchers first matched participants in each group by age and by reading ability such that these two specific factors were the same in each group; thereby, the researchers established control of both factors. Any group differences in recall, then, could not be attributed to age and reading ability, because these factors were the same in each group.

To illustrate how to employ control by matching, we can use the example of controlling intelligence. To use control by matching, we first measure intelligence in a sample of children—we can measure intelligence using the Peabody Picture Vocabulary Test (Dunn, 1979). We then categorize participants based on their intelligence scores and randomly assign the children in each intelligence category to each group, as described in Figure 10.3. In this way, we restrict random assignment to each category of intelligence.

Researchers can also establish control by limiting the types of participants who are included in a study using **control by holding constant**. Using this strategy, we exclude participants who exhibit characteristics that may otherwise differ between groups in

Control by matching and control by holding constant allows researchers to control specific participant characteristics prior to using random assignment.

Figure 10.3 The Procedures for Using Control by Matching

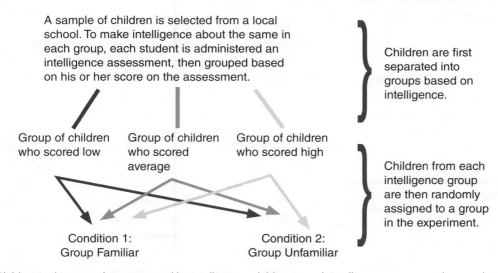

A sample of children is selected from a local school. To make intelligence about the same in each group, each student is administered an intelligence assessment, then grouped based on his or her score on the assessment.

Children are first separated into groups based on intelligence.

Group of children who scored low

Group of children who scored average

Group of children who scored high

Children from each intelligence group are then randomly assigned to a group in the experiment.

Condition 1: Group Familiar

Condition 2: Group Unfamiliar

Children in this example are grouped by intelligence; children in each intelligence group are then randomly assigned to a group in the experiment.

a study. For example, Privitera and Zuraikat (2014) studied how the location of a bowl of apples versus popcorn influenced intake of these foods. Because hunger could affect food intake, the sample was restricted to only those participants who reported not eating within 2 hours of the study—hence, hunger was held constant between groups. The study showed that whatever food was closest to the participant (whether the apples or popcorn) was eaten most. As other examples of control by holding constant, in a study of emotional intelligence, we may use only women to control for sex; in a weight loss study, we may restrict the sample to only those who are obese or to those most motivated to lose weight. In this way, we restrict a sample to include only men or participants who are obese/motivated to lose weight. We then randomly assign participants included in the sample to the different groups. In this way, we hold constant (or make the same) certain participant characteristics between groups.

Control by holding constant is a type of restricted random assignment in which we limit which participants are included in a sample based on characteristics they exhibit that may otherwise differ between groups in a study.

10.4 Variability and the Independent Variable

From a methodological view, the manipulation of the levels of an independent variable and the random assignment of participants to each level or group is the way we control for the possibility that individual differences differ between groups. As an added measure of control, we

> **Error variance** or **error** is a numeric measure of the variability in scores that can be attributed to or is caused by the individual differences of participants in each group.

can also measure individual differences numerically in terms of **error variance**. We can measure the variance or differences between groups and then measure how much of that variance or difference between groups can be attributed to individual differences due to error or random variation.

Random variation is measured by determining the extent to which scores in each group overlap. The more that scores in each group overlap, the larger the error variance; the less that scores overlap between groups, the smaller the error variance. To illustrate error variance, Figure 10.4 shows data for two hypothetical experiments in which there is a 3-point treatment effect between two groups in both experiments; that is, the mean difference between the two groups is 3.0. When scores do not overlap, shown in Figure 10.4a, all scores for the group receiving Treatment A are smaller than scores for the group receiving Treatment B. This result indicates that the manipulation or the different levels of the independent variable likely caused the 3-point treatment effect because individuals at each level, or in each group, are behaving differently.

> A **test statistic** is a mathematical formula that allows researchers to determine the extent to which differences observed between groups can be attributed to the manipulation used to create the different groups.

When scores do overlap, shown in Figure 10.4b, individual differences become a likely explanation for an observed difference between two or more groups in an experiment. Although the same 3-point treatment effect was observed in Figure 10.4b, some participants receiving Treatment B behaved as if they received Treatment A; that is, their scores overlap with the scores of those receiving Treatment A. When scores overlap with those for other groups, it indicates that individual differences may be causing the 3-point treatment effect between groups. Hence, the manipulation that created the two groups is not likely causing the differences between groups when participant responding substantially overlaps from one group to the next.

To measure error variance, and differences between groups, we identify a **test statistic** that is used to make a decision regarding whether an effect observed in a sample is also likely to be observed in a population from which the sample was selected. For this reason, you will find that the categorization of experiments, beginning in Section 10.6, is based upon the type of test statistic used for that experimental situation. Table 10.1 shows each between-subjects experimental design and the parametric test statistic used with each design, to be introduced in this chapter.

> Reducing error variance increases *power*—or likelihood of observing an effect.

Table 10.1 The Type of Between-Subjects Experimental Design and the Corresponding Test Statistic Used With That Design

Experimental Research Design (Between Subjects)	Test Statistic
Two independent samples	Two-independent-sample *t* test
Multiple independent samples	One-way between-subjects analysis of variance

Figure 10.4 A Hypothetical Example of Two Experiments in Which There Is No Overlap (a) in One Experiment and There Is Overlap (b) in Scores Between Groups in the Second Experiment

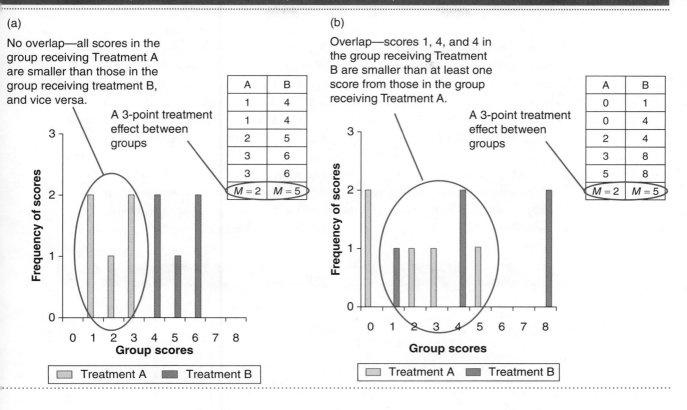

(a)

No overlap—all scores in the group receiving Treatment A are smaller than those in the group receiving treatment B, and vice versa.

A 3-point treatment effect between groups

A	B
1	4
1	4
2	5
3	6
3	6
$M = 2$	$M = 5$

(b)

Overlap—scores 1, 4, and 4 in the group receiving Treatment B are smaller than at least one score from those in the group receiving Treatment A.

A 3-point treatment effect between groups

A	B
0	1
0	4
2	4
3	8
5	8
$M = 2$	$M = 5$

MAKING SENSE—ARE PEOPLE DIFFERENT, OR ARE GROUPS DIFFERENT?

Variability is really an indication of whether people are different or groups are different. If people are different, then individual differences are causing an observed effect. If groups are different, then the manipulation (or the levels of an independent variable) is causing an observed effect. To understand how to decipher between these alternatives, we can ask the following two questions as we work through the same data given in Figure 10.4, now given in Figure 10.5:

1. Are groups different? If yes, then the manipulation is causing the effect.

2. Are people different? If yes, then individual differences are causing an effect.

(Continued)

(Continued)

When viewing a graph of data, we identify all data for one group and look to see how many scores from the other group fall within the range of scores for the group we identified. As illustrated in Figure 10.5, when scores in each group do not overlap (top figure), we can determine that the groups are different because we can clearly divide the scores by group. When the scores from each group do overlap (bottom figure), we can determine that people are different because we cannot clearly divide the scores by group. Using this strategy to interpret data presented graphically can help you decipher how to recognize whether groups are different or people are different.

Keep in mind, however, that the strategy introduced here can only be used to get an idea of whether people are different or groups are different. To determine the actual likelihood that people are different or groups are different, we use statistical analysis in Step 5 of the research process for the between-subjects experimental design (see Figure 10.1). This step is introduced in Sections 10.6 to 10.9.

Figure 10.5 Using Variability to Identify if People Are Different or Groups Are Different

Groups are different. Notice that no persons in Treatment B are behaving as if they are in Treatment A—no scores from Treatment B fall within the shaded region or range of scores for Treatment A. Hence, there is no overlap, and the data can be clearly divided by group.

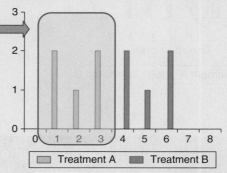

People are different. Notice that three persons in Treatment B are behaving as if they are in Treatment A—three scores from Treatment B fall within the shaded region or range of scores for Treatment A. Hence, people are different because there is a lot of overlap and the data cannot be clearly divided by group.

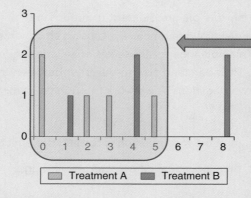

The data given here are the same as those given in Figure 10.4.

10.5 Ethics in Focus: The Accountability of Manipulation

Because the researcher creates or manipulates the levels of an independent variable in an experiment, he or she bears greater responsibility for how participants are treated in each group. For example, Chmelo, Hall, Miller, and Sanders (2009) studied the effects of viewing oneself in a mirror during resistance exercise. In their study, the researchers manipulated the exercise by having participants complete intense resistance exercises each of 3 days, and they manipulated whether a mirror was present or absent during the exercises. Hence, the types of exercises (e.g., crunches, dead lifts, bicep curls) and the intensity of the exercises (e.g., complete until failure) were manipulated.

Manipulating the levels of an independent variable can come with greater ethical responsibility on the part of the researcher. For example, because participants were asked to work out until failure, there was some risk to participants in the study by Chmelo et al. (2009)—and this risk was assumed because the researchers created the exercise conditions. For this reason, precautions to protect each participant were put in place, such as ensuring that participants were regularly active prior to the study and ensuring that participants were observed during each exercise session and allowed sufficient recovery time (i.e., 48 hours) between exercise sessions. These precautions were necessary to minimize risks to participants by making sure that each participant was safe before, during, and after each day of exercise. In this way, manipulating the levels of an independent variable can be associated with greater ethical accountability on the part of the researcher.

LEARNING CHECK 2 ✓

1. State whether each of the following is an example of a natural or a staged manipulation:

   A. A researcher measures the alertness of a student while the lights are off, dimmed, or turned on during a lecture.

   B. A researcher employs a confederate to act calm (Group Calm) or act concerned (Group Concerned) during a mock fire drill. The stress response of participants in each group is measured.

2. True or false: When we use random assignment, we can assume that the individual differences of participants are about the same in each group.

3. A researcher studying love limits his sample to teenage couples who are dating. Is the researcher using control by matching or control by holding constant in this example?

4. When the manipulation of the levels of an independent variable is likely to be causing an effect, should we expect to observe small or large error variance?

Answers: 1. A. Natural manipulation, B. Staged manipulation; 2. True; 3. Control by holding constant; 4. Small error variance.

10.6 Comparing Two Independent Samples

To conduct the between-subjects design, participants are selected in a certain way, and a particular test statistic for two groups is used. The goal in experimentation is to minimize the possibility that individual differences, or that something other than a manipulation, caused differences between groups. Methodologically, we ensure that participants are selected in such a way that random assignment can be used, which will make individual differences about the same in each group. Statistically, we add another level of control by using a test statistic to determine the likelihood that something other than the manipulation caused differences in a dependent measure between groups. Each level of control is described in Table 10.2.

Note that the test statistics introduced in this chapter can also be used in quasi-experiments. However, because the quasi-experiment does not methodologically control for individual differences (i.e., random assignment is not used in a quasi-experiment because the levels of the factor already exist), the design cannot demonstrate cause and effect. Both levels of control (methodological and statistical) are present in the between-subjects experimental design. Therefore, the between-subjects experimental design can demonstrate cause and effect. This section introduces how participants are selected to two groups and how the test statistic is used to analyze measured data.

Selecting Two Independent Samples

Using the between-subjects design, different participants are observed in each group. When participants are observed in this way, the sample is called an **independent sample**. Figure 10.6 shows two ways to select two independent samples, and each way is described in this section.

The first way, shown in Figure 10.6a, is to select a sample from two populations. This type of sampling is commonly used to conduct quasi-experiments for situations in which the levels of a factor are preexisting. For example, suppose we hypothesize that students who pay for their own college education, without financial assistance, will study more. We record the time spent studying in a sample of students who, prior to the study, were paying their tuition with or without

> In an **independent sample**, different participants are independently observed one time in each group.

Table 10.2	Two Levels of Control in Experimentation		
Between-Subjects Experimental Design		**Checklist**	
Level of Control	**How?**	**Quasi-Experiment**	**Experiment**
Methodological	Use Random Assignment		√
Statistical	Compute Test Statistic	√	√

Only when both levels of control are established can we demonstrate cause and effect.

financial assistance. Referring to Figure 10.6a, Population 1 consists of students who pay for their education with financial assistance; Population 2 consists of students who pay for their college education without financial assistance. Each sample is selected from a different population, so each sample constitutes a different group.

The second way to select independent samples, shown in Figure 10.6b, is to select one sample from the same population and randomly assign participants in the sample to two groups. This type of sampling is commonly used in experiments that include randomization, manipulation, and a comparison/control group. The only way to achieve an experiment is to randomly assign participants selected from a single population to different groups. For example, suppose we hypothesize that paying students for earning higher grades will improve their performance on an exam. To test this, we could select a group of students and have them study a word list and test their recall. In one group, participants are paid for better scores, and in a second group, participants are not paid. Referring to Figure 10.6b, the population would be college students, from which each sample was selected and randomly assigned to be paid (Group 1) or not paid (Group 2) for earning grades.

> In an experiment, participants are selected from one population, then randomly assigned to groups.

The Use of the Test Statistic

Once participants have been assigned to groups, we conduct the experiment and measure the same dependent variable in each group. For example, suppose we test the hypothesis that music can inspire greater creativity. Studies are quite common in this area of research (see Kokotsaki, 2011; Newton, 2015; Pool & Odell-Miller, 2011). To test this hypothesis, we can select a sample of participants from a single population and randomly assign them to one of two groups. In Group Music, participants listen to classical music for 10 minutes; in Group No Music, different participants listen to a lecture about music for 10 minutes. Listening to classical music versus a lecture is the manipulation. After the manipulation, participants in both groups are given 5 minutes to write down as many uses as they can think of for a paper clip. If the hypothesis is correct, then Group Music should come up with more practical uses for a paper clip than Group No Music. The number of practical uses for a paper clip, then, is the dependent variable measured in both groups.

To compare differences between groups, we will compute a *test statistic*, which is a mathematical formula that allows us to determine whether the manipulation (music vs. no music) or error variance (other factors attributed to individual differences) is likely to explain differences between the groups. In most cases, researchers measure data on an interval or a ratio scale of measurement. In our example, the number of practical uses for a paper clip is a ratio scale measure. In these situations, when data are interval or ratio scale, the appropriate test statistic for comparing differences between two independent samples is the **two-independent-sample *t* test**. This test statistic follows a common form:

> A **two-independent-sample *t* test**, also called an **independent-sample *t* test**, is a statistical procedure used to test hypotheses concerning the difference in interval or ratio scale data between two group means, in which the variance in the population is unknown.

$$t = \frac{\text{Mean differences between groups}}{\text{Mean differences attributed to error}}$$

Figure 10.6 Two Methods of Selecting Two Independent Samples

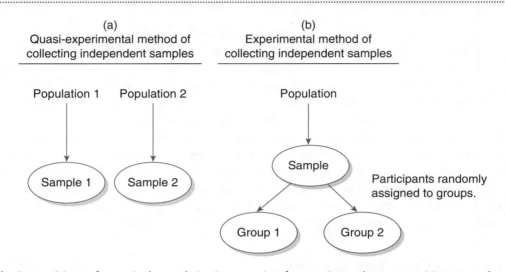

(a)
Quasi-experimental method of
collecting independent samples

(b)
Experimental method of
collecting independent samples

Population 1   Population 2

Sample 1   Sample 2

Population

Sample

Participants randomly
assigned to groups.

Group 1   Group 2

Selecting participants from a single population is appropriate for experiments because participants can then be randomly assigned to different groups.

The numerator of the test statistic is the actual difference between the two groups. For example, suppose that participants in Group Music came up with five practical uses for a paper clip on average, and Group No Music came up with two practical uses on average. The mean difference, then, between the two groups is 3 ($5 - 2 = 3$). We divide the mean difference between two groups by the value for error variance in the denominator. The smaller the error variance, the larger the value of the test statistic will be. In this way, the smaller the error variance, or the less overlap in scores between groups, the more likely we are to conclude that the manipulation, and not factors attributed to individual differences, are causing differences between groups. To illustrate further, we will work through this example using SPSS.

10.7   SPSS in Focus: Two-Independent-Sample *t* Test

In Section 10.4, we used data originally given in Figure 10.4 to illustrate that the more overlap in scores between groups, the larger the error variance. We will use these same data, reproduced in Table 10.3, and assume that they represent the number of practical uses for a paper clip from the classical music and creativity study. We will use SPSS to compute a two-independent-sample *t* test for each data set given in Table 10.3: one test for the no-overlap example, and one test for the overlap example.

1. Click on the **Variable View** tab and enter *Groups* in the **Name column**. In the second row, enter *NoOverlap* in the Name column. In the third row, enter *Overlap*

in the Name column. We will enter whole numbers in each column, so reduce the value to 0 in the **Decimals column** in each row.

2. In the first row (labeled *Groups*), click on the **Values** column and click on the small gray box with three dots. To label the groups, in the **dialog box**, enter *1* in the value cell and *No Music* in the label cell, and then click **Add**. Then enter *2* in the value cell and *Classical Music* in the label cell, and then click **Add**. Select **OK**.

3. Click on the **Data View** tab. In the first column (labeled *Groups*) enter, *1* five times, then *2* five times, which are the codes we entered in Step 2 for each group. In the second column (labeled *NoOverlap*), enter the scores for the No Music group next to the 1s and enter the scores for the Classical Music group next to the 2s for the no-overlap data given in Table 10.3 (left side). In the third column (labeled *Overlap*), enter the scores for the No Music group next to the 1s and enter the scores for the Classical Music group next to the 2s for the overlap data given in Table 10.3 (right side). Figure 10.7 shows how the data should appear.

4. Go to the menu bar and click **Analyze**, then **Compare Means**, and **Independent-Samples T Test** to bring up a dialog box, which is shown in Figure 10.8.

5. Use the arrows to move the data for *NoOverlap* and *Overlap* into the **Test Variable(s):** cell. SPSS will compute a separate *t* test for each of these sets of data. Select *Groups* and use the arrow to move this column into the **Grouping Variable:** cell. Two question marks will appear in that cell.

6. To define the groups, click **Define Groups...** to bring up a new dialog box. Enter *1* in the **Group 1:** box, and enter *2* in the **Group 2:** box, and then click **Continue**. Now a *1* and *2* will appear in the **Grouping Variable** box instead of question marks.

7. Select **OK**, or select **Paste** and click the **Run** command.

Table 10.3   Data to Enter Into SPSS

No-Overlap Example		Overlap Example	
No Music	Classical Music	No Music	Classical Music
1	4	0	1
1	4	0	4
2	5	2	4
3	6	3	8
3	6	5	8
$M = 2$	$M = 5$	$M = 2$	$M = 5$

The data are reproduced from those given in Figure 10.4 (no-overlap example) and Figure 10.5 (overlap example).

Figure 10.7 SPSS Data View for Step 3

Groups	NoOverlap	Overlap
1	1	0
1	1	0
1	2	2
1	3	3
1	3	5
2	4	1
2	4	4
2	5	4
2	6	8
2	6	8

Figure 10.8 SPSS Dialog Box for Steps 4 to 6

Independent-Samples T Test

Test Variable(s):
NoOverlap
Overlap

Options...
Bootstrap...

Grouping Variable:
Groups(1 2)

Define Groups...

OK   Paste   Reset   Cancel   Help

The output table, shown in Table 10.4, gives the results for both data sets; key results are circled and described in the table. Read the first row of each cell because we will assume that the variances were equal between groups. In the Mean Difference column, notice that the mean difference between the two groups is the same for both data sets; the mean difference is –3.0. However, notice in the Std. Error Difference column that the error variance is much smaller for the no-overlap data. The mean difference is the numerator for the test statistic, and the Std. Error Difference (or error variance) is the denominator. If you divide those values, you will obtain the value of the test statistic, given in the t column. The Sig. (2-tailed) column gives the p value, which is the likelihood that individual differences, or anything other than the music manipulation, caused the 3-point effect. The results show that when scores do not overlap between groups, the likelihood that individual differences explain the 3-point effect is $p = .001$; however, when scores do overlap between groups, this likelihood is much larger, $p = .105$.

The criterion in the behavioral sciences is $p \leq .05$. When $p \leq .05$, we conclude that the manipulation caused the effect because the likelihood that anything else caused the effect is less than 5%. When $p > .05$, we conclude that individual differences, or something else, caused the effect because the likelihood is greater than 5% that something else, typically attributed to individual differences, is indeed causing the effect. In this way, the smaller the error variance or overlap in scores between groups, the more likely we are to conclude that differences between groups were caused by the manipulation and not individual differences.

Also given in Table 10.4, the two-independent-sample t test is associated with $N - 2$ degrees of freedom, in which N is the total sample size. We report the results of a t test in a research journal using guidelines given in the *Publication Manual of the American Psychological Association* (APA, 2009). Using these guidelines, we report the results computed here by stating the value of the test statistic, the degrees of freedom (df), and the p value for each t test as shown:

> A two-independent-sample t test showed that classical music significantly enhanced participant creativity when the data did not overlap, $t(8) = -4.743$, $p = .001$; the results were not significant when the data did overlap, $t(8) = -1.826$, $p = .105$.

Table 10.4 SPSS Output Table for the Two-Independent-Sample t Test

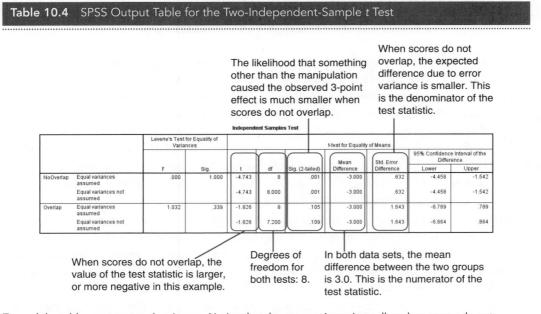

The likelihood that something other than the manipulation caused the observed 3-point effect is much smaller when scores do not overlap.

When scores do not overlap, the expected difference due to error variance is smaller. This is the denominator of the test statistic.

When scores do not overlap, the value of the test statistic is larger, or more negative in this example.

Degrees of freedom for both tests: 8.

In both data sets, the mean difference between the two groups is 3.0. This is the numerator of the test statistic.

To read the table, assume equal variances. Notice that the error variance is smaller when scores do not overlap between groups, thereby making the value of the test statistic larger.

1. In a between-subjects design, are the same or different participants observed at each level of a factor?

2. State whether each of the following is an example of a sampling method used with quasi-experiments or one used with experiments:

   A. A researcher selects a sample of Olympic athletes from the summer and winter Olympic teams to compare differences in motivational styles between these groups of athletes.

   B. A researcher selects a sample of college students, then randomly assigns each student to one of two reading groups and compares comprehension scores in each group.

3. When scores in each group do not overlap, does this mean that the error variance is small or large?

4. True or false: When $p \leq .05$, we conclude that a manipulation caused an effect because the likelihood that anything else caused the effect is less than 5%.

Answers: 1. Different; 2. A. Quasi-experiment, B. Experiment; 3. Small; 4. True.

10.8 Comparing Two or More Independent Samples

Adding groups can allow for more informative conclusions of observed results.

Using the between-subjects design, we can also observe more than two groups, which is often preferred because it can add information that may otherwise be misinterpreted or misunderstood. Consider, for example, Figure 10.9, which summarizes hypothetical well-being scores on a positive social relations subscale of the Ryff Psychological Well-Being Inventory (Ryff, 1989) for three therapy groups, and three comparisons that could have been made if we had chosen to include only two of the three groups. Notice in Comparison A, there is no effect of increasing the intensity of the therapy; in Comparison B, there is a positive effect; in Comparison C, there is a negative effect. By including all three groups, we can see this full pattern emerge. Had we only included two groups, however, we would not have seen this full picture, and we therefore may have made spurious conclusions based on our limited comparisons. Thus, adding groups in a study can often add to the information we have from which conclusions can be drawn, in part, because it increases the number of comparisons we can make between groups.

This section introduces how different participants can be selected to more than two groups and how to use the test statistic to analyze measured data.

Figure 10.9 An Example for How Adding Groups Can Be More Informative

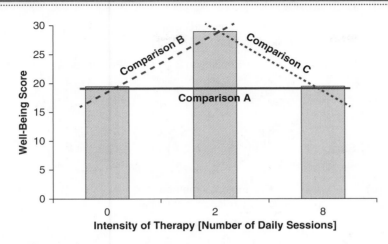

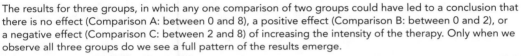

The results for three groups, in which any one comparison of two groups could have led to a conclusion that there is no effect (Comparison A: between 0 and 8), a positive effect (Comparison B: between 0 and 2), or a negative effect (Comparison C: between 2 and 8) of increasing the intensity of the therapy. Only when we observe all three groups do we see a full pattern of the results emerge.

Selecting Multiple Independent Samples

Researchers use similar sampling methods to select different participants to two groups and to multiple groups. The two ways to select different participants to multiple groups are described in Figure 10.10. The first way, shown in Figure 10.10a, is to select a sample from two or more populations. For example, suppose we hypothesize that exercise and food cravings are related, as has been suggested (see Cornier, Melanson, Salzberg, Bechtell, & Tregellas, 2012; Jokisch, Coletta, & Raynor, 2012; McNeil, Cadieux, Finlayson, Blundell, & Doucet, 2015). To test this hypothesis, at a local gym we select patrons who we observe finish an easy, moderate, or intense aerobic workout. Referring to Figure 10.10a, Population 1 consists of patrons who engage in an easy aerobic workout; Population 2 consists of patrons who engage in a moderate aerobic workout; Population *k* consists of patrons who engage in an intense aerobic workout. Each sample is selected from a different population, so each sample constitutes a different group. Because participants determine the group to which they are assigned, this sampling method is commonly used for quasi-experiments.

The second way to select independent samples, shown in Figure 10.10b, is to select one sample from the same population and randomly assign participants in the sample to two or more groups. Using this sampling method, we could select a random sample of patrons at a gym, and then randomly assign the patrons to complete an easy, moderate, or intense aerobic workout. Referring to Figure 10.10b, the population would be gym patrons, from which one sample was selected and randomly assigned to complete an easy (Group 1), moderate (Group 2), or intense (Group *k*) aerobic workout. This sampling method is commonly used for experiments because it makes the random assignment of participants to groups possible.

Figure 10.10 Two Methods of Selecting Multiple Independent Samples

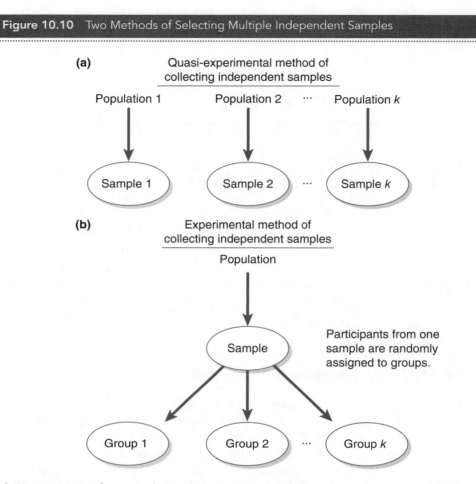

(a) Quasi-experimental method of collecting independent samples

Population 1   Population 2 ··· Population k

Sample 1   Sample 2 ··· Sample k

(b) Experimental method of collecting independent samples

Population

Sample

Participants from one sample are randomly assigned to groups.

Group 1   Group 2 ··· Group k

Selecting participants from a single population is appropriate for experiments because participants can then be randomly assigned to different groups.

The Use of the Test Statistic

Once participants have been assigned to groups, we conduct the experiment and measure the same dependent variable in each group. For example, suppose we want to test the hypothesis that gym patrons will crave more high-fat foods after an intense workout, compared with an easy or moderate aerobic workout. To test this hypothesis, we could create the three exercise levels (easy, moderate, or intense) and randomly assign patrons to each group.

To compare differences between groups, we will compute a *test statistic*, which allows us to determine whether the manipulation (easy, moderate, or intense workout) or error variance (other factors attributed to individual differences) is likely to explain differences between the groups. In most cases, researchers measure data on an interval or a ratio scale of measurement. In our example, the number of high-fat foods chosen is a ratio scale measure. In these situations, when data are interval or ratio scale, the appropriate test statistic for comparing differences among two or more independent samples is the

one-way between-subjects analysis of variance (ANOVA). The term *one-way* indicates the number of factors in a design. In this example, we have one factor or independent variable (type of workout). This test statistic follows a common form:

$$F = \frac{\text{Variability between groups}}{\text{Variability attributed to error}}$$

The **one-way between-subjects ANOVA** is a statistical procedure used to test hypotheses for one factor with two or more levels concerning the variance among group means. This test is used when different participants are observed at each level of a factor and the variance in a given population is unknown.

An ANOVA is computed by dividing the variability in a dependent measure attributed to the manipulation or groups, by the variability attributed to error or individual differences. When the variance attributed to error is the same as the variance attributed to differences between groups, the value of F is 1.0, and we conclude that the manipulation did not cause differences between groups. The larger the variance between groups relative to the variance attributed to error, the larger the value of the test statistic, and the more likely we are to conclude that the manipulation, and not individual differences, is causing an effect or a mean difference between groups.

The one-way between-subjects ANOVA informs us only that the means for at least one pair of groups are different—it does not tell us which pairs of groups differ. For situations in which we have more than two groups in an experiment, we compute **post hoc tests** or "after the fact" tests to determine which pairs of groups are different. Post hoc tests are used to evaluate all possible **pairwise comparisons**, or differences in the group means between all possible pairings of two groups. In the exercise and food cravings experiment, we would use the one-way between-subjects ANOVA to determine if the manipulation (easy, moderate, or intense workout groups) caused the mean number of high-fat foods that participants craved to be different or to vary between groups. We would then compute post hoc tests to determine which pairs of group means were different. To illustrate further, we will work through this research example using SPSS. The data for this example, as well as steps for analyzing these data, are described in Figure 10.11.

A **post hoc test** is a statistical procedure computed following a significant ANOVA to determine which pair or pairs of group means significantly differ. These tests are needed with more than two groups because multiple comparisons must be made.

A **pairwise comparison** is a statistical comparison for the difference between two group means. A post hoc test evaluates all possible pairwise comparisons for an ANOVA with any number of groups.

Reducing error variance increases *power*—or likelihood of observing an effect.

10.9 SPSS in Focus: One-Way Between-Subjects ANOVA

We will use SPSS to compute the one-way between-subjects ANOVA for the data given in Figure 10.11 in Step 1. For these data, we will test the hypothesis that patrons at a gym will crave more high-fat foods after an intense aerobic workout, compared with an easy or moderate aerobic workout. There are two commands that we could use to analyze these data; we will use the One-Way ANOVA command.

1. Click on the **Variable View** tab and enter *Groups* in the **Name column.** In the Values column, click on the small gray box with three dots. To label the groups, in the **dialog box,** enter *1* in the Value cell and *Easy* in the Label cell, then click **Add.** Then enter *2* in the Value cell and *Moderate* in the Label cell, and then click **Add.** Then enter *3* in the Value cell and *Intense* in the Label cell, and then click **Add.** Then click **OK.**

2. Still in the Variable View, enter *Foods* in the Name column in the second row. Reduce the value to 0 in the **Decimals column** for each row.

3. Click on the **Data View** tab. In the first column (labeled *Groups*), enter *1* five times, *2* five times, and *3* five times, which are the codes we entered in Step 2 for each group. In the *Foods* column, enter the data for each group as shown in Figure 10.12a.

4. Go to the menu bar and click **Analyze,** then **Compare Means,** and **One-Way ANOVA** to bring up the dialog box shown in Figure 10.12b.

5. Using the appropriate arrows, move *Groups* into the **Factor:** box. Move *Foods* into the **Dependent List:** box.

6. Click the **Post Hoc** option to bring up the new dialog box shown in Figure 10.12c. Select *Tukey*, which is a commonly used post hoc test. Click **Continue.**

7. Select **OK,** or select **Paste** and click the **Run** command.

The output table, shown in Table 10.5, gives the results for the one-way between-subjects ANOVA. The numerator of the test statistic is the variance between groups, 46.667, and the denominator is the variance attributed to individual differences or error, 2.167. When you divide those two values, you obtain the value of the test statistic, 21.538. The Sig. column gives the *p* value, which in our example shows that the likelihood that anything other than the exercise manipulation caused differences between groups is $p < .001$. We decide that the group manipulation caused the differences when $p < .05$; hence, we decide that the manipulation caused group differences. However, remember that this result does not tell us which groups are different; it tells us only that at least one pair of group means differ significantly.

To determine which groups are different, we conducted post hoc tests, shown in Table 10.6. On the left, you see Easy, Moderate, and Intense labels for the rows. You read the table as comparisons across the rows. The first comparison on the first line in the table is Easy and Moderate. If there is an asterisk next to the value given in the Mean Difference column, then those two groups significantly differ (note that the *p* value for each comparison is also given in the Sig. column for each comparison). The next comparison is Easy and Intense in the top left boxed portion of the table. For all comparisons, the results show that people choose significantly more high-fat foods following an intense workout, compared with a moderate and an easy workout.

Also given in Table 10.5, the one-way between-subjects ANOVA is associated with two sets of degrees of freedom (*df*): one for the variance between groups and one for the variance attributed to error. Using APA (2009) guidelines, we report the results of an ANOVA by stating the value of the test statistic, both degrees of freedom, and the *p* value for the *F* test, and indicate the results of the post hoc test if one was computed as shown:

Step 1: Conduct the one-way between-subjects ANOVA.

Easy	Moderate	Intense
0	4	6
2	3	9
4	3	10
1	6	7
3	4	8
M = 2	M = 4	M = 8

The ANOVA will determine whether at least one of these group means differs from another.

If the test is significant, then conduct post hoc tests; if not, then stop—group means do not differ.

Step 2: Conduct post hoc tests to determine which pairs of means differ.

Easy	Moderate
0	4
2	3
4	3
1	6
3	4
M = 2	M = 4

Moderate	Intense
4	6
3	9
3	10
6	7
4	8
M = 4	M = 8

Easy	Intense
0	6
2	9
4	10
1	7
3	8
M = 2	M = 8

Post hoc tests will make pairwise comparisons—for each pair of means.

If the one-way ANOVA is significant, then the levels of the independent variable are causing at least one pair of means to differ.

A one-way between-subjects ANOVA showed that the number of high-fat foods chosen significantly varied by the type of workout participants completed, $F(2, 12) = 21.538, p < .001$. Participants chose significantly more high-fat foods following a moderate or intense workout compared to an easy workout (Tukey's honestly significant difference, $p \leq .003$).

Figure 10.12   The Data View and Dialog Boxes for Steps 3 to 6

(b) SPSS dialog box for Steps 4 to 5.

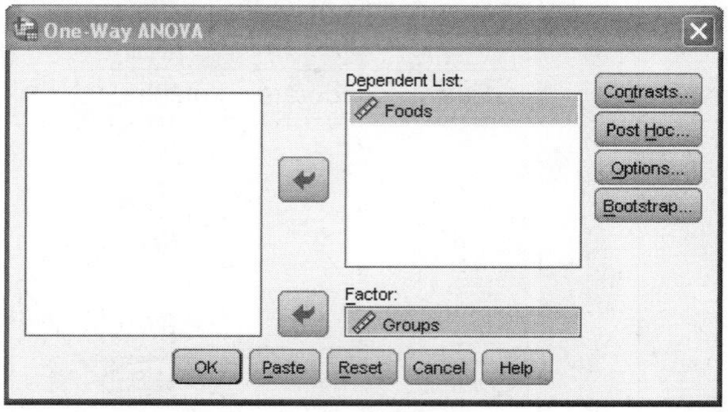

(a) SPSS Data View for Step 3.

Groups	Foods
1	0
1	2
1	4
1	1
1	3
2	4
2	3
2	3
2	6
2	4
3	6
3	9
3	10
3	7
3	8

(c) SPSS dialog box for Step 6.

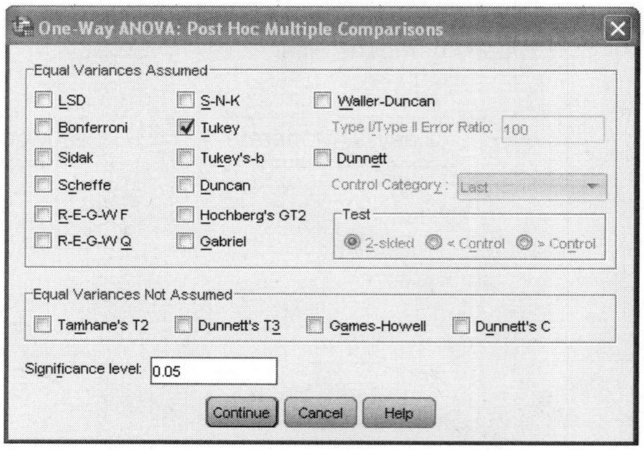

LEARNING CHECK 4 ✓

1. State whether each of the following between-subjects designs is an example of a quasi-experiment or an experiment:

   A. A researcher compares differences in resilience among single, divorced, and married women.

   B. A researcher measures job satisfaction among employees randomly assigned to receive a small, moderate, or large bonus during the holidays.

2. What test statistic is used to compare differences in interval or ratio data between two or more groups to which different participants were assigned?

3. Why do researchers compute post hoc tests?

Answers: 1. A. Quasi-experimental. B. Experimental; 2. The one-way between-subjects ANOVA; 3. To determine which pairs of group means differ significantly following a significant ANOVA.

Table 10.5 SPSS Output Table for the One-Way Between-Subjects ANOVA

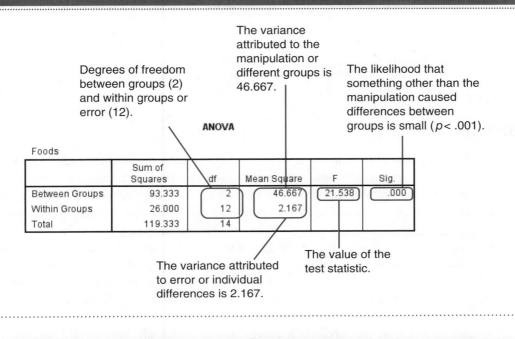

Degrees of freedom between groups (2) and within groups or error (12).

The variance attributed to the manipulation or different groups is 46.667.

The likelihood that something other than the manipulation caused differences between groups is small ($p < .001$).

ANOVA

Foods

	Sum of Squares	df	Mean Square	F	Sig.
Between Groups	93.333	2	46.667	21.538	.000
Within Groups	26.000	12	2.167		
Total	119.333	14			

The variance attributed to error or individual differences is 2.167.

The value of the test statistic.

Table 10.6 SPSS Output Table for the Post Hoc Test

Multiple Comparisons

Dependent Variable: Foods

Tukey HSD

(I) Groups	(J) Groups	Mean Difference (I-J)	Std. Error	Sig.	95% Confidence Interval	
					Lower Bound	Upper Bound
Easy	Moderate	-2.000	.931	.122	-4.48	.48
	Intense	-6.000*	.931	.000	-8.48	-3.52
Moderate	Easy	2.000	.931	.122	-.48	4.48
	Intense	-4.000*	.931	.003	-6.48	-1.52
Intense	Easy	6.000*	.931	.000	3.52	8.48
	Moderate	4.000*	.931	.003	1.52	6.48

*. The mean difference is significant at the 0.05 level.

10.10 Measuring the Dependent Variable

In an experiment, we measure the same dependent variable in each group so that differences in that measure can be compared between groups. While the measures described here can be evaluated using any of the three major categories of research design, they are introduced here to emphasize the importance of making valid and reliable measures in experimentation. Three types of dependent variables commonly measured in the behavioral sciences are as follows:

- Self-report measures
- Behavioral measures
- Physiological measures

Self-Report Measures

The responses of participants using self-report measures can be compared between groups in an experiment. A **self-report measure** is a survey, administered either written or orally, with items (e.g., questions or statements) to which participants respond to indicate their actual or perceived experiences, attitudes, or opinions. The responses in a self-report measure can be coded numerically or given on numeric response scales. In an experiment or another research study, participants are typically given restricted or closed-ended items with numeric response scales to ensure that responses are numeric for later use of a test statistic to compare differences between groups.

> A **self-report measure** is a type of measurement in which participants respond to one or more questions or statements to indicate their actual or perceived experiences, attitudes, or opinions.

Behaviors can be measured using a single item. For example, Svanum and Aiugner (2011) had students complete single-item measures that asked if they completed textbook reading assignments on a scale from 1 (*none*) to 5 (*all of the assigned material*). Although single-item measures are commonly used, multiple-item measures are typically preferred when measuring constructs such as quality of life, depression, self-esteem, and disgust. As an example for such measures, we can measure life satisfaction using the Quality of Life Enjoyment and Satisfaction Questionnaire (Endicott, Nee, Harrison, & Blumenthal, 1993); we can measure depression using the 17-item Hamilton Rating Scale for Depression (Hamilton, 1960; Kalali et al., 2002); we can measure self-esteem using the Rosenberg Self-Esteem Scale (Rosenberg, 1965); and we can measure disgust using the Disgust Propensity and Sensitivity Scale (Cavanagh & Davey, 2000). Each survey or measure includes multiple items to measure a construct or behavior.

The key advantage of using a self-report measure is that it is easy and cost-effective to administer and allows researchers to measure a lot of data in little time. Participants can respond to dozens of restricted items in minutes, providing researchers with a lot of data for a construct or behavior. However, the key disadvantage is that self-report items are often inaccurate. Participants can deliberately lie, be confused by the questions being asked, or simply guess if they do not know how to respond to items in a self-report measure.

> It is important that the dependent variables we measure are valid and reliable.

Behavioral Measures

The behavior of participants can be compared between groups in an experiment. A **behavioral measure** is the observable behavior of participants. How we measure the behavior we will observe mostly depends on how the behavior is operationalized. For example, suppose we test a hypothesis about eating behavior. We could measure how much people eat (number of calories or total weights of foods), how quickly people eat (number of bites or time spent chewing), or how often people eat (number of meals and snacks consumed per day). There are many ways to observe the same behavior, such as in our example of different ways to measure eating behavior.

> A **behavioral measure** is a type of measurement in which researchers directly observe and record the behavior of subjects or participants.

The key advantage of observing behavior is that it is a more direct measure than self-reported behavior. Researchers can directly record the actual frequency, rate, or duration of a behavior they are interested in measuring, instead of relying on participants to self-report their frequency, rate, or duration of a behavior. The key disadvantage, however, is that observing behavior directly can cause substantial ethical problems, such as observing sexual behavior or illegal drug use firsthand. In addition, some aspects of behavior are constructs that do not have obvious behavioral measures, such as self-esteem, which is typically observed using self-report measures.

Physiological Measures

The normal and disordered functioning of the physiological responses of participants can be compared between groups in an experiment. A **physiological measure** is the recorded physical responses of the brain and body in a human or animal. For example, researchers can measure stress and anxiety by measuring cortisol levels in a blood sample or by measuring a galvanic skin response; they can measure sleep and arousal using an electroencephalogram, which records brain activity, or by using an electrooculogram, which monitors eye movements. Other commonly used physiological measures include blood pressure (in systolic pressure over diastolic pressure, or millimeters of mercury), heart rate (in number of beats per minute), or body temperature (in degrees Fahrenheit).

> A **physiological measure** is a type of measurement in which researchers record physical responses of the brain and body in a human or an animal.

The key advantage of physiological measures is that when careful collection procedures are used, these measures are unbiased. Physiological measures are particularly unbiased when they are automatically controlled, such as heart rate, blood pressure, body temperature, and skin conductance. Each physiological measure is an involuntary process of the body. The key disadvantage is largely the expense and training required to operate the equipment needed to make these measurements. Self-report and behavioral measures are often the more affordable option to measure a dependent variable.

10.11 Advantages and Disadvantages of the Between-Subjects Design

The key advantage of using a between-subjects design is that it is the only design that can meet all three requirements of an experiment (randomization, manipulation, and the inclusion of a comparison/control group) to demonstrate cause and effect. In a between-subjects design, we use random assignment to assign different participants to one and only one group. In this way, we can use random assignment, which would otherwise not be possible if the same participants were observed in each group. A second advantage is that the between-subjects design places less of a burden on the participant and the researcher. Observing participants on only one occasion eliminates the problem of attrition or dropout rates, which can ease the burden on researchers because they do not have to track each participant beyond that one observation.

The key disadvantage, however, is that the sample size required to conduct a between-subjects design can be large, particularly with many groups. For example, if we observed 30 participants in each group, then we would need 60 participants in a two-group design ($30 \times 2 = 60$), 90 participants in a three-group design ($30 \times 3 = 90$), and 120 participants in a four-group design ($30 \times 4 = 120$). It can be difficult to recruit the large number of participants needed to conduct a between-subjects design, particularly in small research settings with limited participant pools and funding. In this way, a between-subjects design can sometimes be too impractical, so a researcher will use an alternative design that requires the selection of fewer participants—this alternative research design is described in the next chapter.

> A between-subjects experimental design meets the requirements to demonstrate cause, but this design can require large sample sizes.

LEARNING CHECK 5 ✓

1. Name three types of measurements for a dependent variable.

2. What is the key advantage and disadvantage of using a between-subjects design?

Answers: 1. Self-report measures, behavioral measures, and physiological measures; 2. The key advantage is that participants are observed only once, which allows for the use of random assignment. The key disadvantage is that the sample size required to conduct a between-subjects design can be large, particularly with many groups.

CHAPTER SUMMARY

LO 1 Delineate the between-subjects design and the between-subjects experimental design.

- A **between-subjects design** is a research design in which different participants are observed one time in each group of a research study.
- A **between-subjects experimental design** is an experimental research design in which the levels of a **between-subjects factor** are manipulated, then different participants are randomly assigned to each group or to each level of that factor and observed one time. We follow six steps to use the between-subjects design in an experiment:

1. Obtain a sample.

2. Create two or more groups by manipulating the levels of an independent variable.

3. Use random assignment to select participants to a group.

4. Measure the same dependent variable in each group.

5. Use inferential statistics to compare differences between groups.

6. Make a decision.

LO 2 Distinguish between an experimental group and a control group.

- An **experimental group** is a condition in an experiment in which participants are treated or exposed to a manipulation, or level of the independent variable, that is believed to cause a change in a dependent variable.

- A **control group** is a condition in an experiment in which participants are treated the same as participants in a treatment group, except that the manipulation believed to cause a change in the dependent variable is omitted.

LO 3 Distinguish between a natural and a staged experimental manipulation.

- An **experimental manipulation** is the identification of an independent variable and the creation of two or more groups that constitute the levels of that variable. Two types of experimental manipulations are the following:

  o In a **natural manipulation**, we manipulate a stimulus that can be naturally changed with little effort.

  o In a **staged manipulation**, we manipulate an independent variable that requires the participant to be "set up" to experience some stimulus or event.

LO 4 Explain how random assignment, control by matching, and control by holding constant can make individual differences about the same between groups.

- The random assignment of participants to different groups ensures that participants, and therefore the individual differences of participants, are assigned to groups entirely by chance. When we do this, we can assume that the individual differences of participants in each group are about the same.

- **Restricted random assignment** is a method of controlling differences in participant characteristics between groups in a study by first restricting a sample based on known participant characteristics, then using a random procedure to assign participants to each group. Two strategies of restricted random assignment are the following:

  o In **control by matching**, we assess or measure the characteristic we want to control, group or categorize participants based on scores on that measure, and then use a random procedure to assign participants from each category to a group in the study.

  o In **control by holding constant**, we limit which participants are included in a sample based on characteristics they exhibit that may otherwise differ between groups in a study.

LO 5 Explain why it is important to measure error variance in an experiment.

- **Error variance** or **error** is a numeric measure of the variability in scores that can be attributed to or are caused by the individual differences of participants in each group.

We measure error variance to account for any overlap in scores between groups, which is an indication that differences are occurring by chance because participant behavior is overlapping between groups.

- To measure error variance, and differences between groups, we identify a **test statistic** that allows researchers to determine the extent to which differences observed between groups can be attributed to the manipulation used to create the different groups (i.e., groups are different) or can be attributed to error (i.e., people are different).

LO 6 Identify the appropriate sampling method and test statistic for independent samples to compare differences between two group means.

- Using the between-subjects design, we select an **independent sample**, meaning that different participants are observed in each group. To select participants to an independent sample, we can select two groups from different populations (a quasi-experimental method), or we can sample from a single population, and then randomly assign participants to two groups (an experimental method).
- The appropriate test statistic for comparing differences between two group means for the between-subjects design is the **two-independent-sample t test**. Using this test statistic establishes statistical control of error or differences attributed to individual differences. The larger the value of the test statistic, the more likely we are to conclude that a manipulation, and not error, caused a mean difference between two groups.

LO 7 Identify the appropriate sampling method and test statistic for independent samples to compare differences among two or more group means.

- To select participants to an independent sample with two or more groups, we can select groups from many different populations (a quasi-experimental method), or we can select groups from a single population, and then randomly assign participants to two or more groups (an experimental method).
- The appropriate test statistic for comparing differences between two or more groups using the between-subjects design is the **one-way between-subjects ANOVA**. If the results are significant, then at least one pair of group means are different, and we conduct **post hoc tests** to determine which pairs of group means are significantly different. The larger the value of the test statistic, the more likely we are to conclude that the manipulation, and not error, caused a mean difference between two groups. Using this statistical procedure establishes statistical control of error or differences attributed to individual differences.

LO 8 Identify and give an example of three types of measures for a dependent variable.

- Three types of measures for a dependent variable are **self-report measures** (e.g., items used in a survey), **behavioral measures** (e.g., speed and distance traveled by an athlete), and **physiological measures** (e.g., heart rate or body temperature).

LO 9 Name two advantages and one disadvantage of the between-subjects design.

- The key advantage of using a between-subjects design is that it is the only design that allows for the use of randomization, manipulation, and the inclusion of a comparison/control group, which are required to demonstrate cause and effect. A between-subjects design also places less of a burden on the participant and the researcher because participants are observed (or participate) only one time, and the researcher does not have to track participants over time.
- One disadvantage of a between-subjects design is that the sample size required to conduct this design can be large, particularly with many groups.

LO 10 Compute a two-independent-sample t test and a one-way between-subjects analysis of variance using SPSS.

- SPSS can be used to compute a two-independent-sample t test using the **Analyze, Compare Means**, and **Independent-Samples T Test** options in the menu bar. These actions will display a dialog box that allows you to identify the groups and run the test (for more details, see Section 10.7).
- SPSS can be used to compute the one-way between-subjects ANOVA. Using the **One-Way ANOVA** command, select the **Analyze, Compare Means**, and **One-Way ANOVA** options in the menu bar. These actions will display a dialog box that allows you to identify the variables, choose an appropriate post hoc test, and run the analysis (for more details, see Section 10.9).

KEY TERMS

between-subjects design

between-subjects
  experimental design

between-subjects factor

control

experimental group

treatment group

control group

placebo

experimental manipulation

natural manipulation

staged manipulation

restricted random
  assignment

control by matching

control by holding constant

error variance

error

test statistic

independent sample

two-independent-sample
  t test

independent-sample t test

one-way between-subjects
  ANOVA

post hoc tests

pairwise comparisons

self-report measure

behavioral measure

physiological measure

REVIEW QUESTIONS

1. To conduct a study, a researcher randomly assigns participants to an experimental or a control group and observes each participant one time. Is this study an example of a between-subjects design?

2. State the six steps to conduct a between-subjects experimental design.

3. State which of the following is an example of a natural manipulation and which is an example of a staged manipulation.

   A. A researcher manipulates the lighting in a room during a study session (30, 60, or 120 watts).

   B. A researcher manipulates whether a participant sits next to a polite or a rude confederate in an experimental setting.

4. A researcher selects a sample of female police officers and assigns half of the women to a low-stress group and the other half of the women to a high-stress group, such that all women have an equal probability of being selected to one group or the other. What type of procedure was used to assign women to groups in this example?

5. A researcher studying appetite is concerned that gender differences could be problematic because men and women have very different appetites. What type of restricted random assignment strategy can the researcher use to make sure that an equal number of men and women are represented in the sample? Explain.

6. Based on a visual inspection of the following graph displaying data for two groups in an experiment, is it likely that the manipulation is causing an effect between groups? Explain.

7. How is error variance related to individual differences?

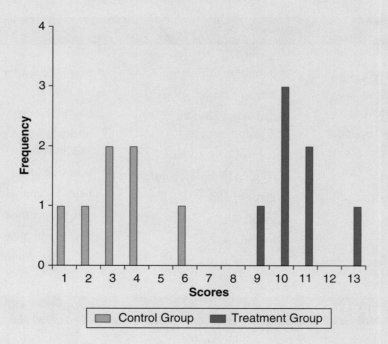

8. State the way of selecting independent samples that is used with experiments, and explain why it is appropriate for an experiment.

9. Name the test statistic for a between-subjects design (1) used to compare differences between two group means, and (2) used to compare differences among two or more group means.

10. In terms of making a decision, what information does the p value indicate?

11. Identify the experimental group and the control group described in the following example:

> To determine how people learn to like the flavors of foods in their diet, participants in a sample were randomly assigned to consume a flavored drink that was either sweetened or unsweetened. Rating of liking for each drink was recorded. It was hypothesized that ratings of liking would be higher for sweetened drinks.

12. A researcher measures stress by recording the heart rate of participants and by asking participants to rate their current stress level on a 5-point scale from 1 (*low stress*) to 5 (*high stress*). What types of measures for the dependent variable were used in this example?

13. A researcher records the number of times a soldier disobeys a direct order. What type of measurement for the dependent variable was used in this example?

14. Why is sample size a potential disadvantage of using a between-subjects design?

ACTIVITIES

1. A few local businesses noticed that their employees are tardy or sick most often on Fridays, compared with any other day of the week. Based on this observation:
   A. Design an experiment using a between-subjects design to test why most employees are tardy or sick on Fridays.
   B. Specify how your design is experimental. In other words, explain how you will use manipulation, randomization, and comparison/control in your design.

2. In studies that use rodents, such as rats or mice, the genetic differences, diets, habitat, environment, and most other aspects of the rodents' lives are mostly identical. How might this level of control make a between-subjects experiment better at controlling for individual differences compared to a similar experiment using human participants?

Identify a problem

- Determine an area of interest.
- Review the literature.
- Identify new ideas in your area of interest.
- Develop a research hypothesis.

Develop a research plan

- Define the variables being tested.
- Identify participants or subjects and determine how to sample them.
- Select a research strategy and design.
- Evaluate ethics and obtain institutional approval to conduct research.

Generate more new ideas

- Results support your hypothesis—refine or expand on your ideas.
- Results do not support your hypothesis—reformulate a new idea or start over.

After reading this chapter, you should be able to:

1 Delineate the within-subjects design and the within-subjects experimental design.

2 Explain why it is important to control for time-related factors using a within-subjects experimental design.

3 Demonstrate the use of counterbalancing and control for timing using a within-subjects experimental design.

4 Identify three sources of variation and explain why one source is removed using the within-subjects design.

5 Identify the appropriate sampling method and test statistic for related samples to compare differences between two group means.

6 Identify the appropriate sampling method and test statistic for related samples to compare differences among two or more group means.

7 Apply a Solomon four-group design for the within-subjects experimental design.

8 Contrast the use of a between-subjects versus a within-subjects design for an experiment.

9 Compute a related-samples *t* test and a one-way within-subjects analysis of variance using SPSS.

Communicate the results

- Method of communication: oral, written, or in a poster.
- Style of communication: APA guidelines are provided to help prepare style and format.

Conduct the study

- Execute the research plan and measure or record the data.

Analyze and evaluate the data

- Analyze and evaluate the data as they relate to the research hypothesis.
- Summarize data and research results.

WITHIN-SUBJECTS EXPERIMENTAL DESIGNS

Suppose you go out for a one-mile run one day with music and the next day without music. You report that running while listening to music on Day 1 made you feel better than running while not listening to music on Day 2. Do you conclude, then, that listening to music while running enhances how good you feel? Suppose you go out on a third day without music and this time feel just as good as when you ran with music. Now does your conclusion change? It should.

The problem described here is a concern when you observe the same participants over time. Specifically, how do you account for the passage of time? In our example, you wake up in the morning on each of two days. On Day 1, you run while listening to music; on Day 2, you run without listening to music and report how good the workout made you feel. Suppose we did this manipulation with a group of participants and find that the workout was reported as making participants feel better on Day 1 when they listened to music while running. What about alternative explanations related to the passage of time? For example, maybe the first run on Day 1 made participants feel sore the following day, so fatigue the following day, and not that they did not listen to music on Day 2, is the reason the second run felt worse. This alternative cannot be ruled out, so we require greater measures of control to account for these alternatives when observing the same participants over time.

In this chapter, we introduce the within-subjects experimental design in which the same participants are observed in each group. Using this design, we take added measures of control to rule out possible factors related to observing the same participants over time. By eliminating time-related factors, we can be more confident that differences observed over time are due to a manipulation (e.g., music vs. no music in our example), and not factors related to the passage of time (e.g., fatigue).

11.1 Conducting Experiments: Within-Subjects Design

A **within-subjects design**, also called a **repeated-measures design**, is a research design in which the same participants are observed one time in each group of a research study.

A **within-subjects experimental design** is an experimental research design in which the levels of a within-subjects factor are manipulated and then the same participants are observed in each group or at each level of the factor. To qualify as an experiment, the researcher must (1) manipulate the levels of the factor and include a comparison/control group, and (2) make added efforts to control for order and time-related factors.

A **within-subjects factor** is a type of factor in which the same participants are observed in each group, or at each level of the factor.

For a between-subjects design, a different set of participants is observed in each group. However, it is not always possible or practical to conduct such a study. In this chapter, we introduce an alternative research design called the **within-subjects design**, which is a research design in which the same participants are observed in each group. Specifically, we will introduce the **within-subjects experimental design,** in which we manipulate the levels of a **within-subjects factor** and then observe the same participants in each group or at each level of the factor. The steps for conducting a within-subjects experimental design are described in Figure 11.1.

Two common reasons that researchers observe the same participants in each group are as follows:

1. To manage sample size. When many groups are observed or when many participants are observed in each group, it is often more practical to observe the same participants in each group. For example, if we observe 30 participants in three groups, then a between-subjects design would require 90 participants (30 × 3 = 90), whereas a within-subjects design would require only 30 participants observed three times.

2. To observe changes in behavior over time, which is often the case for studies on learning or within-participant changes over time. As an example, Badanes, Dmitrieva, and Watamura (2012) studied how brain cortisol levels (a measure of stress) in children changed at different points in time during a full-day child care session. In this study, the only way to make their observations was to measure cortisol levels in each child at multiple times during the day so that changes over time could be compared.

The within-subjects experimental design, described in Figure 11.1, does not meet the randomization requirement for demonstrating cause and effect. We do manipulate the levels of an independent variable and include at least two groups (at least one of which is a comparison or control group) in Steps 2 and 3. However, because the same participants are observed in each group, we cannot use random assignment; we therefore do not use randomization, which is a requirement in an experiment. Step 4 is therefore included as an added measure to control for possible order and time-related factors associated with observing the same participants over time.

In a within-subjects design, the same participants are observed in each group.

Figure 11.1 The Steps Used for a Within-Subjects Experimental Design

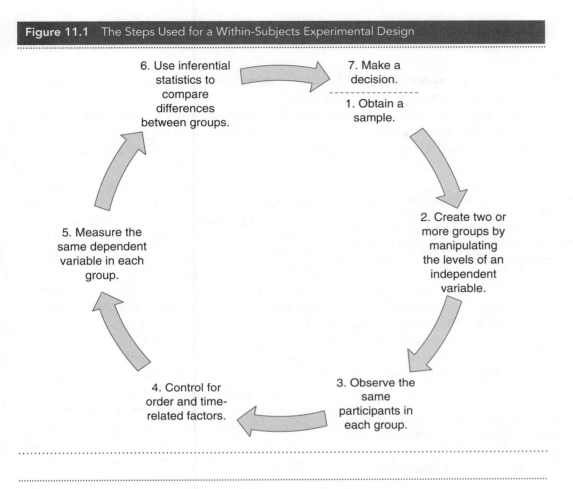

11.2 Controlling Time-Related Factors

Step 4 in Figure 11.1, the step where we control for order and time-related factors, is required for a within-subjects design to qualify as an experiment. The reason Step 4 is required is that when we observe the same participants over time, factors related to observing participants over time can also vary between groups. This is not a problem in a between-subjects design because different participants are observed one time in a group and not over time. When time-related factors covary with the levels of an independent variable (i.e., the manipulation), these factors can then threaten the internal validity of an experiment.

Time-related factors include those introduced in Chapter 6, such as maturation, testing effects, regression toward the mean, attrition, and **participant fatigue**, which occurs when a participant becomes tired of participating further in an experiment. These time-related factors must be controlled or made the same between groups, such that only the levels of the independent variable are different between groups. Again,

> **Participant fatigue** is a state of physical or psychological exhaustion resulting from intense research demands typically due to observing participants too often, or requiring participants to engage in research activities that are too demanding.

the goal here is to conclude that the manipulation is causing differences between groups. Therefore, we need to control for factors that may covary with the manipulation—that is, factors related to observing the same participants over time.

To control for time-related factors, researchers make efforts to control for **order effects**. Order effects occur when the order in which a participant receives different treatments or participates in different groups causes the value of a dependent variable to change. Order effects are observed throughout the literature. For example, consideration must be made for the order in which questions are asked in a survey, which can influence participant responses to items in that survey (Rasinski, Lee, & Krishnamurty, 2012); the order in which different hypothetical situations, such as moral scenarios, are presented can influence the tendency of participants to choose or endorse actions described in one scenario over the other (Schwitzgebel & Cushman, 2012); and, when asked to choose which of two objects we prefer, our preference choice can be influenced by the order in which we are presented with the two alternatives, particularly when the choices vary in magnitude and attractiveness (Englund & Hellström, 2012; Hellström, 2003).

> **Order effects** are a threat to internal validity in which the order in which participants receive different treatments or participate in different groups causes changes in a dependent variable.

To illustrate further, suppose a researcher measures the rate at which children complete each of two behavioral tasks. The goal is to conclude that the two behavioral tasks cause changes in a dependent variable. However, children could use knowledge about one task to help them complete the second task (testing or **carryover effect**); if the tasks were difficult, then the children could have been more fatigued for the second task (fatigue); if there was a lot of time between the two tasks, then the children could have matured by the time they completed the second task (maturation). Any one of these factors could also explain differences between groups unless we control for time-related factors to eliminate these threats to the internal validity of an experiment. To control for these threats to internal validity, researchers can use two strategies:

> **Carryover effects** are a threat to internal validity in which participation in one group "carries over" or causes changes in performance in a second group.

1. Control order (counterbalancing, partial counterbalancing)
2. Control timing

Controlling Order: Counterbalancing

Researchers can control the order in which participants receive different treatments or participate in different groups using a procedure called **counterbalancing**. Using this procedure, we balance or offset the order in which participants receive different treatments or participate in different groups. Two types of counterbalancing are as follows:

> Using a **counterbalancing** procedure, the order in which participants receive different treatments or participate in different groups is balanced or offset in an experiment. Two types of counterbalancing are complete and partial counterbalancing.

1. Complete counterbalancing

2. Partial counterbalancing

Complete counterbalancing is used to balance or offset the different orders in which participants could receive different treatments or participate in different groups. This type of counterbalancing is used when the number of treatments or different groups is small—usually two groups, but not more than three. As an example,

> **Complete counterbalancing** is a procedure in which all possible order sequences in which participants receive different treatments or participate in different groups are balanced or offset in an experiment.

Hill, Williams, Aucott, Thomson, and Mon-Williams (2011) used complete counterbalancing with two groups (exercise program, no exercise program). One group received a classroom-based exercise program in the first week and no program in the second week; that order was reversed for a second group. In this way, the researchers could control for the possibility that the order of group assignment somehow influenced responses in each group.

To calculate the number of possible orders, make the following calculation in which k is the number of treatments or groups:

$$\text{Number of possible order sequences} = k!$$

As k increases, so do the number of possible order sequences. There are 2 possible order sequences when $k = 2$ ($2 \times 1 = 2$); 6 possible order sequences when $k = 3$ ($3 \times 2 \times 1 = 6$); and 24 possible order sequences when $k = 4$ ($4 \times 3 \times 2 \times 1 = 24$). With only 2 or 6 order sequences, researchers could counterbalance every possible order. However, counterbalancing 24 order sequences would be difficult. For example, Figure 11.2 shows how counterbalancing would be used with two groups. Notice that counterbalancing, shown in Figure 11.2b, offsets or balances the possible order sequences in each group. By comparison, counterbalancing 24 possible order sequences would be very difficult. With a larger number of groups, then, researchers use a different type of counterbalancing: partial counterbalancing.

Partial counterbalancing is used to balance or offset some, but not all, possible order sequences in which participants receive different treatments or participate in different groups. This type of counterbalancing is often used when there are three or more groups. The few order sequences that are counterbalanced must be representative of all order sequences that could be counterbalanced. To ensure that the few counterbalanced order sequences are representative of all order sequences, we must ensure the following:

> **Partial counterbalancing** is a procedure in which some, but not all, possible order sequences in which participants receive different treatments or participate in different groups are balanced or offset in an experiment.

- Each treatment or group appears equally often in each position.

- Each treatment or group precedes and follows each treatment or group one time.

Figure 11.2 Counterbalancing With Two Groups or Treatments

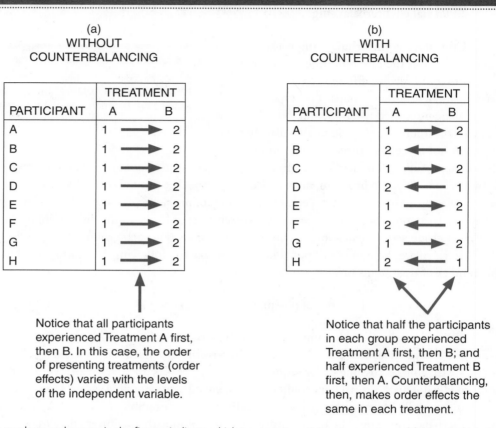

(a)
WITHOUT COUNTERBALANCING

(b)
WITH COUNTERBALANCING

Notice that all participants experienced Treatment A first, then B. In this case, the order of presenting treatments (order effects) varies with the levels of the independent variable.

Notice that half the participants in each group experienced Treatment A first, then B; and half experienced Treatment B first, then A. Counterbalancing, then, makes order effects the same in each treatment.

The numbers and arrows in the figures indicate which treatment participants experienced first and which they experienced second.

With four treatments (A, B, C, and D), we can ensure that a limited number of order sequences are representative of all order sequences, as shown in Figure 11.3. Of the 4 (out of 24 possible) order sequences chosen in Figure 11.3, each treatment occurs one time in each column or position, and each treatment precedes and follows each treatment one time (e.g., AB in row 1, BA in row 3). To use partial counterbalancing, order sequences can be chosen systematically or at random, but the two criteria for selecting representative order sequences must be met. As a special case of partial counterbalancing, we can use a procedure called a **Latin square** to select representative order sequences. This procedure is widely used in the behavioral sciences (for critical reviews, see Cotton, 1993; Reese, 1997) and was used to select the 4 representative order sequences shown in Figure 11.3 (right side). The steps to construct a Latin square are given in Appendix B.2.

A **Latin square** is a matrix design in which a limited number of order sequences are constructed such that (1) the number of order sequences equals the number of treatments, (2) each treatment appears equally often in each position, and (3) each treatment precedes and follows each treatment one time.

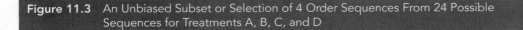

Figure 11.3 An Unbiased Subset or Selection of 4 Order Sequences From 24 Possible Sequences for Treatments A, B, C, and D

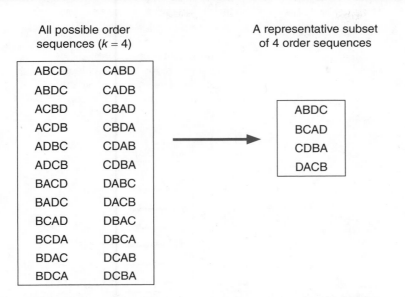

All possible order sequences (*k* = 4)

ABCD	CABD
ABDC	CADB
ACBD	CBAD
ACDB	CBDA
ADBC	CDAB
ADCB	CDBA
BACD	DABC
BADC	DACB
BCAD	DBAC
BCDA	DBCA
BDAC	DCAB
BDCA	DCBA

A representative subset of 4 order sequences

ABDC
BCAD
CDBA
DACB

Notice on the right side that A, B, C, and D occur once in each column or position, and each treatment precedes and follows each treatment one time (e.g., AB in Row 1 and BA in Row 3).

Controlling Timing: Intervals and Duration

Another way to control for threats to internal validity associated with observing the same participants over time is to control timing. Researchers can control timing by controlling the following:

- Interval between treatments or groups

- Total duration of an experiment

> Counterbalancing does not eliminate order effects; rather, it balances these effects, such that they are equal or the same in each group.

MAKING SENSE—COUNTERBALANCING AS A BETWEEN-SUBJECTS FACTOR

Using counterbalancing ensures that the number of possible order sequences is the same in each group. For example, with two groups (A and B), half participate first in Group A, then in Group B; and half participate first in Group B, then in Group A, as shown in Figure 11.4. The order of participation is not a threat to internal validity in this case because the same number of participants in each group have each possible order sequence.

(Continued)

(Continued)

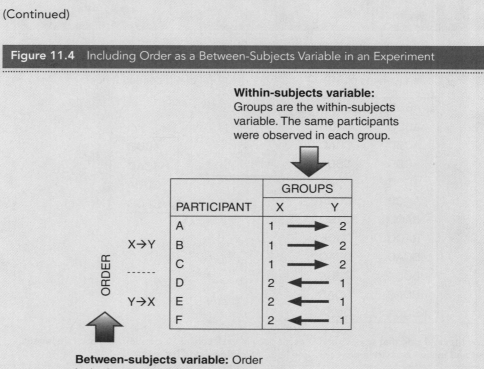

Within-subjects variable: Groups are the within-subjects variable. The same participants were observed in each group.

Between-subjects variable: Order is the between-subjects variable. Half the participants (A, B, C) experienced Group X, then Y, and half (D, E, F) experienced the reverse order: Group Y, then X.

Notice that participants can be grouped based on which order sequence they received (the between-subjects variable).

In some cases, however, there may be reason to believe that one order sequence is associated with larger changes than the other. For example, Privitera, Mulcahey, and Orlowski (2012) measured how much children liked flavors that were sweetened or plain. In this study, one concern was the possibility that having a sweetened drink first could affect participant ratings of the plain drink more so than drinking it plain first and then having it sweetened. In these situations, illustrated in Figure 11.4, researchers can include *order* as a between-subjects factor and the groups (type of drink: sweetened or plain) as a within-subjects factor. In this way, researchers can test whether the order of presenting the drinks causes changes in a dependent variable (e.g., liking for the sweetened drink). The experimental design described here is introduced in greater detail in Chapter 12 for the factorial designs.

We control the interval between treatments or groups to minimize possible testing and carryover effects. We often need to increase the interval between treatments when a treatment causes physiological arousal, such as exercise, to ensure that the arousal settles before giving the next treatment. For example, Chmelo, Hall, Miller, and Sanders (2009) used an exercise manipulation in which participants were given 48 hours between exercise sessions to make sure, in part, that performance in one exercise session did not carry over to the next exercise session.

As another way to control timing, we can control the total duration of an experiment to minimize the total demands placed on participants, which, when great, can lead to participant attrition or fatigue. For example, Privitera, McGrath, Windus, and Doraiswamy (2015) tested how self-control varied for four food types (a dessert, fried food, fruit, and vegetable) across more than 100 trials, with the selection of a smaller portion of a food now versus a larger portion of that same food later constituting a trial. The researchers could have conducted only a few trials per day; however, that would have required weeks or months to complete the study. For this reason, the researchers instead completed all trials in a single experimental session by restricting the duration of each trial to 6 seconds and the duration between each trial to 3 seconds. By doing so, each participant was able to complete all experimental trials in a single session that lasted less than 1 hour—thereby minimizing concerns of participant attrition or participant fatigue.

For a given experiment, we may require very different ways to control timing. However, as a general rule, increasing the interval between treatments or groups, while also minimizing the total duration of an experiment, is often the most effective strategy for minimizing common threats to internal validity that are associated with observing the same participants over time.

> Two ways to control timing are to control the interval between treatments or groups, and to control the total duration of an experiment.

11.3 Ethics in Focus: Minimizing Participant Fatigue

Observing participants over time is mostly problematic or poses potential ethical risks when it leads to participant fatigue, which results from observing participants too often, or requiring participants to engage in research activities that are too demanding. As part of a research protocol, researchers must disclose any potential risks, including those risks related to participant fatigue. To minimize risks related to participant fatigue, we should consider the following precautions, which are the same types of considerations we make to control for timing:

- Minimize the duration needed to complete an experiment. For longer experiments, such as those lasting days or weeks, the researcher must be able to justify or explain why it is absolutely necessary for the experiment to last that long.

- Allow for a reasonable time interval or rest period between treatment presentations. This consideration is particularly important when the treatments involve demanding tasks, such as intense exercise activities or surveys that take a long time to complete.

1. For a within-subjects experimental design, the same participants are observed in each group or at each level of an independent variable. Which requirement of an experiment (manipulation, randomization, or comparison/control) is not met using this design?

2. State two ways that researchers control for order effects.

3. How can researchers ensure that order sequences are representative using partial counterbalancing?

4. State two strategies used to minimize the possible ethical concern of participant fatigue in experiments that use a within-subjects design.

Answers: 1. Randomization (random assignment); 2. Researchers control order and control timing; 3. By ensuring that each treatment or group appears equally often in each position, and each treatment or group precedes and follows each treatment or group one time; 4. Minimize the duration needed to complete an experiment, and allow for a reasonable time interval or rest period between treatment presentations.

11.4 Individual Differences and Variability

Controlling for order effects by using counterbalancing or controlling timing can minimize the threats to internal validity associated with observing the same participants over time. In addition, as described in this section, a within-subjects design can minimize individual differences between groups and reduce variability in an experiment.

Individual Differences

When the same participants are observed in each group, the individual differences of participants are also the same in each group. For example, as shown in Figure 11.5, if we observe five participants in each of two groups, then the individuals who make up those groups are the same. Referring to Figure 11.5, the individual differences that make Hannah, Adam, Aiden, Sam, and Grace unique are the same in each group because these same five individuals are observed in both groups. Hence, when we observe the same participants in each group, we can assume that the individual differences of participants are also the same in each group.

Figure 11.5 A Within-Subjects Design With Five Participants

The same five participants are observed in each group. Hence, the individual differences of participants are also the same in each group.

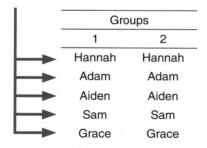

	Groups	
	1	2
	Hannah	Hannah
	Adam	Adam
	Aiden	Aiden
	Sam	Sam
	Grace	Grace

The same five participants (Hannah, Adam, Aiden, Sam, and Grace) are observed in each group.

Sources of Variability

In a within-subjects design, we can measure individual differences as **between-persons variability**; we measure the mean difference caused by the manipulation as **between-groups variability**; we measure the variability in participant responding within each group as **within-groups variability**. Note that individual differences are the same in each group using a within-subjects design. For this reason, we can measure and remove the between-persons variability because we will assume that the value of the between-persons variability is zero—that there is no difference in the individual differences in each group; that is, the individual differences in each group are the same.

The mean difference caused by a manipulation is the between-groups variability. As illustrated in Figure 11.6 for a two-group experiment, this variability is measured by the group means. The groups are the manipulation of the independent variable created by the researcher. For example, suppose the researcher tested how the proximity (close, far) of items in an office influenced how often people used the items. In this example, the groups would be items placed far from a participant (Group Q) and items placed near a participant (Group Z). The data would be the number of items used in each group.

The within-subjects design makes individual differences the same between groups because the same participants are observed in each group.

> **Between-persons variability** is a source of variance in a dependent measure that is caused by or associated with individual differences or differences in participant responses across all groups.
>
> **Between-groups variability** is a source of variance in a dependent measure that is caused by or associated with the manipulation of the levels (or groups) of an independent variable.
>
> **Within-groups variability** is a source of variance in a dependent measure that is caused by or associated with observing different participants within each group.

There are also two other sources that cause variability that have nothing to do with having different groups: between-persons and within-groups variability. These sources of variation are called **error** because they can cause variability but cannot be attributed to having different groups (the manipulation). As illustrated in Figure 11.7 for a two-group experiment, within-groups variability is differences in scores in each group for participants experiencing the same manipulation; between-persons variability is differences in scores between participants across the groups. The sum of these sources of variation is the total error or variability not caused by the manipulation, as illustrated in Figure 11.7.

In a within-subjects design, we assume that the value of the between-persons variability (the variability attributed to individual differences) is equal to zero because we assume that individual differences are the same in each group (i.e., there is no difference). Hence, the total value of error is the within-groups variability in a within-subjects design, thereby making the value of error smaller than if we had added the between-persons

Figure 11.6 Between-Groups Variability for a Hypothetical Sample of Four Participants With Data Given

	Treatments	
Participant	Q	Z
A	3	4
B	0	3
C	2	3
D	3	6
	$M = 2$	$M = 4$

Between-groups variability. The variability caused by the manipulation of the levels of the independent variable.

Error is a source of variance that cannot be attributed to having different groups or treatments. Two sources of error are between-persons and within-groups variability.

variability to compute error. In a within-subjects design, we can represent the calculation of error, or variation not caused by the manipulation, as follows:

$$\text{Error} = \text{Within-Groups Variability} + 0$$

LEARNING CHECK 2 ✓

1. When we observe the same participants in each group, do we assume that the individual differences of participants are the same or different in each group?

2. Which source of variability is attributed to each of the following?

   A. Individual differences

   B. The manipulation

   C. Participant responding within each group

3. In a within-subjects design, why do we assume that the value of the between-persons variability is equal to zero?

Answers: 1. The same; 2. A. Between-persons variability, B. Between-groups variability, C. Within-groups variability; 3. Because we assume that individual differences are the same in each group (i.e., there is no difference).

Figure 11.7   Two Sources of Error for a Sample of Four Participants With Data Given

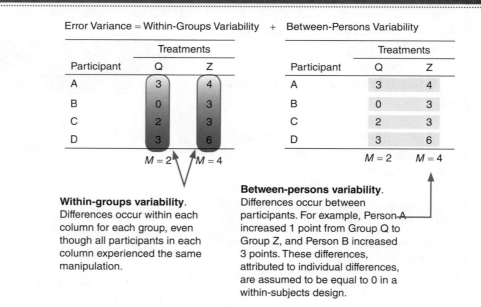

Error Variance = Within-Groups Variability + Between-Persons Variability

Participant	Treatments Q	Z
A	3	4
B	0	3
C	2	3
D	3	6
	$M = 2$	$M = 4$

Participant	Treatments Q	Z
A	3	4
B	0	3
C	2	3
D	3	6
	$M = 2$	$M = 4$

Within-groups variability. Differences occur within each column for each group, even though all participants in each column experienced the same manipulation.

Between-persons variability. Differences occur between participants. For example, Person A increased 1 point from Group Q to Group Z, and Person B increased 3 points. These differences, attributed to individual differences, are assumed to be equal to 0 in a within-subjects design.

The sum of within-groups and between-persons variability is the total value of error. In a within-subjects design, however, we assume that the value of the between-persons variability is equal to 0. Hence, the within-groups variability is the only measure of error in a within-subjects design.

11.5 Comparing Two Related Samples

To conduct the within-subjects design, participants are selected in a certain way, and a particular test statistic for two groups is used. The goal in experimentation is to minimize the possibility that individual differences, or something other than a manipulation, caused differences between groups. Methodologically, we control for order and timing to control for time-related factors associated with observing the same participants in each group. Statistically, we add another level of control by using a test statistic to determine the likelihood that something other than the manipulation caused differences in a dependent measure between groups. Each level of control is described in Table 11.1.

Note that the test statistics introduced in this chapter can also be used in quasi-experiments. However, because the quasi-experiment does not methodologically control for individual differences (i.e., a quasi-experiment lacks a manipulation or control for order effects and timing), the design cannot demonstrate cause and effect. Both levels of control (methodological and statistical) are present in the within-subjects experimental design. Therefore, the within-subjects experimental design can demonstrate cause and effect. Table 11.2 shows each within-subjects experimental design and the test statistic used with each design, to be introduced in this chapter. This section introduces how participants are selected to two groups and how the test statistic is used to analyze measured data.

Selecting Two Related Samples

Using the within-subjects design, the same participants are observed in each group. When participants are observed in this way, the sample is called a **related sample**. The following are two ways to select two related samples, and each way is described in this section:

> In a **related sample**, also called a **dependent sample**, the same or matched participants are observed in each group.

- The same participants are observed in each group.

- Participants are matched, experimentally or naturally, based on the common characteristics or traits that they share.

Table 11.1 Two Levels of Control in Experimentation

Within-Subjects Experimental Design		Checklist	
Level of Control	How?	Quasi-Experiment	Experiment
Methodological	Control Order and Timing		√
Statistical	Compute Test Statistic	√	√

Table 11.2	The Type of Within-Subjects Experimental Design and the Corresponding Test Statistic Used With That Design

Experimental Research Design (Within Subjects)	Test Statistic
Two related samples	Related-samples *t* test
Multiple related samples	One-way within-subjects analysis of variance

As shown in Figure 11.8, we can select one sample from one population and observe that one sample of participants in each group. This type of sampling, used with a *repeated-measures design*, can be used in an experiment only if we manipulate the levels of the independent variable and control for order effects. For example, we can test the research hypothesis that music improves mood among children in grief therapy (see Loewy & Hara, 2002/2007; Thomson, Reece, & Di Benedetto, 2014). To test this hypothesis using an experiment, we could select a sample of children currently in therapy and manipulate whether music is played during a therapy session (music, no music). To counterbalance the order in which participants are assigned to groups, we could play music in one session and no music in a second session for half of the children; the other half of the children would have the reverse order: no music in the first session, then music in the second session. By doing so, we would satisfy Steps 2 to 4 of the within-subjects experimental design, as described in Figure 11.1.

Figure 11.8	Selecting Participants to Two Groups in a Within-Subjects Design

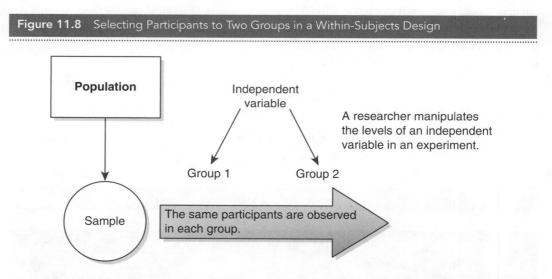

In a within-subjects design, one sample of participants is selected from a population and is observed in each group or at each level of the independent variable.

Another way to select related samples is to match participants based on preexisting characteristics or traits that they share. This type of sampling, called a **matched-samples design**, cannot be used in an experiment because groups are created based on preexisting characteristics of the participants, and not on a manipulation made by the researcher. Hence, a matched-samples design is more often used to select samples for quasi-experiments or nonexperiments.

Using the matched-samples design, participants can be matched as naturally occurring pairs, or they can be matched experimentally based on a common characteristic of interest, as described in Table 11.3. Naturally occurring pairs are matched based on characteristics inherent to each individual. For example, we could match participants by family affiliation (e.g., brothers, sisters), spousal relationship (e.g., husband, wife), or genetics (e.g., identical twins), then test if these matched pairs differ in their attitudes regarding forgiveness.

Experimentally matched pairs are matched based on an experimental matching procedure in which a researcher matches participants based on their scores or responses on a dependent measure. For example, a researcher can measure intelligence, personality type, or education level, then match participants based on their responses or scores on those measures. Once participants are matched, researchers can test if these matched pairs differ in their attitudes regarding forgiveness, for example. Using a matched-samples design, one member of each pair constitutes a group, and the differences in scores for each matched pair are compared.

> A repeated-measures research design can be used in an experiment; a matched-samples design uses a quasi-experimental technique to create groups and is therefore not used in an experiment.

> The **matched-samples design**, also called the **matched-pairs design**, is a within-subjects research design in which participants are matched, experimentally or naturally, based on preexisting characteristics or traits that they share.

Table 11.3 Two Types of Matching in a Matched-Samples Design

Type of Matching	Description	Example
Naturally occurring matched pairs	Participants are matched based on preexisting characteristics inherent to each individual.	Researchers observe pairs of identical twins. The twins then participate in a study in which the differences in scores for each pair of identical twins are compared.
Experimentally matched pairs	Participants are matched based on their scores on a dependent measure for some characteristic of interest.	Researchers measure intelligence in a sample of children, then match them based on their scores. Participants with the two highest scores are paired, then the next two highest scores are paired, and so on. Children then participate in a study in which the differences in scores for each matched pair are compared.

The Use of the Test Statistic

Once participants have been selected, we observe the same participants in each group and also measure the same dependent variable in each group. To illustrate the use of a test statistic, suppose we test the hypothesis that newborns will show a preference for their mother's face (for related research, see Bushnell, 2001; Hendriks, van Rijswijk, & Omtzigt, 2011; Taylor, Slade, & Herbert, 2014). To test this hypothesis, we select a sample of newborns and present them with two types of pictures (a picture of their mother and a picture of a stranger whose facial features match their mother's face, except the face is elongated). The type of picture (mother or stranger) is the manipulation. To be an experiment, we must also counterbalance the order that newborns in each group are presented the pictures, then record the amount of time (in seconds) that newborns orient their head toward each picture. If the hypothesis is correct, we should expect newborns to orient longer toward the picture of their mother.

To compare differences between the picture groups, we compute a *test statistic*, which is a mathematical formula that allows us to determine whether the manipulation (mother vs. stranger) or error variance (other factors attributed to individual differences) is likely to explain differences between the groups. In most cases, researchers measure data on an interval or a ratio scale of measurement. In our example, time spent orienting toward a picture is a ratio scale measure. In these situations, when data are interval or ratio scale, the appropriate test statistic for comparing differences between two related samples is the **related-samples *t* test**. This test statistic follows a common form:

A **related-samples *t* test**, also called a **paired-samples *t* test**, is a statistical procedure used to test hypotheses concerning the difference in interval or ratio scale data for two related samples in which the variance in one population is unknown.

$$t = \frac{\text{Mean differences between groups}}{\text{Mean differences attributed to error}}$$

The numerator of the test statistic is the actual difference between the two groups. For example, suppose that newborns spent 10 seconds orienting toward the picture of their mother and 6 seconds orienting toward the picture of the stranger, on average. The mean difference, then, between the two picture groups is 4 seconds (10 − 6 = 4). We divide the mean difference between two groups by the difference attributed to error in the denominator. In the denominator, we make the value of the between-persons error equal to zero by reducing two columns of data (one column for each group) to one column of difference scores—by subtracting across the rows for each newborn. As illustrated in Figure 11.9, when we reduce a hypothetical data set to one column of difference scores, the between-persons variability is eliminated; that is, it is equal to zero. The result is that the value of error in the denominator of the test statistic will be smaller, thereby making the value of the test statistic larger, than if we did not perform this subtraction procedure. To illustrate how to compute and interpret a related-samples *t* test, we will work through this example using SPSS.

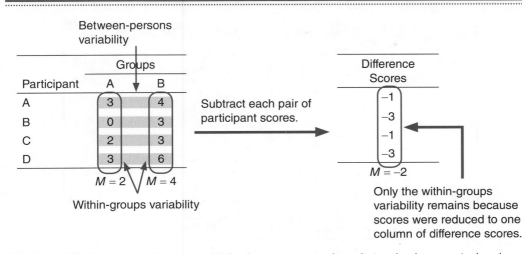

Computing difference scores eliminates variability between persons by reducing the data to a single column of difference scores.

11.6 SPSS in Focus: Related-Samples *t* Test

In Section 11.5, we selected a sample of newborns and presented them with two types of pictures (a picture of their mother and a picture of a stranger). The type of picture (mother or stranger) was the manipulation. To qualify as an experiment, we counterbalanced the order that newborns in each group were presented the pictures, and we recorded the amount of time (in seconds) that newborns oriented toward both pictures. The hypothetical data for a sample of 10 newborns are given in Table 11.4. We will use SPSS to compute a related-samples *t* test for these data.

Table 11.4 The Time (in Seconds) That 10 Newborns Oriented Toward Each of Two Pictures

Type of Picture	
Mother	Stranger
13	9
8	5
10	8
13	7
12	8
6	5
8	7
10	2
11	5
9	4

1. Click on the **Variable View** tab and enter *mother* in the first row, and enter *stranger* in the second row in the Name column. Reduce the value to 0 in the **Decimals column** for each row because we will enter only whole numbers.

2. Click on the **Data View** tab. In the first column, enter the data for each group, same as shown in Table 11.4.

3. Go to the menu bar and click **Analyze**, then **Compare Means**, and **Paired-Samples T Test** to bring up a dialog box, which is shown in Figure 11.10.

4. Click on *mother* and *stranger* in the left box and move them to the right box using the arrow in the middle. Each group should be side by side in the right box.

5. Select **OK**, or select **Paste** and click the **Run** command.

Figure 11.10   SPSS Dialog Box for Steps 3 and 4

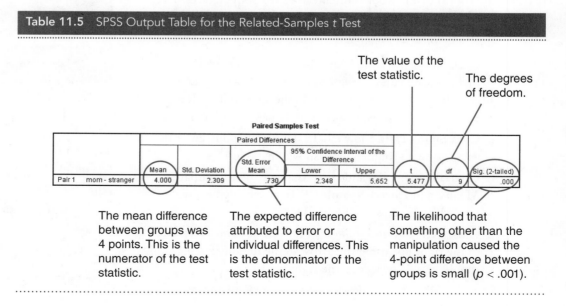

The output table, shown in Table 11.5, gives the results for the related-samples *t* test. The numerator of the test statistic is the mean difference between groups, 4.0, and the denominator is the value attributed to individual differences or error, 0.730. When you divide those two values, you obtain the value of the test statistic, 5.477. The Sig. column gives the *p* value, which in our example shows that the likelihood that anything other than the picture manipulation caused differences between groups is *p* < .001. The criterion for deciding that a manipulation caused differences between groups is typically set at *p* < .05 in the behavioral sciences. Hence, in our example, we conclude that the manipulation of the pictures, and not individual differences, caused newborns to spend significantly more time orienting toward a picture of their mother compared to a picture of a stranger.

Table 11.5   SPSS Output Table for the Related-Samples *t* Test

The value of the test statistic.

The degrees of freedom.

Paired Samples Test

		Paired Differences							
					95% Confidence Interval of the Difference				
		Mean	Std. Deviation	Std. Error Mean	Lower	Upper	t	df	Sig. (2-tailed)
Pair 1	mom - stranger	4.000	2.309	.730	2.348	5.652	5.477	9	.000

The mean difference between groups was 4 points. This is the numerator of the test statistic.

The expected difference attributed to error or individual differences. This is the denominator of the test statistic.

The likelihood that something other than the manipulation caused the 4-point difference between groups is small (*p* < .001).

Also given in Table 11.5, the related-samples t test is associated with $n - 1$ degrees of freedom, in which n is the number of participants. Using American Psychological Association (APA, 2009) guidelines, we report the results of a related-samples t test by stating the value of the test statistic, the degrees of freedom (df), and the p value for the t test as shown:

> A related-samples t test showed that newborns oriented their head longer toward a picture of their mother compared with a picture of a stranger, $t(9) = 5.477, p < .001$.

11.7 Comparing Two or More Related Samples

Using the within-subjects design, we can also observe more than two groups. This section introduces how different participants can be selected to more than two groups and how the test statistic can be used to analyze measured data.

Selecting Multiple Related Samples

Only the repeated-measures design can be used to observe participants in more than two groups. A matched-samples design cannot be used because it is limited to situations in which participants are paired into two groups. As shown in Figure 11.11 using a repeated-measures design, participants are selected from a single population and observed in multiple groups in an experiment.

To illustrate the repeated-measures design with more than two groups, suppose we test the hypothesis that participants will judge the taste of wine based on its price (for related research, see Brentari, Levaggi, & Zuccolotto, 2011; D'Alessandro, & Pecotich, 2013;

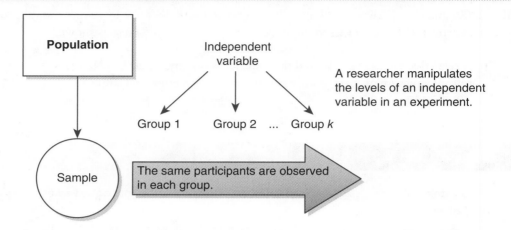

In a within-subjects design, one sample of participants is selected from a population and is observed in each group or at each level of the independent variable.

Piqueras-Fiszman & Spence, 2012). To test this hypothesis, we ask older adults to taste and rate three wines to see if what they are told about the price of those wines will affect their ratings for how much they like the taste of those wines. Adults drink the same wine three times, but they are given different information about the price of each wine before each tasting—they are told that the cost of the wine is inexpensive, moderately expensive, or expensive before each tasting. To be an experiment, we must control for order effects, or the order of presenting the manipulation (whether the wine is described as inexpensive, moderate, or expensive). We hypothesize that ratings for how much the participants like the taste of the wine will be highest for the wine described as being expensive even though all adults actually will consume the same wine each time.

> The repeated-measures, but not the matched-samples, design can be used when the same participants are observed in more than two groups.

The Use of the Test Statistic

To compare differences between groups, we will compute a *test statistic*, which allows us to determine whether the manipulation (describing the wine as inexpensive, moderately expensive, or expensive) or error attributed to individual differences is likely to explain group differences in ratings of liking. In most cases, researchers measure data on an interval or a ratio scale of measurement. In our example, ratings of liking are an interval scale measure. In these situations, when data are interval or ratio scale, the appropriate test statistic for comparing differences among two or more related samples is the **one-way within-subjects analysis of variance (ANOVA)**. This test statistic follows a common form:

$$F = \frac{\text{Variability between groups}}{\text{Variability attributed to error}}$$

ANOVA measures the variance of differences between groups divided by the variance of differences attributed to error or individual differences. Figure 11.12 shows the three sources of variation that are measured by the test statistic. The variance of group means, or *between-groups variability*, is placed in the numerator. There are also two sources of error: variability *between persons* and *within groups*. In the denominator, we will again make the value of the between-persons error equal to zero because the same, not different, participants are observed in each group. We will compute the between-persons variability and remove it from the variability placed in the denominator, thereby leaving only the within-groups variability as the variability attributed to error in the denominator of the test statistic.

The **one-way within-subjects ANOVA** is a statistical procedure used to test hypotheses for one factor with two or more levels concerning the variance among group means. This test is used when the same participants are observed at each level of a factor and the variance in a given population is unknown.

The one-way within-subjects ANOVA informs us only that at least one group is different from another group—it does not tell us which pairs of groups differ. For situations in which we have more than two groups in an experiment, we compute post hoc tests, in the same way that we did for the between-subjects design in Chapter 10. Post hoc tests are used to evaluate all possible pairwise comparisons, or differences between all possible pairings of two group means. In the ratings-of-wine experiment, we would use the one-way within-

Figure 11.12 Three Sources of Variability in a Within-Subjects Design With More Than Two Groups

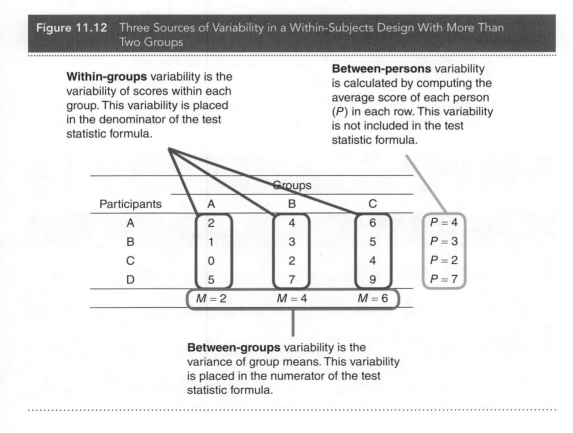

Within-groups variability is the variability of scores within each group. This variability is placed in the denominator of the test statistic formula.

Between-persons variability is calculated by computing the average score of each person (P) in each row. This variability is not included in the test statistic formula.

Between-groups variability is the variance of group means. This variability is placed in the numerator of the test statistic formula.

subjects ANOVA to determine if the manipulation (describing the wine as inexpensive, moderately expensive, or expensive) caused mean ratings of liking to vary between groups. We would then use post hoc tests to determine which pairs of group means were different. To illustrate further, we will work through this example using SPSS.

11.8 SPSS in Focus: One-Way Within-Subjects ANOVA

In Section 11.7, we selected a sample of older adults and had them taste and rate wines that they were told were inexpensive, moderately expensive, or expensive. Suppose we measured liking on a rating scale from 1 (*dislike very much*) to 7 (*like very much*). The hypothetical data for a sample of seven older adults are given in Table 11.6. We will use SPSS to compute the one-way within-subjects ANOVA for these data.

1. Click on the **Variable View** tab and enter *inexpensive* in the **Name column**; enter *moderate* in the Name column below it; enter *expensive* in the Name column below that. Go to the **Decimals column** and reduce the value to 0 for each row because we will enter only whole numbers.

2. Click on the **Data View** tab. Each column is labeled with the label we entered in Step 1. Enter the data for each group in each corresponding column, as shown in Table 11.6.

3. Go to the **Menu bar** and click **Analyze**, then **General Linear Model**, and **Repeated Measures** to bring up the dialog box shown in Figure 11.13a.

4. In the **Within-Subject Factor Name** box, we label the independent variable. Label it *description*, as shown in Figure 11.13a. Below it is a **Number of Levels**

Table 11.6 Hypothetical Data for Seven Participants Each Observed Three Times (at Each Level of the Wine Description Manipulation)

Participant	Description of Wine		
	Inexpensive	Moderate	Expensive
A	2	5	5
B	3	5	6
C	1	4	5
D	4	5	7
E	4	3	6
F	5	4	7
G	2	2	6
	M = 3	M = 4	M = 6

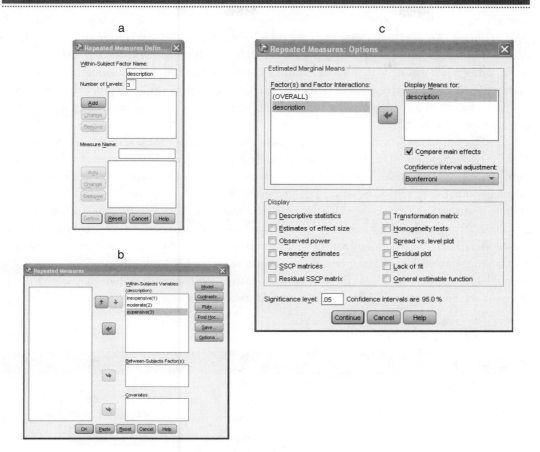

box to enter the number of levels of the independent variable. Enter *3*, which will allow you to select the **Add** option. Click **Add** and **Define** to bring up a new dialog box shown in Figure 11.13b.

5. Using the arrows, move each level of the variable into the **Within-Subjects Variables (description)** box, as shown in Figure 11.13b.

6. Select **Options** and use the arrow to move the *description* variable into the **Display Means for** box. Check the **Compare main effects** option and using the dropdown arrow under the **Confidence interval adjustment:** heading, select **Bonferroni** as the post hoc test as shown in Figure 11.13c. Select **Continue**.

7. Select **OK**, or select **Paste** and click the **Run** command.

The output table, shown in Table 11.7, gives the results for the one-way within-subjects ANOVA. The numerator of the test statistic is the variance caused by having different groups, 16.333, and the denominator is the variance attributed to individual differences or error, 0.944. When you divide those two values, you obtain the value of the test statistic, 17.294. The Sig. column gives the p value, which in our example shows that the likelihood that anything other than the manipulation (i.e., the description of the wine) caused differences between groups is $p < .001$. We decide that the manipulation caused group differences when $p < .05$; hence, in this example, we decide that the price-of-wine manipulation caused differences in liking between groups. However, remember that this result does not tell us which groups are different; it tells us only that at least one pair of the groups significantly differs.

To determine which groups are different, we conducted post hoc tests, shown in Table 11.8. At the left, you see 1 with 2; 3 is placed below the 2. The numbers represent the column numbers. Hence, 1 = inexpensive, 2 = moderately expensive, and 3 = expensive. You read the table as comparisons across the rows. The first comparison in the first row is 1 and 2. If there is an asterisk next to the value given in the mean difference column, then those two groups differ (note that the p value for each comparison is also given in the Sig. column for each comparison). The next comparison is 1 (first row) and 3 (second row) in the top left boxed portion of the table. For all comparisons, the results show that older adults rated the wine as more liked when they were told the wine was expensive, compared with when they were told the wine was inexpensive (Comparison 1 and 3) or moderately expensive (Comparison 2 and 3).

Table 11.7   SPSS Output Table for the One-Way Within-Subjects ANOVA

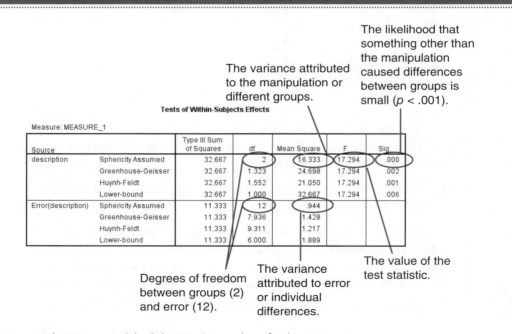

We assume sphericity, so read the Sphericity Assumed row for this test.

Table 11.8 SPSS Output Table for the Post Hoc Test

Pairwise Comparisons

Measure: MEASURE_1

(I) description	(J) description	Mean Difference (I-J)	Std. Error	Sig.[b]	95% Confidence Interval for Difference[b] Lower Bound	Upper Bound
1	2	-1.000	.655	.532	-3.152	1.152
	3	-3.000*	.309	.000	-4.015	-1.985
2	1	1.000	.655	.532	-1.152	3.152
	3	-2.000*	.535	.029	-3.757	-.243
3	1	3.000*	.309	.000	1.985	4.015
	2	2.000*	.535	.029	.243	3.757

Based on estimated marginal means

*. The mean difference is significant at the .05 level.

b. Adjustment for multiple comparisons: Bonferroni.

Also given in Table 11.7, the one-way within-subjects ANOVA is associated with two sets of degrees of freedom (*df*): one for the variance between groups and one for the variance attributed to error. Using APA (2009) guidelines, we report the results of an ANOVA by stating the value of the test statistic, both degrees of freedom (*df*), and the *p* value for the *F* test, and we indicate the results of the post hoc test if one was computed as shown:

> A one-way within-subjects ANOVA showed that ratings of liking for wine depended on how expensive the wine was described as being, $F(2, 12) = 17.294$, $p < .001$. Adults rated the wine as more liked when they were told the wine was expensive, compared to when they were told the wine was inexpensive or moderately priced (Bonferroni, $p \leq .029$).

LEARNING CHECK 4 ✓

1. What test statistic is used to compare differences in interval or ratio data between two or more groups to which the same participants were observed in each group?

2. Why do researchers compute post hoc tests?

3. Which source of variation is computed and removed from the denominator of the test statistic for the one-way within-subjects ANOVA?

Answers: 1. The one-way within-subjects ANOVA; 2. To determine which pairs of group means differ significantly following a significant ANOVA; 3. Between-persons variability.

11.9 An Alternative to Pre-Post Designs: Solomon Four-Group Design

The **Solomon four-group design** is an experimental research design in which different participants are assigned to each of four groups in such a way that comparisons can be made to (1) determine if a treatment causes changes in posttest measure and (2) control for possible confounds or extraneous factors related to giving a pretest measure and observing participants over time.

In a typical pre-post design, we observe one group of participants before and after a treatment is administered. This type of design, however, is quasi-experimental because it lacks an appropriate control group. The **Solomon four-group design** is a combination of the one-group pretest-posttest design and the one-group posttest-only design, with two added control groups that can account for the possibility that confounding variables and extraneous factors have influenced the results.

This design is an experimental solution for the lack of control in one-group pretest-posttest designs (Clark & Shadish, 2008).

A Solomon four-group design utilizes a between-subjects and a within-subjects design to establish control.

To apply the Solomon four-group design, participants are randomly assigned to one of four groups: Two groups are given a treatment, and two groups are not given a treatment. In one treatment group, participants are given a pretest, a treatment, then a posttest, shown in Group A in Figure 11.14; in the second treatment group, participants are given only a treatment, then a posttest, shown in Group C in Figure 11.14. As added controls, two groups are not given a treatment. In one no-treatment group, participants are given a pretest and a posttest without a treatment, shown in Group B in Figure 11.14; in a second no-treatment group, participants are given only a posttest, shown in Group D in Figure 11.14.

Figure 11.14 Solomon Four-Group Design

Group A	Pretest	Treatment	Posttest
Group B	Pretest		Posttest
Group C		Treatment	Posttest
Group D			Posttest

The experimental group is Group A, and the three control groups are included to account for possible confounds or extraneous factors that could be causing differences pre- to posttreatment.

The strength of this design is that multiple comparisons can be made to eliminate the possibility that confounds or extraneous factors are causing differences from pre- to posttreatment. The following comparisons can be made:

- Comparison 1: The difference in pretest-posttest scores for Group A compared to the difference in pretest-posttest scores for Group B. This comparison is the standard comparison made to determine if the inclusion of a treatment caused changes from pretest to posttest.

- Comparison 2 (control): Group A posttest and Group C posttest comparison to determine if including a pretest prior to giving the treatment caused posttest scores to change. If the treatment is causing changes in posttest scores, then posttest scores should not significantly differ between Groups A and C.

- Comparison 3 (control): Group B pretest and Group D posttest to determine if external factors related to observing participants across time could be causing the effect. If the treatment is causing changes in posttest scores (and not just the passage of time), then pretest scores in Group B should not significantly differ from posttest scores in Group D.

- Comparison 4 (control): Group B posttest and Group D posttest to determine if including a pretest caused posttest scores to change, even when no treatment was administered. If the treatment is causing changes in posttest scores, then posttest scores should not significantly differ between Groups B and D.

- Comparison 5 (control): The difference in posttest scores for Groups C and D compared with posttest scores for Groups A and B. We make this comparison to determine if including a pretest had any effect on posttest scores. If the treatment is causing changes in posttest scores, then the difference in posttest scores between Groups C and D should not significantly differ from the difference in posttest scores between Groups A and B.

In all, we make five comparisons. To demonstrate evidence that the treatment caused changes in posttest scores, we should find a significant difference for Comparison 1 and no significant difference for the remaining comparisons. Because the Solomon four-group design includes appropriate control groups, it is regarded as an experimental design, so long as the researcher manipulates the treatment and randomly assigns participants to groups. Note also that the strength of this design is that a within-subjects design (pre-post comparisons) is combined with a between-subjects design (between-group comparisons) to establish control—a comparison of the between-subjects and within-subjects designs is given in Section 11.10.

While the Solomon four-group design is an experimental design capable of controlling for threats to internal validity, its main limitation is the complexity of the design itself. The design requires four groups to which participants must be assigned at random. In research settings with limited funding or in settings in which it is difficult to randomly assign participants to that many groups, this design becomes very difficult to apply. In addition, the statistical analysis needed to make all five comparisons can be rather complex, which often deters researchers from using this design.

11.10 Comparing Between-Subjects and Within-Subjects Designs

The between-subjects design is an experimental research design in which we use randomization, manipulation, and inclusion of a comparison or control group. The within-subjects design is an experimental research design in which we make a manipulation and observe the same participants in each group that was created by the manipulation (i.e., participants serve as their own controls/comparisons). We then control for timing and order effects because randomization is not used. The key advantage of using each type of research design is described in this section.

Between-Subjects Design: Randomization

The between-subjects design allows researchers to randomly assign participants to groups, or to the levels of an independent variable; the within-subjects design does not. The advantage of using random assignment is that it makes individual differences about the same in each group. Participants are observed one time in one group that they were assigned to entirely by chance. We can then measure a dependent variable in each group and compare differences between groups.

Interestingly, the advantage of using random assignment is that participants are observed one time in one group. Yes, random assignment makes individual differences about the same in each group; however, observing the same participants in each group, using a within-subjects design, means that the individual differences of participants are also the same in each group. The problem when we observe the same participants in each group, and do not randomly assign participants to one group, is that we must control for effects resulting from the order in which participants are observed, which can threaten internal validity; this concern is not a problem using a between-subjects design.

Within-Subjects Design: Economizing and Power

The advantage of using a within-subjects design is that fewer participants are required overall (economizing) because the same participants are observed in each group. This is a particular advantage for studying small populations, such as Olympic athletes or children with autism. These groups can be difficult to sample in large numbers, so observing a smaller sample of the same participants in each group can be more practical. In addition, researchers may have limited funding or other limited resources that prevent them from recruiting large samples. In these types of situations, a within-subjects design can be a practical alternative to a between-subjects design to conduct an experiment.

A second advantage of using the within-subjects design is that the test statistic has greater power to detect significant differences between groups (Hampton, 1998). Recall from Chapter 7 that *power* is the likelihood that we can detect an effect, if one exists in a population. In other words, using a within-subjects design, if an effect exists in the population, then we are more likely to detect it (i.e., conclude that a manipulation caused two or more groups to be different) than if we ran a between-subjects analysis on the same data. The reason we have greater power is because of how we compute the test statistics for a within-subjects versus a between-subjects design.

For a between-subjects design, we compute two sources of error: between persons and within groups. We add them up and place the total value in the denominator of the test statistic. Using a within-subjects design, however, we also compute the same two sources of error, but we remove the between-persons variability; that is, we assume its value is equal to zero. Hence, the test statistic for a within-subjects design can detect smaller differences between groups (i.e., lead to a decision that a manipulation caused differences in an experiment) because the denominator of the test statistic is smaller, thereby making the value of the test statistic larger than it would have been if we had included between-persons variability in our calculation of error, as we did for a between-subjects design. Hence, we can represent the test statistic for each experimental design as follows:

$$\text{Between-subjects design}: \frac{\text{Differences or variance between groups}}{\text{Within-groups} + \text{between-persons error}}$$

$$\text{Within-subjects design}: \frac{\text{Differences or variance between groups}}{\text{Within-groups error}}$$

LEARNING CHECK 5 ✓

1. A Solomon four-group design is an experimental design that includes four groups. Describe the procedures for each group.

2. Which type of design, the between-subjects or the within-subjects design, allows for the random assignment of participants to groups?

3. True or false: The between-subjects design has greater power to detect an effect than the within-subjects design.

4. Which type of design, the between-subjects or the within-subjects design, is associated with a smaller value of error variance, assuming the data are the same?

Answers: 1. In one group, participants are given a pretest, a treatment, then a posttest. In a second group, participants are given only a treatment. In a third group, participants are given a pretest and a posttest without a treatment. In a fourth group, participants are given only a posttest. 2. Between-subjects design; 3. False. The within-subjects design has greater power; 4. Within-subjects design.

LO 1 Delineate the within-subjects design and the within-subjects experimental design.

- A **within-subjects design** is a research design in which the same participants are observed one time in each group of a research study.
- A **within-subjects experimental design** is an experimental research design in which the levels of a **within-subjects factor** are manipulated, then the same participants are observed in each group or at each level of the factor. To qualify as an experiment, the researcher must (1) manipulate the levels of the factor and include a comparison/control group, and (2) make added efforts to control for order and time-related factors.

LO 2 Explain why it is important to control for time-related factors using a within-subjects experimental design.

- When we observe the same participants over time, factors related to observing participants over time can also vary between groups. When time-related factors covary with the levels of the independent variable (the manipulation), it can threaten the internal validity of an experiment.
- Time-related factors include maturation, testing effects, regression toward the mean, attrition, **participant fatigue**, and **carryover effects**. For a study to be an experiment, each of these time-related factors must be controlled for, or must be the same between groups, such that only the levels of an independent variable are different between groups.

LO 3 Demonstrate the use of counterbalancing and control for timing using a within-subjects experimental design.

- For the **counterbalancing** procedure, the order in which participants receive different treatments or participate in different groups is balanced or offset in an experiment. Two types of counterbalancing are as follows:

  - Complete counterbalancing, in which all possible order sequences are included in an experiment.
  - Partial counterbalancing, in which some, but not all, possible order sequences are included in an experiment. One example of partial counterbalancing is the **Latin square**.

- We can also control for order effects by controlling timing. We can control the interval between treatments or groups, and the total duration of an experiment. As a general rule, increasing the interval between treatments and minimizing the total duration of an experiment is often the most effective strategy to minimize threats to internal validity that are associated with observing the same participants over time.

LO 4 Identify three sources of variation and explain why one source is removed using the within-subjects design.

- In a within-subjects design, we can measure individual differences as **between-persons variability**. We measure the mean difference caused by the manipulation as **between-groups**

variability. We measure variability in participant responding within each group as **within-groups variability.**

- When the same participants are observed in each group, we assume that the individual differences of participants are also the same in each group. We therefore measure and remove the between-persons variability because we will assume that the value of the between-persons variability is zero—that there is no difference in the individual differences in each group; the individual differences between persons are the same.

LO 5 Identify the appropriate sampling method and test statistic for related samples to compare differences between two group means.

- Using a within-subjects design, the same participants are observed in each group. When participants are observed in this way, the sample is called a **related sample**. There are two ways to select related samples:
  - The **repeated-measures design,** in which we select a sample from one population and observe that one sample of participants in each group. This type of sampling can be used in an experiment when researchers control for order effects and manipulate the levels of the independent variable.
  - The **matched-samples design,** in which participants are matched, experimentally or naturally, based on characteristics or traits that they share. This type of sampling cannot be used in an experiment because groups are created based on preexisting characteristics of the participants, and not on a manipulation made by the researcher.

- The appropriate test statistic for comparing differences between two group means using the within-subjects design is the **related-samples t test.** Using this t test, we divide the mean difference between groups by the value for within-groups error. Because individual differences are the same in each group, the between-persons error is removed by reducing the data to difference scores before computing the test statistic. The larger the value of the test statistic, the more likely we are to conclude that the manipulation, and not error, caused a mean difference between two groups.

LO 6 Identify the appropriate sampling method and test statistic for related samples to compare differences among two or more group means.

- The repeated-measures design is used to observe participants in more than two groups. Using a repeated-measures design, participants are selected from a single population and observed in multiple groups in an experiment.
- The appropriate test statistic for comparing differences between two or more group means using a within-subjects design is the **one-way within-subjects ANOVA.** If the ANOVA is significant, then we conduct *post hoc tests* to determine which pairs of group means are significantly different. Using this test, we divide the variability between groups by the value for within-groups error. Because individual differences are the same in each group, the between-persons error is measured and removed from the

value for error placed in the denominator. The larger the value of the test statistic, the more likely we are to conclude that the manipulation, and not error, caused a mean difference between groups.

LO 7 Apply a Solomon four-group design for the within-subjects experimental design.

- The Solomon four-group design is a combination of the one-group pretest-posttest design and the one-group posttest-only design, with two added control groups that can account for the possibility that confounding variables and extraneous factors have influenced the results.
- To apply the Solomon four-group design, two groups are given a treatment, and two groups are given no treatment. In one treatment group, participants are given a pretest, a treatment, and a posttest; in the other treatment group, participants are given a treatment and a posttest. In one no-treatment group, participants are given a pretest and a posttest without a treatment; in the other no-treatment group, participants are given a posttest only without a treatment. In all, we make five comparisons to demonstrate evidence that a treatment caused changes in a posttest measure.
- Because the Solomon four-group design includes appropriate control groups, it is regarded as an experimental design, so long as the researcher manipulates the treatment and randomly assigns participants to the different groups. The strength of the design is that it is capable of controlling for threats to internal validity; its main limitation is the complexity of the design itself.

LO 8 Contrast the use of a between-subjects versus a within-subjects design for an experiment.

- A between-subjects design allows for the use of random assignment; a within-subjects design does not. The advantage of using random assignment is that we do not need to control for order effects using a between-subjects design; however, we do need to control for order effects using a within-subjects design.
- An advantage of using a within-subjects design is that fewer participants are required overall (economizing) because the same participants are observed in each group. A second advantage of using the within-subjects design is that the test statistic for this design has greater power to detect an effect between groups.

LO 9 Compute a related-samples t test and a one-way within-subjects analysis of variance using SPSS.

- SPSS can be used to compute a related-samples t test using the **Analyze, Compare Means**, and **Paired-Samples T Test** options in the menu bar. These actions will display a dialog box that allows you to identify the groups and run the test (for more details, see Section 11.6).
- SPSS can be used to compute the one-way within-subjects ANOVA using the **Analyze, General Linear Model**, and **Repeated Measures** options in the menu bar. These actions will display a dialog box that allows you to identify the variables, choose an appropriate post hoc test, and run the analysis (for more details, see Section 11.8).

KEY TERMS

within-subjects design

within-subjects
  experimental design

repeated-measures design

within-subjects factor

participant fatigue

order effects

carryover effects

counterbalancing

complete counterbalancing

partial counterbalancing

Latin square

between-persons variability

between-groups variability

within-groups variability

error

related sample

dependent sample

matched-samples design

related-samples t test

paired-samples t test

one-way within-subjects
  ANOVA

Solomon four-group design

REVIEW QUESTIONS

1. Three requirements of an experiment are randomization, manipulation, and the inclusion of a comparison or control group. Which of these requirements is not met when we use the within-subjects design? Explain.

2. What are the two ways that researchers compensate for not using random assignment in a within-subjects experimental design?

3. Explain why each of the following order effects is a threat to internal validity.

    A. Carryover effect

    B. Participant fatigue

4. Explain why partial counterbalancing is often used when three or more groups are included in a within-subjects experimental design.

5. What are two requirements to ensure that the few order sequences that are included using partial counterbalancing are representative of all possible order sequences that could be counterbalanced?

6. State the number of possible order sequences for counterbalancing when the number of treatments is each of the following:

    A. Two treatments

    B. Five treatments

    C. Seven treatments

7. Name two ways that researchers control the timing in an experiment.

8. State whether each of the following is an example of a between-subjects design or a within-subjects design.

    A. A sample of expert chess players is asked to rate the effectiveness of six different playing strategies.

B. A sample of children is randomly assigned to play with one of four types of toys during a reinforcement therapy session.

9. State whether each of the following is an example of a repeated-measures design or a matched-samples design.

A. Researchers measure the number of unforced errors committed by a sample of professional tennis players during each set of a tennis match.

B. Researchers record the amount of time (in minutes) that parent-child pairs spend on social networking sites to test for generational differences between the pairs.

C. Researchers compare perceptions of safety in four different social settings among pairs of participants matched based on emotional stability scores.

10. Name the test statistic used to compare differences between two group means using a within-subjects design. Name the test statistic used to compare differences among two or more group means using a within-subjects design.

11. Which source of variation is removed from the denominator of the test statistic using the within-subjects design? Why is it removed?

12. Using the within-subjects design, what strategy is used to eliminate between-persons variability from the denominator of the test statistic in the following situations?

A. When comparing two group means

B. When comparing two or more group means

13. Explain why the within-subjects design has greater power to detect an effect than the between-subjects design.

ACTIVITIES

1. A clinical psychologist with the U.S. military is concerned that troop morale in war regions is low. She hypothesizes that the greater the number of tours a soldier has served, the worse his or her morale will be. To test this hypothesis:

A. Design an experiment using a within-subjects experimental design to test her hypothesis regarding morale levels and the number of tours a soldier has served.

B. Specify how your design is experimental. In other words, explain how you will use manipulation and comparison/control, and explain how you will control for possible order effects in your design.

2. A Latin square was introduced in this chapter as a type of partial counterbalancing strategy. Refer to the directions for constructing a Latin square given in Appendix B.2 to construct a Latin square to partially counterbalance each of the following:

A. The order sequences for three treatments

B. The order sequences for four treatments

Identify a problem

- Determine an area of interest.
- Review the literature.
- Identify new ideas in your area of interest.
- Develop a research hypothesis.

Develop a research plan

- Define the variables being tested.
- Identify participants or subjects and determine how to sample them.
- Select a research strategy and design.
- Evaluate ethics and obtain institutional approval to conduct research.

Generate more new ideas

- Results support your hypothesis—refine or expand on your ideas.
- Results do not support your hypothesis—reformulate a new idea or start over.

After reading this chapter, you should be able to:

1 Delineate the factorial design from the factorial experimental design.

2 Identify the appropriate sampling method for a factorial design used in an experiment.

3 Identify and describe three types of factorial designs.

4 Distinguish between a main effect and an interaction.

5 Identify main effects and interactions in a summary table and in a graph.

6 Identify the implications of using a quasi-independent factor in a factorial design.

7 Explain how a factorial design can be used to build on previous research, control for threats to validity, and enhance the informativeness of interpretation.

8 Describe the higher-order factorial design.

9 Compute a factorial analysis of variance for the between-subjects, within-subjects, and mixed factorial design using SPSS.

Conduct the study

- Execute the research plan and measure or record the data.

Communicate the results

- Method of communication: oral, written, or in a poster.
- Style of communication: APA guidelines are provided to help prepare style and format.

Analyze and evaluate the data

- Analyze and evaluate the data as they relate to the research hypothesis.
- Summarize data and research results.

FACTORIAL EXPERIMENTAL DESIGNS

Eating foods can make us happy. Indeed, simply seeing foods can make us happy. Many people allow their emotions to regulate how much they eat in order to maintain and promote positive emotion, yet more recent advances show that you do not have to eat food to feel better; seeing color images of foods can also enhance positive emotion (Frank et al., 2010; Privitera, McGrath, Windus, & Doraiswamy, 2015). Indeed, simply viewing comfort foods can enhance positive emotional states, yet intake of these foods in response to emotions has been linked to the rising rates in obesity (Faith, Allison, & Geliebter, 1997; Sanderson, 2010). Studying how food influences emotion is therefore important, yet the nutrient composition of foods can be detailed.

Think of the foods you eat every day. Desserts, such as cakes, ice creams, and pies, are high in fat, but these are also high in sugar. Fried foods, such as chicken wings, pizzas, and fries, are high in fat but low in sugar. Fruits, such as apples, grapes, and strawberries, have no fat but do contain sugar. Vegetables, such as carrots, peas, and potatoes, have low fat and low sugar. In this example, we have identified food groups that vary in fat and sugar content. We could measure emotional changes after viewing images of each type of food to see if emotional changes depend on if foods are high or low in fat and sugar. Here we have identified a study that analyzes two independent variables (fat, sugar) each with two levels (low, high).

Many research studies in the behavioral sciences involve the manipulation of two or more independent variables, similar to the example given here in which the levels of two independent variables were manipulated (fat and sugar). In this chapter, we introduce factorial experimental designs in which participants are observed across the combination of levels of two or more factors.

12.1 Testing Multiple Factors in the Same Experiment

In Chapters 10 and 11, the complexity of the experimental research designs varied in two ways:

1. We changed the levels of one factor. In Chapters 10 and 11, we described tests for differences between two groups and tests for the variance among more than two groups or levels of one factor.

2. We changed how participants were observed. In Chapter 10, we described research designs in which different participants were observed in each group or at each level of one factor (between-subjects experimental design). In Chapter 11, we described research designs in which the same participants were observed in each group or across the levels of one factor (within-subjects experimental design).

For each experimental research design, we manipulated the levels of a factor. Thus, while a factor can be a quasi-independent variable (i.e., a preexisting variable that is not manipulated, such as a person's sex or ethnicity), we manipulate the levels of each factor in an experimental research design. Specifically, in this chapter, we will describe situations in which we manipulate the levels of two factors observed in the same experiment. For example, suppose we record how long (in seconds) it takes participants to complete a brief exam that varies by difficultly level (easy, hard) and type of exam (printed, computerized). As shown in Table 12.1, in this example we have two factors (difficultly level, type of exam) each with two levels. By crossing the levels of the factors, we create four unique groups.

The design shown in Table 12.1 is called a **factorial design**, which is used to compare differences between groups created by combining the levels of two or more factors. Specifically, we will introduce the **factorial experimental design** in which we create groups by manipulating the levels of two or more factors, then observe the same or different participants in each group using experimental procedures of randomization (for a between-subjects factor) and using control for timing and order effects (for a within-subjects factor). In this chapter, we will only discuss situations in which participants are observed at each level of both factors, which is called a **complete factorial design**. For the example shown in Table 12.1, this means that we will describe situations in which we observe participants in each group (or in each cell in the table).

A **factorial design** is a research design in which participants are observed across the combination of levels of two or more factors.

A **factorial experimental design** is a research design in which groups are created by manipulating the levels of two or more factors, then the same or different participants are observed in each group using experimental procedures of randomization (for a between-subjects factor) and using control for timing and order effects (for a within-subjects factor).

A **complete factorial design**, or **completely crossed design**, is a factorial design in which each level of one factor is combined or crossed with each level of the other factor, with participants observed in each cell or combination of levels.

Table 12.1 A Factorial Research Design With Two Factors (Gender, Attractiveness)

		Type of Exam	
		Printed	Computerized
Difficulty Level	Easy	Participants complete an easy exam that is printed	Participants complete an easy exam that is computerized
	Hard	Participants complete a hard exam that is printed	Participants complete a hard exam that is computerized

In this example, combining the levels of each factor creates four unique groups, which are described in the cells of the table. For this example, in each cell, we record the time (in seconds) that it takes participants to complete an exam.

12.2 Selecting Samples for a Factorial Design in Experimentation

Using the factorial experimental design, we manipulate the levels of each independent variable. For a between-subjects factor, we would then use random assignment to observe different participants in each group. For a within-subjects factor, we would observe the same participants in each group (i.e., we would not use random assignment) and control for timing and order effects. Regardless of the type of factor we manipulate, the sampling procedure for a factorial design used in an experiment follows the form illustrated in Figure 12.1.

As illustrated in Figure 12.1, we can select one sample from the same population, then assign the same or different participants to groups created by combining the levels of two or more factors or independent variables. This type of sampling is commonly used in experiments because we can include randomization, manipulation, and a comparison or control group. For example, suppose we hypothesize that ratings of athletic ability by an athlete will vary depending on the type of feedback (positive, negative) and the type of feedback delivery (written, in-person) he or she receives following a staged exercise. To test this hypothesis, we can select a sample of athletes and have them complete the mock exercise.

We then need to create the groups by combining the levels of each independent variable. In this example, we have two levels of each factor, so we have 2 × 2 = 4 groups. We identify a factorial design by the number of levels for each factor. Hence, in this example, we have a 2 × 2 factorial design, as illustrated in Figure 12.1. How participants are assigned to each group depends on if we manipulate the levels of a within-subjects factor or the levels of a between-subjects factor. This next step to assign participants to groups is described in Section 12.3.

A factorial experimental design is used when we manipulate the levels of two or more independent variables to create groups.

In a factorial experimental design, the levels of both factors must be manipulated, and experimental procedures must be used to assign or observe participants in each group.

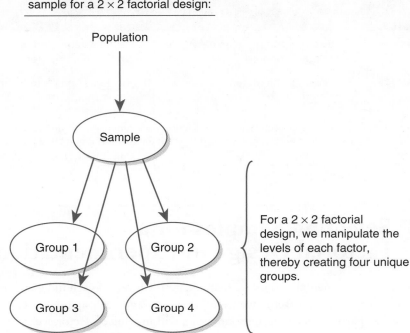

Experimental method of selecting a
sample for a 2 × 2 factorial design:

Population

Sample

Group 1   Group 2

Group 3   Group 4

For a 2 × 2 factorial
design, we manipulate the
levels of each factor,
thereby creating four unique
groups.

To be an experiment, the researcher must manipulate the levels of two or more factors and observe participants at each combination of levels or in each group.

12.3 Types of Factorial Designs

The factorial design can include between-subjects factors, within-subjects factors, or both. In this section we will introduce three types of factorial designs for situations in which the levels of two factors are manipulated, using an example to illustrate each type. The three types of factorial designs introduced in this section are the following:

- Between-subjects design (a design in which all factors are between-subjects factors)

- Within-subjects design (a design in which all factors are within-subjects factors)

- Mixed factorial design (a design with at least one between-subjects factor and at least one within-subjects factor)

Between-Subjects Factorial Designs

We use a **between-subjects factorial design** when we observe different participants in each group created by combining the levels of at least two factors. Hence, once we select the sample, we assign different participants to each group. To illustrate the between-subjects factorial design, consider an experiment conducted by Privitera and Creary (2013), which is illustrated in Table 12.2. In this study, researchers recorded how proximity (near, far) and visibility (visible, not visible) influenced how much fruit participants consumed. For the between-subjects factorial design to be an experiment, the researchers must have done each of the following:

> A **between-subjects factorial design** is a research design in which the levels of two or more between-subjects factors are combined to create groups, meaning that different participants are observed in each group.

1. Manipulate the levels of each factor. In this example, the researchers manipulated the proximity and visibility of the food from the participant. Proximity was manipulated by placing the bowl of fruits within arms reach (near) or 2 meters from participants (far). Visibility was manipulated by placing the fruits in an open bowl (visible) or in a bowl with a lid placed over it (not visible).

2. Cross the levels of the two factors to create the groups. In this example, we have two factors, each with two levels. If we cross the levels of each factor, then we have $2 \times 2 = 4$ groups.

3. Randomly assign different participants to each group. Then compare group differences in the dependent variable (amount consumed in calories).

The researchers in this experiment predicted that participants' consumption would be greatest when the bowl of fruits was close to them (near) and they could see the fruits in the bowl (visible). As shown in Table 12.2, this hypothesis was supported, as reported in their published study, in that consumption of the fruits was greatest in Group Near-Visible.

Using the between-subjects factorial design, we can determine the total number of participants (N) in an experiment by multiplying the sample size by the number of levels for

Table 12.2 An Experiment in Which the Proximity (Near, Far) and the Visibility (Visible, Not Visible) of a Bowl of Fruits Were Manipulated

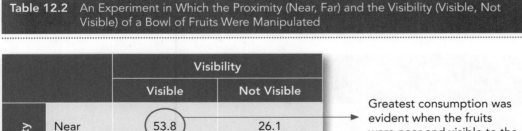

Greatest consumption was evident when the fruits were near and visible to the participant.

The cells in the table represent the groups created by combining the levels of each factor. Using the between-subjects factorial design, different participants are observed in each cell or group. Data and design are adapted from those reported by Privitera and Creary (2013).

In a between-subjects factorial design, we combine the levels of two or more between-subjects factors.

each factor. In this experiment, we had two factors, each with two levels. Suppose that 10 participants were observed in each group in this example. In this case, then, the total number of participants in the experiment would be as follows:

$$N = 10 \times 2 \times 2 = 40 \text{ participants}$$

Within-Subjects Factorial Designs

We use a **within-subjects factorial design** when we observe the same participants in each group created by combining the levels of at least two factors. To illustrate a within-subjects factorial design, consider an experiment conducted by Dishman, Thomson, and Karnovsky (2009), which is illustrated in Table 12.3. In this study, researchers measured the activity levels of captive ring-tailed lemurs (*Lemur catta*) in each of four environments that varied by the visibility of food (openly presented, hidden) and arrangement of food (aggregated, scattered). For the within-subjects factorial design to be an experiment, the researchers must have done each of the following:

> A **within-subjects factorial design** is a research design in which the levels of two or more within-subjects factors are combined to create groups, meaning that the same participants are observed in each group.

In a within-subjects factorial design, we combine the levels of two or more within-subjects factors.

1. Manipulate the levels of each factor. In this example, the researchers manipulated the visibility and arrangement of food in an environment.

2. Cross the levels of the two factors to create the groups. In this example, we have two factors, each with two levels. If we cross the levels of each factor, then we have $2 \times 2 = 4$ groups.

Table 12.3 A Within-Subjects Factorial Design in Which the Visibility of Food (Openly Presented, Hidden) and the Arrangement of Food (Aggregated, Scattered) in an Environment Were Manipulated

		Visibility of Food	
		Openly Presented	Hidden
Arrangement of Food	Aggregated	12	15
	Scattered	14	22

Greatest activity levels observed when food was scattered and hidden.

The cells in the table represent the groups created by combining the levels of each factor. Using the within-subjects factorial design, the same subjects are observed in each cell or group. Data and design are adapted from those reported by Dishman et al. (2009).

3. Control for order effects due to observing the same subjects in each group or in each environment in this example. Then compare group differences in the dependent variable (activity levels).

The researchers in this experiment hypothesized that lemurs would be more active in an enriched environment, which they describe as an environment in which food is hidden and scattered in the environment. As shown in Table 12.3 using hypothetical data based on the pattern of findings in their experiment, this hypothesis was supported in that activity levels were greatest in Group Hidden-Scattered.

Using the within-subjects factorial design, the total number of participants or subjects (*N*) in an experiment is equal to the sample size in each group because the same participants or subjects are observed in each group. In this experiment, eight lemurs were observed in each group, so the total number of subjects was eight.

Mixed Factorial Designs

We use a **mixed factorial design** when we create groups by crossing the levels of at least one between-subjects factor and one within-subjects factor. To illustrate a mixed factorial design, consider an experiment conducted by Ling and Xuejun (2011), which is illustrated in Table 12.4. In this study, researchers tested how two factors affected the ability to code memories using a 2 × 2 mixed factorial design, with preexposure to target stimuli (preexposure, no preexposure) varied between subjects and attentional demand required during a word rating task (standard, high) varied within subjects. For the mixed factorial design to be an experiment, the researchers must have done each of the following:

> A **mixed factorial design** is a research design in which different participants are observed at each level of a between-subjects factor and also repeatedly observed across the levels of the within-subjects factor.

1. Manipulate the levels of each factor. In this example, the researchers manipulated whether participants were preexposed to the target stimuli and the attentional demand required during the task.

2. Cross the levels of the two factors to create the groups. In this example, we have two factors each with two levels. If we cross the levels of each factor, then we have 2 × 2 = 4 groups.

3. Randomly assign different participants to each level of the between-subjects factor (preexposure to target stimuli).

4. Control for order effects due to observing the same participants at each level of the within-subjects factor (attentional demand required during the task). Then compare group differences in the dependent variable (memory recall).

In a mixed factorial design, we combine the levels of at least one between-subjects factor and one within-subjects factor.

Using the mixed factorial design, the total number of participants or subjects (*N*) in an experiment is equal to the sample size times the number of levels of the between-subjects factor. Suppose that 30 participants were randomly assigned to each level of the

Table 12.4 A Mixed Factorial Design

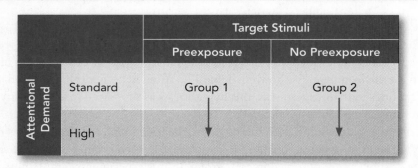

		Target Stimuli	
		Preexposure	No Preexposure
Attentional Demand	Standard	Group 1	Group 2
	High	↓	↓

With preexposure to a target stimulus (preexposure, no preexposure) as the between-subjects factor and the attentional demand required during the task (standard, high) as the within-subjects factor. Using a mixed factorial design, the same subjects were observed in each level of the within-subjects factor. Design is adapted from that reported by Ling and Xuejun (2011).

between-subjects factor (preexposure to target stimuli). In this case, then, the total number of participants in the experiment would be as follows:

$$N = 30 \times 2 = 60 \text{ participants each observed two times}$$

12.4 Ethics in Focus: Participant Fatigue and Factorial Designs

When the same participants are observed in multiple groups, the researcher must show that the greater demands on the participants do not cause undue harm or place an undue burden on the participants. The need to ease the burden on the participants is especially important for a factorial design because the number of groups created by combining the levels of at least two factors can be large. Two concerns are of particular importance for a factorial design:

1. The larger the number of levels combined to create the groups, the greater the demands on the participants. For a 3 × 3 within-subjects factorial design, for example, we would observe the same participants in nine groups. Simply observing the same participants nine times can place undue burden on a participant, particularly if the experiment takes weeks or months to complete.

2. The greater the demands in each group, the greater the burden on the participants. For example, if we observe the same participants in different physical exercise groups, then we would be concerned about participant fatigue. To address this concern, we could ensure that a medical professional was present during the experiment, for example, to protect the participants in case one or more does fatigue. How we address the concerns will depend on the type of demands placed on participants in each group.

1. True or false: In order to manipulate the levels of each factor in a factorial design, we must select a sample from at least two or more different populations.

2. A researcher conducts a 4 × 2 factorial design with 10 participants observed in each group. How many participants are needed to conduct this experiment if the researcher conducts each of the following designs?

   A. A between-subjects factorial design

   B. A within-subjects factorial design

   C. A mixed factorial design in which the first variable is a within-subjects factor

   D. A mixed factorial design in which the second variable is a within-subjects factor

3. Which type of factorial design includes the manipulation of a between-subjects factor and a within-subjects factor?

> In a factorial design, we need to be concerned with participant fatigue when we use a within-subjects design and when the demands in each group are great.

Answers: 1. False. We must select one sample from a single population; 2. A. 80 participants, B. 10 participants, C. 20 participants, D. 40 participants; 3. A mixed factorial design.

12.5 Main Effects and Interactions

The goal in experimentation is to minimize the possibility that individual differences, or something other than a manipulation, caused differences between groups. Methodologically, we use different strategies depending on whether we manipulate the levels of a between-subjects factor or a within-subjects factor. For a between-subjects factor, we ensure that participants are selected in such a way that random assignment can be used. For a within-subjects factor, we observe the same participants in each group and control for timing and order effects.

Statistically, we also control for individual differences by using a test statistic to determine the likelihood that something other than the manipulation of two factors caused differences in a dependent measure between groups. The test statistic commonly used for a factorial design is the **two-way analysis of variance (ANOVA)**, which is used for data that are measured on an interval or a ratio scale. The formula for this test statistic follows the same general structure as that defined for the one-way ANOVAs in Chapters 10 and 11. The general structure of the two-way ANOVA is as follows:

> A **two-way ANOVA** is a statistical procedure used to analyze the variance in a dependent variable between groups created by combining the levels of two factors.

$$F = \frac{\text{Variance between groups}}{\text{Variance attributed to error}}$$

Note that the test statistic introduced in this chapter can also be used in quasi-experiments. However, because the quasi-experiment does not methodologically control for individual differences (i.e., a quasi-experiment lacks a manipulation, randomization, or control

> A **two-way factorial design** is a research design in which participants are observed in groups created by combining or crossing the levels of two factors.

for timing and order effects), the design cannot demonstrate cause and effect. Both levels of control (methodological and statistical) must be present for the factorial research design to be an experiment and therefore demonstrate cause and effect.

In this section, we will introduce the factorial design in which the levels of two factors are manipulated, as is illustrated in Tables 12.2 to 12.4. When the levels of two factors (A and B) are combined to create groups, the design is specifically called a **two-way factorial design**. Using this design, we can identify three sources of variation:

1. Two main effects (one for Factor A and one for Factor B)

2. One interaction (the combination of levels of Factors A and B)

3. Error variance (variability attributed to individual differences)

We make three independent statistical tests using the two-way factorial design. To show how the sources of variation relate to a research hypothesis, we will work with an example in which we manipulate two factors (studying for a quiz and attending class) and measure quiz scores (the dependent variable) to answer the following three questions:

- Did manipulating the levels of Factor A (a main effect) cause differences between groups? Example: Does studying for a quiz result in higher quiz scores? (See Table 12.5.)

- Did manipulating the levels of Factor B (a main effect) cause differences between groups? Example: Does attending class result in higher quiz scores? (See Table 12.5.)

- Did combining the levels of Factor A and Factor B to create groups (the interaction) cause differences between groups? Example: Does the combination of studying for a quiz and attending class result in higher quiz scores? (See Table 12.6.)

In this example, Factor A is whether students studied for a quiz (no, yes), and Factor B is their class attendance (high, low). In this section, we will identify each source of variation and show how measuring each source allows researchers to answer each of the questions identified for each factor.

Main Effects

In a factorial design, we can look at the effects of each factor separately. The extent to which the levels of a single factor cause changes in a dependent variable is called a **main effect**. Using this definition, we also tested for main effects using the one-way ANOVAs in Chapters 10 and 11 because we tested for the effects at each level of a single factor.

For a 2 × 2 factorial design, we can illustrate main effects in the row and column totals of a 2 × 2 table summary. To illustrate, suppose the data in Table 12.5 are quiz scores, in which Factor A is whether students studied for a quiz (no, yes) and Factor B is their

Table 12.5 Main Effects

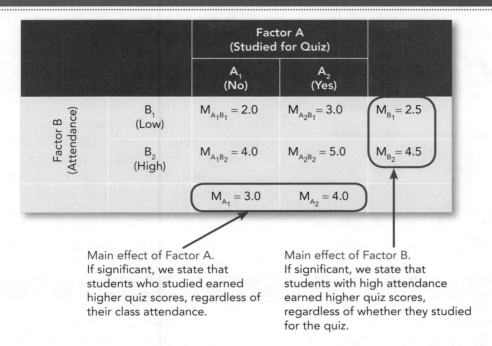

		Factor A (Studied for Quiz)		
		A_1 (No)	A_2 (Yes)	
Factor B (Attendance)	B_1 (Low)	$M_{A_1B_1} = 2.0$	$M_{A_2B_1} = 3.0$	$M_{B_1} = 2.5$
	B_2 (High)	$M_{A_1B_2} = 4.0$	$M_{A_2B_2} = 5.0$	$M_{B_2} = 4.5$
		$M_{A_1} = 3.0$	$M_{A_2} = 4.0$	

Main effect of Factor A. If significant, we state that students who studied earned higher quiz scores, regardless of their class attendance.

Main effect of Factor B. If significant, we state that students with high attendance earned higher quiz scores, regardless of whether they studied for the quiz.

The main effect for each factor reflects the difference between the row and column totals in the table. There are two main effects (one for Factor A and one for Factor B) in a two-way factorial design.

class attendance (high, low). Table 12.5 identifies each main effect and shows how each would be interpreted, if significant. Notice that we interpret a significant main effect similar to the interpretation of significant results using the one-way ANOVAs.

A significant main effect indicates that group means significantly vary across the levels of one factor, independent of the second factor. In a table summary, such as that given in Table 12.5, we compare the variance of row and column means to interpret the main effects. To compute the test statistic for each main effect, we place the between-groups variance for one factor in the numerator and the error variance in the denominator. Referring to the table summary, the test statistic for the main effect of Factor A is as follows:

A **main effect** is a source of variation associated with mean differences across the levels of a single factor.

In a table summary, a main effect is a measure of how the row and column means differ across the levels of a single factor.

In a two-way factorial design there are two main effects: one for Factor A and one for Factor B.

$$F = \frac{\text{Variance of column means}}{\text{Variance attributed to error}}$$

The test statistic for the main effect of Factor B is as follows:

$$F = \frac{\text{Variance of row means}}{\text{Variance attributed to error}}$$

Interactions

The changes in a dependent variable across the levels of a single factor are called a main effect.

In a factorial design, we can also look at the effects of combining the levels of two factors to create groups. The extent to which groups created by combining the levels of two factors cause changes in a dependent variable is called an A × B interaction. An **interaction** is unique to the factorial design in that it allows us to determine if changes in a dependent variable across the levels of one factor depend on the level of the second factor we look at.

An **interaction** is a source of variation associated with how the effects of one factor are influenced by, or depend on, the levels of a second factor.

In a table summary, an interaction is a measure of how cell means at each level of one factor change across the levels of a second factor.

For a 2 × 2 factorial design, we can illustrate the interaction in the cells of a 2 × 2 table summary. To illustrate, the quiz data where Factor A is whether students studied for a quiz (no, yes) and Factor B is their class attendance (high, low) are given again in Table 12.6. Table 12.6 identifies two ways to interpret the interaction, if significant. For each interpretation, we look across the levels of one

Table 12.6 Interaction

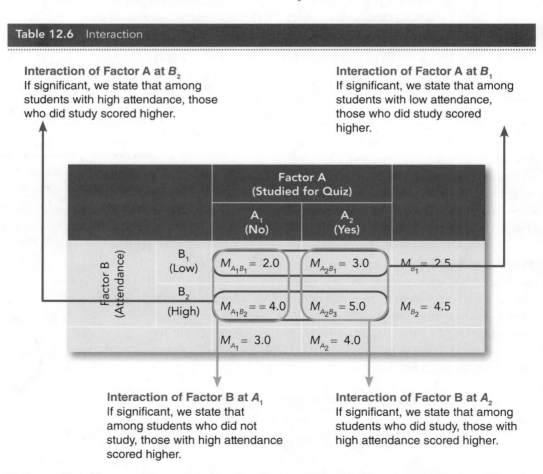

Interaction of Factor A at B_2
If significant, we state that among students with high attendance, those who did study scored higher.

Interaction of Factor A at B_1
If significant, we state that among students with low attendance, those who did study scored higher.

Interaction of Factor B at A_1
If significant, we state that among students who did not study, those with high attendance scored higher.

Interaction of Factor B at A_2
If significant, we state that among students who did study, those with high attendance scored higher.

The interaction reflects the difference between the cell means in the table. There is one interaction with two ways to interpret it. Each way to interpret the interaction in a two-way factorial design is described in the table.

factor at each level of the second factor. Which interpretation we use to describe the interaction depends largely on how we want to describe the data.

A significant interaction indicates that group means significantly vary across the combined levels of two factors. In a table summary, such as that given in Table 12.6, we compare the variance of cell means to interpret an interaction. To compute the test statistic for an interaction, we place the between-groups variance for the interaction in the numerator and the error variance in the denominator. Referring to the table summary, the test statistic for the interaction is as follows:

$$F = \frac{\text{Variance of cell means}}{\text{Variance attributed to error}}$$

The change in a dependent variable across the combined levels of two factors is called an interaction.

Error

To compute the test statistic, we divide the variance between groups by the variance attributed to error for each main effect test and the interaction. Each main effect

Table 12.7 Error Variance

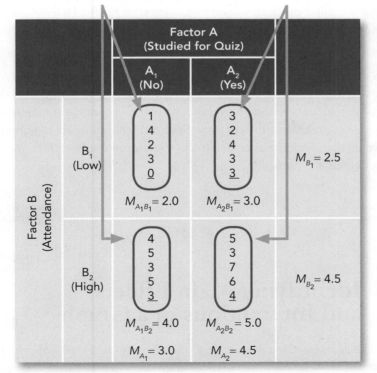

Error variance, or individual differences in participant scores in each cell.

In a two-way factorial design, error variance is a measure of the individual differences, or differences in participant scores, within each cell in the table.

test and the interaction test are separate hypothesis tests. Like all previous tests, error variance is largely attributed to individual differences. It is a measure to account for the fact that people are different or behave as individuals, regardless of the group to which they are assigned.

The variance attributed to error in a factorial design is associated with differences in participant scores within each cell, called *within-groups variability* (also defined in Chapter 11). To illustrate error in a factorial design, suppose the quiz scores data were from a study with five participants observed in each group or cell in the table summary. Table 12.7 shows the same quiz scores data, except that the individual scores of each participant in each group are listed. Notice that participants in each group do not always respond the same, even if they are in the same group. For example, all students in the no-attendance, low-study group had a different quiz score even though they were in the same group. Having different groups cannot explain this variability. For this reason, we calculate the within-groups variability in each group and place that value for error in the denominator of the test statistic.

LEARNING CHECK 2 ✓

1. What are the three effects about which researchers test a hypothesis using the two-way factorial design?

2. Name the statistical procedure used to analyze data for the factorial design with two factors.

3. The variance attributed to error in a factorial design is associated with differences in _____ within each cell.

4. A researcher tests whether the lighting (dull, bright) and background noise (low, high) in a classroom influence student performance on an exam. He conducts a two-way factorial design to analyze the data and finds a significant effect of lighting, with higher scores when the lighting was bright. Is the effect described in this study an example of a main effect or an interaction?

Answers: 1. A main effect of Factor A, a main effect of Factor B, and an A × B interaction; 2. The two-way ANOVA; 3. participant scores; 4. Main effect.

12.6 Identifying Main Effects and Interactions in a Graph

A main effect and an interaction can be evident when the cell means in a table summary are plotted in a graph. Keep in mind, however, that even if a graph shows a possible main effect or interaction, the use of a test statistic is still needed to determine whether a main effect or an interaction is significant. In other words, we use the test statistic to determine if our manipulation of the two factors caused the observed pattern we plotted in a graph. In this section, we look at how three types of outcomes appear graphically for a two-way factorial design.

Graphing Only Main Effects

One possible outcome is to observe only main effects. For the main effects, we would observe changes at the levels of one factor, independent of the changes in a second factor. Consider, for example, a factorial design in which we manipulate whether the setting (familiar, unfamiliar) and the duration (1 hour, 2 hours) of a treatment influence its effectiveness to reduce (lower) social anxiety. When the main effects are significant, we look at the row and column means to describe the effect. Figure 12.2 shows how a graph would appear when main effects are significant: Figure 12.2a depicts a main effect of duration only; Figure 12.2b depicts a main effect of duration and a main effect of setting, but no interaction.

> The group means in a table summary can be graphed to identify the main effects.

Figure 12.2 The Data and Graph of the Cell Means for One Main Effect Only (a) and Two Main Effects, But No Interaction (b)

(a) Data showing a main effect of duration only.

		Setting		ROW MEANS
		Familiar	Unfamiliar	
Duration	1 Hour	8	8	8
	2 Hours	4	4	4
	COLUMN MEANS	6	6	

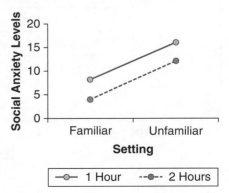

(b) Data showing a main effect of both factors (duration and setting), but no interaction.

		Setting		ROW MEANS
		Familiar	Unfamiliar	
Duration	1 Hour	8	16	12
	2 Hours	4	12	8
	COLUMN MEANS	6	14	

Graphing a Main Effect and an Interaction

Another possible outcome is to observe an interaction and also at least one main effect. To identify an interaction, we graph the cell means and look to see if the lines in the graph are parallel. A possible interaction is evident when the lines are not parallel. Keep in mind that it is not required that the lines actually touch or cross over to show evidence of a possible interaction; as long as the lines are not parallel, a possible interaction is evident. To illustrate, consider again the example of a factorial design in which we manipulate whether the setting (familiar, unfamiliar) and the duration (1 hour, 2 hours) of a treatment influence its effectiveness to reduce social anxiety. Figure 12.3a depicts a main effect of setting (lower anxiety levels observed in the familiar setting regardless of the duration of the treatment) and an interaction. The interaction qualifies the main effect in that it identifies that the main effect alone does not tell the whole story, so to speak. The interaction shows that anxiety levels were

> The group means in a table summary can be graphed to identify an interaction.

Figure 12.3 The Data and Graph of the Cell Means for One Main Effect and an Interaction (a), and an Interaction But No Main Effects (b)

(a) Data showing a main effect of setting and a Setting × Duration interaction.

		Setting		ROW MEANS
		Familiar	Unfamiliar	
Duration	1 Hour	7	7	7
	2 Hours	2	12	7
	COLUMN MEANS	5	9	

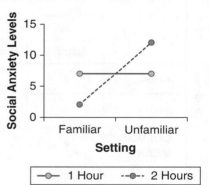

(b) Data showing a Setting × Duration interaction, but no main effects.

		Setting		ROW MEANS
		Familiar	Unfamiliar	
Duration	1 Hour	12	6	9
	2 Hours	6	12	9
	COLUMN MEANS	9	9	

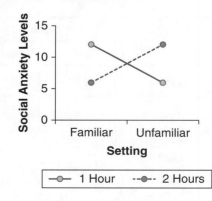

lower in the familiar setting for the two-hour treatment (2 vs. 12) but not for the one-hour treatment in which anxiety levels were actually the same in each setting (7 vs. 7). Thus, stating that anxiety levels are lower in a familiar setting (shown by the main effect) is not the whole story. Instead, spending 2 hours in a familiar setting lowers anxiety; spending 1 hour in that same setting does not affect anxiety at all (shown by the interaction). Notice in Figure 12.3a that the lines are not parallel, which indicates a possible interaction.

Graphing Only an Interaction

Another possible outcome is to observe only an interaction. For the interaction, we expect to observe that changes in a dependent variable for one factor depend on which level of the second factor we look at. Consider again the example of a factorial design in which we manipulate whether the setting (familiar, unfamiliar) and the duration (1 hour, 2 hours) of a treatment influence its effectiveness to reduce social anxiety. Figure 12.3b depicts an interaction only—the 1-hour treatment resulted in lower social anxiety levels in the unfamiliar setting, whereas the 2-hour treatment resulted in lower social anxiety levels in the familiar setting. No main effects are evident in Figure 12.3b because the row means and column means do not differ. Notice in Figure 12.3b that the lines are not parallel, which indicates a possible interaction.

LEARNING CHECK 3 ✓

1. Which effect, a main effect or an interaction, can be identified in the row means and column means of a table summary?

2. The following graph summarizes the results of a study that manipulated the caloric density (low, high) and type of food (dessert, snack, meal) consumed in a buffet. Is an interaction evident? If no, then explain your answer.

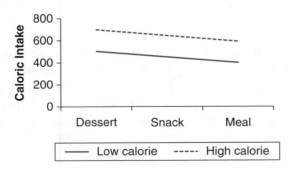

3. Which effect, a main effect or an interaction, is identified in the cell means of a table summary?

Answers: 1. A main effect; 2. No, because the lines are parallel; 3. An interaction.

12.7 Including Quasi-Independent Factors in an Experiment

In this chapter, we have described the factorial design using examples for how the design is used in an experiment. In other words, both factors were manipulated in each example, such that participants could be randomly assigned to groups, or the same participants could be observed in each group and the researcher could then control for order effects (e.g., use counterbalancing; see Chapter 11). Hence, in each example, we manipulated the levels of two independent variables. Because the manipulation of an independent variable is a requirement for demonstrating cause and effect, each example thus far is one that could be used in an experiment.

The factorial design, however, can also be used when we include preexisting or quasi-independent factors. When all factors in a factorial design are quasi-experimental, the design is not an experiment because no factor is manipulated. For example, if we measure

> A **participant variable** is a quasi-independent or preexisting variable that is related to or characteristic of the personal attributes of a participant.

health scores among participants of different sexes (male, female) and health insurance status (insured, uninsured), then the study is a quasi-experiment because the participants determined their group assignment; both factors were preexisting. We would still use a factorial design to analyze the health scores, but we would not conclude that one or both factors caused changes in the dependent variable (health scores). Instead, we could only conclude that these factors were related to or associated with observed changes because the study conducted is a quasi-experiment.

When at least one factor in a factorial design is manipulated (an independent variable), the design is typically called an experiment, even if a quasi-independent variable is included in the design. Often, researchers will include a quasi-independent variable called a **participant variable** in an experiment when it relates to the hypothesis being tested. Participant variables are typically demographic characteristics—that is, characteristics of the participants in a study. Examples of participant variables include intelligence level, age, gender, race, ethnicity, education level, personality type, and body weight.

> An effect of a quasi-independent variable shows that the factor is related to changes in a dependent variable. It does not demonstrate cause and effect because the factor is preexisting.

When a quasi-independent variable is included in a factorial design, we do not show cause and effect for any effect that involves that quasi-independent factor. Instead, we conclude that the levels of a quasi-independent variable are related to or associated with changes in a dependent variable. To illustrate how to interpret the effects of a factorial design with a quasi-independent variable, consider a 2 × 2 mixed factorial design similar to that conducted by Salvy, Coelho, Kieffer, and Epstein (2007) used to test the hypothesis that children would eat more in the presence of others. To test this hypothesis, researchers manipulated whether elementary school–aged children ate alone or with other children (social context). A quasi-independent participant variable was also included to see how it related to the results (participant weight: lean, overweight). The design of this experiment is illustrated in Table 12.8.

The results of the study by Salvy et al. (2007) showed a significant main effect of participant weight and a Participant Weight × Social Context interaction. In this example, both effects involved the quasi-independent factor (participant weight). Hence, neither effect shows cause and effect. Instead, the advantage of including the preexisting factor

Interaction of social context among lean children. Lean children ate more in a group than alone.

Interaction of social context among overweight children. Overweight children ate more when alone than in a group.

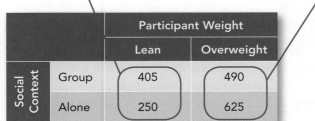

The approximate mean amount consumed (in kilocalories) is given for each group in the cells of the table. The interaction of social context is also interpreted at each level of participant weight. Data and design are adapted from those reported by Salvy et al. (2007).

(participant weight) is to test the generality of their findings across the levels of the quasi-independent variable. For example, to interpret the interaction, researchers concluded that overweight children ate more when eating alone compared with in a group; by contrast, lean children ate more in a group than when eating alone. Hence, because the researchers included the quasi-independent factor (participant weight), they determined that their manipulation (eating alone or in a group) generalized to lean children (who ate more in a group than alone) and differently to overweight children (who ate more alone than in a group).

12.8 Reasons for Including Two or More Factors in an Experiment

There are many reasons why we would want to manipulate or observe the levels of two or more factors in the same experiment. One overarching reason for conducting a factorial design is that so many effects in nature are "conditional" or "depend on" other factors (i.e., they are interactive). For example, obesity interacts with other factors such as dietary history, mental health, and exercise. As another example, income level interacts with other factors such as socioeconomic status, education level, and motivation. A factorial design is thus well suited to help us understand "effects" by studying how two or more factors interact to produce those effects. Beyond this key overarching reason, in this section we describe three additional and important reasons for adding factors to an experiment:

- To build on previous research
- To control for threats to validity
- To enhance the informativeness of interpretation

Table 12.9 Hypothetical Findings for an Experiment with One Factor

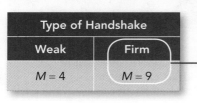

Type of Handshake	
Weak	**Firm**
$M = 4$	$M = 9$

The results support the hypothesis because the most positive evaluations were given for vignettes describing an interviewee giving a firm handshake.

Building on Previous Research

One reason for adding factors to an experiment is to replicate a previous finding and also in the same design demonstrate a novel or new finding. Although it is important to determine whether a previous finding can be replicated, that alone is redundant because the experiment shows the same finding that someone else already showed. Not only is it important to replicate previous findings, but it is also important to build on or add to what the previous findings showed.

To illustrate how we can add factors in a factorial design to build on previous findings, suppose a researcher tested the hypothesis that individuals who give a firm handshake will receive more positive evaluations during employment interviews (such as a similar hypothesis tested by Stewart, Dustin, Barrick, & Darnold, 2008; see also Bernieri & Petty, 2011). To test this hypothesis, a researcher randomly assigned participants to read a vignette describing an interviewee. Participants were then asked to rate how positively they would evaluate the interviewee described in the vignette. In one group, the vignette described the interviewee as giving a weak handshake at the beginning and end of the interview; in a second group, the interviewee was described as giving a firm handshake at the beginning and end of the interview. To support the hypothesis we would expect participants in the firm handshake group to have more positive evaluations of the interviewee, as shown in Table 12.9.

> Factorial designs allow you to build on previous research by replicating a previous result while also demonstrating a new result in the same design.

To replicate the result shown in Table 12.9 and build upon this finding, we could state our own hypothesis that individuals who give a firm handshake will receive more positive evaluations during employment interviews particularly when they shake hands with the interviewer at the beginning and end of an interview. To test this hypothesis we again include the type of handshake factor (weak, firm) and add the new factor (time of handshake: beginning only, end only, beginning and end of interview) to build upon this finding. In this example, shown with hypothetical data in Table 12.10, we have a 2×3 factorial design with six total groups or versions of the vignette. Table 12.10 shows where in a table summary we can replicate the previous findings for the two groups that are identical to those in Table 12.9, and it also shows where in a table summary we can show support for our new hypothesis by adding the second factor. In this way, we can replicate a previous finding, and we can demonstrate a new finding in the same design because we add a second factor to the design.

Controlling for Threats to Validity

A second reason for adding factors to an experiment is to control for possible threats to validity, which includes all of those introduced in Chapter 6 (e.g., history and maturation,

Table 12.10 Hypothetical Findings for a Two-Way Factorial Design

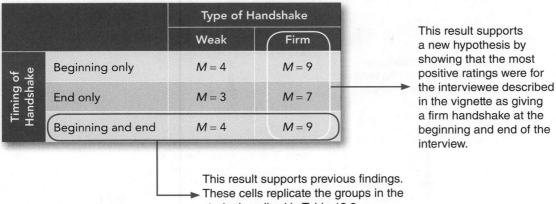

		Type of Handshake	
		Weak	Firm
Timing of Handshake	Beginning only	M = 4	M = 9
	End only	M = 3	M = 7
	Beginning and end	M = 4	M = 9

This result supports a new hypothesis by showing that the most positive ratings were for the interviewee described in the vignette as giving a firm handshake at the beginning and end of the interview.

This result supports previous findings. These cells replicate the groups in the study described in Table 12.9.

This design replicates results shown in Table 12.9, and also builds on this hypothesis by demonstrating a new effect.

testing and regression effects, participant attrition, and other environmental factors) as well as those introduced in Chapter 11 (e.g., participant fatigue, order effects, and carryover effects). For example, suppose we measured liking for an unsweetened drink and a sweetened drink (similar to the example given in Chapter 11 in the Making Sense section). Because this is a within-subjects design, one possible threat to internal validity is the order in which participants are given the drinks (sweetened, then unsweetened; vs. unsweetened, then sweetened). To control for this threat to internal validity, we can include *order* as a between-subjects variable. The structure of this design is given in Figure 12.4. The results shown in Figure 12.4 demonstrate the effect of interest and demonstrate that order did not influence ratings of liking—this is shown because the order in which participants were given the drinks was included as a factor in the study.

> To control for threats to internal validity, these threats can be included as factors in a factorial design.

Likewise, we can control for just about any other threat to internal validity by including it as a factor in a factorial design. Factors added to control for threats to validity can be inherent to the individual, such as gender (men, women) or health status (lean, overweight, obese); or these factors can be inherent to the research setting or structure, such as the time of day (morning, afternoon, evening) that a study is conducted or the lab room that a participant was observed in, if observations were made in more than one room. In this way, we can use the factorial design to test at least one factor of interest, while also controlling for possible threats to validity by including these threats as factors in the design.

Enhancing the Informativeness of Interpretation

A third reason for adding factors to an experiment is that a factorial design can be more informative than a single-factor design because it allows us to analyze the effects of two or more factors simultaneously. In addition to the two advantages already stated, the factorial design allows us to analyze an effect that can only be analyzed using

> Factorial designs are more informative in that they allow us to observe the interaction of two or more factors.

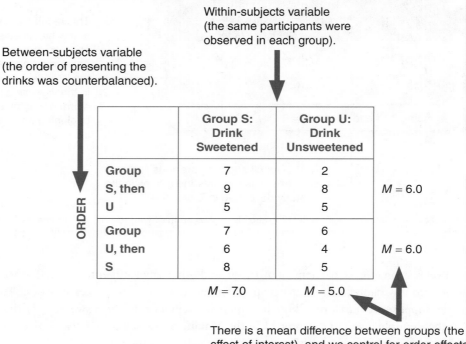

Between-subjects variable (the order of presenting the drinks was counterbalanced).

Within-subjects variable (the same participants were observed in each group).

ORDER

	Group S: Drink Sweetened	Group U: Drink Unsweetened	
Group S, then U	7 9 5	2 8 5	$M = 6.0$
Group U, then S	7 6 8	6 4 5	$M = 6.0$
	$M = 7.0$	$M = 5.0$	

There is a mean difference between groups (the effect of interest), and we control for order effects by showing that ratings did not differ at each level of order.

Notice that there is no mean difference in ratings at each level of order. Hence, we controlled for order effects (showed no difference), while also showing a mean difference between the groups of interest.

this design: the interaction. Hence, we can analyze changes in a dependent variable across the levels of a single factor (the main effects), and we can also analyze how multiple factors interact to cause changes in a dependent variable (the interaction) in the same design. In this way, an analysis using a factorial design is more informative than research designs that analyze the effects of only one factor at a time—in that only a factorial design can demonstrate an interaction effect.

12.9 Higher-Order Factorial Designs

In this chapter, we used the two-way factorial design to illustrate how to conduct experiments using this design. However, factorial designs are not limited to testing only two factors. When a factorial design includes more than two factors, it is called a **higher-order factorial design.**

The "way" of a factorial design indicates the number of factors being combined or crossed to create groups. In the two-way factorial design, we cross two factors to create groups; in a three-way factorial design, we cross three factors. The number of factors we cross to create groups is the number of "ways" of a factorial design. One consequence of adding factors is that the number of possible effects we could observe also increases. For example, in a three-way factorial design, we could observe any combination of 3 main effects, 2 two-way interactions, and 1 three-way interaction. The three-way interaction is called a **higher-order interaction** because it shows that the combination of levels of more than two factors is associated with changes in a dependent variable. To show how the number of possible effects increases as we increase the number of factors in a factorial design, Table 12.11 lists the possible main effects and interactions for a three-way and a four-way factorial design.

> A **higher-order factorial design** is a research design in which the levels of more than two factors are combined or crossed to create groups.
>
> A **higher-order interaction** is an interaction for the combination of levels of three or more factors in a factorial design.

Interpreting a higher-order interaction can be challenging, although a three-way interaction can be readily interpreted—to graph such a finding, we would need to plot the data on three axes, however. For example, we may observe a three-way interaction in which participant ratings of attractiveness vary by the gender (male, female), body type (lean, overweight), and type of food eaten (healthy, unhealthy) of the person being rated. To plot one data point, we would record, for example, that a male (one axis) who is lean (a second axis) and eating a healthy food (a third axis) is rated as 7 on an attractiveness measure. A four-way interaction or higher is very difficult to interpret because the number of axes needed to plot the data makes it difficult to understand exactly what the interaction is showing. For this reason, researchers will often limit the number of factors in a factorial design to two or three, if possible, to avoid the possibility of observing higher-order interactions with four or more factors.

> Higher-order factorial designs allow us to observe the effects of three or more factors in the same design.

Table 12.11 The Possible Main Effects and Interactions in Three-Way and Four-Way Factorial Designs

	Three-Way Factorial Design	Four-Way Factorial Design
Main Effects	A, B, C	A, B, C, D
Two-Way Interactions	A × B, B × C, A × C	A × B, B × C, C × D, A × C, A × D, B × D
Three-Way Interactions	A × B × C	A × B × C, B × C × D, A × B × D, A × C × D
Four-Way Interactions	—	A × B × C × D

LEARNING CHECK 4 ✓

1. How are our conclusions in a factorial design limited when the design includes at least one quasi-independent factor?

2. A researcher replicated a previous finding and also demonstrates a new finding in the same factorial design. Which reason for adding factors to an experiment does this statement illustrate?

3. A researcher measures the time it takes college students to complete a cognitive task after receiving positive or negative feedback. Because the class year of participants (freshman, sophomore, junior, or senior) may influence how students respond to the feedback, class year was included as a second factor. Which reason for adding factors to an experiment does this statement illustrate?

4. What is a higher-order interaction?

Answers: 1. When a quasi-independent factor is included in a factorial design, we do not show cause and effect for any effect that includes that quasi-independent factor; 2. Building on previous research; 3. Controlling for threats to validity; 4. A higher-order interaction is an interaction for the combination of levels of three or more factors in a factorial design.

12.10 SPSS in Focus: General Instructions for Conducting a Factorial ANOVA

We can use SPSS to compute a factorial design with any number of within-subjects factors and between-subjects factors. To demonstrate how to use SPSS, we will use an example similar to a clever study design used by Wansink and Kim (2005). In this example, suppose we vary the type (stale, fresh) and bag size (small, large) of popcorn during a movie presentation. Thus, we are using a 2×2 factorial design. Using the data given in Table 12.12, we will compute a two-way ANOVA assuming both factors are between-subjects factors, then recompute the data assuming both factors are within-subjects factors, using SPSS.

Factorial Designs With Only Between-Subjects Factors

The following are procedures for using SPSS when two factors (type of popcorn and bag size) are between-subjects factors, meaning that different participants are observed in each group created by crossing the levels of two factors.

1. Click on the **Variable View** tab and enter *popcorn* in the **Name column**; enter *bagsize* in the Name column below it; enter *dv* in the Name column below that. Reduce the value to 0 in the **Decimals column** for each row because we will enter only whole numbers.

Table 12.12 Amount of Popcorn Consumed for Three Participants in Each Group or Cell

		Bag Size	
		Small	Large
Popcorn	Stale	20, 21, 23	24, 26, 23
	Fresh	23, 22, 21	29, 25, 26

2. In the row named *popcorn*, click on the small gray box with three dots in the **Values** column. In the **dialog box**, enter *1* in the value cell and *stale* in the label cell, and then click **Add**. Then enter *2* in the value cell and *fresh* in the label cell, and then click **Add**. Select **OK**.

3. In the row named *bagsize*, follow the same directions stated in Step 2, except enter *1* for *small* and enter *2* for *large*.

4. Click on the **Data View** tab. Enter the codes for each factor and the data for each group as shown in Figure 12.5a.

5. Go to the menu bar and click **Analyze**, then **General Linear Model**, and **Univariate** to display a dialog box.

6. Use the appropriate arrows to move *popcorn* and *bagsize* into the **Fixed Factor(s):** box. Move the dependent variable, *dv*, into the **Dependent Variable:** box, as shown in Figure 12.5b.

7. Select **OK**, or select **Paste** and click the **Run** command.

The SPSS output table, shown in Table 12.13, shows only a significant main effect of bag size ($p = .003$). Hence, participants ate more popcorn when it was served in a large bag, regardless of whether it was stale or fresh. Note that additional steps to compute post hoc tests are required to analyze an interaction, if significant. Because the interaction was not significant in our example ($p > .05$), we will not compute post hoc tests here.

Figure 12.5 Data Entry for Step 4 (a), and the Dialog Box for Step 6 (b)

a

popcorn	bagsize	dv
1	1	20
1	1	21
1	1	23
1	2	24
1	2	26
1	2	23
2	1	23
2	1	22
2	1	21
2	2	29
2	2	25
2	2	26

b

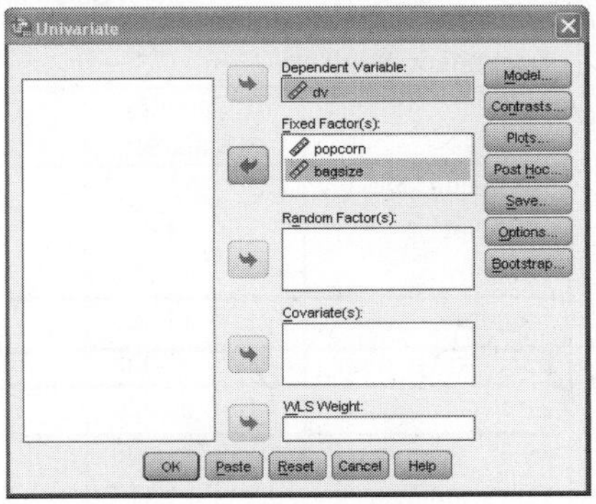

Also given in Table 12.13, the factorial ANOVA is associated with two sets of degrees of freedom (*df*): one for the variance between groups (either for a main effect or for an interaction) and one for the variance attributed to error. The computation of degrees of freedom can change substantially depending on how participants are observed (between subjects vs. within subjects) and the number of factors observed. Using American Psychological Association (APA, 2009) guidelines, we can report the results of any factorial ANOVA by stating the value of the test statistic, both degrees of freedom, and the *p* value for each significant hypothesis test. In our example, only one main effect was significant, so we can report that result as shown:

> A between-subjects factorial ANOVA showed a significant main effect of bag size, $F(1, 8) = 17.633$, $p = .003$, with participants consuming more food in a large bag compared with a small bag, regardless of whether the food was stale or fresh.

Factorial Designs With at Least One Within-Subjects Factor

The following are procedures for using SPSS when both factors (type of popcorn and bag size) are within-subjects factors, meaning that the same participants are observed in each group or in each cell in the summary table. The procedures described here show how to handle within-subjects factors using SPSS in a factorial design.

Table 12.13 SPSS Output Table With the Rows for the Main Effect of Bag Size and Error Circled

Degrees of freedom for the main effect of bag size (1) and error (8).

The likelihood that something other than the manipulation of bag size is causing differences between the levels of this factor is low ($p = .003$).

Tests of Between Subjects Effects

Dependent Variable: dv

Source	Type III Sum of Squares	df	Mean Square	F	Sig.
Corrected Model	52.917[a]	3	17.639	7.056	.012
Intercept	6674.083	1	6674.083	2669.633	.000
popcorn	6.750	1	6.750	2.700	.139
bagsize	44.083	1	44.083	17.633	.003
popcorn * bagsize	2.083	1	2.083	.833	.388
Error	20.000	8	2.500		
Total	6747.000	12			
Corrected Total	72.917	11			

a. R Squared = .726 (Adjusted R Squared = .623)

The numerator (44.083) and denominator (2.500) of the test statistic for the main effect of bag size.

The value of the test statistic for the main effect of bag size (17.633).

1. Click on the **Variable View** tab and enter *stalesmall* in the **Name column**; enter *stalelarge* in the Name column below it; enter *freshsmall* in the Name column below that; and enter *freshlarge* in the Name column below that. In the **Decimals column**, reduce the value to 0 for each row.

2. Click on the **Data View** tab. In each column, enter the data for each appropriate cell, as shown in Figure 12.6a.

3. Go to the menu bar and click **Analyze**, then **General Linear Model**, and **Repeated Measures** to display a dialog box. Enter *popcorn* in the **Within-Subjects Factor Name** box, and *2* in the **Number of Levels** box below it. Click **Add**. Enter *bagsize* in the **Within-Subjects Factor Name** box, and *2* in the **Number of Levels** box below it. Click **Add**. Figure 12.6b shows how this dialog box appears if entered correctly.

4. Click **Define** to display a new dialog box. As shown in Figure 12.6c, move the levels for *popcorn* and *bagsize* into the **Within-Subjects Variables** box because both factors are within-subjects factors in this example.

5. Select **OK**, or select **Paste** and click the **Run** command.

Figure 12.6 Data Entry for Step 2 (a), the Dialog Box Used to Define Within-Subjects Factors in Step 3 (b), the Dialog Box for Step 4 (c)

a

stalesmall	stalelarge	freshsmall	freshlarge
20	24	23	29
21	26	22	25
23	23	21	26

b

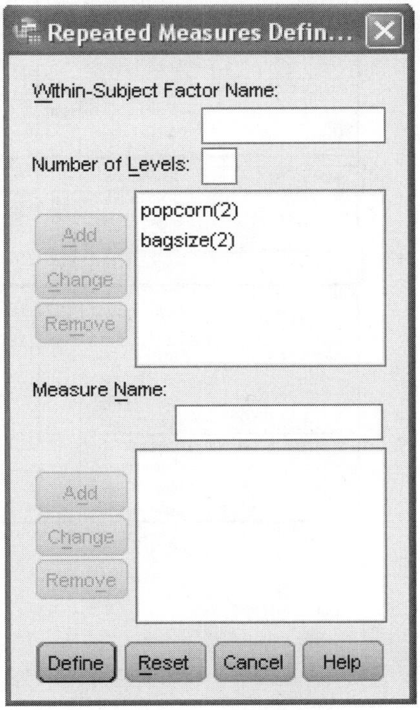

c

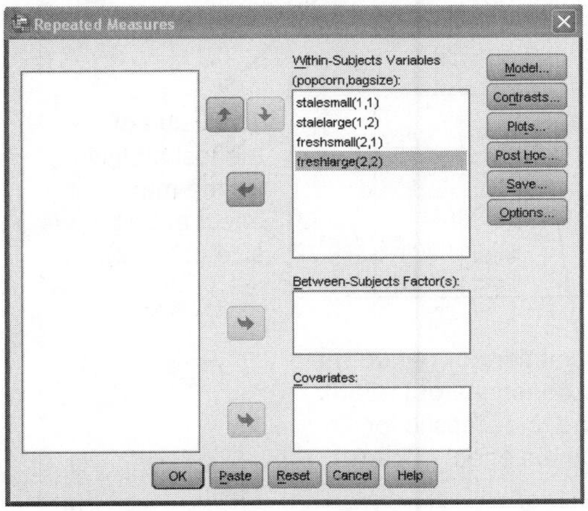

The SPSS output table, shown in Table 12.14, shows only a significant main effect of bag size ($p = .034$). Again, participants ate more popcorn when it was served in a large bag, regardless of whether it was stale or fresh. Note that additional steps to compute post hoc tests are required to analyze an interaction, if significant. Because the interaction was not significant in our example ($p > .05$), we will not compute post hoc tests here.

Using APA (2009) guidelines, we again report the results of any factorial ANOVA by stating the value of the test statistic, both degrees of freedom, and the p value for each significant hypothesis test. In our example, only one main effect was again significant, so we can report that result as shown:

> A within-subjects factorial ANOVA showed a significant main effect of bag size, $F(1, 2) = 27.842$, $p = .034$, with participants consuming more food in a large bag compared with a small bag, regardless of whether the food was stale or fresh.

Table 12.14 SPSS Output Table With the Rows for the Main Effect of Bag Size and Error Circled

Degrees of freedom for the main effect of bag size (1) and error (2).

The likelihood that something other than the manipulation of bag size is causing differences between the levels of this factor is low ($p = .034$).

Tests of Within-Subjects Effects

Measure: MEASURE_1

Source		Type III Sum of Squares	df	Mean Square	F	Sig.
popcorn	Sphericity Assumed	6.750	1	6.750	1.421	.355
	Greenhouse-Geisser	6.750	1.000	6.750	1.421	.355
	Huynh-Feldt	6.750	1.000	6.750	1.421	.355
	Lower-bound	6.750	1.000	6.750	1.421	.355
Error(popcorn)	Sphericity Assumed	9.500	2	4.750		
	Greenhouse-Geisser	9.500	2.000	4.750		
	Huynh-Feldt	9.500	2.000	4.750		
	Lower-bound	9.500	2.000	4.750		
bagsize	Sphericity Assumed	44.083	1	44.083	27.842	.034
	Greenhouse-Geisser	44.083	1.000	44.083	27.842	.034
	Huynh-Feldt	44.083	1.000	44.083	27.842	.034
	Lower-bound	44.083	1.000	44.083	27.842	.034
Error(bagsize)	Sphericity Assumed	3.167	2	1.583		
	Greenhouse-Geisser	3.167	2.000	1.583		
	Huynh-Feldt	3.167	2.000	1.583		
	Lower-bound	3.167	2.000	1.583		
popcorn * bagsize	Sphericity Assumed	2.083	1	2.083	.676	.497
	Greenhouse-Geisser	2.083	1.000	2.083	.676	.497
	Huynh-Feldt	2.083	1.000	2.083	.676	.497
	Lower-bound	2.083	1.000	2.083	.676	.497
Error(popcorn*bagsize)	Sphericity Assumed	6.167	2	3.083		
	Greenhouse-Geisser	6.167	2.000	3.083		
	Huynh-Feldt	6.167	2.000	3.083		
	Lower-bound	6.167	2.000	3.083		

The value of the test statistic for the main effect of bag size (27.842).

The numerator (44.083) and denominator (1.583) of the test statistic for the main effect of bag size.

LO 1 Delineate the factorial design from the factorial experimental design.

- A **factorial design** is a research design in which participants are observed in groups created by combining the levels of two or more factors.
- A **factorial experimental design** is a research design in which groups are created by manipulating the levels of two or more factors, then the same or different participants are observed in each group using experimental procedures of randomization (for a between-subjects factor) and using control for timing and order effects (for a within-subjects factor).

LO 2 Identify the appropriate sampling method for a factorial design used in an experiment.

- The appropriate sampling method for a factorial design used in an experiment is to select one sample from the same population, then randomly assign the same or different participants to groups created by combining the levels of two or more factors. This type of sampling is used in experiments because we can include randomization, manipulation, and a comparison or control group.

LO 3 Identify and describe three types of factorial designs.

- **Between-subjects design** (a design in which all factors are between-subjects factors). Using this design, we manipulate the levels of both factors, cross the levels of each factor to create groups, and randomly assign different participants to each group.
- **Within-subjects design** (a design in which all factors are within-subjects factors). Using this design, we manipulate the levels of both factors, cross the levels of each factor to create groups, and control for order effects due to observing the same participants in each group.
- **Mixed factorial design** (a design with at least one between-subjects factor and one within-subjects factor). Using this design, we manipulate the levels of both factors, cross the levels of each factor to create groups, randomly assign different participants to each level of the between-subjects factor, and control for order effects due to observing the same participants at each level of the within-subjects factor.
- We identify any type of factorial design by the number of levels of each factor. We find the number of groups in a factorial design by multiplying the levels of each factor. For example, a 3×4 factorial design has two factors, one with three levels and one with four levels, and with $3 \times 4 = 12$ groups. How participants are assigned to each group depends on whether we manipulate the levels of a within-subjects factor or the levels of a between-subjects factor.

LO 4 Distinguish between a main effect and an interaction.

- A **main effect** is a source of variation associated with mean differences across the levels of a single factor. In a two-way factorial design, there are two possible main effects (one for each factor).

- An **interaction** is a source of variation associated with the variance of group means across the combination of levels of two factors. In a table summary, an interaction is a measure of how cell means at each level of one factor change across the levels of a second factor.
- The test statistic used to analyze the main effects and interactions in a **two-way factorial design** is the **two-way ANOVA**. The two-way ANOVA is used for factorial designs that measure data on an interval or a ratio scale.

LO 5 Identify main effects and interactions in a summary table and in a graph.

- The group means in a table summary can be graphed to identify a main effect, an interaction, or both. A main effect is evident when changes in a dependent variable vary across the levels of a single factor. An interaction is evident when changes in a dependent variable across the levels of one factor depend on which level of the second factor you analyze. Note that even if a graph shows a possible main effect or interaction, only the test statistic can determine if a main effect or an interaction is significant.

LO 6 Identify the implications of using a quasi-independent factor in a factorial design.

- The factorial design can be used when we include quasi-independent factors. When all factors in a factorial design are quasi-experimental, the design is not an experiment because no factor is manipulated; the design is a quasi-experiment. When at least one factor in a factorial design is manipulated (i.e., an independent variable), then the design is typically called an experiment; however, any effects involving the quasi-independent variable cannot demonstrate cause—only effects of the experimentally manipulated variable can demonstrate cause.

LO 7 Explain how a factorial design can be used to build on previous research, control for threats to validity, and enhance the informativeness of interpretation.

- An overarching reason for conducting a factorial design is that so many effects in nature are "conditional" or "depend on" other factors (i.e., they are interactive). A factorial design is also used for the following three important reasons:
  o To replicate a previous finding and also to demonstrate a novel or new finding in the same design. Although it is important to determine whether a previous finding can be replicated, this alone is redundant, so it is important to also build on previous research findings.
  o To control for possible threats to validity. One way to control for possible threats to validity is to add these possible threats as factors in a factorial design.
  o To enhance the informativeness of interpretation. The factorial design is more informative because it allows us to analyze the effects of two or more factors simultaneously, which leads to the analysis of an effect that is unique to the factorial design: the interaction. In this way, an analysis using a factorial design is more informative than research designs that analyze the effects of only one factor at a time.

LO 8 Describe the higher-order factorial design.

- A **higher-order factorial design** is a research design in which the levels of more than two factors are combined or crossed to create groups. The higher-order factorial design allows researchers to analyze **higher-order interactions** for the combination of levels of three or more factors. Because a higher-order interaction is difficult to interpret, researchers will often try to limit the number of factors in a factorial design to two or three, if possible.

LO 9 Compute a factorial analysis of variance for the between-subjects, within-subjects, and mixed factorial design using SPSS.

- SPSS can be used to analyze factorial designs that include only between-subjects factors by using the **Analyze, General Linear Model**, and **Univariate** options in the menu bar. These actions will display a dialog box that allows you to identify the variables, choose an appropriate post hoc test for the main effects, and run the analysis (for more details, see Section 12.10).
- SPSS can be used to analyze factorial designs that include at least one within-subjects factor by using the **Analyze, General Linear Model**, and **Repeated Measures** options in the menu bar. These actions will display a dialog box that allows you to identify the variables, choose an appropriate post hoc test for the main effects, and run the analysis (for more details, see Section 12.10).

KEY TERMS

factorial design	design	main effect
factorial experimental design	within-subjects factorial design	interaction
complete factorial design	mixed factorial design	participant variable
completely crossed design	two-way ANOVA	higher-order factorial design
between-subjects factorial	two-way factorial design	higher-order interaction

REVIEW QUESTIONS

1. How are groups created using the factorial design?

2. A researcher conducts a 3 × 6 complete factorial design. (A) How many factors are in this design? (B) How many groups are in this design?

3. Describe the sampling method used to select participants for a factorial design in an experiment.

4. What type of factorial design is described in each of the following situations?

   A. The same participants are observed in each group.

   B. The same participants are observed at each level of one factor and repeatedly observed across the levels of a second factor.

   C. Different participants are observed in each group.

5. Using the following table summarizing the cell, column, and row means for a 2 × 2 factorial design, answer the following questions:

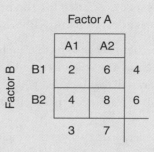

   A. Which means (row, column, or cell means) indicate a main effect for Factor A?

   B. Which means (row, column, or cell means) indicate a main effect for Factor B?

   C Which means (row, column, or cell means) indicate an A × B interaction?

6. A researcher measures performance on a recognition test in a sample of preschool children shown pictures of food items that differ based on familiarity (familiar, unfamiliar) and labeling (labeled, not labeled). Identify the main effect or interaction depicted in the following graphical summary of the study.

7. A researcher conducts a 3 × 2 factorial design with 15 participants observed in each group. How many participants are needed to conduct this experiment if the researcher conducts each of the following designs?

   A. Between-subjects factorial design

   B. Within-subjects factorial design

   C. A mixed factorial design in which the first factor is a within-subjects factor

   D. A mixed factorial design in which the second factor is a within-subjects factor

8. A social scientist has male and female participants read a vignette describing a person performing an immoral act for reasons of either preservation, protection, or self-gain. Participants rated the morality of the person described in the vignette. Identify the quasi-independent variable in this design.

9. A researcher has participants who are experienced or inexperienced with using computers complete a computer task that is either easy or difficult. He records stress levels among participants and finds a significant main effect of experience. He concludes that having experience with using computers causes participants to have lower stress levels compared with those who are inexperienced. Explain why this conclusion is inappropriate.

10. State three reasons for including two or more factors in an experiment.

11. How many factors are crossed in (A) a two-way factorial design and (B) a four-way factorial design?

12. Describe the following terms:

   A. Higher-order factorial design

   B. Higher-order interaction

ACTIVITIES

1. Conduct a literature review by searching an online database (e.g., PsycINFO) and typing in keywords to search for factorial designs. From your search, choose any two factorial designs that interest you the most. For the purposes of this activity, you should choose designs with only two or three factors so that you can more readily understand the design. Complete the following assignment:

   A. Identify each factor and the number of levels of each factor. Also state whether each factor is an independent variable or a quasi-independent variable.

   B. Identify if the design is a between-subjects, within-subjects, or mixed factorial design. If you choose a mixed factorial design, then also identify the between-subjects factor(s) and within-subjects factor(s).

   C. State the main effects and interactions found in each study you chose. Use the variable names to identify each effect. For example, state "a main effect of imagery" and not "a main effect of one factor."

2. A researcher conducts a one-factor experiment and shows that children are more afraid in dark rooms compared with well-lit rooms. Suppose you hypothesize that children will be less afraid of the dark room if a grown-up "checks" the room with them to show them it is safe. Complete the following assignment:

   A. Construct a summary table that adds this second factor, *checking*, to test your hypothesis.

   B. Enter hypothetical data in the table consistent with what your hypothesis predicts should occur. Identify whether you expect to observe a main effect or an interaction. Construct a graph from the table that displays the effect that is predicted by your hypothesis.

ANALYZING, INTERPRETING, AND COMMUNICATING RESEARCH DATA

Identify a problem

- Determine an area of interest.
- Review the literature.
- Identify new ideas in your area of interest.
- Develop a research hypothesis.

Develop a research plan

- Define the variables being tested.
- Identify participants or subjects and determine how to sample them.
- Select a research strategy and design.
- Evaluate ethics and obtain institutional approval to conduct research.

Generate more new ideas

- Results support your hypothesis—refine or expand on your ideas.
- Results do not support your hypothesis—reformulate a new idea or start over.

After reading this chapter, you should be able to:

1. State two reasons why it is important to summarize data.

2. Define descriptive statistics and explain how they are used to describe data.

3. Identify and construct tables and graphs for frequency distributions.

4. Identify and appropriately use the mean, median, and mode to describe data.

5. Identify and appropriately use the variance and standard deviation to describe data.

6. Define and apply the empirical rule.

7. Identify and construct graphs used to display group means and correlations.

8. Use Cronbach's alpha and Cohen's kappa to estimate reliability.

9. Compute the mean, median, mode, variance, and standard deviation using SPSS.

10. Compute two measures of reliability using SPSS: Cronbach's alpha and Cohen's kappa.

Conduct the study

- Execute the research plan and measure or record the data.

Communicate the results

- Method of communication: oral, written, or in a poster.
- Style of communication: APA guidelines are provided to help prepare style and format.

Analyze and evaluate the data

- Analyze and evaluate the data as they relate to the research hypothesis.
- Summarize data and research results.

ANALYSIS AND INTERPRETATION: EXPOSITION OF DATA

"Crunching the numbers" is a common phrase typically used to describe the large-scale processing or analysis of numeric data. The phrase is often used to imply that by "crunching the numbers," the numbers themselves will make more sense or be values that we can use. For example, sports analysts "crunch the numbers" to create rankings of teams or players based on the large-scale analysis of statistics so that we can more easily see or appreciate how the teams or players rank against each other. While the analysis itself may be complex, the output or result is a simple-to-understand ranking that lists the teams or players in order of how good they are.

In the same way a sports analyst crunches the numbers to make sense of sports data, a scientist crunches the numbers to make sense of data collected during a research study. Typically researchers make sense of their data by relating them to their hypothesis. For example, suppose we test the hypothesis that knowledge of organic foods can predict ecofriendly behaviors—meaning behaviors that are good for the environment such as recycling or buying fuel-efficient cars. To test this hypothesis, we can measure the number of organic foods that participants correctly recognize and use statistical analysis to see how this knowledge relates to the participants' ecofriendly behaviors. The analysis itself may be complex, but we can relate the results to our hypothesis by "crunching the numbers." Hence, if the analysis shows support for our hypothesis, then we can state clearly that the pattern of data shows that as knowledge of organic foods increases, so do the ecofriendly behaviors of participants. Hence, the hypothesis is supported.

In this chapter, we will introduce many ways in which researchers summarize data sets using descriptive statistics, which are procedures used to summarize, organize, and make sense of a set of scores, typically presented graphically, in tabular form (in tables), or as summary statistics (single values). Using descriptive statistics, we can "crunch the numbers" to more clearly relate our data to the hypotheses we test.

13.1 Descriptive Statistics: Why Summarize Data?

Anytime you conduct a study, it is important to report the data. To report the data, you typically do not disclose each individual score or measure. Instead, you summarize the data because this is a clearer way to present them. A clear presentation of the data is necessary because it allows the reader to critically evaluate the data you are reporting.

To illustrate the usefulness of summarizing data, Table 13.1a shows the number of apple slices consumed by each of 48 participants when a bowl of apple slices was placed near or far from where each participant was seated—the data given are actual data from a study published by Privitera and Creary (2013). The listing in Table 13.1a is not particularly helpful because you cannot see at a glance how the number of apple slices consumed compares between groups. A more meaningful arrangement of the data is to place them in a summary table that shows the total number of apple slices consumed per group. When the data are arranged in this way, as shown in Table 13.1b, you can see at a glance that many more apple

Table 13.1 Arranging Data in a Frequency Distribution

(a)

Bowl of Apple Slices			
Placed Near Participant		Placed Far From Participant	
10	2	0	4
5	2	1	0
3	10	0	2
5	0	4	0
6	2	0	0
0	2	1	0
5	5	2	0
5	3	1	0
4	1	2	3
9	2	0	2
10	0	3	0
10	5	0	0

(b)

Groups	Total Number of Apple Slices Consumed
Near	106
Far	25

A list of the number of apple slices consumed by 24 participants in each of two groups (a) and a summary table for the total number of apple slices consumed in each group (b).

slices were consumed when the bowl was placed near the participant than when the bowl was placed far from the participant. In all, there are two common reasons why we summarize data using descriptive statistics:

- To clarify what patterns were observed in a data set at a glance. It is more meaningful to present data in a way that makes the interpretation of the data clearer.

- To be concise. When publishing an article, many journals have limited space, which requires that the exposition of data be concise. The presentation in Table 13.1b takes up much less space to summarize the same data given in Table 13.1a and is therefore more concise.

Before we summarize data in a figure or table, we often need to explore or review the data to identify possible omissions, errors, or other anomalies (Abelson, 1995; Hoaglin, Mosteller, & Tukey, 1991; Privitera, 2015; Tukey, 1977). We can apply this step as we measure the data for each participant or after all data have been recorded. However, this step, if used, must be applied before the data are analyzed statistically or displayed in a figure or table. Figure 13.1 illustrates where this step can be applied in the research process based on the steps of the scientific method first given in Figure 1.1 in Chapter 1.

As an example for applying an exploratory analysis, consider that for the study summarized in Table 13.1, each participant was given a bowl that contained 10 apple slices. Therefore, if we found that a value larger than 10 was recorded for a participant, then that

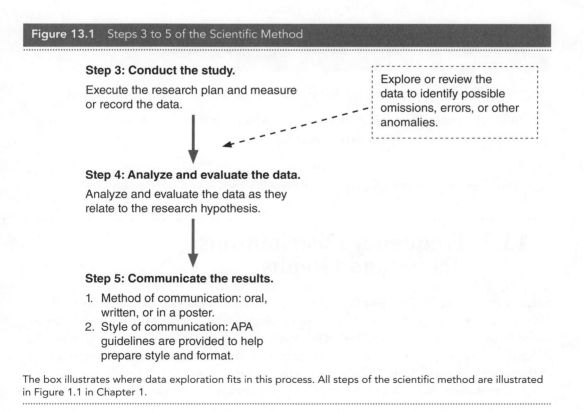

Figure 13.1 Steps 3 to 5 of the Scientific Method

Step 3: Conduct the study.

Execute the research plan and measure or record the data.

Explore or review the data to identify possible omissions, errors, or other anomalies.

Step 4: Analyze and evaluate the data.

Analyze and evaluate the data as they relate to the research hypothesis.

Step 5: Communicate the results.

1. Method of communication: oral, written, or in a poster.
2. Style of communication: APA guidelines are provided to help prepare style and format.

The box illustrates where data exploration fits in this process. All steps of the scientific method are illustrated in Figure 1.1 in Chapter 1.

entry must have been an error and thus would have been removed before further analysis. Likewise, we could review the data for missing values, and we could check that values for one group were not mistakenly recorded for another group. The advantage of exploring or reviewing data before reporting them is to make sure that all errors have been removed from the data before further analysis is conducted.

Using the steps illustrated in Figure 13.1, Step 4 of the scientific method is introduced in this chapter and Chapter 14; Step 5 is introduced in Chapter 15. In all, there are two common ways in which we can analyze a data set: We can describe it, and we can make decisions about how to interpret it. In this chapter, we will introduce how to describe data; in Chapter 14, we will introduce how to make decisions about data.

> **Descriptive statistics** are procedures used to summarize, organize, and make sense of a set of scores or observations, typically presented graphically, in tabular form (in tables), or as summary statistics (single values).

> Descriptive statistics summarize data to make sense or meaning of the measurements we make.

To describe data, we use **descriptive statistics**, which are procedures used to summarize, organize, and make sense of a set of scores, typically presented graphically, in tabular form (in tables), or as summary statistics (single values). Summary statistics include the mean, median, mode, variance, and frequencies. How to calculate and graph these values is described in this chapter. Also, keep in mind that descriptive statistics are used to describe numeric data. Therefore, we can use descriptive statistics only with quantitative, but not qualitative, research designs. In this chapter, we begin with how to display and summarize frequencies or counts.

LEARNING CHECK 1 ✓

1. What are two common reasons that we summarize data using descriptive statistics?

2. Descriptive statistics make sense of data by presenting them in a table. What are two other ways to present descriptive statistics?

Answers: 1. To clarify what patterns were observed in a data set at a glance, and to be concise; 2. Graphically or as summary statistics.

....

13.2 Frequency Distributions: Tables and Graphs

Suppose you scored 90% on your first statistics exam. How could you determine how well you did compared with the rest of the class? One meaningful arrangement to answer this question would be to place the data in a table that lists the ranges of exam scores in one column and the frequency of exam scores for each grade range in a second column. When scores are arranged in this way, as shown in Table 13.2b, it is clear that an exam score of 90% is excellent—only three other students fared as well or better, and most students in the class had lower scores.

Table 13.2 Arranging Data in a Frequency Distribution

(a)

Exam Scores	
90%	80%
59%	72%
64%	84%
77%	87%
88%	60%
78%	66%
94%	78%
96%	73%
65%	81%
79%	55%

(b)

Exam Scores (%)	Frequency
90–99	3
80–89	5
70–79	6
60–69	4
50–59	2

A list of 20 exam scores (a) and a summary of the frequency of scores from that list (b).

A **frequency** is the number of times or how often a category, score, or range of scores occurs. In this section, we will describe the types of tables and graphs used to summarize frequencies. Tables and graphs of frequency data can make the presentation and interpretation of data clearer. In all, this section will help you appropriately construct and accurately interpret many of the tables and graphs used to summarize frequency data in behavioral research.

> A **frequency** is a value that describes the number of times or how often a category, score, or range of scores occurs.

Frequency Distribution Tables

One way to describe frequency data is to count how often a particular score or range of scores occurs using a **frequency distribution table**. In a frequency distribution table, we list each score or range of scores in one column and list the corresponding frequencies for each score or range of scores in a second column. Table 13.3 shows three ways to summarize data in this way.

We can summarize the frequency, stated as $f(x)$, of a continuous variable, a discrete variable,

> A **frequency distribution table** is a tabular summary display for a distribution of data organized or summarized in terms of how often a category, score, or range of scores occurs.
>
> A frequency distribution table can be used to summarize (1) the frequency of each individual score or category in a distribution or (2) the frequency of scores falling within defined ranges or intervals in a distribution.

or a categorical variable, and we can summarize the frequency of data that are grouped into intervals or listed as individual scores. To illustrate, Table 13.3a lists continuous data in intervals by summarizing the time in seconds to complete a task (the continuous variable) among a sample of college students. Table 13.3b lists the frequency of discrete data as individual scores by summarizing quiz scores (the discrete variable) for students in a college class. Table 13.3c lists the frequency of categorical data by summarizing the number of students in each class year (the categorical variable) at a small school. In each display, the sum of all frequencies (in the right column) equals the total number of observations or counts made.

The type of data measured determines whether to group data into intervals or leave data as individual scores or categories. We group data when many different scores are recorded, as shown in Table 13.3a for the time (in seconds) it took participants to complete a task. When data are grouped, it is recommended that the number of intervals ranges between 5 and 20. Fewer than 5 intervals can provide too little summary; more than 20 intervals can be too confusing.

We leave data as individual scores when only a few possible scores are recorded, as shown in Table 13.3b for quiz scores ranging in whole units from 0 to 4. For data that are categorical, we also identify each individual category, as shown in Table 13.3c for college year.

Frequency Distribution Graphs

The same information conveyed in a frequency distribution table can also be presented graphically. To present frequency data graphically, we list the categories, scores, or intervals of scores on the *x*-axis (the horizontal axis) and the frequency in each category, for each score, or in each interval on the *y*-axis (the vertical axis) of a graph. The type of graph we use to describe frequency data depends on whether the data are continuous or discrete.

Continuous data are often summarized graphically using a histogram. The **histogram** is a graph that lists continuous data that are grouped into intervals along the horizontal scale (*x*-axis) and lists the frequency of scores in each interval on the vertical scale (*y*-axis). To illustrate, Figure 13.2 displays a frequency distribution table and a corresponding histogram for the number of traffic stops made over a period of time along a dangerous stretch of roadway. Notice that each bar in the histogram represents the frequency of traffic stops made in each interval.

Discrete data are often summarized using a bar chart or a pie chart. A **bar chart**, or **bar graph**, is like a histogram, except that the bars do not touch. The separation between bars reflects the separation or "break" between the whole numbers or categories being summarized. Figure 13.3 displays a bar chart for the number or frequency of students who are majors in psychology, education, or biology at a small school. To summarize these same data as percents, a **pie chart**

Table 13.3 Frequency Distribution Tables for Continuous, Discrete, and Categorical Variables

(a)

Time (in seconds)	f(x)
50–59	4
40–49	9
30–39	12
20–29	13
10–19	7
0–9	5
Total Participants	**50**

(b)

Quiz Scores	f(x)
4	5
3	7
2	8
1	6
0	4
Total Participants	**30**

(c)

College Year	f(x)
Senior	12
Junior	15
Sophomore	28
Freshman	20
Total Participants	**75**

Continuous data grouped into intervals (a), discrete data listed as individual scores (b), and categorical data given as individual categories (c).

can be a more effective display (Hollands & Spence, 1992, 1998). Using a pie chart, we split the data into sectors that represent the relative proportion of counts in each category. The larger a sector, the larger the percent of scores in a given category. To illustrate, Figure 13.3 also displays a pie chart for the percent of students in each of three academic majors. Notice in the pie chart that larger percentages take up a larger portion of the pie.

> A **pie chart** is a graphical display in the shape of a circle that is used to summarize the relative percent of discrete and categorical data into sectors.

13.3 Measures of Central Tendency

Descriptive statistics often used to describe behavior are those that measure **central tendency**. Measures of central tendency are single values that have a "tendency" to be at or near the "center" of a distribution. Although we lose some meaning anytime we reduce a set of data to a

Figure 13.2 Summarizing Data in a Histogram

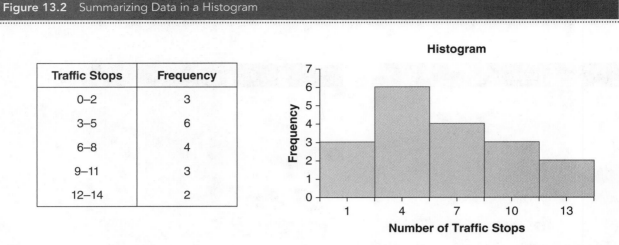

Traffic Stops	Frequency
0–2	3
3–5	6
6–8	4
9–11	3
12–14	2

A grouped frequency distribution table (left) and a histogram (right) for the number of traffic stops along a dangerous stretch of roadway.

Figure 13.3 Summarizing Data in a Bar Chart and a Pie Chart

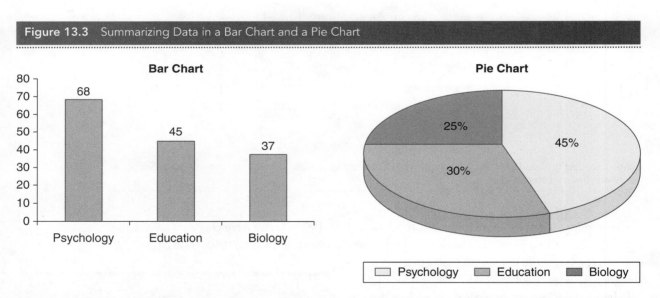

A bar chart (left) giving the frequency of students in each of three academic majors at a small college, and a pie chart (right) giving the percentage of students in each major. The same data are summarized in each graphical display.

single score, statistical measures of central tendency ensure that the single score meaningfully represents a data set. In this section, we will introduce three measures of central tendency:

- The mean
- The median
- The mode

The Mean

One way to describe behavior is to compute the average score in a distribution, called the *mean*. Because researchers in the behavioral sciences rarely select data from an entire population, we will introduce the **sample mean**, represented as *M*. To compute a sample mean, we sum all scores in a distribution (Σx) and divide by the number of scores summed (*n*).

The sample mean is the balance point of a distribution. The balance point is not always at the exact center of a distribution, as this analogy will demonstrate. Pick up a pen with a cap and remove the cap. Then place the pen sideways on your index finger until it is balanced and parallel with the floor. Once you have steadied the pen, your finger represents the balance point of the distribution of the weight of that pen. In the same way, the mean is the balance point of a distribution of data. Now, put the cap back on the pen and balance it again on your index finger. To balance the pen, you must move your finger toward the side with the cap, right? Now your finger is not at the center of the pen but closer to the cap. In the same way, the mean is not necessarily the middle value; it is the value that balances an entire distribution of numbers.

Using the sample mean as an appropriate measure of central tendency depends largely on the type of distribution and the scale of measurement of the data. The sample mean is typically used to describe data that are normally distributed and measures on an interval or ratio scale. Each is described here.

> Measures of **central tendency** are statistical measures for locating a single score that tends to be near the center of a distribution and is most representative or descriptive of all scores in a distribution.

> The **sample mean** is the sum of all scores (Σx) divided by the number of scores summed (*n*) in a sample, or in a subset of scores selected from a larger population.

- The **normal distribution** is a distribution in which half of the scores fall above the mean, median, and mode, and half fall below these measures. Hence, the mean, median, and mode are all located at the center of a normal distribution, as illustrated in Figure 13.4. In cases in which the mean is approximately equal to all other measures of central tendency, the mean is used to summarize the data. We could choose to summarize a normal distribution with the median or mode, but the mean is most often used because all scores are included in its calculation (i.e., its value is most reflective of all of the data).

> A **normal distribution** is a theoretical distribution with data that are symmetrically distributed around the mean, the median, and the mode.

- The mean is used for data that can be described in terms of the *distance* that scores deviate from the mean. After all, the mean balances a distribution of values. For this reason, data that are described by the mean should meaningfully convey differences (or deviations) from the mean. Differences between two scores are meaningfully conveyed for data on an interval or ratio scale only. Hence, the mean is an appropriate measure of central tendency used to describe interval and ratio scale data.

> The mean typically describes interval and ratio scale data that are normally distributed.

Figure 13.4   The Normal Distribution

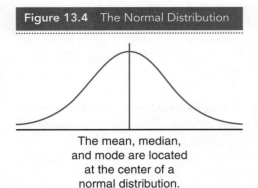

The mean, median, and mode are located at the center of a normal distribution.

The **median** is the middle value in a distribution of data listed in numeric order.

A **skewed distribution** is a distribution of scores that includes outliers or scores that fall substantially above or below most other scores in a data set.

The median typically describes ordinal data and distributions that are skewed.

The Median

Another measure of central tendency is the **median**, which is the middle value or midpoint of a distribution in which half of all scores fall above and half fall below its value. To explain the need for another measure of central tendency, imagine you measure the following set of scores: 2, 3, 4, 5, 6, 6, and 100. The mean of these scores is 18 (add up the seven scores and divide by 7). Yet the score of 100 is an outlier in this data set, which causes the mean value to increase so much that the mean fails to reflect most of the data—its value ($M = 18$) is larger than the values of all scores, except one. For these data, the mean can actually be misleading because its value shifts toward the value of that outlier. In this case, the median will be more reflective of all data because it is the middle score of data listed in numeric order. For these data, the median is 5.

Using the median as an appropriate measure of central tendency also depends largely on the type of distribution and the scale of measurement of the data. The median is typically used to describe data that have a **skewed distribution** and measures on an ordinal scale. Each is described here.

- Some data can have outliers that skew or distort a data set. As an example, U.S. income is typically skewed, with very few people earning substantially higher incomes than most others in the population. Income, then, is skewed. Outliers in a data set will distort the value of a mean, making it a less meaningful measure for describing all data in a distribution. For example, the median (middle) income in the United States is approximately $52,000 (Noss, 2014), whereas the mean (average) income would be much larger than this because the income of billionaires (the outliers) would be included in the calculation. Hence, the median is used to describe skewed data sets because it is most representative of all data for these types of distributions.

- The median is used to describe ranked or ordinal data that convey *direction* only. For example, the fifth person to finish a task took longer than the first person to finish a task; an individual with a bachelor's degree is more educated than an individual with an associate's degree. In both examples, the ordinal data convey direction (greater than or less than) only. For ordinal data, the *distance* (or deviation) of scores from their mean is not meaningful, so the median is used to describe central tendency.

The Mode

Another measure of central tendency is the **mode**, which is the value that occurs most often. The mode is a count; no calculations or formulas are necessary to compute a mode. The mode can be used to describe data in any distribution, so long as one or more scores occur most often. However, the mode is rarely used as the sole way to describe data and is typically reported with other measures of central tendency, such as the mean and median. The mode is typically used to describe data in a modal distribution and measures on a nominal scale. Each is described here.

| A **mode** is the value in a data set that occurs most often or most frequently. |

- So long as a distribution has a value that occurs most often—that is, a mode—the mode can be used as a measure of central tendency. Modal distributions can have a single mode, such as a normal distribution (the mode and the mean are reported together) or a skewed distribution (the mode and the median are reported together). A distribution can also have two or more modes, in which case each mode is reported either with the mean or with the median.

- The mode is used to describe nominal data that identify something or someone, nothing more. Because a nominal scale value is not a *quantity*, it does not make sense to use the mean or median to describe these data. The mode is used instead. For example, the mean or median season of birth for patients with schizophrenia is not very meaningful or sensible. However, describing these nominal data with the mode is meaningful by saying, for example, that most patients with schizophrenia are born in winter months. Anytime you see phrases such as *most often*, *typical*, or *common*, the mode is being used to describe these data.

The mode typically describes nominal data and any distribution with one or more modes.

Table 13.4 summarizes the discussion presented here for when it is appropriate to use each measure of central tendency.

Table 13.4 Appropriately Using Measures of Central Tendency

Measure of Central Tendency	Shape of Distribution	Measurement Scale
Mean	Normal	Interval, ratio
Median	Skewed	Ordinal
Mode	Modal	Nominal

Appropriately use each measure of central tendency to describe data based on the shape of the distribution and the measurement scale of the data.

13.4 Measures of Variability

Measures of central tendency inform us only of scores that tend to be near the center of a distribution, but they do not inform us of all other scores in a distribution, as illustrated in Figure 13.5. The most common procedure for locating all other scores is to identify the

> **Variability** is a measure of the dispersion or spread of scores in a distribution and ranges from 0 to +∞.

> Variability can be 0 or greater than 0; a negative variability is meaningless.

mean (a measure of central tendency) and then compute the **variability** of scores from the mean. By definition, variability can never be negative: Variability ranges from 0 to +∞. If four students receive the same score of 8, 8, 8, and 8 on an assessment, then their scores do not vary because they are all the same value—the variability is 0. However, if the scores were 8, 8, 8, and 9, then they do vary because at least one score differs from the others. Thus, either scores do not vary (variability is 0), or scores do vary (variability is greater than 0). A negative variability is meaningless. In this section, we will introduce three key measures of variability:

- Range

- Variance

- Standard deviation

The Range

One measure of variability is the **range**. The range is the difference between the largest value (*L*) and smallest value (*S*) in a data set. The formula for the range can be stated as follows:

$$\text{Range} = L - S.$$

> **Range** is the difference between the largest (*L*) value and the smallest (*S*) value in a data set.

The range is most informative for data sets without outliers. For example, suppose you measure five scores: 1, 2, 3, 4, and 5. The range of these data is 5 − 1 = 4. In this example, the range gives a fair description of the variability of these data. Now suppose your friend also measures five scores: 2, 4, 6, 8, and 100. The range of these data is 100 − 2 = 98 because the outlier is the largest value in the data set. In this example, a range of 98 is misleading because only one value is greater than 8.

Figure 13.5 What We Do Not Know About a Distribution Even When We Know the Mean

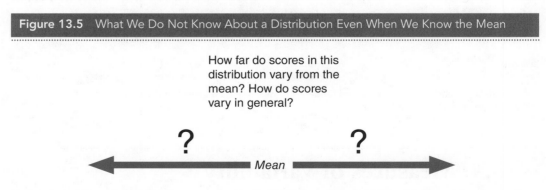

How far do scores in this distribution vary from the mean? How do scores vary in general?

Mean

Notice that while we know the mean score in this distribution, we know nothing of the remaining scores. By computing measures of variability, we can determine how scores vary around the mean and how scores vary in general.

One way to resolve the problem of outliers when computing range is to compute an **interquartile range (IQR)**. An IQR is the range of scores in a distribution between the first quartile (Q_1) and the third quartile (Q_3). Quartiles split data into four equal parts (each containing 25% of the data). Hence, the IQR is the range of scores, minus the top and bottom 25% of scores, in a distribution. The top 25% of scores are above Q_3 (the 75th percentile); the bottom 25% of scores are below Q_1 (the 25th percentile). To compute an IQR, we therefore subtract the first quartile (Q_1) from the third quartile (Q_3):

> The **interquartile range (IQR)** is the range of values between the third (Q_3) and the first (Q_1) quartiles of a data set.

$$IQR = Q_3 - Q_1.$$

Although the range provides a simple measure of variability, the range accounts for only two values (the largest value and smallest value) in a distribution. Whether the data set has five scores or 5 million scores, calculations of the range consider only the largest value and smallest value in that distribution. The range in a data set of $n = 3$ may be very informative, but a typical data set for human participant research can be in the hundreds or even thousands. For this reason, many researchers favor other measures of variability to describe data sets.

The Variance

One measure of variability is the **sample variance**, represented as s^2. The variance is a measure of the average squared distance that scores deviate from the mean. A deviation is a measure of distance. For example, if the mean is 10 and you score 15, then your score is a deviation (or distance) of 5 points above the mean. To compute variance, we square this deviation, which would represent the distance of 15 from 10 as $5^2 = 25$ points. We could subtract all scores from the mean and sum the values in order to find the distance that all scores deviate from the mean. However, using this procedure will always result in a solution equal to 0. For this reason, we square each deviation, and then sum the squared deviations, which gives the smallest solution greater than 0 for determining the distance that scores deviate from the mean. To avoid a 0 solution, then, researchers square each deviation, then sum, which is represented by the **sum of squares (SS)**:

> The **sample variance** is a measure of variability for the average squared distance that scores in a sample deviate from the sample mean.
>
> The **sum of squares (SS)** is the sum of the squared deviations of scores from the mean and is the value placed in the numerator of the sample variance formula.

$$SS = \Sigma \, (x - M)^2$$

To find the average squared distance of scores from the mean, we then divide by the number of scores subtracted from the mean. However, dividing by the number of scores, or sample size, will underestimate the variance of scores in a population. The solution is to divide by one less than the number of scores or deviations summed. Doing so ensures that the sample variance will equal the variance in the population on average. When we subtract one from the sample size, the resulting value is called the **degrees of freedom (*df*) for sample variance**, which can be represented as follows:

$$df = n - 1$$

Hence, the formula for sample variance is the following:

$$s^2 = \frac{SS}{df}$$

An advantage of the sample variance is that its interpretation is clear: The larger the sample variance, the farther that scores deviate from the mean on average. However, one limitation of the sample variance is that the average distance of scores from the mean is squared. To find the distance (and not the squared distance) of scores from the mean, we need a new measure of variability called the standard deviation.

The Standard Deviation

To find the average distance that scores deviate from the mean, called the standard deviation, we take the square root of the variance. Mathematically, square rooting is a correction for having squared each deviation to compute the variance. The formula for the **sample standard deviation (SD)** can be represented as follows:

$$SD = \sqrt{s^2} = \sqrt{\frac{SS}{df}}$$

The advantage of using standard deviation is that it provides detailed information about a distribution of scores, particularly for scores in a normal distribution. Using the *Chebyshev theorem*, which is a theorem devised by the Russian mathematician Pafnuty Chebyshev, we can determine that at least 99% of all scores will fall within 10 standard deviations of the mean for any type of distribution with any shape.

The standard deviation is most informative, however, for the normal distribution. For a normal distribution, over 99% of all scores will fall within three standard deviations of the mean. We can use the **empirical rule** to identify the percent of scores that fall within one, two, and three standard deviations of the mean. The name, *empirical rule*, comes from the word *empiricism*, meaning "to observe," because many of the behaviors that researchers observe are approximately normally distributed. The empirical rule, then, is an approximation—the percentages at each standard deviation are correct, give or take a few fractions of a standard deviation. Nevertheless, this rule is critical because of how specific it is for describing behavior. The empirical rule identifies the following:

- At least 68% of all scores fall within one standard deviation of the mean.

- At least 95% of all scores fall within two standard deviations of the mean.

- At least 99.7% of all scores fall within three standard deviations of the mean.

To illustrate how useful the empirical rule is, consider how we can apply it to a sample data set and can come to some immediate conclusions about the distribution of scores. Suppose we measure creativity scores in a sample with a mean of 20 ($M = 20$) and a standard deviation of 4 ($SD = 4$). If the data were normally distributed, then the data would be distributed as shown in Figure 13.6, with at least 68% of scores falling between 16 and 24, at least 95% of scores falling between 12 and 28, and at least 99.7% of scores falling between 8 and 32. Hence, without knowing the scores for each individual in the sample, we still know a lot about this sample. When the data are normally distributed, we can use the sample mean and standard deviation to identify the distribution of almost all scores in a sample, which makes both measures (M and SD) very informative when used together.

> In a normal distribution, most scores fall within one standard deviation of the mean, and almost all scores fall within three standard deviations of the mean.

Figure 13.6 The Empirical Rule

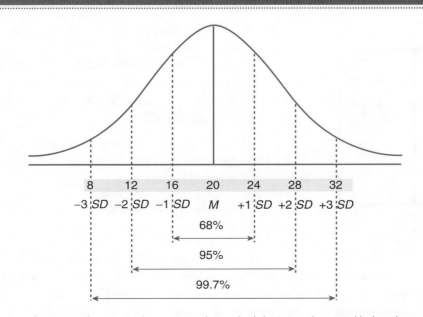

The proportion of scores under a normal curve at each standard deviation above and below the mean. The data are distributed as 20 ± 4 (M ± SD).

13.5 SPSS in Focus: Central Tendency and Variability

| Table 13.5 | Time (in seconds) That It Took 20 Participants to Write Down 10 Uses for a Paper Clip on a Creativity Test |

32	18	45	32
18	20	27	21
19	40	25	34
38	32	31	37
33	48	18	40

| Table 13.6 | SPSS Output Table for Computing Measures of Central Tendency and Variability |

Statistics

memory

N	Valid	20
	Missing	0
Mean		30.40
Median		32.00
Mode		18[a]
Std. Deviation		9.361
Variance		87.621

a. Multiple modes exist. The smallest value is shown

We can use SPSS to compute measures of central tendency (e.g., mean, median, and mode) and measures of variability (e.g., variance and standard deviation). In this section, we will use SPSS to compute the mean, median, mode, variance, and standard deviation for the following example. Suppose a researcher gives students a creativity test. Students are given a paper clip, and the time (in seconds) it takes them to list 10 uses for the paper clip is recorded. Faster times are presumed to reflect greater creativity. Using the data given in Table 13.5, we will use SPSS to analyze these data.

1. Click on the **Variable View** tab and enter *creativity* in the **Name column**. Go to the **Decimals column** and reduce that value to 0 because we will enter only whole numbers.

2. Click on the **Data View** tab and enter the 20 values in the column labeled *creativity*.

3. Go to the menu bar and click **Analyze, Descriptive Statistics**, and **Frequencies** to bring up a dialog box.

4. In the **dialog box**, select the *creativity* variable and click the arrow in the center. This will move *creativity* into the box labeled **Variable(s)** to the right. Make sure the option to display frequency tables is not selected, and then select **Statistics** to bring up another dialog box.

5. In the dialog box, select **Mean, Median**, and **Mode** to the right; select **Std. deviation** and **Variance** to the left. Select **Continue**.

6. Select **OK**, or select **Paste** and click the **Run** command.

The SPSS output table, shown in Table 13.6, displays the mean, median, mode, variance, and standard deviation for these creativity data. If multiple modes exist, SPSS will list the value for the smallest mode and place a superscript *a* next to that modal value to indicate that more than one mode exists.

1. State whether the mean, median, or mode should be used to describe the data for each of the following examples.

    A. The data are skewed.

    B. The data have two modes.

    C. The data are categorical.

    D. The data are on a ratio scale.

    E. The data are on an ordinal scale.

    F. The mean, median, and mode are equal.

2. Can variability be negative?

3. A researcher measures scores in a sample with a normal distribution of 32 ± 2 ($M \pm SD$). State the cutoffs in this distribution within which each of the following is true:

    A. At least 68% of scores lie within this distribution.

    B. At least 95% of scores lie within this distribution.

    C. At least 99.7% of scores lie within this distribution.

Answers: 1. A. Median, B. Mode, C. Mode, D. Mean, E. Median, F. Mean; 2. No; 3. A. Between 30 and 34, B. Between 28 and 36, C. Between 26 and 38.

13.6 Graphing Means and Correlations

Graphs can be used to display group means for one or more factors, which is particularly useful when differences in a dependent variable are compared between groups. Graphs also summarize correlational data in which we plot data points for two variables. This section introduces graphs for each type of data.

Graphing Group Means

We can graph a mean for one or more groups using a graph with lines or bars to represent the means. By convention, we use a bar graph when the groups on the x-axis (horizontal axis) are represented on a nominal or ordinal scale; we use a line graph when the groups on the x-axis are represented on an interval or ratio scale.

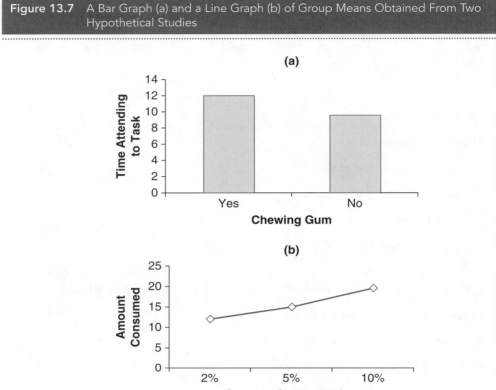

To use a bar graph, we list the groups on the x-axis and use bars to represent the means along the y-axis (vertical axis). As an example of a bar graph to display group means, Figure 13.7a displays the mean time (in seconds) attending to a task among students chewing or not chewing gum. To use a line graph, we similarly list the groups on the x-axis and instead use dots connected by a single line to represent the means along the y-axis. As an example of a line graph to display group means, Figure 13.7b displays the mean amount consumed (in milliliters) of a flavor mixed with a concentration of 2%, 5%, or 10% sucrose.

We can also use bar graphs and line graphs to summarize the means for two or more factors. For example, in Chapter 12, we displayed the means for the levels of two factors (duration and setting) to identify main effects and interactions in Figures 12.2 and 12.3. To construct those graphs, we followed the same rules as described in this section: We listed the groups on the x-axis, and we used lines to represent the means along the y-axis in those figures. These same rules can be applied to graph group means for just about any number of groups or factors.

Graphing Correlations

We can graph a correlation using a **scatter plot** (also defined in Chapter 8), which is a graphical display of discrete data points (x, y). To plot a data point, you first move across the x-axis, and then move up or down the y-axis to mark or plot each pair of (x, y) data points.

A *correlation*, introduced in Chapter 8, is a statistic used to measure the strength and the direction of the linear relationship between two factors. The relationship between two factors can be evident by the pattern of data points plotted in a scatter plot.

> A **scatter plot** is a graphical display of discrete data points (x, y) used to summarize the relationship between two factors.

When the values of two factors change in the same direction, the two factors have a positive correlation. To illustrate, Figure 13.8a shows a scatter plot of a positive correlation between body image satisfaction and exercise. Notice that as the number of minutes of exercise increase, so do ratings of body image satisfaction; as the minutes of exercise decrease, so do ratings of body image satisfaction. In a scatter plot, the pattern of a positive correlation appears as an ascending line.

When the values of two factors change in the opposite direction, then the two factors have a negative correlation. To illustrate, Figure 13.8b shows a scatter plot of a negative correlation between class absences and quiz grades. Notice that as the number of absences increase, quiz grades decrease; as the number of absences decrease, quiz grades increase. In a scatter plot, the pattern of a negative correlation appears as a descending line.

Figure 13.8   A Scatter Plot of a Positive Correlation (a) and a Negative Correlation (b) Obtained From Two Hypothetical Studies

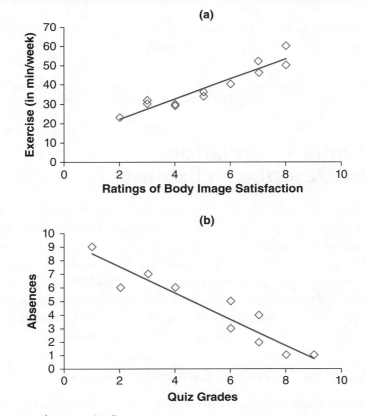

The solid lines represent the regression lines.

1. A researcher records the number of dreams that 50 college freshman students recalled during the night prior to a final exam. What type of graph or graphs would be appropriate to summarize this frequency distribution? Explain.

Number of Dreams	f(x)
4	16
3	14
2	18
1	7
0	5

2. Which type of graphical display for frequency data is used to summarize continuous data?

3. A researcher reports that cell phone use while driving is negatively correlated with attention to driving tasks. What type of graph should the researcher use to summarize the correlation?

4. For what types of data do we use a bar graph to plot group means? For what types of data do we use a line graph to plot group means?

Answers: 1. A bar chart or pie chart because the data are discrete; 2. A histogram; 3. A scatter plot; 4. We use a bar graph when the groups are represented on a nominal or ordinal scale, and we use a line graph when the groups are represented on an interval or ratio scale.

13.7 Using Correlation to Describe Reliability

We can also describe the consistency of data using a correlation to describe the data. In Section 4.5 of Chapter 4, we introduced three types of reliability for the consistency, stability, or repeatability of one or more measures or observations: test-retest reliability, internal consistency, and interrater reliability. We use a correlational measure to identify the extent to which we have established or demonstrated each type of reliability. In this section, we will specifically describe the correlational measure for internal consistency using Cronbach's alpha, and the correlational measure for interrater reliability using Cohen's kappa. This section introduces the formula and analysis of each reliability measure.

Cronbach's Alpha (Internal Consistency)

Internal consistency is a measure of reliability used to determine the extent to which multiple items used to measure the same variable are related. This type of measure is useful to analyze, for example, the reliability of a questionnaire or survey that consists of multiple items used to measure the same construct. If participants rated six items that all measure romantic love, then we should expect the responses

> **Cronbach's alpha** is a measure of internal consistency that estimates the average correlation for every possible way that a measure can be split in half.

for each item to be the same or similar because all items measure the same thing. If we then split the items in half (3 and 3), we should expect each half or set of three responses to be related or similar. This type of analysis is computed using **Cronbach's alpha** (Cronbach, 1951), which is used to estimate the average correlation for every possible way that a measure can be split in half. The formula for Cronbach's alpha is as follows:

$$\text{Cronbach's alpha} = \left(\frac{n}{n-1}\right)\left(\frac{\sigma_x^2 - \Sigma\sigma_Y^2}{\sigma_x^2}\right)$$

In the formula, n is the number of items, σ_x^2 is the variance for the total scores across all items, and $\Sigma\sigma_Y^2$ is the sum of the variances for each item calculated one item at a time. Using this formula, Cronbach's alpha is a measure of split-half reliability in that it analyzes the correlation for every possible way to split the test in half. The result is an average correlation for all possible ways to split a measure in half. Cronbach's alpha is like a proportion of variance in that values range between 0 and 1.0, with higher values indicating a stronger correlation or relationship between items on the test.

Cohen's Kappa (Interrater Reliability)

Interrater reliability (IRR) is the extent to which two or more raters of the same behavior or event are in agreement with what they observed. The most straightforward way to measure IRR is to divide the number of agreements between two raters by the total number of observations that were rated. We could then multiply the fraction by 100 to convert it to a percent. As an example, we could compute the IRR of ratings for the raters described in Table 13.7 as follows:

$$\frac{9 \text{ agreements}}{12 \text{ total observations}} \times 100 = 75\% \text{ agreement}$$

One limitation of computing IRR this way is that the value could be inflated by chance or error if, for example, the two raters accidentally rated different behaviors, but still made similar ratings. A more conservative estimate of IRR that takes the possibility of error into account is

> **Cohen's kappa** is a measure of interrater reliability that estimates the level of agreement between two raters, while taking into account the probability that the two raters agree by chance or error.

Cohen's kappa (Cohen, 1961). The following is the formula for Cohen's kappa, in which P_A is the percent agreement and P_E is the percent expected by error:

$$\text{Cohen's kappa} = \frac{P_A - P_E}{1 - P_E}$$

Table 13.7 The Independent Ratings of Two Raters During 12 Observation Periods

Observation	Rater 1	Rater 2	Agreement?
1	Yes	Yes	√
2	No	No	√
3	Yes	Yes	√
4	No	Yes	—
5	No	No	√
6	No	No	√
7	Yes	No	—
8	Yes	Yes	√
9	Yes	Yes	√
10	Yes	No	—
11	No	No	√
12	Yes	Yes	√

In this example, the two raters agreed on 9 of 12 observation periods. √ indicates agreement.

Cronbach's alpha is a measure for internal consistency reliability; Cohen's kappa is a measure for interrater reliability.

In the formula, P_E is computed by multiplying the probability of saying yes and no for each rater, then summing each probability. For the ratings shown in Table 13.7, for example, Rater 1 said *yes* 7 times in 12 observation periods ($7 \div 12 = 0.583$); Rater 2 said *yes* 6 times in 12 observation periods ($6 \div 12 = 0.500$). The probability, then, that both raters said *yes* is $(0.583) \times (0.5000) = 0.292$ or 29.2%.

Similarly, Rater 1 said *no* 5 times in 12 observation periods ($5 \div 12 = 0.417$); Rater 2 said *no* 6 times in 12 observation periods ($6 \div 12 = 0.500$). The probability, then, that both raters said *no* is $(0.417) \times (0.5000) = 0.209$ or 20.9%. By summing each probability, we obtain the overall probability that two raters agree by chance or error: $P_E = 29.2\% + 20.9\% = 50.1\%$, which makes the following the value of Cohen's kappa:

$$\text{Cohen's kappa} = \frac{75\% - 50.1\%}{1 - 50.1\%} = 50\% \text{ agreement}$$

13.8 SPSS in Focus: Cronbach's Alpha and Cohen's Kappa

Cronbach's alpha and Cohen's kappa can be computed using SPSS. In this section, we will use SPSS to compute both measures of reliability.

Cronbach's Alpha

Cronbach's alpha is used to determine the internal consistency of a set of scores or measures. As an example, Table 13.8 lists actual data for a subset of participants who completed 13 items for a scale used to estimate the daily intake of fat in people's diets, called the estimated daily intake scale for fat (EDIS-F; Privitera & Freeman, 2012). The items for the scale are given in Table 13.9. We will use SPSS to analyze the data given in Table 13.8.

1. Click on the **Variable View** tab and enter $q1$ in the **Name column**. In the cell below, enter $q2$, then $q3$, and so on until you reach $q13$. Hence, 13 rows will be active. Go to the **Decimals column** in each row and reduce the value to 0 because we will enter only whole numbers.

2. Click on the **Data View** tab and enter the 20 values for each item, in the same way that they are entered in Table 13.8.

Table 13.8 Actual Responses for 20 Participants on the 13 Items of the EDIS-F

Participant	Q1	Q2	Q3	Q4	Q5	Q6	Q7	Q8	Q9	Q10	Q11	Q12	Q13
A	5	2	3	4	4	2	2	2	2	2	3	2	3
B	7	6	6	7	3	6	6	6	7	7	6	6	5
C	6	2	2	5	2	1	1	4	4	1	3	4	4
D	5	4	1	5	3	3	4	4	2	3	3	5	4
E	6	2	2	4	2	2	2	5	2	4	1	3	4
F	5	5	4	5	2	2	3	7	6	2	4	4	3
G	6	4	5	6	4	4	4	5	4	6	4	5	4
H	4	4	4	4	3	4	4	5	4	1	4	3	5
I	5	6	5	5	4	4	4	5	3	5	5	6	4
J	5	5	2	5	5	6	3	5	2	5	4	5	5
K	6	6	1	6	6	3	6	1	3	6	6	5	5
L	6	4	1	6	5	5	4	2	2	3	2	4	4
M	4	5	2	3	3	3	6	4	4	3	3	3	2
N	4	5	2	4	4	4	4	6	4	4	4	5	5
O	7	7	1	7	7	7	7	7	7	7	1	7	6
P	3	3	3	4	3	3	3	5	2	1	3	4	2
Q	7	6	2	5	5	1	6	4	2	4	6	7	3
R	7	3	5	5	4	3	6	4	2	1	6	2	2
S	5	6	2	6	5	6	6	6	4	5	5	3	4
T	5	5	2	4	6	4	4	4	2	3	4	6	5

For a study published by Privitera and Freeman (2012).

Table 13.9	The 13 Items for the EDIS-F
Item	**Statement**
1	I tend to enjoy eating high-fat flavorful foods in a meal.
2	I tend to eat foods that are low in fat, even desserts.
3	I tend to snack on cakes, cookies, or brownies when I am hungry.
4	I tend to crave foods that are high in fat.
5	I tend to eat high-fat meals each day.
6	I tend to snack on healthier, low-fat food options.
7	I generally tend to consume a low-fat diet.
8	I tend to avoid desserts that are too fattening.
9	When I crave a snack, I typically seek out high-fat foods.
10	I tend to eat fast foods, especially when I am in a rush.
11	I like consuming high-fat foods that are flavorful.
12	I typically will eat a snack, even when only high-fat foods are available.
13	I generally tend to enjoy consuming a high-fat diet.

Source: Privitera & Freeman, 2012.

3. Go to the menu bar and click **Analyze, Scale,** and **Reliability Analysis** to bring up a dialog box.

4. In the **dialog box,** select all 13 items and click the arrow in the center. This will move all items into the box labeled **Items** to the right. Select **Statistics** to bring up another dialog box.

5. In the dialog box, select **Item, Scale,** and **Scale if item deleted** to the left. Select **Continue**.

6. Select **OK**, or select **Paste** and click the **Run** command.

The SPSS output table, shown in Table 13.10 (top), displays the value of Cronbach's alpha for the 13-item EDIS-F, alpha =.848. We use alpha to determine the items that are most related. For this reason, we also want to see if removing one of the 13 items will increase the value of alpha—meaning that removing the item increases the internal consistency of the scale; that is, removing the item makes the scale more reliable. To check this, we look at the last column in Table 13.10 (bottom) to see if any values for alpha are larger than .848. If so, then removing that corresponding item will increase the value of alpha. In this example, notice that removing *q3* will increase the value of alpha to .865; removing *q8* will increase the value

Reliability Statistics

Cronbach's Alpha	N of Items
.848	13

Value of alpha increases if item is deleted. Choose the item that increases alpha the most.

Item-Total Statistics

	Scale Mean if Item Deleted	Scale Variance if Item Deleted	Corrected Item-Total Correlation	Cronbach's Alpha if Item Deleted
q1	48.00	126.000	.394	.844
q2	48.90	109.568	.812	.817
q3	50.65	132.239	.077	.865
q4	48.40	119.411	.716	.829
q5	49.40	121.411	.449	.841
q6	49.75	112.197	.622	.829
q7	49.15	112.766	.625	.829
q8	48.85	123.818	.318	.850
q9	50.00	115.158	.544	.835
q10	49.75	102.934	.760	.816
q11	49.55	126.682	.243	.854
q12	48.95	116.050	.590	.832
q13	49.45	123.103	.511	.838

For the subset of data in this example, removing q3, q8, and q11 will increase the value of alpha. The next step is to remove the item that increases alpha the most (q3) and rerun the analysis with the remaining items.

of alpha to .850; removing *q11* will increase the value of alpha to .854. The next step is to remove the item that increases alpha the most. In this case, we remove *q3* and then rerun the analysis with the remaining 12 items. We repeat these steps until the removal of any further items does not increase the value of alpha.

Cohen's Kappa

Cohen's kappa is used to determine the extent to which two or more raters of the same behavior or event are in agreement with what they observed. As an example, we will analyze the same data given in Table 13.7, which is rearranged in Table 13.11a, to compute Cohen's kappa using SPSS.

1. Click on the **Variable View** tab and enter *Rater1* in the **Name column**. In the cell below, enter *Rater2*, and in the cell below that enter *Count*. Go to the **Decimals column** in each row and reduce the value to 0 because we will enter only whole numbers.

2. To code rater agreement, click on the small gray box with three dots in the **Values** column for *Rater1*. In the **dialog box**, enter *1* in the value cell and *Yes* in the label cell, and then click **Add**. Then enter *2* in the value cell and *No* in the label cell, and then click **Add**. Enter the same codes for *Rater2: 1 = Yes*, and *2 = No*. Select **OK**.

3. Click on the **Data View** tab. For the *Rater1* column, enter *1, 1, 2, 2* down the column. For the *Rater 2* column, enter *1, 2, 1, 2* down the column. In the *Count* column, enter the corresponding observed frequencies, as shown in Table 13.11b.

4. In the menu bar, click **Data**, then **Weight cases** to display a dialog box. Select **Weight cases by** and move *Count* into the **Frequency Variable:** cell, as shown in Figure 13.9. Select **OK**.

5. Go to the menu bar and click **Analyze**, then **Descriptive Statistics**, then **Crosstabs** to bring up a dialog box.

6. Using the arrows, move *Rater1* into the **Row(s)** box and move *Rater2* into the **Column(s)** box. Click **Statistics** to display another dialog box. In the dialog box, select **Kappa** and click **Continue**.

7. Select **OK**, or select **Paste** and click the **Run** command.

The SPSS output table, shown in Table 13.12, displays the value of Cohen's kappa = .500, which is the same value we computed in Section 13.7 by hand. Also given in Table 13.12 is the significance of the reliability. For two raters to show reliably similar ratings, the last column should show a significance of less than .05, meaning that there is less than a 5% chance that the two raters' agreements occurred by chance. In this example, the significance is. 079, which is greater than 5%. Hence, we conclude that agreement between the two raters is not reliable.

Table 13.11 Rearrangement of Data for Agreement Between Two Raters

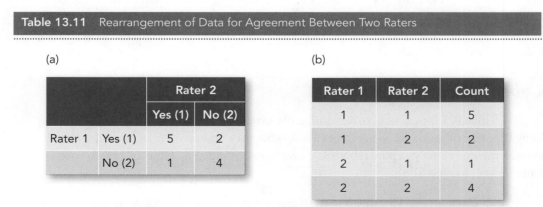

(a)

		Rater 2	
		Yes (1)	No (2)
Rater 1	Yes (1)	5	2
	No (2)	1	4

(b)

Rater 1	Rater 2	Count
1	1	5
1	2	2
2	1	1
2	2	4

Agreement between two raters with data arranged to match up agreements (yes, yes; no, no) and disagreements (yes, no; no, yes) (a), and the corresponding data view arrangement of these same data in SPSS (b).

Figure 13.9 SPSS Dialog Box for Step 4

Weight Cases

Rater1
Rater2

○ Do not weight cases
◉ Weight cases by

Frequency Variable:
Count

Current Status: Do not weight cases

[OK] [Paste] [Reset] [Cancel] [Help]

Table 13.12 SPSS Output Table for Cohen's Kappa

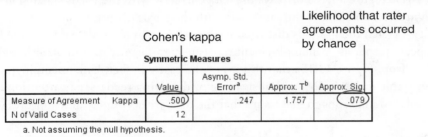

Cohen's kappa

Likelihood that rater agreements occurred by chance

Symmetric Measures

	Value	Asymp. Std. Error[a]	Approx. T[b]	Approx. Sig.
Measure of Agreement Kappa	.500	.247	1.757	.079
N of Valid Cases	12			

a. Not assuming the null hypothesis.

b. Using the asymptotic standard error assuming the null hypothesis.

LEARNING CHECK 4 ✓

1. For each of the following descriptions, name the appropriate statistical measure of reliability.

   A. The extent to which multiple items consistently measure the same thing

   B. The extent to which two raters are in agreement

2. State the statistic used to describe each of the following types of reliability:

   A. Interrater reliability

   B. Internal consistency

Answers: 1. A. Cronbach's alpha, B. Cohen's kappa; 2. A. Cohen's kappa, B. Cronbach's alpha.

13.9 Ethics in Focus: Deception Due to the Distortion of Data

It was Mark Twain who once said *there are lies, damned lies, and statistics.* His statement identified that statistics can be deceiving—and so can interpreting them. Descriptive statistics are used to inform us. Therefore, being able to identify statistics and correctly interpret what they mean is an important part of the research process. Presenting data can be an ethical concern when the data are distorted in any way, whether on accident or intentionally. The distortion of data can occur for data presented graphically or as summary statistics. How the presentation of data can be distorted is described in this section.

When a graph is distorted, it can deceive the reader into thinking differences exist, when in truth differences are negligible (Frankfort-Nachmias & Leon-Guerrero, 2006; Good & Hardin, 2003; Privitera, 2016). Three common distortions to look for in graphs are (1) displays with an unlabeled axis, (2) displays with one axis altered in relation to the other axis, and (3) displays in which the vertical axis (*y*-axis) does not begin with 0. As an example of how a graphical display can be distorted, Figure 13.10 displays a line graph for U.S. unemployment rates in 2011. Figure 13.10a displays the data correctly with the *y*-axis starting at 0%; Figure 13.10b displays the same data with the *y*-axis distorted and beginning at 8.2%. When the graph is distorted in this way, it can make the slope of the line appear steeper as if unemployment rates are significantly declining, although it is clear from Figure 13.10a that this is not the case—in fact, U.S. unemployment rates were rather stable in 2011. To avoid misleading or deceiving readers, pay attention to how data are displayed in graphs to make sure that the data are accurately and appropriately presented.

> Data presentation must not be distorted in order to prevent misleading interpretations of data.

Distortion can also occur when presenting summary statistics. Two common distortions to look for with summary statistics are when data are omitted or differences are described in a way that gives the impression of larger differences than really are meaningful in the data. It can sometimes be difficult to determine if data are misleading or have been omitted, although some data should naturally be reported together. Means and standard deviations should be reported together; correlations and proportions should be reported with sample size; standard error should be reported anytime data are recorded in a sample. When these data are omitted or not reported together, it can lead to erroneous conclusions. For example, if we report that 75% of those surveyed preferred Product A to Product B, you may be inclined to conclude that Product A is a better product. However, if you were also informed that only four people were sampled, then 75% may not seem as convincing. Anytime you read a claim about results in a study, it is important to refer back to the data to confirm the extent to which the data support the claim being made by the author or authors of a study.

Figure 13.10 Two Graphical Displays for the Same Data

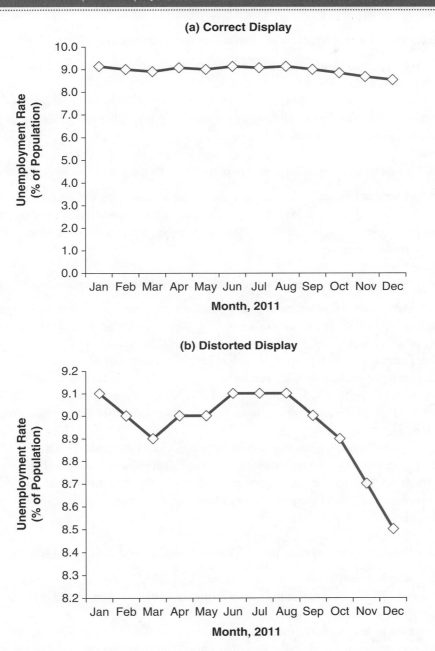

(a) Correct Display

(b) Distorted Display

(a) This graph is a correct display and (b) this is a display that is distorted because the *y*-axis does not begin at 0%. Data are of actual unemployment rates in the United States in 2011 (U.S. Bureau of Labor Statistics, 2013).

CHAPTER SUMMARY

LO 1 State two reasons why it is important to summarize data.

- It is important to summarize data in order (1) to clarify what patterns were observed in a data set at a glance and (2) to be concise.
- It is more meaningful to present data in a way that makes the interpretation of the data clearer. Also, when publishing an article, many journals have limited space, which requires that the exposition of data be concise.

LO 2 Define descriptive statistics and explain how they are used to describe data.

- **Descriptive statistics** are procedures used to summarize, organize, and make sense of a set of scores or observations. Descriptive statistics are presented graphically, in tabular form (in tables), or as summary statistics (e.g., mean, median, mode, variance, and standard deviation).

LO 3 Identify and construct tables and graphs for frequency distributions.

- A **frequency distribution table**, which lists scores or categories in one column and the corresponding frequencies in a second column, can be used to summarize (1) the frequency of each individual score or category in a distribution or (2) the frequency of scores falling within defined ranges or intervals in a distribution.
- A frequency distribution table can be presented graphically by listing the categories, scores, or intervals of scores on the x-axis (the horizontal axis) and the frequency in each category, for each score, or in each interval on the y-axis (the vertical axis) of a graph.
- The type of graph we use to describe frequency data depends on whether the factors being summarized are continuous or discrete. Continuous data are displayed in a **histogram**. Discrete and categorical data are displayed in a **bar chart** or **pie chart**. To summarize data as percents, a **pie chart** can be a more effective display than a bar chart.

LO 4 Identify and appropriately use the mean, median, and mode to describe data.

- The **sample mean** is the sum of all scores (Σx) divided by the number of scores summed (n) in a sample. The mean is used to describe data that are normally distributed and on an interval or ratio scale of measurement.
- The **median** is the middle value in a distribution of data listed in numeric order. The median is used to describe data that are skewed and data on an ordinal scale of measurement.
- The **mode** is the value that occurs most often or at the highest frequency in a distribution. The mode is used to describe distributions with one or more modes and categorical data on a nominal scale of measurement.

LO 5 Identify and appropriately use the range, variance, and standard deviation to describe data.

- The **range** is the difference between the largest value (L) and smallest value (S) in a data set. One way to resolve the problem of outliers when computing range is to compute an **interquartile range (IQR)**, which is the range of scores in a distribution between the first quartile (Q_1) and the third quartile (Q_3).
- The **sample variance** is a measure of variability for the average squared distance that scores in a sample deviate from the sample mean. The sample variance is associated with $n - 1$ **degrees of freedom (*df*)** and is computed by dividing the **sum of squares (SS)** by *df*. The larger the sample variance, the farther that scores deviate from the mean, on average. One limitation of sample variance is that the average distance of scores from the mean is squared. To find the deviation or distance of scores from the mean, we take the square root of the variance, called the **standard deviation**.

LO 6 Define and apply the empirical rule.

- For normal distributions, the **empirical rule** states that 68% of scores fall within one standard deviation, 95% of scores fall within two standard deviations, and 99.7% of scores fall within three standard deviations of the mean.

LO 7 Identify and construct graphs used to display group means and correlations.

- We can graph a mean for one or more groups using a graph with lines or bars to represent the means. By convention, we use a bar graph when the groups on the *x*-axis (horizontal axis) are represented on a nominal or ordinal scale; we use a line graph when the groups on the *x*-axis are represented on an interval or ratio scale.
- We graph correlations using a scatter plot. To plot a data point, you first move across the *x*-axis, and then move up or down the *y*-axis to mark or plot each pair of (x, y) data points. In a scatter plot, the pattern of a positive correlation appears as an ascending line; the pattern of a negative correlation appears as a descending line.

LO 8 Use Cronbach's alpha and Cohen's kappa to estimate reliability.

- **Cronbach's alpha** is a measure of internal consistency that estimates the average correlation for every possible way that a measure can be split in half. The higher the value of Cronbach's alpha, the stronger the correlation or relationship between items on the same measure.
- **Cohen's kappa** is a measure of interrater reliability that measures the level of agreement between two raters, while taking into account the probability that the two raters agree by chance or error. The higher the value of Cohen's kappa, the stronger the interrater reliability.

LO 9 Compute the mean, median, mode, variance, and standard deviation using SPSS.

- SPSS can be used to compute the mean, median, mode, variance, and standard deviation by using the **Analyze, Descriptive Statistics**, and **Frequencies** options in the menu bar. These actions will bring up a dialog box that will allow you to identify the variable and select the **Statistics** option to select each descriptive statistic (for more details, see Section 13.5).

LO 10 Compute two measures of reliability using SPSS: Cronbach's alpha and Cohen's kappa.

- SPSS can be used to compute Cronbach's alpha by using the **Analyze, Scale**, and **Reliability Analysis** options in the menu bar. These actions will display a dialog box that allows you to identify items on the scale, and choose the **Statistics** option to identify the value of Cronbach's alpha for the **Scale** and **Scale if item deleted** (for more details, see Section 13.8).

- SPSS can be used to compute Cohen's kappa by using the **Analyze, Descriptive Statistics**, and **Crosstabs** options in the menu bar. These actions will display a dialog box that allows you to identify the raters and run the analysis. A **Weight cases** option must also be selected from the Menu bar (for more details, see Section 13.8).

KEY TERMS

descriptive statistics

frequency

frequency distribution table

histogram

bar chart

bar graph

pie chart

central tendency

sample mean

normal distribution

median

skewed distribution

mode

variability

range

interquartile range (IQR)

sample variance

sum of squares (SS)

degrees of freedom (df) for sample variance

sample standard deviation (SD)

empirical rule

scatter plot

Cronbach's alpha

Cohen's kappa

REVIEW QUESTIONS

1. Which of the following words *best* describes descriptive statistics?

   A. Generalize

   B. Summarize

   C. Inference

   D. Decision making

2. In a study on romantic relationships, 240 romantically involved men were asked to choose their preference for an ideal night out with their partner. The frequency of men choosing (1) dinner and a movie, (2) a sporting event, (3) gambling/gaming, or (4) going out for drinks was recorded. Should these frequency data be grouped into intervals? Why or why not?

3. Below is an incomplete frequency distribution table for the number of mistakes made during a series of military combat readiness training exercises. Fill in the missing values for A, B, and C in the table.

Number of mistakes	Frequency
6–A	1
B–5	3
0–2	C
	N = 16

4. The following seasons of birth were recorded for a sample of patients with schizophrenia: winter, spring, spring, fall, summer, winter, fall, winter, winter, spring, winter, spring, winter, winter, summer, spring, winter, winter, fall, spring.

   A. Construct a bar chart.

   B. Why is a histogram not appropriate for summarizing these data?

5. The following graphs depict the mean time spent attending to an abstract painting among art majors from each class year. Which of the following graphs is most appropriate? Why?

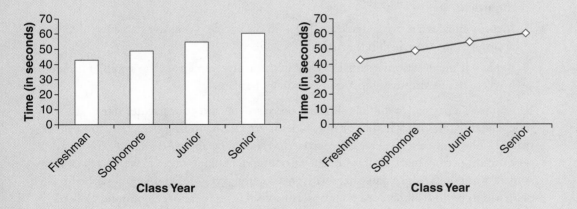

6. Name the type of graph used to describe a correlation.

7. Name the statistic used to identify (A) internal consistency and (B) interrater reliability.

8. A researcher recorded the following data: 4, 3, 6, 7, 6, 8, 10, 15, and 13. State whether each of the following values is the mean, median, or mode for these data.

   A. 6

   B. 7

   C. 8

9. Which measure of central tendency, the mean, median, or mode, is most appropriate to describe each of the following variables based on its scale of measurement?

   A. The time, in seconds, it takes participants to complete a graded assignment

   B. The blood type (A, B, AB, and O) of patients in a hospital setting

   C. The rankings of college academic programs in psychology

10. State two measures of variability. Which measure of variability is a measure of the average distance that scores deviate from their mean?

11. Which measure of variability is typically reported with the mean?

12. State the empirical rule for normally distributed data.

ACTIVITIES

1. Descriptive statistics are used in science, both in the literature and in the popular media. As an exercise, read through local newspapers, online news sources (e.g., CNN, NBC, or ABC), and popular magazines (e.g., *People*, *Time*, or *National Geographic*). Choose one article from a newspaper, one from an online source, and one from a magazine; then complete the following assignment:

   A. Cite the authors, the title or webpage of the article, and the date/year/source of the article.

   B. Identify the descriptive statistics included in the article. Were the statistics appropriately described in the article? Explain.

   C. Explain if the descriptive statistics used in the article supported the arguments made in it. Were the descriptive statistics misleading? Explain.

2. Pair up with a partner to do the following exercise. You and your partner must independently observe whether or not students are talking during one class. You will make 12 observations. Each observation period should be about 10 seconds. After each observation period, mark *yes* if a student was observed talking during class; mark *no* if a student was not. Create a data sheet with two columns (yes, no) and 12 rows (one for each observation period) and record your observations. Using these data, compute Cohen's kappa to determine the interrater reliability of the observations made.

Identify a problem

- Determine an area of interest.
- Review the literature.
- Identify new ideas in your area of interest.
- Develop a research hypothesis.

Develop a research plan

- Define the variables being tested.
- Identify participants or subjects and determine how to sample them.
- Select a research strategy and design.
- Evaluate ethics and obtain institutional approval to conduct research.

Generate more new ideas

- Results support your hypothesis—refine or expand on your ideas.
- Results do not support your hypothesis—reformulate a new idea or start over.

Communicate the results

- Method of communication: oral, written, or in a poster.
- Style of communication: APA guidelines are provided to help prepare style and format.

Conduct the study

- Execute the research plan and measure or record the data.

Analyze and evaluate the data

- Analyze and evaluate the data as they relate to the research hypothesis.
- Summarize data and research results.

After reading this chapter, you should be able to:

1   Define inferential statistics and explain why they are necessary.
2   Describe the process of null hypothesis significance testing (NHST).
3   Distinguish between Type I and Type II errors and define power.
4   Distinguish between parametric and nonparametric tests and choose an appropriate test statistic for research designs with one and two factors.
5   Distinguish between a chi-square goodness-of-fit test and a chi-square test for independence.
6   Identify and describe the following effect size measures: Cohen's *d*, eta squared, the coefficient of determination, and Cramer's *V*.
7   Distinguish between a point estimate and an interval estimate and explain how estimation relates to the significance and effect size of an outcome.
8   Distinguish between the precision and the certainty of an interval estimate.
9   Compute a chi-square goodness-of-fit test and a chi-square test for independence using SPSS.

chapter
fourteen

ANALYSIS AND INTERPRETATION: MAKING DECISIONS ABOUT DATA

Each day you make decisions. When you wake up, you decide what to wear for the day based on the clothes available in your closet or drawers; you decide what to eat based on the food available in your kitchen or on a menu; you decide how fast to drive based on posted speed limits; you decide to take notes and attend classes based on how important the class is to you; you even decided whether to read this vignette likely based on the readings assigned by your professor in a syllabus. You make all sorts of decisions each day from the little ones described here to the monumental ones, such as when you make a marriage proposal or buy a house.

In science, we systematically record data, and we make decisions on the basis of these data as well. The decisions we make in science often relate to the populations we are interested in. However, researchers select samples to understand behavior in a population. We therefore must make decisions or inferences about populations we are interested in based solely on the data recorded in a sample. To make these decisions we use inferential statistics, which are statistical procedures that allow us to *infer* or generalize observations made with samples to the larger population from which they were selected. Ultimately, scientists use inferential statistics to be confident that the observations made in a sample will also be observed in the larger population.

Throughout this book, we have been introduced to many inferential statistics beginning in Chapter 5. In this chapter, we will take a closer look at how to decide which inferential statistics to use to analyze data based on what we know about a population and the data recorded. We will organize the use of these statistics to better understand why we are using them in various research situations.

14.1 Inferential Statistics: What Are We Making Inferences About?

As illustrated in Figure 14.1, we select a sampling method in Step 2 of the research process to select a portion of all members of a group of interest in a population. In Chapter 5, we explained that researchers select samples because they do not have access to all individuals in a population. For example, in this book we have tested hypotheses concerning eating patterns in U.S. residents, wine tasting in adults aged 21 years or older, reading ability in children, exercise in physically active adults, behavioral therapies in patients with psychosis, and memory or attention in college students. In each research study, we did not select all persons in the group of interest. In fact, it would be absurd to consider doing so—imagine selecting all U.S. residents, for example, to conduct a study.

> **Inferential statistics** are procedures that allow researchers to *infer* or generalize observations made with samples to the larger population from which they were selected.

In Step 4 of the research process, we often use **inferential statistics** to analyze and evaluate the data because we are interested in describing the population of interest based on data measured in a sample. To illustrate the usefulness of inferential statistics, suppose we select a sample of patients with psychosis to test the hypothesis that a new behavioral therapy is effective. We select a sample of 20 patients, conduct the behavioral therapy study, and find that it was effective for the patients in our sample. However, we are interested in describing whether this behavioral therapy is effective for *all* patients with psychosis, and not just those patients in our sample. Here, we can use inferential statistics to determine whether the results we observed in our sample are likely to also be observed in the population of *all* patients with psychosis. Hence, inferential statistics allow us to use data measured in a sample to draw conclusions about the larger population of interest, which would not otherwise be possible without inferential statistics.

> We use inferential statistics to make decisions about characteristics in a population based on data measured in a sample.

Null Hypothesis Significance Testing

Inferential statistics include a diverse set of tests of statistical significance more formally known as *null hypothesis significance testing* (NHST). To use NHST, we begin by stating a **null hypothesis**, which is a statement about a population parameter, such as the population mean, that is assumed to be true but contradicts the research hypothesis. In other words, we begin by assuming we are wrong. We then conduct a study to determine if we can reject the null hypothesis, thereby providing support for our own claim.

> The **null hypothesis**, stated as the *null*, is a statement about a population parameter, such as the population mean, that is assumed to be true. The null hypothesis is a starting point. We will test whether the value stated in the null hypothesis is likely to be true.

To illustrate the use of NHST, suppose we state the research hypothesis that a new therapy will reduce symptoms of depression. To use NHST, we begin by stating a null hypothesis that the new therapy does *not* reduce symptoms of depression. We then conduct a study to determine if that assumption can be rejected. If we reject the

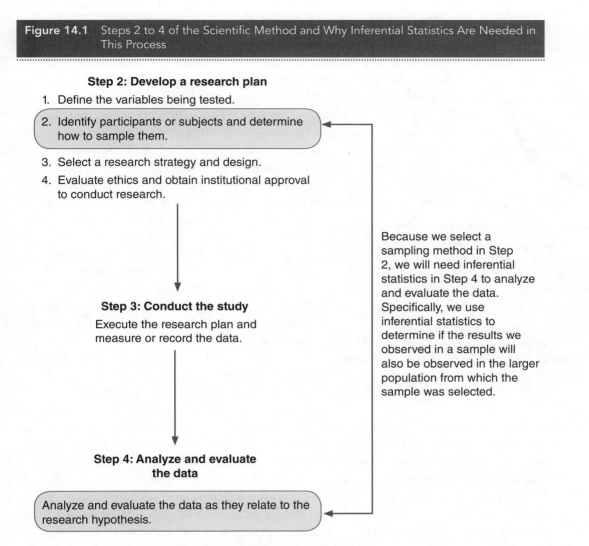

Figure 14.1 Steps 2 to 4 of the Scientific Method and Why Inferential Statistics Are Needed in This Process

Step 2: Develop a research plan

1. Define the variables being tested.
2. Identify participants or subjects and determine how to sample them.
3. Select a research strategy and design.
4. Evaluate ethics and obtain institutional approval to conduct research.

Step 3: Conduct the study

Execute the research plan and measure or record the data.

Step 4: Analyze and evaluate the data

Analyze and evaluate the data as they relate to the research hypothesis.

Because we select a sampling method in Step 2, we will need inferential statistics in Step 4 to analyze and evaluate the data. Specifically, we use inferential statistics to determine if the results we observed in a sample will also be observed in the larger population from which the sample was selected.

All steps of the scientific method are illustrated in Figure 1.1 in Chapter 1.

null hypothesis, then we have shown support for the alternative, which is our claim that the behavioral therapy does, in fact, reduce symptoms of depression. At this point, we need a criterion upon which to decide whether to reject or retain the null hypothesis.

The null hypothesis and the criteria used can be applied to an analogy in a criminal courtroom. The prosecutor begins a trial because he or she "hypothesizes" that the defendant is guilty. However, to begin the trial, we do not assume guilt; instead, a jury assumes the defendant is innocent—the assumption of innocence is the null hypothesis. The prosecutor then conducts a trial to show that the null hypothesis should be rejected "beyond reasonable doubt," which is the criterion upon which jurors decide whether a defendant is guilty or not guilty. In a research study, the criterion is a probability value for the likelihood of obtaining the data in a sample if the null hypothesis were true for the population.

Using the Criterion and Test Statistic to Make a Decision

If our goal is to describe the mean behavior in a population based upon observations made in a sample, then it is important to know exactly how informative the sample mean is; in the behavioral sciences, we are most often testing hypotheses about mean changes or differences in behavior. In other words, what does the sample mean tell us about the population mean? Two important characteristics make the sample mean particularly informative and thus useful for NHST. First, it is an **unbiased estimator** of the population mean, meaning that if we select a sample at random from a population, on average, the sample mean will equal the population mean. Second, all other possible sample means we could select from a given population are approximately normally distributed, which is characterized by the **central limit theorem**. The advantage of knowing this is that we can identify the probability or likelihood of selecting any sample mean from a population by applying the empirical rule described in Chapter 13 (p. 436).

To illustrate the informativeness of the sample mean, suppose we select all possible samples of two people from a population of three people (A, B, C) who scored an 8, 5, and 2, respectively, on some assessment—thus, the mean in the population is 5. If we select all possible samples of a certain size from this population, then we should find that the sample mean is equal to 5 on average (unbiased estimator) and all other possible sample means we could select from this population are normally distributed (central limit theorem). Notice in Figure 14.2 (also given in Table 5.2, p. 151) that this is exactly what we find in our example: on average, the same mean equals the population mean (both equal 5) and the means for all other possible samples we could select are normally distributed. Knowing this, we can therefore use a sample mean selected at random to test the likelihood of selecting that sample mean, if what we think is the value of a population mean (stated in a null hypothesis) is true. If it is very unlikely, then we can reject the value stated in the null hypothesis; if it is likely, then we can retain it.

To establish a criterion for a decision (to choose whether or not the reject a null hypothesis), we state a **level of significance** for a test. The level of significance for most studies in behavioral science is .05 or 5%. When the likelihood of obtaining a sample outcome is less than 5% if the null hypothesis were true, we reject the null hypothesis because the sample outcome would be unlikely to occur (less than 5% likely) if the null hypothesis were true. When the likelihood of obtaining a sample outcome is greater than 5% if the null hypothesis were true, we retain the null

> An **unbiased estimator** is any sample statistic obtained from a randomly selected sample that equals the value of its respective population parameter on average.
>
> The **central limit theorem** explains that regardless of the distribution of scores in a population, the sampling distribution of sample means selected at random from that population will approach the shape of a normal distribution, as the number of samples in the sampling distribution increases.

> The **level of significance**, or **significance level**, is a criterion of judgment upon which a decision is made regarding the value stated in a null hypothesis. The criterion is based on the probability of obtaining a statistic measured in a sample if the value stated in the null hypothesis were true.

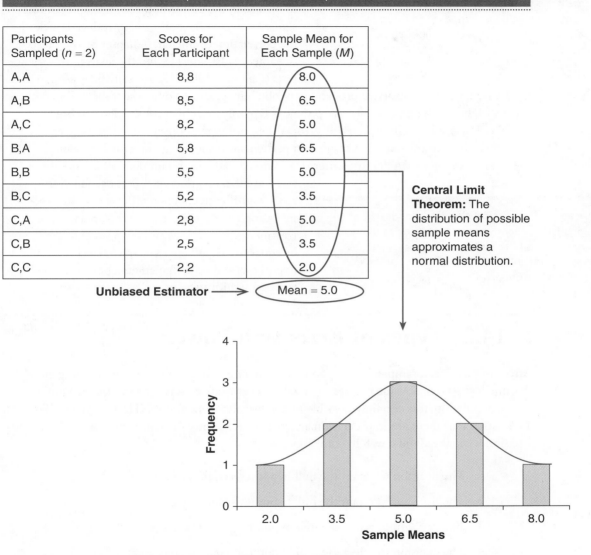

Figure 14.2 The Participants, Individual Scores, and Sample Mean for Each Possible Sample of Size 2 From This Population of Size 3

Participants Sampled ($n = 2$)	Scores for Each Participant	Sample Mean for Each Sample (M)
A,A	8,8	8.0
A,B	8,5	6.5
A,C	8,2	5.0
B,A	5,8	6.5
B,B	5,5	5.0
B,C	5,2	3.5
C,A	2,8	5.0
C,B	2,5	3.5
C,C	2,2	2.0

Unbiased Estimator ⟶ Mean = 5.0

Central Limit Theorem: The distribution of possible sample means approximates a normal distribution.

The example given here shows that the sample mean is an *unbiased estimator* and follows the *central limit theorem*.

hypothesis because the sample outcome would be likely to occur (greater than 5% likely) if the null hypothesis were true.

To determine the likelihood or probability of obtaining a sample outcome, if the value stated in the null hypothesis is true, we compute a **test statistic.** The test statistic is a mathematical formula

A **test statistic** is a mathematical formula that allows researchers to determine the likelihood of obtaining sample outcomes if the null hypothesis were true. The value of the test statistic can be used to make a decision regarding the null hypothesis.

A **p value** is the probability of obtaining a sample outcome if the value stated in the null hypothesis were true. The p value is compared to the level of significance to make a decision about a null hypothesis.

used to determine how far a sample outcome deviates or varies from the outcome that is assumed to be true in the null hypothesis. Examples of test statistics include those already introduced, such as the correlation coefficient (Chapter 8), the *t* tests (Chapters 5, 10, and 11), and the analysis of variance tests (Chapters 10–12). A test statistic is used to find the *p* value, which is the actual probability of obtaining a sample outcome if the null hypothesis is true. In the SPSS output tables, the *p* value is typically given in a column labeled **Sig.**

The *p* value is interpreted as error. When differences observed in a sample are attributed to error (or random variation in participant responding), error is large, and the *p* value is larger than .05 (the criterion). When $p > .05$, we retain the null hypothesis and state that an effect or difference failed to reach **significance**. When differences observed in a sample are attributed to a manipulation or treatment, error is low, and the *p* value is less than or equal to .05. When $p \leq .05$, we reject the null hypothesis and state that an effect or difference reached significance.

Significance, or **statistical significance**, describes a decision made concerning a value stated in the null hypothesis. When the null hypothesis is rejected, we reach significance. When the null hypothesis is retained, we fail to reach significance.

14.2 Types of Error and Power

Anytime we select a sample from a population, there is some probability of sampling error inasmuch as *p* is some value greater than 0. Because we are observing a sample and not an entire population, it is certainly possible that a decision made using NHST is wrong. Table 14.1 shows that there are four decision alternatives regarding the truth and falsity of the decision we make about a null hypothesis:

1. The decision to retain the null hypothesis could be correct.

2. The decision to retain the null hypothesis could be incorrect.

3. The decision to reject the null hypothesis could be correct.

4. The decision to reject the null hypothesis could be incorrect.

We investigate each decision alternative in this section. Because we will observe a sample, and not a population, it is impossible to know for sure the truth in a population. So for the sake of illustration, we will assume we know this. This assumption is labeled as "Truth in the Population" in Table 14.1.

Decision: Retain the Null Hypothesis

When we decide to retain the null hypothesis, we can be correct or incorrect. The correct decision, called a *null result* or a *null finding*, is to retain a true null hypothesis. This

Table 14.1 Four Decision Alternatives in NHST

Decision

Truth in the Population		Retain the Null	Reject the Null
	True	CORRECT	TYPE I ERROR
	False	TYPE II ERROR	CORRECT **POWER**

A decision can be either correct (correctly reject or retain null hypothesis) or incorrect (incorrectly reject or retain null hypothesis).

is usually an uninteresting decision because the decision is to retain what we already assumed: that the value stated in a null hypothesis is correct. For this reason, null results alone are rarely published in behavioral research.

> A **Type II error** is a "false negative" finding. It is the probability of retaining a null hypothesis that is actually false. This means the researcher is reporting no effect in the population, when in truth there is an effect.

The incorrect decision is to retain a false null hypothesis. This decision is an example of a **Type II error**, which equates to a "false negative" finding. With each test we make, there is always some probability that the decision could be a Type II error. In this decision, we decide to retain previous notions of truth that are in fact false. Although it is an error, we still changed nothing; we retained the null hypothesis. We can always go back and conduct more studies.

> A Type II error is a "false negative" finding.

Decision: Reject the Null Hypothesis

When we decide to reject the null hypothesis, we can be correct or incorrect. The incorrect decision is to reject a true null hypothesis, which is a **Type I error**, which equates to a "false positive" finding. With each test we make, there is always some probability that our decision is a Type I error. A researcher who makes this error decides to reject previous notions of truth that are in fact true. The goal in NHST is to avoid this error by starting with the assumption that the null hypothesis is correct, thereby placing the burden on the researcher to show evidence that the null hypothesis is indeed false. To demonstrate evidence that leads to a decision to reject the null hypothesis, the research must reach significance ($p < .05$); that is, we must show that the likelihood of committing a Type I error by rejecting the null hypothesis is less than 5%.

> A **Type I error** is a "false positive" finding. It is the probability of rejecting a null hypothesis that is actually true. Researchers directly control for this error by stating the level of significance.

The correct decision is to reject a false null hypothesis. In other words, we decide that the null hypothesis is false when it is indeed false. This decision is called the **power**

The **power** in hypothesis testing is the probability of rejecting a false null hypothesis. Specifically, power is the probability that we will detect an effect if an effect actually exists in a population.

A Type I error is a "false positive" finding.

of the decision-making process because it is the decision we aim for. Remember that we are testing the null hypothesis because we think it is wrong. The greater the power, the more likely it is that we will detect an effect, if it really exists. Deciding to reject a false null hypothesis, then, is the power, inasmuch as we learn the most about populations when we accurately reject false notions of truth. This decision is the most publishable outcome in behavioral research.

LEARNING CHECK 1 ✓

1. Suppose a population mean is equal to 1.5. If we select a sample at random from this population, on average, we expect the sample mean will equal what value?

2. What are the two decisions a researcher can make, each of which could be correct or incorrect?

3. A researcher states that adult supervision during playtime significantly reduced aggressive behavior among children in her sample ($p = .12$). Is this conclusion appropriate at a .05 level of significance?

4. Which type of error, Type I or Type II, is associated with a decision to reject the null hypothesis?

5. What is the power of the decision-making process?

Answers: 1. 1.5 (the sample mean is an unbiased estimator); 2. Reject the null hypothesis and retain the null hypothesis; 3. No, because the *p* value is greater than .05; 4. Type I error; 5. The probability of correctly rejecting a false null hypothesis.

14.3 Parametric Tests: Applying the Decision Tree

Parametric tests are significance tests that are used to test hypotheses about parameters in a population in which the data in the population are normally distributed and measured on an interval or ratio scale of measurement.

We apply NHST to analyze a data set in Step 4 of the research process, as illustrated in Chapter 1 and in Figure 14.1 in this chapter. The most common tests of significance are **parametric tests,** which are significance tests used to test hypotheses about parameters in a population in which each of the following is true:

- Data in the population are normally distributed.

- Data are measured on an interval or ratio scale of measurement.

Parametric tests are commonly applied to analyze behavioral data because most behavioral phenomena are approximately normally distributed and most behavioral data can be measured on an interval or ratio scale. Parametric tests are used for interval and ratio data because differences are meaningful on these scales. Therefore, analyzing mean differences between groups is also meaningful—this is the computation made by the test statistics for each parametric test listed in Figure 14.3. Also, many of the physical and behavioral phenomena that researchers study are normally distributed, with very few people at the extremes of behavior relative to the general population. For example, if we measure blood pressure or insulin levels in the body, we can identify that most people will fall within a normal or typical range, a few will have abnormally low levels, and a few will have abnormally high levels; if we measure activity levels, we will identify that most people are moderately active, a few are very active (such as Olympic athletes), and a few are sedentary.

If many groups are observed, then to use parametric tests we must also make the assumption that the variance in the population for each group is approximately the same or equal. Hence, parametric tests require assumptions concerning mean differences between groups, assuming that the variances in each group are about the same. In this section, we will describe how to choose between the following parametric tests in various research situations: the t tests, analyses of variance (ANOVAs), correlation, and regression—each test has already been introduced with an explanation for how to compute each test using SPSS.

t *Tests and ANOVAs*

We introduced the t tests and ANOVAs in Chapters 5, 10, 11, and 12 for tests concerning the mean difference between one or more groups. Again, to use parametric tests, we must measure interval/ratio data from populations with data that are normally distributed and have similar variances. If these criteria are met, then parametric tests are appropriate for analyzing the data. Choosing an appropriate parametric test depends largely on how participants were observed (between subjects or within subjects) and how many factors and groups were included in a research design. Figure 14.3 shows how to choose each parametric test for different research situations.

We use parametric tests for any case in which one or more groups or factors are observed to include experiments, quasi-experiments, and nonexperiments. An advantage of using parametric tests to analyze data is that the test statistics provide statistical control of individual error variation that cannot be explained by the levels of a factor. However, also keep in mind that we cannot draw causal conclusions without the methodological control that can only be attained in an experiment—that is, randomization (or control of order effects if the same participants are observed across groups), manipulation (of the levels of an independent variable), and the inclusion of a control or comparison group. Consequently, quasi-experiments and nonexperiments have research designs for which parametric tests can establish statistical control, but because these research designs lack methodological control, they fail to demonstrate cause and effect.

Parametric Tests for One and Two Factors With Interval/Ratio Data

The chapter in which each test was introduced is given in parentheses next to the name for each test.

Correlation and Regression

We also introduced in Chapter 8 parametric tests concerning the extent to which two factors are related (correlation) and the extent to which we can use known values of one factor to predict values of a second factor (linear regression). For these tests, we do not manipulate the levels of a factor to create groups; instead, we treat each factor like a dependent variable and measure its value for each participant in a study. The correlation coefficient and linear regression do provide statistical control of individual error variation that cannot be explained by the two factors. However, research designs that require these statistics are typically not experimental and thus lack the methodological control needed to demonstrate cause and effect.

To choose a correlation, we need to know the scale of measurement of the data. For a parametric test, we use the *Pearson correlation coefficient* for data measured on an interval or ratio scale. Other coefficients have been derived from the Pearson correlation coefficient for situations in which at least one factor is not measured on an interval/ratio scale. The *Spearman correlation coefficient* is used to examine the relationship between two factors measured on an ordinal scale; the *phi correlation coefficient* is used to examine the relationship between two factors measured on a nominal scale; the *point-biserial correlation coefficient* is used to examine the relationship between two factors when one factor is dichotomous (nominal) and a second factor is continuous (interval or ratio scale). Each alternative correlation coefficient was mathematically derived from, and is therefore equal to, the Pearson formula. For this reason, the Pearson correlation coefficient can be used to analyze data on any scale because its value will equal the value of the other coefficients—with some minor adjustments needed for data on ordinal and nominal scales, adjustments that SPSS will make automatically when you enter the data.

Similarly, choosing an appropriate linear regression model will require that we know the scale of measurement of the data. In addition, we need to know how many predictor variables we will include in the model. For one predictor variable, we use *linear regression*. For two or more predictor variables, we use *multiple regression*. Choosing an appropriate regression model can also depend on whether the research question is exploratory or confirmatory. The details of an exploratory and confirmatory factor analysis, however, go beyond the scope of this book and can be very complex—resources for applying factor analyses using regression models can be found in many upper-level textbooks (see Bollen, 1989; Child, 1990; Schumacker & Lomax, 1996; Weisberg, 2005).

> The Spearman, point-biserial, and phi correlation coefficients are mathematically equivalent to the Pearson correlation coefficient.

LEARNING CHECK 2 ✓

1. State the three assumptions or criteria that must be met to conduct a parametric test for a set of data.

2. In a research study, one group of tasters was asked to taste and rate the sweetness of four different energy drinks on an interval scale measure. State the appropriate parametric test to analyze the data for this hypothetical study.

3. Which correlation coefficient is used to analyze data on an interval or ratio scale?

Answers: 1. Data in the population are normally distributed, data are measured on an interval or ratio scale, and the variance of data in the population for each group is approximately the same or equal when many groups are observed; 2. One-way within-subjects ANOVA; 3. Pearson correlation coefficient.

14.4 Nonparametric Tests: Applying the Decision Tree

When the distribution in the population is not normally distributed and when data are measured on an ordinal or nominal scale, we apply **nonparametric tests** to analyze data in Step 4 of the research process (see Figure 14.1). Nonparametric tests are tests of significance that can be used to test hypotheses about parameters in a population in which each of the following is true:

- Data in the population can have any type of distribution.

- Data are measured on a nominal or ordinal scale of measurement.

Nonparametric tests are often called *distribution-free tests* because the shape of the distribution in the population can be any shape. The reason that the variance and therefore the shape of a distribution in the population does not

> **Nonparametric tests** are significance tests that are used to test hypotheses about data that can have any type of distribution and to analyze data on a nominal or ordinal scale of measurement.

matter is that a test statistic for nonparametric tests will not measure variance to determine significance. Likewise, because variance is not computed in nonparametric test statistics, these tests can also be used to analyze ordinal and nominal data, which are scales in which the variance is not meaningful. In this section, we will describe how to choose between nonparametric tests for ordinal and nominal data.

Tests for Ordinal Data

Nonparametric tests for ordinal data are used as alternatives to parametric tests, which require that data be measured on an interval or ratio scale. Choosing an appropriate nonparametric test depends largely on how participants were observed (between subjects or within subjects) and the number of groups in the research design. Figure 14.4 shows how to choose each nonparametric test for ordinal data for different research situations.

The structure of the decision tree for choosing an appropriate nonparametric test for ordinal data is similar to that for parametric tests with one factor—note the overlap between Figures 14.2 and 14.3 for one factor. We can require the use of nonparametric tests in two common situations. In the first situation, the data may be on an interval or ratio scale but are not normally distributed, which is an assumption that must be met for parametric tests. In these situations, we convert the data to ranks (ordinal data) and use the nonparametric alternative test to analyze the data. In the second situation, we record ranked data in which case the variability of ranks (ordinal data) is not meaningful and so a nonparametric test is required.

The specific analysis of each nonparametric test for ordinal data given in Figure 14.4 is beyond the scope of this book (for a full description of the analysis for each test, see Privitera, 2015). However, these tests can be readily computed in SPSS by using the **Analyze**, **Nonparametric Tests**, and **Legacy Dialogs** options in the menu bar. These options will display a menu that allows you to select and compute each nonparametric test for ordinal data given in Figure 14.4.

Figure 14.4   A Decision Tree for Choosing Nonparametric Tests for Ordinal Data

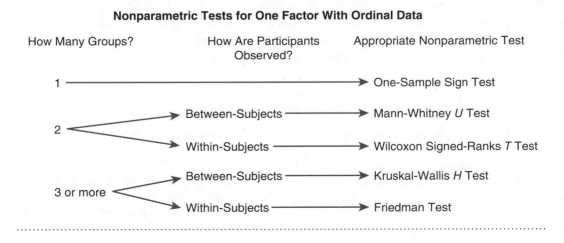

Nonparametric Tests for One Factor With Ordinal Data

How Many Groups?	How Are Participants Observed?	Appropriate Nonparametric Test
1		One-Sample Sign Test
2	Between-Subjects	Mann-Whitney *U* Test
	Within-Subjects	Wilcoxon Signed-Ranks *T* Test
3 or more	Between-Subjects	Kruskal-Wallis *H* Test
	Within-Subjects	Friedman Test

Tests for Nominal (Categorical) Data

Nonparametric tests can also be used to analyze nominal or categorical data. For these research situations, we count the frequency of occurrence in two or more categories for one or two factors. Variance is meaningless in these research situations because it is meaningless to analyze the variance of a single count or frequency in each category—variance cannot be computed for a single value. The nonparametric tests used to analyze nominal (categorical) data are called the *chi-square tests*.

For one categorical factor, we analyze the extent to which frequencies observed fit well with frequencies expected using the **chi-square goodness-of-fit test**. To illustrate a research situation in which we use this nonparametric test, we will count the frequency of soccer players kicking the ball to the left, center, or right during a penalty kick in a professional tournament (for similar research on playing tactics, see Bar-Eli, Azar, Ritov, Keidar-Levin, & Schein, 2007; Lago-Ballesteros, Lago-Peñas, & Rey, 2012). If we want to determine if players have a bias for one side, then we begin by assuming that an equal number or proportion of kicks will be directed to the left, right, and center. If we observe 90 penalty kicks, then we expect 30 kicks in each location. The chi-square goodness-of-fit test is used to determine if the proportion of kicks we observe in each location fits well with this expectation. If it fits well, then there is no bias, and the result will not reach significance. If it does not fit well, then there is a bias, and the result will reach significance. Using SPSS to analyze and interpret the result, we will continue with this same research example in the next section using a sample data set.

> The **chi-square goodness-of-fit test** is a statistical procedure used to determine whether observed frequencies at each level of one categorical variable are similar to or different from frequencies expected.

> A chi-square goodness-of-fit test is used to determine how well a set of observed frequencies fits with what was expected.

We can also analyze the extent to which frequencies observed across the levels of two nominal (categorical) factors are related or independent using the **chi-square test for independence**. When two factors are related, such as activity levels and depression (yes, no), the frequencies displayed in a summary table will vary across the cells, as shown in Table 14.2a. When two factors are independent (not related), such as a preference (Coke or Pepsi) and depression (yes, no), the frequencies in a summary table will be the same or similar, as shown in Table 14.2b.

> The **chi-square test for independence** is a statistical procedure used to determine whether frequencies observed at the combination of levels of two categorical variables are similar to or different from frequencies expected.

To illustrate a research situation in which we use this nonparametric test, we can test if the location that soccer players kicked the ball (left, center, right) during a penalty kick in a professional tournament depended on which direction the goalie dove to block the kick (left, center, right). If it is independent, then the location that a player kicked the ball will not be related to the direction the goalie dove to block the kick, and the result will not reach significance. If it is dependent or related, then the location that a player kicked the ball will be related to the direction the goalie dove to block the kick, and the result will reach significance. Using SPSS to analyze and interpret the result, we will continue with this same research example in the next section using a sample data set.

> A chi-square test for independence is used to determine if frequencies at the levels of two categorical variables are independent or related.

(a) Dependent relationship
(Two factors are related.)

Frequencies vary
across the cells.

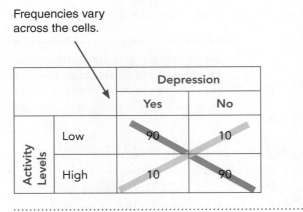

(b) Independent relationship
(Two factors are not related.)

Frequencies do not
vary across the cells.

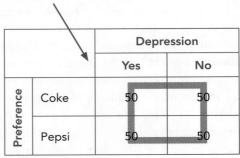

14.5 SPSS in Focus: The Chi-Square Tests

SPSS can be used to compute the chi-square tests. In this section, we will use SPSS to compute a chi-square goodness-of-fit test and a chi-square test for independence.

Chi-Square Goodness-of-Fit Test

In Section 14.4, we used a research situation in which we counted the frequency of soccer players kicking the ball to the left, center, or right during a penalty kick in a professional tournament. We wanted to determine if players have a bias for one side, so we began by assuming that an equal proportion of kicks will be directed to the left, right, and center. Hypothetical data are given in Table 14.3, which is based on actual data published by Bar-Eli et al. (2007). We will use SPSS to analyze these data using a chi-square goodness-of-fit test.

1. Click on the **Variable View** tab and enter *direction* in the **Name column**; enter *count* in the Name column below it. Go to the **Decimals column** and reduce the value to 0 for both rows.

2. To code the *direction* variable, click on the small gray box with three dots in the **Values** column. In the **dialog box**, enter *1* in the value cell and *left* in the label cell, and click **Add**; then enter *2* in the value cell and *center* in the label cell, and click **Add**; then enter *3* in the value cell and *right* in the label cell. Click **Add**. Select **OK**.

Table 14.3 The Frequency Observed (top row) and the Frequency Expected Assuming an Equal Proportion of Kicks to Each Side (bottom row)

	Penalty Kick Direction		
	Left	Center	Right
Observed Frequency	29	26	35
Expected Frequency	30	30	30

$N = 90$

3. Click on the **Data View** tab. In the *direction* column, enter a *1* in the first cell, *2* in the cell below it, and *3* in the cell below that. In the *count* column, enter the corresponding observed frequencies: Enter *29* in the first cell, enter *26* in the cell below it, and enter *35* in the cell below that.

4. Go to the menu bar and click **Data** and **Weight cases** to display a dialog box. Select **Weight cases by** and move *count* into the **Frequency Variable** cell. Select **OK**.

5. Go to the menu bar and click **Analyze**, and **Nonparametric Tests**, **Legacy Dialogs**, and **Chi-square** to display another dialog box.

6. Using the arrows, move *direction* into the **Test Variables List** box. In the **Expected Values** box, the default setting in SPSS is that we expect the same expected frequency at each level of the categorical variable. Because this is the case for this example, we leave the default setting.

7. Select **OK**, or select **Paste** and click the **Run** command.

The SPSS output table, shown in Table 14.4, gives the results of the chi-square goodness-of-fit test. The top table displays the observed and expected frequencies, which are the same as those given in Table 14.3. The bottom table lists the value of the chi-square test statistic, symbolized as χ^2; the degrees of freedom, which are equal to the number of category levels minus one ($3 - 1 = 2$); and the *p* value. One assumption that must be met to use a chi-square test is that the expected frequency in each category should be equal to at least 5—this assumption is met, as confirmed below the bottom table in the SPSS output.

To make a decision, we use the same criteria as parametric tests. In this example, the *p* value is greater than .05 ($p = .497$); our decision is to retain the null hypothesis. We conclude that the frequencies observed fit well with the frequencies expected. Using American Psychological Association (APA, 2009) guidelines, we report the results of a chi-square test by stating the value of the test statistic, degrees of freedom, and *p* value as shown:

A chi-square goodness-of-fit test showed that soccer players in a professional tournament do not show a side preference during a penalty kick, $\chi^2(2) = 1.40, p = .497$.

Table 14.4 The SPSS Output Table for a Chi-Square Goodness-of-Fit Test

The observed and expected frequencies are the same as those shown in Table 14.3.

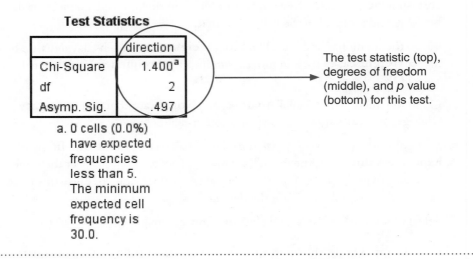

direction

	Observed N	Expected N	Residual
left	29	30.0	-1.0
center	26	30.0	-4.0
right	35	30.0	5.0
Total	90		

Test Statistics

	direction
Chi-Square	1.400[a]
df	2
Asymp. Sig.	.497

a. 0 cells (0.0%) have expected frequencies less than 5. The minimum expected cell frequency is 30.0.

The test statistic (top), degrees of freedom (middle), and *p* value (bottom) for this test.

Chi-Square Test for Independence

In Section 14.4, we also used a research situation in which we tested if the location that soccer players kicked the ball (left, center, right) during a penalty kick in a professional tournament depended on which direction the goalie dove to block the kick (left, center, right). We wanted to determine if the location that a player kicked the ball is related to the direction the goalie dove to block the kick. Hypothetical data for this research situation are given in Table 14.5, which is based on actual data published by Bar-Eli et al. (2007). We will use SPSS to analyze these data using a chi-square test for independence.

1. Click on the **Variable View** tab and enter *kicker* in the **Name column**; enter *goalie* in the Name column below it; enter *count* in the Name column below that. Go to the **Decimals column** and reduce the value to 0 for all rows.

2. To code the *kicker* variable, click on the small gray box with three dots in the **Values** column for *kicker*. In the **dialog box**, enter *1* in the value cell and *left* in the label cell, and click **Add**; enter *2* in the value cell and *center* in the label cell, and click **Add**; enter *3* in the value cell and *right* in the label cell, and click **Add**. Select **OK**.

3. To code the *goalie* variable, click on the small gray box with three dots in the **Values** column for *goalie*. In the **dialog box**, enter *1* in the value cell and *left* in the label cell, and click **Add**; enter *2* in the value cell and *center* in the label cell, and click **Add**; enter *3* in the value cell and *right* in the label cell, and click **Add**. Select **OK**.

4. Click on the **Data View** tab. Enter the data as shown in Figure 14.5. Note that the counts line up across the row with the corresponding counts in each cell.

5. Go to the menu bar and click **Data**, then **Weight cases** to display a dialog box. In the dialog box, click **Weight Cases by** and move *count* into the **Frequency Variable** cell. Select **OK**.

6. Go to the menu bar and click **Analyze**, **Descriptive statistics**, and **Crosstabs** to display a dialog box.

7. Using the arrows, move *kicker* into the **Row(s)** box and move *goalie* into the **Column(s)** box. Click **Statistics…** to display another dialog box. In the dialog box, select **Chi-square**, and then click **Continue**.

8. Select **OK**, or select **Paste** and click the **Run** command.

The SPSS output table, shown in Table 14.6, gives the results of the chi-square test for independence. The first row in the table lists the value of the chi-square test statistic, the degrees of freedom, and the *p* value for the test. Again, a chi-square test requires that the

Table 14.5 The Observed Frequency of Penalty Kicks to the Left, Center, and Right When the Goalie Dove to the Left, Center, and Right

| | | Goalie Jump Direction | | | |
		Left	Center	Right	Totals
Penalty Kick Direction	Left	54	1	37	92
	Center	41	10	31	82
	Right	46	7	59	112
	Totals	141	18	127	$N = 286$

Row and column totals are also given. These data are based on those reported by Bar-Eli et al. (2007).

Figure 14.5   SPSS Data View for Step 4

	kicker	goalie	count
1	1	1	54
2	1	2	1
3	1	3	37
4	2	1	41
5	2	2	10
6	2	3	31
7	3	1	46
8	3	2	7
9	3	3	59

expected frequency in each category should be equal to at least 5—this assumption is met, as confirmed below the SPSS output table.

To make a decision, we use the same criteria as parametric tests. In this example, the p value is less than .05 ($p = .006$); our decision is to reject the null hypothesis. We conclude that the location that a soccer player kicks the ball is related to the direction that a goalie jumps to block it. To determine the nature of the relationship, we refer back to the data in Table 14.5. Using APA (2009) guidelines, we can report the results of a chi-square test by stating the value of the test statistic, degrees of freedom, and p value as shown:

Table 14.6   The SPSS Output Table for a Chi-Square Test for Independence

Chi-Square Tests

	Value	df	Asymp. Sig. (2-sided)	
Pearson Chi-Square	14.589[a]	4	.006	The test statistic (left), degrees of freedom (middle), and p value (right) for this test.
Likelihood Ratio	15.663	4	.004	
Linear-by-Linear Association	5.050	1	.025	
N of Valid Cases	286			

a. 0 cells (0.0%) have expected count less than 5. The minimum expected count is 5.16.

A chi-square test for independence showed that the location that a soccer player kicks the ball during a penalty kick is related to the direction that a goalie jumps to block it, $\chi^2(4) = 14.589$, $p = .006$. The pattern of data shows that soccer players are likely to kick the ball in the opposite direction that a goalie jumps to block it.

LEARNING CHECK 3 ✓

1. State the nonparametric alternative test for each of the following parametric tests:

   A. One-sample t test

   B. Two-independent-sample t test

   C. One-way between-subjects ANOVA

2. State whether a chi-square goodness-of-fit test or a chi-square test for independence is the appropriate nonparametric test for the following example: A health psychologist compares the number of students who are lean, healthy, overweight, and obese at a local school to expected proportions in each category.

3. A researcher makes the decision to reject the null hypothesis using a chi-square test for independence. Does this decision mean that two factors are independent or related?

Answers: 1. A. One-sample sign test, B. Mann-Whitney U Test, C. Kruskal-Wallis H Test; 2. Chi-square goodness-of-fit test; 3. The two factors are related.

14.6 Effect Size: How Big Is an Effect in the Population?

We use NHST to determine if the results observed in a sample are likely to also occur in the population from which that sample was selected. In other words, we use NHST to determine if an effect exists in a population. An **effect** is a term used to describe the mean difference or discrepancy between what was observed in a sample and what was expected in the population as stated by the null hypothesis. When we reject a null hypothesis, an effect is significant and therefore does exist in a population; when we retain a null hypothesis, an effect is not significant and therefore does not exist in a population. The decision using NHST, however, only indicates if an effect exists but does not inform us of the size of that effect in the population.

> An **effect** is a mean difference or discrepancy between what was observed in a sample and what was expected to be observed in the population (stated by the null hypothesis).
>
> **Effect size** is a statistical measure of the size or magnitude of an observed effect in a population, which allows researchers to describe how far scores shifted in a population, or the percent of variance in a dependent variable that can be explained by the levels of a factor.

To determine the size of an effect in a population, we compute an estimate called **effect size**, which is a measure of the size of an observed effect in a population. Effect size can describe how far scores shifted in a population, or it can describe the proportion of variance in a dependent variable that can be explained or accounted for by the levels of a factor. Effect size is often reported with many parametric and nonparametric tests for significance. Table 14.7 lists common tests for significance and the corresponding effect size measure reported with each test. The following effect size measures listed in Table 14.7 are described in this section:

NHST indicates if an effect exists in a population; effect size indicates the size of an effect in a population.

- Cohen's d

- Proportion of variance: η^2, R^2

- Proportion of variance: Cramer's V

Cohen's d

When one or two groups are observed, we can describe effect size as a shift or mean difference between groups in a population using a measure called **Cohen's d** (Cohen, 1988). Cohen's d estimates the size of a shift in the population as the number of standard deviations that scores shifted. In the formula for Cohen's d, the numerator is the sample mean difference— either between two groups or between a sample and a population mean for one group. The denominator is the sample standard deviation for one group or the pooled (averaged) sample standard deviation for two groups. The formula for Cohen's d can be represented using the following standard form:

Cohen's d is a measure of effect size in terms of the number of standard deviations that mean scores shifted above or below the population mean stated by the null hypothesis. The larger the value of d, the larger the effect in the population.

$$d = \frac{\text{Sample mean difference}}{\text{Sample standard deviation}}$$

Cohen's d is used with the t tests. In each case, there is no effect size when $d = 0$, with larger values for d indicating a larger effect size in the population. We interpret the value of d in terms of standard deviations. The positive or negative sign indicates only the direction of an effect in the population. For example, if $d = +.36$, then scores shifted .36 standard deviations above the value stated in a null hypothesis; if $d = -.36$, then scores shifted .36 standard deviations below the value stated by a null hypothesis.

The size of an effect can be described as small, medium, or large. Conventions for interpreting the size of an effect using Cohen's d are identified by **Cohen's conventions**, which are given in Table 14.8 under the d column heading. In our example, we would describe $d = \pm.36$ as a medium effect size.

Cohen's conventions, or **effect size conventions**, are standard rules for identifying small, medium, and large effects based on typical findings in behavioral research.

Table 14.7 Measures of Effect Size That Correspond to Common Tests for Significance

Test for Significance	Effect Size	
	Corresponding Effect Size Measure	**Interpretation of Effect Size Measure**
t tests	Cohen's *d*	Its value represents the number of standard deviations that scores shift or fall above or below a value stated in a null hypothesis.
ANOVAs	η^2	Its value represents the proportion of variance in a dependent variable that can be explained by the levels of a factor.
Correlation and Regression	R^2	Its value represents the proportion of variance in values of one factor that can be explained by changes in the values of a second factor.
Chi-Square Test for Independence	Cramer's *V*	Same as R^2

The interpretation is also given for each effect size measure.

Proportion of Variance: η^2, R^2

An alternative measure of effect size is **proportion of variance**. Proportion of variance is a measure of effect size in terms of the proportion or percent of variability in a dependent variable that can be explained or accounted for by the levels of a factor or treatment. This type of effect size estimate is used when a study includes more than two groups or applies a correlational research design.

> **Proportion of variance** is a measure of effect size in terms of the proportion or percent of variability in a dependent variable that can be explained or accounted for by the levels of a factor or treatment.

To estimate proportion of variance with ANOVA, we compute a measure called **eta squared**, symbolized as η^2. Sometimes, a partial estimate of eta squared is reported for a within-subjects design. The value of eta squared can range between 0 and 1.0 and is interpreted as a proportion or percentage. For example, if $\eta^2 = .04$, then 4% of the variability in a dependent variable can be explained by the levels of a factor. The formula for eta squared can be represented using the following standard form:

> **Eta squared** (η^2) is a measure of proportion of variance used to describe effect size for data analyzed using ANOVA.

$$\eta^2 = \frac{\text{Variability between groups}}{\text{Total variability}}$$

The size of an effect for eta squared can be described as trivial, small, medium, or large. Conventions for interpreting the size of an effect using eta squared are given in Table 14.8 under the $\eta^2 = R^2$ column heading. In our example, then, we would describe $\eta^2 = .04$ as a small effect size based on the conventions given in Table 14.8.

> The **coefficient of determination** (R^2) is a measure of proportion of variance used to describe effect size for data analyzed using a correlation coefficient or regression. The coefficient of determination is mathematically equivalent to eta squared.

A measure of proportion of variance that is used with a correlation or regression analysis is a measure called the **coefficient of determination**, symbolized as R^2. The coefficient of determination is the square of the *correlation coefficient*, r, and its value can range from 0 to 1.0. For example, in Chapter 8 we determined that the correlation between mobile phone use and perceived stress is $r = .54$. Therefore, the coefficient of determination is $R^2 = (.54)^2 = .29$. To interpret R^2, we state that 29% of the variability in perceived stress can be explained by mobile phone use.

The coefficient of determination is mathematically equivalent to eta squared. For this reason, the size of an effect for R^2 can be described as trivial, small, medium, or large using the same conventions given in Table 14.8 under the $\eta^2 = R^2$ column heading. In our example, then, we would describe $R^2 = .29$ as a large effect size based on the conventions given in Table 14.8.

> The coefficient of determination is mathematically equivalent to eta squared: $\eta^2 = R^2$.

Proportion of Variance: Cramer's V

A measure of proportion of variance that is used with a chi-square test for independence is a measure called **Cramer's V**. Its value can range from 0 to 1.0 and is interpreted the same as the coefficient of determination. For example, in Section 14.5 we computed the chi-square test for independence and determined that the location that a soccer player directs a penalty kick is related to the direction that a goalie jumps to block it,

Table 14.8 The Size of an Effect Using Cohen's *d*, Eta Squared (η^2), and the Coefficient of Determination (R^2)

Description of Effect	*d*	$\eta^2 = R^2$
Trivial	—	$\eta^2, R^2 < .01$
Small	$d < 0.2$	$.01 < \eta^2, R^2 < .09$
Medium	$0.2 < d < 0.8$	$.09 < \eta^2, R^2 < .25$
Large	$d \geq 0.8$	$\eta^2, R^2 \geq .25$

Eta squared and the coefficient of determination are mathematically equivalent.

$\chi^2 = 14.589$. Cramer's V for this example is $V = .16$, which can be computed using SPSS by selecting the **Phi and Cramer's V** option in Step 7 of the steps given in Section 14.5 for computing the chi-square test for independence.

> **Cramer's V** is a measure of proportion of variance that is used as an estimate of effect size for the chi-square test for independence.

To describe the size of the effect as small, medium, or large, we follow the conventions given in Table 14.9. To interpret Cramer's V, we need to identify the factor with the smaller degrees of freedom, $df_{smaller}$. The degrees of freedom for a factor are the number of categories for a factor, minus one. In our example, there were three categories for each factor (left, center, and right). Hence, the smaller degrees of freedom in our example are 2. We can therefore describe $V = .16$ as a small effect size based on the conventions given in Table 14.9.

Table 14.9 Effect Size Conventions for Cramer's V

$df_{smaller}$	Effect Size		
	Small	Medium	Large
1	0.10	0.30	0.50
2	0.07	0.21	0.35
3	0.06	0.17	0.29

Each value represents the smallest value for a given effect size category.

LEARNING CHECK 4 ✓

1. _____ is a statistical measure of the size of an observed effect in a population, which allows researchers to describe how far scores shifted in a population, or the percent of variance in a dependent variable that can be explained by the levels of a factor.

2. What measure of proportion of variance is used to estimate effect size when data are analyzed using ANOVA?

3. Eta squared is mathematically equivalent to what other measure of proportion of variance?

4. What test for significance uses Cramer's V to estimate effect size?

Answers: 1. Effect size; 2. Eta squared; 3. The coefficient of determination; 4. The chi-square test for independence.

14.7 Estimation: What Are the Possible Values of a Parameter?

Estimation is a statistical procedure in which a sample statistic is used to estimate the value of an unknown population parameter. Two types of estimation are point estimation and interval estimation.

As an alternative to NHST, we can also learn more about a parameter (e.g., a population mean) without ever stating a null hypothesis. This approach requires only that we set limits for the possible values of a population parameter within which it is likely to be contained. The goal of this alternative approach, called **estimation**, is the same as that in significance testing—to learn more about the value of a mean or mean difference in a population of interest. To use estimation, we select a sample, measure a sample mean or mean difference, and then use that sample mean or mean difference to estimate the value of a population parameter.

We use estimation to estimate the possible value of a parameter in a population.

We measure two types of estimates using estimation: a point estimate and an interval estimate. A **point estimate** is a sample mean for one group or mean difference between two groups. We use the sample mean (the statistic) to estimate the population mean (the parameter). An **interval estimate**, called the **confidence interval**, is the range of possible values for the parameter stated within a given **level of confidence**, which is the likelihood that a population mean is contained within that given interval.

A **point estimate** is a sample statistic (e.g., a sample mean) that is used to estimate a population parameter (e.g., a population mean).

An **interval estimate**, called the **confidence interval (CI)**, is the interval or range of possible values within which an unknown population parameter is likely to be contained.

Level of confidence is the probability or likelihood that an interval estimate will contain the value of an unknown population parameter (e.g., a population mean).

Interval estimates are reported as a point estimate ± interval estimate. For example, you may read that 53% ± 3% of Americans believe that evolution is true, 34% ± 3% believe in ghosts, or 38% ± 3% believe that professional athletes are good role models for children. The ±3%, called the *margin of error*, is added to and subtracted from the point estimate to find the **confidence limits** of an interval estimate. If we add and subtract 3% from each point estimate, we can be confident that 50% to 56% of Americans believe evolution is true, 31% to 37% believe in ghosts, and 35% to 41% believe professional athletes are good role models for children, on average. Exactly how confident we are depends on the level of confidence, which is determined by the researcher. Typical levels of confidence are stated at 80%, 95%, or 99% in behavioral research.

Confidence limits are the upper and lower boundaries of a confidence interval given within a specified level of confidence.

14.8 Confidence Intervals, Significance, and Effect Size

A confidence interval states the range of possible values for a population parameter (e.g., a population mean) at a specified level of confidence. The process of computing a confidence interval is related to the process we used to retain or reject a null hypothesis using NHST. In fact, we can use the information conveyed by a confidence interval to determine the significance of an outcome. We apply the following rules to identify the significance of an outcome:

1. If the null hypothesis were inside a confidence interval, the decision would have been to retain the null hypothesis (not significant).

2. If the null hypothesis were outside the confidence interval, the decision would have been to reject the null hypothesis (significant).

An interval estimate is reported as the point estimate ± the interval estimate.

We can therefore compare a confidence interval with the decision for a significance test. To illustrate, we will revisit the related-samples t test computed in Chapter 11. In that study, we tested if infants would spend more time orienting their head toward a picture of their mother or a picture of a stranger (i.e., a picture of their mother that was distorted to look like a stranger). We tested the null hypothesis that there was no difference in time spent orienting toward a picture. Hence, if the null hypothesis were true, we would expect a mean difference of 0 seconds. In our study, however, we decided to reject the null hypothesis and concluded that children spent significantly more time orienting toward a picture of their mother. The SPSS output displaying the results of this related-samples t test is reproduced in Table 14.10.

The output in SPSS for a t test will give the results of the t test and also give the 95% confidence interval for that test by default. Referring to Table 14.10, the mean difference between groups (mother, stranger) is 4.0—this is the point estimate. The confidence limits for the 95% confidence interval are 2.348 and 5.652. As expected, we find that the value stated in the null hypothesis (mean difference = 0) falls outside the confidence interval for a test in which we chose to reject the null hypothesis. Hence, a mean difference of 0 is not one of the possible values contained within the confidence interval for the mean difference in the population. Using APA (2009) guidelines, we report a confidence interval by stating the level of confidence, the sample mean, and the confidence limits as shown:

Newborns oriented their heads 4.0 seconds longer toward a picture of their mother compared to a picture of a stranger (95% CI 2.35 to 5.65).

We can also interpret effect size using the confidence limits of a confidence interval. The effect size for a confidence interval is a range or interval in which the

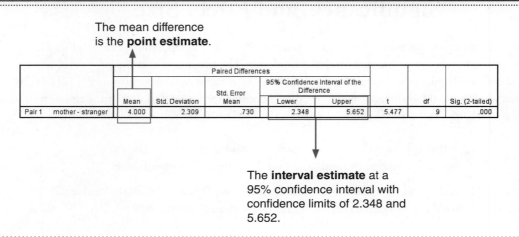

The mean difference is the **point estimate**.

		Paired Differences						
		Mean	Std. Deviation	Std. Error Mean	95% Confidence Interval of the Difference		t	df	Sig. (2-tailed)
					Lower	Upper			
Pair 1	mother - stranger	4.000	2.309	.730	2.348	5.652	5.477	9	.000

The **interval estimate** at a 95% confidence interval with confidence limits of 2.348 and 5.652.

The significance and effect size of an outcome can be determined based on the confidence interval identified at a specified level of confidence.

lower effect size estimate is the difference between the value stated in the null hypothesis and the lower confidence limit; the upper effect size estimate is the difference between the value stated in the null hypothesis and the upper confidence limit. Effect size can then be interpreted in terms of a shift in the population when the value of the null hypothesis is outside a given confidence interval. In our example, we can therefore state effect size as follows: Newborns in the population spent between 2.35 and 5.65 seconds longer orienting toward a picture of their mother compared with a picture of a stranger. This effect size is also illustrated in Figure 14.6.

14.9 Issues for Interpretation: Precision and Certainty

When we use estimation to identify a confidence interval, we often refer to the precision and the certainty of the interval. The *precision* of an estimate is determined by the range of the confidence interval: The smaller the range of an interval, the more precise the estimate. The *certainty* of an estimate is determined by the level of confidence: The larger the level of confidence, the more certain the estimate. Therefore, we can use the following rules to identify the precision and certainty of a confidence interval:

1. Decreasing the level of confidence increases the precision of an estimate.

2. Increasing the level of confidence increases the certainty of an estimate.

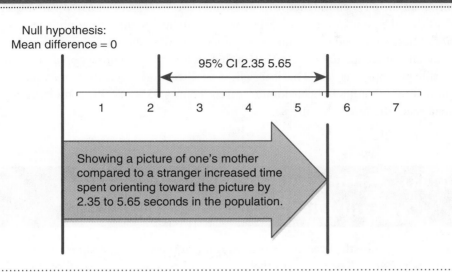

Null hypothesis:
Mean difference = 0

95% CI 2.35 5.65

1   2   3   4   5   6   7

Showing a picture of one's mother compared to a stranger increased time spent orienting toward the picture by 2.35 to 5.65 seconds in the population.

To illustrate these rules, Figure 14.7 displays the 80% and the 95% levels of confidence for the mother preference study we evaluated in Section 14.8. The upper and lower confidence limits at each level of confidence are given in the figure. Rule 1 indicates that the smaller the level of confidence, the more precise the estimate. The 80% confidence interval is the smaller level of confidence and is also more precise because it estimates the narrowest range within which the mean difference in the population is likely to be contained.

Figure 14.7   The 80% and 95% Confidence Intervals for the Mother Preference Study

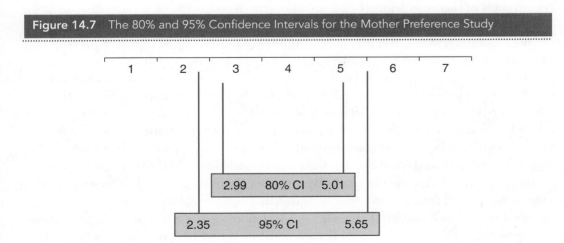

1   2   3   4   5   6   7

2.99   80% CI   5.01

2.35   95% CI   5.65

Notice that the lower the level of confidence, the more precise the estimate, but the less certain we are that the confidence interval contains the actual population mean.

Rule 2 indicates that the larger the level of confidence, the more certain the estimate. The 95% confidence interval is the larger level of confidence and is associated with greater certainty than the 80% confidence interval because we are 95%, compared with 80%, confident that the population mean difference is contained within the confidence interval specified. These rules lead to an important implication regarding the precision and certainty of a confidence interval: To be more certain that an interval contains a population parameter, we typically give up precision. This is usually a sacrifice most researchers are willing to make in that most studies in behavioral research report a 95% or 99% confidence interval in published scientific research journals.

14.10 Ethics in Focus: Full Disclosure of Data

When reporting statistical results, it is important to report data as thoroughly, yet concisely, as possible. Keep in mind that, as the author, you will have all of the data in front of you. However, the reader will not. The reader will only know as much information as you provide. You need to make sure that the data you report in an article are thorough enough that they tell the whole story. For example, suppose you report that a treatment for a behavioral disorder is effective. To support your claim, you provide all significant data, including test statistics and effect size showing that the treatment is effective. However, suppose that your data also show that the treatment is effective for men, but not women. If you fail to provide all data for this outcome, then your report is misleading because you are selectively omitting data that could indicate limitations in the effectiveness of the treatment.

Evidence of the failure to report all data can be found in the published peer-reviewed literature, with a strong commitment by peer-review journal editors to prevent this from happening (Bauchner & Fontanarosa, 2012). Chan, Hróbjartsson, Haahr, Gøtzsche, and Altman (2004), for example, reported in the *Journal of the American Medical Association* that failure to report all data is particularly a problem for clinical trial research in which outcomes reported can mean the difference between life and death for patients. The researchers reviewed over 100 published journal articles and found alarming discrepancies in reporting. They found that many nonsignificant results were not reported, and up to 50% to 65% of trials included outcomes that were incompletely reported in some way, such as missing p values or effect size estimates that could be used in meta-analysis. The researchers suggest that clinical trials research may be biased, and many studies may likely overestimate the benefits of an intervention. This conclusion is important in that it is based on the finding that researchers were not fully reporting data, particularly data that were not significant. To avoid problems in trusting the outcomes reported in a paper, the simple solution is to always fully disclose data.

1. Identify two types of estimates for a population parameter.

2. A researcher compares health scores in a sample to the general health score known in the population and reports the following confidence interval: 95% CI −0.69 to 4.09. If the null hypothesis stated that there was no difference in health scores between the sample and the population, then what would the decision likely have been for a significance test? Explain.

3. What is the difference between the precision and the certainty of a confidence interval?

4. True or false: Selectively omitting data can lead to misleading interpretations of data.

Answers: 1. Point estimate and interval estimate; 2. Retain the null hypothesis because the null hypothesis value of a mean difference equal to 0 is contained within the stated confidence interval; 3. The precision of an estimate is determined by the range of the confidence interval, whereas the certainty of an estimate is determined by the level of confidence; 4. True.

CHAPTER SUMMARY

LO 1 Define inferential statistics and explain why they are necessary.

- **Inferential statistics** are procedures that allow researchers to *infer* or generalize observations made with samples to the larger population from which they were selected.
- Inferential statistics allow researchers to use data recorded in a sample to draw conclusions about the larger population of interest—this would not be possible without inferential statistics.

LO 2 Describe the process of null hypothesis significance testing (NHST).

- To use NHST, we begin by stating a **null hypothesis**, which is a statement about a population parameter, such as the population mean, that is assumed to be true but contradicts the research hypothesis.
- Two important characteristics make the sample mean particularly informative, and thus useful for NHST. First, it is an **unbiased estimator** of the population mean, meaning that if we select a sample at random from a population, on average, the sample mean will equal the population mean. Second, all other possible sample means we could select from a population are approximately normally distributed, which is characterized by the **central limit theorem**. These characteristics allow us to justify selecting a sample mean at random to test the likelihood of selecting that sample mean, if what we think is the value of a population mean (stated in a null hypothesis) is true.

- To establish a criterion for a decision, we state a **level of significance** for a test. The level of significance for most studies in behavioral science is .05. To determine the likelihood or probability of obtaining a sample outcome, if the value stated in the null hypothesis is true, we compute a **test statistic**. A test statistic is used to find the *p* **value**, which is the actual probability of obtaining a sample outcome if the null hypothesis is true. We reject the null hypothesis when $p \leq .05$; an effect reached **significance.** We retain the null hypothesis when $p > .05$; an effect failed to reach significance.

LO 3 Distinguish between Type I and Type II errors and define power.

- A **Type I error** is the probability of rejecting a null hypothesis that is actually true. Researchers control for this type of error by stating a level of significance, which is typically set at .05. A **Type II error** is the probability of retaining a null hypothesis that is actually false, meaning that the researcher reports no effect in the population, when in truth there is an effect.
- **Power** is the probability of rejecting a false null hypothesis. Specifically, power is the probability that we will detect an effect if it actually exists in a population.

LO 4 Distinguish between parametric and nonparametric tests and choose an appropriate test statistic for research designs with one and two factors.

- **Parametric tests** are significance tests that are used to test hypotheses about parameters in a population in which the data are normally distributed and measured on an interval or ratio scale of measurement.
- **Nonparametric tests** are significance tests that are used to test hypotheses about data that can have any type of distribution and to analyze data on a nominal or ordinal scale of measurement.
- Choosing an appropriate parametric and nonparametric test can depend largely on how participants were observed (between subjects or within subjects), how many factors and groups were included in a research design, and the type of research question being asked.

LO 5 Distinguish between a chi-square goodness-of-fit test and a chi-square test for independence.

- A **chi-square goodness-of-fit test** is a statistical procedure used to determine whether observed frequencies at each level of one categorical variable are similar to or different from the frequencies we expected at each level of the categorical variable. If frequencies observed fit well with frequencies expected, the decision will be to retain the null hypothesis; if frequencies observed do not fit well with frequencies expected, the decision will be to reject the null hypothesis.
- A **chi-square test for independence** is a statistical procedure used to determine whether frequencies observed at the combination of levels of two categorical variables are similar to frequencies expected. If two factors are independent, the decision will be to retain the null hypothesis; if two factors are related, the decision will be to reject the null hypothesis.

LO 6 Identify and describe the following effect size measures: Cohen's *d*, eta squared, the coefficient of determination, and Cramer's *V*.

- **Effect size** is a statistical measure of the size of an observed effect in a population, which allows researchers to describe how far scores shifted in a population, or the percent of variance in a dependent variable that can be explained by the levels of a factor.
- **Cohen's *d*** is a measure of effect size in terms of the number of standard deviations that mean scores shift above or below a population mean. The larger the value of *d*, the larger the effect in the population. Cohen's *d* is an effect size measure used with the one-sample, two-independent-sample, and related-samples *t* tests.
- When ANOVA is used to analyze data, **eta squared** (η^2) is used to estimate effect size as the proportion of variance in a dependent variable that can be explained or accounted for by the levels of a factor. When a correlation or regression is used to analyze data, the **coefficient of determination** (R^2) is used to estimate effect size. The coefficient of determination is mathematically equivalent to eta squared.
- **Cramer's *V*** is used to estimate effect size when data are analyzed using the chi-square test for independence and is interpreted the same as the coefficient of determination.

LO 7 Distinguish between a point estimate and an interval estimate and explain how estimation relates to the significance and effect size of an outcome.

- To use **estimation**, we set limits for the possible values of a population parameter within which the parameter is likely to be contained. Two types of estimates are a **point estimate** (a sample mean or mean difference) and an **interval estimate** (the range of possible values for a parameter stated with a given level of confidence).
- An effect would be significant if the value stated in a null hypothesis were outside the limits of a confidence interval; an effect would not be significant if the value were contained within the limits of a confidence interval.
- The effect size for a confidence interval is stated as a range or interval, in which the lower effect size estimate is the difference between the value stated in a null hypothesis and the lower confidence limit; the upper effect size estimate is the difference between the value stated in a null hypothesis and the upper confidence limit. Effect size can then be interpreted in terms of a shift in the population when the value of the null hypothesis is outside a specified confidence interval.

LO 8 Distinguish between the precision and the certainty of an interval estimate.

- The precision of an estimate is determined by the range of the confidence interval. The certainty of an estimate is determined by the level of confidence. To be more certain that an interval contains a population parameter, we typically give up precision.

LO 9 Compute a chi-square goodness-of-fit test and a chi-square test for independence using SPSS.

- SPSS can be used to compute the chi-square goodness-of-fit test using the **Analyze**, **Nonparametric Tests**, and **Chi-square** options in the menu bar. These actions will display a dialog box that allows you to identify the groups and run the test. A **Weight Cases** option must also be selected from the menu bar (for more details, see Section 14.5).
- SPSS can be used to compute the chi-square test for independence using the **Analyze**, **Descriptive Statistics**, and **Crosstabs** options in the menu bar. These actions will display a dialog box that allows you to identify the groups and run the analysis. A **Weight Cases** option must also be selected from the menu bar (for more details, see Section 14.5).

KEY TERMS

inferential statistics	Type I error	effect size conventions
null hypothesis	power	proportion of variance
unbiased estimator	parametric tests	eta squared
central limit theorem	nonparametric tests	coefficient of determination
level of significance	chi-square goodness-of-fit test	Cramer's V
significance level		estimation
test statistic	chi-square test for independence	point estimate
p value	effect	interval estimate
significance	effect size	confidence interval
statistical significance	Cohen's d	level of confidence
Type II error	Cohen's conventions	confidence limits

REVIEW QUESTIONS

1. State whether each of the following describes the use of null hypothesis significance testing (NHST), effect size, or confidence intervals.

    A. The range of values within which a parameter is likely to be contained

    B. An analysis used to determine whether or not an effect exits in the population

    C. The mean shift of scores in the population

2. Which decision, to reject a null hypothesis or retain a null hypothesis, is associated with a finding that an outcome *reached significance*?

3. A study showed that children who snack between meals consumed significantly fewer calories in each meal. If $p = .02$, is this conclusion appropriate for NHST at a .05 level of significance? Explain.

4. The type of error associated with a decision to reject the null hypothesis is _____; the type of error associated with a decision to retain the null hypothesis is _____.

5. State three assumptions or criteria that must be met to conduct a parametric test of significance.

6. Which nonparametric test for ordinal data is an alternative to the related-samples t test?

7. A local brewery brews 40% Half Pint, 40% XXX, and 20% Dark Night premium lagers. To determine if production fits well with actual preferences for the lagers, a sample of adult consumers of legal drinking age were asked to choose their favorite lager, and the proportion of those choosing each lager was compared with brewing proportions. Which chi-square test is appropriate to analyze significance in this study?

8. A psychologist reports the following results for a related-samples t test: The results showed that married couples report similar ratings of marital satisfaction, $t(5) = 1.581$, $p = .175$.

   A. What are the degrees of freedom for this test?

   B. How many participants were observed in this study?

   C. Did the test statistic reach significance? Explain.

9. A researcher finds that the religious affiliation of a parent is related to the religious affiliation of the parent's child, $\chi^2(9) = 16.96$, $p = .049$.

   A. What are the degrees of freedom for this test?

   B. Is this test a chi-square goodness-of-fit test or a chi-square test for independence?

   C. Did the test statistic reach significance? Explain.

10. A researcher reports that studying increases student confidence ($d = .45$). Using Cohen's conventions, describe the size of this effect as being small, medium, or large.

11. True or false: Eta squared and the coefficient of determination are mathematically equivalent.

12. Two professors teach the same class. The mean grade in Professor G's class is 80% (95% CI 72% to 88%); the mean grade in Professor P's class is 76% (95% CI 68% to 84%). In which class is the confidence interval more precise? In which class is the confidence interval more certain?

13. What is the decision for a hypothesis test (significant or not significant) if the value stated in a null hypothesis would have been each of the following?

   A. Inside a stated confidence interval

   B. Outside a stated confidence interval

1. Suppose you hypothesize that people who think they are intoxicated will show signs of intoxication, even if they did not consume alcohol.

   A. Choose a research design to test your hypothesis.

   B. Create a hypothetical set of data that would be observed if it showed support for your hypothesis and use SPSS to analyze the data using an appropriate test statistic.

   C. Describe the results of your statistical analysis and include one estimate of effect size in your description.

2. State your own hypothesis in any area of research of interest to you and follow Items A, B, and C from Activity Question 1. Make sure you state a hypothesis that can be tested using one of the many test statistics described in this chapter and throughout this book.

Identify a problem

- Determine an area of interest.
- Review the literature.
- Identify new ideas in your area of interest.
- Develop a research hypothesis.

Develop a research plan

- Define the variables being tested.
- Identify participants or subjects and determine how to sample them.
- Select a research strategy and design.
- Evaluate ethics and obtain institutional approval to conduct research.

Generate more new ideas

- Results support your hypothesis—refine or expand on your ideas.
- Results do not support your hypothesis—reformulate a new idea or start over.

After reading this chapter, you should be able to:

1 Identify three methods of communication among scientists.

2 Describe three elements of communication.

3 Apply APA writing style and language guidelines for writing a manuscript.

4 Apply APA formatting requirements for writing a manuscript.

5 Apply APA guidelines for writing and organizing a literature review article.

6 Delineate how results are reported for a qualitative versus a quantitative research design.

7 State APA guidelines for identifying the authorship of published scientific work.

8 Identify guidelines for effectively presenting a poster.

9 Identify guidelines for effectively giving a professional talk.

Conduct the study

- Execute the research plan and measure or record the data.

Communicate the results

- Method of communication: oral, written, or in a poster.
- Style of communication: APA guidelines are provided to help prepare style and format.

Analyze and evaluate the data

- Analyze and evaluate the data as they relate to the research hypothesis.
- Summarize data and research results.

COMMUNICATING RESEARCH: PREPARING MANUSCRIPTS, POSTERS, AND TALKS

Communicating what was found in a research study is just as important as the finding itself. Albert Einstein said, "If you can't explain it simply, you don't understand it well enough." Being able to communicate what you found, then, is important inasmuch as it not only allows others to understand what you found but also makes clear to others that you understand the finding as well. In this way, your ability to effectively communicate in science can reflect your fundamental credibility as an author.

As a student, you can appreciate fully the value of communicating ideas. In the classroom, you often categorize professors as being good or bad teachers based on how well they could explain or make sense of the material being taught in class. Professors who made sense of difficult material in class often receive higher ratings than professors who are obviously knowledgeable but unable to effectively communicate that knowledge in the classroom. In a similar way, a scientist has the responsibility to make sense of the findings or ideas discovered in a research study. After all, it is of little value to be unable to communicate new knowledge to others. In fact, Einstein himself believed that "any fool can know. The point is to understand." Communicating research findings, then, can be as important as the discovery itself.

In this chapter, we will introduce the methods of communication in research: manuscripts, posters, and talks. Throughout this chapter, we focus largely on how to effectively communicate ideas using each method and we provide tips and strategies to help you in your own work. Following the guidelines described in this chapter can give you the tools you need to effectively appeal your ideas to a diverse audience and allow you to present yourself as an authoritative, credible, and engaging communicator.

15.1 Elements of Communication

Oral and written reports can exist for long periods of time and contribute to a large body of knowledge in the behavioral sciences. Scientific research is a collaborative effort in which groups of researchers from different universities and institutions across the globe converge to describe their research and interpretations on a topic. Common methods of communication for researchers include publishing their work in a peer-reviewed journal and participating in some of the many conferences held each year all over the world, in which researchers gather to report their most current findings in a poster or introduce their new ideas in a talk. When a manuscript is published in a peer-reviewed journal, it is integrated into the accepted scientific body of knowledge and made available for criticism and review by other scientists who accept or reject the ideas presented in that publication. Likewise, a poster or talk can open the lines of communication between scientists in a way that allows them to share ideas to facilitate a more grounded understanding of a topic in the behavioral sciences.

Writing a manuscript for publication, presenting a poster, and preparing a talk are three key methods of communication among scientists. In this chapter, we introduce the American Psychological Association (APA, 2009) style for formatting and writing manuscripts, and we provide tips and strategies for presenting a poster and giving a talk. First, we introduce three basic elements of communication: the speaker (or author), the audience, and the message. Each element of communication is also summarized in Table 15.1 at the end of this section.

> Three methods of communication are to publish a manuscript, present a poster, and prepare a talk.

The Speaker or Author

As a speaker or author, you are responsible for mediating a communication. How you communicate will be important in how your message is received by an audience. For a manuscript, it is important to communicate using the following APA guidelines:

1. Use first person and third person appropriately. In APA style, use the first person to discuss research steps rather than anthropomorphizing the work. For example, a study cannot "manipulate" or "hypothesize"; you and your coauthors, however, can (e.g., "We manipulated the levels of the variable..." or "We hypothesized that changes would occur..."). Also use first-person singular (i.e., "I") if you are a sole author; use first-person plural (i.e., "we") when referring to work you completed with many authors. Use the third person, however, to foreground the research. For example, state, "The results indicate..." and *not* "We found evidence..." to report the findings of a study—the study, not the authors, elicits data. The most important suggestion is to be clear and avoid confusion in your writing. For example, "We are facing an obesity epidemic..." may leave the reader wondering whether *we* refers to the authors of the article, to community members, or to some other group. In these cases, *we* can still be an appropriate referent with a simple rewrite (e.g., "As Americans, *we* are facing

an obesity epidemic…"), or the third person can be used (e.g., "Americans are facing an obesity epidemic…").

2. Use past, present, and future tense appropriately. To describe previous research, use past tense. For example, state, "The data showed that…" or "Previous work demonstrated that…" to describe published or completed work. Also use past tense to describe your results for completed work, such as "Scores increased from Time 1 to Time 2" or "The data were significant." In the discussion, you can use present tense to describe current work, such as "To address these concerns, we are conducting several follow-up studies." Use future tense to describe events or work that will occur or be completed at a later time.

3. Use an impersonal writing style. A research manuscript is not a novel, so avoid the use of literary devices beyond what is necessary. For example, avoid using colloquial devices such as "over the top" (in place of "exaggerated") and avoid jargon such as "techy" (in place of "technologically savvy"). Also, use language appropriately. For example, to give a reason for an event or method use "because" and not "since" (e.g., "male participants were excluded *because*…") because "since" indicates the passage of time (e.g., "These studies have not been replicated *since* before 2000"). As another example, to describe something that does not refer to a location, use "in which" and not "where" (e.g., "participants completed a survey *in which* all items pertained to…") because "where" indicates a location (e.g., "Participants were situated at the back of a room, *where* a series of items were located").

4. Reduce biased language. The author can use unbiased language in two ways. First, follow APA guidelines for using unbiased language, as discussed in greater detail in Section 15.2, with examples given in Table 15.2. For example, people with a disorder should be characterized as a person and not by their disorder. To avoid bias, we state "Participants with depression" instead of "Depressed participants," for example. Second, do not use language in a manuscript that would be offensive to others, particularly our colleagues and fellow researchers. For example, to describe the limitations in another study, state, "Gender *was not included* as a factor" instead of "Previous researchers *completely ignored* gender as a factor in their study."

5. Give credit where appropriate. The APA provides specific guidelines for citing sources that are published in the *Publication Manual of the American Psychological Association* (APA, 2009). Anytime you cite work that is not your own, make sure you give proper credit to the author of that work using these APA guidelines. Further details for properly citing sources are given in Section 15.3 in this chapter and also in Appendix A.

6. The perspective of writing using APA style is that the author reports about findings in a research study; the author does not tell about his or her research. In other words, it is the research itself, and not the researcher, that is the focus of the

report. The goal of communication is to persuade others based upon the methods and findings in a research report, and not by catchy literary devices or the actions of the researcher. While this goal also applies to poster presentations and talks, we do make one exception: It is preferred that the speaker uses primarily first person in these forums because posters and talks are interactive. The speaker communicates in real time to other researchers, so using first person more often can be more natural in these settings. Otherwise, the remaining guidelines should be followed to present a poster or give a talk.

The Audience

The audience is any individual or group with whom you intend to communicate. Although scientific data may often be completed at a level that is difficult to understand, it is often the case that the audience is more diverse than many authors recognize. For any scientific work, the authors should consider the following audiences who are likely to read their report:

1. Scientists and professionals. Scientists are those who work in university or laboratory settings. Professionals are those who work in industry or hospitals. These groups are interested in the methods and procedures of your work, as well as your ideas and interpretations of the outcomes. Scientists and professionals are educated in your field or general discipline. They can also often be among the most critical audiences to evaluate the contributions of your research and ideas because they are often in the best position, in terms of funding and resources, to challenge your results and interpretations and to produce their own research to demonstrate the validity of their challenges. Because these groups tend to be the most critical of a research study, most authors tend to write or speak mostly to these groups.

2. College students. It is likely that more students read scientific reports and attend poster sessions and talks each year than those with terminal and professional degrees. Doctoral graduate students, for example, must complete a dissertation and spend many years and endless hours integrating a body of research to develop a research idea and conduct a study worthy of earning a doctoral degree. Undergraduate students often review articles in published works as part of class assignments or attend conferences to gain experience needed for acceptance to graduate programs. College students are likely to be your largest audience and yet they have less background or understanding of the topic being communicated than scientists and professionals. Providing sufficient background of the research topic and defining or operationalizing key factors in a research study can facilitate an understanding of your work among this group.

3. The general public (laypersons). Many persons in the general public can find and read your work. For example, when parents learn that a member of their family has a behavioral disorder, they can use problem-focused coping strategies to learn

more about what is known of a disorder and the potential treatment options for that disorder. In these cases, it is useful to make an effort to communicate data effectively such that this general nonscientific audience can also understand the gist or importance of the findings of a given report.

The audiences with which we share our ideas and works are often larger than we recognize. Consider also that there is a growing popularity in the publication of open-access articles, such as those in open-access peer-reviewed journals published by BioMed Central and Scientific Research Publishing. Open-access articles are peer-reviewed works that are freely available to scientists, professionals, students, and the general public. The direction of publication, then, is to expand the size of an audience by enhancing how accessible research is, which makes it more pertinent than ever for the author or speaker to effectively communicate to this broader audience.

The Message

The author or speaker communicates the message, which is any information regarding the design, analyses, interpretations, and new ideas contributed by a completed research project or literature review. The message is important inasmuch as an audience understands it. To effectively communicate a message, we should consider the following guidelines:

1. The message should be novel. A novel idea is one that is original or new. You must be able to explain and demonstrate in your work how your ideas add to or build upon the scientific literature. If you can demonstrate what we learn from your ideas, then your ideas are novel.

2. The message should be interesting. An interesting idea can potentially benefit society, test a prediction, or develop areas of research in which little is known. Peer-reviewed journals have a readership, and your idea must appeal to those who read that journal if you are to publish your ideas.

3. The message should be informative. An informative message is one that provides a thorough description of a work. For example, the literature should be fully reviewed, the details of research procedures should be fully described, and all data measured in a study should be fully reported. Hence, do not omit information that would be otherwise informative to an audience to determine the extent to which a work is novel and interesting.

For a speaker or author to effectively communicate a message to an audience, it is important to consider the three elements of communication described in this section. The implication of each element suggests that delivering an appropriate, novel, interesting, and informative message to a broad audience will significantly enhance the effectiveness of the communication of a work. Table 15.1 summarizes each element of communication described in this section.

Table 15.1 Three Elements of Communication

Elements of Communication	General Characteristics
The speaker or author	Use appropriate verb tense. Use an impersonal writing style. Reduce biased language. Give credit where appropriate.
The audience	Scientists and professionals. College students. The general public (laypeople).
The message	The message should be novel. The message should be interesting. The message should be informative.

LEARNING CHECK 1 ✓

1. State three methods of communication.

2. State three elements in communication.

3. True or false: Delivering an appropriate, novel, interesting, and informative message to a broad audience will significantly enhance the effectiveness of the communication of a work.

Answers: 1. Publish a manuscript, present a poster, or prepare a talk; 2. The speaker or author, the audience, and the message; 3. True.

15.2 Writing a Manuscript: Writing Style and Language

The most critical method of communication is to publish a work in a peer-reviewed journal, which is any publication that is subjected to a peer review. A **peer review** is a procedure used by scientific journals in which a manuscript or work is sent to peers or experts in that area to review the work and determine its scientific value or worth regarding publication. Only upon acceptance from these peer reviewers will a work be published in a peer-reviewed journal. The peer review process is demanding because of the high rejection rates

Peer review is a procedure used by the editors of scientific journals in which a manuscript or work is sent to peers or experts in that area to review the work and determine its scientific value or worth regarding publication.

of works submitted to a journal for consideration for publication. Many of these journals reject from 75% to 85% or more of the manuscripts they receive each year. For this reason, publishing a work in a peer-reviewed journal is regarded as a high achievement in the scientific community.

An **APA-style manuscript** is a document that is created using the writing style format detailed in the *Publication Manual of the American Psychological Association*, typically for the purposes of having the work considered for publication in a peer-reviewed journal.

To submit a work for consideration for publication in a peer-reviewed journal, we prepare a document called an **APA-style manuscript.** An APA-style manuscript is a document that is created using the formatting style detailed in the *Publication Manual of the American Psychological Association* (APA, 2009), abbreviated as the *Publication Manual.* APA style is required by over 1,000 research journals worldwide and across disciplines. The *Publication Manual* provides guidelines for writing an APA-style manuscript and should always be referred to when writing a manuscript using this writing style.

Accuracy in a scientific report is important because it reflects the credibility of the author.

In this section, and in Sections 15.3 and 15.4, we will introduce the writing style described in the *Publication Manual.* This chapter is meant to be an overview of writing using APA style. For a more exhaustive description of this writing style, please refer to the *Publication Manual.* In this section, we introduce four general writing guidelines: Be accurate; be comprehensive, yet concise; be conservative; and be appropriate.

Be Accurate

When writing an APA-style manuscript, or any type of paper for that matter, the sources you cite, the interpretations you provide, the data you report, and the grammar and writing you present must be accurate. Accuracy in a manuscript is important because it reflects the credibility of the author. Writing a manuscript with even just one error can damage the credibility of the author and, depending on how serious the mistake, can lead the audience to question the accuracy of other aspects of the report, even when the other parts of the work are accurate. Keep in mind that to be able to persuade others of the value of a work, the researcher must have credibility with the audience. Losing credibility due to mistakes is often avoidable and is seen as the result of sloppy writing and poor revision. To avoid this problem, we can apply a common method: proofread a paper or manuscript, put it down for a day or two, proofread it again, then let a friend or colleague proofread it before making final changes. This method can be used to eliminate many errors that may have been otherwise overlooked or ignored.

Be Comprehensive, Yet Concise

Being comprehensive means that you include enough information in your report that the reader is able to critically evaluate its contribution to the scientific literature. For a primary research study, for example, this means that the author fully discloses the procedures used and clearly identifies the hypotheses tested and why it was important to test those hypotheses. Being concise means that the author fully discloses his or her study in as few words as possible. It means that the author only makes arguments that are needed to support his or her hypotheses, and the author describes only as many details about the procedures and data so as to allow another author to replicate his or her design. Being comprehensive, yet concise, is important because it makes the manuscript easier to follow—it provides a full report, while also focusing only on information needed to make arguments and report the procedures and data. The following are four common strategies used to be comprehensive, yet concise, using APA style:

- Abbreviate where appropriate. Any terms that can be abbreviated or have a common abbreviation should be abbreviated after their first use. For example, to describe participants who exhibit high dietary restraint, we spell out *high dietary restraint* on first use with an abbreviation given in parentheses, and all subsequent references to the term can be abbreviated as HDR. For example, on first use we state, "Only participants exhibiting high dietary restraint (HDR) were..." On subsequent uses we only use the abbreviation HDR. Other common abbreviations include seconds (s), grams (g), compare (cf.), and post meridiem (p.m.), which are used to make the writing more concise.

- Display data in a figure or table. A figure or table can be particularly helpful when large data sets are reported. For example, to describe participant characteristics, we can report them in the text or in a table. The more characteristics to report, the more concise (and clear) it will be to summarize these characteristics in a table and not in the text. Likewise, any data analyses that are relevant to the hypotheses being tested should be described in a table or figure. In the text, you would only refer the reader to that figure or table. For example, you can state, "The groups all showed a significant increase in responding, as shown in Figure 1." The data for this result would then be given in the figure and not in the text.

- Avoid using unnecessary words and avoid using the passive voice: Write efficiently. At a macro-level, read through your paper and if you can remove a word, phrase, or sentence without losing the meaning of your content, then delete it. At a micro-level, preferentially use an active voice within each sentence because the passive voice often tends to be unnecessary or too wordy. For example, to describe your results in the passive voice, you could write, "Significance *was shown* in the analysis." However, the active voice is less wordy; it is thus more concise. We could revise this sentence to state, "The analysis *showed* significance." Here, we reduce a six-word sentence to a four-word sentence.

- Keep the writing focused. In other words, introduce only those ideas and research needed to persuade the reader of the value of your work or research hypotheses. For example, you may hypothesize that integrating technology in the classroom will improve student grades. In your literature review, then, you should review what we know about classrooms that integrate technology, student learning outcomes related to the use of technology, and how that literature relates to the hypotheses you are testing. You should not introduce any ideas or research other than that directly related to your hypothesis. Likewise, you should only display data in a figure or table that are directly related to your hypothesis and otherwise briefly summarize data that are not directly related to your hypothesis. Focused writing makes it easier for the reader to evaluate the value of your work.

- Do not repeat information. When you read over your own work, ask yourself: Does this sentence add information? If not, then delete it. When you introduce more than one study in a single report, ask yourself: Are the procedures in this study different from those I already introduced? If not, then do not introduce the procedures again; instead, refer the reader to where the procedures were originally introduced. For example, suppose you conduct two experiments using the same research design. In Experiment 1, introduce the full research design; for the second experiment, state, "same as those described for Experiment 1" for all procedures that repeat those already introduced. We avoid repetition in writing to make the writing style more concise. Being comprehensive, yet concise, is important because the space or the number of pages available in printed peer-reviewed journals is limited. To be published in peer-reviewed journals, then, many journal editors require that a manuscript fully describe a study that was conducted while also taking up as few printed pages as possible.

> Clearly state all essential information in as few words as possible.

Be Conservative

As part of any scientific writing style, it is important to be conservative in your claims and interpretations. In other words, do not generalize beyond the data or overstate your conclusions. For example, suppose we observe that women were significantly more willing to offer to help a bystander than men. An appropriately conservative conclusion is that women were more helpful in the experimental situation in our study. That is all we observed: helping behavior. We should not generalize beyond these specific observations. In other words, a statement like "Women were nicer than men" is inappropriate. We did not measure *niceness*; we measured *helping*. We can speculate about whether our observations indicate that women are nicer than men, but we must make it clear that this is just a speculation and that more research is required. As a general rule, do not make claims about anything that you did not directly measure or observe, or that others have not directly measured or observed. Be cautious in your writing. The strengths of your study will be in what you observed, so it is your observations, and not your speculations, that should be the focus of your interpretations in a manuscript.

> Do not generalize your claims or interpretations beyond the data; do not overstate your conclusions.

Be Appropriate

The *Publication Manual* provides detailed guidelines for using appropriate and unbiased language. Some of the guidelines in the *Publication Manual* are given in Table 15.2. The importance of using appropriate and unbiased language is to ensure that you do not offend those who read your work or those who are the subject of your work. For example, in the sixth row of Table 15.2, we find that it is biased to refer to individuals or groups by their disorder. Hence, it is biased to write "A sample of autistic patients were studied" because we are identifying the group by its disorder. Instead, we should write "A sample of patients with autism were studied." It may seem like a subtle change, but in the first sentence, we identified the group as being defined by its disorder, which could be viewed as offensive. In the revised sentence, we identified autism as one characteristic of this group, which is more appropriate and less biased.

Table 15.2 Examples for Using Unbiased Language

Do Not Use:	Instead Use:
"homosexuals"	"gay men and lesbians"
"sexual preference"	"sexual orientation"
"men" (referring to all adults)	"men and women"
"black" or "white" (referring to social groups)	"Black" or "White" (capitalized)
ethnic labels (e.g., "Oriental")	geographical labels (e.g., "Asian" or "Asian American")
"victims" or "disordered" (to characterize people)	"people with _____" (e.g., "People with autism")
"case"	"patient"
"sex" (referring to a culture or social role)	"gender"
"gender" (referring to biology)	"sex"
"subjects" (referring to humans)	"participants"
"participants" (referring to animals)	"subjects"

Adapted from the Publication Manual (APA, 2009).

LEARNING CHECK 2 ✓

1. What is a peer review?

2. Why is it important to be accurate?

3. State four common strategies used to be comprehensive yet concise using APA style.

4. A researcher measured grades on an exam in two classes and concluded that students in Class 2 scored higher and so must have enjoyed the class more. Is this a conservative conclusion? Explain.

5. Why is it important to use appropriate and unbiased language?

Answers: 1. A peer review is a procedure used by the editors of scientific journals in which a manuscript or work is sent to peers or experts in that area to review the work and determine its scientific value or worth regarding publication; 2. Because it reflects the credibility of the author; 3. Abbreviate where appropriate, display data in a figure or table, keep the writing focused, and do not repeat information; 4. No, because the researcher measured exam grades and did not measure enjoyment; 5. To ensure that you do not offend those who read your work or those who are the subject of your work.

15.3 Elements of an APA-Style Manuscript

Using APA style is as much an editorial style as it is a writing style. The elements of an APA-style manuscript are structured so that the manuscript can be readily typeset and converted to a published document. Having a formatting style that is readily converted to a published document is convenient for editors who, upon acceptance following a peer review, will publish the manuscript in their journal. An APA-style manuscript is organized into the following major sections, each of which is described in this section:

- **Title page.** The title page is always the first page and includes a running head, the title, a list of the author or authors, affiliations, and an author note with the contact information of the primary (contact) author.

- **Abstract.** The abstract is always the second page and provides a brief written summary of the purpose, methods, and results of a work or published document in 150 to 250 words.

- **Main body.** The main body begins on page 3 of a manuscript. The main body is divided into subsections and most often includes the following main subheadings: (1) an introduction section that includes a literature review and identification of research hypotheses; (2) a method section that describes the participants, surveys and materials, procedures, and analyses; (3) a results section that fully discloses the data measured and statistical outcomes observed; and (4) a discussion section that provides an evaluation of the design, the data, and the hypotheses.

- **References.** The references page always follows the main body on a new page. All sources cited in the manuscript are listed in alphabetical order in APA format in this section.

- **Footnotes** (if any). Footnotes are used to provide additional content (such as clarification about a procedure or outcome) or acknowledge copyright permissions. Many manuscripts are written without needing a footnotes section; however, if this section is included in the manuscript, then it should immediately follow the references section.

- **Tables** (if any). Tables can be included, often to summarize participant data or data analyses. Each table is given on a separate page after the references section (or after the footnotes section if included). Table captions are included above or below each table on each page.

- **Figures** (if any). Figures can be included, often to summarize data analyses or illustrate a research procedure. Each figure is given on a separate page following the tables. Figure captions are included above or below each figure on each page.

- **Appendices** (if any). In some cases there may be supplemental materials, such as surveys, illustrations, or instructions for using complex equipment. Many manuscripts are written without needing an appendix; however, if this section is included, then it should be at the end of the manuscript.

Next we will review the sections that are most often included in a manuscript: the title page, abstract, main body (introduction, methods and results, and discussion), and references. As an illustration for each section of an APA manuscript, we will use a manuscript that was completed by an undergraduate student at St. Bonaventure University under the advisement of the first author. This manuscript has since been accepted for publication in a peer-reviewed journal (Privitera & Creary, 2013), and a follow-up to this study was subsequently published (Privitera & Zuraikat, 2014). For more detailed APA guidelines including creating margins, page numbers, and running heads, refer to Appendix A, which gives an APA writing guide (A.1), an APA guide to grammar, punctuation, and spelling (A.2), and a full sample APA-style manuscript from a study that was published in a peer-reviewed scientific journal (A.3).

Title Page

The title page allows an editor to identify the individuals and affiliations of those who have significantly contributed to the work being described in the manuscript. This page is often the only page in which authors identify themselves, which can allow editors at many journals to send out a manuscript for an anonymous peer review by omitting the title page before sending the rest of the manuscript to reviewers. All required parts of a title page are illustrated in Figure 15.1.

The title page is the first page of a manuscript and includes the title, authors, affiliations, and author note.

The title page includes a running head in all capital letters that is a maximum of 50 characters, and the first page number is aligned to the right. All subsequent pages will also have a running head, but the words "Running Head" will be omitted. In addition to a running head, we include the title, author or authors, affiliations, and author note, which are centered on the title page. The title should be no more than 12 words, although it can exceed this total if needed to convey important information to the potential reader. The author note should include the contact information for only one author who is deemed the contact author, or the author with whom the editor (and readers of the research, if it is published) will correspond regarding the manuscript.

Abstract

The abstract, shown in Figure 15.2, is the second page and provides a brief written summary of the purpose, methods, and results of a work or published document in 150 to 250 words. The words "Running Head" are removed from the header on this page and all other pages of the manuscript. The structure of an abstract can differ depending on the type of study being described. For APA manuscripts that describe primary research (i.e., the conduct of an experiment or research study), the following components should be described in an abstract:

- An opening sentence of the hypothesis or research problem being tested.

- A description of participants (e.g., number, sex, or age) if pertinent to outcomes. For animal research, the genus and species can be given.

Running Head: PROXIMITY, VISIBILITY, AND INTAKE   1

Proximity and Visibility of Fruits and Vegetables Influences Intake in a Kitchen Setting

Faris M. Zuraikat and Heather E. Creary

Saint Bonaventure University

Author Note

Correspondence regarding this article should be addressed to Gregory J. Privitera, Department of Psychology, Saint Bonaventure University, 3261 West State Street, St. Bonaventure, New York, 14778. E-mail: gprivite@sbu.edu

The running head is in capital letters and appears left in the header. It is a maximum of 50 characters.

Author Note is centered, and each paragraph where it is cited.

Manuscript pages are numbered at the top right of every page.

The title, author or authors, and affiliations are centered. The title is a maximum of 12 words if possible. Use "and," not the ampersand symbol (&), before the last author.

- The essential structure or procedures of the research design used.
- The basic findings, which can include p values, confidence intervals, or effect sizes.
- A one- or two-sentence conclusion indicating the implications or applications of the research outcomes.

An abstract can be the most important paragraph in your manuscript because many potential readers, if not interested in your research after reading the abstract, will not be likely to read on. For this reason, make sure you use keywords in your abstract that will appeal to potential readers and words you anticipate that potential readers would use as keywords in online searches. Following these suggestions can help get your work noticed by potential readers.

An abstract is a brief summary of the purpose, methods, and results of a work in 150 to 250 words.

Introduction

The introduction begins on page 3 with the title restated on the first line. On the second line, indent the first paragraph and begin the introduction. An introduction must clearly communicate what makes your ideas novel and interesting in about two to three pages. Your ideas should be novel inasmuch as they build on previous research. Your ideas should be interesting inasmuch as they appeal to the readership of the journal to which you submit your work. The structure of an introduction should use the following organization:

Figure 15.2 An APA-Style Abstract

"Abstract" is centered on the top line. The paragraph below it is not indented.

The body of the abstract describes the hypotheses, participants, research design, basic findings, and implications in 150 to 250 words.

Italicize and center a list of 4 to 5 keywords.

Abstract

The hypothesis that participants will eat more fruits (apples) and vegetables (carrots) if they are made more proximate and visible was tested using a 2 × 2 between-subjects design. Proximity was manipulated by placing fruits and vegetables in a bowl at a table where participants sat (near) or 2 m from the table (far). Visibility was manipulated by placing fruits and vegetables in an opaque bowl that was covered (not visible) or in a clear bowl that was open (visible). The results showed that placing apples and carrots in closer proximity to participants increased intake of these healthy foods. Making these foods more visible increased intake of apples, but not carrots, possibly because fruits taste sweet and so may be more visually appealing. Regardless, these data are the first to demonstrate experimentally that the proximity and visibility of healthy foods can influence intake of these foods.

Keywords: proximity, visibility, fruits, vegetables, for convenience

- Introduce the problem and explain why it is important to conduct new research to address the problem. For example:
  - "The impact of environmental factors on food intake and consumption volume is of particular interest to researchers because such factors can lead to overeating and potential risks of obesity." In this first sentence of the introduction illustrated in Figure 15.3, we identified the problem (the impact of environmental factors on food intake) and why it is important to conduct research to address this problem (because environmental factors can lead to overeating and potential risks of obesity).

- Integrate previous research that is relevant to the research you are conducting to address the problem. You must thoroughly review the literature and include any and all research that could impact the validity of your claims and the value of your research. Providing appropriate credit is the responsibility of each author and contributes to the growth of scientific understanding across studies and disciplines. Also keep in mind the following suggestions:

Figure 15.3 Excerpt From an APA-Style Introduction

The introduction begins on page 3 with the running head.

The title is centered on page 1.

The introduction begins on page 2 and is indented.

Use an ampersand (&) to give a reference in parentheses; use the word "and" when a reference is given in the text.

Proximity and Visibility of Fruits and Vegetables Influences Intake in a Kitchen Setting

The impact of environmental factors on food intake and consumption volume is of particular interest to researchers because such factors can lead to overeating and potential risks of obesity (Swinburn, Sacks, McPherson, Finegood, Moodie, & Gortmaker, 2011). Environmental factors that influence consumption volume include the portion sizes of foods in a meal (Wansink & Kim, 2005; Krim, Roe, & Rolls, 2004), mere exposure to foods (Pliner, 1982; Birch & Marlin, 1982), sensory characteristics of foods (Bell, Roe & Rolls, 2003; Kral, 2006), reward and punishment (Hendy, 1999; Batsell & Brown, 2002), cognition (Capaldi, Owens, & Privitera, 2006), social context (Birch, Zimmerman, & Hind, 1980), time of day (Rozin & Tuorila, 1993), and other factors related to family, society, culture, and media influences (see Privitera, 2008). Two factors that can cova...

food from an individ...

example, foods serve...

is more proximate a...

In an early inve...

intake, Terry and Be...

obese families, but i...

Herman Hackett, an...

and consumed less w...

participants being

The results in these previous studies raise an important question for dieters and health professionals alike: Does the proximity and visibility of fruits and vegetables also influence intake of healthier foods? Fruits and vegetables do not require preparation to eat and are often not wrapped, meaning that we should find that proximate and visible fruits and vegetables are consumed more. An early study using survey data suggests that the more proximate and visible parents make fruits and vegetables, the more elementary school children will eat them (Hearn, Baranowski, Baranowski, Doyle, Smith, Lin, & Resnicow, 1998). To date, these findings have not been supported using an experimental research design, and of the studies using experimental designs to test food. In the present study, we adapted the experimental design used by Wansink et al. (2006) to determine whether the proximity and visibility of apples (fruit) and carrots (vegetable) in a kitchen setting influences intake of these healthier foods using a between-subjects design. A between-subjects design was used to minimize demand characteristics caused by changing the location of the experimental foods.

The beginning of the introduction on page 3 and the last paragraph of the introduction on page 5 are shown in the figure.

- o Do not review the history of your topic; review only those articles that directly impact your claims and research. Do not describe details of those works that are not pertinent to your work.
- o Cite all sources appropriately. In the text, use "and" to separate the last author; in parentheses, use the ampersand symbol (&).
- o Although you must be concise in your writing, make sure that your writing can be clearly understood by the audience to which you are writing.

- State the hypotheses being tested and the research design being used to address the problem. State how you plan to address the problem in a way that will build upon (not repeat) the literature. For example:

  - o "To date… of the studies using experimental designs to test proximity and visibility, all have used junk food or candies as the test food. In the present study, we adapted the experimental design… to determine whether the proximity and visibility of apples (fruit) and carrots (vegetable) in a kitchen setting influences intake of these healthier foods using a between-subjects design." In this sentence, in the last paragraph of the introduction for the manuscript illustrated in Figure 15.3, we identified the hypothesis tested (proximity and visibility of fruits and vegetables influence intake) and the research design used (between-subjects design). We also identified how we will build upon the literature (by using fruits and vegetables, and not junk foods, as test foods). Notice that by including information about our hypothesis, the rationale for the hypothesis being tested is also implied (to advance our understanding for how visibility and proximity influence intake of fruits and vegetables). If the rationale for a hypothesis is not clearly implied, you should state it directly.

In an introduction, state a problem, review pertinent literature, and state why the problem is important, and how it will be addressed.

Method and Results

The "Method" section immediately follows the introduction. As shown in Figure 15.4, we bold and center "Method" on the line below the last line of the introduction. On the next line we indent and begin the "Method" section. The "Method" section is divided with many subheadings. The major subheadings—"Participants," "Procedures," "Data Analyses," and "Results"—are described here and illustrated in Figure 15.4.

- The "Participants" subheading is flush left and bold, as shown in Figure 15.4. The "Participants" section should include full details of the participants, such as age, weight, and height. The specific characteristics of participants can be listed in a table or in the text. Also, state how participants in the sample compare to the target population of interest, which sampling method was used to select the participants, and how the total number of participants was determined.

- The "Procedures" subheading follows the "Participants" section and is flush left and bold, as shown in Figure 15.4. The "Procedures" section must describe how participants were treated with enough information so as to allow the reader to fully replicate the procedures. When portions of the procedures make the writing more concise and easier to follow if presented apart from the "Procedures"

influences intake of these healthier foods using a between-subjects design. A between-subjects design was used to minimize demand characteristics caused by changing the location of the experimental foods.

Method

The experiment was separated into two variations. In Variation 1, the location of a bowl of apples (fruit) was manipulated using one sample. In Variation 2, the location of a bowl of carrots (vegetable) was manipulated using a different sample. In all, a total of 96 participants ($n = 48$ per variation) were observed in this study. Otherwise, all procedures described here were identical in each variation.

Participants

A total of 96 participants (24 men, 72 women) were recruited through university classroom visits and sign-up sheets. In Variation 1, participant

ch

po

ch

ate within two hours of the study were excluded from data analyses. The university's Institutional Review Board approved the procedures for this study.

Setting and Stimuli

Kitchen setting. All experimental foods were consumed in a kitchen

se

Procedures

pa

an

All procedures were conducted in a laboratory setting between 2:00 p.m

an

the

lo

we

x

to

Data Analyses

bo

In each variation, a 2×2 between-subjects analysis of variance (ANOVA) was computed with proximity (near, far) and visibility (yes, no) as between-subject factors. Gender and BMI were added as factors to determine whether these factors influenced intakes. A Tukey's HSD was used as the post hoc test where appropriate. All tests were conducted at a .05 level of significance.

to

the

Results

tal

Variation 1 (apples). A Proximity × Visibility interaction was significant, $F(3, 44) = 4.75$, $p < .04$ ($R^2 = .10$). As shown in Figure 1, participants consumed the most apples when they were both convenient and visible (6.0 vs. 1.6, Tukey's HSD, $p < .001$). A main effect of proximity, $F(1, 44) = 25.46$, $p < .001$ ($R^2 = .37$), and a main effect of visibility, was significant, and showed that more apples were consumed when they were placed in closer proximity to the participant.

fo

pa

cl

pa

op

Left margin notes:

ter "Method" in d on the line below last line of the oduction (not on a arate page).

ce "Participants," h left and in d, on the line ow the last line he "Method" tion.

lude a ocedures" tion, flush left d in bold, on line below "Participants" tion. If portions be more arly presented er their own ding—e.g., escription of veys or, in this e, a setting d foods—then so before the ocedures" tion as shown.

d "Data alyses," flush left d in bold. This tion is optional ome journals required by er journals.

esults" is tered in bold. statistical tcomes are orted in this tion.

subheading, this is acceptable. If portions of the "Procedures" section are introduced separately, then give that portion its own subheading before the "Procedures" section, as shown in Figure 15.4 for describing a unique kitchen setting and food stimuli.

- The "Data Analyses" subheading follows the "Procedures" section and is flush left and bold, as shown in Figure 15.4. This section is not required using APA style; however, it is required by many journals that use APA-style formatting. If this section is required, then indicate the statistical tests and criterion used for each analysis that will be reported in the "Results" section that follows.

- The "Results" subheading follows the "Procedures" section and is centered and bold, as shown in Figure 15.4. Fully report all statistical outcomes in this section; however, make sure you place particular emphasis on the results that specifically address the research hypothesis being tested. Report the group means and standard deviations of measured outcomes and the test statistic, significance, effect size, and confidence intervals for statistical outcomes using APA style. Be thorough in the exposition of data, yet provide only enough detail in this section to help the reader understand how the outcomes reported relate to the hypotheses that were tested. Note that sample APA-style write-ups for statistical results have been provided throughout this book.

Discussion

The "Discussion" heading is centered and bolded on the line below the last line of the "Results" section, as shown in Figure 15.5. On the next line, indent the first paragraph and begin the discussion. In the discussion, you will evaluate and interpret the outcomes in your study. Do not use the discussion to restate points that were already made in the manuscript; instead, use the discussion to build upon or facilitate a stronger interpretation and understanding of the problem that was studied. The structure of a discussion should use the following organization:

- Clearly state whether the findings lend support or nonsupport for the hypothesis that was tested. Briefly explain where in the data the support or nonsupport was observed. For example:
  - In the last sentence of the first paragraph of the discussion in Figure 15.5, the authors state a clear message of support and nonsupport for their research hypothesis: "For vegetables, then, the hypothesis tested here was only partly supported in that no effect of visibility was observed."

- Give context for how your findings fit with previously published studies (studies that were likely first described in the introduction). For example:
  - In the second paragraph of the discussion in Figure 15.5, the authors give the following explanation for how their results could fit with previously published studies: "One likely explanation... is that apples may be more visually appealing than carrots because sweet-tasting foods are more visually appealing than bitter-tasting foods, and there is evidence to support such an explanation."

The "Method" section is divided into four main subheadings: "Participants," "Procedures" (can be further divided into subheadings), "Data Analyses" (may be optional), and "Results."

Figure 15.5   Excerpts From an APA-Style "Discussion" Section

that participants ate (1.4 vs. 0.3). Intakes did not significantly differ by gender or BMI across groups ($p > .65$ for all tests).

Discussion

The hypothesis that making fruits and vegetables more proximate and visible will increase intake of these foods was tested. For fruits, participants consumed more apples when they were made more proximate and visible, i.e., in an open clear bowl within arms reach of the participant. For vegetables, however, participants consumed more carrots only when they were made, pre proximate (within arms reach of the participant). For vegetables, then, the hypothesis tested here was only partly supported in that no effect of visibility was observed.

Center "Discussion" in bold on the line below the last line of the "Results" section.

Include a statement of support and nonsupport of the hypothesis tested.

PROXIMITY, VISIBILITY, AND INTAKE   10

Describe how findings relate to previously published studies.

Identify potential limitations.

Summarize and provide commentary on the importance of the research findings.

One likely explanation for the different results observed for apples and carrots is that apples may be more visually appealing than carrots because sweet-tasting foods are more visually appealing than bitter-tasting foods, and there is evidence to support such an explanation (see Capaldi & Privitera, 2008; Privitera, 2008). Also, participants knew the fruits or vegetables were fresh and good to eat because foods were served from fresh sealed packages in front of each participant. Whether the results would be different if fruits and vegetables were placed in a bowl before participants entered the room, or if the setting was different, such as in a workplace or office setting, cannot be determined here.

At present, these results extend survey findings with parents and children (Hearn et al., 1998) and experimental findings with adults (Painter et al., 2002; Wansink et al., 2006) by showing the first data to demonstrate experimentally that the proximity and visibility of fruits (apples) and vegetables (carrots) in a kitchen setting influences intake of these healthier foods. In all, these results show that overeating may be food for health, so long as the environment consists of fruits and vegetables in the most proximate and visible locations.

- Identify potential limitations of your research and methods, imprecision of measures that may have biased the pattern of results observed, and any potential threats to internal or external validity. It is important to be conservative; identify what could be improved to make the reader more confident in the findings you observed. For example:

  o In the second paragraph of the discussion in Figure 15.5, the authors also identify a potential limitation for their study: "Whether the results would be different if fruits and vegetables were placed in a bowl before participants entered the room, or if the setting was different, such as in a workplace or office setting, cannot be determined here."

- Provide a brief summary or commentary on the importance of your findings, as shown in the last paragraph of the discussion in Figure 15.5. In a sentence or two, state how your findings are novel (build upon what is known in the literature) and interesting (to the readership of the journal to which you are submitting your work). You can also speculate as to what new directions of research could be pursued, given the results you observed, and the implications for such research.

References

The "References" heading begins on a separate page after the "Discussion" section. The word "References" is centered and bolded at the top of the page, and each source that was cited in the manuscript is listed in alphabetical order in this section, as shown in Figure 15.6. The appropriate citation for almost any type of source is provided in the *Publication Manual*. The most common sources cited are journal articles, books, and book chapters. We will describe the appropriate citation for each type of source in this section. For any other type of source, refer to the *Publication Manual*.

To cite a journal article, list the author or authors, year of publication in parentheses, title of the article, name of the journal in italics, volume number in italics, issue number in parentheses (only if the journal is paginated by issue, not by volume), pages in the article, and digital object identifier (doi)—in that order. If a doi or an issue number is not available for an in-print article, then each can be omitted. The following citation is an example of a journal article reference (note that each reference in Figure 15.6 is for a journal article):

Privitera, G. J., & Dickinson, E. K. (2015). Control your cravings: Self-control varies by eating attitudes, sex, and food type among Division I collegiate athletes. *Psychology of Sport and Exercise*, *19*, 18–22. doi:10.1016/j.psychsport.2015.02.004

To cite an entire book, list the author or authors, year of publication, title of the book with edition number in parentheses (if applicable), city and state of publication, and name of the publisher. For example, the following is an APA reference for the most recent

In a "Discussion" section evaluate and interpret how the outcomes in a study relate to the problem or hypothesis that was tested.

Figure 15.6 APA-Style "References" Section

Center "References" on the top line of a separate page.

Each reference is listed in alphabetical order, and the format for each reference is a hanging indent.

Always use the ampersand (&) symbol for listing the last author of a multiple-author reference.

Use the *Publication Manual* to find the correct citation for any type of reference. Note that all references shown here are for journal articles.

PROXIMITY, VISIBILITY, AND INTAKE   11

References

Baumgartner, E., & Laghi, F. (2012). Affective responses to movie posters: Differences
    between adolescents and young adults. *International Journal of Psychology, 47,*
    154–160. doi:10.1080/00207594.2011.597398

Dalton, M., Blundell, J., & Finlayson, G. (2010). Effect of BMI and binge eating on food
    reward and energy intake: Further evidence for a binge eating subtype of obesity.
    Obesity Facts, 6, 348–359. doi:10.1159/000354599

Drewnowski, A. (2004). Obesity and the food environment: Dietary energy density and
    diet costs. *American Journal of Preventative Medicine, 27,* 154–162.
    doi:10.1016/j.amepre.2004.06.011

Epstein, L. H., Leddy, J. J., Temple, J. L., & Faith, M. S. (2007). Food reinforcement and
    eating: A multilevel analysis. *Psychological Bulletin, 133,* 884–906.
    doi:10.1037/0033–2909.133.5.884

---

edition of the *Publication Manual*; the second reference is for a book publication that is not published in editions:

> American Psychological Association. (2009). *Publication manual of the American Psychological Association* (6th ed.). Washington, DC: Author.
>
> Brookes, G., Pooley, J. A., & Earnest, J. (2015). *Terrorism, trauma and psychology: A multilevel victim perspective of the Bali bombings.* New York, NY: Routledge/Taylor & Francis Group.

> The "References" section is an alphabetical list of all sources cited in a manuscript.

Many books are edited and not authored, meaning different authors contribute a chapter to a book that is then edited or assembled by a few of those contributors. For an edited book, then, it is very likely that a specific chapter in that book, and not the entire book, was the source you used. To cite a book chapter, list the author or authors of the book chapter, year of publication in parentheses, name of chapter, name of the editor or editors of the book with "Eds." given in parentheses after all names are listed, title of the book in italics, page numbers of the book chapter in parentheses, city and state of publication, and name of the publisher. If the book chapter is available electronically, then you can include the doi or uniform resource locator (URL). As an example, the following is a book chapter reference with a chapter contributed by two authors in a book with four editors:

> Fanselow, M. S., & Sterlace, S. R. (2014). Pavlovian fear conditioning: Function, cause, and treatment. In F. K. McSweeney, E. S. Murphy, F. K. McSweeney, E. S. Murphy (Eds.), *The Wiley Blackwell handbook of operant and classical conditioning* (pp. 117–141). Hoboken, NJ: Wiley-Blackwell. doi:10.1002/9781118468135.ch6

LEARNING CHECK 3 ✓

1. What is the maximum number of characters for a running head? What is the maximum number of words for a title?

2. What is the word limit for an abstract?

3. What are the four main sections of the main body of an APA-style manuscript?

4. In what order and with what type of formatting are references listed in a references section?

Answers: 1. The maximum is 50 characters for a running head, and 12 words for a title; 2. Between 150 and 250 words; 3. The introduction, methods, results, and discussion sections; 4. References are listed in alphabetical order using a hanging indent format.

15.4 Literature Reviews

An APA-style manuscript is typically written to report the findings of primary research, which is research conducted by the authors of a manuscript. However, it is also common to report on a review of literature in the form of a synthesis of previous articles or as a meta-analysis (Galvan, 2006). These types of reports, called **literature review articles**, are often submitted for publication in peer-reviewed journals as well. Because a literature review article follows a different organization from reports of primary research, we will introduce the unique organization of a literature review article in this section.

A **literature review article** is a written comprehensive report of findings from previously published works about a problem in the form of a synthesis of previous articles or as a meta-analysis.

A literature review article is a written comprehensive report of findings from previously published works in a specified area of research in the form of a synthesis of previous articles or as a meta-analysis. A literature review article can be chosen by research area (e.g., the motivational salience of primary rewards) or by a specific theme in an area of research (e.g., the use of a conditioned place preference design to study the motivational salience of primary rewards). The goal of a literature review article is to organize, integrate, and evaluate published works about a problem and to consider progress made toward clarifying that problem.

To write a literature review article, we include a title page, an abstract, a literature review (main body), and references. If footnotes, tables, figures, or appendices are included, then we can place them at the end of the manuscript following the references section using the same order introduced in Section 15.3. Two sections in a literature review article that differ from a manuscript or report of primary research are the abstract and the main body. In the abstract, identify the problem and give a synopsis of the evaluations made in the literature review using the same formatting and word count limits identified in Section 15.3. To write the main body, use the following organization:

- Identify the problem and how it will be evaluated. Identify the topic, keywords used to search for articles in that topic, and what search engines you used to find articles. Identify anything in your method of selecting articles that could bias the evaluations made in the literature review.

- Integrate the literature to identify the state of the research. In other words, identify what is known and what is not known. Be clear on how far we have advanced on an understanding of the problem being reviewed.

- Identify how findings and interpretations in the published literature are related or consistent, or are inconsistent, contradictory, or flawed. How confident can we be in what is known? For a meta-analysis, report effect sizes for the findings of many studies. Be critical of the samples used, the research designs implemented, and the data and interpretations made to address the problem.

- Consider the progress made in an area of research and potential next steps toward clarifying the problem. Identify what is not known and possible methods or advancements in technology that could be used to clarify the problem further.

The main body or literature review is the primary section of a literature review article. The entire review of the literature is contained in this one section. The main body or literature portion of the manuscript can have any headings and subheadings to organize the ideas and evaluations presented in the review. Major headings should be bold and flush left, with the text for that section beginning on the line below the major heading. In all, we can use the analogy of a puzzle to describe a literature review: It is an attempt to fit many puzzle pieces together, with the many articles published in a given area of research being the puzzle pieces in this analogy.

15.5 Reporting Observations in Qualitative Research

In Chapter 7 we introduced the qualitative research design as a method used to make nonnumeric observations, from which conclusions are drawn without the use of statistical analysis. The implication of not using statistical analysis is that the "Results" section in an APA-style manuscript is replaced with an "Analysis" section. A "Results" section in a quantitative study reports the statistical outcomes of the measured data; an "Analysis" section in a qualitative study provides a series of interpretations and contributes a new perspective or generates the possibility that many different perspectives can explain the observations made. For a qualitative analysis, then, the "Analysis" section is written as a narrative, and not as a report of statistical outcomes.

The "Results" section in an APA-style manuscript is replaced with an "Analysis" section for qualitative research designs.

Qualitative research is typically not directed by a hypothesis. In other words, researchers do not state a hypothesis and then limit their observations to measure only phenomena that are related to that hypothesis. Instead, qualitative researchers often use interviews, participant observation techniques, and field notes and allow participants to ask their own questions during the time that participants are observed. To analyze observations that are descriptive (i.e., written in words) and often guided by the questions that participants ask, researchers evaluate the *trustworthiness* of their observations, as introduced in Chapter 7 (see Table 7.2). Although this is certainly not an exhaustive list of differences, the following are two key differences in writing an APA-style manuscript for qualitative versus quantitative research:

- The introduction and the "Method" section in a qualitative report argue ways of examining a problem in a way that often leaves open many alternatives that were anticipated or not anticipated by the authors. This is unlike quantitative research, in which the introduction narrows in on one or more stated hypotheses upon which the "Method" section outlines what will be observed to test those hypotheses.

- In a qualitative report, a narrative is constructed in an "Analysis" section to describe what was observed. A "Discussion" section, then, evaluates possible explanations for those observations with little effort to generalize beyond the specific observations made. This is unlike quantitative research in which statistical outcomes are reported in a "Results" section. A "Discussion" section then focuses on whether the data showed support or nonsupport for the hypotheses tested.

For most qualitative research, the goal is to describe the experiences of an individual or a small group. The structure of the manuscript, then, takes the form of a narrative that leaves open many possible explanations and evaluates the extent to which those observations are trustworthy.

15.6 Ethics in Focus: Credit and Authorship

Authorship of a peer-reviewed work is a great achievement. In psychology, we expect the order of authorship to reflect the relative contributions of those listed as authors. The first author of a manuscript is the individual who contributed the most, with each subsequent author making relatively fewer contributions. Authors listed on the title page of a manuscript should be listed in order of their "relative scientific or professional contributions" (APA, 2010, p. 11) to the work being submitted to an editor or reviewer, and not based on their status or institutional position.

The challenges of authorship are in defining what constitutes "relative scientific or professional contributions." Is it the person who conducted the research, wrote the manuscript, developed the research hypothesis, or created the research design? Is it about the relative value of the ideas shared to contribute to the work, or is it in the time spent to complete the work? There is no one answer that can resolve what constitutes more or less "relative scientific or professional contributions." The APA suggests that to resolve any concerns regarding authorship, all potential authors should talk about publication credit as early as possible. Agreeing on the order of authorship prior to completing the work can facilitate less disagreement regarding the order of authorship later in the publication process.

LEARNING CHECK 4 ✓

1. What is the goal of a literature review?

2. What is reported in an "Analysis" section for a qualitative research study?

3. According to the APA, authors listed on the title page of a manuscript should be listed in order of their _____.

Answers: 1. The goal of a literature review is to organize, integrate, and evaluate published works about a problem and to consider progress made toward clarifying that problem; 2. An "Analysis" section in a qualitative study provides, in narrative form, a series of interpretations and contributes a new perspective or generates the possibility that many different perspectives can explain the observations made; 3. relative scientific or professional contributions.

15.7 Presenting a Poster

Aside from writing a manuscript, researchers and professionals often communicate by presenting a **poster**, which is a concise description of a research study in a display of text boxes, figures, and tables shown on a single large page. A poster is an eye-catching and engaging display that is typically presented during a **poster session** at a professional conference, such as those held annually by the APA,

> A **poster** is a concise description of a research study in the form of a display of text boxes, figures, and tables on a single large page.
>
> A **poster session** is a 1- to 4-hour time slot during which many authors stand near their poster ready and open to answer questions or talk about their work with interested attendees.

or at smaller venues. A poster session is a 1- to 4-hour time slot during which many authors stand near their poster ready and open to answer questions or talk about their work with interested attendees. To present a poster, you must submit an abstract of your work before the submission deadline of a conference. Upon acceptance of the abstract, you will receive a poster session time to present your poster.

Poster sessions can be exciting because researchers often present their most current work—so current that it has yet to be published in a peer-reviewed journal. For this reason, poster sessions can often give researchers a preview of the type of research that could be published in the coming year and generate many new ideas and directions for advancing research. Although thousands of poster sessions are held each year, the APA does not provide specific guidelines for creating posters. For this reason, the display of posters at conferences and professional meetings can vary quite a bit from poster to poster. Although the APA does not provide specific guidelines, we can identify many strategies you can use to get your poster noticed using the following suggestions adapted, in part, from Block (1996):

- Keep the title short. The title should clearly identify the topic of your poster and should be the largest font size you use. If needed, shorten the title in order to increase the font size of the title.

- Do not use a small font size, and use a consistent font type. The font size should not be smaller than 20 points, and the font type should be the same for the entire poster (except possibly the title). Larger font size and consistent font type is good because it makes a poster easy to read from at least 4 feet away.

- Use colorful figures and borders. A colorful display is eye-catching; however, keep the color simple by using solid colors throughout.

- Display the logo for your school affiliation (optional). Displaying your school logo is a point of pride and a way to advertise to others where the research was conducted.

- Place each text box or section in a logical order. The sections in a poster include the title, the abstract or overview, the method and results, figures and tables, conclusions or implications, and a list of key references. Try to organize each section, moving from left to right, in the same way that it would be presented in an APA-style manuscript.

- Make sure the poster takes less than 5 minutes to read. A poster does not need to be comprehensive; it needs to give enough information such that the reader can understand the gist of what you did and what you found.

- Avoid technical jargon. Do not assume that everyone in the audience is an expert. Avoid using words that are specific to your area of research, or if you do use these words, then define them in your poster. Make the poster accessible to a large audience.

- Always stand near the poster, but not directly in front of it. Stay near the poster to let people know that you are available to answer questions or talk about what you did, and stand away from it so that all patrons can clearly see the poster. Also, wait for the audience to address you with questions, and be respectful when you do respond to questions.

- Bring supportive materials, such as reprints or a printed copy of the poster itself, to give to attendees. This gives people something to bring home that will remind them of the poster you presented. Also, bring business cards so people can contact you if they have any follow-up questions after the poster session.

Most authors now use a single slide in Microsoft® PowerPoint to create their poster. Directions for using this software to create a poster are given in Appendix A.4. Sample posters that have been presented at professional conferences are also provided in Appendix A.4. Learning how to create a poster and following the suggestions provided in this section can help you make a strong impression at a poster session.

15.8 Giving a Professional Talk

The third method of communication introduced in this chapter is a professional talk. A talk is typically given in a formal setting. Graduate students often present their current work in brown-bag sessions to members of their department. At a doctoral level, researchers can be invited to present their work in a talk at conferences and professional meetings. The advantage of giving a talk is that the presenter is likely the only presenter or one of only a few presenters for the hour or so that the talk is given. By contrast, hundreds or thousands of authors present a poster in a single poster session. For this reason, giving a professional talk can be a great way to reach an engaged audience and promote your research, identify the scientific merits of your research, and even get people excited about your research.

There are many good suggestions for giving a professional talk. The following is a list of eight suggestions for giving an effective talk:

- Arrive early and be prepared. Being on time is the same as being late. You will need time to prepare, practice, and set up any technology, such as Microsoft® PowerPoint, needed to give the talk. As a general rule, always arrive about 30 minutes early to make sure everything is prepared so that you can start on time.

- Dress appropriately. Be aware of the audience and forum in which you are presenting. Try not to overdress (too formal) or underdress (too informal), but, when in doubt, overdress.

- Introduce yourself. Begin any talk with a brief introduction. State your name, affiliation, and general area of interest in an effort to relate to the audience and help the listeners understand who you are.

- Begin with an attention-grabber. A great talk captures the attention of an audience. Begin with a story, a short video clip, an exercise, a demonstration, or fun facts that get the audience interested to hear more. For example, if you give a talk on addiction, you could begin by describing a special case of a patient with the addiction and symptoms you plan to talk about.

- Use technology to facilitate your talk; do not read from it. Many presentations are given using Microsoft® PowerPoint. Do not read the slides verbatim; it reflects poorly on your preparedness and level of understanding of the topic of your talk. Instead, use only a few bulleted words on each slide, talk in your own words, and refer only to the slides as a reference for the order in which you present the topics of your talk. The more you engage the audience (and not the slides), the more effective the talk will be.

- Keep the talk focused. A talk is typically given within a specified time limit that is usually not more than 1 hour. Practice giving your talk often and keep to that script as closely as possible during the talk. Stay on topic so that you can stay on time. If an audience member asks an off-topic question or a question that will take too much time to answer, then let the individual know that the question is important to you and that it may be best for you to answer that question at the end of the talk. This allows you to show respect for the audience member and also allows you to keep the talk on topic and on time.

- Follow through with questions. Many questions can be answered during or immediately after a talk. However, if you do not know an answer to a question or did not get a chance to answer a specific question, then offer to take down the contact information of the person who asked the question so that you can follow up later with an answer. Make sure you follow through.

- Always end with references and acknowledgments. The speaker may have been invited to talk, and many people often help a speaker prepare a talk, so these people should be acknowledged. In addition, any work cited in the talk should be recognized at the end of the talk. If the talk is given using Microsoft® PowerPoint slides, then the final slide should list the references and acknowledgments.

The best advice of all is to relax and enjoy the moment. Public speaking tends to be stressful for many people. Breathe deeply, squeeze a stress ball, or tell yourself a joke. Do anything to relax and overcome any anxiety or stress you may be experiencing prior to a talk. For most talks, the audience is voluntary; by being present at your talk, your listeners have already expressed an interest in your topic. Following the guidelines described in this section, you can give a talk that appeals to your audience and allows you to present yourself as an authoritative, yet engaged, speaker.

LEARNING CHECK 5 ✓

1. What is a poster session?

2. What guidelines does the APA provide for creating a poster?

3. What is the advantage of giving a professional talk compared to presenting a poster?

Answers: 1. A poster session is a 1- to 4-hour time slot during which many authors stand near their poster ready and open to answer questions or talk about their work with interested attendees; 2. None; 3. The advantage of giving a talk is that, unlike in a poster session, the speaker is likely the only presenter or one of only a few presenters at the time the talk is given.

LO 1 Identify three methods of communication among scientists.

- Three methods of communication among scientists are to publish a manuscript, present a poster, and give a talk.

LO 2 Describe three elements of communication.

- Three elements in communication are the speaker or author, the audience, and the message. The speaker or author uses first person and third person appropriately; uses past, present, and future tense appropriately; uses an impersonal writing style; reduces biased language; and gives credit where appropriate. The audience includes scientists and professionals, college students, and the general public. The message should be novel (contribute new findings or new ideas), interesting (to the readership of the work), and informative.

LO 3 Apply APA writing style and language guidelines for writing a manuscript.

- To submit a work for consideration for publication in a peer-reviewed journal, we prepare an **APA-style manuscript** using the writing style format described in the *Publication Manual*. Four writing and language guidelines for writing an APA-style manuscript are to be accurate; comprehensive, yet concise; conservative; and appropriate. To be comprehensive, yet concise, apply the following suggestions: Abbreviate where appropriate, display data in a figure or table, keep the writing focused, and do not repeat information.

LO 4 Apply APA formatting requirements for writing a manuscript.

- An APA-style manuscript is formatted or organized into the following major sections: title page, abstract, main body (includes introduction, methods, results, and discussion), references, footnotes (if any), tables (if any), figures (if any), and appendices (if any).

- A title page is on page 1 and includes the title, authors, affiliations, and author note. On page 2, the abstract provides a brief written summary of the purpose, methods, and results of a work or published document in 150 to 250 words. On page 3, the main body begins with the title on line 1, and the introduction begins on line 2. The introduction states a problem and why it is important to address, reviews the pertinent literature, and states how the problem will be addressed. The "Method" section is divided into four main subheadings: "Participants," "Procedures" (can be further divided into subheadings), "Data Analyses" (may be optional), and "Results." The "Discussion" section evaluates and interprets how the outcomes in a study relate to the problem that was tested. The "References" section, which begins on a new page, is an alphabetical list of all sources cited in a manuscript.

LO 5 Apply APA guidelines for writing and organizing a literature review article.

- A **literature review article** is a written comprehensive report of findings from previously published works about a problem in the form of a synthesis of previous articles or as a meta-analysis. To write the main body of a literature review:

  o Identify the problem and how it will be evaluated.
  o Integrate the literature to identify the state of the research.
  o Identify how findings and interpretations in the published literature are related or consistent, or are inconsistent, contradictory, or flawed.
  o Consider the progress made in an area of research and potential next steps toward clarifying the problem.

LO 6 Delineate how results are reported for a qualitative versus a quantitative research design.

- The "Results" section is replaced with an "Analysis" section in a qualitative research study, which provides a series of interpretations and contributes a new perspective or generates the possibility that many different perspectives can explain the observations made. The "Analysis" section is written as a narrative, and not as a report of statistical outcomes.

- In a qualitative report, the introduction and the "Method" section argue approaches to examining a problem in a way that often leaves open many alternatives that were anticipated or not anticipated by the authors. In the "Analysis" section, a narrative is used to describe what was observed, and the "Discussion" section evaluates possible explanations for those observations with little effort to generalize beyond the specific observations made.

LO 7 State APA guidelines for identifying the authorship of published scientific work.

- According to the APA, authors listed on the title page of a manuscript should be listed in order of their "relative scientific or professional contributions." The APA suggests that to resolve any concerns regarding authorship, all potential authors should talk about publication credit as early as possible.

LO 8 Identify guidelines for effectively presenting a poster.

- A **poster** is a concise description of a research study in the form of a display of text boxes, figures, and tables on a single large page. A poster is presented at a conference or professional meeting in a **poster session**, which is a 1- to 4-hour time slot during which many authors stand near their poster ready and open to answer questions or talk about their work with interested attendees.

- The APA does not provide specific guidelines for creating and presenting posters; however, using the following suggestions is advisable: Keep the title short, do not use small font size and use a constant font type, use colorful figures and borders, display the logo for your school affiliation, place each text box or section in a logical order, make sure the poster takes less than 5 minutes to read, avoid technical jargon, always stand near the poster but not directly in front of it, and bring supportive materials.

LO 9 Identify guidelines for effectively giving a professional talk.

- Giving a professional talk can be a great way to promote your research and get people excited about your work. The following is a list of eight suggestions for giving an effective talk: Arrive early and be prepared, dress appropriately, introduce yourself, begin with an attention-grabber, use technology to facilitate your talk, keep the talk focused, follow through with questions, and always end with references and acknowledgments.

KEY TERMS

peer review

APA-style manuscript

literature review article

poster

poster session

REVIEW QUESTIONS

1. State three methods of communication among scientists.

2. State three elements of communication.

3. Scientific journals use a peer review process to determine whether to accept or reject a manuscript for publication. What is peer review?

4. State the writing and language guideline for writing an APA-style manuscript (be accurate; be comprehensive, yet concise; be conservative; or be appropriate) that is described by each of the following:

   A. Proofread your manuscript before submitting it.

   B. Abbreviate where appropriate.

   C. Do not generalize beyond the data.

   D. Capitalize the word "Black" to refer to a social or ethnic group.

5. State the major sections in an APA-style manuscript in order of how each section should appear in the manuscript.

6. A researcher reports that students spent significantly more time attending to a passage given in color than when it was presented in black and white, $t(30) = 4.16, p < .05$. In which section of an APA-style manuscript do we report this outcome?

7. What information is conveyed in the introduction of an APA-style manuscript?

8. What sections constitute the first two pages of an APA-style manuscript?

9. What is the goal of a literature review?

10. In a qualitative report, the "Results" section is omitted and replaced with what section?

11. At what stage in the publication process should potential authors talk about publication credit?

12. How should the sections in a poster be organized, moving from left to right?

ACTIVITIES

1. Conduct a literature search and choose one article that interests you. After reading the article, write a three- to four-page paper that identifies whether each of the following was a strength or weakness in the introduction and discussion sections of the article, and give an example to support each argument:

   A. Did the introduction: Describe the problem and explain why it is important to conduct new research to address the problem? Integrate previous research that is relevant to the research conducted to address the problem? State the hypotheses being tested and the research design being used to address the problem?

   B. Did the discussion: State whether the findings lend support or nonsupport for the hypothesis that was tested? Give context for how the findings fit with previously published studies? Identify potential limitations of the research and methods, imprecision of measures that may have biased the pattern of results observed, and any potential threats to internal or external validity? Provide a broad summary or commentary on the importance of the findings?

2. Conduct a literature review and find one article that interests you. Create a poster for the study that is described in the article by applying the suggestions introduced for creating posters in Section 15.7.

APPENDIX A

APA-Style Writing, Sample Manuscript, and Posters

A.1 Essentials for Writing APA-Style Research Papers

Writing an APA-style manuscript can be challenging and intimidating for many students. Whether submitting a paper for publication or for a class assignment, following APA guidelines is important for helping you to become a better writer. Writing an APA-style manuscript for a class is more than just an assignment—being proficient can help you well beyond the classroom. APA guidelines are widely accepted rules for writing proficiently, and are used across disciplines. Understanding and applying these guidelines is therefore a worthwhile endeavor.

APA guidelines provided in the *Publication Manual of the American Psychological Association* (APA, 2009), which we refer to hereafter as the *Publication Manual*, cover many aspects of writing style and these guidelines are not always conventional. As one example, in the English language, the word *data* can be treated as singular (e.g., the data *is* compelling) or plural (e.g., the data *are* compelling). Although the singular usage of this word is widely used in the United States, the APA treats *data* as the plural of *datum* (as defined in Chapter 1). Keeping up with these many guidelines can be difficult—yes, even for scientists.

This appendix provides a useful guide for following some of the most essential rules provided in the *Publication Manual*. Obviously, you should always refer to the *Publication Manual* if you have any questions, but this four-page guide alone can help you effectively gain points and score better on your APA papers because it summarizes many common issues related to APA writing style and language. This summary is based on feedback from dozens of professors across the country and it is focused on the areas in writing where students often lose the most points. So please photocopy this guide, highlight it, laminate it, and refer to it as you write your papers.

Note: The information provided in these notes is based on the writing style provided in the *Publication Manual* (APA, 2009). These notes provide the essentials for writing just about any type of research report using the APA writing style format, but they are not a substitute for the *Publication Manual*. If there is any doubt regarding APA writing style, please consult the *Publication Manual*.

Abbreviations

The use of abbreviations is largely the judgment of the author. Overuse can make the text too confusing, and underuse can make the text less concise.

LATIN ABBREVIATIONS

Use abbreviations in parentheses. Use English translations in text. One exception is made for *et al.* (and others) when citing a source (e.g., "Privitera et al. (2013) showed . . . "). Examples with translations include:

cf. (compare)	i.e. (that is)	viz. (namely)
e.g. (for example)	vs. (versus)	etc. (and so forth)

UNITS OF MEASUREMENT AND TIME

The following units of time should never be abbreviated: day, week, month, and year. With units of time, abbreviate *hour* (hr), *minute* (min), *millisecond* (ms), *nanosecond* (ns), and *second* (s). Use an abbreviation when a number accompanies a measure (e.g., 5 m), but not without (e.g., "measured in meters"). Report measurements in metric units (e.g., not inches or feet). Do not add *s* for plural units (e.g., 5 meters is 5 m). More examples include:

mm (millimeter)	cm (centimeter)	lb (pound)
p.m. (post meridiem)	ml (milliliter)	L (liter)
a.m. (ante meridiem)	g (gram, gravity)	mg (milligram)

Never begin a sentence with a lowercase abbreviation (such as *e.g.*) or a symbol that stands alone (such as α).

Use of Numbers

Use numerals to express:

1. Numbers 10 and above and decimals (e.g., 0.25): Use a zero before decimals, unless it is a value that cannot be greater than 1 (e.g., correlations and proportions).
2. All numbers in the abstract.
3. Numbers that represent a fractional or decimal quantity, proportion, percentile, or mathematical function (e.g., "8% of students" or "4 times more likely").
4. Time (e.g., 1 hr or 11:00 a.m.), dates (e.g., January 1, 2000), age (e.g., 3-month-olds), scores on a scale (e.g., "mean score was 3 on a 5-point scale"), and exact sums of money (e.g., $4.12).
5. Numbers that indicate a specific row or column in a table (e.g., "row 2 column 1"), or that are placed in a numbered series (Figure 1 or rank 1).
6. A list of four or more numbers (e.g., "students viewed 0, 2, 4, or 8 objects").

Use words to express:

1. Numbers below 10, except when displayed in a figure or table, or preceding a unit of measurement (e.g., 5 m).
2. Approximations for days, months, and years (e.g., "about two days ago" or "almost three months ago").
3. Common fractions when used as adjectives (e.g., two-thirds majority).

Periods, Commas, and Capitalization

Do not use periods to abbreviate units of measurement, time, routes of administration (e.g., IV indicates intravenous), degree titles (e.g., MA, PhD), or organization titles (e.g., APA).

Do not use commas to separate parts of a measure (e.g., 2 lb 4 oz). Use commas before the final conjunction in lists (e.g., time, money, and resources), with numbers larger than three digits (e.g., 1,000), with a reference citation (e.g., Privitera, 2016), with exact dates (e.g., "March 30, 2015," but not "March 2015"), and for lists within the text (e.g., "choices were (a) low, (b) moderate, and (c) high").

Capitalize nouns preceding a number, but not preceding a variable (e.g., Session 1 or session *x*); capitalize references to specific terms or groups (e.g., write "the control group," but also write "Control Group A," or write "the independent variables," but also write "Independent Variable 1"); capitalize the first word following a colon only if the clause that follows is a complete sentence (e.g., "They identified two potential causes: One cause was environmental, and the second was biological"); and capitalize all words of four letters or more in a heading, subheading, or title (e.g., "Research Methods for the Behavioral Sciences").

Hyphens and Prefixes

Hyphens for compound words (e.g., using *makeover*, *make over*, or *make-over*) and prefixes can be tricky. Refer to the dictionary when in doubt. APA style follows *Webster's Collegiate* in most cases. Also, use the Grammar Guide provided in the study guide that accompanies this book.

The following prefixes will require a hyphen: *all-* (e.g., all-knowing), *ever-* (e.g., ever-present), *quasi-* (e.g., quasi-experimental), *half-* (e.g., half-witted), *ex-* (e.g., ex-girlfriend), and *self-* (e.g., self-fulfilling).

Avoiding Biased Language

The general rule here is to avoid language that may be perceived as offensive. Use a respectful tone (e.g., "Smith et al. did not account for . . . ," not "Smith et al. completely ignored . . ."). Use *subjects* when referring to animals observed in a study; use *participants* to refer to humans observed in a study.

Refer to the Guidelines for Unbiased Language at www.apastyle.org/manual/supplement as a more complete guide.

GENDER

Gender is a cultural term referring to social roles; *sex* refers to biology. Avoid sexist bias (e.g., referring to "the nurse" as "she" or using *fireman* instead of *firefighter*).

AGE

Always report an age range (e.g., "17 to 24 years," not "under 24 years"). *Boy* and *girl* are used to refer to persons under the age of 12 years. *Young man* and *young woman* are used to refer to persons aged 13–17 years. *Man* and *woman* are used to refer to adults 18 years or older; and the term *older person* is preferred to *elderly* when referring to persons over 65 years of age.

SEXUALITY

Use *gay men* and *lesbians* or *bisexual individuals*, not *homosexuals*. Use *sexual orientation*, not *sexual preference*.

ETHNICITY

Capitalize *Black* and *White* when referring to social groups. Use geographic locations, not ethnic labels (e.g., use *Asian* or *Asian American*, not *Oriental*). When possible, identify persons by nation of origin (e.g., *Chinese*, *Japanese*, *Korean*).

DISABILITIES

Avoid language that objectifies a person's condition (e.g., *autistic*, *dyslexic*, *bedridden*). Avoid negative labels (e.g., *disordered*) and slurs (e.g., *retard*, *cripple*). Place the focus on the individual, not the disability (e.g., say "persons with dyslexia," not "dyslexics").

Data and Statistics

Do not present the equation for a statistic in common use (e.g., a t statistic). If it is uncommon and essential to the paper, then write it in line with the text when possible.

The descriptive statistics (e.g., mean, standard deviation) should enhance the informativeness of the paper—so they should allow a reader to determine the effect size or confidence interval, if possible. If descriptive statistics are given in a table or figure, do not restate them in the text, but indicate in which table or figure they are given.

Means in the text are reported as M (SD) or $M \pm SD$. Do not use the symbol M in text (e.g., say "the means were . . . ," not "the Ms were . . . ").

To report a statistic (e.g., t test or F test), include enough information for the reader to fully understand the analysis. The information needed varies from statistic to statistic.

The general form for reporting an inferential statistic is "statistic (df) = obtained value, p value." Always include a space after an arithmetic operator and sign (e.g., =, <, >, +, −).

If the test is one-tailed, then indicate this in parentheses following the p value. Include an estimate for effect size when possible for significant effects.

To report a confidence interval, state "([percentage] CI [lower limit, upper limit])"—for example, "(95% CI [1.2, 3.5])." The level of confidence (i.e., the percentage) must be clearly stated.

N typically indicates the total number of subjects or participants in a study, whereas n typically indicates the number in each group (or limited portion) of the sample.

Use the symbol for percent when followed by a numeral (e.g., "30% of the variance . . . "); use *percentage* when a number is not given (e.g., "the percentage of time . . . ").

Quotations and Italics

Use double quotation marks (e.g., "text") to:

1. Introduce ironic, slang, or coined terms (e.g., It was a "normal" day). However, only use quotation marks the first time the word is used.

2. Include the title of an article or chapter of a book in the text (e.g., The author of the article "Probability Theory" makes some interesting points . . .).

3. Reproduce test material verbatim
   (e.g., The item was "How often do you _____?").

Use italics to:

1. Identify the anchors for a scale (e.g., "Ratings were given from 1 (*not at all*) to 5 (*all the time*)").

2. Cite a linguistic example (e.g., "This study distinguishes between *fair* and *equal* treatment of . . . ").

3. Introduce technical jargon (e.g., "The frequency of *token count* words . . . ").

4. Include the title of a book in the text
   (e.g., "The author of the book *Research Methods for the Behavioral Sciences* is developing . . . ").

Block quotations are given in a separate paragraph for quotations of 40 or more words. Do not place block quotations in quotation marks. For example:

Privitera (2015) explains the following:

> Success is really not something you can easily measure; it is an outcome that is inherent to the dreams and expectations within our mind. What we imagine in our mind as being successful is our own success—no one else can define success for you, except you. (p. 193)

Use single quotation marks (e.g., 'text') within double quotation marks for text that was enclosed in double quotation marks in the original source (e.g., Privitera (2015) believes that "It is important for students to 'become extraordinary' by striving to achieve things they never thought possible" (p. 193)).

Citations in Text

- For a single author, the surname and year must be cited if referencing another work (e.g., "Kelly (2006) found . . . " or "In 2006, Kelly found . . . ").

- For two authors, the surname for each author and the year must be stated each time a work is cited in the text (e.g., "Jones and Smith (2010) initiated . . . " or "In 2010, Jones and Smith initiated . . . ").

- For three to five authors, the surname for each author and the year must be stated the first time. Any other citation should state the first author followed by *et al.* and the year (e.g., for the first citation state, "Woods, Peters, and Martin (2007) found . . .," and for all remaining citations state, "Woods et al. (2007) found . . . ").

- For six or more authors all citations give the surname of the first author followed by *et al.* then the year.

- When multiple first authors are cited in the same parentheses, they should appear in alphabetical order by the first author's surname (not by publication year), in the same way that they appear in the reference list (e.g., " . . . and this hypothesis has support (Albert, 2003; Jonas, 1999; Jones, 2007)").

- Cite two or more works by the same author in order of publication year. Do not restate the author's name for each citation within parentheses (e.g., Walter, 2003, 2007).

- Use alphabetical suffixes (e.g., a, b, c) to differentiate between works published in the same year by the same author (e.g., Douglas 2000a, 2000b).

- For works that have been accepted for publication, but not yet published, state "in press" for the publication year.

- To cite a specific portion of a work (e.g., pages, chapter, figure, or table) include the additional information (e.g., Hughes et al., 2006, p. 32).

- To cite a source secondhand (meaning that you got the citation from another source and not the original), make this clear by stating "as cited in" (e.g., "According to Karl Popper (1959), as cited in Platt (1964), there is no such thing as proof in science").

- Cite a personal communication (e.g., e-mail, personal interview, or phone call) in the text only, not in the reference list. Include the name of the communicator and the exact date if possible (e.g., R. J. Smith, personal communication, June, 12, 2001).

Note that material that is *reprinted* appears in its exact original form; material that is *adapted* is modified to make it suitable for a new purpose.

Citations in a Reference List

All references cited in the text must be cited in a reference list at the end of a paper or article (except personal communications, because these are regarded as "unrecoverable data").

Reference lists are not numbered and are listed in alphabetical order by letter. For this ordering, a space precedes a letter (e.g., Mann, W. J., precedes Manning, A. J.). Some additional rules include:

1. Same-author references are listed by publication year, beginning with the earliest year.

2. When multiple entries have the same first-author surname, one-author references precede multiple-author references (e.g., Gill, T. (2006) precedes Gill, T., & Bond, R. (2002)).

3. Alphabetize group authors (e.g., an institution or agency) by the full official name for the group (e.g., order by American Psychological Association, not APA).

A.2 Grammar, Punctuation, and Spelling (GPS) Writing Guide

American Psychological Association, or APA, writing style is important to learn. In Chapter 15, the use of APA style is described and many tips are provided to help you improve your APA writing. However, without proper grammar, punctuation, and spelling, even the best APA style can appear sloppy. For this reason, we briefly describe the following basic features of writing in this guide that are consistent with the use of APA writing rules:

- Nouns and pronouns
- Verbs
- Adjectives and adverbs
- Prepositions
- Commas
- Colons and semicolons
- Apostrophes
- Quotation marks
- Hyphens
- Sentence structure
- Spelling

Because this guide is written to support the use of APA style, we will focus on aspects of writing that are consistent with APA style. Hence, this writing guide is like your GPS of writing using APA style; that is, it will get your writing where it needs to be—to a college level. This guide is thorough, yet it is also a brief overview of the essentials in writing properly. Using this guide can certainly help you improve your grades on papers, particularly those that require an APA writing style.

Nouns and Pronouns

A noun is used to name or identify a person, place, thing, quality, or action. A pronoun takes the place of a noun, noun phrase, or noun clause. A brief list of rules for using nouns and pronouns appropriately is given here.

USE OF CAPITALIZATION

There are many capitalization rules for nouns and pronouns. Some are straightforward and some vary depending on how words are used in a sentence. The following is a list of fundamental capitalization rules:

Rule 1: Capitalize the first word in a sentence.

- <u>The</u> experiment was a success.

Rule 2: Capitalize the pronoun *I*.

- If only <u>I</u> had considered that alternative.

Rule 3: Capitalize family relationships only when used as proper names.

- She loves her <u>Uncle</u> Bob more than her other <u>uncles</u>.
- He came home to see <u>Father</u>, although his <u>father</u> was not home.

Rule 4: Capitalize proper nouns such as people, places, and organizations.

- Supreme Court, Buffalo Bills, Alcoholics Anonymous, U.S. Marine Corps, Ellicottville Brewing Company, New York City.

Rule 5: Capitalize titles that precede names.

- We asked <u>Sergeant Major</u> Privitera for comment; however, the <u>sergeant major</u> was not available for comment.

Rule 6: Capitalize names of countries and nationalities and capitalize the adjective describing a person from that country or nationality.

- She was born in <u>Canada</u>, which makes her a <u>Canadian</u>.
- There was an <u>Austrian</u> who found refuge in <u>Finland</u>.

Rule 7: Capitalize all words except for short prepositions in books, articles, and songs.

- One of his most significant books was <u>*Beyond Freedom and Dignity*</u>.

Rule 8: Capitalize the names of gods, deities, religious figures, and books, except for nonspecific use of the word *god*.

- His faith called for him to worship only one <u>god</u>, so he prayed to <u>God</u> daily.
- Capitalize religious books such as the <u>Holy Bible</u> or <u>Koran</u> and deities such as <u>Buddha</u> or <u>Jesus Christ</u>.

Rule 9: Capitalize *North*, *South*, *East*, and *West* as regional directions, but not as compass directions.

- A sample was selected at a college in the <u>Northeast</u>.
- The habitat was located a few minutes <u>east</u> of the river.

Rule 10: Capitalize the days of the week, months, and holidays, and capitalize the seasons only when used in a title.

- His favorite season was <u>fall</u>, which is when he enrolled in college for the <u>Fall</u> 2013 semester.

- He did not attend class on <u>Wednesday</u>, which was <u>Halloween</u>. In <u>November</u>, he did not miss a class.

Rule 11: Capitalize historical eras, periods, and events, but not century numbers.

- The <u>Great Depression</u> occurred in the <u>twentieth</u> century and was a difficult time for many <u>Americans</u>.

Rule 12: Capitalize the first word after a colon only when the clause following the colon is a complete sentence.

- The experiment was conducted to learn about human behavior: the outcome.

- The lecturer gave an important lesson: To learn about human behavior means that we advance human understanding.

USE OF PRONOUNS AND PRONOUN CASE

Rule 1: Pronouns should agree in number. In other words, if the pronoun replaces a singular noun, then use a singular pronoun. Note that words such as *everybody*, *anybody*, *anyone*, *someone*, *neither*, *nobody*, and *each* are singular words that take singular pronouns.

- A participant was read an informed consent that <u>he or she</u> signed. (NOT: A participant was read an informed consent that <u>they</u> signed.)

- Everybody had 30 seconds to finish <u>his or her</u> test. (NOT: Everybody had 30 seconds to finish <u>their</u> test.)

Rule 2: Pronouns should agree in person. When you use first person (*I, we*), second person (*you*), or third person (*he, she, they*), be consistent. Don't switch from one person to the other.

- When <u>we</u> are working, <u>we</u> should have time to relax afterward. (NOT: When <u>we</u> are working, <u>you</u> should have time to relax afterward.)

Rule 3: Pronouns should be clearly identified.

- It is important that <u>the executive team</u> gets the decision correct. [NOT: It is important that <u>they</u> get the decision correct. (Who are "they"?)]

- Students completed a test and quiz, then placed <u>the test and quiz</u> face down when they were finished. [NOT: Students completed a test and quiz, then placed <u>it</u> face down when they were finished. (Is "it" referring to the test, the quiz, or both?)]

Here, we will list some additional rules pertaining to pronoun case use. To begin, keep in mind that pronouns have three cases:

Subjective case (pronouns used as subject)

I, you, he, she it, we, they, who

Objective case (pronouns used as objects of verbs or prepositions)

Me, you, him, her, it, us, them, whom

Possessive case (pronouns used to express ownership)

My (mine), your (yours), his/her (his/hers), it (its), our (ours), their (theirs), whose

Rule 4: Some pronouns do not change case or form.

That, these, those, which

Rule 5: Use the subjective and objective case appropriately for formal and informal writing.

Formal writing: In the subjective case, "It is I." In the objective case, "To whom am I speaking?"

Informal writing: In the subjective case, "Who am I speaking with?" In the objective case, "It is me."

Rule 6: When making comparisons, use *than*, *as*, *compared to*, or *versus (vs.)*.

The effect was larger in the experimental group <u>than</u> in the control group. [NOT: The effect was larger in the experimental group. (Larger than what?)]

The effect was larger in the experimental group <u>compared to</u> the control group.

Self-reports were as truthful <u>as</u> possible.

Scores were comparable in the experimental <u>versus</u> the control group.

Verbs

A verb is used to describe an action or occurrence or identify a state of being. A brief list of rules for using verbs appropriately is given here. There are six basic tenses you should be familiar with:

Simple present: We conclude

Present perfect: We have concluded

Simple past: They concluded

Past perfect: They had concluded

Future: They will conclude

Future perfect: They will have concluded

The challenge in sequencing tenses usually occurs with the perfect tenses. Perfect tenses are formed by adding an auxiliary or auxiliaries, which most commonly take the forms of *has*, *have*, *had*, *be*, *can*, *do*, *may*, *must*, *ought*, *shall*, and *will*. We will use the common forms identified here.

VERB TENSES

Rule 1: Present perfect designates actions that have occurred and are ongoing and consists of a past participle with *has* or *have*.

Simple past: We attended school for four years.

Present perfect: We have attended school for four years.

The simple past implies that "we" are finished attending school; the present perfect implies that "we" are still attending school.

Rule 2: Infinitives also have perfect tense forms when combined with auxiliaries, even when used with verbs that identify the future, such as *hope*, *intend*, *expect*, and *plan*. When the perfect tense is used with verbs that identify the future, the perfect tense sets up the sequence by identifying the action that began and was completed before the action of the main verb.

- The researcher had expected to observe the result. (In this example, the action, "had expected," began and was completed before the action of the main verb, "to observe the result.")

Rule 3: Past perfect indicates an action completed in the past before another action begins.

- Simple past: The scientist developed research protocols and later used them to conduct research.
- Past perfect: The scientist used research protocols that he had developed.

In each example, the research protocols were developed before they were used to conduct research.

- Simple past: The technician fixed the apparatus when the inspector arrived.
- Past perfect: The technician had fixed the apparatus when the inspector arrived.

The simple past indicates that the technician waited until the inspector arrived to fix the apparatus; the past perfect indicates that the technician had already fixed the apparatus by the time the inspector arrived.

Rule 4: Future perfect indicates an action that will have been completed at a specified time in the future.

- Simple future: Friday I will finish my homework.
- Future perfect: By Friday, I will have finished my homework.

The simple future indicates that the homework will be completed specifically on Friday; the future perfect indicates that the homework will be completed at any time leading up to Friday.

IRREGULAR VERBS

Regular verbs consist of the present/root form, the simple past form, and the past participle form. Regular verbs have an ending of *-ed* added to the present/root form for both the simple past and past participle form. Irregular verbs are identified as verbs that do not follow this pattern.

To help you identify the form of irregular verbs, the list here consists of the present/root form, the simple past form, and the past participle form of 60 irregular verbs.

Present	Past	Past Participle	Present	Past	Past Participle
be	was, were	been	lay	laid	laid
become	became	become	lead	led	led
begin	began	begun	leave	left	left
bring	brought	brought	let	let	let
build	built	built	lie	lay	lain
catch	caught	caught	lose	lost	lost
choose	chose	chosen	make	made	made
come	came	come	meet	met	met
cut	cut	cut	quit	quit	quit
deal	dealt	dealt	read	read	read
do	did	done	ride	rode	ridden
drink	drank	drunk	run	ran	run
eat	ate	eaten	say	said	said
fall	fell	fallen	see	saw	seen
feed	fed	fed	seek	sought	sought
feel	felt	felt	send	sent	sent
find	found	found	sleep	slept	slept
forget	forgot	forgotten	speak	spoke	spoken
forgive	forgave	forgiven	spend	spent	spent
get	got	gotten	stand	stood	stood
give	gave	given	take	took	taken
go	went	gone	teach	taught	taught
grow	grew	grown	tell	told	told
have	had	had	think	thought	thought
hear	heard	heard	throw	threw	thrown

(Continued)

Present	Past	Past Participle	Present	Past	Past Participle
hide	hid	hidden	understand	understood	understood
hold	held	held	wear	wore	worn
keep	kept	kept	win	won	won
know	knew	known	write	wrote	written

Active and Passive Voice

Active voice: Verbs in an active voice show the subject or person acting. The active voice is often a more concise writing style. For this reason, many writers feel that the active voice should be the primary voice of an author.

Passive voice: Verbs in the passive voice show something else acting on the subject or person. This voice is often used only when needed but is usually not the primary voice of an author.

To distinguish between the active and passive voice, we will use two examples for each:

Example 1: Active voice: The graduate student *ended* the study.

Passive voice: The study *was ended* by the graduate student.

Example 2: Active voice: The analysis *showed* significance.

Passive voice: Significance *was shown* in the analysis.

Indicative, Imperative, and Subjective Mood

The **indicative mood** indicates a fact or opinion. Most verbs we use are in the indicative mood.

Examples: The doctor *was* here.

I *am* working late.

She *will bring* her notes.

The **imperative mood** expresses commands or requests. The subject of sentences that use the imperative mood is *you*, although it is not directly stated in the sentence.

Examples: *Be* to class on time.

Turn to page 32 in your book.

Bring your calculator to the exam.

Although it is not directly stated, in each example it is understood that <u>you</u> be to class on time, <u>you</u> turn to page 32 in your book, and <u>you</u> bring your calculator to the exam.

The **subjunctive mood** shows something contrary to fact. To express something that is not principally true, use the past tense or past perfect tense; when using the verb *to be* in the subjunctive mood, always use *were* rather than *was*.

Examples: If the inspector *were* here . . . (Implied: but he is not)

I wish we *had tested* the sample first. (Implied: but we did not)

You would have preferred *to be* in class. (Implied: but you were not)

Adjectives and Adverbs

Adjectives modify nouns in some way. Adverbs modify verbs, adjectives, or other adverbs in some way. A description of each type of modifier with examples is given in this section.

ADJECTIVES

Adjectives modify nouns in some way. For example:

- He was given a survey. (*Survey* is a noun. We know that participants were given the survey; we don't know anything else about the survey.)

- He was given a *brief* survey. (*Survey* is a noun. *Brief* is an adjective. The adjective modifies the noun; we now know the kind of survey completed: a *brief* survey.)

Adjectives can answer the following questions:

- Which? (e.g., "The *third* floor." Which floor? The third floor.)

- How many? (e.g., "*Six* students were absent." How many students? Six students.)

- What kind? (e.g., "The student took a *makeup* exam." What kind of exam? A makeup exam.)

ADVERBS

Adverbs modify verbs, adjectives, or other adverbs in some way. Adverbs most often answer the question: How? For example:

- She *studied quietly*. (*Quietly* is an adverb that modifies the verb *studied*. How did she study? Quietly.)

- The professor was *very* fair. (*Fair* is an adjective that modifies the noun *professor*. *Very* is an adverb that modifies the adjective *fair*. How fair is the professor? Very fair.)

Many adverbs have an *-ly* ending. Some examples: *abruptly, absolutely, beautifully, briskly, brutally, cheerfully, delicately, endlessly, expertly, firmly, lightly, literally, quietly, quickly, randomly, really, slowly, successfully, tremendously, wholeheartedly, willfully, willingly.*

- She was a *tremendously* successful researcher. (*Successful* is an adjective that modifies the noun *researcher*. *Tremendously* is an adverb that modifies the adjective *successful*. How successful was the researcher? Tremendously successful.)

Some adverbs indicate the place or location of an action. Some examples: *everywhere, here, in, inside, out, outside, somewhere, there*.

- The class relocated *upstairs*. (*Upstairs* is an adverb that modifies the verb *relocated*. Where did the class relocate? Upstairs.)

Some adverbs indicate when, how often, or what time an action occurred. Some examples: *always, daily, early, first, last, later, monthly, never, now, often, regularly, usually, weekly*.

- Participants were observed *daily*. (*Daily* is an adverb that modifies the verb *observed*. How often were participants observed? Daily.)

Some adverbs indicate to what extent an action or something was done. Some examples: *almost, also, enough, only, quite, rather, so, too, very*.

- The room was *quite* comfortable. (*Comfortable* is an adjective that modifies the noun *room*. *Quite* is an adverb that modifies the adjective *comfortable*. To what extent was the room comfortable? Quite comfortable.)

A Versus An

Using *a* or *an* in a sentence depends on the phonetic (sound) representation of the first letter in a word, not on the orthographic (written) representation of the letter. If the first letter makes a vowel-like sound, then use *an*; if the first letter makes a consonant-like sound, then use *a*. The following are some basic rules for using *a* or *an*:

Rule 1: *A* goes before a word that begins with a consonant. For example:

- <u>A</u> study
- <u>A</u> replication
- <u>A</u> limitation

Rule 2: *An* goes before a word that begins with a vowel. For example:

- <u>An</u> analysis
- <u>An</u> increase
- <u>An</u> effect

Exception 1: Use *an* before an unsounded *h* in which a vowel follows the first letter. The *h* has no audible sound in its phonetic representation; therefore, we use *an* because the first audible sound is a vowel (e.g., "<u>an</u> honest mistake" or "<u>an</u> honorable life").

Exception 2: Use *a* when *u* makes the same sound as *y* (e.g., "<u>a</u> U.S. sample" or "a united team") or *o* makes the same sound as *w* (e.g., "<u>a</u> one-day trial").

Prepositions

A preposition is a word or phrase typically used before a substantive that indicates the relation of the substantive to a verb, an adjective, or another substantive. A preposition functions as a modifier to a verb, noun, or adjective and generally expresses a spatial, temporal, or other type of relationship. Many forms of prepositions are discussed in this section.

PREPOSITIONS FOR TIME AND PLACE

Prepositions are used to identify **one point in time**.
On is used with days of the week and with a specific calendar day.

- The school week begins *on* Monday.
- My birthday is *on* March 30.

At is used with *noon*, *night*, *midnight*, and time of day.

- Class begins *at* noon.
- The stars come out *at* night.
- The deadline is *at* midnight.
- The test will be administered *at* 4:30 p.m.

In is used with *afternoon* and seasons, months, and years.

- He awoke *in* the afternoon.
- The study was conducted *in* spring.
- Snowfall was recorded *in* February.
- He earned his college degree *in* 2012.

Prepositions are used to identify an **extended period of time** using the following prepositions: *since*, *for*, *by*, *from*, *until*, *within*, and *during*.

- It has been two years *since* the last cohort was observed.
- Participants were observed *for* two weeks.
- The deadline has been extended *by* two hours.
- The study continued *from* morning *until* night.
- A research protocol must be completed *within* three years.
- I am always focused *during* class.

Prepositions are used to identify a **place**, or refer to a **location relative to a given point**.
To identify a **place**, use *in* to refer to the point itself, use *inside* to indicate something contained, use *on* to indicate a surface, and use *at* to indicate a specific place/location or general vicinity.

- Animal subjects were housed *in* steel cages.

- He placed his notes *inside* the folder.

- The student left his exam *on* the desk.

- Assistance was available *at* the help desk.

To identify a **location relative to a given point**, use *over* or *above* for a location higher than a point; use *under*, *underneath*, *beneath*, or *below* to identify a location lower than a point; use *near*, *by*, *next to*, *between*, *among*, *behind*, or *opposite* to identify a location close to a point.

- The flask is *above* the cabinet.

- The survey was *beneath* the consent form.

- The child hid *underneath* the table.

- The confederate was *behind* the participant.

- The field was located *between* two oak trees.

PREPOSITIONS FOR DIRECTION OR MOVEMENT

The prepositions *to*, *onto*, and *into* can be used to identify movement toward something. The basic preposition of a direction toward a goal is *to*. When the goal is physical, such as a destination, *to* implies movement toward the goal.

- The mouse ran *to* the cheese.

- The newlyweds flew *to* Paris.

When the goal is not physical, such as an action, *to* marks a verb and is used as an infinitive.

- The student went *to* see her teacher.

- The professor hurried *to* attend the conference.

The preposition *onto* indicates movement toward a surface, whereas the preposition *into* indicates movements toward the interior of a volume.

- The athlete jumped *onto* the platform.

- The solution was poured *into* the container.

Note that *to* can be optional for *onto* and *into* because *on* and *in* can have a directional meaning when used with verbs of motion. The compound preposition (*onto*, *into*) indicates the completion of an action, whereas the simple preposition (*on*, *in*) indicates the position of a subject as a result of that action.

- The shot went *into* the basket OR The shot went *in* the basket.

- The fossils washed up *onto* the shore OR The fossils washed up *on* the shore.

Research Methods for the Behavioral Sciences

Note that some verbs that indicate direction or movement express the idea that some physical object or subject is situated in a specific place. In these cases, some verbs use only *on*, whereas others can use *on* or *onto*. The following is an example in which *on* and *onto* can be distinguished:

- The pilot landed the aircraft [*on* or *onto*] the runway. (In this case, the pilot lands the aircraft toward a surface, i.e., the runway.)
- The aircraft landed *on* [not *onto*] the runway. (In this case, the plane itself is situated on a specific surface, i.e., on the runway.)

Note also that *to* suggests movement toward a specific destination, whereas *toward* suggests movement in a general direction, without necessarily arriving at a destination.

- The student went *to* the exit during the fire drill. (The exit is the destination; note that *to* implies that the student does not actually go *through* the exit; the exit is the destination.)
- The student went *toward* the exit during the fire drill. (The student was headed in the direction of the exit, but may not have reached or gone through the exit.)

PREPOSITIONS FOR INTRODUCING OBJECTS OF VERBS

Use *of* with *approve* and *consists*.

- She did not approve *of* his behavior.
- The solution consists *of* sugar water.

Use *of* or *about* with *dream* and *think*.

- I dream [*of* or *about*] making the world a better place.
- Can you think [*of* or *about*] a solution to the problem?

Use *at* with *laugh*, *stare*, *smile*, and *look*.

- I had to laugh *at* the joke.
- I tend to stare *at* the screen.
- I saw you smile *at* me.
- I look *at* a map to find directions.

Use *for* with *call*, *hope*, *look*, *wait*, and *watch*.

- I may need you to call *for* help.
- We will hope *for* reliable results with this new test.
- Can we look *for* a solution to the problem?
- Can you wait *for* me to return?
- He must watch *for* the signal before proceeding.

Commas

Using punctuation correctly requires that we distinguish between an independent clause and a dependent clause. An *independent clause* is a passage that is a complete sentence that has a subject and a verb. A *dependent clause* is a passage that also has a subject and a verb, but is an incomplete sentence. In this section, we will identify when it is and is not appropriate to use punctuation with independent and dependent clauses.

The following is a brief list of eight rules for **when to use commas**:

Rule 1: Use commas to separate independent clauses that are joined by coordinating conjunctions (e.g., *and*, *but*, *or*, *nor*, *so*, *yet*).

- The study was complete, *but* the data were not analyzed.
- The analysis showed significance, *yet* the results were difficult to interpret.

Note: DO NOT use a comma between the two verbs or verb phrases in a compound predicate.

- The baseball player ran on the bases *and* slid to home. (Do not use a comma because *and* separates two verbs—*ran* [on bases] and *slid* [to home].)
- The researcher explained the expectations and procedures *and* began the study. (Do not use a comma before the last *and* because it separates two verb phrases—*explained the expectations* and *began the study*.)

Rule 2: Use commas after introductory clauses that come before the main clause. The following is a list of common words used to start an introductory clause that should be followed by a comma: *although*, *after*, *as*, *because*, *if*, *when*, *while*, *since*, *however*, *yes*, *well*.

- *After* a short break, participants had no trouble completing the task.
- *While* the student studied, his roommate was playing loud music.
- *As* stated earlier, human behavior can be understood using the scientific process.
- *Yes*, the findings do support the hypothesis.

Note: DO NOT use a comma if the introductory clause follows the main clause (except for cases of extreme contrast).

- Participants had no trouble completing the task *after* a short break. (Do not use a comma.)
- The student was in a great mood, *although* he failed out of college. (Failing out of college is an extreme contrast to being in a great mood; use a comma.)

Rule 3: Use commas to separate three or more elements or words written in a series.

- The categories of research design are experimental, nonexperimental, and quasi-experimental.

- The food environment was contrived to appear open, hidden, or clustered.
- The researcher gave a participant, who volunteered for the study, who completed all interviews, and who followed all procedures, a debriefing form.

Rule 4: Use commas to enclose clauses, phrases, and words in the middle of a sentence that are not essential to the meaning of the sentence.

- His research, *which was completed many years ago*, was published just this year.
- The verdict, *on the other hand*, did not satisfy the family.
- The patient, *however*, was not ready to be released.

Note: To identify a clause, phrase, or word that is not essential to the meaning of a sentence, follow these three guidelines. Enclose the clause, phrase, or word in commas if:

- It could be omitted and the sentence still makes sense,
- It would otherwise interrupt the flow of words in the original sentence, or
- It could be moved to a different part of the sentence, and the sentence would still make sense.

Rule 5: Use commas to separate two or more coordinate adjectives but not two or more noncoordinate adjectives to describe the same noun.

- Participation in the experimental group required *intense*, *rigorous* skills. (The sentence uses coordinate adjectives [*intense*, *rigorous*], so a comma is used.)
- The student wore a *green woolly* sweater. (The sentence uses noncoordinate adjectives [*green*, *woolly*], so no comma is used.)
- He was prepared for the *cold*, *chilly*, *snowy winter* weather. (There are three coordinate adjectives [*cold*, *chilly*, *snowy*] with a comma used to separate each, and one noncoordinate adjective [*winter*] with no comma used.)

Note: To identify coordinate adjectives used to describe the same noun, follow these two guidelines. The adjectives are coordinate and a comma is used if:

- The sentence still makes sense when the adjectives are written in reverse order, or
- The sentence still makes sense when *and* is written between the adjectives.

Rule 6: Use a comma near the end of a sentence to indicate a distinct pause or to separate contrasted coordinate elements.

- The study showed evidence of clinical significance, not statistical significance.
- The student seemed frustrated, even angry.
- The research findings were an important advancement, almost landmark.

Rule 7: Use commas to separate geographical names, items in dates (except month and day), titles in names, and addresses (except street number and name).

- The author was raised in East Aurora, New York.

- November 10, 2015, will be the 240th birthday of the U.S. Marine Corps.

- Ivan Pavlov, PhD, was a Noble Prize winner.

- The White House is located at 1600 Pennsylvania Avenue, Washington, DC.

Rule 8: Use a comma to shift between the main discourse and a quotation but not when the quotation is part of the main discourse.

- The parent told his child, "Every moment I am with you is the greatest moment of my life."

- Telling your child to "live every moment as if it is your last" can be inspirational. (No comma is used because the quoted material is part of the main discourse.)

Colons and Semicolons

Colons and semicolons are used to mark a major division in a sentence, typically to bring together two or more ideas into one enumeration. This section describes many rules for appropriately using colons and semicolons.

COLONS

A colon is used to divide the main discourse of a sentence from an elaboration, summation, or general implication of the main discourse. A colon is also used to separate numbers, such as hours and minutes, and a ratio or proportion. The following is a list of five rules for appropriately using colons.

Rule 1: Use a colon before statements that introduce a formal passage or list.

- Three topics are described in this guide: grammar, punctuation, and spelling.

- To do well in this class: Take notes! Read the book! Study often!

Note: DO NOT use a colon after a preposition or linking verb.

- Three topics described in this guide *are* grammar, punctuation, and spelling. (*Are* is a linking verb used in place of the colon.)

- You can do well in this class *by* taking notes, reading the book, and studying often. (*By* is used to link "doing well" with the three criteria listed for doing well.)

Rule 2: Use a colon (in place of a comma) before long or formal direct quotations.

- The German-born American physicist Albert Einstein once *said:* "I am neither especially clever nor especially gifted. I am only very, very curious." (A colon is used to separate the passage from the quoted material; note that a comma can also be used in place of the colon to separate the passage from the quoted material.)

Rule 3: Use a colon before formal appositives.

- Most citizens polled identified the same issue as their main concern: the economy. (A colon introduces an appositive.)

- One class was his favorite in college: psychology. (A colon introduces an appositive.)

Rule 4: Use a colon between independent clauses when the second clause restates or supports the same idea as the preceding clause.

- Scientists are not infallible: On occasion, they can, without intention, misinterpret, mislead, or misrepresent the data they publish. (The second clause expands on and supports the preceding clause.)

- Any idea you develop must be testable: An idea must lead to specific predictions that can be observed under specified conditions. (The second clause expands on and supports the preceding clause.)

Note: To be concise, DO NOT restate the same idea unless it serves to expand on or further illustrate the content in the preceding clause.

Rule 5: Use a colon to separate numbers, such as hours and minutes, and a ratio or proportion.

The deadline was set at *9:00* p.m.

The chances of winning the game were *4:1*. (A ratio can also be stated as *4 to 1* without the colon.)

SEMICOLONS

A semicolon is used to divide the main discourse of a sentence and to balance two contrasted or related ideas. The following is a list of three rules for appropriately using semicolons.

Rule 1: Use a semicolon to separate two independent clauses not connected by a coordinating conjunction.

- Each participant chose the second option; it was the preferred option.

- She finished her exam in one hour; I completed my exam in half that time.

- The laboratory was contrived; it was designed to look like a day care center.

Note: DO NOT overuse semicolons for Rule 1. As a general rule, only apply Rule 1 when using a comma in place of a period allows for an easier transition between two complete sentences or independent clauses. As an example, for the sentences below, the transition between the sentences is not made easier by using the semicolon.

- INCORRECT: From a broad view, science is any systematic method of acquiring knowledge apart from ignorance; *from* a stricter view, science is specifically the acquisition of knowledge using the scientific method.

- CORRECT: From a broad view, science is any systematic method of acquiring knowledge apart from ignorance. *From* a stricter view, science is specifically the acquisition of knowledge using the scientific method.

Rule 2: Use a semicolon before a transitional connective or conjunctive adverb that separates two main clauses. Examples of conjunctive adverbs are *consequently*, *besides*, *instead*, *also*, *furthermore*, *therefore*, *however*, *likewise*, *hence*, *nevertheless*, *in addition*, and *moreover*.

- His hypothesis has support; *however*, his statements go beyond the data.

- It was the best product on the market; *yet*, it was overpriced.

- The student was not distracted; *instead*, she was focused.

Note: The same caution applies here regarding the use of semicolons and periods. Only use a semicolon for Rule 2 when using a comma in place of a period allows for an easier transition between two complete sentences or independent clauses.

Rule 3: Use semicolons between items that have internal punctuation in a series or sequence.

- The members of the editorial board are William James, editor-in-chief; Ivan Pavlov, associate editor; B. F. Skinner, associate editor; and Chris Thomas, editorial assistant. (A semicolon is used to "break up" the commas used to separate the names from the titles of each editor.)

- Over the next four years, our conference will be held in Buffalo, New York; Chicago, Illinois; Washington, DC; and Seattle, Washington. (A semicolon is used to "break up" the commas used to separate the names of each city and state.)

Apostrophes

An apostrophe is used to form possessives of nouns, to indicate missing letters with contractions, and to show plurals of lowercase letters. Each type of use for an apostrophe is briefly described in this section.

FORMING POSSESSIVES OF NOUNS

An apostrophe is used for the possessive. To see if you need to form the possessive of a noun, make the phrase an "of the" phrase. If the "of the" phrase makes sense, then use an apostrophe—except if the noun after *of* is a building or room, an object, or a piece of furniture.

- The patient's file = the file *of the* patient ("of the" makes sense; apostrophe needed)

- The study's outcome = the outcome *of the* study ("of the" makes sense; apostrophe needed)

- The day's end = the end *of the* day ("of the" makes sense; apostrophe needed)

- The laboratory corridor = the corridor of the laboratory ("of the" makes sense; however, no apostrophe is needed because "the laboratory" is a building or room)

Note: DO NOT use apostrophes with possessive pronouns because possessive pronouns already show possession. For example:

- His lab (NOT: His' lab)
- The team made its quota. (NOT: The team made it's quota. *Its* is a possessive pronoun meaning "belonging to it"; *it's* is a contraction meaning "it is.")

In addition, do not use an apostrophe with units of time. For example:

- The study was two hours long. (NOT: The study was two hours' long.)

The following is a list of five rules for when to use an apostrophe for the possessive:

Rule 1: Add *'s* to the singular form of a word, even if it ends in -*s*.

- The researcher's conclusions
- The student's grade
- James's application

Rule 2: Add *'s* to words in which the plural form does not end in -*s*.

- The nuclei's activity
- The stimuli's presence
- The people's choice

The following is a brief list of words with a plural form that does not end in *s*. Follow Rule 2 for the plural form of these words.

Singular	Plural
Alumna	Alumnae
Alumnus	Alumni
Child	Children
Criterion	Criteria
Curriculum	Curricula
Datum	Data
Dice	Die
Foot	Feet
Focus	Foci
Fungus	Fungi
Man	Men
Mouse	Mice
Nucleus	Nuclei
Person	People
Phenomenon	Phenomena
Stimulus	Stimuli
Woman	Women

Rule 3: Add ' to the end of plural nouns that end in *s*:

- The countries' independence
- The universities' collaboration

Rule 4: Add *'s* to the singular form of compound words and hyphenated nouns.

- The scapegoat's rationale
- The rattlesnake's bite
- The editor-in-chief's decision

Rule 5: Add *'s* to the last noun to show joint possession of an object.

- Tom and Jerry's house
- Denver and Miami's football game

INDICATING MISSING LETTERS WITH CONTRACTIONS

Apostrophes are used in contractions to indicate that letters are missing when two words are combined—for example, *it's* (it is), *don't* (do not), *could've* (could have). However, contractions are NOT used with APA style. For this reason, we will not introduce the use of apostrophes in detail greater than that identified in this paragraph.

SHOWING PLURALS OF LOWERCASE LETTERS

Rule for lowercase letters: Add *'s* to form the plural of lowercase letters.

- Mind your *p's* and *q's*. (Lowercase letters need apostrophe.)
- In sports, it is all about the *w's*. (Lowercase letter needs apostrophe.)

Note: Apostrophes indicating the plural form of capitalized letters, numbers, and symbols are NOT needed. For example:

- Two *MVPs* were selected.
- All students earned *As* and scored in the *90s* on the exam.
- Many *&s* were used in the reference list.

Quotation Marks

Quotation marks are most often used to set off or represent exact spoken or written language, typically from another source. For this reason, using quotation marks correctly is one practical way to avoid plagiarism. Quotations can also be used for other purposes not related to citing other sources. In this section, we will describe many of the rules for quotation mark use.

As a general rule, always open and close quoted material with quotation marks. Hence, quotation marks should always be used in pairs. Quotation marks are used for direct quotations; not indirect quotations. The APA manual provides complete instructions on how to properly cite references in text with and without quotation marks—and therefore for direct and indirect quotation use, respectively.

Keep in mind also that overuse of quotation marks can be poor practice because it gives the impression that the ideas expressed in a paper are not primarily coming from the author or writer. For this reason, make sure to use direct quotations sparingly. If you can simply summarize a work, results, or other details in the text, then paraphrase; that is, use indirect quotations. Only use direct quotations for material or language in which paraphrasing would diminish its importance (e.g., a quote from a famous author or figure such as that given in a speech, a definition for a key term, or an important work or policy).

Note for all examples below that the period or comma punctuation always comes before the final quotation mark. Follow this punctuation rule when using quotation marks.

Rule 1: Capitalize the first letter of a direct quote when the quoted material is a complete sentence.

- The author stated, "A significant outcome is not proof of an effect; a significant outcome indicates evidence of an effect."

- While he did have a viable program of research, it was another researcher who said, "High power may be the most essential factor for a program of research to be viable."

Rule 2: DO NOT capitalize the first letter of a direct quote when the quoted material is a fragment sentence or is integrated as part of an original sentence.

- The students behaved during class because the professor made clear that "self-discipline and control" were important to be successful in his class.

- These findings support the assertion that "it is not all about the calories" when it comes to understanding hunger and fullness.

Rule 3: If the quoted material is a complete sentence and is broken up, then capitalize the first part of the sentence but not the second part.

- "Isolating confounding variables," he said, "is important when conducting an experiment." (Note that two pairs of quotations are used when one quote is broken into two parts.)

Rule 4: Use single quotation marks to enclose quotes within another quotation.

- The participant replied, "He told me that 'I was being too strict' as a parent." (The single quotation marks indicate quotes from a secondary source and not those of the speaker specifically being quoted in double quotation marks.)

Rule 5: You may omit portions of a quote, typically to be more concise, by replacing the omitted words with an ellipsis.

- **Original Quote**: "An experiment with an increased sample size should be able to detect an effect, if one exists, because it is associated with greater power."
- **Revised Quote**: "An experiment with an increased sample size . . . is associated with greater power."

Rule 6: You may add words to quoted material, typically to improve clarity, by enclosing the added words in brackets.

- **Original Quote**: He explained, "At that time, I handed out the survey."
- **Revised Quote**: He explained, "At that time [when participants arrived], I handed out the survey."

Rule 7: Use quotation marks for the definition of a key term if quoted from another source. DO NOT use quotation marks for the key term; instead, use italics or boldface to identify the to-be-defined term.

- *Science* is "the acquisition of knowledge through observation, evaluation, interpretation, and theoretical explanation."

Rule 8: Quotation marks—not used for direct quotes—can indicate words used ironically or even comically.

- It was an awful game at the "Super" Bowl. ("Super" Bowl is an ironic name for the game if the game itself was awful.)
- The sprinter "ran away" from the competition. (This phrase could be construed as funny because "run away" has a double meaning in this context—it relates to winning a competition and the fact that the competition involved running.)

Hyphens

A hyphen can be used to separate words or phrases. The following six rules can be applied and are generally accepted for using hyphens correctly.

Rule 1: Use a hyphen to join two or more words serving as a single adjective that precedes a noun.

- The *well-known* study. (The adjective [*well-known*] precedes the noun [*study*]; use a hyphen to combine the words *well* and *known*.)
- The *clear-headed* researcher. (The adjective [*clear-headed*] precedes the noun [*researcher*]; use a hyphen to combine the words *clear* and *headed*.)

Rule 2: DO NOT use a hyphen to join two or more words serving as a single adjective that follow a noun.

- The study was *well known*. (The adjective [*well known*] follows the noun [*study*]; DO NOT use a hyphen.)

- The researcher was *clear headed*. (The adjective [*clear headed*] follows the noun [*researcher*]; DO NOT use a hyphen.)

Rule 3: Use a hyphen to join letters that may otherwise cause confusion.

- They were asked to *re-sign* the form. (*Re-sign* is "to sign again" whereas *resign* is "to give up" or "to accept as inevitable.")

- We had to *re-cover* the solution. (*Re-cover* is "to cover again" whereas *recover* is "to restore" or "to regain.")

Rule 4: Use a hyphen for prefixes [*ex-* (meaning "former"), *self-*, *all-*, *half-*, *quasi-*]; for suffixes [*-elect*, *-like*, *-typical*]; and between a prefix and a capitalized word (such as a proper noun) or number.

- Prefixes: ex-husband, self-aware, all-knowing, half-asleep, quasi-experimental.

- Suffixes: president-elect, playoff-like atmosphere, schizoid-typical behavior.

- Between a prefix and a capitalized word or number: anti-American, mid-1900s.

Rule 5: Use a hyphen to join multiword compounds (with few exceptions), usually even if the multiword compound precedes or follows the noun.

- His response was *matter-of-fact*.

- The *next-to-last* student was chosen to participate.

Rule 6: Use a hyphen to join compound numbers.

- *Thirty-six* students took the exam.

- A total of *twenty-two* participants dropped out of the study.

Rule 6a: Using APA style, it is necessary to express a number in words when:

- The number is less than 10, except when displayed in a figure or table, or preceding a unit of measurement (e.g., 5 m).

- The number is the first word in a sentence (e.g., Thirty-eight participants were observed), except if the sentence is in the abstract, in which case it is recommended to avoid starting a sentence with a number (all numbers are expressed as numerals in an abstract).

- Approximating days, months, and years (e.g., "about two days ago," or "almost three months went by").

- The number expresses a common fraction when used as an adjective (e.g., two-thirds majority).

Sentence Structure

Sentence structure is the grammatical arrangement of words into sentences. In addition to words, sentences can also include numbers and individual letters or symbols.

Sentence structure is important in that good structure strengthens the flow of ideas in a written work and makes it easier for the reader to correctly understand what is written. In this section, we introduce fundamental rules of sentence structure not yet discussed in this basic writing guide.

SUBJECT-VERB AGREEMENT

Rule 1: Use a plural verb when the subject of a sentence consists of two or more nouns or pronouns connected by *and*; use a singular verb when nouns or pronouns are linked with *or*.

- Jack *and* Jill <u>are</u> in the lab. (Plural)

- His work *or* your work <u>is</u> going to win the prize. (Singular)

Rule 2: When the subject of a sentence consists of two or more nouns or pronouns connected by *or*, the verb must agree with the part of the subject that is closer to the verb in the sentence.

- The graduate students *or* a researcher <u>runs</u> the study. (The "researcher" [singular] is the part of the subject that is closest to the verb *runs*.)

- A researcher *or* the graduate students <u>run</u> the study. (The "graduate students" [plural] are the part of the subject that is closest to the verb *run*.)

Rule 3: A verb must agree with the subject, not with the noun or pronoun in the clause.

- One of the hypotheses <u>is</u> correct. (*One* is singular and is the subject.)

- The hypotheses <u>are</u> both correct. (*Hypotheses* is plural and is the subject.)

- The book, including all appendices, <u>was</u> easy to read. (*Book* is singular and is the subject.)

- The women, even those who did not volunteer, <u>were</u> cooperative. (*Women* is plural and is the subject.)

Rule 4: The following words are singular and require a singular verb: *anybody*, *anyone*, *each*, *everybody*, *everyone*, *no one*, *nobody*, *somebody*, and *someone*.

- *Each* of the students <u>is</u> responsible.

- *Nobody* <u>is</u> leaving.

- *Everybody* <u>has</u> arrived.

Rule 5: Use a singular verb for nouns that imply more than one person but are considered singular, such as *class*, *committee*, *family*, *group*, and *team*.

- The *group* <u>is</u> ready for therapy.

- The *committee* <u>has</u> made a decision.

Rule 6: Use a singular verb when *either* or *neither* is the subject.

- *Neither* of us <u>was</u> aware of what happened.
- *Either* of them <u>is</u> culpable.

Rule 7: The following expressions do not change the number of the subject or the verb: *with*, *together with*, *including*, *accompanied by*, *in addition to*, *along with*, and *as well*.

- The sailor, *along with* his mates, <u>is</u> excited for the trip. (The subject is *the sailor* [singular], so the verb is also singular.)
- The cofounders, *together with* an outside supporter, <u>are</u> pleased with the outcome. (The subject is *the cofounders* [plural], so the verb is also plural.)

Rule 8: The expression *the number* is followed by a singular verb; the expression *a number* is followed by a plural verb.

- *The number* of participants required <u>is</u> substantial. (Singular)
- *A number* of attendees <u>are</u> being honored today. (Plural)

Rule 9: Use a singular verb with sums of money or periods/durations of time.

- The *$20* <u>is</u> for a parking fee.
- *Ten years* <u>is</u> a long time to continue a study.

Rule 10: The verb agrees with what follows *there is*, *there are*, *here is*, and *here are* when a sentence begins with one of these terms.

- There <u>is</u> *a question*. (Singular)
- There <u>are</u> *many participants*. (Plural)
- Here <u>is</u> *an example*. (Singular)
- Here <u>are</u> *a few examples*. (Plural)

SENTENCE FRAGMENTS

Sentence fragments are incomplete sentences. Fragments should always be avoided in academic writing, even if the fragment follows clearly from the preceding main clause. For example:

- The study took longer than expected. Which is why we ended it early. (The second sentence is a fragment. If read alone, we are left asking, "What was ended early?")

Possible revisions to make the fragment a complete sentence:

1. The study took longer than expected, which is why we ended it early. (*It* now clearly refers back to *the study*.)
2. We ended the study early because it took longer than expected. (*It* now clearly refers back to *the study*.)

Many sentence fragments are written as main clauses but lack a main verb or a subject. A sentence fragment with no subject often begins with a preposition. An example for each case is given here. Again, avoid sentence fragments and use only complete sentences in academic writing.

A fragment with **no main verb**:

- A study with three independent variables.

Possible revisions to make the fragment a complete sentence by adding a main verb:

1. A study <u>was conducted</u> with three independent variables.

2. Participants <u>completed</u> a study with three independent variables.

A fragment with **no subject**:

- For making the most of a difficult situation, Jim got promoted.

Possible revisions to make the fragment a complete sentence:

1. Making the most of a difficult situation got Jim promoted. (Removed *for* [the preposition].)

2. Jim got promoted for making the most of a difficult situation. (The sentence was rearranged so that it ends with the prepositional phrase.)

DANGLING MODIFIERS

A dangling modifier is a word or phrase that modifies a word not clearly stated in a sentence. Many strategies can be used to correct sentences with dangling modifiers. The key is to ask *who* did an action. Two examples are given here.

- Dangling modifier: Having completed all preparations, the door was opened. [Who completed all preparations? "Having completed" expresses action, but the doer is not the door (the subject of the main clause): A door does not finish preparations. The phrase before the comma, then, is a dangling modifier.]

To correct the sentence we can name the doer of the action as the subject of the main clause:

- Having completed all preparations, the researcher opened the door. [In this sentence, the doer of the action (completing all preparations) seems logically to be the researcher (identified in the main clause). The sentence is good, and it does not have a dangling modifier.]

Alternatively, we can combine the phrase and main clause into one sentence without a comma:

- The researcher opened the door after completing all preparations. [Again, the doer of the action (completing all preparations) seems logically to be the researcher in this sentence. The sentence is good, and it does not have a dangling modifier.]

Many other strategies can be used to clarify *who* is doing the action. In all, you should be able to clearly identify *who* is doing an action described in a sentence. If the doer of an action is unclear in a sentence, then revise the sentence to make this clear.

PARALLEL SENTENCE STRUCTURE

A parallel structure implies that the sentence uses consistent words and phrases. Here, we give two rules to help you identify and use parallel sentence structure.

Rule 1: Do not mix forms of elements or words in a list, such as elements or words ending in *-ing*, *-ly*, and *-ed*.

- INCORRECT: The athletics test involved throwing, blocking, tackling, and making maneuvers. (Not parallel; the last word changes the *-ing* form.)
- CORRECT: The athletics test involved throwing, blocking, tackling, and maneuvering. (Parallel; all words in the set end in the same *-ing* form.)

Rule 2: A parallel structure that begins with clauses must keep on with clauses.

- INCORRECT: Participants were told to arrive 15 minutes early for the study, to complete all forms, and that they should dress appropriately. (Not parallel; the last underlined clause changes pattern or form.)
- CORRECT: Participants were told to arrive 15 minutes early for the study, to complete all forms, and to dress appropriately. (Parallel; all clauses have the same form or pattern.)

Spelling

In this final section of the guide we will review commonly misspelled words in English. Students often take spelling for granted because Microsoft® Office software includes a spell-check feature. However, many words can be improperly used in a sentence yet be spelled correctly. For example, consider "She was *hosing* around" versus "She was horsing around." In the first sentence, an *r* is missing from the word *horsing*; however, both spellings are a correct word. As another common example consider "He came *form* nowhere" versus "He came *from* nowhere." In the first sentence, the order of *o* and *r* is reversed in the word *from*; the spellings of each word, however, are correct—it is the meaning of each word that is different. Mistakes that are not caught by spell-check also often occur when we drop or forget to add letters to the beginning (e.g., *[un]necessary*, *[mis]used*) or ending (e.g., *common[ly]*, *play[s]*, *grant[ed]*, *no[t]*) of otherwise correctly spelled words. It can be easy to miss or overlook mistakes such as those given as examples here. Make sure you carefully proofread your work before you submit it to try to catch these types of silly and unnecessary mistakes.

Also a concern is misspellings caused by a misunderstanding of the meanings of words used in a sentence. Grammatical and spelling errors often occur because we improperly use words we think are being used correctly. Common examples include *that* versus *which*, *accept* versus *except*, and *then* versus *than*. Mistakes in the use of these words can be difficult to overcome because the author can often "think" the use of these words is correct when in fact it is wrong. To help clarify some of the most common grammatical and spelling errors in English, the following table lists 26 words that are commonly misused. How each word is used in a sentence (as a noun, verb, etc.) and definitions for each word are given, along with examples, if needed, to further clarify the correct meanings and uses of the words.

Words	Meaning
accept/except	*accept:* (verb) to receive something; to join, consent, or enter into agreement *except:* (verb) to exclude or leave out; (preposition) not including; other than
affect/effect	*affect:* (noun) emotion or desire; (verb) to influence or act upon *effect:* (noun) the result of a consequence, action; (verb) to bring about or implement
afterward/afterword	*afterward:* (adverb) at a later time; subsequently *afterword:* (noun) a concluding section in a book or work
already/all ready	*already:* (adverb) by an implied or specified time; now; so soon; e.g., It is break <u>already</u> [by this time]. *all ready:* (adjective) completely prepared; e.g., The study was <u>all ready</u> [completely prepared] to begin.
alright/all right	*alright:* (adjective, adverb) to be satisfactory or acceptable; e.g., The evidence is <u>alright</u> [satisfactory]. *all right:* (adjective, adverb) without doubt; accurate or acceptable; e.g., The evidence is <u>all right</u> [accurate]. Note: In English, alright is not widely accepted as a word, so avoid its use.
altogether/all together	*altogether:* (adverb) entirely; completely; e.g., The event was <u>altogether</u> [entirely] successful. *all together:* (adverb) collectively; at the same time; e.g., We completed the study <u>all together</u> [collectively].
among/between	*among:* (preposition) surrounded by; being a member in a larger set *between:* (adverb) at, into, or across a space separating two points in position or time
amount/number	*amount:* (noun) a quantity; (verb) a total when added to together *number:* (noun) an arithmetic or countable value; (verb) to comprise or amount to
assure/ensure/insure	*Assure:* (verb) to make secure or certain; to put the mind at rest *Ensure:* (verb) to make secure or certain; to put the mind at rest [assure, ensure: same meanings] *Insure:* (verb) to guarantee persons or property from risk

Words	Meaning
breath/breathe	*breath:* (noun) An ability to inhale and exhale air, oxygen, etc.; exhalation that can be seen, smelled, or heard *breathe:* (verb) to take air into the lungs and exhale it; to be or seem to be alive
cite/site	*cite:* (noun) a citation; (verb) to quote *site:* (noun) a spatial location or position of interest; (verb) to fix or build [something] in a particular location
compliment/complement	*compliment:* (noun) a polite express of praise; (verb) to praise or congratulate *complement:* (noun) something that completes or makes perfect; (verb) to enhance or improve in some way; to make perfect
counsel/council	*counsel:* (noun) advice; (verb) to give [someone] advice *council:* (noun) a body or assembly of persons convened for consultation, deliberation, or advice
everyone/every one	*everyone:* (pronoun) every person [in a group]; e.g., On this day, <u>everyone</u> [every person] agreed. *every one:* (pronoun) each one; The awardee thanked <u>every one</u> [each person] at the ceremony. Note: In English, everyone and everybody can be used interchangeably and mean the same thing.
few/little	*few:* (noun) a minority of people; (adjective) a small number of *little:* (adjective) small in size, amount, or degree; (adverb) to a small extent
its/it's	*its:* (pronoun) forms the possessive case of it; belonging to it, e.g., The board had <u>its</u> meeting. *it's:* contraction of "it is"; Note: Using APA style, always write out "it is."
lose/loose	*lose:* (verb) to be deprived of; cease or fail to retain *loose:* (verb) to set free; release; (adjective) not firmly in place; able to be detached
many/much	*many:* (noun) the majority of people; (adjective) a large number of people *much:* (adverb) to a great extent; (adjective) a large amount [in quantity]
mute/moot	*mute:* (noun) a person who cannot speak; (verb) to reduce or soften sound; (adjective) temporarily speechless *moot:* (verb) to raise or suggest for discussion; (adjective) a subject of debate, dispute, or uncertainty
past/passed	*past:* (noun) a previous time; (adjective) gone by and no longer exists; (adverb) to pass from one side [of something] to another; (preposition) on a further side of [something] *passed:* (verb) move or lie in a specific direction or position
principle/principal	*principle:* (noun) a fundamental truth, rule, or belief that governs individual/group behavior *principal:* (noun) person with highest authority or importance; (adjective) most important

(Continued)

(Continued)

Words	Meaning
that/which	*that:* (pronoun, adjective, adverb, conjunction) used to identify key information about something or someone; e.g., It was in this study <u>that</u> researchers first discovered . . . [*That* allows for a clear transition and flow of key information in the sentence.] *which:* (pronoun) used to specify information related to something previously mentioned or from a definite set; e.g., The landmark study, <u>which</u> was conducted in the 1950s . . . [The information that follows which relates back to the study]; e.g., There are so many classes I like; <u>which</u> do I choose? [*Which* refers to a choice based on a definite set or availability of classes.] Note: Which is usually preceded by a comma; that does not take a comma.
then/than	*then:* (adverb) at a given time; after that; next; soon afterward *than:* (conjunction) introduces a comparison; expresses an exception or contrast
there/they/their/they're	*there:* (adverb) in, at, or to a place or position; e.g., <u>Go there</u> to take your turn. *they:* (pronoun) something or someone previously mentioned or easily identified; e.g., <u>They</u> get a turn. *their:* (adjective) forms the possessive case of *they*; e.g., It is <u>their</u> turn. *they're:* contraction of "they are"; Note: Using APA style, always write out "they are."
who/whose/who's	*who:* (pronoun) used to identify a person or people; introduces a clause that gives greater detail about a person or people; e.g., <u>Who</u> has the next turn?; e.g., The student <u>who</u> went out of turn. *whose:* (adjective) forms the possessive case of *who*; e.g., <u>Whose</u> turn is it? *who's:* contraction of "who is"; Note: Using APA style, always write out "who is."
you/your/you're	*you:* (pronoun) refers to the person who is being addressed; e.g., <u>You</u> have a degree. *your:* (adjective) forms the possessive case of you; e.g., It is <u>your</u> degree. *you're:* contraction of "you are"; Note: Using APA style, always write out "you are."

A.3 Sample APA-Style Manuscript

Writing an APA-style manuscript is unique. The general format for a submitted APA-style manuscript is restated here (from that originally stated in Chapter 15):

- **Title page.** Page 1; includes title, author(s), affiliations, and author note with contact information of primary author.

- **Abstract** (defined in Chapter 2). Page 2; a brief overview of the manuscript no more than 250 words.

- **Main body.** Includes many subheadings beginning on page 3. (1) The introduction section includes a literature review and identification of research hypotheses. (2) The method section includes a description of participants, materials and apparatus, procedures, and analyses. (3) The results section includes a summary of data and the statistical analyses used. (4) The discussion section includes an interpretation and evaluation of the data and how these relate to the research hypotheses.

- **References.** A complete list of all references for each source cited in the manuscript, on a separate page.

- **Tables** (if any). Each table is given on a separate page following the references. The tables are inserted into the main body upon publication of a manuscript. Table notes are included with each table.

- **Figures** (if any). Each figure is given on a separate page following the tables. The figures are inserted into the main body upon publication of a manuscript. Figure captions are included with each figure. Note: Keep in mind that you are submitting papers for class to your professor, and not an editor. So your professor may want you to insert figures and tables in the main body of the text.

For multiple experiments, the main body is modified a bit. The order of the main body for multiple experiments is (1) "Introduction" heading; (2) "General Method" heading (for methods common to all experiments); (3) "Experiment 1" heading, with "Method" (specific to only that experiment), "Results," and "Discussion" subheadings; (4) "Experiment 2" heading with the same subheadings, and so on for all experiments; and (5) "General Discussion" heading (this gives an overall summary for all experiments). Using APA style, main headings are centered, whereas subheadings are left aligned on the page. In sum, the only change is in the main body to allow for multiple experiments to be included.

To write an APA-style manuscript, you can refer also to the sample manuscript provided here, which is adapted from a manuscript published in 2015 in the *Journal of Attention Disorders*, and was featured in June 2015 in the *Wall Street Journal*. The research reported in this sample manuscript was completed at the time by two professors (Dr. Gregory Privitera and Dr. Stacy Bender) and two undergraduate students (Jaela Agnello and Shelby Walters). Please feel free to use this sample manuscript to guide your own writing.

The running head is an abbreviated title in all capital letters and appears flush left on the top of every page. It should be a maximum of 50 characters, and pages are numbered at the top right of each page.

Randomized Feedback About Diagnosis Influences Significance of Adult ADHD Assessment

Gregory J. Privitera[1], Jaela E. Agnello[1], Shelby A. Walters[1], and Stacy L. Bender[2]

[1]Saint Bonaventure University, Department of Psychology, Saint Bonaventure, NY, USA.
[2]University of Rochester Medical Center, Rochester, NY, USA.

The title is centered on the top half of the title page and not longer than 12 words.

Each author is listed with institutional affiliation given below. Use "and," not the ampersand symbol (&), before listing the last author.

Author Note

Correspondence should be directed to: Dr. Gregory Privitera, Department of Psychology, St. Bonaventure University, 3261 West State Street, St. Bonaventure, NY 14778, USA. Tel. +1 (716) 375-2488; e-mail: gprivite@sbu.edu.

The author note includes full contact or affiliation information, including any changes since the study was completed, and disclaimers, acknowledgments, and other pertinent information.

Abstract

An experiment was conducted to test the hypothesis that feedback about an ADHD diagnosis influences how a nonclinical sample scores on the Adult ADHD Self-Report Scale (ASRS) screener. In all, 54 participants who scored below clinical significance on the ASRS in a pretest, i.e., marked fewer than 4 of 6 items found to be most predictive of symptoms consistent with clinical diagnosis of adult ADHD, completed the assessment again one week later in a posttest with "negative," "positive," or no feedback written on the posttest to indicate how participants scored on the pretest. Results showed that 8 of 10 participants who scored in the clinical significance range for ADHD in the posttest were those who received positive feedback. Scores for the positive feedback group increased most from pretest to posttest for inattentive domain items. Results suggest that patient beliefs prior to a diagnostic screening can influence ASRS self-report ratings.

Keywords: ADHD, adolescence, beliefs, inattention, psychometrics

The abstract begins on a new page. It is 250 words at most with no paragraph indentation. The heading "Abstract" is centered; the remaining text is left aligned.

Keywords are search terms that should be embedded in the abstract to make it more searchable.

Randomized Feedback About Diagnosis Influences Significance
of Adult ADHD Assessment

Attention Deficit Hyperactivity Disorder (ADHD) is a neurodevelopmental
chronic mental health disorder associated with substantial physical, behavioral,
cognitive, and social impairments throughout the lifespan (American Psychiatric
Association, 2000; Barkley, 2006; Barkley, Fischer, Smallish, & Fletcher, 2002; Faraone
& Antshel, 2008). About 4.4% of the adult U.S. population, or about 9 million adults,
are estimated to have ADHD (Faraone & Biederman, 2005; Kessler et al., 2006). The
primary screening tool used by clinicians to make decisions regarding ADHD diagnosis
in adults is self-report (Wender, Wolf, & Wasserstein, 2001), which is a method believed
to underestimate the incidence of the disorder (Murphy & Schachar, 2000; Zucker,
Morris, Ingram, Morris, & Bakeman, 2002).

The extent to which ADHD is under or overdiagnosed in adolescents has long been
investigated (Desgranges, Desgranges, & Karsky, 1995; Kessler et al., 2006), with most
research focused on the ability of therapists to properly identify sex differences in the
expression of ADHD (Gaub & Carlson, 1997; Gershon, 2002), to properly adhere to diagnostic
criteria in the *Diagnostic and Statistical Manual of Mental Disorders* (4th ed.; DSM-IV;
Bruchmüller, Margraf, & Schneider, 2012), and to be aware of the heritability of ADHD
(Able, Johnston, Adler, & Swindle, 2007; Waite & Ramsay, 2010). However, little effort has
been focused on the extent to which patient beliefs about their diagnosis prior to a diagnostic
assessment influences diagnosis.

Recent evidence suggests that self-reports, which are commonly used as screening tools
to help clinicians make decisions regarding ADHD diagnosis with adolescents and

adults, are less diagnostically sensitive than informant reports in assessing ADHD

symptoms (Sibley et al., 2012; Sibley et al., in press). The evidence suggests that young

adults with ADHD tend to underreport symptoms and young adults without ADHD tend

to overreport symptoms using self-report assessments (Barkley et al., 2002; Sibley et

al., 2010). In fact, Sibley et al. (in press) suggest that the use of self-report measures in

assessing ADHD is so inconsistent that it adds little benefit compared to parent reports

alone. Therefore, it would be beneficial to identify potential factors that contribute to

inconsistencies in self-reports in order to alleviate the problems associated with using

these measures to reliably screen for ADHD.

One possible factor contributing to inconsistent patient self-reports is patient

beliefs about diagnosis. Concerns regarding the influence of self-beliefs on the

expression of ADHD symptoms have been raised (Bell, Long, Garvan, & Bussing,

2011). Studies show that negative stigmas held by teachers and parents can negatively

influence the behavior and self-efficacy of children (Eisenburg & Schneider, 2007;

Madon, Guyll, Spoth, & Willard, 2004). For children with ADHD, teachers and parents

can often hold more negative perceptions of the abilities of these children compared

to those without ADHD, even when no child differences exist (Eisenburg et al., 2007).

Given that adults can hold negative stigmas that change their behavior toward children

known to be diagnosed with ADHD, it is certainly possible that young adults may

likewise be influenced by their perceptions or beliefs of their own diagnosis. If true,

then these beliefs could contribute to the purported inconsistent self-reports of

young adults using these self-report assessments (Barkley et al., 2002; Sibley

et al., 2010).

In this experiment, we tested for the first time the hypothesis that self-beliefs prior

to ADHD assessment can influence self-report ratings. In this experiment, we used the

World Health Organization (WHO) Adult ADHD Self-Report Scale (ASRS) screener (Adler et al., 2006; Kessler et al., 2005; Kessler et al., 2007), which is commonly used in clinical practice[1]

Each subheading for the method section is left aligned in bold type. Subheadings can vary. This manuscript includes "Participants," "Measure," "Procedures," and "Statistical Analyses."

The method section follows introduction. The text "Method" centered bold type

Method

Participants

A sample of undergraduate college students enrolled in introductory level psychology courses were recruited using classroom visits. A final sample was selected who had no prior knowledge of, diagnosis, treatment, or other medical or clinical history of a mental or behavioral disorder, as determined in a preliminary medical and demographic survey. Participants also completed the WHO Adult ADHD Self-Report Scale (ASRS) screener (Kessler et al., 2005), which was used to select participants and establish baseline scores on this screener. Of the 74 participants who completed this screener, 54 participants scored below clinical significance on the ASRS screener (see *ASRS Measure* section) and were therefore selected to participate in this experiment. For the 54 participants, key additional characteristics were: 24 women, 30 men; 63% White, 37% Black; age: $M = 20.4$, SD = 1.2 years. The university's Institutional Review Board approved the procedures for this study.

Statement of IRB approval is appropriate.

Measure

The ASRS is a valid and reliable screener that is commonly used in clinical practice to screen for ADHD in adults (Adler et al., 2006; Kessler et al., 2007). The ASRS screener is used to determine the likelihood of diagnosis for ADHD with 18-items on the following 5-point scale: 0 (*never*), 1 (*rarely*), 2 (*sometimes*), 3 (*often*), and 4 (*very often*). The ASRS screener can be used to determine clinical significance of diagnosis by scoring 6-items found to be the most predictive of symptoms consistent with clinical

Use numerals to express scores on a scale. Rating scale descriptions or anchors are italicized.

Capi name tests scale The "scre is no capit

diagnosis of adult ADHD (Adler et al., 2006; Kessler et al., 2007). Clinical significance is identified when a participant scores in the clinical range (i.e., has symptoms highly consistent with adult ADHD) on at least 4 of these 6 items. To also identify the frequency of symptoms, scores were summed for all items and for each domain: Inattentive domain (sum questions 1-4, 7-8), and hyperactive/impulsive domain (sum questions 5-6, 12-18). Each method of scoring the ASRS was applied here.

Procedures

Participants completed the ASRS in a pretest and again one week later in a posttest. The ASRS pretest was taken at the time of participant selection (see Participants section). The 54 participants who scored below clinical significance on the ASRS constituted our sample. These participants were matched based on their ASRS pretest scores and randomly assigned to one of three feedback manipulation groups, such that the same proportion of men and women from each ethnic category were assigned to each group and ASRS pretest scores were identical between groups.

One week following the initial ASRS pretest, participants were brought back for a follow-up session. All participants who completed the pretest returned for the one-week follow-up session. In that session, participants received the ASRS with the order of items reversed to minimize testing effects. In this session, all groups were told that they were taking a follow-up test that was different from their pretest and that the results of their pretest were indicated on the back of their follow-up test, if those scores were available. Participants were then randomly assigned to one of three feedback manipulation groups. Group Negative had "Negative" written on their follow-up test to indicate that they did not have symptoms consistent with ADHD diagnosis. Group Positive was deceived and had "Positive" written on their follow-up test to indicate that they did have symptoms

ze
of
when
re
s
nouns.

consistent with ADHD diagnosis, which was not true. Group No Feedback received no feedback about their pretest scores. The feedback was written down instead of spoken to standardize the delivery of feedback between groups and reduce the likelihood of demand characteristics.

After completing the ASRS posttest, all participants confirmed in a follow-up survey that they felt the feedback given was honest. All participants were then debriefed and told the true purpose of the study, thanked for their time, and dismissed. Differences between pretest and posttest scores on the ASRS were compared.

Statistical Analysis

A Kruskal Wallace H Test was used to compare the number of participants in each group who scored in the clinical significance range on the ASRS. Using this test, we tested the null hypothesis that the distribution of those scoring in the clinical significance range was the same in each group. Because the ASRS was taken at two times, test-retest reliability was computed using a binomial test. Like the pretest, no participants should score at or above clinical significance on the follow-up test. However, for the binomial test we tested the null hypothesis test that the proportion of participants scoring at or above clinical significance in each group is .05, to allow for the standard .05 error rate. All tests were conducted at a .05 level of significance.

An analysis of variance (ANOVA) with groups, gender and race as factors was also computed for three dependent measures: difference scores (pretest-posttest) in the attentive domain, in the hyperactive/impulsive domain, and totals for the sum of all 18 items. If significant, 95% confidence intervals (CIs) were drawn around the difference scores for each group. A significant difference was identified when the difference scores did not envelop zero.

Capitalize all words of four or more letters in a heading, subheading, or title.

Results

The distribution of those scoring in the clinical significance range (i.e., those

having symptoms highly consistent with adult ADHD) was not equal between groups,

χ^2 (2) = 11.81, p = .003. Group Positive showed a significantly higher proportion

of participants scoring in the clinical significance range on the posttest (8/18;

44%) compared to both other groups. A binomial test showed that this result was

significantly disproportionate, p < .001, and therefore would fail to meet criteria

needed to establish test-retest reliability. By comparison, Group Negative and Group

No Feedback had only one participant in each group score in the clinical significance

range on the posttest (1/18; 6%). A binomial test showed that this result matches

expected proportions, p = .60, and therefore does meet criteria needed to establish test-

retest reliability.

An ANOVA showed that changes from pre- to posttest were significant for total

scores on the ASRS, F(2,53) = 3.85, p = .03 (R^2 = .13), and for scores in the inattentive

domain, F(2,53) = 6.00, p = .005 (R^2 = .19), but no significance was evident for scores in

the hyperactive/impulsive domain, p = .36. 95% CIs were drawn for scores on the ASRS.

As shown in Figure 1, total scores significantly increased from pre- to posttest only for

Group

Positive (95% CI 0.19 9.03). For Group Positive, scores significantly increased in the

inattentive domain (95% CI 1.89 6.56), but not in the hyperactive/impulsive domain. All

other CIs enveloped zero and so no further significant differences were evident. No effects

of gender or race were significant (*p* > .35 for all tests).

<<Insert Figure 1 About Here>>

Values between 0 and 1 that can be larger than 1 include a 0 in the ones place; if the value cannot be larger than 1, then the ones place is blank.

The discussion section follows the results section.

The term "Discussion" is centered in bold type.

Discussion

This experiment was conducted to test the hypothesis that feedback about an ADHD diagnosis influences how a nonclinical sample scores on an Adult ADHD Self-Report Scale (ASRS) screener. In this experiment, all participants scored below clinical significance on the ASRS in a pretest and had no history of ADHD or any other mental or behavioral disorder. When participants received no feedback or were informed that they did not show symptoms consistent with ADHD diagnosis, ASRS scores were consistent in a posttest and the screener met criteria needed to establish test-retest reliability. However, when participants were deceived and informed that they did have symptoms consistent with ADHD diagnosis, ASRS scores were remarkably unreliable, with 8 of 18 participants scoring in the clinically significant range of the ASRS in a posttest, despite scoring below clinical significance in a pretest one week earlier.

The results presented here illuminate that positive feedback about having a disorder can increase inconsistencies in ASRS scores. In this study, we manipulated participant self-beliefs by giving positive feedback, negative feedback, or no feedback prior to the ASRS retest. The manipulation check showed that all participants found the feedback to be honest. Therefore, we surmise that participants receiving the positive feedback changed their self-belief of their own likelihood of diagnosis, which led to the greater inconsistency in ASRS ratings from time 1 to time 2. These findings suggest that one possible reason that adults without ADHD can overreport symptoms is that they have self-beliefs regarding their own likelihood of disorder. Because patients are often told of their possibility of having ADHD or are inherently convinced they have the disorder prior to assessment (Guyll, Madon, Prieto, & Scherr, 2010; Weisler & Goodman, 2008), one possible implication is that positive feedback given prior to assessment may lead many patients to overreport their symptoms (Barkley et al., 2002; Sibley et al., 2010), thereby leading to the possibility of overdiagnosing the disorder in these cases.

Use "et al." to abbreviate multiple-author citations that were already cited in the manuscript.

Interestingly, participants in our study overreported symptoms in the inattentive domain in the posttest, but not in the hyperactive/impulsive domain. These findings are consistent with studies showing that the inattentive domain is prominent in adults and that hyperactive/impulsive symptoms can decline significantly with age, even if these symptoms were expressed in childhood (Biederman, Mick, & Faraone, 2000; Millstein, Wilens, Biederman, & Spencer, 1997). Inattentive symptoms are also more strongly related to academic performance than hyperactive/impulsive symptoms (Gordon et al., 2006), which may explain why college students in our study specially overreported symptoms in this domain.

The extent to which these findings can be applied to patients who express ADHD or can be controlled in a clinical setting cannot be determined here. However, the results do show that self-beliefs regarding the likelihood of having ADHD can lead young adults without ADHD to overreport their symptoms, potentially leading to overdiagnosis in these cases. These findings provide one likely explanation for why self-report measures to assess adult ADHD can be diagnostically insensitive (Sibley et al., 2012; Sibley et al., in press) inasmuch as patient beliefs prior to diagnostic assessment influence ASRS self-report ratings and therefore decrease the reliability of those ratings.

References

Able, S., Johnston, J., Adler, L. A., & Swindle, R. (2007). Functional and psychosocial impairment in adults with undiagnosed ADHD. *Psychological Medicine, 37*, 97–107. doi:10.1017/S0033291706008713

Adler, L. A., Spencer, T., Faraone, S. V., Kessler, R. C., Howes, M. J., Biederman, J., & Secnik, K. (2006). Validity of pilot adult ADHD self-report scale (ASRS) to rate adult ADHD symptoms. *Ann Clin Psychiatry, 18*, 145–148. doi:10.1080/10401230600801077

American Psychiatric Association. (2000). *Diagnostic and statistical manual of mental disorders* (4th ed., text rev.). Washington, DC: Author.

Barkley, R. A. (2006). *Attention-deficit hyperactivity disorder: A handbook for diagnosis and treatment* (3rd ed.). New York, NY: Guilford Press.

Barkley, R. A., Fischer, M., Smallish, L., & Fletcher, K. (2002). Young adult outcome of hyperactive children: Adaptive functioning in major life activities. *Journal of Abnormal Psychology, 111*, 279–289. doi:10.1037/0021843X.111.2.279.

Bell, L., Long, S., Garvan, C., & Bussing, R. (2011). The impact of teacher credentials on ADHD stigma perceptions. *Psychology in the Schools, 48*, 184–197. doi:10.1002/pits.20536

Biederman, J., Mick, E., & Faraone, S. V. (2000). Age-dependent decline of symptoms of attention deficit hyperactivity disorder: Impact of remission definition and symptom type. *American Journal of Psychiatry, 157*, 816–818. doi:10.1176/appi.ajp.157.5.816

Bruchmüller, K., Margraf, J., & Schneider, S. (2012). Is ADHD diagnosed in accord with diagnostic criteria? Overdiagnosis and influence of client gender on diagnosis. *Journal of Consulting and Clinical Psychology, 80*, 128–138. doi:10.1037/a0026582

The reference section follows discuss section "Refere is cente bold typ a sepa page. E referen is listed alphabe order, a the form for each referen a "hang indent." Always use the ampers (&) syn for listin last aut of a mu author referen

Desgranges, K., Desgranges, L., & Karsky, K. (1995). Attention deficit disorder: Problems with preconceived diagnosis. *Child & Adolescent Social Work Journal, 12*, 3–17. doi:10.1007/BF01876136

Eisenberg, D., & Schneider, H. (2007). Perceptions of academic skills of children diagnosed with ADHD. *Journal of Attention Disorders, 10*, 390–397. doi:10.1177/1087054706292105

Faraone, S. V., & Antshel, K. (2008). Diagnosing and treating attention-deficit/hyperactivity disorder in adults. *World Psychiatry, 7*, 131–136.

Faraone, S. V., & Biederman, J. (2005). What is the prevalence of adult attention deficit/ hyperactivity disorder? Results of a population screen of 966 adults. *Journal of Attention Disorders, 9*, 384–391. doi:10.1177/1087054705281478

Gaub, M., & Carlson, C. L. (1997). Gender differences in ADHD: A meta-analysis and critical review. Journal of the *American Academy of Child & Adolescent Psychiatry, 36*, 1036–1045. doi:10.1097/00004583199708000-00011

Gershon, J. (2002). A meta-analytic review of gender differences in ADHD. *Journal of Attention Disorders, 5*, 143–154. doi:10.1177/108705470200500302

Gordon, M., Antshel, K., Faraone, S., Barkley, R., Lewandowski, L., Hudziak, J. J., … Cunningham, C. (2006). Symptoms versus impairment: The case for respecting DSM-IV's Criterion D. *Journal of Attention Disorders, 9*, 465–475.

Guyll, M., Madon, S., Prieto, L., & Scherr, K. C. (2010). The potential roles of self-fulfilling prophecies, stigma consciousness, and stereotype threat in linking Latino/a ethnicity and educational outcomes. *Social Issues, 66*, 113–130. doi:10.1111/ j.1540-4560.2009.01636.x

Kessler, R. C., Adler, L., Gruber, M. J., Sarawate, C. A., Spencer, T., & Van Brunt, D. L. (2007). Validity of the World Health Organization adult ADHD self-report scale (ASRS) screener in a representative sample of health plan members. *International Journal of Methods in Psychiatric Research, 16*, 52–65. doi:10.1002/mpr.208

Kessler, R. C., Adler, L., Barkley, R., Biederman, J., Conners, C., Demler, O., ... Zaslavsky, A. M. (2006). The prevalence and correlates of adult ADHD in the United States: Results from the National Comorbidity Survey Replication. *American Journal of Psychiatry, 163*, 716–723. doi:10.1176/appi.ajp.163.4.716

Kessler, R. C., Adler, L., Ames, M., Demler, O., Faraone, S., Hiripi, E., ... Walters, E. E. (2005). The World Health Organization Adult ADHD Self-Report Scale (ASRS): A short screening scale for use in the general population. *Psychological Medicine, 35*, 245–256. doi:10.1017/S0033291704002892

Madon, S., Guyll, M., Spoth, R., & Willard, J. (2004). Self-fulfilling prophecies: The synergistic accumulative effect of parents' beliefs on children's drinking behavior. *Psychological Science, 15*, 837–845. doi:10.1111/j.0956-7976.2004.00764.x

Millstein, R. B., Wilens, T. E., Biederman, J., & Spencer, T. J. (1997). Presenting ADHD symptoms and subtypes in clinically referred adults with ADHD. *Journal of Attention Disorders, 2*, 159–166. doi:10.1177/108705479700200302

Murphy, P., & Schachar, R. (2000). Use of self-ratings in the assessment of symptoms of attention deficit hyperactivity disorder in adults. *American Journal of Psychiatry, 157*, 1156–1159.

Sibley, M. H., Pelham Jr., W. E., Gnagy, E. M., Waxmonsky, J. G., Waschbusch, D. A., Derefinko, K. J. ... Huriyan, A. B. (in press). When diagnosing ADHD in young adults emphasize informant reports, DSM items, and impairment. *Journal of Consulting and Clinical Psychology*. doi:10.1037/a0029098

Sibley, M. H., Pelham Jr., W. E., Molina, B. S. G., Gnagy, E., Waschbusch, D. A., Garefino, A. C., ... Karch, K. M. (2012). Diagnosing ADHD in adolescence. *Journal of Consulting and Clinical Psychology, 80*, 139–150. doi:10.1037/a0026577

Sibley, M. H., Pelham Jr., W. E., Molina, B. S. G., Waschbusch, D. A., Gnagy, E., Babinski, D. E., & Biswas, A. (2010). Inconsistent self-report of delinquency by adolescents and young adults with ADHD. J *Abnorm Child Psych, 38*, 645–656. doi:10.1007/s10802-010-9404-3

Waite, R., & Ramsay, J. R. (2010). Adults with ADHD: Who are we missing? *Issues in Mental Health Nursing, 31*, 670–678. doi:10.3109/01612840.2010.496137

Weisler, R. H., & Goodman, D. W. (2008). Assessment and diagnosis of adult ADHD: Clinical challenges and opportunities for improving patient care. *Primary Psychiatry, 15*, 53–64.

Wender, P. H., Wolf, L. E., & Wasserstein, J. (2001). Adults with ADHD: An overview. *Annals of the New York Academy of Sciences, 931*, 1–16. doi:10.1111/j.1749-6632.2001.tb05770.x

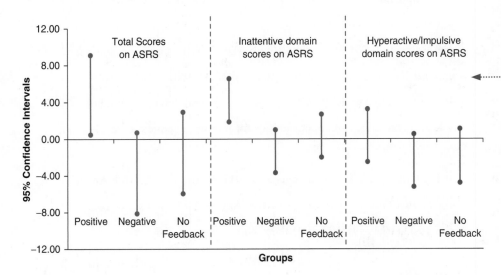

Figure 1. The 95% confidence intervals by group for differences pretest to posttest on all 18-items of the ASRS (total scores), on the inattentive domain items (sum questions 1-4, 7-8), and on the hyperactive/impulsive domain items (sum questions 5-6, 12-18). Difference scores were multiplied times (-1) so that larger differences indicated greater predictive symptoms of adult ADHD. Difference scores significantly increased for Group Positive for total scores and for scores in the inattentive domain. CIs for all other groups enveloped zero.

NOTE
tables
figure
includ
a sep
page
end c
manu
in ord
of the
appe
in the
of the
manu
Table
prece
figure
both
inclu
manu

A.4 Poster Template and Sample Poster

As stated in Chapter 15, presenting a poster is one way of communicating research. APA-style posters are typically presented during poster sessions held by professional organizations or local colleges. A poster session is a 1- to 4-hour time slot where many posters are displayed in a room for any person in attendance to observe and ask questions of an author who is standing nearby his or her poster.

One of the most common and professional ways to create a poster is using Microsoft® PowerPoint. This section shows you how to create a poster template using Microsoft PowerPoint (version 2007, 2010). Earlier and more recent versions can, of course, be used to create posters but will require somewhat different selections in the menu bar. To begin, open up Microsoft PowerPoint and follow these directions. In the menu bar, select Design, then Page Setup (for version 2013, select Design, Slide Size, then Custom Slide Size…). These steps will bring up the following dialog box shown here, which should appear basically the same regardless of which version you are using:

The size of the poster can vary. If you present a poster at an APA conference, then the poster board surface area is 4 feet × 6 feet; full instructions for preparing a poster for the APA conference can be found at http://www.apa.org/convention/poster-instructions.pdf. On this poster board surface, we can choose any number of poster sizes. For our example, we will use the following dimensions: 36 × 48 inches (or 3 feet high × 4 feet wide). To do this, plug in the values shown in the dialog box.

To insert text boxes, go to Insert, then Text Box, in the menu bar (repeat this as often as needed). Each text box can be used to summarize different parts of your study (abstract, methods, deign, results, conclusions, etc.). To align the text boxes, it is useful to use the grid line feature. To do this, go to the menu bar and select View, then check the Gridlines box to superimpose a grid on your slide with 1-inch squares. Make sure you leave 1-inch margins on each side of your poster. When you have completed the poster, simply uncheck the gridlines box and the squares will disappear.

This appendix includes (1) a template for how a poster can be prepared for a class or student research project and (2) a sample poster that was presented at the Eastern Psychological Association conference, and later published in the *Journal of Attention Disorders* in 2015. The sample poster follows a similar organization to the template also given here to give you a sense of how to apply the format of the template to summarize a research study. Although posters can have many different looks, one common requirement of a poster is that it is typically organized in chronological order from left to right—the same way a person would read words or sentences on a page to read a story. Hence, start with the abstract or rationale for a study to the left of the poster, then describe the study in order of the research process (from the procedures to the results and discussion) moving to the right of the poster.

Insert the Title Here

Insert Authors Here

Insert the name and location of university or college affiliation

Overview

Insert summary of research project. Do not simply copy and past your abstract....

Statistical Analysis

Insert summary results using statistical values....

- Name the statistical test(s) you used to analyze your data.
- State (in APA format) the test statistic and *p*-value for each test. Each test statistic should have its own bullet.

Summary & Implications

Insert conclusions and implications here...

- Give general conclusions first. Make sure these conclusions relate back to your hypothesis. Don't generalize beyond your data. Use a separate bullet for each conclusion.
- State any major limitations for your study. Briefly (in a sentence or two at most) explain how the limitations influence your conclusions.
- Finally, give a one or two sentence overview for how your results compare with what you expected/what has been shown in the published literature.

Methods and Design

Insert summary of methods and design, including the following sections...

Participants:

Research Design:

Materials/Measures:

Procedures:

Results

Insert summary of results without using technical jargon...

*Use a table or figure to make sense of your data.

Just insert the table or figure into this text box and include a figure/table caption.

References

List key references here...

- References should follow APA format and be in alphabetical order.
- Only list main references here.

Randomized Feedback About Diagnosis Influences Statistical and Clinical Significance of Self-Report ADHD Assessment in Adults

Shelby A. Walters, Jaela E. Agnello, Gregory J. Privitera, and Stacy L. Bender

Overview

- The hypothesis that feedback about an ADHD diagnosis influences how a nonclinical sample scores on the Adult ADHD Self-Report Scale (ASRS) screener
- Participants were a sample of college students ranging in age from 18 to 23 years.
- Participants were given the adult ADHD self-report scale (ASRS)
- In Group Negative ADHD participants were told they exhibited no symptoms of ADHD according to the assessment
- Group Positive ADHD participants were told that they did exhibit symptoms of ADHD according to the assessment
- Group No Feedback, were not given any feedback

Methods and Design

Participants:

- 54 undergraduate university students, both men and women, participated in the study
- Key additional characteristics were 24 women, 30 men; 63% White, 37% Black; and age: $M=20.4$, $SD=1.2$ years
- A demographic questionnaire was distributed to participants before the pre-test; those who were clinically diagnosed with ADHD or scored in the ADHD diagnostic range of the ASRS were omitted from the study
- Participants were not clinically diagnosed with ADHD
- The University's Institutional Review Board approved the procedures for this study.

Research Design:

- A between-subjects design was used with 3 groups

Measures:

- The ASRS was used to measure for symptoms of ADHD
- Scoring was based on the frequency of symptoms
- Part A of the ASRS was scored

Procedures:

- Students completed a demographic questionnaire, pre-test of the ASRS, and consent form
- Participants were randomly assigned to one of three manipulation groups in order to decrease likelihood of testing effects
- Group No Feedback, the participants were told nothing. Group Negative was told pretest scores did indicate symptoms of ADHD. Group Positive was told pretest scores indicated symptoms of ADHD
- Post-tests were scored the same as the pre-tests and participants scoring in the ADHD range on the ASRS were recorded
- Once all items were completed, participants were debriefed and dismissed

Statistical Analysis

- The dependent variable was the number of participants exhibiting ADHD after the manipulation
- The independent variable were the groups: positive, negative, and no feedback
- All tests were conducted at a 0.05 level of significance

I. Is clinical significance reliable?

- The Kruskal Wallis H-test was used to assess clinical significance by identifying group differences
  - Tested if the rates of false positives were the same in each group
- Binominal test was used as post hoc for Kruskal-Wallis H-test to look at group differences

III. Did scores statistically change?

- One-way ANOVA
  - Computed for difference scores in the attentive domain, in the hyperactive/impulsive domain, and the totals for the sum of all 18 items
  - If significant, 95% confidence intervals drawn around the difference scores for each group

Results

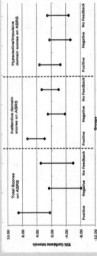

Figure 1. 95% confidence intervals by group for differences pretest to posttest on all 18-items of the ASRS (total scores), on the inattentive domain items (sum questions 1-4,7-8), and on the hyperactive/impulsive domain items (sum questions 5-6, 12-18). Difference scores significantly increased for Group Positive for total scores and for scores in the inattentive domain.

- Each group consisted of 18 participants ($n=18$)
- Distribution of those scoring in the clinical significance range was not equal between groups: Group Negative and Group No Feedback both had a mean rank of 24.00 while Group Positive had a mean rank of 34.50
- The H statistic revealed there was a significant difference between the groups.
  - $\chi^2 = 11.805$, $p = 0.003$, $df = 2$.
- There was 1/18 participants that scored in the ADHD range of the ASRS post-test for Group Negative and Group No Feedback in which the binominal test showed that this result matched expected proportions
- Group Positive had 8/18 participants who scored in the ADHD range of the ASRS post-test in which the binominal test showed that this result did not match expected proportions
- ANOVA showed that Group Positive scores significantly increased in the inattentive domain, but not the hyperactive/impulsive domain

Summary & Implications

- When participants received no feedback or were informed that they did not have symptoms consistent with ADHD diagnosis, ASRS scores were consistent in a posttest and the screener met criteria needed to establish test-retest reliability
- When participants were deceived about symptoms consistent with ADHD diagnosis, ASRS scores were unreliable despite scoring below clinical significance in the pretest
- These findings suggest that one possible reason that adults without ADHD can overreport symptoms is that they have self-beliefs regarding their own likelihood of the disorder
- Participants in our study overreported symptoms in the inattentive domain in the posttest, but not in the hyperactive/impulsive domain
- These findings are consistent with studies showing that the inattentive domain is prominent in adults and that hyperactive/impulsive symptoms can decline significantly with age

References

Garnier-Dykstra, L. M., Pinchevsky, G. M., Caldeira, K. M., Vincent, K. B., & Arria, A. M. (2010). Self-reported adult attention-deficit/hyperactivity disorder symptoms among college students. *American College Health*, 59(2), 133-136.

Kessler, R. C., Adler, L.., Ames, M., Demler, O., Faraone, S., Hiripi, E., Howes, M. J., Jin, R., Secnik, K., Spencer, T., Ustun, T. B., & Walters, E. E. (2005). The world health organization adult ADHD self-report scale (ASRS): A short screening scale for use in the general population. *Psychological Medicine*, 35, 245-256. doi: 10.1017/S0033291704002892.

Gayil, M., Madon, S., Prieto, L., & Scherr, K. C. (2010). The potential roles of self-fulfilling prophecies, stigma consciousness, and stereotype threat in linking Latino/a ethnicity and educational outcomes. *Social Issues*, 66, 113-130. doi: 10.1111/j.1540-4560.2009.01636.x

APPENDIX B

Instructions for Randomizing and Counterbalancing

B.1 Random Numbers Table

Randomization, defined in Chapter 6, is used to ensure that confounding variables operate entirely by chance in a research study. Two strategies of randomization are random sampling and random assignment. Random sampling ensures that all participants are selected to participate for a study at random; random assignment ensures that all participants in a study are assigned to groups or treatments at random. The random number table can be used to accomplish both strategies of randomization. In this brief appendix, we show you how to use the random number table.

Participant Order	Random Number
1	15
2	2
3	33
4	32
5	14
6	1
7	28
8	26
9	7
10	20

Random Sampling

Suppose you have a pool of 10 people from which you select 8 participants to be in your study. To *randomly select* 8 participants from this pool of 10 people, first list all 10 people in any order (participants are listed in numerical order in the table above), then go to the random number table and begin at a random spot in the table. For example, you can drop a coin on the random list of numbers and begin with the number it falls on. Starting with this number, read across or down the list. In the example above, we began with the first number in the upper left corner and read down. Now a random number has been assigned to each person. Finally, you can choose 8 participants with the lowest number (e.g., participants 1, 2, 5, 6, 7, 8, 9, 10) or largest number (participants 1, 3, 4, 5, 7, 8, 9, 10) to be in the sample. Both will produce a random sample of participants from the pool of 10 people.

Random Assignment

To *randomly assign* participants to any number of groups, first list (in any order) all participants in your study (again, participants are listed in numerical order in the table above) and then go to the random number table and begin at a random spot in the table. In this example, we will use the same random list of numbers used in the previous example for random sampling. If we have two groups, then to randomly assign participants to groups, you can assign participants with the lowest five scores to Group 1 (participants 6, 2, 9, 5, 1) and the highest five scores to Group 2 (participants 10, 8, 7, 4, 3), or vice versa. For more information about using randomization, visit www.randomizer.org or visit www.random.org.

Table B.1 Random Number Table

15	2	40	24	26	12	32	38	46	46	14	18	9	49	6
2	48	10	21	10	49	10	13	2	25	10	6	1	14	4
33	23	35	43	17	35	4	44	5	45	29	46	31	19	37
32	44	39	44	14	41	36	41	15	47	3	41	43	43	0
14	11	41	30	37	0	47	28	49	13	8	15	26	4	48
1	38	42	17	22	45	27	37	7	1	26	44	16	39	10
28	26	3	34	33	2	33	33	45	28	25	35	2	48	42
26	21	31	13	46	46	44	46	26	15	18	5	18	45	8
7	24	7	7	24	37	16	16	16	38	38	38	8	30	14
20	35	47	14	34	4	29	1	30	39	1	25	4	33	17
8	26	44	20	34	3	10	1	6	7	12	37	8	29	34
48	43	2	7	35	25	30	37	27	36	11	19	14	32	5
41	2	47	9	45	17	16	34	39	8	21	18	11	11	45
43	27	18	19	3	6	41	32	34	22	36	5	1	38	27
28	19	22	42	1	48	22	2	10	3	2	28	2	15	42
21	31	29	27	26	23	42	6	2	1	41	44	38	28	19

47	33	17	11	43	20	35	49	24	39	16	6	48	45	41
20	13	42	24	40	39	23	3	41	19	30	10	24	48	8
14	9	7	45	48	0	9	38	15	44	42	17	47	14	33
39	37	28	21	29	29	31	22	22	35	38	16	6	37	11

15	10	47	1	20	16	25	13	4	30	5	24	7	26	40
31	35	1	48	34	35	36	43	44	9	32	4	28	42	34
22	20	20	2	33	41	41	12	0	7	33	12	47	19	43
26	15	6	40	4	39	44	40	43	12	34	21	27	14	23
40	21	32	39	25	24	47	0	19	48	49	44	10	24	19
6	42	24	10	19	7	7	44	16	44	30	28	48	33	18
10	19	31	47	1	36	12	22	25	39	41	48	5	18	39
16	18	26	20	7	43	17	37	41	46	13	17	13	37	9
28	13	12	22	21	48	38	25	49	15	1	45	2	4	48
46	44	8	32	31	22	18	28	42	49	44	41	4	46	13

31	33	9	42	30	38	45	17	24	15	36	9	28	29	16
30	45	13	48	6	44	4	42	18	19	24	2	7	11	18
43	10	4	0	21	25	26	44	32	13	20	1	4	7	12
32	24	28	23	10	19	11	47	23	42	48	39	8	23	3
16	40	14	20	26	49	44	19	16	47	0	29	37	13	34
37	39	5	49	12	45	16	1	26	16	29	48	1	47	47
26	19	0	18	43	5	40	30	42	20	6	0	38	9	29
39	31	29	32	5	12	33	2	48	37	43	17	36	25	42
23	26	23	26	3	17	28	28	1	4	35	10	47	4	45
10	47	16	3	36	1	21	27	10	29	19	8	21	22	23

40	20	38	26	9	10	33	28	47	25	32	4	18	33	18
42	24	26	14	39	34	49	41	12	23	24	37	41	18	5
38	10	24	12	8	23	16	3	3	38	20	26	14	30	30
37	35	14	23	42	31	30	39	44	29	15	9	37	16	36
46	47	12	19	32	35	36	10	4	42	41	38	19	27	19
43	9	4	46	31	2	7	26	2	24	1	19	4	14	8
5	48	2	33	28	27	48	48	20	47	9	40	1	40	35
11	42	9	37	21	44	21	21	22	43	45	13	22	19	46
27	6	20	34	37	47	47	7	24	31	19	31	30	13	22
6	8	37	6	10	7	24	9	1	28	29	44	38	43	34

44	10	48	37	38	33	45	5	2	15	17	5	12	26	3
17	41	43	6	19	45	35	35	13	3	24	15	8	44	30
41	34	10	1	9	29	23	21	35	28	36	3	15	8	16
30	30	41	38	41	15	29	20	32	18	8	7	9	12	41
19	15	20	40	44	1	14	15	28	39	28	1	34	17	18
38	24	40	14	22	23	28	19	38	26	33	25	49	46	9

2	35	27	8	16	22	49	47	25	4	5	12	19	5	12
40	9	9	17	21	4	17	1	27	14	4	4	42	2	0
7	39	29	13	28	37	27	7	44	47	15	47	0	45	47
26	8	13	47	47	26	6	25	36	21	19	31	21	47	6

13	14	47	35	45	23	17	48	24	18	22	25	47	30	46
5	35	36	34	12	2	19	2	42	42	20	41	9	2	35
31	12	37	46	48	31	9	0	26	10	47	20	34	14	19
43	6	30	18	23	29	28	1	4	49	45	43	35	41	26
39	4	15	11	3	13	35	43	18	47	0	44	15	45	6
35	21	17	42	4	37	48	8	14	36	39	42	17	39	31
40	33	13	12	37	33	37	13	40	27	43	34	26	28	2
29	31	2	45	7	26	6	29	48	14	19	18	24	7	10
48	1	24	10	0	22	41	19	6	8	4	0	43	46	34
6	0	49	22	34	48	27	37	31	26	24	37	44	36	48

31	47	34	10	24	19	47	17	3	15	31	5	24	1	9
38	18	48	9	28	48	7	40	11	9	2	45	20	37	36
42	15	36	49	2	2	20	31	9	31	38	36	31	39	42
28	25	43	31	11	45	22	34	19	21	16	9	38	26	13
29	14	14	39	12	14	2	3	28	19	21	47	6	0	33
6	39	33	46	38	46	38	12	21	18	39	23	5	7	32
16	22	2	48	6	3	15	23	49	12	29	37	13	23	48
36	44	16	34	0	35	0	9	47	3	32	29	21	16	49
8	17	35	42	17	39	44	37	22	36	36	13	39	41	41
10	21	46	32	41	47	36	44	41	43	26	49	1	29	2

41	45	22	49	48	3	40	8	46	16	8	22	18	47	1
36	20	21	17	18	42	3	38	12	49	13	24	12	39	40
17	38	38	13	4	29	27	21	4	42	11	12	9	11	44
9	32	42	3	22	16	14	40	30	19	24	21	5	1	19
42	1	3	22	11	22	15	6	42	6	15	36	2	44	15
24	6	27	37	10	24	45	43	28	31	27	29	17	43	47
35	33	6	38	5	27	43	29	43	11	33	16	34	21	6
30	7	35	47	13	4	17	17	7	37	3	37	40	46	41
6	12	28	30	42	43	26	25	19	3	25	39	29	28	0
26	14	5	31	0	15	25	42	24	33	9	2	33	20	23

16	43	21	13	42	19	30	34	29	18	39	34	29	22	32
49	49	7	10	15	24	18	35	2	49	6	42	30	33	41
2	34	42	46	23	48	13	27	45	40	0	6	1	6	47
0	20	12	34	48	21	37	6	42	22	38	7	18	13	46
11	7	32	3	31	5	35	3	30	14	36	10	22	49	14
35	12	47	37	39	26	45	12	11	17	20	37	16	17	8

44	18	1	33	14	34	38	23	3	9	42	9	47	19	38
6	19	27	35	17	29	6	2	41	30	44	48	42	46	37
37	28	22	26	12	31	42	4	19	34	12	15	44	28	40
32	30	15	29	6	37	29	17	40	45	9	21	38	45	3

30	30	12	28	21	11	1	22	28	27	34	40	34	31	7
37	38	37	31	8	14	9	45	49	20	35	26	33	19	1
4	48	16	11	27	40	8	17	42	9	45	16	40	10	0
1	33	23	14	6	27	41	37	11	8	36	10	36	5	30
8	7	41	45	33	46	46	41	23	10	22	17	23	2	8
23	44	20	4	44	16	48	25	10	37	31	25	13	22	6
25	41	4	22	26	25	35	40	13	14	40	20	44	18	19
2	20	34	19	16	48	7	49	3	28	42	45	14	38	42
24	23	8	5	36	7	17	4	15	3	5	12	4	11	41
35	46	48	18	39	21	12	26	12	22	39	8	21	6	22

38	40	47	42	24	46	32	31	24	7	28	13	28	8	24
16	23	16	27	42	17	31	13	16	10	14	15	14	37	39
29	35	29	43	20	14	23	25	7	32	34	4	41	31	6
33	7	25	21	19	36	40	27	36	46	30	38	9	33	32
35	12	34	45	0	6	38	10	2	25	25	28	36	39	12
43	13	42	18	17	35	9	30	28	29	42	9	19	48	17
9	17	15	22	8	9	48	33	15	47	38	49	45	5	2
32	3	7	5	44	25	43	37	27	27	37	11	17	44	23
1	24	4	44	38	7	8	23	44	2	49	46	38	0	1
40	16	10	2	41	11	18	36	6	18	44	5	10	9	36

B.2 Constructing a Latin Square

In Chapter 11, we introduced the *within-subjects design*, which is a research design in which the same participants are observed in each group. One drawback of this design is that random assignment is not possible because the same participants are assigned to all groups. Thus, for this design to qualify as an experiment, the researcher must manipulate the levels of an independent variable, include a control or comparison group, and take added measures to control for time-related factors.

> A **Latin square** is a matrix design in which a limited number of order sequences are constructed such that (1) the number of order sequences chosen equals the number of treatments, (2) each treatment appears equally often in each position, and (3) each treatment precedes and follows each treatment one time.

One added measure of control for order is *counterbalancing*, which is used to minimize order effects so that the order of presenting treatments, or the order in which participants are assigned to groups, does not systematically vary with the levels of an independent variable.

However, in many cases the number of groups or treatments in a study is simply too large to fully counterbalance the design. In these cases, it is often best to use partial counterbalancing, which can be accomplished using a **Latin square** (defined here and also in Chapter 11). A Latin square is a partial counterbalancing procedure used to select an unbiased set of order sequences when it is difficult to counterbalance all order sequences in a research design.

An unbiased order sequence is one in which (1) each treatment appears equally often in each position, and (2) each treatment precedes and follows each treatment one time. A Latin square meets both requirements and also ensures that the number of order sequences chosen equals the number of groups or treatments. The following procedures can be used to construct a Latin square with an even and an odd number of groups or treatments (k).

Constructing a Latin Square (When k Is Even)

The following directions are for constructing a Latin square with an even number of groups or treatments (k).

1. Label your treatments alphabetically—so ABCD for four treatments, ABCDEF for six treatments, ABCDEFGH for eight treatments, and so on. We will work through an example for eight groups or treatments. This will make it easier for you to see the overall pattern for ordering.

2. Determine the order sequence for row 1 using the following ordering, in which L is the "last" group or treatment alphabetically:

A, B, L, C, L-1, D, L-2, E

For eight groups or treatments, then, L is treatment H (the last letter), L-1 is treatment G (the next-to-last treatment), and L-2 is treatment F (the third-to-last treatment). These procedures require you to take treatments at the end and insert them into different positions. Hence, with eight treatments, the first row or order sequence is as follows:

Row 1: ABHCGDFE

3. To determine the remaining rows or order sequences, increase one letter at each position of the previous row. The last letter in a row reverts to A because it cannot be increased. In our example, for the second row, A becomes B at the first position, B becomes C at the second position, H becomes A at the third position, and so on:

Row 2: BCADHEGF

For the third row, B becomes C at the first position; C becomes D at the second position; A becomes B at the third position, and so on:

Row 3: CDBEAFHG

Continue this to complete the Latin square with eight rows or order sequences, which is equal to k (the number of groups or treatments).

4. Construct the Latin square. In our example, we have eight groups or treatments, so we will have eight rows or order sequences. Hence, the 8 × 8 Latin square for this example is as follows:

```
A B H C G D F E
B C A D H E G F
C D B E A F H G
D E C F B G A H
E F D G C H B A
F G E H D A C B
G H F A E B D C
H A G B F C E D
```

The eight rows constitute an unbiased random order sequence for observing participants in each group or treatment. Now you can observe participants in each order sequence to control for order effects.

Constructing a Latin Square (When k Is Odd)

With an odd number of groups or treatments (k), it is not possible to construct an unbiased order sequence because there will be an odd number of rows. The solution is to basically construct two Latin squares so that the total number of rows or order sequences is even. We will work through an example with five treatments (A, B, C, D, E):

1. Latin square 1: Follow Steps 1–4 given above. This produces the following Latin square (we recommend that you try this on your own):

```
A B E C D
B C A D E
C D B E A
D E C A B
E A D B C
```

2. Latin square 2: Create a second square that reverses the order for each row in the first square. So you will have a total of 10 rows. Here is the first Latin square (top five rows) given with the second Latin square (bottom five rows):

```
A B E C D
B C A D E
C D B E A
D E C A B
E A D B C

D C E B A
E D A C B
A E B D C
B A C E D
C B D A E
```

This basically produces a Latin rectangle. The 10 rows constitute an unbiased random order sequence for observing participants in each group or treatment in that each treatment appears equally often in each position, and each treatment precedes and follows each treatment two times. Now you can observe participants in each order sequence to control for order effects.

APPENDIX C

SPSS General Instructions Guide and Statistical Tables

C.1 General Instructions Guide for Using SPSS

The *General Instructions Guidebook*, referred to here as GIG, provides standardized instructions for using SPSS to enter and analyze data. Most instructions provided in the GIG are also given in the book chapters. The GIG provides general instructions for using SPSS without the use of a specific example. Although many more instructions for using SPSS are given in the book, the instructions in the GIG are focused on tests for significance computed with various research designs in the behavioral sciences.

   Where applicable, instructions are given with reference to which SPSS in Focus section in the book illustrates the use of the directions within the context of an example. Note that the term *independent variable* is used where appropriate in the GIG. Anytime this term is used, the term *quasi-independent variable* can be used in its place. To keep the step-by-step directions as concise as possible, only the term *independent variable* or *factor* is used. The GIG first reviews the procedures for entering data for between-subjects and within-subjects factors and is then organized as follows:

Parametric Tests

- *t* tests
  - One-sample *t* test
  - Two-independent-sample *t* test
  - Related-samples *t* test

- One-way ANOVAs
  - One-way between-subjects ANOVA
  - One-way within-subjects ANOVA

- Factorial ANOVAs
  - Two-way between-subjects ANOVA
  - Two-way within-subjects ANOVA
  - Two-way mixed factorial ANOVA

- Correlation and regression
  - Pearson correlation
  - Analysis of regression

Nonparametric Tests

- Tests for nominal data
  - Chi-square goodness-of-fit test
  - Chi-square test for independence

- Tests for ordinal data
  - Wilcoxon signed-ranks *t* test
  - Mann-Whitney *U* test
  - Kruskal-Wallis *H* test
  - Friedman test

In Chapter 4, Section 4.9 (SPSS in Focus, p. 122) of this book, we introduced entering data for a within-subjects factor and a between-subjects factor. A within-subjects factor is a factor in which the same participants are observed at each level of the factor. A between-subjects factor is a factor in which different participants are observed at each level of the factor. Here, we will first review instructions for entering and defining each type of factor, which will be needed for entering data with each type of parametric and nonparametric statistical test taught in this book.

ENTERING DATA FOR WITHIN-SUBJECTS FACTORS

Enter data by column:

1. Open the **Variable View** tab. In the **Name column**, enter each variable name (one variable per row).

2. Go to the **Decimals column** and reduce that value to the degree of accuracy of the data.

3. Open the **Data View** tab. You will see that each variable is now the title for each column. Enter the data for each variable in the appropriate column.

ENTERING DATA FOR BETWEEN-SUBJECTS FACTORS

Enter data by row (this requires *coding* the grouped data):

1. Open the **Variable View** tab. Enter the variable name in the first row and a name for the dependent variable in the second row.

2. Go to the **Decimals column** and reduce that value to 0 for the first row. This is because the values in this column will be coded. Reduce the Decimals column in the second row to the degree of accuracy of the data.

3. Go to the **Values column** in the first row and click on the small gray box with three dots. In the **dialog box**, enter a number in the **Value cell** and the name of each level of the independent variable in the **Label cell**. After each entry select **Add**. Repeat these steps for each level of the independent variable and then select **OK**. The data are now coded as numbers.

4. Open the **Data View** tab. In the first column, enter each number so that it equals the number of scores in each level. For example, if you measure five scores at each level of the independent variable, then you will enter each number (or code) five times in the first column. In the second column, enter the values for the dependent variable. These values should match up with the levels of the independent variable you coded.

Parametric Tests

t Tests

ONE-SAMPLE T TEST

*This exercise is illustrated in **Chapter 5, Section 5.9** (SPSS in Focus, p. 155), of this book.

1. Click on the **Variable View** tab and enter the variable name in the **Name column**. In the **Decimals column**, reduce the value to the degree of accuracy of the data.

2. Click on the **Data View** tab and enter the values for the variable in the first column.

3. Go to the **menu bar** and click **Analyze, Compare Means**, and **One-Sample T Test** to bring up a dialog box.

4. In the **dialog box**, select the variable name and click the arrow in the middle to move it to the **Test Variable(s):** box.

5. State the null value in the **Test Value:** box. The value is 0 by default.

6. Select **OK**, or select **Paste** and click the **Run** command.

TWO-INDEPENDENT-SAMPLE T TEST

*This exercise is illustrated in **Chapter 10, Section 10.7** (SPSS in Focus, p. 330), of this book.

1. Click on the **Variable View** tab and enter the independent variable in the **Name column**. In the second row, enter the name of the dependent variable in the Name column. Reduce the value to 0 in the **Decimals column** in the first row and to the degree of accuracy of the data in the second row.

2. Code the levels of the independent variable listed in the first row in the **Values** column.

3. In the **Data View** tab, in the first column enter each number so that it equals the number of scores in each level. For example, if you measure five scores in each group (or level), then enter each numeric code five times in the first column. In the second column, enter the values for the dependent variable so that they correspond with the code for each group.

4. Go to the **menu bar** and click **Analyze, Compare Means**, and **Independent-Samples T Test** to bring up a dialog box.

5. Using the arrows to move the variables, select the dependent variable and place it in the **Test Variable(s):** box; select the independent variable and move it into the **Grouping Variable:** box. Two question marks will appear in the Grouping Variable box.

6. Now click **Define Groups**. . . to bring up a new dialog box. Place the numeric code for each group in the spaces provided and then click **Continue**. The numeric codes should now appear in the Grouping Variable box (instead of question marks).

7. Select **OK**, or select **Paste** and click the **Run** command.

RELATED-SAMPLES T TEST

*This exercise is illustrated in **Chapter 11, Section 11.6** (SPSS in Focus, p. 367), of this book.

1. Click on the **Variable View** tab and enter the name of the first level of the independent variable in the Name column in the first row; enter the name of the second level of the independent variable in the second row. Reduce the **Decimals column** value in both rows to the degree of accuracy of the data.

2. Click on the **Data View** tab. List the data for each level of the independent variable. Make sure the scores for each related pair are matched in each row.

3. Go to the **menu bar** and click **Analyze, Compare Means**, and **Paired-Samples T Test** to bring up a dialog box.

4. In the **dialog box**, select each level of the independent variable in the left box and move them to the right box using the arrow in the middle. The variables should be side by side in the box to the right.

5. Select **OK**, or select **Paste** and click the **Run** command.

One-Way ANOVAs

ONE-WAY BETWEEN-SUBJECTS ANOVA

*This exercise is illustrated in **Chapter 10, Section 10.9** (SPSS in Focus, p. 337), of this book.

Compute this test using the **One-Way ANOVA** command:

1. Click on the **Variable View** tab and enter the name of the independent variable in the **Name column**. Go to the **Decimals column** for this row and reduce the value to 0 (because this variable will be coded). In the second row, enter the name of the dependent variable in the Name column. Reduce the **Decimals column** value in the second row to the degree of accuracy of the data.

2. Code the levels of the independent variable listed in the first row in the **Values** column.

3. In the **Data View** tab, in the first column enter each coded value so that it equals the number of scores in each level. For example, if you measure five scores in each group (or level), then enter each numeric code five times in the first column. In the second column, enter the values for the dependent variable so that they correspond with the codes for each group.

4. Go to the **menu bar** and click **Analyze, Compare Means**, and **One-Way ANOVA** to bring up a dialog box.

5. Using the appropriate arrows, move the independent variable into the **Factor:** box. Move the dependent variable into the **Dependent List:** box.

6. Click the **Post Hoc** option to bring up a new dialog box. Select an appropriate post hoc test and click **Continue**.

7. Select **OK**, or select **Paste** and click the **Run** command.

Compute this test using the **GLM Univariate** command:

1. Follow Steps 1–3 for using the One-Way ANOVA command.

2. Go to the **menu bar** and click **Analyze, General Linear Model**, and **Univariate** to bring up a dialog box.

3. Using the appropriate arrows, move the independent variable into the **Fixed Factor(s):** box. Move the dependent variable into the **Dependent Variable:** box.

4. Select the **Post Hoc. . .** option to bring up a new dialog box, which will again give you the option to perform post hoc comparisons so long as you move the independent variable into the **Post Hoc Tests for:** box. Select an appropriate post hoc test and click **Continue**.

5. Select **OK**, or select **Paste** and click the **Run** command.

ONE-WAY WITHIN-SUBJECTS ANOVA

*This exercise is illustrated in **Chapter 11, Section 11.8** (SPSS in Focus, p. 372), of this book.

1. Click on the **Variable View** tab and enter the name of each level of the independent variable in the **Name column**. One level (or group) should be listed in each row. Go to the **Decimals column** and reduce the value to 0 for each row to the degree of accuracy of the data.

2. Click on the **Data View** tab. Now each column is labeled with each level of the independent variable. Enter the data for each respective column.

3. Go to the **menu bar** and click **Analyze, General Linear Model**, and **Repeated Measures** to bring up a dialog box.

4. In the **Within-Subject Factor Name** box, label or give a name for the repeated measure factor (or independent variable). Below it you will see a **Number of Levels** box. Here, SPSS is asking for the number of levels for the independent variable. Enter the number and the **Add** option will illuminate. Click Add and you will see the independent variable with the number of levels in parentheses. Click **Define** to bring up a new dialog box.

5. In the **dialog box**, use the appropriate arrows to move each column into the **Within-Subjects Variables (cues)** box.

6. Then select **Options** to bring up a new dialog box. To compute effect size, use the arrow to move the independent variable into the **Display Means for:** box. Then check the **Compare main effects** option. Using the dropdown arrow under the **Confidence interval adjustment** heading select an appropriate post hoc test. Then select **Continue**.

7. Select **OK**, or select **Paste** and click the **Run** command.

Factorial ANOVAs

TWO-WAY BETWEEN-SUBJECTS ANOVA

*This exercise is illustrated in **Chapter 12, Section 12.10** (SPSS in Focus, p. 410), of this book.

1. Click on the **Variable View** tab and enter the name of each independent variable (one in each row) in the **Name column**; in the third row, enter a name for the dependent variable in the Name column. Reduce the value to 0 in the **Decimals column** for the first two rows (for both independent variables). In the Decimals column, reduce the value to the degree of accuracy of the data for the third row.

2. Code the levels of both independent variables listed in the first two rows in the **Values** column.

3. In the **Data View** tab, in the first column enter each coded value so that it equals the number of scores in each level. Do the same in the second column (for the second independent variable). The two columns create the cells. For example, if the first two columns in the row read 1, 1, then this tells SPSS that any data entered in the third column come from a cell that combines the first level of each

factor. In the second column, enter the values for the dependent variable; make sure the data correspond to each cell.

4. Go to the **menu bar** and click **Analyze, General Linear Model,** and **Univariate** to bring up a dialog box.

5. Use the appropriate arrows to move the factors (or independent variables) into the **Fixed Factor(s):** box. Move the dependent variable into the **Dependent Variable:** box.

6. Finally, click **Options** to bring up a new dialog box. In the **Factor(s) and Factor Interactions** box, move the two main effects and interaction into the **Display Means for:** box by using the arrow. Click **Continue.**

7. Select **Post Hoc. . .** to bring up another dialog box. Use the arrow to bring both main effects from the **Factor(s)** box into the **Post Hoc Tests for:** box. Select an appropriate pairwise comparison for the main effects and select **Continue.** [Note: SPSS does not perform simple effect tests. If you get a significant interaction, you will have to conduct these tests separately.]

8. Select **OK,** or select **Paste** and click the **Run** command.

TWO-WAY WITHIN-SUBJECTS ANOVA

*This exercise is illustrated in **Chapter 12, Section 12.10** (SPSS in Focus, p. 410), of this book.

1. Click on the **Variable View** tab and enter the names of each group created by combining the levels of two independent variables (one group in each row) in the **Name column.** In the **Decimals column,** reduce the value to the degree of accuracy of the data for each row in which a group was entered.

2. Click on the **Data View** tab. In each column, enter the data that correspond to each group (in each column).

3. Go to the **menu bar** and click **Analyze, General Linear Model,** and **Repeated Measures** to display a dialog box. Enter the name of the first factor in the **Within-Subjects Factor Name** box, and enter the number of levels for that factor in the **Number of Levels** box below it. Click **Add.** Follow these same instructions for the second factor.

4. Click **Define** to display a new dialog box. Move the levels for each factor into the **Within-Subjects Variables** box.

5. To compute post hoc tests for the main effects, select **Options** and move each factor into the **Display Means for:** box. Check mark the **Compare main effects** box and select your post hoc test from the drop down menu below the **Confidence interval adjustment** heading. [Note: SPSS does not perform simple effect tests. If you get a significant interaction, you will have to conduct these tests separately.]

6. Select **OK,** or select **Paste** and click the **Run** command.

TWO-WAY MIXED FACTORIAL ANOVA

*This exercise is illustrated in **Chapter 12, Section 12.10** (SPSS in Focus, p. 410), of this book.

1. Click on the **Variable View** tab and enter the name of the between-subjects factor in the first row in the **Name column** and reduce the **Decimals column** to 0 (because this variable will be coded). In the remaining rows, enter each level of the within-subjects factor; each level should be listed in each row in the **Name column**. In the **Decimals column**, reduce the value to the degree of accuracy of the data.

2. Code the levels of the between-subjects factor listed in the first row in the **Values** column.

3. In the **Data View** tab, in the first column enter each coded value for the between-subjects factor so that it equals the number of scores in each level. In each column for the within-subjects factor, enter the data that correspond to each group in each column.

4. Go to the **menu bar** and click **Analyze, General Linear Model**, and **Repeated Measures** to display a dialog box. Enter the name of the within-subjects factor in the **Within-Subjects Factor Name** box, and enter the number of levels for that factor in the **Number of Levels** box below it. Click **Add**.

5. Click **Define** to display a new dialog box. Move the levels for the within-subjects factor into the **Within-Subjects Variables** box. Move the name of the between-subjects factors into the **Between-subjects factor(s)** box.

6. To compute post hoc tests for the main effects, select **Options** and move each factor into the **Display Means for:** box. Check mark the **Compare main effects** box and select your post hoc test from the dropdown menu below the **Confidence interval adjustment** heading. [Note: SPSS does not perform simple effect tests. If you get a significant interaction, you will have to conduct these tests separately.]

7. Select **OK**, or select **Paste** and click the **Run** command.

Correlation and Regression

PEARSON CORRELATION COEFFICIENT

*This exercise is illustrated in **Chapter 8, Section 8.11** (SPSS in Focus, p. 266), of this book.

1. Click on the **Variable View** tab and enter the first variable name in the **Name column**; and enter the second variable name in the Name column below it. Go to the **Decimals column** and reduce the value to the degree of accuracy of the data for each row.

2. Click on the **Data View** tab. Enter the data for each variable in the appropriate columns.

3. Go to the **menu bar** and click **Analyze, Correlate**, and **Bivariate** to bring up a dialog box.

4. Using the arrows, move both variables into the **Variables** box.

5. Select **OK**, or select **Paste** and click the **Run** command.

ANALYSIS OF REGRESSION

*This exercise is illustrated in **Chapter 8, Section 8.11** (SPSS in Focus, p. 266), of this book.

1. Click on the **Variable View** tab and enter the predictor variable name in the **Name column**; and enter the criterion variable name in the Name column below it. Go to the **Decimals column** and reduce the value in both rows to the degree of accuracy for the data.

2. Click on the **Data View** tab. Enter the data for the predictor variable (X) in the first column. Enter the data for the criterion variable (Y) in the second column.

3. Go to the **menu bar** and click **Analyze, Regression**, and **Linear** to bring up a dialog box.

4. Use the arrows to move the predictor variable into the **Independent(s)** box; move the criterion variable into the **Dependent** box.

5. Select **OK**, or select **Paste** and click the **Run** command.

Nonparametric Tests

Tests for Nominal Data

CHI-SQUARE GOODNESS-OF-FIT TEST

*This exercise is illustrated in **Chapter 14, Section 14.5** (SPSS in Focus, p. 472), of this book.

1. Click on the **Variable View** tab and enter the nominal variable name in the **Name column** in the first row; and enter *frequencies* in the Name column below it. Go to the **Decimals column** and reduce the value to 0 for both rows.

2. Code the levels for the nominal variable listed in the first row in the **Values** column.

3. Click on the **Data View** tab. In the first column, list each coded value one time. In the second column, list the corresponding observed frequencies for each coded level of the nominal variable.

4. Go to the menu bar and click **Data** and **Weight cases** to bring up a dialog box. In the new dialog box, click **Weight cases by** and move *frequencies* into the **Frequency Variable** cell. Select **OK**.

5. Go to the **menu bar** and click **Analyze, Nonparametric tests**, and **Chi-square** to bring up a new dialog box.

6. Using the arrows, move the nominal variable into the **Test Variables List** box. In the **Expected Values** box, notice that we have two options: We can assume all categories (or expected frequencies) are equal, or we can input the frequencies for each cell. If the expected frequencies are equal, then leave this alone; if they are not equal, then enter the expected frequencies one at a time and click **Add** to move them into the cell.

7. Select **OK**, or select **Paste** and click the **Run** command.

CHI-SQUARE TEST FOR INDEPENDENCE

*This exercise is illustrated in **Chapter 14, Section 14.5** (SPSS in Focus, p. 472), of this book.

1. To organize the data, write out the contingency table so that one variable is listed in the row and another in the column. Click on the **Variable View** tab and in the **Name column** enter the name of the *row* variable in the first row; and enter the name of the *column* variable in the second row. In the third row, enter *frequencies* in the Name column. Reduce the value to 0 in each row in the **Decimals column**.

2. Code the levels for both nominal variables listed in the first two rows in the **Values** column.

3. In the **Data View** tab, we need to set up the cells by row and column. For the *row* variable, enter each coded value equal to the number of levels for the *column* variable. For example, if the *row* variable has two levels and the *column* variable has three levels, then list 1, 1, 1, 2, 2, 2 in the first column of the Data View. Set up the cells in the second column by listing the levels in numeric order across from each level of the *row* variable. Using the same example, list 1, 2, 3, 1, 2, 3 in the second column. The two columns create the cells. For example, if the first two columns list 1, 1 across the row, then this tells SPSS that any data entered in the third column come from a cell that combines the first level of each factor. List the corresponding observed frequencies for each cell in the third column.

4. Go to the menu bar and click **Data** and **Weight cases** to bring up a dialog box. In the new dialog box, click **Weight cases by** and move *frequencies* into the **Frequency Variable** cell. This tells SPSS that the frequencies you enter are those for each row-column combination. Select **OK**.

5. Go to the **menu bar** and click **Analyze, Descriptive statistics**, and **Crosstabs** to bring up a dialog box.

6. Using the arrows, move the *row* variable into the **Row(s)** box and move the *column* variable into the **Column(s)** box. Click **Statistics**. . . to open a new dialog box.

7. Select **Chi-square** in the top left. To compute effect size select **Phi and Cramer's V** in the box labeled **Nominal**. Click **Continue**.

8. Select **OK**, or select **Paste** and click the **Run** command.

Tests for Ordinal Data

WILCOXON SIGNED-RANKS T TEST

*The directions for this test are not given in this book but are illustrated as an alternative to parametric tests in Figure 14.4 (p. 470) of the book.

1. Click on the **Variable View** tab and enter the name of the first level of the independent variable in the name column in the first row; enter the name of the second level of the independent variable in the second row. Reduce the **Decimals column** value in both rows to the degree of accuracy of the data.

2. Click on the **Data View** tab. List the data for each level of the independent variable. Make sure the scores for each related pair are matched in each row.

3. Go to the **menu bar** and click **Analyze, Nonparametric tests**, and **2 Related Samples**. . . to bring up a dialog box.

4. In the **dialog box**, select each level of the independent variable in the left box and move them to the right box using the arrow in the middle. The variables should be side by side in the box to the right. In the **Test Type** box, make sure that only the box next to **Wilcoxon** is checked.

5. Select **OK**, or select **Paste** and click the **Run** command.

MANN-WHITNEY U TEST

*The directions for this test are not given in this book but are illustrated as an alternative to parametric tests in Figure 14.4 (p. 470) of the book.

1. Click on the **Variable View** tab and enter the independent variable in the **Name column**. In the second row, enter the name of the dependent variable in the Name column. Reduce the value to 0 in the **Decimals column** in the first row and to the degree of accuracy of the data in the second row.

2. Code the levels for the independent variable listed in the first row in the **Values** column.

3. In the **Data View** tab, in the first column enter each number so that it equals the number of scores in each level. For example, if you measure five scores in each group (or level), then enter each numeric code five times in the first column. In the second column, enter the values for the dependent variable so that they correspond with the code for each group.

4. Go to the **menu bar** and click **Analyze, Nonparametric Tests**, and **2 Independent Samples** to bring up a dialog box.

5. Notice that **Mann-Whitney U** is selected by default. Using the arrows, move the dependent variable into the **Test Variable List** box and the independent variable into the **Grouping Variable** box. Click **Define Groups. . .** to open a new dialog box. Place the numeric code for each group in the spaces provided and then click **Continue**.

6. Select **OK**, or select **Paste** and click the **Run** command.

KRUSKAL-WALLIS H TEST

*The directions for this test are not given in this book but are illustrated as an alternative to parametric tests in Figure 14.4 (p. 470) of the book.

1. Click on the **Variable View** tab and enter the name of the independent variable in the **Name column**. Go to the **Decimals column** for this row and reduce the value to 0 (since this variable will be coded). In the second row enter the name of the dependent variable in the Name column. Reduce the **Decimals column** value in the second row to the degree of accuracy of the data.

2. Code the levels for the independent variable listed in the first row in the **Values** column.

3. In the **Data View** tab, in the first column enter each coded value so that it equals the number of scores in each level. For example, if you measure five scores in each group (or level), then enter each numeric code five times in the first column. In the second column, enter the values for the dependent variable so that they correspond with the codes for each group.

4. Go to the **menu bar** and click **Analyze, Nonparametric Tests**, and **k Independent Samples** to bring up a dialog box.

5. Notice that **Kruskal-Wallis H** is selected by default. Using the arrows, move the dependent variable into the **Test Variable List** box and the independent variable into the **Grouping Variable** box. Click **Define Groups. . .** to open a new dialog box. Enter the range of codes (i.e., the smallest and largest number used to code the levels of the independent variable). Select **Continue**.

6. Select **OK**, or select **Paste** and click the **Run** command.

FRIEDMAN TEST

*The directions for this test are not given in this book but are illustrated as an alternative to parametric tests in Figure 14.4 (p. 470) of the book.

1. Click on the **Variable View** tab and enter the name of each level of the independent variable in the **Name column**. One level (or group) should be listed

in each row. Go to the **Decimals column** and reduce the value to the degree of accuracy of the data.

2. Click on the **Data View** tab. Now each column is labeled with each level of the independent variable. Enter the data for each respective column.

3. Go to the **menu bar** and click **Analyze, Nonparametric Tests,** and **k Related Samples** to bring up a dialog box.

4. Notice that **Friedman** is selected by default. Use the arrows to move each column into the **Test Variables** box.

5. Select **OK**, or select **Paste** and click the **Run** command.

C.2 Statistical Tables

Table C.1   Critical Values for the *t* Distribution

Table entries are values of *t* corresponding to proportions in one tail or in two tails combined.

	Proportion in One Tail					
	0.25	0.10	0.05	0.025	0.01	0.005
	Proportion in Two Tails Combined					
df	0.50	0.20	0.10	0.05	0.02	0.01
1	1.000	3.078	6.314	12.706	31.821	63.657
2	0.816	1.886	2.920	4.303	6.965	9.925
3	0.765	1.638	2.353	3.182	4.541	5.841
4	0.741	1.533	2.132	2.776	3.747	4.604
5	0.727	1.476	2.015	2.571	3.365	4.032
6	0.718	1.440	1.943	2.447	3.143	3.707
7	0.711	1.415	1.895	2.365	2.998	3.499
8	0.706	1.397	1.860	2.306	2.896	3.355
9	0.703	1.383	1.833	2.262	2.821	3.250
10	0.700	1.372	1.812	2.228	2.764	3.169
11	0.697	1.363	1.796	2.201	2.718	3.106
12	0.695	1.356	1.782	2.179	2.681	3.055
13	0.694	1.350	1.771	2.160	2.650	3.012
14	0.692	1.345	1.761	2.145	2.624	2.977
15	0.691	1.341	1.753	2.131	2.602	2.947
16	0.690	1.337	1.746	2.120	2.583	2.921

	Proportion in One Tail					
	0.25	0.10	0.05	0.025	0.01	0.005
	Proportion in Two Tails Combined					
df	0.50	0.20	0.10	0.05	0.02	0.01
17	0.689	1.333	1.740	2.110	2.567	2.898
18	0.688	1.330	1.734	2.101	2.552	2.878
19	0.688	1.328	1.729	2.093	2.539	2.861
20	0.687	1.325	1.725	2.086	2.528	2.845
21	0.686	1.323	1.721	2.080	2.518	2.831
22	0.686	1.321	1.717	2.074	2.508	2.819
23	0.685	1.319	1.714	2.069	2.500	2.807
24	0.685	1.318	1.711	2.064	2.492	2.797
25	0.684	1.316	1.708	2.060	2.485	2.787
26	0.684	1.315	1.706	2.056	2.479	2.779
27	0.684	1.314	1.703	2.052	2.473	2.771
28	0.683	1.313	1.701	2.048	2.467	2.763
29	0.683	1.311	1.699	2.045	2.462	2.756
30	0.683	1.310	1.697	2.042	2.457	2.750
40	0.681	1.303	1.684	2.021	2.423	2.704
60	0.679	1.296	1.671	2.000	2.390	2.660
120	0.677	1.289	1.658	1.980	2.358	2.617
∞	0.674	1.282	1.645	1.960	2.326	2.576

Source: Table III of R.A. Fisher and F. Yates, *Statistical Tables for Biological, Agricultural and Medical Research*, 6th ed. London: Longman Group Ltd., 1974 (previously published by Oliver and Boyd Ltd., Edinburgh). Adapted and reprinted with permission of the Addison Wesley Longman Publishing Co.

Table C.2 Critical Values for the *F* Distribution

Critcial values at a .05 level of significance are given in lightface type.
Critcial values at a .01 level of significance are given in boldface type.

Degrees of Freedom Denominator	Degrees of Freedom Numerator											
	1	**2**	**3**	**4**	**5**	**6**	**7**	**8**	**9**	**10**	**20**	**∞**
1	161 **4052**	200 **5000**	216 **5403**	225 **5625**	230 **5764**	234 **5859**	237 **5928**	239 **5928**	241 **6023**	242 **6056**	248 **6209**	254 **6366**
2	18.51 **98.49**	19.00 **99.00**	19.16 **99.17**	19.25 **99.25**	19.30 **99.30**	19.33 **99.33**	19.36 **99.34**	19.37 **99.36**	19.38 **99.38**	19.39 **99.40**	19.44 **99.45**	19.5 **99.5**
3	10.13 **34.12**	9.55 **30.92**	9.28 **29.46**	9.12 **28.71**	9.01 **28.24**	8.94 **27.91**	8.88 **27.67**	8.84 **27.49**	8.81 **27.34**	8.78 **27.23**	8.66 **26.69**	8.5 **26.1**
4	7.71 **21.20**	6.94 **18.00**	6.59 **16.69**	6.39 **15.98**	6.26 **15.52**	6.16 **15.21**	6.09 **14.98**	6.04 **14.80**	6.00 **14.66**	5.96 **14.54**	5.80 **14.02**	5.6 **13.5**
5	6.61 **16.26**	5.79 **13.27**	5.41 **12.06**	5.19 **11.39**	5.05 **10.97**	4.95 **10.67**	4.88 **10.45**	4.82 **10.27**	4.78 **10.15**	4.74 **10.05**	4.56 **9.55**	4.37 **9.02**
6	5.99 **13.74**	5.14 **10.92**	4.76 **9.78**	4.53 **9.15**	4.39 **8.75**	4.28 **8.47**	4.21 **8.26**	4.15 **8.10**	4.10 **7.98**	4.06 **7.87**	3.87 **7.39**	3.67 **6.88**
7	5.59 **13.74**	4.74 **9.55**	4.35 **8.45**	4.12 **7.85**	3.97 **7.46**	3.87 **7.19**	3.79 **7.00**	3.73 **6.84**	3.68 **6.71**	3.63 **6.62**	3.44 **6.15**	3.23 **5.65**
8	5.32 **11.26**	4.46 **8.65**	4.07 **7.59**	3.84 **7.01**	3.69 **6.63**	3.58 **6.37**	3.50 **6.19**	3.44 **6.03**	3.39 **5.91**	3.34 **5.82**	3.15 **5.36**	2.93 **4.86**
9	5.12 **10.56**	4.26 **8.02**	3.86 **6.99**	3.63 **6.42**	3.48 **6.06**	3.37 **5.80**	3.29 **5.62**	3.23 **5.47**	3.18 **5.35**	3.13 **5.26**	2.93 **4.80**	2.71 **4.31**
10	4.96 **10.04**	4.10 **7.56**	3.71 **6.55**	3.48 **5.99**	3.33 **5.64**	3.22 **5.39**	3.14 **5.21**	3.07 **5.06**	3.02 **4.95**	2.97 **4.85**	2.77 **4.41**	2.54 **3.91**
11	4.84 **9.65**	3.98 **7.20**	3.59 **6.22**	3.36 **5.67**	3.20 **5.32**	3.09 **5.07**	3.01 **4.88**	2.95 **4.74**	2.90 **4.63**	2.86 **4.54**	2.65 **4.10**	2.40 **3.60**
12	4.75 **9.33**	3.89 **6.93**	3.49 **5.95**	3.26 **5.41**	3.11 **5.06**	3.00 **4.82**	2.92 **4.65**	2.85 **4.50**	2.80 **4.39**	2.76 **4.30**	2.54 **3.86**	2.30 **3.36**
13	4.67 **9.07**	3.80 **6.70**	3.41 **5.74**	3.18 **5.20**	3.02 **4.86**	2.92 **4.62**	2.84 **4.44**	2.77 **4.30**	2.72 **4.19**	2.67 **4.10**	2.46 **3.67**	2.21 **3.17**
14	4.60 **8.86**	3.74 **6.51**	3.34 **5.56**	3.11 **5.03**	2.96 **4.69**	2.85 **4.46**	2.77 **4.28**	2.70 **4.14**	2.65 **4.03**	2.60 **3.94**	2.39 **3.51**	2.13 **3.00**
15	4.54 **8.68**	3.68 **6.36**	3.29 **5.42**	3.06 **4.89**	2.90 **4.56**	2.79 **4.32**	2.70 **4.14**	2.64 **4.00**	2.59 **3.89**	2.55 **3.80**	2.33 **3.36**	2.07 **2.87**

	Degrees of Freedom Numerator											
	1	2	3	4	5	6	7	8	9	10	20	∞
16	4.49 **8.53**	3.63 **6.23**	3.24 **5.29**	3.01 **4.77**	2.85 **4.44**	2.74 **4.20**	2.66 **4.03**	2.59 **3.89**	2.54 **3.78**	2.49 **3.69**	2.28 **3.25**	2.01 **2.75**
17	4.45 **8.40**	3.59 **6.11**	3.20 **5.18**	2.96 **4.67**	2.81 **4.34**	2.70 **4.10**	2.62 **3.93**	2.55 **3.79**	2.50 **3.68**	2.45 **3.59**	2.23 **3.16**	1.96 **2.65**
18	4.41 **8.28**	3.55 **6.01**	3.16 **5.09**	2.93 **4.58**	2.77 **4.25**	2.66 **4.01**	2.58 **3.85**	2.51 **3.71**	2.46 **3.60**	2.41 **3.51**	2.19 **3.07**	1.92 **2.57**
19	4.38 **8.18**	3.52 **5.93**	3.13 **5.01**	2.90 **4.50**	2.74 **4.17**	2.63 **3.94**	2.55 **3.77**	2.48 **3.63**	2.43 **3.52**	2.38 **3.43**	2.15 **3.00**	1.88 **2.49**
20	4.35 **8.10**	3.49 **5.85**	3.10 **4.94**	2.87 **4.43**	2.71 **4.10**	2.60 **3.87**	2.52 **3.71**	2.45 **3.56**	2.40 **3.45**	2.35 **3.37**	2.12 **2.94**	1.84 **2.42**
21	4.32 **8.02**	3.47 **5.78**	3.07 **4.87**	2.84 **4.37**	2.68 **4.04**	2.57 **3.81**	2.49 **3.65**	2.42 **3.51**	2.37 **3.40**	2.32 **3.31**	2.09 **2.88**	1.81 **2.36**
22	4.30 **7.94**	3.44 **5.72**	3.05 **4.82**	2.82 **4.31**	2.66 **3.99**	2.55 **3.76**	2.47 **3.59**	2.40 **3.45**	2.35 **3.35**	2.30 **3.26**	2.07 **2.83**	1.78 **2.31**
23	4.28 **7.88**	3.42 **5.66**	3.03 **4.76**	2.80 **4.26**	2.64 **3.94**	2.53 **3.71**	2.45 **3.54**	2.38 **3.41**	2.32 **3.30**	2.28 **3.21**	2.04 **2.78**	1.76 **2.26**
24	4.26 **7.82**	3.40 **5.61**	3.01 **4.72**	2.78 **4.22**	2.62 **3.90**	2.51 **3.67**	2.43 **3.50**	2.36 **3.36**	2.30 **3.25**	2.26 **3.17**	2.02 **2.74**	1.73 **2.21**
25	4.24 **7.77**	3.38 **5.57**	2.99 **4.68**	2.76 **4.18**	2.60 **3.86**	2.49 **3.63**	2.41 **3.46**	2.34 **3.32**	2.28 **3.21**	2.24 **3.13**	2.00 **2.70**	1.71 **2.17**
26	4.22 **7.72**	3.37 **5.53**	2.98 **4.64**	2.74 **4.14**	2.59 **3.82**	2.47 **3.59**	2.39 **3.42**	2.32 **3.29**	2.27 **3.17**	2.22 **3.09**	1.99 **2.66**	1.69 **2.13**
27	4.21 **7.68**	3.35 **5.49**	2.96 **4.60**	2.73 **4.11**	2.57 **3.79**	2.46 **3.56**	2.37 **3.39**	2.30 **3.26**	2.25 **3.14**	2.20 **3.06**	1.97 **2.63**	1.67 **2.10**
28	4.20 **7.64**	3.34 **5.45**	2.95 **4.57**	2.71 **4.07**	2.56 **3.76**	2.44 **3.53**	2.36 **3.36**	2.29 **3.23**	2.24 **3.11**	2.19 **3.03**	1.96 **2.60**	1.65 **2.07**
29	4.18 **7.60**	3.33 **5.42**	2.93 **4.54**	2.70 **4.04**	2.54 **3.73**	2.43 **3.50**	2.35 **3.33**	2.28 **3.20**	2.22 **3.08**	2.18 **3.00**	1.94 **2.57**	1.63 **2.04**
30	4.17 **7.56**	3.32 **5.39**	2.92 **4.51**	2.69 **4.02**	2.53 **3.70**	2.42 **3.47**	2.34 **3.30**	2.27 **3.17**	2.21 **3.06**	2.16 **2.98**	1.93 **2.55**	1.61 **2.01**
31	4.16 **7.53**	3.30 **5.36**	2.91 **4.48**	2.68 **3.99**	2.52 **3.67**	2.41 **3.45**	2.32 **3.28**	2.25 **3.15**	2.20 **3.04**	2.15 **2.96**	1.92 **2.53**	1.60 **1.89**
32	4.15 **7.50**	3.29 **5.34**	2.90 **4.46**	2.67 **3.97**	2.51 **3.65**	2.40 **3.43**	2.31 **3.26**	2.24 **3.13**	2.19 **3.02**	2.14 **2.93**	1.91 **2.51**	1.59 **1.88**

| | Degrees of Freedom Numerator | | | | | | | | | | | |
	1	2	3	4	5	6	7	8	9	10	20	∞
33	4.14 **7.47**	3.28 **5.31**	2.89 **4.44**	2.66 **3.95**	2.50 **3.63**	2.39 **3.41**	2.30 **3.24**	2.23 **3.11**	2.18 **3.00**	2.13 **2.91**	1.90 **2.49**	1.58 **1.87**
34	4.13 **7.44**	3.28 **5.29**	2.88 **4.42**	2.65 **3.93**	2.49 **3.61**	2.38 **3.39**	2.29 **3.22**	2.23 **3.09**	2.17 **2.98**	2.12 **2.89**	1.89 **2.47**	1.57 **1.86**
35	4.12 **7.42**	3.27 **5.27**	2.87 **4.40**	2.64 **3.91**	2.49 **3.59**	2.37 **3.37**	2.29 **3.20**	2.22 **3.07**	2.16 **2.96**	2.11 **2.88**	1.88 **2.45**	1.56 **1.85**
36	4.11 **7.40**	3.26 **5.25**	2.87 **4.38**	2.63 **3.89**	2.48 **3.57**	2.36 **3.35**	2.28 **3.18**	2.21 **3.05**	2.15 **2.95**	2.11 **2.86**	1.87 **2.43**	1.55 **1.84**
37	4.11 **7.37**	3.25 **5.23**	2.86 **4.36**	2.63 **3.87**	2.47 **3.56**	2.36 **3.33**	2.27 **3.17**	2.20 **3.04**	2.14 **2.93**	2.10 **2.84**	1.86 **2.42**	1.54 **1.83**
38	4.10 **7.35**	3.24 **5.21**	2.85 **4.34**	2.62 **3.86**	2.46 **3.54**	2.35 **3.32**	2.26 **3.15**	2.19 **3.02**	2.14 **2.92**	2.09 **2.83**	1.85 **2.40**	1.53 **1.82**
39	4.09 **7.33**	3.24 **5.19**	2.85 **4.33**	2.61 **3.84**	2.46 **3.53**	2.34 **3.30**	2.26 **3.14**	2.19 **3.01**	2.13 **2.90**	2.08 **2.81**	1.84 **2.39**	1.52 **1.81**
40	4.08 **7.31**	3.23 **5.18**	2.84 **4.31**	2.61 **3.83**	2.45 **3.51**	2.34 **3.29**	2.25 **3.12**	2.18 **2.99**	2.12 **2.88**	2.07 **2.80**	1.84 **2.37**	1.51 **1.80**
42	4.07 **7.27**	3.22 **5.15**	2.83 **4.29**	2.59 **3.80**	2.44 **3.49**	2.32 **3.26**	2.24 **3.10**	2.17 **2.96**	2.11 **2.86**	2.06 **2.77**	1.82 **2.35**	1.50 **1.78**
44	4.06 **7.24**	3.21 **5.12**	2.82 **4.26**	2.58 **3.78**	2.43 **3.46**	2.31 **3.24**	2.23 **3.07**	2.16 **2.94**	2.10 **2.84**	2.05 **2.75**	1.81 **2.32**	1.49 **1.76**
60	4.00 **7.08**	3.15 **4.98**	2.76 **4.13**	2.53 **3.65**	2.37 **3.34**	2.25 **3.12**	2.17 **2.95**	2.10 **2.82**	2.04 **2.72**	1.99 **2.63**	1.75 **2.20**	1.39 **1.60**
120	3.92 **6.85**	3.07 **4.79**	2.68 **3.95**	2.45 **3.48**	2.29 **3.17**	2.18 **2.96**	2.09 **2.79**	2.02 **2.66**	1.96 **2.56**	1.91 **2.47**	1.66 **2.03**	1.25 **1.38**
∞	3.84 **6.63**	3.00 **4.61**	2.60 **3.78**	2.37 **3.32**	2.21 **3.02**	2.10 **2.80**	2.01 **2.64**	1.94 **2.51**	1.88 **2.41**	1.83 **2.32**	1.57 **1.88**	1.00 **1.00**

(Left axis label: Degrees of Freedom Denominator)

Source: The entries in this table were computed by the author.

Table C.3 Critical Values for the Pearson Correlation

To be significant, the sample correlation, *r*, must be greater than or equal to the critical value in the table.

	Level of Significance for One-Tailed Test			
	.05	.025	.01	.005
	Level of Significance for Two-Tailed Test			
df = n − 2	.10	.05	.02	.01
1	.988	.997	.9995	.9999
2	.900	.950	.980	.990
3	.805	.878	.934	.959
4	.729	.811	.882	.917
5	.669	.754	.833	.874
6	.622	.707	.789	.834
7	.582	.666	.750	.798
8	.549	.632	.716	.765
9	.521	.602	.685	.735
10	.497	.576	.658	.708
11	.476	.553	.634	.684
12	.458	.532	.612	.661
13	.441	.514	.592	.641
14	.426	.497	.574	.623
15	.412	.482	.558	.606
16	.400	.468	.542	.590
17	.389	.456	.528	.575
18	.378	.444	.516	.561
19	.369	.433	.503	.549
20	.360	.423	.492	.537
21	.352	.413	.482	.526
22	.344	.404	.472	.515
23	.337	.396	.462	.505
24	.330	.388	.453	.496
25	.323	.381	.445	.487
26	.317	.374	.437	.479
27	.311	.367	.430	.471
28	.306	.361	.423	.463
29	.301	.355	.416	.456
30	.296	.349	.409	.449
35	.275	.325	.381	.418
40	.257	.304	.358	.393
45	.243	.288	.338	.372
50	.231	.273	.322	.354
60	.211	.250	.295	.325
70	.195	.232	.274	.302
80	.183	.217	.256	.283
90	.173	.205	.242	.267
100	.164	.195	.230	.254

Source: Table VI of R.A. Fisher and F. Yates, *Statistical Tables for Biological, Agricultural and Medical Research*, 6th ed. London: Longman Group Ltd., 1974 (previously published by Oliver and Boyd Ltd., Edinburgh). Adapted and reprinted with permission of the Addison Wesley Longman Publishing Co.

Table C.4 Critical Values of Chi-Square (χ^2)

df	Level of Significance	
	$\alpha = .05$	$\alpha = .01$
1	3.84	6.64
2	5.99	9.21
3	7.81	11.34
4	9.49	13.28
5	11.07	15.09
6	12.59	16.81
7	14.07	18.48
8	15.51	20.09
9	16.92	21.67
10	18.31	23.21
11	19.68	24.72
12	21.03	26.22
13	22.36	27.69
14	23.68	29.14
15	25.00	30.58
16	26.30	32.00
17	27.59	33.41
18	28.87	34.80
19	30.14	36.19
20	31.41	37.47
21	32.67	38.93
22	33.92	40.29
23	35.17	41.64
24	36.42	42.98
25	37.65	44.31
26	38.88	45.64
27	40.11	46.96
28	41.34	48.28
29	42.56	49.59
30	43.77	50.89
40	55.76	63.69
50	67.50	76.15
60	79.08	88.38
70	90.53	100.42

Source: From Table IV of R.A. Fisher and F. Yates, *Statistical Tables for Biological, Agricultural and Medical Research*, 6th ed. London: Longman Group Ltd., 1974. Reprinted with permission of the Addison Wesley Longman Ltd.

GLOSSARY

This glossary includes all of the key terms that were defined in each chapter. The number in parentheses following each definition indicates the chapter or appendix where the term was defined.

ABA design   See *reversal design* (9).

Abstract   A brief written summary of the purpose, methods, and results of an article, a chapter, a book, or another published document. The length of an abstract can vary; however, abstracts are usually 250 words or less (2).

Accessible population   The portion of the target population that can be clearly identified and directly sampled from (5).

Anchors   Adjectives that are given to describe the end points of a rating scale to give the scale greater meaning (8).

Anonymity   A protection of individual identity in which the identity of a participant remains unknown throughout a study, even to those involved in a study (3).

APA-style manuscript   A document that is created using the writing style format detailed in the *Publication Manual of the American Psychological Association*, typically for the purposes of having the work considered for publication in a peer-reviewed journal (15).

Applied research   Uses the scientific method to answer questions concerning practical problems with potential practical solutions (1).

Archival research   A type of existing data design in which events or behaviors are described based on a review and analysis of relevant historical or archival records (7).

Assent   The consent of a minor or other legally incapable person to agree to participate in research only after receiving an appropriate explanation in reasonably understandable language (3).

Attrition   A possible threat to validity in which a participant does not show up for a study at a scheduled time or fails to complete the study (6).

Authority   A method of knowing accepted as fact because it was stated by an expert or respected source in a particular subject area (1).

Bar chart   A graphical display used to summarize the frequency of discrete and categorical data using bars to represent each frequency (13).

Bar graph   See *bar chart* (13).

Baseline phase (A)   A phase in which a treatment or manipulation is absent (9).

Basic research   Uses the scientific method to answer questions that address theoretical issues about fundamental processes and underlying mechanisms related to the behaviors and events being studied (1).

Basic time series design   A quasi-experimental research design in which a dependent variable is measured at many different points in time in one group before and after a treatment that is manipulated by the researcher is administered (9).

Behavior categories   The specific types of behaviors that researchers want to measure in the research setting, and they are typically organized as a list of examples that "count" in each category or for each type of behavior (7).

Behavioral measure   A type of measurement in which researchers directly observe and record the behavior of subjects or participants (10).

Belmont Report   A published document that recommends three principles for the ethical conduct of research with human participants: respect for persons, beneficence, and justice (3).

Beneficence   An ethical principle listed in the Belmont Report that states that it is the researcher's responsibility to minimize the potential risks and maximize the potential benefits associated with conducting a research study (3).

Between-groups variability   A source of variance in a dependent measure that is caused by or associated with the manipulation of the levels (or groups) of an independent variable (11).

Between-persons variability   A source of variance in a dependent measure that is caused by or associated with individual differences or differences in participant responses across all groups (11).

Between-subjects design   A research design in which different participants are observed one time in each group or at each level of a factor (10).

Between-subjects experimental design   An experimental research design in which the levels of a between-subjects factor are manipulated, then different participants are randomly assigned to each group or to each level of that factor and observed one time (10).

Between-subjects factor   A type of factor in which different participants are observed in each group, or at each level of the factor (10).

Between-subjects factorial design   A research design in which the levels of two or more between-subjects factors are combined to create groups, meaning that different participants are observed in each group (12).

Bipolar scales   Response scales that have points above (positive values) and below (negative values) a zero point (8).

Carryover effects   A threat to internal validity in which participation in one group "carries over" or causes changes in performance in a second group (11).

Case history   An in-depth description of the history and background of the individual, group, or organization observed. A case history can be the only information provided in a case study for situations in which the researcher does not include a manipulation, a treatment, or an intervention (7).

Case study   The qualitative analysis of an individual, a group, an organization, or an event used to illustrate a phenomenon, explore new hypotheses, or compare the observations of many cases (7).

Ceiling effect   A range effect where scores are clustered at the high end of a scale (4).

Central limit theorem   Regardless of the distribution of scores in a population, the sampling distribution of sample means selected at random from that population will approach the shape of a normal distribution, as the number of samples in the sampling distribution increases (14).

Central tendency   Statistical measures for locating a single score that tends to be near the center of a distribution and is most representative or descriptive of all scores in a distribution (13).

Changing-criterion design   A single-case experimental design in which a baseline phase is followed by successive treatment phases in which some criterion or target level of behavior is changed from one treatment phase to the next. The participant must meet the criterion of one treatment phase before the next treatment phase is administered (9).

Chi-square goodness-of-fit test   A statistical procedure used to determine whether observed frequencies at each level of one categorical variable are similar to or different from frequencies expected (14).

Chi-square test for independence   A statistical procedure used to determine whether frequencies observed at the combination of levels of two categorical variables are similar to or different from frequencies expected (14).

Citation bias   A misleading approach to citing sources that occurs when an author or authors cite only evidence that supports their view and fail to cite existing evidence that refutes their view (2).

Closed-ended item   See *restricted item* (8).

Cluster sampling   A method of sampling in which subgroups or clusters of individuals are identified in a population, and then a portion of clusters that are representative of the population are selected such that all individuals in the selected clusters are included in the sample. All clusters that are not selected are omitted from the sample (5).

Coding   The procedure of converting a categorical variable to numeric values (4).

Coefficient of determination   A measure (R^2) of proportion of variance used to describe effect size for data analyzed using a correlation coefficient or regression. The coefficient of determination is mathematically equivalent to eta squared (14).

Cohen's conventions   Standard rules for identifying small, medium, and large effects based on typical findings in behavioral research (14).

Cohen's *d*   A measure of effect size in terms of the number of standard deviations that mean scores shifted above or below the population mean stated by the null hypothesis. The larger the value of *d*, the larger the effect in the population (14).

Cohen's kappa   A measure of interrater reliability that estimates the level of agreement between two raters, while taking into account the probability that the two raters agree by chance or error (13).

Cohort   A group of individuals who share common statistical traits or characteristics, or experiences within a defined period (9).

Cohort effect   A threat to internal validity in which differences in the characteristics of participants in different cohorts or age groups confound or alternatively explain an observed result (9).

Cohort-sequential design   A developmental research design that combines longitudinal and cross-sectional techniques by observing different cohorts of participants over time at overlapping times (9).

Collective case study   A type of case study used to compare observations of many cases (7).

Complete counterbalancing   A procedure in which all possible order sequences in which participants receive different treatments or participate in different groups are balanced or offset in an experiment (11).

Complete factorial design   A factorial design in which each level of one factor is combined or crossed with each level of the other factor, with participants observed in each cell or combination of levels (12).

Completely crossed design   See *complete factorial design* (12).

Confederate   A co-researcher or actor who pretends to be a participant in a research study for the purposes of scientific investigation (3).

Confidence interval (CI)   See *interval estimate* (14).

Confidence limits   The upper and lower boundaries of a confidence interval given within a specified level of confidence (14).

Confidentiality   A protection of individual identity in which the identity of a participant is not made available to anyone who is not directly involved in a study. Those involved in a study, however, are able to identify participant information (3).

Confirmational strategy   A method of testing a theory or hypothesis in which a positive result confirms the predictions made by that theory or hypothesis (2).

Confound   An unanticipated variable not accounted for in a research study that could be causing or associated with observed changes in one or more measured variables (6, 8).

Confound variable   See *confound* (6, 8).

Construct   A conceptual variable that is known to exist but cannot be directly observed (4).

Construct validity   The extent to which an operational definition for a variable or construct is actually measuring that variable or construct (4).

Content analysis   A type of existing data design in which the content of written or spoken records of the occurrence of specific events or behaviors is described and interpreted (7).

Content validity   The extent to which the items or contents of a measure adequately represent all of the features of the construct being measured (4).

Continuous variable   A variable measured along a continuum at any place beyond the decimal point, meaning that it can be measured in whole units or fractional units (4).

Contrived setting   A location or site arranged to mimic the natural setting within which a behavior of interest normally occurs, in order to facilitate the occurrence of that behavior (7).

Control   (a) The manipulation of a variable and (b) holding all other variables constant. When control is low, neither criterion is met; when control is high, both criteria are met (6, 10).

Control by holding constant   A type of restricted random assignment in which we limit which participants are included in a sample based on characteristics they exhibit that may otherwise differ between groups in a study (10).

Control by matching   A type of restricted random assignment in which we assess or measure the characteristic we want to control, group or categorize participants based on scores on that measure, and then use a random procedure to assign participants from each category to a group in the study (10).

Control group   A condition in an experiment in which participants are treated the same as participants in an experimental group, except that the manipulation believed to cause a change in the dependent variable is omitted (10).

Control time series design   A basic or interrupted time series quasi-experimental research design that also includes a nonequivalent control group that is observed during the same period of time as a treatment group, but does not receive the treatment (9).

Convenience sampling   A method of sampling in which subjects or participants are selected for a research study based on how easy or convenient it is to reach or access them and based on their availability to participate (5).

Correlation coefficient   A statistic used to measure the strength and direction of the linear relationship, or correlation, between two factors. The value of r can range from -1.0 to $+1.0$ (8).

Correlational research design   The measurement of two or more factors to determine or estimate the extent to which the values for the factors are related or change in an identifiable pattern (8).

Counterbalancing A procedure in which the order in which participants receive different treatments or participate in different groups is balanced or offset in an experiment. Two types of counterbalancing are complete and partial counterbalancing (11).

Covariance The extent to which the values of two factors (X and Y) vary together. The closer data points fall to the regression line, the more the values of two factors vary together (8).

Cover story A false explanation or story intended to prevent research participants from discovering the true purpose of a research study (3).

Cramer's V A measure of proportion of variance that is used as an estimate of effect size for the chi-square test for independence (14).

Criterion-related validity The extent to which scores obtained on some measure can be used to infer or predict a criterion or expected outcome (4).

Criterion variable The to-be-predicted variable (Y) with unknown values that can be predicted or estimated, given known values of the predictor variable (8).

Cronbach's alpha A measure of internal consistency that estimates the average correlation for every possible way that a measure can be split in half (13).

Cross-sectional design A developmental research design in which participants are grouped by their age and participant characteristics are measured in each age group (9).

Data (plural) Measurements or observations that are typically numeric (1).

Data points The x- and y-coordinates for each plot in a scatter plot (8).

Datum (singular) A single measurement or observation, usually called a *score* or *raw score* (1).

Debriefing The full disclosure to participants of the true purpose of a study, typically given at the end of a study (3).

Deception A strategy used by researchers in which participants are deliberately mislead concerning the true purpose and nature of the research being conducted. Deception can be active (deliberately untruthful) or passive (omission of key information) (3).

Deductive reasoning A "top-down" type of reasoning in which a claim (a hypothesis or theory) is used to generate ideas or predictions and make observations (2).

Degrees of freedom (*df*) for sample variance One less than the sample size, or $n - 1$ (13).

Demand characteristic Any feature or characteristic of a research setting that may reveal the hypothesis being tested or give the participant a clue regarding how he or she is expected to behave (4).

Dependent sample See *related sample* (11).

Dependent variable The variable that is believed to change in the presence of the independent variable. It is the "presumed effect" (6).

Descriptive statistics Procedures used to summarize, organize, and make sense of a set of scores or observations, typically presented graphically, in tabular form (in tables), or as summary statistics (single values) (13).

Determinism An assumption in science that all actions in the universe have a cause (7).

Disconfirmational strategy A method of testing a theory or hypothesis in which a positive result disconfirms the predictions made by that theory or hypothesis (2).

Discrete variable A variable measured in whole units or categories that are not distributed along a continuum (4).

Double-barreled items   Survey items that ask participants for one response to two different questions or statements (8).

Double-blind study   A type of research study in which the researcher collecting the data and the participants in the study are unaware of the conditions that participants are assigned (4).

Duplication   The republication of original data that were previously published (3).

Duration method   A method used to quantify observations made in a study by recording the amount of time or duration that participants engage in a certain behavior during a fixed period of time (7).

Ecological validity   The extent to which results observed in a study will generalize across settings or environments (6).

Effect   A mean difference or discrepancy between what was observed in a sample and what was expected to be observed in the population (stated by the null hypothesis) (14).

Effect size   A statistical measure of the size or magnitude of an observed effect in a population, which allows researchers to describe how far scores shifted in a population, or the percentage of variance in a dependent variable that can be explained by the levels of a factor (7, 14).

Effect size conventions   See *Cohen's conventions* (14).

Empirical generalization   The extent to which results in a survey or another research study are consistent with data obtained in previous research studies (8).

Empirical rule   A rule for normally distributed data that states that at least 99.7% of data fall within three standard deviations of the mean; at least 95% of data fall within two standard deviations of the mean; at least 68% of data fall within one standard deviation of the mean. (13)

Empiricism   A method of knowing based on one's experiences or observations (1).

Error   A source of variance that cannot be attributed to having different groups or treatments. Two sources of error are between-persons and within-groups variability (10, 11).

Error variance   A numeric measure of the variability in scores that can be attributed to or is caused by the individual differences of participants in each group (10).

Estimation   A statistical procedure in which a sample statistic is used to estimate the value of an unknown population parameter. Two types of estimation are point estimation and interval estimation (14).

Eta squared   A measure (η^2) of proportion of variance used to describe effect size for data analyzed using ANOVA (14).

Ethnography   The qualitative analysis of the behavior and identity of a group or culture as it is described and characterized by the members of that group or culture (7).

Evaluation apprehension   A type of participant reactivity in which a participant is overly apprehensive (4).

Event sampling   A strategy used to manage an observation period by splitting a fixed period of time into smaller intervals of time, and then recording a different behavior in each time interval (7).

Existing data design   The collection, review, and analysis of any type of existing documents or records, including those that are written or recorded as video, as audio, or in other electronic form (7).

Expectancy effects   Preconceived ideas or expectations regarding how participants should behave or what participants are capable of doing. Expectancy effects can often lead to experimenter bias (4).

Experiment   The methods and procedures used in an experimental research design to specifically control the conditions under which observations are made in order to isolate cause-and-effect relationships between variables (6).

Experimental group See *treatment group* (10).

Experimental manipulation The identification of an independent variable and the creation of two or more groups that constitute the levels of that variable (10).

Experimental mortality See *attrition* (6).

Experimental realism The extent to which the psychological aspects of a research setting are meaningful or feel real to participants (6).

Experimental research design The use of methods and procedures to make observations in which the researcher fully controls the conditions and experiences of participants by applying three required elements of control: randomization, manipulation, and comparison/control (6).

Experimenter bias The extent to which the behavior of a researcher or experimenter intentionally or unintentionally influences the results of a study (4).

Exploratory case study A type of case study used to explore or generate hypotheses for later investigation (7).

External factor of a construct An observable behavior or event that is presumed to reflect the construct itself (4).

External validity The extent to which observations made in a study generalize beyond the specific manipulations or constraints in the study (6).

Fabrication To concoct methods or data that misrepresent aspects of a research study with the intent to deceive others (3).

Face validity The extent to which a measure for a variable or construct appears to measure what it is purported to measure (4).

Factor See *independent variable* (6).

Factorial design A research design in which participants are observed across the combination of levels of two or more factors (12).

Factorial experimental design A research design in which groups are created by manipulating the levels of two or more factors, then the same or different participants are observed in each group using experimental procedures of randomization (for a between-subjects factor) and using control for timing and order effects (for a within-subjects factor) (12).

Field experiment An experiment that takes place in an environment within which the behavior or event being observed would naturally operate (6).

File drawer problem A type of publication bias in which researchers have a tendency to file away studies that show negative results, knowing that most journals will likely reject them (2).

Floor effect A range effect where scores are clustered at the low end of a scale (4).

Frequency A value that describes the number of times or how often a category, score, or range of scores occurs (13).

Frequency distribution table A tabular summary display for a distribution of data organized or summarized in terms of how often a category, score, or range of scores occurs (13).

Frequency method A method used to quantify observations made in a study by counting the number of times a behavior occurs during a fixed or predetermined period of time (7).

Full-text article Any article or text that is available in its full or complete published version (2).

Full-text database Any online database that makes full-text articles available to be downloaded electronically as a PDF or in another electronic format (2).

Generation effect   See *cohort effect* (9).

Heterogeneous attrition   A possible threat to internal validity in which rates of attrition are different between groups in a study (6).

Higher-order factorial design   A research design in which the levels of more than two factors are combined or crossed to create groups (12).

Higher-order interaction   An interaction for the combination of levels of three or more factors in a factorial design (12).

Histogram   A graphical display used to summarize the frequency of continuous data that are distributed in numeric intervals using bars connected at the upper limits of each interval (13).

History effect   A possible threat to internal validity in which an unanticipated event co-occurs with a treatment or manipulation in a study (6).

Homogeneous attrition   A threat to population validity in which rates of attrition are about the same in each group (6).

Hypothesis   A specific, testable claim or prediction about what you expect to observe given a set of circumstances (1, 2).

Hypothetical construct   See *construct* (4).

Illustrative case study   A type of case study used to investigate rare or unknown phenomena (7).

Independent sample   A type of sample in which different participants are independently observed one time in each group (10).

Independent-sample *t* test   See *two-independent-sample* t *test* (10).

Independent variable   The variable that is manipulated in an experiment. The levels of the variable remain unchanged (or "independent") between groups in an experiment. It is the "presumed cause" (6).

Individual differences   The unique characteristics of participants in a sample that can differ from one participant to another (6).

Individual sampling   A strategy used to manage an observation period by splitting a fixed period of time into smaller intervals of time, and then recording the behaviors of a different participant in each time interval (7).

Inductive reasoning   A "bottom-up" type of reasoning in which a limited number of observations or measurements (i.e., data) are used to generate ideas and make observations (2).

Inferential statistics   Procedures that allow researchers to *infer* or generalize observations made with samples to the larger population from which they were selected (14).

Informed consent   A signed or verbal agreement in which participants state they are willing to participate in a research study after being informed of all aspects of their role in the study (3).

Institutional animal care and use committee (IACUC)   A review board that consists of at least one veterinarian, one scientist with experience using animals, and one public member from the community. These members review for approval animal research protocols submitted by researchers prior to the conduct of any research. Every institution that receives federal funding must have an IACUC (3).

Institutional review board (IRB)   A review board with at least five members, one of whom comes from outside the institution. These members review for approval research protocols submitted by researchers prior to the conduct of any human participant research. Every institution that receives federal funding must have an IRB (3).

Instrumentation   A possible threat to internal validity in which the measurement of the dependent variable changes due to an error during the course of a research study (6).

Interaction   A source of variation associated with how the effects of one factor are influenced by, or depend on, the levels of a second factor (12).

Internal consistency   A measure of reliability used to determine the extent to which multiple items used to measure the same variable are related (4).

Internal validity   The extent to which a research design includes enough control of the conditions and experiences of participants that it can demonstrate a single unambiguous explanation for a manipulation—that is, cause and effect (6).

Interobserver reliability   See *interrater reliability (IRR)* (4).

Interquartile range (IQR)   The range of values between the third (Q_3) and first (Q_1) quartiles of a data set (13).

Interrater reliability (IRR)   A measure for the extent to which two or more raters of the same behavior or event are in agreement with what they observed (4).

Interrupted time series design   A quasi-experimental research design in which a dependent variable is measured at many different points in time in one group before and after a treatment that naturally occurred (9).

Interval estimate   The interval or range of possible values within which an unknown population parameter is likely to be contained (14).

Interval method   A method used to quantify observations made in a study by dividing an observational period into equal intervals of time, and then recording whether or not certain behaviors occur in each interval (7).

Interval scales   Measurements that have no true zero and are distributed in equal units (4).

Interviewer bias   The tendency for the demeanor, words, or expressions of a researcher to influence the responses of a participant when the researcher and the participant are in direct contact (8).

Intuition   A method of knowing based largely on an individual's hunch or feeling that something is correct (1).

Justice   An ethical principle listed in the Belmont Report that states that all participants should be treated fairly and equitably in terms of receiving the benefits and bearing the risks in research (3).

Laboratory experiment   An experiment that takes place in a laboratory setting in which the researcher has greatest control over variables, regardless of whether it is made to look natural or not (6).

Latency method   A method used to quantify observations made in a study by recording the time or duration between the occurrences of behaviors during a fixed period of time (7).

Latin square   A matrix design in which a limited number of order sequences are constructed such that (1) the number of order sequences equals the number of treatments, (2) each treatment appears equally often in each position, and (3) each treatment precedes and follows each treatment one time (11, B.2).

Level of confidence   The probability or likelihood that an interval estimate will contain the value of an unknown population parameter (e.g., a population mean) (14).

Level of significance   A criterion of judgment upon which a decision is made regarding the value stated in a null hypothesis. The criterion is based on the probability of obtaining a statistic measured in a sample if the value stated in the null hypothesis were true (14).

Levels of a factor   The specific conditions or groups created by manipulating that factor (6).

Likert scale   A numeric response scale used to indicate a participant's rating or level of agreement with a question or statement (8).

Linear regression　A statistical procedure used to determine the equation of a regression line to a set of data points and to determine the extent to which the regression equation can be used to predict values of one factor, given known values of a second factor in a population (8).

Literature review　A systematic search for and recording of information identified in the general body of published scientific knowledge (2).

Literature review article　A written comprehensive report of findings from previously published works about a problem in the form of a synthesis of previous articles or as a meta-analysis (15).

Longitudinal design　A developmental research design used to study changes across the life span by observing the same participants at different points in time and measuring the same dependent variable at each time (9).

Magnitude　The size of the change in a dependent measure observed between phases of a design. The larger the magnitude of changes in a dependent measure between each phase, the higher the internal validity of a research design (9).

Main effect　A source of variation associated with mean differences across the levels of a single factor (12).

Manipulation check　A procedure used to check or confirm that a manipulation in a study had the effect that was intended (4).

Matched-pairs design　See *matched-samples design* (11).

Matched-samples design　A within-subjects research design in which participants are matched, experimentally or naturally, based on preexisting characteristics or traits that they share (11).

Maturation　A possible threat to internal validity in which a participant's physiological or psychological state changes over time during a study (6).

Median　The middle value in a distribution of data listed in numeric order (13).

Meta-analysis　A type of existing data design in which data are combined, analyzed, and summarized across a group of related studies to make statistically guided decisions about the strength or reliability of the reported findings in those studies (7).

Mixed factorial design　A research design in which different participants are observed at each level of a between-subjects factor and also repeatedly observed across the levels of the within-subjects factor (12).

Mode　The value in a data set that occurs most often or most frequently (13).

Multiple-baseline design　A single-case experimental design in which a treatment is successively administered over time to different participants, for different behaviors, or in different settings (9).

Mundane realism　The extent to which a research setting physically resembles or looks like the natural or real-world environment being simulated (6).

Natural manipulation　The manipulation of a stimulus that can be naturally changed with little effort (10).

Natural setting　A location or site where a behavior of interest normally occurs (7).

Naturalistic observation　The observation of behavior in the natural setting where it is expected to occur, with limited or no attempt to overtly manipulate the conditions of the environment where the observations are made (7).

Negative correlation　A negative value of *r* that indicates that the values of two factors change in different directions, meaning that as the values of one factor increase, values of the second factor decrease (8).

Nominal scales　Measurements in which a number is assigned to represent something or someone. Numbers on a nominal scale are often coded values (4).

Nonequivalent control group   A control group that is matched upon certain preexisting characteristics similar to those observed in a treatment group, but to which participants are not randomly assigned. In a quasi-experiment, a dependent variable measured in a treatment group is compared to that in the nonequivalent control group (9).

Nonequivalent control group posttest-only design   A quasi-experimental research design in which a dependent variable is measured following a treatment in one group and also in a nonequivalent control group that does not receive the treatment (9).

Nonequivalent control group pretest-posttest design   A quasi-experimental research design in which a dependent variable is measured in one group of participants before (pretest) and after (posttest) a treatment and that same dependent variable is also measured at pretest and posttest in another nonequivalent control group that does not receive the treatment (9).

Nonexperimental research design   The use of methods and procedures to make observations in which the behavior or event is observed "as is" or without an intervention from the researcher (6).

Nonparametric tests   Significance tests that are used to test hypotheses about data that can have any type of distribution and to analyze data on a nominal or ordinal scale of measurement (14).

Nonprobability sampling   A category of sampling in which a sample is selected from the accessible population. Nonprobability sampling methods are used when it is not possible to select individuals directly from the target population (5).

Nonresponse bias   A bias in sampling in which a number of participants in one or more groups choose not to respond to a survey or request to participate in a research study (5).

Normal distribution   A theoretical distribution with data that are symmetrically distributed around the mean, the median, and the mode (13).

Null   See *null hypothesis* (14).

Null hypothesis   A statement about a population parameter, such as the population mean, that is assumed to be true. The null hypothesis is a starting point. We will test whether the value stated in the null hypothesis is likely to be true (14).

Nuremberg Code   The first international code for ethical conduct in research consisting of 10 directives aimed at the protection of human participants (3).

One-group posttest-only design   A quasi-experimental research design in which a dependent variable is measured for one group of participants following a treatment (9).

One-group pretest-posttest design   A quasi-experimental research design in which the same dependent variable is measured in one group of participants before (pretest) and after (posttest) a treatment is administered (9).

One-sample t test   A statistical procedure used to test hypotheses concerning the mean of interval or ratio data in a single population with an unknown variance (5).

One-way between-subjects ANOVA   A statistical procedure used to test hypotheses for one factor with two or more levels concerning the variance among group means. This test is used when different participants are observed at each level of a factor and the variance in a given population is unknown (10).

One-way within-subjects ANOVA   A statistical procedure used to test hypotheses for one factor with two or more levels concerning the variance among group means. This test is used when the same participants are observed at each level of a factor and the variance in a given population is unknown (11).

Open-ended item   A question or statement in a survey that allows the respondent to give any response in his or her own words, without restriction (8).

Operational definition   A description of some observable event in terms of the specific process or manner by which it was observed or measured (1).

Order effects   A threat to internal validity in which the order in which participants receive different treatments or participate in different groups causes changes in a dependent variable (11).

Ordinal scales   Measurements that convey order or rank only (4).

Outcome validity   The extent to which the results or outcomes observed in a study will generalize across different but related dependent variables (6).

Outlier   A score that falls substantially above or below most other scores in a data set (8).

p **value**   The probability of obtaining a sample outcome if the value stated in the null hypothesis is true. The *p* value is compared to the level of significance to make a decision about a null hypothesis (14).

Paired-samples *t* test   See *related samples* t *test* (11).

Pairwise comparison   A statistical comparison for the difference between two group means. A post hoc test evaluates all possible pairwise comparisons for an ANOVA with any number of groups (10).

Parametric tests   Significance tests that are used to test hypotheses about parameters in a population in which the data are normally distributed and measured on an interval or ratio scale of measurement (14).

Parsimony   A canon of science that states that, all else being equal, simpler explanations should be preferred to more complex ones (2).

Partial counterbalancing   A procedure in which some, but not all, possible order sequences in which participants receive different treatments or participate in different groups are balanced or offset in an experiment (11).

Partially open-ended item   A question or statement in a survey that includes a few restricted answer options and then a last one that allows participants to respond in their own words in case the few restricted options do not fit with the answer they want to give (8).

Participant   A term used to describe a human who volunteers to be subjected to the procedures in a research study (5).

Participant expectancy   A type of participant reactivity in which a participant is overly cooperative (4).

Participant fatigue   A state of physical or psychological exhaustion resulting from intense research demands typically due to observing participants too often, or requiring participants to engage in research activities that are too demanding (11).

Participant observation   A method of observation in which researchers participate in or join the group or culture that they are observing (7).

Participant pool   A group of accessible and available participants for a research study. In college or university settings, a participant pool is created using policies that require students to participate in academic research, typically as a condition for receiving grades or credits in introductory-level classes (5).

Participant reactivity   The reaction or response participants have when they know they are being observed or measured (4).

Participant reluctance   A type of participant reactivity in which a participant is overly antagonistic (4).

Participant variable   A quasi-independent or preexisting variable that is related to or characteristic of the personal attributes of a participant (12).

Pearson correlation coefficient   A coefficient used to measure the direction and strength of the linear relationship of two factors in which the data for both factors are on an interval or a ratio scale of measurement (8).

Peer review   A procedure used by the editors of scientific journals in which a manuscript or work is sent to peers or experts in that area to review the work and determine its scientific value or worth regarding publication (3, 15).

Peer-reviewed journal A type of publication that specifically publishes scientific articles, reviews, or commentaries only after the work has been reviewed by peers or scientific experts who determine its scientific value or worth regarding publication. Only after acceptance from peer reviewers will a work be published (2).

Phase A series of trials or observations made in one condition (9).

Phenomenology The qualitative analysis of the conscious experiences of phenomena from the first-person point of view of the participant (7).

Physiological measure A type of measurement in which researchers record physical responses of the brain and body in a human or an animal (10).

Pie chart A graphical display in the shape of a circle that is used to summarize the relative percent of discrete and categorical data into sectors (13).

Pilot study A small preliminary study used to determine the extent to which a manipulation or measure will show an effect of interest (4).

Placebo An inert substance, surgery, or therapy that resembles a real treatment but has no real effect (10).

Plagiarism An individual's use of someone else's ideas or work that is represented as the individual's own ideas or work (3).

Point estimate A sample statistic (e.g., a sample mean) that is used to estimate a population parameter (e.g., a population mean) (14).

Population A set of *all* individuals, items, or data of interest about which scientists will generalize (1).

Population validity The extent to which results observed in a study will generalize to the population from which a sample was selected (6).

Positive correlation A positive value of r that indicates that the values of two factors change in the same direction: As the values of one factor increase, values of the second factor also increase; as the values of one factor decrease, values of the second factor also decrease (8).

Post hoc test A statistical procedure computed following a significant ANOVA to determine which pair or pairs of group means significantly differ. These tests are needed with more than two groups because multiple comparisons must be made (10).

Poster A concise description of a research study in the form of a display of text boxes, figures, and tables on a single large page (15).

Poster session A 1- to 4-hour time slot during which many authors stand near their poster ready and open to answer questions or talk about their work with interested attendees (15).

Power The probability in hypothesis testing of rejecting a false null hypothesis. Specifically, power is the probability that we will detect an effect if an effect actually exists in a population (7, 14).

Predictor variable The variable (X) with values that are known and can be used to predict values of another variable (8).

Primary source Any publication in which the works, ideas, or observations are those of the author (2).

Probability sampling A category of sampling in which a sample is selected directly from the target population. Probability sampling methods are used when the probability of selecting each individual in a population is known and every member of the population has an equal chance of being selected (5).

Proportion of variance A measure of effect size in terms of the proportion or percent of variability in a dependent variable that can be explained or accounted for by the levels of a factor or treatment (14).

Proportionate quota sampling   A type of quota sampling used when the proportions of certain characteristics in a target population are known. Using this type of quota sampling, subjects or participants are selected such that the known characteristics or demographics are proportionately represented in the sample (5).

Proportionate stratified random sampling   A type of stratified sampling in which a proportionate number of participants are sampled from each subgroup such that the sample resembles proportions in the population of interest (5).

Pseudoscience   A set of procedures that are not scientific, and it is part of a system or set of beliefs that try to deceptively create the impression that the knowledge gained represents the "final say" or most reliable knowledge on its subject matter (1).

Publication bias   The tendency for editors of peer-reviewed journals to preferentially accept articles that show positive results and reject those that show only negative results (2).

Qualitative research   Uses the scientific method to make nonnumeric observations, from which conclusions are drawn without the use of statistical analysis (1, 7).

Qualitative research design   See *qualitative research* (1, 7).

Qualitative variable   Varies by class. A qualitative variable is often a category or label for the behaviors and events researchers observe, and so describes nonnumeric aspects of phenomena (4).

Quantitative research   Uses the scientific method to record observations as numeric data. Most research conducted in the behavioral sciences is quantitative (1).

Quantitative variable   Varies by amount. A quantitative variable is measured as a numeric value and is often collected by measuring or counting (4).

Quasi-experimental research design   The use of methods and procedures to make observations in a study that is structured similar to an experiment, but the conditions and experiences of participants lack some control because the study lacks random assignment, includes a preexisting factor (i.e., a variable that is not manipulated), or does not include a comparison/control group (6, 9).

Quasi-independent variable   A variable with levels to which participants are not randomly assigned and that differentiates the groups or conditions being compared in a research study. Because the levels of the variable are preexisting, it is not possible to randomly assign participants to groups (6, 9).

Quota sampling   A method of sampling in which subjects or participants are selected based on known or unknown criteria or characteristics in the target population (5).

Random assignment   A random procedure used to ensure that participants in a study have an equal chance of being assigned to a particular group or condition (6).

Random digit dialing   A strategy for selecting participants in telephone interviews by generating telephone numbers to dial or call at random (8).

Random sampling   A random procedure used to ensure that participants have an equal chance of being selected to participate in a study. Also called *random selection* (6).

Random selection   See *random sampling* (6).

Randomization   The use of methods for selecting individuals to participate in a study and assigning them to groups such that each individual has an equal chance of being selected to participate and assigned to a group (6).

Range   The difference between the largest (*L*) value and the smallest (*S*) value in a data set (13).

Range effect   A limitation in the range of data measured in which scores are clustered to one extreme (4).

Rationalism   A method of knowing that requires the use of reasoning and logic (1).

Ratio scales Measurements that have a true zero and are equidistant (4).

Raw score A single measurement or observation; see also *datum, score* (1).

Regression See *linear regression* (8).

Regression line The best-fitting straight line to a set of data points. A best-fitting line is the line that minimizes the distance that all data points fall from it (8).

Regression toward the mean A change or shift in a participant's performance toward a level or score that is closer to or more typical of his or her true potential or mean ability on some measure, after previously scoring unusually high or low on the same measure (6).

Related sample A type of sample in which the same or matched participants are observed in each group (11).

Related-samples *t* test A statistical procedure used to test hypotheses concerning the difference in interval or ratio scale data for two related samples in which the variance in one population is unknown (11).

Reliability The consistency, stability, or repeatability of one or more measures or observations (4).

Repeated-measures design See *within-subjects design* (11).

Replication The reproduction of research procedures under identical conditions for the purposes of observing the same phenomenon (3).

Representative sample A sample in which the characteristics of individuals or items in the sample resemble those in a target population of interest (5).

Research design The specific methods and procedures used to answer a research question (6).

Research ethics Identifies the actions that researchers must take to conduct responsible and moral research (3).

Research hypothesis A specific, testable claim or prediction about what you expect to observe given a set of circumstances (1).

Research method See *scientific method* (1).

Research protocol A proposal, submitted by a researcher to an IRB, outlining the details of a study he or she wishes to complete and how he or she will address potential ethical concerns. Only upon approval by an IRB is a researcher allowed to conduct his or her study, and all researchers are bound to follow the protocol once it is approved (3).

Respect for persons An ethical principle listed in the Belmont Report that states that participants in a research study must be autonomous agents capable of making informed decisions concerning whether to participate in research (3).

Response rate The portion of participants who agree to complete a survey among all individuals who were asked to complete the survey (8).

Response set The tendency for participants to respond the same way to all items in a survey when the direction of ratings is the same for all items in the survey (8).

Restricted item A question or statement in a survey that includes a restricted number of answer options to which participants must respond (8).

Restricted random assignment A method of controlling differences in participant characteristics between groups in a study by first restricting a sample based on known participant characteristics, then using a random procedure to assign participants to each group. Two strategies of restricted random assignment are control by matching and control by holding constant (10).

Restriction of range   A problem that arises when the range of data for one or both correlated factors in a sample is limited or restricted, compared with the range of data in the population from which the sample was selected (8).

Reversal design   A single-case experimental design in which a single participant is observed before (A), during (B), and after (A) a treatment or manipulation (9).

Reverse causality   A problem that arises when the direction of causality between two factors can be in either direction (8).

Reverse coded item   An item that is phrased in the semantically opposite direction of most other items in a survey and is scored by coding or entering responses for the item in reverse order from how they are listed (8).

Risk-benefit analysis   A type of analysis in which the researcher anticipates or weighs the risks and benefits in a study (3).

Sample   A set of *selected* individuals, items, or data taken from a population of interest (1).

Sample mean   The sum of all scores (Σx) divided by the number of scores summed (n) in a sample, or in a subset of scores selected from a larger population (13).

Sample standard deviation (SD)   A measure of variability for the average distance that scores in a sample deviate from the sample mean and is computed by taking the square root of the sample variance (13).

Sample variance   A measure of variability for the average squared distance that scores in a sample deviate from the sample mean (13).

Sampling bias   A bias in sampling in which the sampling procedures employed in a study favor certain individuals or groups over others (5).

Sampling error   The extent to which sample means selected from the same population differ from one another. This difference, which occurs by chance, is measured by the standard error of the mean (5).

Sampling frame   See *accessible population* (5).

Sampling with replacement   A strategy used with simple random sampling in which each individual selected is replaced before the next selection to ensure that the probability of selecting each individual is always the same (5).

Sampling without replacement   A nonrandom sampling strategy most often used by behavioral researchers in which each individual selected is not replaced before the next selection (5).

Scales of measurement   Rules for how the properties of numbers can change with different uses (4).

Scatter diagram   See *scatter plot* (8).

Scatter gram   See *scatter plot* (8)

Scatter plot   A graphical display of discrete data points (x, y) used to summarize the relationship between two factors (8, 13).

Science   The acquisition of knowledge through observation, evaluation, interpretation, and theoretical explanation (1).

Scientific integrity   The extent to which a researcher is honest and truthful in his or her actions, values, methods, measures, and dissemination of research (3).

Scientific method   A set of systematic techniques used to acquire, modify, and integrate knowledge concerning observable and measurable phenomena (1).

Score   A single measurement or observation; see also *datum, raw score* (1).

Secondary source   Any publication that refers to works, ideas, or observations that are not those of the author (2).

Selection bias   See *sampling bias* (5).

Selection differences   Any differences, which are not controlled by the researcher, between individuals who are selected from preexisting groups or groups to which the researcher does not randomly assign participants (9).

Selective deposit   The process by which existing records are selectively recorded or deposited into document files that can be accessed for analysis (7).

Selective survival   The process by which existing records survive or are excluded/decay over time (7).

Self-report measure   A type of measurement in which participants respond to one or more questions or statements to indicate their actual or perceived experiences, attitudes, or opinions (10).

Sensitivity of a measure   The extent to which a measure can change or be different in the presence of a manipulation (4).

Significance   Describes a decision made concerning a value stated in the null hypothesis. When the null hypothesis is rejected, we reach significance. When the null hypothesis is retained, we fail to reach significance (14).

Significance level   See *level of significance* (14).

Simple quota sampling   A type of quota sampling used when little is known about the characteristics of a target population. Using this type of quota sampling, an equal number of subjects or participants are selected for a given characteristic or demographic (5).

Simple random sampling   A method of sampling subjects and participants such that all individuals in a population have an equal chance of being selected and are selected using sampling with replacement (5).

Simple stratified random sampling   A type of stratified random sampling that involves selecting an equal number of participants in each subgroup (5).

Single-case experimental design   An experimental research design in which a participant serves as his or her own control and the dependent variable measured is analyzed for each individual participant, and is not averaged across groups or across participants (9).

Skewed distribution   A distribution of scores that includes outliers or scores that fall substantially above or below most other scores in a data set (13).

Solomon four-group design   An experimental research design in which different participants are assigned to each of four groups in such a way that comparisons can be made to (1) determine if a treatment causes changes in posttest measure and (2) control for possible confounds or extraneous factors related to giving a pretest measure and observing participants over time (11).

Stability   The consistency in the pattern of change in a dependent measure in each phase of a design. The more stable or consistent changes in a dependent measure are in each phase, the higher the internal validity of a research design (9).

Staged manipulation   The manipulation of an independent variable that requires the participant to be "set up" to experience some stimulus or event (10).

Standard error of the mean   The standard deviation of a sampling distribution of sample means. It is the standard error or distance that sample mean values can deviate from the value of the population mean (5).

Statistical power   The likelihood that data in a sample can detect or discover an effect in a population, assuming that the effect does exist in the population of interest (7).

Statistical significance   See *significance* (14).

Stratified random sampling   A method of sampling in which a population is divided into subgroups or strata; participants are then selected from each subgroup using simple random sampling and are combined into one overall sample (5).

Structured setting   See *contrived setting* (7).

Subject   A term used to describe a nonhuman that is subjected to procedures in a research study and to identify the names of research designs (5).

Subject pool   See *participant pool* (5).

Sum of squares (SS)   The sum of the squared deviations of scores from the mean and is the value placed in the numerator of the sample variance formula (13).

Survey   A series of questions or statements, called items, used in a questionnaire or an interview to measure the self-reports or responses of respondents (8).

Survey research design   The use of a survey, administered either in written form or orally, to quantify, describe, or characterize an individual or a group (8).

Systematic sampling   A method of sampling in which the first participant is selected using simple random sampling, and then every nth person is systematically selected until all participants have been selected (5).

Target population   All members of a group of interest to a researcher (5).

Temporal validity   The extent to which results observed in a study will generalize across time and at different points in time (6).

Tenacity   A method of knowing based largely on habit or superstition (1).

Test-retest reliability   The extent to which a measure or observation is consistent or stable at two points in time (4).

Test statistic   A mathematical formula that allows researchers to determine the likelihood of obtaining sample outcomes if the null hypothesis were true. The value of the test statistic can be used to make a decision regarding the null hypothesis. The test statistic also allows researchers to determine the extent to which differences observed between groups can be attributed to the manipulation used to create the different groups (10, 14).

Testing effect   The improved performance on a test or measure the second time it is taken due to the experience of taking the test (6).

Theoretical generalization   The extent to which results in a survey or another research study are consistent with predictions made by an existing theory (8).

Theory   A broad statement used to account for an existing body of knowledge and also provide unique predictions to extend that body of knowledge. A theory is not necessarily correct; instead, it is a generally accepted explanation for evidence, as it is understood (2).

Time sampling   A strategy used to manage an observation period by splitting a fixed period of time into smaller intervals of time, and then making observations during alternating intervals until the full observation period has ended (7).

Treatment group   A condition in an experiment in which participants are treated or exposed to a manipulation, or level of the independent variable, that is believed to cause a change in the dependent variable (10).

True zero   The value 0 truly indicates nothing on a scale of measurement (4).

Trustworthiness   The credibility, transferability, dependability, and confirmability of a qualitative analysis (7).

Two-independent-sample *t* test   A statistical procedure used to test hypotheses concerning the difference in interval or ratio scale data between two group means, in which the variance in the population is unknown (10).

Two-way ANOVA   A statistical procedure used to analyze the variance in a dependent variable between groups created by combining the levels of two factors (12).

Two-way factorial design   A research design in which participants are observed in groups created by combining or crossing the levels of two factors (12).

Type I error   A "false positive" finding. It is the probability of rejecting a null hypothesis that is actually true. Researchers directly control for this error by stating the level of significance (14).

Type II error   A "false negative" finding. It is the probability of retaining a null hypothesis that is actually false. This means the researcher is reporting no effect in the population, when in truth there is an effect (14).

Unbiased estimator   Any sample statistic obtained from a randomly selected sample that equals the value of its respective population parameter on average (14).

Unobtrusive observation   A technique used by an observer to record or observe behavior in a way that does not interfere with or change a participant's behavior in a research setting (7).

Validity   The extent to which a measurement for a variable or construct measures what it is purported or intended to measure (4).

Variability   A measure of the dispersion or spread of scores in a distribution and ranges from 0 to $+\infty$ (13).

Variable   Any value or characteristic that can change or vary from one person to another or from one situation to another (1, 4).

Within-groups variability   A source of variance in a dependent measure that is caused by or associated with observing different participants within each group (11).

Within-subjects design   A research design in which the same participants are observed one time in each group of a research study (11).

Within-subjects experimental design   An experimental research design in which the levels of a within-subjects factor are manipulated, then the same participants are observed in each group or at each level of the factor. To qualify as an experiment, the researcher must (1) manipulate the levels of the factor and include a comparison/control group, and (2) make added efforts to control for order and time-related factors (11).

Within-subjects factor   A type of factor in which the same participants are observed in each group, or at each level of the factor (11).

Within-subjects factorial design   A research design in which the levels of two or more within-subjects factors are combined to create groups, meaning that the same participants are observed in each group (12).

REFERENCES

Abar, C., & Turrisi, R. (2008). How important are parents during the college years? A longitudinal perspective of *indirect* influences parents yield on their college teens' alcohol use. *Addictive Behaviors, 33,* 1360–1368. doi:10.1016/j.addbeh.2008.06.010

Abelson, R. P. (1995). *Statistics as principled argument.* Hillsdale, NJ: Erlbaum.

Acevedo, B. P., & Aron, A. (2009). Does a long-term relationship kill romantic love? *Review of General Psychology, 13,* 59–65. doi:10.1037/a0014226

Albert, U., Salvi, V., Saracco, P., Bogetto, P., & Maina, G. (2007). Health-related quality of life among first-degree relatives of patients with obsessive-compulsive disorder in Italy. *Psychiatric Services, 58,* 970–976. doi:10.1176/appi.ps.58.7.970

Alvarez, S. D., & Schneider, J. (2008). One college campus's need for a safe zone: A case study. *Journal of Gender Studies, 17,* 71–74. doi:10.1080/09589230701838461

American Psychological Association. (1953). *Ethical principles of psychologists.* Washington, DC: Author.

American Psychological Association. (2009). *Publication manual of the American Psychological Association* (6th ed.). Washington, DC: Author.

American Psychological Association. (2010). *Ethical principles of psychologists and code of conduct.* Washington, DC: Author.

American Psychological Association. (2012). *Guidelines for ethical conduct in the care and use of nonhuman animals in research.* Washington, DC: Author. Retrieved from http://www.apa.org/science/leadership/care/guidelines.aspx

American Psychological Association. (2013a). *APA databases: PsycARTICLES.* Retrieved from http://www.apa.org/pubs/databases/psycarticles/index.aspx

American Psychological Association. (2013b). *APA databases: PsycINFO.* Retrieved from http://www.apa.org/psycinfo/

American Society for the Prevention of Cruelty to Animals. (1996). *"Regarding Henry": A "Bergh's-eye" view of 140 years at the ASPCA.* Retrieved from http://www.aspca.org/about-us/history.html

Anderson, E. A. (1976). The chivalrous treatment of the female offender in the arms of the criminal justice system. *Social Problems, 23,* 349–357.

Antonietti, A., Cocomazzi, D., & Iannello, P. (2009). Looking at the audience improves music appreciation. *Journal of Nonverbal Behavior, 33,* 89–106. doi:10.1007/s10919-008-0062-x

Badanes, L. S., Dmitrieva, J., & Watamura, S. E. (2012). Understanding cortisol reactivity across the day at child care: The potential buffering role of secure attachments to caregivers. *Early Childhood Research Quarterly, 27,* 156–165. doi:10.1016/j.ecresq.2011.05.005

Balk, D. E., Walker, A. C., & Baker, A. (2010). Prevalence and severity of college student bereavement examined in a randomly selected sample. *Death Studies, 34,* 459–468. doi:10.1080/07481180903251810

Bar-Eli, M., Azar, O. H., Ritov, I., Keidar-Levin, Y., & Schein, G. (2007). Action bias among elite soccer goalkeepers: The case of penalty kicks. *Journal of Economic Psychology, 28,* 606–621. doi:10.1016/j.joep.2006.12.001

Barfield, R. C., & Kane, J. R. (2009). Balancing disclosure of diagnosis and assent for research in children with HIV. *Journal of the American Medical Association, 300,* 576–578. doi:10.1001/jama.300.5.576

Barnett, N. P., Wei, J., & Czachowski, C. (2009). Measured alcohol content in college party mixed drinks. *Psychology of Addictive Behaviors, 23,* 152–156. doi:10.1037/ a0013611

Baruch, Y. (1999). Response rate in academic studies: A comparative analysis. *Human Relations, 52,* 421–438. doi:10.1177/001872679905200401

Baruch, Y., & Holtom, B. C. (2008). Survey response rate levels and trends in organizational research. *Human Relations, 61,* 1139–1160. doi:10.1177/0018726708094863

Bauchner, H., & Fontanarosa, P. B. (2012). Update on JAMA's policies on conflicts of interest, trial registration, embargo, and data timeliness, access, and analysis. *JAMA, 308,* 186–188. doi:10.1001/jama.2012.7926

Baumgartner, E., & Laghi, F. (2012). Affective responses to movie posters: Differences between adolescents and young adults. *International Journal of Psychology, 47,* 154–160. doi:10.1080/0020759 4.2011.597398

Bernieri, F. J., & Petty, K. N. (2011). The influence of handshakes on first impression accuracy. *Social Influence, 6,* 78–87. doi:10.1080/15534510.2011.566706

Betz, N. E., Klein, K. L., & Taylor, K. M. (1996). Evaluation of a short form of the career decision-making self-efficacy scale. *Journal of Career Assessment, 4,* 47–57. doi:10.1177/106907279600400103

Bianchi, A., & Phillips, J. G. (2005). Psychological predictors of problem mobile phone use. *Cyberpsychology & Behavior, 8,* 39–51. doi:10.1089/cpb.2005.8.39

Bjørkedal, E., & Flaten, M. A. (2011). Interaction between expectancies and drug effects: An experimental investigation of placebo analgesia with caffeine as an active placebo. *Psychopharmacology, 215,* 537–548. doi:10.1007/s00213-011-2233-4

Blair, E., & Zinkhan, G. M. (2006). Nonresponse and generalizability in academic research. *Journal of the Academy of Marketing Science, 34,* 4–7. doi:10.1177/0092070305283778

Block, S. M. (1996). Do's and don'ts of poster presentation. *Biophysical Journal, 71,* 3527–3529.

Bollen, K. A. (1989). *Structural equations with latent variables.* New York, NY: Wiley.

Brach, T. (2015). Healing traumatic fear: The wings of mindfulness and love. In V. M. Follette, J. Briere, D. Rozelle, J. W. Hopper, & D. I. Rome (Eds.), *Mindfulness-oriented interventions for trauma: Integrating contemplative practices* (pp. 31–42). New York, NY: Guilford Press.

Bradley, M. M., & Lang, P. J. (1994). Measuring emotion: The Self-Assessment Manikin and the semantic differential. *Journal of Behavior Therapy & Experimental Psychiatry, 25,* 49–59. doi:10.1016/0005-7916(94)90063-9

Brentari, E., Levaggi, R., & Zuccolotto, P. (2011). Pricing strategies for Italian red wine. *Food Quality And Preference, 22,* 725-732. doi:10.1016/j.foodqual.2011.06.001

Brookes, G., Pooley, J. A., & Earnest, J. (2015). *Terrorism, trauma and psychology: A multilevel victim perspective of the Bali bombings.* New York, NY: Routledge/Taylor & Francis Group.

Bushnell, I. W. R. (2001). Mother's face recognition in newborn infants: Learning and memory. *Infant and Child Development, 10,* 67–74. doi:10.1002/icd.248

Butler, L. H., & Correia, C. J. (2009). Brief alcohol intervention with college student drinkers: Face-to-face versus computerized feedback. *Psychology of Addictive Behaviors, 23,* 163–167. doi:10.1037/a0014892

Calnan, M., Smith, D., & Sterne, J. A. C. (2006). The publication process itself was the major cause of publication bias in genetic epidemiology. *Journal of Clinical Epidemiology, 59,* 1312–1318. doi:10.1016/j.jclinepi.2006.05.002

Campbell, D. T., & Stanley, J. C. (1966). *Experimental and quasi-experimental designs for research.* Chicago, IL: Rand McNally.

Capaldi, E. D., Hunter, M. J., & Privitera, G. J. (2004). Odor of taste stimuli in conditioned "taste" aversion learning. *Behavioral Neuroscience, 118,* 1400–1408. doi:10.1037/0735-7044.118.6.1400

Capaldi, E. D., & Privitera, G. J. (2008). Decreasing dislike for sour and bitter in children and adults. *Appetite, 50,* 139–145. doi:10.1016/j.appet.2007.06.008

Cavanagh, K., & Davey, G. C. L. (2000). *The development of a measure of individual differences in disgust.* Paper presented to the British Psychological Society.

Centers for Disease Control and Prevention. (2011). *U.S. Public Health Service Syphilis Study at Tuskegee: The Tuskegee timeline.* Atlanta, GA: Author. Retrieved from http://www.cdc.gov/tuskegee/timeline.htm

Chan, A. W., Hróbjartsson, A., Haahr, M. T., Gøtzsche, P. C., & Altman, D. G. (2004). Empirical evidence for selective reporting of outcomes in randomized trials: Comparison of protocols to published articles. *Journal of the American Medical Association, 291,* 2457–2465. doi:10.1001/jama.291.20.2457

Chapman, C. A., Struhsaker, T. T., Skorupa, J. P., Snaith, T. V., & Rothman, J. M. (2010). Understanding long-term primate community dynamics: Implications of forest change. *Ecological Applications, 20,* 179–191. doi:10.1890/09-0128.1

Chen, X. L., Dai, X. Y., & Dong, Q. (2008). A research of Aitken Procrastination Inventory applied to Chinese college students. *Chinese Journal of Clinical Psychology, 16,* 22–23. doi:10.1016/j.paid.2010.02.025

Child, D. (1990). *The essentials of factor analysis* (2nd ed.). London, England: Cassel Educational Limited.

Chmelo, E. A., Hall, E. E., Miller, P. C., & Sanders, K. N. (2009). Mirrors and resistance exercise, do they influence affective responses? *Journal of Health Psychology, 14,* 1067–1074. doi:10.1177/1359105309342300

Christensen, L. (1988). Deception in psychological research: When is its use justified? *Personality and Social Psychology Bulletin, 14,* 664–675. doi:10.1177/0146167288144002

Clark, M. H., & Shadish, W. R. (2008). Solomon Four Group Design. In P. J. Lavrakas (Ed.), *Encyclopedia of survey research methods* (pp. 830–831). Thousand Oaks, CA: SAGE.

Cohen, J. (1961). A coefficient of agreement for nominal scales. *Educational and Psychological Measurement, 20,* 37–46. doi:10.1177/001316446002000104

Cohen, J. (1988). *Statistical power analysis for the behavioral sciences.* Hillsdale, NJ: Erlbaum.

Cohen, S., & Williamson, G. (1988). Perceived stress in a probability sample of the United States. In S. Spacapam & S. Oskamp (Eds.), *The social psychology of health* (pp. 31–67). Newbury Park, CA: SAGE.

Cohn, M. A., Fredrickson, B. L., Brown, S. L., Mikels, J. A., & Conway, A. M. (2009). Happiness unpacked: Positive emotions increase life satisfaction by building resilience. *Emotion, 9,* 361–368. doi:10.1037/a0015952

Cooke, M., Holzhauser, K., Jones, M., Davis, C., & Finucane, J. (2007). The effects of aromatherapy massage with music on the stress and anxiety levels of emergency nurses: Comparison between summer and winter. *Journal of Clinical Nursing, 16,* 1695–1703. doi:10.1111/j.1365-2702.2007.01709.x

Cooper, H., & Rosenthal, R. (1980). Statistical versus traditional procedures for summarizing research findings. *Psychological Bulletin, 87,* 442–449. doi:10.1037/0033-2909.87.3.442

Cooper, J. O., Heron, T. E., & Heward, W. L. (1987). *Applied behavior analysis* (1st ed.). Columbus, OH: Merrill.

Cooper, J. O., Heron, T. E., & Heward, W. L. (2007). *Applied behavior analysis* (2nd ed.). Upper Saddle River, NJ: Prentice Hall.

Corcos, E., & Willows, D. M. (2009). Processing words varying in personal familiarity (based on reading and spelling) by poor readers and age-matched and reading-matched controls. *Remedial and Special Education, 30,* 195–206. doi:10.1177/0741932508315377

Cornier, M. A., Melanson, E. L., Salzberg, A. K., Bechtell, J. L., & Tregellas, J. R. (2012). The effects of exercise on the neuronal response to food cues. *Physiology & Behavior, 105,* 1028–1034. doi:10.1016/j.physbeh.2011.11.023

Cotton, J. W. (1993). Latin square designs. In L. K. Edwards (Ed.), *Applied analysis of variance in behavioral science* (pp. 147–196). New York, NY: Marcel Dekker.

Crisp, R. J., & Turner, R. N. (2009). Can imagined interactions produce positive perceptions? Reducing prejudice through simulated social contact. *American Psychologist, 64,* 231–240. doi:10.1037/a0014718

Cronbach, L. J. (1951). Coefficient alpha and the internal structure of tests. *Psychometrika, 16,* 297–334.

Curry, S. J., Mermelstein, R. J., & Sporer, A. K. (2009). Therapy for specific problems: Youth tobacco cessation. *Annual Review of Psychology, 60,* 229–255. doi:10.1146/annurev.psych.60.110707.163659

D'Alessandro, S., & Pecotich, A. (2013). Evaluation of wine by expert and novice consumers in the presence of variations in quality, brand and country of origin cues. *Food Quality and Preference, 28,* 287–303. doi:10.1016/j.foodqual.2012.10.002

Daniulaityte, R., Falck, R., Li, L., Nahhas, R. W., & Carlson, R. G. (2012). Respondent-driven sampling to recruit young adult non-medical users of pharmaceutical opioid: Problems and solutions. *Drug and Alcohol Dependence, 121,* 23–29. doi:10.1016/j.drugalcdep.2011.08.005

Dickersin, K. (1990). The existence of publication bias and risk factors for its occurrence. *Journal of the American Medical Association, 263*, 1385–1389. doi:10.1001/jama.1990.03440100097014

Dijk, C., de Jong, P. J., & Peters, M. L. (2009). The remedial value of blushing in the context of transgressions and mishaps. *Emotion, 9*, 287–291. doi:10.1037/a0015081

Dillman, D. A. (2000). *Mail and Internet surveys: The tailored design method* (2nd ed.). New York, NY: Wiley.

Dishman, D. L., Thomson, D. M., & Karnovsky, N. J. (2009). Does simple feeding enrichment raise activity levels of captive ring-tailed lemurs (*Lemurs catta*)? *Applied Animal Behaviour Science, 116*, 88–95. doi:10.1016/j.applanim.2008.06.012

Dukes, E., & McGuire, B. E. (2009). Enhancing capacity to make sexuality-related decisions in people with an intellectual disability. *Journal of Intellectual Disability Research, 53*, 727–734. doi:10.1111/j.1365-2788.2009.01186.x

Dunn, L. M. (1979). *Peabody picture vocabulary test.* Minneapolis, MN: American Guidance Service.

Dunn, R., & Dunn, K. (1978). *Teaching students through their individual learning styles: A practical approach.* Reston, VA: Reston.

Educational Resource Information Center. (n.d.). *About the ERIC collection.* Retrieved from http://www.eric.ed.gov/ERICWebPortal/resources/html/collection/about_collection.html

Edwards, S. J. L., Kirchin, S., & Huxtable, R. (2004). Research ethics committees and paternalism. *Journal of Medical Ethics, 30*, 88–91. doi:10.1136/jme.2002.000166

Endicott, J., Nee, J., Harrison, W., & Blumenthal, R. (1993). Quality of life enjoyment and satisfaction questionnaire: A new measure. *Psychopharmacology Bulletin, 29*, 321–326.

Englund, M. P., & Hellström, Å. (2012). If you have a choice, you have trouble: Stimulus valence modulates presentation-order effects in preference judgment. *Journal of Behavioral Decision Making, 25*, 82–94. doi:10.1002/bdm.714

Engqvist, L., & Frommen, J. G. (2008). Double-blind peer review and gender publication bias. *Animal Behaviour, 76*, e1–e2. doi:10.1016/j.anbehav.2008.05.023

Errami, M., & Garner, H. (2008). A tale of two citations. *Nature, 451*, 397–399. doi:10.1038/451397a

Faith, M. S., Allison, D. B., & Geliebter, A. (1997). Emotional eating and obesity: Theoretical considerations and practical recommendations. In S. Dalton (Ed.), *Overweight and weight management: The health professional's guide to understanding and practice* (pp. 439–465). Gaithersburg, MD: Aspen.

Fanselow, M. S., & Sterlace, S. R. (2014). Pavlovian fear conditioning: Function, cause, and treatment. In F. K. McSweeney & E. S. Murphy (Eds.), *The Wiley Blackwell handbook of operant and classical conditioning* (pp. 117–141). Hoboken, NJ: Wiley-Blackwell. doi:10.1002/9781118468135.ch6

Fareedi, M. A., Prasant, M. C., Safiya, T., Nashiroddin, M., & Sujata, P. (2011). Dental anxiety: A review. *Indian Journal of Community Psychology, 7*, 198–203.

Ferguson, C. J. (2010). Blazing angels or resident evil? Can violent video games be a force for good? *Review of General Psychology, 14*, 68–81. doi:10.1037/a0018941

Festinger, D. S., Marlowe, D. B., Croft, J. R., Dugosh, K. L., Arabia, P. L., & Benasutti, K. M. (2009). Monetary incentives improve recall of research consent information: It pays to remember. *Experimental and Clinical Psychopharmacology, 17*, 99–104. doi:10.1037/a0015421

Fischer, K., & Jungermann, H. (1996). Rarely occurring headaches and rarely occurring blindness: Is rarely=rarely? *Journal of Behavioral Decision Making, 9*, 153–172. doi:10.1002/(SICI)1099-0771(199609)9:3<153::AID-BDM222>3.0.CO;2-W

Fisher, R. A. (1925). *Statistical methods for research workers.* Edinburgh, Scotland: Oliver & Boyd.

Fisher, R. A. (1935). *The design of experiments.* Edinburgh, Scotland: Oliver & Boyd.

Flory, J., & Emanuel, E. (2004). Interventions to improve research participants' understanding in informed consent for research: A systematic review. *Journal of the American Medical Association, 292*, 1593–1601. doi:10.1001/jama.292.13.1593

Frank, R. H. (1988). *Passions within reason: The strategic role of the emotions.* New York, NY: Norton.

Frank, R. H. (2001). Cooperation through emotional commitment. In R. M. Nesse (Ed.), *Evaluation and the capacity for commitment* (pp. 57–76). New York, NY: Russell Sage.

Frank, S., Laharnar, N., Kullmann, S., Veit, R., Canova, C., Hegner, Y. L., Fritsche, A., & Preissl, H. (2010). Processing of food pictures: Influence of hunger, gender and calorie content. *Brain Research, 1350*, 159–166. doi:10.1016/j.brainres.2010.04.030

Frankfort-Nachmias, C., & Leon-Guerrero, A. (2006). *Social statistics for a diverse society*. Thousand Oaks, CA: Pine Forge Press.

Galvan, J. (2006). *Writing literature reviews: A guide for students of the behavioral sciences* (3rd ed.). Glendale, CA: Pyrczak.

Gao, X., Hamzah, S. H., Yiu, C. Y., McGrath, C., & King, N. M. (2013). Dental fear and anxiety in children and adolescents: Qualitative study using YouTube. *Journal of Medical Internet Research, 15*, 285-295. doi:10.2196/jmir.2290

Garcia, J., Kimeldorf, D. J., & Koelling, R. A. (1955). A conditioned aversion toward saccharin resulting from exposure to gamma radiation. *Science, 122*, 157–158.

Gardner, M. (1957). *Fads and fallacies in the name of science*. New York, NY: Dover Publications. (Expanded version of his *In the Name of Science*, 1952.)

Gentry, J. A., & Luiselli, J. K. (2008). Treating a child's selective eating through parent implemented feeding intervention in the home setting. *Journal of Developmental and Physical Disabilities, 20*, 63–70. doi:10.1007/s10882-007-9080-6

Goldkamp, J. S. (2008). Missing the target and missing the point: "Successful" random assignment but misleading results. *Journal of Experimental Criminology, 4*, 83–115. doi:10.1007/s11292-008-9052-6

Good, P. I., & Hardin, J. W. (2003). *Common errors in statistics (and how to avoid them)*. New York, NY: Wiley.

Gow, K. M. (2006). Skipping out on the dentist. *Australian Journal of Clinical & Experimental Hypnosis, 34*, 98–100.

Grabe, M. E., Trager, K. D., Lear, M., & Rauch, J. (2006). Gender in crime news: A case study test of the chivalry hypothesis. *Mass Communication & Society, 9*, 137–163. doi:10.1207/s15327825mcs0902_2

Greitemeyer, T. (2009). Effects of songs with prosocial lyrics on prosocial thoughts, affect, and behavior. *Journal of Experimental Social Psychology, 45*, 186–190. doi:10.1016/j.jesp.2008.08.003

Guba, E. G., & Lincoln, Y. S. (1989). *Fourth generation evaluation*. Thousand Oaks, CA: SAGE.

Hadfield, G., Howse, R., & Trebilcock, M. J. (1998). Information-based principles: Biotechnology is influenced not only by their perceptions about the magnitude for rethinking consumer protection policy. *Journal of Consumer Policy, 21*, 131–169.

Hamilton, M. (1960). A rating scale for depression. *Journal of Neurology, Neurosurgery, and Psychiatry, 163*, 28–40.

Hampton, J. (1998). Between-subjects versus within-subjects designs. In J. Nunn (Ed.), *Laboratory psychology: A beginner's guide* (pp. 15–38). Hove, England: Psychology Press/Erlbaum (UK) Taylor & Francis.

Haney, C., & Zimbardo, P. G. (1977). The socialization into criminality: On becoming a prisoner and a guard. In J. L. Tapp & T. L. Levine (Eds.), *Law, justice, and the individual in society: Psychological and legal issues* (pp. 198–223). New York, NY: Holt, Rinehart & Winston.

Hannover, B., & Kühnen, U. (2002). "The clothing makes the self" via knowledge activation. *Journal of Applied Social Psychology, 32*, 2513–2525. doi:10.1111/j.1559- 1816.2002.tb02754.x

Hansson, S. O. (2015). *The Stanford encyclopedia of philosophy: Science and pseudoscience*. Retrieved from http://plato.stanford.edu/entries/pseudo-science/

Harrison, M. A. (2011). College students' prevalence and perceptions of text messaging while driving. *Accident Analysis and Prevention, 43*, 1516–1520. doi:10.1016/j.aap.2011.03.003

Hartford, K., Carey, R., & Mendonca, J. (2007). Sampling bias in an international Internet survey of diversion programs in the criminal justice system. *Evaluation & the Health Professions, 30*, 35–46. doi:10.1177/0163278706297344

Hawkley, L. C., Thisted, R. A., & Cacioppo, J. T. (2009). Loneliness predicts reduced physical activity: Cross-sectional & longitudinal analyses. *Health Psychology, 28*, 354–363. doi:10.1037/a0014400

Hayes, S. C. (1981). Single-case research designs and empirical clinical practice. *Journal of Consulting & Clinical Psychology, 49*, 193–211.

Hellström, Å. (2003). Comparison is not just subtraction: Effects of time- and space-order on subjective stimulus difference. *Perception & Psychophysics, 65*, 1161–1177.

Hendriks, A. W., van Rijswijk, M., & Omtzigt, D. (2011). Holding-side influences on infant's view of mother's face. *Laterality: Asymmetries of Body, Brain and Cognition, 16*, 641–655. doi:10.1080/13576500903468904

Hermans, R. C. J., Larsen, J. K., Herman, C. P., & Engels, R. (2008). Modeling of palatable food intake in female young adults: Effects of perceived body size. *Appetite, 51,* 512–518. doi:10.1016/j.appet.2008.03.016

Hermans, R. C. J., Salvy, S. J., Larsen, J. K., & Engels, R. (2012). Examining the effects of remote-video confederates on young women's food intake. *Eating Behaviors, 13,* 246–251. doi:10.1016/j.eatbeh.2012.03.008

Hill, L. J. B., Williams, J. H. G., Aucott, L., Thomson, J., & Mon-Williams, M. (2011). How does exercise benefit performance on cognitive tests in primary-school pupils? *Developmental Medicine & Child Neurology, 53,* 630–635. doi:10.1111/j.1469-8749.2011. 03954.x

Hoaglin, D. C., Mosteller, F., & Tukey, J. W. (1991). *Fundamentals of exploratory analysis of variance.* New York, NY: Wiley.

Hollands, J. G., & Spence, I. (1992). Judgments of change and proportion in graphical perception. *Human Factors, 34,* 313–334.

Hollands, J. G., & Spence, I. (1998). Judging proportions with graphs: The summation model. *Applied Cognitive Psychology, 12,* 173–190. doi:10.1002/(SICI)1099-0720(199804)12:2<173:: AID-ACP499>3.0.CO;2-K

Holman, E. W. (1975). Immediate and delayed reinforcers for flavor preferences in rats. *Animal Learning & Behavior, 6,* 91–100.

Hondagneu-Sotelo, P. (2002). Families on the frontier: From *braceros* in the fields to *braceras* in the home. In M. M. Suarez-Orozco & M. M. Paez (Eds.), *Latinos: Remaking America* (pp. 259–273). Berkeley, CA: University of California Press.

Horne, J. A. (1988). *Why we sleep: The functions of sleep in humans and other mammals.* Oxford, England: Oxford University Press.

Horton, S. (2009). A mother's heart is weighed down with stones: A phenomenological approach to the experience of transitional motherhood. *Culture, Medicine, and Psychiatry, 33,* 21–40. doi:10.1007/s11013-008-9117-z

Howard, G. S., Hill, T. L., Maxwell, S. E., Baptista, T. M., Farias, M. H., Coelho, C., Coulter-Kern, M., & Coulter-Kern, R. (2009). What's wrong with research literatures? And how to make them right. *Review of General Psychology, 13,* 146–166. doi:10.1037/a0015319

Howard, G. S., Lau, M. Y., Maxwell, S. E., Venter, A., Lundy, R., & Sweeny, R. M. (2009). Do research literatures give correct answers? *Review of General Psychology, 13,* 116–121. doi:10.1037/a0015468

ITHAKA. (2013). *JSTOR.* Retrieved from http://www.jstor.org/

Jha, V., Quinton, N. D., Bekker, H. L., & Roberts, T. E. (2009). What educators and students really think about using patients as teachers in medical education: A qualitative study. *Medical Education, 43,* 449–456. doi:10.1111/j.1365-2923.2009.03355.x

Jokisch, E., Coletta, A., & Raynor, H. A. (2012). Acute energy compensation and macronutrient intake following exercise in active and inactive males who are normal weight. *Appetite, 58,* 722–729. doi:10.1016/j.appet.2011.11.024

Kalali, A. H., Williams, J. B., Kobak, K. A., Engelhardt, N., Evans, K. R., Olin, J., Pearson, J. D., Rothman, M., & Bech, P. (2002). The new GRID HAM-D pilot testing and international field trials. *International Journal of Neuropsychopharmacology, 5,* S147.

Kaptchuk, T. J. (1998). Powerful placebo: The dark side of the randomized controlled trial. *Lancet, 351,* 1722–1725.

Kennedy, C. H. (1993). *Sexual Consent and Education Assessment.* Philadelphia, PA: Drexel University.

Khuder, S. A., Milz, S., Jordan, T., Price, J., Silvestri, K., & Butler, P. (2007). The impact of a smoking ban on hospital admissions for coronary heart disease. *Preventive Medicine, 45,* 3–8. doi:10.1016/j.ypmed.2007.03.011

Kline, R. B. (2008). *Becoming a behavioral science researchers A guide to producing research that matters.* New York, NY: Guilford Press.

Kokotsaki, D. (2011). Student teachers' conceptions of creativity in the secondary music classroom. *Thinking Skills and Creativity, 6,* 100–113. doi:10.1016/j.tsc.2011.04.001

Komorita, S. S., & Graham, W. K. (1965). Number of scale points and the reliability of scales. *Educational and Psychological Measurement, 25,* 987–995.

Kramer, A. D. I., Guillory, J. E., & Hancock, J. T. (2014). Experimental evidence of massive-scale emotional contagion through social networks. *Proceedings of the National Academy of Sciences U S A, 111*, 8788–8790. doi:10.1073/pnas.1320040111

Krefting, L. (1991). Rigor in qualitative research: The assessment of trustworthiness. *American Journal of Occupational Therapy, 45*, 214–222. doi:10.5014/ajot.45.3.214

Kunze, A. E., Arntz, A., Kindt, M. (2015). Fear conditioning with film clips: A complex associative learning paradigm. *Journal of Behavior Therapy and Experimental Psychiatry, 47*, 42–50. doi:10.1016/j.jbtep.2014.11.007

Lago-Ballesteros, J., Lago-Peñas, C., & Rey, E. (2012). The effect of playing tactics and situational variables on achieving score-box possessions in a professional soccer team. *Journal of Sports Sciences, 30*, 1455–1461. doi:10.1080/02640414.2012.712715

Langer, A., Cangas, A., Salcedo, E., & Fuentes, B. (2012). Applying mindfulness therapy in a group of psychotic individuals: A controlled study. *Behavioural and Cognitive Psychotherapy, 40*, 105–109. doi:10.1017/ S1352465811000464

Langlois, J. H., Kalakanis, L., Rubenstein, A. J., Larson, A., Hallam, M., & Smoot, M. (2000). Maxims or myths of beauty? A meta-analytic and theoretical review. *Psychological Bulletin, 126*, 390–423. doi:10.1037//0033-2909.126.3.390

LaRose, R., & Tsai, H. S. (2014). Completion rates and non-response error in online surveys: Comparing sweepstakes and pre-paid cash incentives in studies of online behavior. *Computers In Human Behavior, 34*, 110–119. doi:10.1016/j.chb.2014.01.017

Levitt, J. T., Malta, L. S., Martin, A., Davis, L., & Cloitre, M. (2007). The flexible applications of a manualized treatment for PTSD symptoms and functional impairment related to the 9/11 World Trade Center attack. *Behaviour Research and Therapy, 45*, 1419–1433. doi:10.1016/j.brat.2007.01.004

Liesegang, T. J., Albert, D. M., & Schachat, A. P. (2008). Not for your eyes: Information concealed through publication bias. *American Journal of Ophthalmology, 146*, 638–640. doi:10.1016/j.ajo.2008.07.034

Likert, R. (1932). A technique for the measurement of attitude. *Archives of Psychology, 140*, 55.

Lincoln, Y. S., & Guba, E. G. (1985). *Naturalistic inquiry.* Beverly Hills, CA: SAGE.

Ling, P., & Xuejun, B. (2011). The effect of target pre-exposure on event-based prospective memory. *Psychological Science (China), 34*, 538–545.

Ling, R., Bertel, T. F., & Sundsøy, P. R. (2012). The socio-demographics of texting: An analysis of traffic data. *New Media & Society, 14*, 281–298. doi:10.1177/1461444811412711

Lipkus, I. M. (2007). Numeric, verbal and visual formats of conveying health risks: Suggested best practices and future recommendations. *Medical Decision Making, 27*, 696–713. doi:10.1177/ 0272989X07307271

Loewy, J. V., & Hara, A. F. (2007). *Caring for the caregiver: The use of music and music therapy in grief and trauma.* Silver Spring, MD: American Music Therapy Association. (Original work published 2002)

Lollar, D., & Talley, R. C. (2014). Mental health caregiving: A call to professional providers, family caregivers, and individuals with mental health challenges. In R. C. Talley, G. L. Fricchione, & B. G. Druss (Eds.), *The challenges of mental health caregiving: Research, practice, policy* (pp. 225–229). New York, NY: Springer Science + Business Media.

Long, T. C., Errami, M., George, A. C., Sun, Z., & Garner, H. R. (2009). Responding to possible plagiarism. *Science, 323*, 1293–1294. doi:10.1126/science.1167408

Machin, D., & Thornborrow, J. (2003). Branding and discourse: The case of Cosmopolitan. *Discourse & Society, 14*, 453–471. doi:10.1177/0957926503014004003

Magazine Publishers of America. (2013). *Consumer marketing.* Retrieved from http://www.magazine.org/ insights-resources/research-publications/guides-studies

Mahner, M. (2007). Demarcating science from non-science. In T. Kuipers (Ed.), *Handbook of the philosophy of science: General philosophy of science – focal issues* (pp. 515–575). Amsterdam: Elsevier.

Matell, M. S., & Jacoby, J. (1971). Is there an optimal number of alternatives for Likert scale items? Study 1: Reliability and validity. *Educational and Psychological Measurement, 31*, 657–674. doi:10.1177/001316447103100307

Maynard, B. R., Kjellstrand, E. & Thompson, A. M. (2014). A randomized trial of the effects of Check n' Connect on dropout and academic performance. *Research on Social Work Practice, 23*, 1–14. doi: 1177/1049731513497804

Mazur, D. J., & Merz, J. F. (1994). How age, outcome severity, and scale influence general medicine clinic patients' interpretations of verbal probability terms. *Journal of General Internal Medicine, 9*, 268–271. doi:10.1007/BF02599654

McCallum, J. M., Arekere, D. M., Green, B. L., Katz, R. V., & Rivers, B. M. (2006). Awareness and knowledge of the U.S. Public Health Service syphilis study at Tuskegee: Implications for biomedical research. *Journal of Health Care for the Poor and Underserved, 17*, 716–733. doi:10.1353/hpu.2006.0130

McCambridge, J. (2007). A case study of publication bias in an influential series of reviews of drug education. *Drug and Alcohol Review, 26*, 463–468. doi:10.1080/09595230701494366

McIntyre, S. H., & Munson, J. M. (2008). Exploring cramming: Student behaviors, beliefs, and learning retention in the Principles of Marketing course. *Journal of Marketing Education, 30*, 226–243. doi:10.1177/0273475308321819

McLaughlin, K. (2003). Agency, resilience and empowerment: The dangers posed by a therapeutic culture. *Practice, 15*, 45–58. doi:10.1080/09503150308416918

McNeil, J., Cadieux, S., Finlayson, G., Blundell, J. E., & Doucet, É. (2015). The effects of a single bout of aerobic or resistance exercise on food reward. *Appetite, 84*, 264–270. doi:10.1016/j.appet.2014.10.018

McNemar, Q. (1946). Opinion-attitude methodology. *Psychological Bulletin, 43*, 289–374.

Mellor, J. M., Rapoport, R. B., & Maliniak, D. (2008). The impact of child obesity on active parental consent in school-based survey research on healthy eating and physical activity. *Evaluation Review, 32*, 298–312. doi:10.1177/0193841X07312682

Milgram S. (1963). Behavioral study of obedience. *Journal of Abnormal Social Psychology, 67*, 371–378. doi:10.1037/ h0040525

Milgrom, P., Mancl, L., King, B., & Weinstein, P. (1995). Origins of childhood dental fear. *Behaviour Research and Therapy, 33*, 313–319. doi:10.1016/0005-7967(94)00042-I

Miller, F. G., Wendler, D., & Swartzman, L. C. (2005). Deception in research on the placebo effect. *PLoS Medicine, 2*, e262. doi:10.1371/journal.pmed.0020262

Minamimoto, T., La Camera, G., & Richmond, B. J. (2009). Measuring and modeling the interaction among reward size, delay to reward, and satiation level on motivation in monkeys. *Journal of Neurophysiology, 101*, 437–447. doi:10.1152/jn. 90959.2008

Moon, M., & Hoffman, C. D. (2000). References on men and women in psychology (1887–1997): PsycINFO as an archival research tool. *Psychology of Men and Masculinity, 1*, 16–20. doi:10.1037/1524-9220.1.1.16

Morgan, E. S., Umberson, K., & Hertzog, C. (2014). Construct validation of self-reported stress scales. *Psychological Assessment, 26*, 90–99. doi:10.1037/a0034714

Muliira, J. K., Nalwanga, P. B., Muliira, R. S., & Nankinga, Z. (2012). Knowledge, perceived risks and barriers to testicular self-examination among male university students in Uganda. *Journal of Men's Health, 9*, 36–44. doi:10.1016/j.jomh.2011.11.004

Murdock, K. K., Gorman, S., & Robbins, M. (2015). Co-rumination via cellphone moderates the association of perceived interpersonal stress and psychosocial well-being in emerging adults. *Journal of Adolescence, 38*, 27–37. doi:10.1016/j.adolescence.2014.10.010

Mutz, R., Bornmann, L., & Daniel, H. (2012). Does gender matter in grant peer review? An empirical investigation using the example of the Austrian science fund. *Zeitschrift Für Psychologie, 220*, 121–129. doi:10.1027/2151-2604/a000103

Nagels, A., Kircher, T., Steines, M., Grosvald, M., & Straube, B. (2015). A brief self-rating scale for the assessment of individual differences in gesture perception and production. *Learning and Individual Differences, 39*, 73–80. doi:10.1016/j.lindif.2015.03.008

National Commission for the Protection of Human Subjects of Biomedical and Behavioral Research. (1979, April 18). *The Belmont Report: Ethical principles and guidelines for the protection of human subjects of research*. Retrieved from http://www.hhs.gov/ohrp/humansubjects/guidance/belmont.html

National Research Council. (2011). *Guide for the care and use of laboratory animals* (8th ed.). Washington, DC: National Academies Press.

Newton, H. B. (2015). The neurology of creativity: Focus on music. In C. Charyton (Ed.), *Creativity and innovation among science and art: A discussion of the two cultures* (pp. 3–52). New York, NY: Springer-Verlag Publishing.

Noss, A. (2014). *Household Income: 2013, American Community Survey Briefs*. Retrieved from https://www.census.gov/content/dam/Census/library/publications/2014/acs/acsbr13-02.pdf

Ogden, C. L., Lamb, M. M., Carroll, M. D., & Flegal, K. M. (2010). Obesity and socioeconomic status in children: United States 1988–1994 and 2005–2008. NCHS data brief no 51. Hyattsville, MD: National Center for Health Statistics.

Oldham, J. (2011). When is a placebo not a placebo? *Journal of Psychiatric Practice, 17*, 383. doi:10.1097/01.pra.0000407960.04110.b8

Office of Research Integrity. (2011a). *Avoiding plagiarism, self-plagiarism, and other questionable writing practices: A guide to ethical writing*. Retrieved from http://ori.dhhs.gov/education/products/plagiarism/plagiarism.pdf

Office of Research Integrity. (2011b). *Handling misconduct*. Retrieved from http://ori.dhhs.gov/misconduct/cases

Olson, C. M., Rennie, D., Cook, D., Dickersin, K., Flanagin, A., Hogan, J. W., Zhu, Q., Reiling, J., & Pace, B. (2002). Publication bias in editorial decision making. *Journal of the American Medical Association, 287*, 2825–2828. doi:10.1001/jama.287.21.2825

Painter, J. E., Wansink, B., & Hieggelke, J. B. (2002). How visibility and convenience influence candy consumption. *Appetite, 38*, 237–238. doi:10.1006/appe.2002.0485

Parascandola, M., Hawkins, J., & Danis, M. (2002). Patient autonomy and the challenge of clinical uncertainty. *Kennedy Institute of Ethics Journal, 12*, 245–264. doi:10.1353/ken.2002.0018

Parker, I. (2005). *Qualitative psychology: Introducing radical research*. New York, NY: Open University Press.

Pate, R. R., Stevens, J., Webber, L. S., Dowda, M., Murray, D. M., Young, D. R., & Going, S. (2009). Age-related change in physical activity in adolescent girls. *Journal of Adolescent Health, 44*, 275–282. doi:10.1016/j.jadohealth. 2008.07.003

Phillips, T. (2008). Age-related differences in identity style: A cross-sectional analysis. *Current Psychology, 27*, 205–215. doi:10.1007/s12144-008-9035-9

Piqueras-Fiszman, B., & Spence, C. (2012). The weight of the bottle as a possible extrinsic cue with which to estimate the price (and quality) of the wine? Observed correlations. *Food Quality and Preference, 25*, 41–45. doi:10.1016/j.foodqual.2012.01.001

Platt, J. R. (1964). Strong inference: Certain systematic methods of scientific thinking may produce much more rapid progress than others. *Science, 146*, 347–353.

Pliner, P. (1982). The effects of mere exposure on liking for edible substances. *Appetite, 3*, 283–290.

Pollak, O. (1950). *The criminality of women*. Philadelphia, PA: University of Pennsylvania Press.

Pool, J., & Odell-Miller, H. (2011). Aggression in music therapy and its role in creativity with reference to personality disorder. *Arts in Psychotherapy, 38*, 169–177. doi:10.1016/j.aip.2011.04.003

Popper, K. R. (1959). *The logic of scientific discovery*. New York, NY: Basic Books.

Privitera, G. J. (2008a, February). Decreasing dislike for sour and bitter in children and adults. *International Fruit & Vegetable Alliance (IFAVA) Scientific Newsletter, 4*.

Privitera, G. J. (2008b). *The psychological dieter: It's not all about the calories*. Lanham, MD: University Press of America.

Privitera, G. J. (2015). *Statistics for the behavioral sciences* (2nd ed.). Thousand Oaks, CA: SAGE.

Privitera, G. J. (2016). *Essential Statistics for the Behavioral Sciences*. Thousand Oaks, CA: SAGE.

Privitera, G. J., Agnello, J. E., Walters, S. A., & Bender, S. L. (2015). Randomized feedback about diagnosis influences statistical and clinical significance of self-report ADHD assessment in adults. *Journal of Attention Disorders, 19*, 447–451. doi:10.1177/1087054712461178

Privitera, G. J., & Creary, H. E. (2013). Proximity and visibility of fruits and vegetables influences intake in a kitchen setting among college students. *Environment & Behavior, 45*, 876–886. doi:10.1177/0013916512442892

Privitera, G. J., & Dickinson, E. K. (2015). Control your cravings: Self-control varies by eating attitudes, sex, and food type among Division I collegiate athletes. *Psychology of Sport and Exercise, 19*, 18–22. doi:10.1016/j.psychsport.2015.02.004

Privitera, G. J., & Freeman, C. S. (2012). Validity and reliability of an estimated daily intake scale for fat. *Global Journal of Health Science, 4*, 36–41. doi:10.5539/gjhs.v4n2p36

Privitera, G. J., McGrath, H. K., Windus, B. A., & Doraiswamy, P. M. (2015). Eat now or later: Self-control as an overlapping cognitive mechanism of depression and obesity. *PLoS ONE, 10,* e0123136. doi:10.1371/journal.pone.0123136

Privitera, G. J., Mulcahey, C. P., & Orlowski, C. M. (2012). Human sensory preconditioning in a flavor preference paradigm. *Appetite, 59,* 414–418. doi:10.1016/j.appet.2012.06.005

Privitera, G. J., Phillips, T. E., Zuraikat, F. M., & Paque, R. (2015). Emolabeling increases healthy food choices among grade school children in a structured grocery aisle setting. *Appetite, 92,* 173–177. doi:10.1016/j.appet.2015.05.024

Privitera, G. J., & Wallace, M. (2011). An assessment of liking for sugars using the estimated daily intake scale. *Appetite, 56,* 713–718. doi:10.1016/j.appet.2011.02.008

Privitera, G. J., & Zuraikat, F. M. (2014). Proximity of foods in a competitive food environment influences consumption of a low calorie and a high calorie food. *Appetite, 76,* 175–179. doi:10.1016/j.appet.2014.02.004

Purser, G. (2009). The dignity of job-seeking men: Boundary work among immigrant day laborers. *Journal of Contemporary Ethnography, 38,* 117–139. doi:10.1177/0891241607311867

Quisenberry, P. N. (2015). Texting and driving: Can it be explained by the general theory of crime? *American Journal of Criminal Justice, 40,* 303–316. doi:10.1007/s12103-014-9249-3

Rasinski, K. A., Lee, L., & Krishnamurty, P. (2012). Question order effects. In H. Cooper, P. M. Canic, D. L. Long, A. T. Painter, D. Rindskopf, & K. J. Sher (Eds.), *APA handbook of research methods in psychology: Foundations, planning, measures, and psychometrics* (Vol. 1, pp. 229–248). Washington, DC: American Psychological Association.

Rector, T. S. (2008). How should we communicate the likelihood of risks to inform decisions about consent? *IRB: Ethics & Human Research, 30,* 15–18.

Reese, H. W. (1997). Counterbalancing and other uses of repeated-measures Latin-square designs: Analyses and interpretations. *Journal of Experimental Child Psychology, 64,* 137–158. doi:10.1006/jecp.1996.2333

Reese, R. J., & Miller, C. D. (2006). Effects of a university career development course on career decision-making self-efficacy. *Journal of Career Assessment, 14,* 252–266. doi:10.1177/1069072705274985

Reid, S. C., Kauer, S. D., Dudgeon, P., Sanci, L. A., Shrier, L. A., & Patton, G. C. (2009). A mobile phone program to track young people's experiences of mood, stress and coping: Development and testing of the mobile type program. *Social Psychiatry and Psychiatric Epidemiology, 44,* 501–507. doi:10.1007/s00127-008-0455-5

Resnick, J. H., & Schwartz, T. (1973). Ethical standards as an independent variable in psychological research. *American Psychologist, 28,* 134–139.

Robinson, T. N., Borzekowski, D. L. G., Matheson, D. M., & Kraemer, H. C. (2007). Effects of fast food branding on young children's taste preference. *Archives of Pediatrics & Adolescent Medicine, 161,* 792–797. doi:10.1001/archpedi.161.8.792

Robinson-Cimpian, J. P. (2014). Inaccurate estimation of disparities due to mischievous responders: Several suggestions to assess conclusions. *Educational Researcher, 43,* 171–185. doi:10.3102/0013189X14534297

Roemmich, J. N., Lambiase, M. J., Lobarinas, C. L., & Balantekin, K. N. (2011). Interactive effects of dietary restraint and adiposity on stress-induced eating and the food choice of children. *Eating Behaviors, 12,* 309–312. doi:10.1016/j.eatbeh.2011.07.003

Rolls, B.J. (2014). What is the role of portion control in weight management? *International Journal of Obesity, 38,* S1–S8. doi:10.1038/ijo.2014.82

Rosenberg, M. (1965). *Society and the adolescent self-image.* Princeton, NJ: Princeton University Press.

Rosenthal, R. (1984). Meta-analytic procedures for social research. *Applied Social Research Methods* (Vol. 6). Beverly Hills, CA: SAGE.

Rosmarin, D. H., Krumrei, E. J., & Andersson, G. (2009). Religion as a predictor of psychological distress in two religious communities. *Cognitive Behaviour Therapy, 38,* 54–64. doi:10.1080/16506070802477222

Ryff, C. D. (1989). Happiness is everything, or is it? Explorations on the meaning of psychological well-being. *Journal of Personality and Social Psychology, 57,* 1069–1081.

Salvy, S. J., Coelho, J. S., Kieffer, E., & Epstein, L. H. (2007). Effects of social contexts on overweight and normal-weight children's food intake. *Physiology & Behavior, 92*, 840–846. doi:10.1016/j.physbeh.2007.06.014

Sanderson, S. C. (2010). Obesity risk. In K. P. Tercyak (Ed.), *Handbook of genomics and the family: Psychosocial context for children and adolescents* (pp. 329–343). New York, NY: Springer Science + Business Media.

Sarkar, R., Klein, J., & Krüger, S. (2008). Aripiprazole augmentation in treatment-refractory obsessive-compulsive disorder. *Psychopharmacology, 197*, 687–688. doi:10.1007/s00213-008-1091-1

Schredl, M., Fricke-Oerkermann, L., Mitschke, A., Wiater, A., & Lehmkuhl, G. (2009). Longitudinal study of nightmares in children: Stability and effect of emotional symptoms. *Child Psychiatry & Human Development, 40*, 439–449. doi:10.1007/s10578-009-0136-y

Schumacker, R. E., & Lomax, R. G. (1996). *A beginner's guide to structural equation modeling.* Mahwah, NJ: Erlbaum.

Schwitzgebel, E., & Cushman, F. (2012). Expertise in moral reasoning? Order-effects on moral judgment in professional philosophers and non-philosophers. *Mind & Language, 27*, 135–153. doi:10.1111/j.1468-0017.2012.01438.x

Scott, C. K., Sonis, J., Creamer, M., & Dennis, M. L. (2006). Maximizing follow-up in longitudinal studies of traumatized populations. *Journal of Traumatic Stress, 19*, 757–769. doi:10.1002/jts.20186

Shepherd, R. M., & Edelmann, R. J. (2007). Social phobia and the self-medication hypothesis: A case study approach. *Counseling Psychology Quarterly, 20*, 295–307. doi:10.1080/ 09515070701571756

Sherif, M., Harvey, O. J., White, B. J., Hood, W. R., & Sherif, C. W. (1988). *The Robber's Cave experiment: Intergroup conflict and cooperation.* Middletown, CT: Wesleyan University Press. (Original work published 1961)

Shih, T., & Fan, X. (2008). Comparing response rates from web and mail surveys: A meta-analysis. *Field Methods, 20*, 249–271. doi:10.1177/1525822X08317085

Shook, N. J., & Fazio, R. H. (2008). Interracial roommate relationships: An experimental field test of the contact hypothesis. *Psychological Science, 19*, 717–723. doi:10.1111/j.1467-9280.2008.02147.x

Sieber, J. E. (2007). Respect for persons and informed consent: A moving target. *Journal of Empirical Research on Human Research Ethics, 2*, 1–2. doi:10.1525/jer.2007.2.3.1

Siebers, R., & Holt, S. (2000). Accuracy of references in five leading medical journals. *Lancet, 356*, 1445. doi:10.1016/S0140-6736(05)74090-3

Stevens, S. S. (1946). On the theory of scales of measurement. *Science, 103*, 677–680.

Stewart, A. E., & St. Peter, C. C. (2004). Driving and riding avoidance following motor vehicle crashes in a non-clinical sample: Psychometric properties of a new measure. *Behaviour Research and Therapy, 42*, 859–879. doi:10.1016/S0005-7967(03)00203-1

Stewart, G. L., Dustin, S. L., Barrick, M. R., & Darnold, T. C. (2008). Exploring the handshake in employment interviews. *Journal of Applied Psychology, 93*, 1139–1146. doi:10.1037/0021-9010.93.5.1139

Stoop, I. (2015). Nonresponse in comparative studies: Enhancing response rates and detecting and minimizing nonresponse bias. In U. Engel, B. Jann, P. Lynn, A. Scherpenzeel, & P. Sturgis (Eds.), *Improving survey methods: Lessons from recent research* (pp. 351–362). New York, NY: Routledge/Taylor & Francis Group.

Su, D., Esqueda, O. A., Li, L., & Pagán, J. A. (2012). Income inequality and obesity prevalence among OECD countries. *Journal of Biosocial Science, 44*, 417–432. doi:10.1017/S002193201100071X

Svanum, S., & Aigner, C. (2011). The influences of course effort, mastery and performance goals, grade expectancies, and earned course grades on student ratings of course satisfaction. *British Journal of Educational Psychology, 81*, 667–679. doi:10.1111/j.2044-8279.2010.02011.x

Tamboukou, M. (2014). Archival research: Unravelling space/time/matter entanglements and fragments. *Qualitative Research, 14*, 617–633. doi:10.1177/1468794113490719

Taylor, D. (2002). The appropriate use of references in a scientific research paper. *Emergency Medicine, 14*, 166–170. doi:10.1046/j.1442-2026.2002.00312.x

Taylor, G., Slade, P., & Herbert, J. S. (2014). Infant face interest is associated with voice information and maternal psychological health. *Infant Behavior & Development, 37*, 597-605. doi:10.1016/j.infbeh.2014.08.002

Taylor, J. E. (2008). Driving phobia consequent to motor vehicle collisions. In M. P. Duckworth, T. Iezzi, & W. T. O'Donohue (Eds.), *Motor vehicle collisions: Medical, psychosocial, and legal consequences* (pp. 389–416). San Diego, CA: Academic Press.

Taylor, J. E., & Sullman, M. J. M. (2009). What does the Driving and Riding Avoidance Scale (DRAS) measure? *Journal of Anxiety Disorders, 23*, 504–510. doi:10.1016/j.janxdis.2008.10.006

Thomée, S., Härenstam, A., & Hagberg, M. (2011). Mobile phone use and stress, sleep disturbances, and symptoms of depression among young adults—a prospective cohort study. *BMC Public Health, 11*, 66–76. doi:10.1186/1471-2458-11-66

Thomson, C. J., Reece, J. E., & Di Benedetto, M. (2014). The relationship between music-related mood regulation and psychopathology in young people. *Musicae Scientiae, 18*, 150–165. doi:10.1177/1029864914521422

Thompson, R. A., & Sherman, R. (2010). *Eating disorders in sport.* New York, NY: Routledge/Taylor & Francis Group.

Trials of War Criminals before the Nuremberg Military Tribunals under Control Council Law No. 10, Vol. 2, 181–182. Washington, DC: U.S. Government Printing Office, 1949.

Tukey, J. W. (1977). *Exploratory data analysis.* Reading, MA: Addison-Wesley.

Umberson, D., Thomeer, M. B., & Williams, K. (2013). Family status and mental health: Recent advances and future directions. In C. S. Aneshensel, J. C. Phelan, & A. Bierman (Eds.), *Handbook of the sociology of mental health* (2nd ed.) (pp. 405–431). New York, NY: Springer Science + Business Media.

U.S. Bureau of Labor Statistics. (2013). *Databases, tables & calculators by subject.* Retrieved from http://data.bls.gov/timeseries/LNS14000000

U.S. Department of Health and Human Services. (2007). *Guidance on reviewing and reporting unanticipated problems involving risks to subjects or others and adverse events.* Retrieved from http://www.hhs.gov/ohrp/policy/advevntguid.html

U.S. National Library of Medicine. (2013). *Databases, resources & APIs.* Retrieved from http://wwwcf2.nlm.nih.gov/nlm_eresources/eresources/search_database.cfm

Verma, I. M. (2014). Editorial expression of concern and correction. *Proceedings of the National Academy of Sciences U S A, 111*, 10779. doi:10.1073/pnas.1412583111

Vrangalova, Z. (2015). Does casual sex harm college students' well-being? A longitudinal investigation of the role of motivation. *Archives of Sexual Behavior, 44*, 945–959. doi:10.1007/s10508-013-0255-1

Wansink, B., & Kim, J. (2005). Bad popcorn in big buckets: Portion size can influence intake as much as taste. *Journal of Nutrition Education and Behavior, 37*, 242–245. doi: 10.1016/S1499-4046(06)60278-9

Wansink, B., Painter, J. E., & Lee, Y.-K. (2006). The office candy dish: Proximity's influence on estimated and actual consumption. *International Journal of Obesity, 30*, 871–875. doi:10.1038/sj.ijo.0803217

Weisberg, S. (2005). *Applied linear regression.* Hoboken, NJ: Wiley.

Wendler, D., & Miller, F. G. (2004). Deception in pursuit of science. *Archives of Internal Medicine, 164*, 597–600.

White, J. M., Wampler, R. S., & Winn, K. I. (1998). In identity style inventory: A revision with a sixth-grade reading level (ISI-6G). *Journal of Adolescent Research, 13*, 223–245. doi:10.1177/0743554898132007

Willson, V. L. (1981). Time and the external validity of experiments. *Evaluation and Program Planning, 4*, 229–238. doi:10.1016/0149-7189(81)90024-0

Wing, V. C., & Shoaib, M. (2008). Contextual stimuli modulate extinction and reinstatement in rodents self-administering intravenous nicotine. *Psychopharmacology, 200*, 357–365. doi:10.1007/s00213-008-1211-y

Wolf, M., Sedway, J., Bulik, C. M., & Kordy, H. (2007). Linguistic analyses of nature written language: Unobtrusive assessment of cognitive style in eating disorders. *International Journal of Eating Disorders, 40*, 711–717. doi:10.1002/eat. 20445

Wolkin, A., Sanfilipo, M., Angrist, B., Duncan, E., Wieland, S., Wolf, A. P., Brodie, J. D., Cooper, T. B., & Laska, E. (1994). Acute d-amphetamine challenge in schizophrenia: Effects of cerebral glucose utilization and clinical symptomatology. *Biological Psychiatry, 36*, 317–325. doi:10.1016/0006-3223(94)90629-7

Young, M. M., Wohl, M. J. A., Matheson, K., Baumann, S., & Anisman, H. (2008). The desire to gamble: The influence of outcomes on the priming effects of a gambling episode. *Journal of Gambling Studies, 24*, 275–293. doi:10.1007/s10899-008-9093-9

Zigmond, M. J., & Fischer, B. A. (2002). Beyond fabrication and plagiarism: The little murders of everyday science: Commentary on "Six Domains of Research Ethics" (K. D. Pimple). *Science and Engineering Ethics, 8*, 229–234.

Zimbardo, P. G. (1975). On transforming experimental research into advocacy for social change. In M. Deutsch & H. Hornstein (Eds.), *Applying social psychology: Implications for research, practice, and training* (pp. 33–66). Hillsdale, NJ: Erlbaum.

Zöllner, F. (1860). Ueber eine neue Art von Pseudoskopie und ihre Beziehungen zu den von Plateau und Oppel beschrieben Bewegungsphaenomenen. *Annalen der Physik, 186*, 500–525.

INDEX

In this index *f* represents figures and *t* represents tables.